Census Substitutes & State Census Records

♦♦ 3rd Edition ♦♦

Volume 5
Western / Pacific States & Nationwide Chapter

by
William Dollarhide

Copyright © 2020 – Updated May 2021.
William W. Dollarhide and Leland K. Meitzler
All rights reserved.

No part of this book may be reproduced in any form without permission in writing from the author or publisher except in brief quotations in articles and reviews.

Published by Family Roots Publishing Co., LLC
PO Box 1682
Orting, WA 98360-1682
www.familyrootspublishing.com

Library of Congress Control Number: 2020934867

ISBN (Paperback): 978-1-62859-292-4
ISBN (eBook): 978-1-62859-293-1

Recommended Citation:
Census Substitutes & State Census Records, 3rd Edition,
Volume Five – Western / Pacific States & Nationwide Chapter,
by William Dollarhide, publ. Family Roots Publishing Co., LLC, Orting, WA, 303 pages, 2020. Updated May 2021.

Printed in the United States of America

Contents – Vol. 5
Western / Pacific States & Nationwide Chapter

State Finder – Vols. 1 to 5 6
   Foreword 7
   Introduction 9
   Table 1: Non-State Census States 13
   Table 2: State Census States – AL-MI 14
   Table 2: State Census States – MN-WY 15
   Table 3: State Censuses in Common Years 16
   Table 4: Availability of Federal Censuses for each State 17

Vol. 5 States
   Alaska 19
   Hawaii 37
   California 57
   Nevada 107
   Oregon 121
   Washington 141
   Idaho 163
   Montana 189
   Wyoming 205

Nationwide Chapter
   PART 1: Maps, Descriptions and Internet Access for the
              U.S. Federal Censuses, 1790-1950 217
   PART 2: U.S. Census Substitutes 259

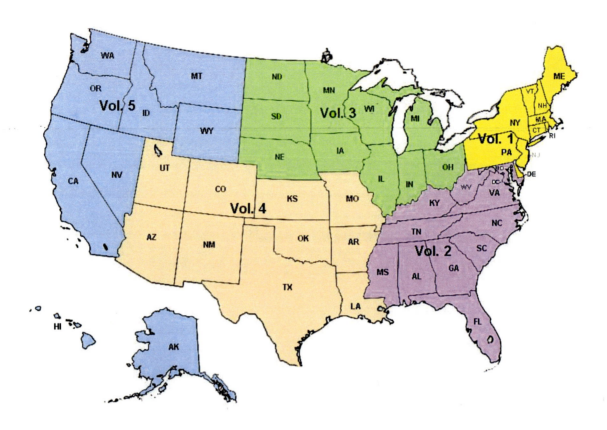

State Finder, Vols. 1-5

States	Vol.	Page
Alabama	2	233
Alaska	5	19
Arizona	4	213
Arkansas	4	75
California	5	57
Colorado	4	239
Connecticut	1	145
Delaware	1	223
District of Columbia	2	58
Florida	2	277
Georgia	2	193
Hawaii	5	37
Idaho	5	163
Illinois	3	119
Indiana	3	91
Iowa	3	179
Kansas	4	41
Kentucky	2	113
Louisiana	4	123
Maine	1	19
Maryland	2	19
Massachusetts	1	91

States	Vol.	Page
Michigan	3	43
Minnesota	3	225
Mississippi	2	259
Missouri	4	19
Montana	5	189
Nebraska	3	243
Nevada	5	107
New Hampshire	1	63
New Jersey	1	191
New Mexico	4	191
New York	1	173
North Carolina	2	145
North Dakota	3	273
Ohio	3	19
Oklahoma	4	101
Oregon	5	121
Pennsylvania	1	205
Rhode Island	1	133
South Carolina	2	177
South Dakota	3	261
Tennessee	2	161
Texas	4	169

States	Vol.	Page
Utah	4	261
Vermont	1	77
Virginia	2	79
Washington	5	141
West Virginia	2	97
Wisconsin	3	159
Wyoming	5	205

US Territories	Vol.	Page
Caribbean Region	1	245
Puerto Rico	1	246
US Virgin Islands	1	251
Panama Canal Zone	1	256
Pacific Region	1	259
Guam	1	260
No. Mariana Islands	1	262
American Samoa	1	264
The Philippines	1	268

US Nationwide	Vol.	Page
1790-1950 Maps / Descr.	5	217
US Census Substitutes	5	259

Foreword
by Leland K. Meitzler

In late 2003 Bill Dollarhide came by my office and asked if I had any ideas for *Genealogy Bulletin* articles. As it turned out, I had just finished organizing materials for a lecture on state and territorial census records and had a file folder full of data I had collected over the years on my desk. I suggested he put something together on that subject and gave him the file to review. After looking through my file, Bill decided that we needed to identify the many substitutes to censuses (statewide tax lists, voter registration lists, and such), as he quickly noted that a number of states didn't take any state or territorial censuses at all. Bill began compiling a bibliography of not only extant state and territorial censuses, but substitute lists as well.

Researched and compiled by region, he added timelines of historical references to show the jurisdictions in place at the time of each census. Compiling the material by region was a logical way to go, as we quickly realized that in most cases, it would have been very difficult to write about one state without writing about those surrounding it. So, if you start with Maine, for example, the adjoining state of New Hampshire would be the next chapter, then Vermont, Massachusetts, and so on.

Much of the data found in the two-volume First Edition (2008) was initially published in serial form in the old *Genealogy Bulletin (1983-2006)*. That said, the District of Columbia, for which there are many excellent sources, was never published. Also never published was The Oregon Country chapter. However, both chapters were included in the First Edition.

In the three-volume Second Edition (2016), numerous online sources were added, reflecting the ongoing efforts of both public and private companies to digitize relevant records.

In this new five-volume Third Edition (2020), the Northeastern States (Volume 1) adds seven (7) U.S. Territories for the first time. In addition, the *Western & Pacific States (*Volume 5) has an all-new *Maps, Descriptions, and Internet Access for the U.S. Federal Censuses, 1790-1950;* followed by an updated *U.S. Census Substitutes* chapter. Each of the 50 states & DC in this 3rd Edition has many more citations for newly added online databases and recently digitized microfilm collections – in just three years, the number went from 3,865 to 8,067 hyperlinks.

Bill also spent countless hours compiling tabulated charts that may be worth the cost of this book all by themselves. The first, found on page 13, is a chart for the non-state census states. There happens to be 13 of them (including the District of Columbia). This chart lists the states and the years covered by census substitutes. The second chart, found on pages 14-15, lists the 38 states that have extant colonial, pre-statehood, territorial, and state censuses, complete with the census year, and an indication if the census is available online as of the date of publication. The third chart, found on page 16, shows in graphic form the states that had censuses taken in common years – "on the fives." Census dates for some states are within a range. The fourth chart, on page 17, shows the availability of federal censuses for all states, 1790-1950.

Note that the title of this series of volumes is *Census Substitutes & State Census Records,* which reflects the fact that the volumes really contain a list of census substitutes, with state censuses turning out to be in the minority. Substitutes outnumber censuses by a factor of ten to one! However, the state censuses identified in this series are by far the most complete lists of

Colonial, Territorial, or State Censuses published to date.

State and Territorial Censuses have long fascinated me. Many were taken in order to get congress to allow statehood. Some territories would take censuses on a nearly annual basis, in the attempt to show that they had the population base necessary to justify statehood.

Other states, like New York, had authorization of non-federal censuses written into their state constitutions. New York was one of the most prolific when it came to state censuses, as it produced numerous schedules, most falling on the ubiquitous "fives." Today we have extant New York censuses for 1825, 1835, 1845, 1855, 1865, 1875, 1892, 1905, 1915, and 1925. Some of the early years are not complete, but what is available is certainly useful. The 1925 New York census was taken as well as any other, and the population returns are largely legible and complete. However, the census was wrought with scandal, leaving New Yorkers with a taste of bitterness for such things. To make a long story short, it seems that the New York Secretary of State, a former Dean of Home Economics at Syracuse University, Florence Elizabeth Smith Knapp, took nepotism to a whole new level. As the state official in charge of the 1925 census, she put family and friends on the payroll, and while this wasn't illegal, most of these folks did little or nothing to earn their salaries. Even her 74-year old mother, Ella Smith, enjoyed a non-working stint as an assistant supervisor. Florence's stepdaughter, Clara Blanche Knapp, a professor at Middlebury College in Vermont, was on the payroll for over $5,000 in income, while never leaving the state of Vermont. Moreover, checks written to both Ella and Blanche seemed to have been endorsed into Florence E.S. Knapp's bank account. Numerous other family members and friends were paid substantial sums for non-work. In 1928, Mrs. Knapp finally went on trial for her misdeeds, and found guilty of first-degree grand larceny for misappropriation of state funds. She served 30 days in the Albany Jail. She could have gotten 10 years. So ended the brief political career of the first woman ever to be elected to state-wide office in New York. So also ended the state censuses of New York State.

Iowa, Kansas, Rhode Island, Florida, North Dakota, and South Dakota also took censuses up through 1925. South Dakota and Florida even took censuses in 1935 and 1945! The real value of state censuses is found in the numerous schedules enumerated in the mid-nineteenth century. Thirty-eight states took non-federal censuses that are still extant today.

And then there are the substitutes. They are of prime importance, since 12 states, as well as the District of Columbia, took no state censuses at all. And even if your ancestors lived in a state where censuses were taken "on the fives," census substitutes are helpful, especially if the family was on the move.

Although Mr. Dollarhide has used all kinds of substitutes throughout this volume, more attention has been given to tax lists, voter registration rolls, vital records, directories, statewide probate indexes, land records, and even military censuses, than most others. These records are often easily accessible and using this guide, you will be able to quickly find them for your own use. You are in for a treat, so sit back and look up the states of your ancestors. You will find information on records you never knew existed. Then… go get the records, and happy hunting!

Leland K. Meitzler
Publisher

Introduction
Census Substitutes & State Census Records

Census Substitutes are those name lists derived from tax lists, directories, military lists, land ownership lists, voter registrations, and other compilations of names of residents for an entire state, or part of a state. A census substitute can be used to determine the names of residents in a given area when a federal or state census is missing. Moreover, a census substitute can be used as an alternative name list; confirming, contradicting, or adding to information found in a federal or state census.

This book identifies at least ten times the number of Census Substitute titles than any previous work ever published. All states are represented with significant alternative name lists – name lists that stop time for a certain year and place and name the residents of a certain place. Since all of these name lists are specific to a certain year, they are listed within each state category in chronological order. Incorporated into the lists are any State Census titles – a reference to a state census taken for a specific year.

Federal vs. State Censuses

Federal Censuses have their origins in the constitutional provision for apportionment of the U.S. House of Representatives. The first federal census was taken in 1790, and beginning about the same time, state censuses were conducted for the same reason, that is, apportionment of the various state legislatures.

Although the primary purpose of all censuses was to simply count the population, beginning with the first federal census of 1790, more information than a simple tally was added. This included the name and age of a person and progressively more details about a household for each subsequent census year. State censuses followed this same pattern.

State censuses usually add even more information than the federal censuses, and as a result, they are premier genealogical resources. Except in cases where a federal census is lost, state census records are not substitutes for the federal censuses – state censuses were almost always taken between federal census years, and usually add unique information and details about a household not found in a federal census. If a state census exists between federal census years, it may add marginally to the knowledge one gains about a family. But, more often, it will add critical information, such as more exact dates of birth, marriages, deaths; plus, additional children, different residences, other relatives living with a family; and more.

Non-State Census States

Thirteen (13) states (including DC) have never conducted a state-sponsored census. For these Non-State Census States, this review attempts to identify as many census substitutes as possible. In some cases, the census substitutes are for a single county within a state, and by listing multiple county name lists for about the same time period, regional coverage is achieved.

For an overview of the Non-State Census States, see Table 1 (page 13) showing the years for which census substitutes exist. More detail for each census substitute year indicated on the table is covered in the bibliographic sections.

State Census States

Thirty-eight (38) states have conducted censuses separate from the federal censuses. The number of censuses taken by each of the State Census States ranges from one (1) census year, e.g., the 1852 California; to twenty-four (24) census years, e.g., the 1792-1866 Mississippi territorial/state censuses. For this review, all of the state-sponsored censuses are identified, plus, to a lesser degree than the non-state census states, census substitutes available. See Table 2 (pages 14-15) for an overview of the State Census States, the year for each surviving census for a state; and an indication of which specific years are now available online as digitized databases.

Locating the Extant State Census Records

Generally, state censuses were conducted from the time of territorial status or early statehood up until about 1905, but a few continued until 1925, 1935, or 1945. The last state censuses taken by any of the states was in 1945 (Florida and South Dakota). Due to budget restraints, the Depression Era of the 1930s was a contributing factor to states ending their census-taking endeavors. Eventually, all states of the Union stopped using the population figures from state censuses and began using the federal census figures for apportionment of their state legislatures.

While the surviving federal census manuscripts are all located mostly in one repository (the National Archives), state census manuscripts are spread across the country in the various state archives or local repositories. The accessibility of state censuses may be just as good as federal censuses – but one needs to know where they are located first.

Beginning in 1941, the U.S. Bureau of the Census issued a bibliographic report attempting to identify all known state censuses, those undertaken by the various states separate from the federal censuses since 1790.[1] Prepared by Henry J. Dubester of the Library of Congress, the report was the first known attempt to research all of the state constitutions and subsequent laws related to state censuses for all of the states. The Dubester report sought, first, to identify what state censuses had ever been authorized by a state constitution or legislature; and second, to identify what census manuscripts still survive. The identification of extant state censuses was very incomplete, due to the war and under-funding of the project.

However, Dubester's review of each state's constitutional provisions for taking state censuses still stands as the best overview of what state censuses were ever authorized. The report cites the specific articles of the state constitutions or the actual state laws relating to censuses for all states.

Unfortunately, the fact that a state legislature authorized a state census does not mean one was actually taken. For example, the State Constitution of California of 1849 authorized a census in the years 1852 and 1855 and each ten years thereafter, all for the purpose of apportionment of its state legislature. Yet, only one was ever taken, that for 1852. Later, the California Constitution of 1879 provided that the decennial national census serve as the basis for legislative apportionment.[2]

This was fairly typical of all states. Even in those states for which several decades of state censuses now survive, they eventually got out of the census business, turning to the federal decennial censuses to determine apportionment. For example, New York took state censuses from 1825 and every ten years thereafter until 1925, yet, in 1938, New York decided to use the federal decennial censuses thereafter.[3]

Since the Dubester report, there have been several attempts to list all known state censuses, where they are located, and the contents of the census name lists. All of these attempts differ dramatically, because some of the lists rely on the Dubester report, which may have been accurate in identifying which state censuses were ever authorized but was not nearly complete in identifying the extant manuscripts of state census records. For example, Table 4-8 of *The Source*,[4] seems to use the census years cited in the Dubester report for "authorized state censuses" rather than those actually extant. There are lists of state censuses for each state in *The Red Book*,[5] but are only a slight improvement over those found in *The Source*. And, several Internet sites offer lists of state censuses, all of which seem to take data previously published in the *Source* or *The Red Book*, and similar publications.

Based on survey results from all states, the Family History Library prepared a two-volume publication, *U.S. State and Special Census Register: A Listing of Family History Library Microfilm Numbers,* compiled by G. Eileen Buckway and Fred Adams, a revised edition published by the FHL in 1992 (FHL book 973 X2 v. 1 & 2, and fiche #6104851 (vol. 1) and #6104852 (vol. 2). This is a very good guide to military censuses, school censuses, and special censuses of American Indian tribes. As a guide to state censuses, however, the list is incomplete. Since the results of the surveys from each of the states were only partially successful, there are many omissions.

Clearly, the best list of state censuses to date is Ann S. Lainhart, *State Census Records*, published by Genealogical Publishing Co., Inc., Baltimore, in 1992. The book identifies state censuses in 43 states, including 5 states without state censuses (but have major state-wide census substitutes available). For the 38 state census states, the lists generally do not include colonial or pre-territorial censuses. With a few exceptions, census substitutes such as those compiled from tax lists, voter registration lists, military lists, or other name sources, are also not included. Still, Lainhart's book stands as the most complete list ever done.

At the time when most of the previous state census lists were put together, there were some research tools unavailable to the authors. Today, the Internet as a resource for finding place-specific records is overwhelming. And, special tools such as the Periodical Source Index (PERSI)[6] which indexes articles in over 11,000 different genealogical periodicals (by subject, place, and surname) gives a big boost to the task of finding references to relevant articles using keywords such as "state census," "territorial census," or "tax list." In addition, the State Archives and/or State Libraries where obscure census originals and substitute name lists reside often have a website with an online searchable catalog.

For any genealogical research project, it helps to be close to the Family History Library (FHL) in Salt Lake City. But from any place where a researcher has access to the Internet, the FamilySearch™ online catalog as a genealogical research tool has no equal. Searching for published state censuses and census substitutes in the FHL catalog will not bring up every extant resource, but it is more complete than any other library in the world.

The Evolution of Regional Chapters to State Chapters

In the 2008 First Edition of this work, the two volumes had chapters for six (6) Eastern Regions and five (5) Western Regions of the United States.

For the 2016 Second Edition, the three volumes included an Eastern volume with five (5) regions; the Central Volume had three (3) regions; and the Western volume had four (4) regions; plus, an all-new Nationwide Chapter was added to the Western volume. A timeline for each region was prepared to put the area into a historical perspective from a genealogist's point of view.

This 2020 Third Edition was expanded to five volumes, each volume a region of the United States. Therefore, the content of each state's review now includes much of the content that was done at the regional level in the earlier editions, e.g., there is now a Timeline specific to each state.

The organization of the state bibliographic lists has changed as well. The Second Edition had six (6) listings for bibliographic entries, including State Resource Centers, FamilySearch.org, Ancestry.com, and others. This Third Edition has just one (1) listing where all databases from any provider are presented in chronological order.

About PERSI

PERSI (PERiodical Source Index) is a digitized database project of the Allen County Public Library (ACPL), Fort Wayne, IN. Since 1986, the PERSI extractors have indexed article titles, places, and surnames from over 11,000 genealogical & historical periodicals. The PERSI database is currently available online through the FindMyPast.com subscription website.

A number of printed articles found in periodicals were included in the state bibliography listings that follow. The Fort Wayne library has an online order form for requesting a printed copy of any article indexed in the PERSI database, see http://genealogycenter.org/docs/default-source/resources/articlerequest.pdf?sfvrsn=2.

Federal Censuses

Since the Second Edition was published in 2016, the digital images of all federal censuses 1790-1940 became accessible to the public via the online FHL Catalog. It is now possible to view the digital images for any state's federal censuses separate from the various databases at FamilySearch.org, Ancestry.com, et al, and this meant adding the URL link for each state's digitized federal censuses in the state chapters.

The Nationwide Chapter (Vol. 5) was completely reorganized into Part 1: *Maps, Descriptions, and Internet Access for the U.S. Federal Censuses, 1790-1950;* and Part 2: *U.S. Census Substitutes.* To review the federal censuses in more detail, refer to *The Census Book*[7] for each census year. The new 2019 *Census Book* has a detailed review of published federal censuses online, 1790-1950.

The maps of the changing county boundaries for all of the states shown in *Map Guide to the U.S. Federal Census, 1790-1920*[8] should also be helpful for reviewing substitute or state census years between federal census years.

- bill$hide

Notes:

1. *State Censuses: An Annotated Bibliography of Censuses of Population Taken After the Year 1790 by States and Territories of the United States*, prepared by Henry J. Dubester, Chief, Census Library Project, Library of Congress, published Washington, DC, by United States Department of Commerce, Bureau of the Census, 1941, rev. 1948.

2. Dubester, *State Censuses*, p. 3.

3. Dubester, *State Censuses*, p. 50.

4. *The Source: A Guidebook of American Genealogy*, first edition, edited by Arlene Eakle and Johni Cerny, published by Ancestry, Inc., Salt Lake City, 1984.

5. *The Red Book: American State, County & Town Sources*, edited by Alice Eichholz, rev. ed., published by Ancestry, Inc., Salt Lake City, UT, 1992.

6. Allen County Public Library, *Periodical Source Index (PERSI)*, updated semi-annually. [database online at various contracted websites] Original data: Allen County Public Library. Periodical Source Index, Fort Wayne, IN: Allen County Public Library Foundation, 1985- .

7. *The Census Book: Facts, Schedules & Worksheets for the U.S Federal Censuses,* by William Dollarhide, publ. Family Roots Publishing Co., Orting, WA, 2019, 245 pages. See www.familyrootspublishing.com/store/product_view.php?id=3643

8. *Map Guide to the U.S. Federal Censuses, 1790-1920,* by William Thorndale and William Dollarhide, published by Genealogical Publishing Co., Inc., Baltimore, 1987-2016.

Table 1 – Non-State Census States. The following 13 states (including DC) have never conducted a state-sponsored census (or no state census survives). Census Substitutes for each state are shown for a range of years. Refer to the bibliographic listings for details about each.

State	Terr.	State	Years for which Census Substitutes are Available
Alaska	1912	1959	1870, 1873, 1878, 1885, 1887, 1890-1895, 1902-1912, 1905, 1908-1914, 1910- 1929, 1913-1916, 1917-1918, 1947, 1950, 1959-1986, and 1960-1985.
Delaware	—	1787	1609-1888, 1646-1679, 1680-1934, 1682-1759, 1684-1693, 1726, 1755, 1759, 1779, 1782, 1785, 1790, 1800, 1807, 1850-1860, and 1862-1872.
District* of Columbia	1801	1871*	1803, 1807, 1818, 1867, 1878, 1885, 1888, 1894, 1897, 1905-1909, 1912-1913, 1915, 1917, 1919, and 1925.
Idaho	1863	1890	1863, 1865-1874, 1871-1881, 1880, 1890, 1911-1937, 1911-1950, and 1930.
Kentucky	—	1792	1773-1780, 1774-1796, 1780-1909, 1781-1839, 1782-1787, 1782-1875, 1787, 1787-1811, 1787-1875, 1788-1875, 1789-1882, 1792-1830, 1792-1913, 1792-1796, 1793-1836, 1794-1805, 1794-1817, 1795, 1796-1808, 1797-1866, 1800, 1820-1900, 1851-1900, 1859-1860, 1860-1936, 1861-1865, 1862-1866, and 1895- 1896.
Montana	1864	1889	1860, 1856-1993, 1864-1872, 1868-1869, 1868-1929, 1870, 1880, 1870-1957, 1872- 1900, 1879-1880, 1881-1928, 1881-2000, 1891-1929, 1894, 1913, 1906- 1917, 1909- 1910, 1917-1918, 1921, and 1930-1975.
New Hampshire	—	1788	1648, 1709. 1723, 1736, 1740, 1763, 1767, 1775, 1776, 1779, 1789, 1795-1816, 1797, 1802, 1803, 1821, 1826, 1833, 1836, 1838, 1849, 1855 & 1865 MA, 1860, 1862-1866, 1903, and 1902-1921
Ohio	1787	1803	1787-1840, 1787-1871, 1788-1799, 1788-1820, 1790, 1800-1803, 1801-1814, 1801-1824, 1802, 1803-1827, 1804, 1807, 1810, 1812, 1816-1838, 1816-1838, 1825, 1827, 1832-1850, 1833-1994, 1835, 1846-1880, 1851-1900, 1851-1907, and 1907.
Pennsylvania	—	1787	1682-1950, 1759, 1680-1938, 1680s-1900s, 1760s-1790s, 1700s, 1780, 1798, 1740- 1900, 1887-1893, and 1870.
Texas	—	1845	1736-1838, 1700s-1800s, 1756-1830s, 1782-1836, 1809-1836, 1814-1909, 1821-1846, 1826, 1826-1835, 1820s-1846, 1820-1829, 1826-1836, 1829-1836, 1830-1839, 1835, 1835-1846, 1836, 1836-1935, 1837-1859, 1840-1849, 1840, 1846, 1837-1910, 1851-1900, 1858, 1861-1865, 1863, 1865-1866, 1867, 1874, 1882-1895, 1884, 1889-1894, 1890, 1914, 1917-1918, 1896-1948, and 1964-1968.
Vermont	—	1791	1770s-1780s, 1700s-1800s, 1654-1800, 1710-1753, 1721-1800, 1770-1832, 1771, 1782, 1788, 1793, 1796-1959, 1800s-1870, 1807, 1813, 1815, 1816, 1827-1833, 1828, 1832, 1843, 1852-1959, 1855-1860, 1861-1866, 1865, 1869, 1871-1908, 1874, 1880-1881, 1881-1882, 1882-1883, 1883-1884, 1884, 1887-1888, 1888, 1889, and 1895-1924.
Virginia	—	1788	1600s-1700s, 1600s, 1619-1930, 1623-1990, 1623-1800, 1632-1800, 1654-1800, 1704-1705, 1720, 1736-1820, 1740, 1744-1890, 1760, 1769-1800, 1779, 1779-1978, 1779-1860, 1782-1785, 1785, 1787, 1809-1848, 1810, 1815, 1828-1938, 1835, 1835-1941, 1840, 1861, 1861-1865, 1852, 1853-1896, and 1889-1890.
West Virginia	—	1863	1600s-1900s, 1777-1850, 1787, 1782-1907, 1782-1850, 1782-1860, 1782, 1783-1900, 1783-1850, 1785-1850, 1787,1850, 1789-1850, 1792-1850, 1797-1899, 1797-1851, 1799-1850, 1800, 1801-1850, 1810, 1811-1850, 1862-1866, 1863-1900, and 1899-1900.

From *Census Substitutes & State Census Records* by William Dollarhide, published by Family Roots Publishing Co., Orting WA

Table 2 – State Census States – Alabama to Michigan

The following 38 states have state-sponsored censuses available:

State	Year a Terr.	Year a State	Years for which State Censuses are available (underlined year = an online database is available)	Notes
Alabama	1817	1819	**Colony:** 1706 1721 1764 1785 1786-1803 **AL Territory:** 1801* 1808* 1809* 1810* 1816* 1818 **State:** <u>1820</u>** 1821 1823 1832 1838 1844 <u>1850</u>** <u>1855</u> <u>1866</u>.	* as part of MS Terr. ** separate from federal.
Arizona	1863	1912	**AZ Territory:** 1831 <u>1864</u> <u>1866</u> <u>1867</u>* <u>1869</u>* <u>1874</u>* <u>1876</u>* <u>1882</u>*	*1-2 counties only
Arkansas	1819	1836	**Colony:** 1686-1791 **AR Territory:** <u>1814</u>* <u>1823</u> <u>1827</u> <u>1829</u> 1833 1835 **State:** 1838 1854 1865	* as part of MO Terr.
California	—	1850	**Colony:** <u>1790</u> <u>1790-1796</u> 1822 1834 1836 1837 **State:** <u>1852</u> only	
Colorado	1861	1876	**CO Territory:** 1861 1866* **State:** <u>1885</u>	* 2 counties only
Connecticut	--	1788	**Colony:** 1762 **State:** <u>1917</u>*	* Military census, males over 16
Florida	1822	1845	**Colony:** 1759 1763-1779 1783-1814 **FL Territory:** <u>1825</u> 1838 **State:** 1845** 1855 1864* <u>1867</u> <u>1875</u> <u>1885</u> 1895 <u>1935</u> <u>1945</u>	* Military census ** Statehood census
Georgia	—	1788	1800 federal* **State:** Partial lists only: 1827 <u>1838</u> <u>1845</u> 1852 1859 1879 1890 federal** <u>1890</u> (statewide reconstruction).	* Oglethorpe Co only ** Washington Co only
Hawaii	1900	1959	**Kingdom of Hawaii:** 1840-1866 1878 1890 1896	
Illinois	1809	1818	**IL Territory:** <u>1810</u> **State:** <u>1818</u> <u>1820</u>* <u>1825</u> <u>1830</u>* <u>1835</u> <u>1840</u>* <u>1845</u> <u>1855</u> <u>1865</u>.	* separate from federal
Indiana	1800	1816	**IN Territory:** <u>1807</u>. **State:** A few townships only: 1857 1871 1877 1883 1889 1901 1913 1919 1931	
Iowa	1838	1846	As part of **WI Territory:** <u>1836</u> **IA Territory:** <u>1838</u> **State:** <u>1844</u> <u>1845</u> <u>1847</u> <u>1849</u> <u>1851</u> <u>1852</u> <u>1853</u> <u>1854</u> <u>1856</u> <u>1859</u> <u>1873</u> <u>1875</u> <u>1885</u> <u>1888</u> <u>1893</u> <u>1895</u> <u>1896</u> <u>1897</u> <u>1905</u> <u>1915</u> <u>1925</u>	
Kansas	1854	1861	**KS Territory:** <u>1855</u> <u>1856</u> <u>1857</u> <u>1858</u> <u>1859</u> **State:** <u>1865</u> <u>1875</u> <u>1885</u> <u>1895</u> <u>1905</u> <u>1915</u> <u>1925</u>	
Louisiana	1809	1812	**Orleans District:** 1804 **State:** 1833 1837 1890 federal*	*Ascension Parish only
Maine	—	1820	<u>1837</u> only.	
Maryland	—	1788	<u>1776</u> <u>1778</u> <u>1783</u>*	* Tax list
Massachusetts	—	1788	<u>1855</u> <u>1865</u>	
Michigan	1805	1837	**MI Territory:** <u>1827</u> <u>1834</u> **State:** <u>1837</u> <u>1845</u> <u>1854</u> <u>1864</u> <u>1874</u> <u>1884</u> <u>1894</u>	

From *Census Substitutes & State Census Records* by William Dollarhide, published by Family Roots Publishing Co., Orting WA

Table 2 – State Census States – Minnesota to Wyoming

Continuation of states with state-sponsored censuses available:

State	Year a Terr.	Year a State	Years for which State Censuses are available (underlined year = an online database is available)	Notes
Minnesota	1849	1858	**MN Territory:** 1849 1853 1855 1857* **State:** 1865 1875 1885 1895 1905	* special federal
Mississippi	1798	1817	**Colony:** 1792** **MS Territory:** 1801 1805 1809 1810 1813 1815 1816 1817 **State:** 1818 1820* 1822 1823 1824 1825 1830* 1837 1840* 1841 1845 1850* 1853 1857 1866	* separate from federal ** Natchez District only
Missouri	1805	1821	**Colony:** 1752 1791 1797 **MO Territory:** 1817 1818 1819 **State:** 1844* 1845* 1846* 1852* 1856* 1864* 1868* 1876**	* 1-2 counties only ** 28 counties
Nebraska	1854	1867	**NE Territory:** 1854 1855 1856 1865 **State:** Lancaster & Cass Co Only: 1874 1875 1876 1877 1878 1881 1882 1883 1884 1885	
Nevada	1861	1864	**NV Territory:** 1861 1862 1863 **State:** 1864 1875	
New Jersey	—	1787	1855 1865 1875* 1885 1895 1905 1915	* a few townships only
New Mexico	1850	1912	**Colony:** 1600 1750 1790 **Territory:** 1885	
New York	—	1788	1825 1835 1845 1855 1865 1875 1892 1905 1915 1925	
North Carolina	—	1789	**Pre-statehood:** 1784 -1787.	
North Dakota	1861*	1889	**Dakota Territory:** 1885 **State:** 1905 (statistics only) 1915 1925	* Dakota Territory
Oklahoma	1890	1907	**OK Territory:** 1890* **State:** 1907 federal (Seminole Co. only)	* separate from federal
Oregon	1848	1859	**OR Provisional Territory:** 1842 1843 1845 1846 **OR Territory:** 1849 1853 1854 1855 1856 1857 1858 1859 **State:** 1865* 1875* 1885* 1895* 1905	* indexes for a few counties only
Rhode Island	—	1790	1865 1875 1885 1905 1915 1925 1935	
South Carolina	—	1788	1829 1839 1869 1875	
South Dakota	1861*	1889	**Dakota Territory:** 1885 **State:** 1895 1905 1915 1925 1935 1945	* Dakota Territory
Tennessee	1790*	1796	**Southwest Territory:** 1790 (Reconstructed) **State:** 1891 (partial)	
Utah	1850	1896	**UT Territory:** 1856 only.	
Washington	1853	1889	**WA Territory:** 1851* 1856 1857 1858 1859 1861 1871 1879 1881 1883 1885 1887 **State:** 1891 1892 1894 1898	* As part of Oregon Territory.
Wisconsin	1836	1848	**WI Territory:** 1836 1838 1842 1846 1847 **State:** 1855 1865 1875 1885 1895 1905	
Wyoming	1868	1890	**WY Territory:** 1869 1885*.	*1 county only

From *Census Substitutes & State Census Records* by William Dollarhide, published by Family Roots Publishing Co., Orting, WA

Table 3 – State Censuses Taken in Common Years. As a means of comparing state censuses taken by the 38 state census states, this table shows the common years for which many states conducted a state census. Many were done in years ending in "5." Census dates for some states are within a range, e.g., within 3 years of 1825, are indicated in the 1825 column.

	1815	1825	1835	1845	1855	1865	1875	1885	1895	1905	1915	1925	1935	1945
Alabama	•	•	•	•	•	•								
Arizona						•								
Arkansas	•	•	•		•	•								
California					•									
Colorado						•			•					
Connecticut											•			
Florida		•			•		•	•	•			•	•	•
Georgia		•	•	•	•		•							
Hawaii					•			•	•		•			
Illinois		•	•	•	•									
Indiana					•			•	•		•			
Iowa				•	•	•		•	•	•	•	•	•	
Kansas					•		•	•	•	•	•	•	•	
Louisiana			•											
Maine					•									
Maryland														
Massachusetts					•	•								
Michigan			•	•	•	•	•	•	•					
Minnesota					•	•	•	•	•	•	•			
Mississippi	•	•	•	•	•	•								
Missouri					•	•	•	•						
Nebraska						•	•	•	•					
Nevada						•	•							
New Jersey					•	•	•	•	•	•	•			
New Mexico									•					
New York		•	•	•	•	•	•		•	•	•	•		
No. Carolina														
No. Dakota								•		•	•	•		
Oklahoma									•	•				
Oregon				•	•	•	•	•	•	•				
Rhode Island							•	•	•	•	•	•	•	
So. Carolina		•	•			•	•							
So. Dakota								•	•	•	•	•	•	•
Tennessee								•						
Utah					•									
Washington						•		•	•	•				
Wisconsin			•		•	•	•	•	•	•				
Wyoming						•								
No. of States:	3	8	12	11	21	20	17	16	16	11	9	7	3	2

From *Census Substitutes & State Census Records* by William Dollarhide, published by Family Roots Publishing Co., Orting WA

Table 4 - Availability of Federal Censuses for each State

State	Year a Terr	Year a State	1790	1800	1810	1820	1830	1840	1850	1860	1870	1880	1890	1900	1910	1920	1930	1940	1950
Alabama	1817	1819				lost	•	•	•	•	•	•	lost	•	•	•	•	•	•
Alaska (to US 1867)	1912	1959					No census taken, District of Alaska, 1870, 1880, or 1890 →				--	--	--	•	•	•	•	•	•
Arizona	1863	1912									•	•	lost	•	•	•	•	•	•
Arkansas	1819	1836					lost	•	•	•	•	•	lost	•	•	•	•	•	•
California (to US 1848)	—	1850							•	•	•	•	lost	•	•	•	•	•	•
Colorado	1861	1876									•	•	lost	•	•	•	•	•	•
Connecticut	—	1788	•	•	•	•	•	•	•	•	•	•	lost	•	•	•	•	•	•
Delaware	—	1787	•	•	•	•	•	•	•	•	•	•	lost	•	•	•	•	•	•
Distr. of Columbia	1801	—		•	•	•	•	•	•	•	•	•	lost	•	•	•	•	•	•
Florida	1822	1845								•	•	•	lost	•	•	•	•	•	•
Georgia	—	1788	lost	lost	lost	•	•	•	•	•	•	•	lost	•	•	•	•	•	•
Hawaii (to US 1898)	1900	1959												•	•	•	•	•	•
Idaho	1863	1890									•	•	lost	•	•	•	•	•	•
Illinois	1809	1818				part	•	•	•	•	•	•	lost	•	•	•	•	•	•
Indiana	1800	1816			lost	lost	•	•	•	•	•	•	lost	•	•	•	•	•	•
Iowa (* part of WI Terr.)	1838	1846						•*	•	•	•	•	lost	•	•	•	•	•	•
Kansas	1854	1861								•	•	•	lost	•	•	•	•	•	•
Kentucky (*Distr. of VA)	—	1791	lost*	lost	•	•	•	•	•	•	•	•	lost	•	•	•	•	•	•
Louisiana (*OrleansTer)	1809	1812			•*	•	•	•	•	•	•	•	lost	•	•	•	•	•	•
Maine (*Distr. of MA)	—	1820	•*	•*	•*	•	•	•	•	•	•	•	lost	•	•	•	•	•	•
Maryland	—	1788	•	•	•	•	•	•	•	•	•	•	lost	•	•	•	•	•	•
Massachusetts	—	1788	•	•	•	•	•	•	•	•	•	•	lost	•	•	•	•	•	•
Michigan	1805	1837				lost	•	•	•	•	•	•	lost	•	•	•	•	•	•
Minnesota	1849	1858			MN Terr. had a special federal census in 1857 →				•	•	•	•	lost	•	•	•	•	•	•
Mississippi	1798	1817			lost	lost	•	•	•	•	•	•	lost	•	•	•	•	•	•
Missouri	1805	1821			lost	lost	•	•	•	•	•	•	lost	•	•	•	•	•	•
Montana	1864	1889									•	•	lost	•	•	•	•	•	•
Nebraska	1854	1867								•	•	•	lost	•	•	•	•	•	•
Nevada	1861	1864									•	•	lost	•	•	•	•	•	•
New Hampshire	—	1788	•	•	•	•	•	•	•	•	•	•	lost	•	•	•	•	•	•
New Jersey	—	1787	lost	lost	lost	lost	•	•	•	•	•	•	lost	•	•	•	•	•	•
New Mexico	1850	1912							•	•	•	•	lost	•	•	•	•	•	•
New York	—	1788	•	•	•	•	•	•	•	•	•	•	lost	•	•	•	•	•	•
North Carolina	—	1789	•	•	•	•	•	•	•	•	•	•	lost	•	•	•	•	•	•
North Dakota*	1861	1889			*1860, 1870, 1880 as part of Dakota Territory →					•	•	•	lost	•	•	•	•	•	•
Ohio (*NW Terr.)	1787	1803		* lost	lost	•	•	•	•	•	•	•	lost	•	•	•	•	•	•
Oklahoma	1890	1907		1 month prior to statehood in 1907, Oklahoma Territory had a special federal census									lost	•	•	•	•	•	•
Oregon	1848	1859							•	•	•	•	lost	•	•	•	•	•	•
Pennsylvania	—	1787	•	•	•	•	•	•	•	•	•	•	lost	•	•	•	•	•	•
Rhode Island	—	1790	•	•	•	•	•	•	•	•	•	•	lost	•	•	•	•	•	•
South Carolina	—	1788	•	•	•	•	•	•	•	•	•	•	lost	•	•	•	•	•	•
South Dakota*	1861	1889			*1860, 1870, 1880 as part of Dakota Territory →					•	•	•	lost	•	•	•	•	•	•
Tennessee (*SW Terr)	1790	1796	* tally	lost	lost	part	•	•	•	•	•	•	lost	•	•	•	•	•	•
Texas (to US 1845)	—	1845							•	•	•	•	lost	•	•	•	•	•	•
Utah	1850	1896							•	•	•	•	lost	•	•	•	•	•	•
Vermont	—	1791	•	•	•	•	•	•	•	•	•	•	lost	•	•	•	•	•	•
Virginia	—	1788	lost	lost	•	•	•	•	•	•	•	•	lost	•	•	•	•	•	•
Washington	1853	1889									•	•	lost	•	•	•	•	•	•
West Virginia	—	1863			Part of Virginia, 1790-1860						•	•	lost	•	•	•	•	•	•
Wisconsin	1836	1848						•	•	•	•	•	lost	•	•	•	•	•	•
Wyoming	1868	1890									•	•	lost	•	•	•	•	•	•

From *Census Substitutes & State Census Records* by William Dollarhide, published by Family Roots Publishing Co., Orting WA

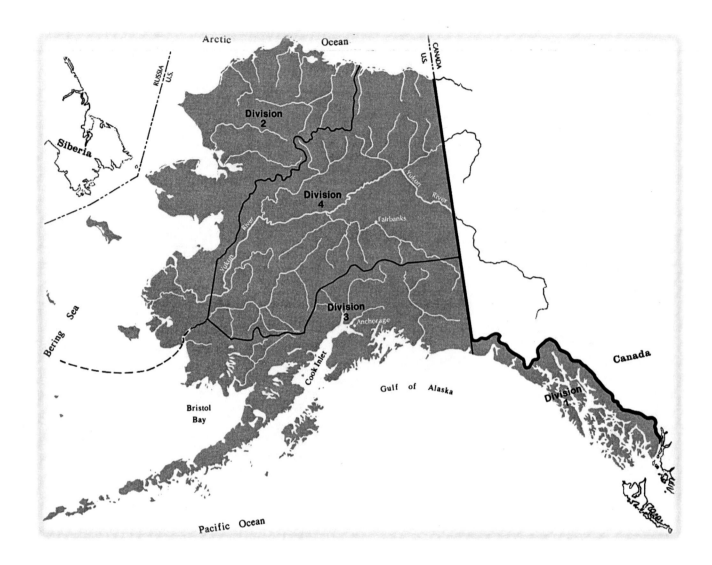

Alaska Census Jurisdictions, 1910-1940. A U.S. possession since 1867, no federal census was taken in the District of Alaska in 1870. The 1880 and 1890 were conducted with statistical summaries only. The first federal census taken with full name lists was in 1900. The District of Alaska was divided into two census divisions in 1900: 1) the Northern District was the Yukon drainage and north to the Arctic Ocean. 2) The Southern District was everything south, including Southeastern Alaska. The only state without counties, Alaska's census divisions were designated by the U.S. Census Bureau, as shown on the map above. The map shows the census division beginning in 1910. Alaska became a territory in 1912, and the same divisions were used again for the 1920, 1930, and 1940 federal censuses. The divisions were the same as the four Alaska court districts: **Juneau District 1** (Southeastern); **Nome District 2** (North, Barrow, et al); **Anchorage District 3** (Gulf of Alaska, Bristol Bay, Aleutians); and **Fairbanks District 4** (Yukon Basin). **Map Source:** Pages 25, *Map Guide to the U.S. Federal Censuses, 1790-1920,* by William Thorndale and William Dollarhide.

Alaska
Censuses & Substitute Name Lists

Historical Timeline for Alaska, 1725-1959

1725. Tsar Peter the Great of Russia commissioned a Danish sea captain, Vitus Bering, to explore the Northwest coast of North America. Bering is credited with the official discovery of Alaska, the first reliable information on the land, and the establishment of Russia's claim to Northwestern North America. Although the Russians visited Alaska frequently with seal and fishing expeditions, the first attempts at colonization did not begin until 1784.

1774-1791. Charles III of Spain, fearing Russian expansion, sent several expeditions north from Mexico to Alaska, intent on claiming the entire area for Spain. But their visits were fleeting, and no colonies or settlers were established at any of their stops. Few traces of the Spanish expeditions remain in Alaska except for a few placenames, such as Malaspina Glacier and Valdez.

1778. While searching for the elusive Northwest Passage, British explorer Captain James Cook explored the waterway (Cook Inlet) that downtown Anchorage now borders. Captain Cook's maps of North America proved for the first time that Asia and North America were separate continents. His maps became the standard for world navigation in the North Pacific for the next hundred years.

1784. Grigory Ivanovich Shelekhov, a Siberian fur merchant, established the first permanent Russian settlement at Three Saints Bay, on Kodiak Island. His wife, Natalya, was the first European woman in Russian America.

1795. The first Russian Orthodox Church was established at Kodiak.

1799. Alexander Baranov established the Russian post known today as Old Sitka; the trade charter from the Tsar granted exclusive trading rights to the new Russian America Company for a period of twenty years.

1821. The Russian trading charter was renewed and extended the area of the Russian claim to the 51st parallel. Meanwhile, the British-owned Hudson's Bay Company was trying to gain a foothold in the Alaska fur trade. In 1821 they made a deal with the Russian America Company, leasing land south of Cape Spenser. The British were a presence in Alaska for the next 30 years.

1823. President James Monroe issued the *Monroe Doctrine*, seeking to exclude European intervention in the New World. It was clearly aimed at Russia and Spain, countries still clamoring to gain more involvement in the Americas.

1824. Russia and the U.S. signed a treaty accepting 54 degrees 4 minutes as the southern boundary of Russian America. Also in 1824, the Russians began explorations of mainland Alaska that led to the discovery of the Nushagak, Kuskokwim, Yukon, and Koyokuk Rivers.

1857. The beginning of the end for the Russian America Company – the company was suffering from financial problems and the Tsar was threatening to revoke their charter. The company had been beaten by the Hudson's Bay Company in the fur trade. The British company had better and cheaper items to trade with the natives for furs. The Russian America company tried new business ventures, such as coal mining, whaling, and ice trading, but failed at all of them. The company lost wealth and power before the first gold discoveries in Alaska. Gold mining was destined to replace fur trading as Alaska's main economic activity.

1867. Apr. Financial struggles forced Russia to sell Russian America to the United States. Negotiated by U.S. Secretary of State William Seward, the purchase price for what is now Alaska was $7.2 million, or about 2 cents an acre. Alaska's value was not appreciated by most Americans, many calling it "Seward's Folly." The treaty was approved by Congress on 9 April 1867, and the United States flag was raised on 18 October 1867 (now called Alaska Day, a legal holiday). The rest of the U.S. may have forgotten William Seward, but in Alaska, Seward's Day (another legal holiday) is celebrated every year on the last Monday of March.

1867. Oct. While the United States and most of Europe recognized the Gregorian Calendar, Russia had still not made the change in 1867. The Gregorian Calendar had been in effect in British North America since the British officially changed from the Julian to Gregorian in 1752. On the day Alaska became part of the U.S., the change from the Julian Calendar to the Gregorian Calendar caused Alaska residents to have Friday, October 6, 1867 followed by Friday, October 18, 1867. They also had their shortest year. In 1867, Alaska's year began on March 25th and ended on December 31st.

1868-1959. In 1868 Congress designated the Russian America purchase as the **Department of Alaska**, under the command of U.S. Army Major General Jefferson C. Davis. Alaska was ruled by a military command until 1884, when it became the **District of Alaska.** As a district, Alaska had a civil government similar to that of the District of Columbia at the time. Alaska did not have a Governor or Legislature until 1912, when it became the **Territory of Alaska**. And, Alaska sent its first voting members to Congress after it became the **State of Alaska** in 1959.

1870. Although Alaska was a U.S. possession from 1867, a federal census for 1870 was not conducted there – except for a military tally of some of the inhabitants. Censuses exist for several local Alaskan jurisdictions from 1870 to 1880, many done as part of U.S. Government surveys of the seal and fishing industries. Any extant name lists are included in the bibliography that follows.

1872. Gold was discovered near Sitka and in British Columbia.

1880. Richard Harris and Joseph Juneau discovered gold on the Gastineau Channel, with the aid of Kowee, a local clan leader. Soon after, the town of Juneau was founded.

1880-1900. Federal Censuses came to Alaska in 1880, followed by 1890, but both were apparently statistical summaries only, since no name lists have been found. Without counties as the basic census units, the U.S. Census Bureau had to be creative in parceling out enumeration districts. The first full federal census was for 1900, which survives. In that year, the Census Bureau divided Alaska into Northern (Arctic), Southern (Kodiak Kuskokwim, Nushagak, Aleutian-Unalaska), and Southeastern (Sitka, Juneau) districts.

1896. Dawson City (Canada) was founded on the Yukon River at the mouth of the Klondike River. Gold was discovered on nearby Bonanza Creek, and Dawson City became the epicenter of the Klondike Gold Rush that followed.

1897-1900. Klondike Gold Rush. The main Gold Rush claims were on the Canadian length of the Yukon River. At the time, the easiest method of getting to Dawson City was a steamboat trip from the Bering Sea to the mouth of the Yukon River, across the length of Alaska, and into Yukon Territory. While the Yukon River was iced over, overland routes began at Skagway or Dyea over the Boundary Mountains by foot, and then a long sled-dog trek to the Yukon and into Dawson City.

1898. Skagway was the largest city in Alaska.
- work started on the White Pass and Yukon Railroad.
- Congress appropriated money for a telegraph from Seattle to Sitka.
- The Nome gold rush started.

1910-1940. In the 1910, 1920, 1930, and 1940 federal censuses, Alaska was enumerated using four judicial districts, indicated by the location of the district courthouse as Division 1 (Juneau), Division 2 (Nome), Division 3 (Anchorage), and Division 4 (Fairbanks). See the map on page 18.

1912. Alaska became a U.S. Territory. Alaska's population was at 29,500 Eskimos, Indians and Aleuts; 4,300 "Caucasian Alaskans" and 26,000 Cheechakos (newcomers).

1913. The first Alaska Territorial Legislature convened. The first law enacted granted women voting rights.

1914. Congress authorized the construction of the Alaska Railroad, clearing the way for the only railroad owned and operated by the U.S. government. The city of Anchorage was born as the main railroad construction campsite.

1924. After a Supreme Court ruling, Congress granted Native Americans U.S. citizenship and the right to vote. As a result of this act, the number of qualified voters in Alaska doubled over night.

1942. The Japanese invaded Alaska's Aleutian Islands. As part of the defense of the West Coast, the Alaska Highway was built in the amazingly short time of eight months and 12 days, linking Anchorage and Fairbanks with the rest of the nation. Anchorage entered the war years with a population of 7,724 and emerged with 43,314 residents.

1955. A Constitutional Convention opened at the University of Alaska.

1959. The Alaska statehood measure passed Congress in late 1958. President Eisenhower signed the statehood bill on January 3, 1959, and Alaska entered the Union as the 49th state.

Alaska Digital Archives

The Alaska Digital Archives is a consortium of Alaska's most important historical repositories, and presents a wealth of historical photographs, albums, oral histories, moving images, maps, documents, physical objects, and other materials. The images, documents, and historical artifacts are from libraries, museums, and archives throughout the state of Alaska. To search the combined collections for a name or place, see http://vilda.alaska.edu/index.php.

The source of all historical materials available online at Alaska's Digital Archives comes from the following contributing partners. From the main Digital Archives site, access one of these sources for more details about their collections:

Alaska State Library – Historical Collections. Established in 1900, the Alaska Historical Collections in the Alaska State Library in Juneau is a major repository for historical manuscripts, photographs, newspapers, maps, books, and other publications, along with significant personal collections.

UAA/APU Archives and Special Collections. The University of Alaska Anchorage / Alaska Pacific University Consortium Library collects, preserves, and makes available for research records that document Alaska's past and present.

University of Alaska Fairbanks. The University's Alaska and Polar Regions Collections contain one of the world's largest collections of historic photographs, manuscripts, moving images, rare books, maps, oral histories, and printed materials pertaining to Alaska and the Polar regions.

Anchorage Museum. The Anchorage Museum at the Rasmuson Center (Downtown Anchorage) is a world-class museum which seeks to preserve, exhibit and interpret the art and history of Alaska and the circumpolar North.

Alaska State Museum – Juneau. The Alaska State Museum was established in 1900, when an Act of Congress created the Historical Library and Museum for the District of Alaska. The purpose of the Museum was to collect, preserve and exhibit objects from the territory.

Alaska State Museum - Sheldon Jackson Museum – Sitka. Sheldon Jackson Museum was founded in 1888 to house an exceptional collection of Alaska Native ethnographic material, most of which had been gathered by Presbyterian missionary and General Agent of Education for Alaska, the Rev. Dr. Sheldon Jackson. In 1985, the state purchased the Sheldon Jackson Museum.

Seward Community Library Museum. The mission of the Seward Community Library Association is to support and enhance literacy in its community, provide educational opportunities through scholarships and other programs, support library functions, and encourage community-wide involvement in cultural activities for all ages.

University of Alaska Museum of the North. This Fairbanks museum's 1.4 million natural and cultural history specimens represent millions of years of biological diversity and more than 11,000 years of cultural traditions in the North. These collections provide the foundation for the Museum's research, education and exhibition programs.

Alaska State Library – Document Collection. Includes a selection of state and federal documents at the Juneau facility.

Community Curated Micro Collection Project. Selected materials from Alaskan communities and small Alaskan institutions.

Alaska Moving Image Preservation Association. The AMIPA was organized as a private non-profit corporation in 1991 in Anchorage. In 2004, AMIPA entered into a preservation partnership with the UAA/APU Consortium Library; moved into offices on the 3rd floor of the library; and during the spring of 2005 installed its 17,000-item collection into modern film and magnetic media vaults adjacent to the office space.

Sitka Tribe of Alaska & Sitka Historical Society. The Sitka Tribal Library provides rare tribal documents, recordings and historical photographs; the Sitka Historical Museum has exhibits, photographs, artifacts, and archives related to Sitka's Tlingit, Russian, and American history, and particularly, the period surrounding and following Alaska's 1867 transfer from Russia.

Alaska State Archives. The state archives in Juneau is the repository for original territorial and state government records that document Alaska's history. Its records date back to 1873, just after the U.S. purchased Alaska from Russia.

Igiugig. The village of Igiugig has joined with Alaska's Digital Archives to share glimpses of their past.

Petersburg Public Library. Photos of people, collections, and details.

Alaska Resources Library and Information Services (ARLIS). This collection of almost 600 photos was a joint project between ARLIS and University of Alaska Anchorage Archives staff, on behalf of Alaska Department of Fish and Game (ADF&G).

Bibliography
Alaska Censuses & Substitutes

Alaska's political and census jurisdictions date back to the time of the Klondike Gold Rush when all of Alaska became dominated politically by the mining industries. Fearing that more local government meant more local taxes, the Alaska mining industries yielded their political influence in the creation of Alaska Territory to their benefit. For example, the act of 1912 making Alaska a territory prohibited the creation of counties without the approval of Congress. None were ever created, and Alaska remains the only state in the Union without counties.

Today, Alaskan local municipalities function through boroughs, cities, and village governments; and various area-wide units such as judicial, election, school, recorder, and public utility districts. The eighteen Alaskan boroughs can cover large areas but are not analogous to counties, since they have the legislative powers of municipal governments, and they do not cover the entire state.

Alaska has never conducted a state-sponsored census, before or after statehood. The U.S. Census Bureau currently treats the Alaska boroughs as "county-equivalents" for the purpose of enumerating the population but had to create an "Unorganized Borough" for the areas not covered within an organized borough. Six of Alaska's cities have merged themselves into cities-boroughs.

With the diverse local governments, the census substitutes found in Alaska are not typical of other states with many countywide name lists. But the unique local Alaska governments still provide a good array of name lists that can be used by family historians to locate the name, date, and place of residence for an Alaskan ancestor. In addition to the federal censuses taken in Alaska, there were numerous valuable substitute name lists, which are listed below in chronological order:

◆ ◆ ◆ ◆ ◆

1732-1867. *History of Russian America* **[Printed Book],** by Obshchei Redakt and N. N. Bolkhovitinova, written mostly in Russian, published by a Russian Institute, 3 vols., Includes bibliographical references and indexes. Details the history of Russian exploration and colonization of Alaska, the formation and history of the Russian-American Company, and the sale of Alaska to the United States in 1867. Text in Russian, with some in English. Contents: vol. 1: The establishment of Russian America, 1732-1799; vol. 2: The Russian-American Company, 1799-1825; vol. 3. Russian America: from its height to its decline, 1825-1867. FHL book 979.8 H2i v. 1-3.

1784-1867. *History of the Russian Colonization in America* **[Printed Book],** written in Russian by A. D. Drudzo and R. V. Kinzhalov, published Moscow, 1994, 379 pages. FHL book 947 W2d.

1741-1867. *Russian America: A Biographical Dictionary* **[Printed Book],** by Richard A. Pierce, published by Limestone Press, Kingston, Ontario, 1990, 555 pages. Table of contents serves as an index. Biographies deal largely with Russian immigrants to Alaska, 1741-1867. Canada and other areas are also represented. FHL book 979.8 D3p.

1792-1970. *Census Alaska: Numbers of Inhabitants* **[Microfiche],** from the originals compiled by Alden M. Rollins, published by the University of Anchorage Library, Anchorage, AK, 1978. This study in the population growth of Alaska from the time of the Russian American Company gives names of divisions and subdivisions and lists numbers at each place but does not name residents. Filmed by the Arctic Environmental Information Data Center, 1986, 3 fiches, FHL fiche #6332869.

1816-1959. *Alaska, Vital Records* **[Online Database],** digitized and indexed at the FamilySearch.org website. Source: Alaska State Archives. Index and digital images of birth, marriage, death and divorce records from Alaska. There is a first name/surname search option for the entire database, or browse through the images organized by these locations: Aleutian Islands, Bethel Precinct, Chandalar Precinct, Chichagof Precinct, Circle Precinct, Douglas, Eagle, Fairbanks, Forty Mile Precinct, Fort Yukon, Gold Precinct, Goodnews Bay, Homer, Hoonah, Hyder, Juneau, Juneau and Douglas, Karluk, Kenai, Ketchikan, Killisnoo, Kodiak, Kodiak Precinct, Koyukuk Precinct, Manley Hot Springs, Noatak-Kobuk Precinct, Nome, Nulato Precinct, Palmer, Petersburg, Point Hope, Salchaket, Seldovia, Seward, Sitka, Tanana Precinct, Tenakee, Tok, Tolovana, Unga Prct, Wade Hampton Precinct, and Yakutat. The earliest records (ca1816) all seem to be from Sitka. This database has 63,254 records. See www.familysearch.org/search/collection/2216300.

1818-1863. *Alaska, Vital Records* **[Online Database],** digitized and indexed at the Ancestry.com website. This appears to be an updated version of the Alaska State Archives Vital Records database, but only Ancestry.com is listed as the source. This collection includes birth, marriage, and death records from Alaska that took place between the years 1818 and 1963. Birth records typically appear on pre-printed forms or registers. Depending on the individual form used you may find: Name of Child, Birth Date, Birthplace, Names, Ages, Birthplaces, and Residences of Parents. Death records typically appear on pre-printed forms or index cards. Depending on the individual form used you may find: Name of the Deceased, Date and Place of Death, Date and Place of Burial, Cause of Death, and Names of Parents. This database has 125,215 records: https://search.ancestry.com/search/db.aspx?dbid=61458.

1845-1917. *Alaska, Russian Orthodox Church Records* **[Digital Capture],** from the originals at the AK State Archives, Juneau, AK. Digitized by FamilySearch International, 2014. To access the digital images, see the online FHL catalog: www.familysearch.org/search/catalog/2442350.

1850-1950. *Biographies of Alaska-Yukon Pioneers* **[Printed Book],** compiled and edited by Ed Ferrell, Contains brief biographies which are arranged in alphabetical order by surname, published by Heritage Books, Bowie, MD, 1994-2000, 5 vols, FHL book 979.8 D3f v1-5.

1867-1889. See *Index to Baptisms, Marriages and Deaths in the Archives of the Russian Orthodox Greek Catholic Church in Alaska, 1867-1889* **[Microfilm & Digital Capture],** filmed by the Library of Congress, Washington, DC, 1 roll, FHL film #14450902. To access the digital images, see the online FHL catalog: www.familysearch.org/search/catalog/476503.

- See also, *Cook Inlet Deaths Copied from Greek Church Records, 1867-1912* **[Digital Capture],** by Father Kashevaroff, from a copy at the AK State Archives, Juneau, AK. Digitized by FamilySearch International, 2018. To access the digital images, see the online FHL catalog: www.familysearch.org/search/catalog/2827995.

1866-1998. *Guide to Alaska Newspapers on Microfilm* **[Printed Book & Online PDF File],** a 301-page guide with 994 entries with holdings information and chronologies for Alaskan newspaper locations, compiled by the Alaska State Library. Copies of the guide were distributed to libraries and museums throughout Alaska, to other state libraries and to the Library of Congress. Most of the microfilm listed in the publication is available for use through Interlibrary Loan. Contact your local library to initiate a request. Or, for a look at the Alaska Historical Collections of the Alaska State Library see
http://library.state.ak.us/hist/hist.html.
- The *Guide to Alaska Newspapers on Microfilm* is one of several downloadable PDF files at the site.

1867-1935. *Alaska People Index* **[Printed Book],** by Connie Bradbury, David A. Hales, and Nancy Lesh, published as No. 203, Alaska Historical Commission Studies in History, Anchorage, AK, 3 vols., FHL book 979.8 D32b.

1867-1972. *Chronology and Documentary Handbook of the State of Alaska* **[Printed Book],** by Ellen Lloyd Trover, state editor, William F. Swindler, series editor. Includes surname index. Contains a chronology of historical events in Alaska, a biographical dictionary, and outline of the state constitution and selected documents pertinent to Alaskan history. Published as No. 2: Chronologies and Documentary Handbooks of the States, by Oceana Publications, Inc., 1972, 112 pages. See FHL book 979.8 H2t.

1867-1987. *120 Years of Alaska Postmasters* **[Printed Book],** by Ora B. Dickerson. Contains an alphabetical list of post offices, showing name of each postmaster and date of appointment or change. Publ. C. J. Cammarata, Scotts, MI, 1989, 75 pages, FHL book 979.8 U2d.

1869-1993. See *Alaska Newspaper Archives, 1869-1993* **[Online Database],** digitized and indexed at the GenealogyBank.com website, historic newspapers are available for Anchorage, Fairbanks, Fort Adams, Healy, Juneau, Nome, and Sitka. See the search screen: www.genealogybank.com/gbnk/newspapers/explore/USA/Alaska.

✓ **1870-1880 NOTE.** No federal census for 1870 or 1880 was conducted in Alaska. But local censuses exist for several Alaskan jurisdictions from 1870 into the 1890s, many done as part of U.S. Government surveys of the seal and fishing industries.

1870-1907. *Alaska [Local] Census Records* **[Printed Index],** edited by Ronald Vern Jackson and Gary Ronald Teeples, published by Accelerated Indexing Systems, 1976, 68 pages. FHL book 979.8 X22j.

1870. *Enumeration of Sitka, Alaska Territory* **[Microfilm},** from the original published 1871, Government Printing Office. Some persons enumerated were Aleut Indians. Reproduced from Letter from the Secretary of War, in Relation to the Territory of Alaska (House of Representatives Executive Document no. 5, 42nd Congress, 1st Session), published in the Serial Set of U.S. government documents, v. 1470. Filmed by the Genealogical Society of Utah, 1976, 1 roll, FHL film #982047. To see if this microfilm was digitized yet, see the online FHL catalog:
www.familysearch.org/search/catalog/45962.

1870-1873. See *Resident Natives of St. Paul Island, Alaska, July 1, 1870: Taken From Philip Volkov's Lists, August 8, 1873* **[Microfilm],** from a photocopy of original published by the Government Printing Office, 1884. Reproduced from Report on the Seal islands of Alaska (House of Representatives Miscellaneous Documents, vol. 13 no 42, pt. 8), published in the Serial Set of U.S. government documents, vol. 2136. Filmed by the Genealogical Society of Utah, 1976, 1 roll, FHL film #982047. To see if this microfilm was digitized yet, see the online FHL catalog:
www.familysearch.org/search/catalog/205605.

1878. *Census of Unalaska and Aleutian Villages, Alaska, March 1878* **[Microfilm & Digital Capture],** from a typescript of a government document. Includes the Aleutian Islands and the mainland Aleut Indian villages of Belkovsky, Nicholayevsk and Protossoff (also known as Morzovoy). FHL book 979.84 X2p. Filmed by the Genealogical Society of Utah, 1973, 1 roll, FHL film #908376. To access the digital images, see the online FHL catalog:
www.familysearch.org/search/catalog/214871.

1880. *Census of Sitka, Alaska Territory: Taken April 25, 1880* **[Microfilm],** by Commander L. A. Beardslee, U.S.N., from the originals published by Government Printing Office, 1882. Reproduced from Reports of Captain L. A. Beardslee, U. S. Navy, relative to affairs in Alaska, (Senate Executive Document No. 71, 47th

Congress, 1st session), published in the Serial Set of U. S. Government documents, vol. 1989. Includes only those inhabitants who were U. S. citizens by birth or naturalization, not the Aleut Indians who became citizens by treaty. Filmed by the Genealogical Society of Utah, 1976, 1 roll, FHL film #982047. To see if this microfilm was digitized yet, see the online FHL catalog:
www.familysearch.org/search/catalog/47626.

1881-1889. *Roster of Ellsworth Post No. 2: Department of Washington and Alaska, Grand Army of the Republic, Organized January 11th, 1881* **[Photocopy],** from the original printed in 1889, Schwab Bros., Portland, OR, 9 pages, FHL book 979 M2r.

1883-1978. *Alaska, Wills and Probate Records* **[Online Database],** digitized and indexed at the Ancestry.com website. Source: Sitka Precinct, Probate Records, Sitka Probate Court. Index records for related person are brief, but for the deceased person each index record includes: Name, Probate date, Probate place, Inferred death year, Inferred death place, and Item description. A Table of Contents identifies the number of papers by category. This database has 376 records:
https://search.ancestry.com/search/db.aspx?dbid=9042.

1884-1974. *Who's Who in Alaska Politics: A Biographical Dictionary of Alaskan Political Personalities, 1884-1974* **[Printed Book],** compiled by Evangeline Atwood and Robert N. DeArmond, publ. Binford & Mort, Portland, OR, 1997, 109 pages, see FHL book 979.8 N2a.

1884-1960. *Alaska, District Court Criminal Docket* **[Digital Capture],** from the originals at the AK State Archives, Juneau, AK. Digitized by FamilySearch International, 2015. To access the digital images, see the online FHL catalog:
www.familysearch.org/search/catalog/2552252.

1884-1991. *Alaska Naturalization Records* **[Online Database],** digitized and indexed at FamilySearch.org. Source: National Archives microfilm series M1788. Includes Petitions, Declarations of Intentions, and Naturalization Certificates. This database has 4,822 records, see
www.familysearch.org/search/collection/2513103.

1885. *Approximate Census of Eskimos at the Cape Smythe Village: Weights and Measures of the Eskimos of Cape Smythe and Point Barrow* **[Microfilm],** from a photocopy of original published by the Government Printing Office, 1885. Reproduced from Report of the International Polar Expedition to Point Barrow, Alaska (House of Representatives Executive Document no. 44, 48th Congress, 2nd session), published in the Serial Set of U.S. government documents, vol. 2298. Filmed by the Genealogical Society of Utah, 1976, 1 roll, FHL film #982047. To see if this microfilm was digitized yet, see the online FHL catalog:
www.familysearch.org/search/catalog/38555.

1885-1887. See *The Alaskan, November 1885-March 1887: Newspaper Excerpts of Genealogical and Historical Interest* **[Printed Book],** edited by Elizabeth Richardson, publ. E.S. Richardson, Ward Cove, AK, 1997, 150 pages, FHL book 979.82/S1 B39r.
- See also, *Subject Index to the Alaskan, 1885-1907, a Sitka Newspaper* **[Printed Book & Digital Version],** by Robert DeArmond for the AK State Library, 1974, 107 pages, FHL book 979.82 B32. To access the digital version, see the online FHL catalog:
www.familysearch.org/search/catalog/480991.

1885-1960. *Guide to the Probate Records for Alaska* **[Printed Book],** includes a surname index giving the precinct in which the probate case was administered, and an index to probate case files, arranged by precinct, then alphabetically by surname. Published by the Alaska State Archives, Juneau, AK, 2000, 271 pages, FHL book 979.8 P22g.

1887. *Tsimshian History Project: First Census of the Original Pioneers, Family Groups* **[Microfiche],** from originals by the Tsimshian Studies Institute of Metlakatla, 7 pages. FHL book 979.8 A1 No. 6. Filmed by the Genealogical Society of Utah, 1991, 1 roll, FHL film #6093468.

1886-1986. *Have Gospel Tent Will Travel: The Methodist Church in Alaska Since 1886* **[Printed Book],** by Bea Shepard and Claudia Kelsey, published by Conference Council on Ministries, Alaska Missionary, 1986, 207 pages. See FHL book 979.8 K2s.

1889-1999. *Alaska's Kenai Peninsula Death Records and Cemetery Inscriptions* **[Printed Book],** compiled by Kenai Totem Tracers; Index compiled by Virginia Walters, publ. 1999, 53 pages, see FHL book 979.83 V3ktt.

1890-1895. See *Census of the Pribilof Islands of Alaska for 1890, 1891, 1892, 1893, 1894 and 1895; Births, Deaths, and Marriages on the Pribilof Islands, 1 June 1892 - 31 May 1893; 1 June 1893 - 31 May 1895* **[Microfilm],** from a photocopy of original published Government Printing Office, 1898, 60 pages. Reproduced from Seal and Salmon Fisheries and General Resources of Alaska, in Four Volumes. Volume 1 (House of Representatives Document no. 92, pt. 1, 55th Congress, 1st session), published in the Serial Set of U.S. government documents, vol. 3576. Filmed by the Genealogical Society of Utah, 1976, 1 roll, FHL film #982047. To see if this microfilm was digitized yet, see the online FHL catalog: www.familysearch.org/search/catalog/205654.

1890-1899. *Index to Baptisms, Marriages, and Deaths in the Archives of the Russian Orthodox Greek Catholic Church in Alaska* **[Microfilm & Digital Capture],** filmed by the Library of Congress, Washington, DC. 1st filming: FHL film #944197 (microfilm only). 2nd filming: FHL film #1445902 (with link to digital images). To access the digital images, see the online FHL catalog: www.familysearch.org/search/catalog/16240.

1890s. *Alaskana Catholica: A History of the Catholic Church in Alaska* **[Printed Book],** by Louis L. Renner, published by Arthur H. Clark, Spokane, WA, 2005, 702 pages. See FHL book 979.8 K2rl.

1894-1983. *Alaska's Kenai Peninsula Death Records and Cemetery Inscriptions* **[Printed Book],** compiled and published by Kenai Totem Tracers, Kenai, AK, 1983, 146 pages. Includes index. See FHL book 979.83 V3k.

1895-1967. *Who's Who in Alaska* **[Printed Book],** compiled by John I. Eichman, published by the author, 1967, 21 pages. See FHL book 979.8 D36e.

1897-1900. *The Alaska-Yukon Gold Book: A Roster of the Progressive Men and Women Who Were the Argonauts of the Klondike Gold Stampede* **[Printed Book]** compiled, edited and published by Sourdough Stampede Association, Inc., Seattle, WA 1930, 147 pages, FHL book 910.H2so. Also on microfilm, see FHL film #1598025.

1897-1900. *Gold Rush Women* **[Printed Book],** by Claire Rudolf Murphy and Jan G. Haigh. Includes index. Contains biographical sketches of women pioneers who went to Alaska and the Yukon Territory during the gold rush beginning in 1897. Published by Alaska Northwest Books, Portland, OR, 1997, 126 pages. See FHL book 979.8 D3m.

1896-1914. *How to Find Your Gold Rush Relative: Sources on the Klondike and Alaska Gold Rushes* **[Printed Booklet],** compiled by R. Bruce Parham. Contains a list of record sources and repositories compiled for the Alaska Gold Rush Centennial Task Force, locating information about pioneers and individuals who were in the north during the Klondike and Alaska gold rushes. Published by the National Archives, Pacific Alaska Region, Anchorage, AK, 1997, 10 pages, FHL book 979.8 A1 No. 12.

1897. *Alaska and the Klondike Gold Fields: Containing a Full Account of the Discovery of Gold and Practical Instructions for Fortune Seekers* **[Microfilm],** from an original book published by National Publishing, Philadelphia, 1897, 566 pages. Filmed by the Genealogical Society of Utah, 1978, 1 roll, FHL film #1036076. To see if this microfilm was digitized yet, see the online FHL catalog: www.familysearch.org/search/catalog/7360.

1897. *The Gold Fields of the Klondike: Fortune Seeker's Guide to the Yukon Region of Alaska and British America: The Story as told by Ladue Berry, Phiscator and Other Gold Finders* **[Printed Book],** from the original book published in 1897 by A.N. Marquis & Co., Chicago; reprinted 1994 by Clairedge, Whitehorse, Yukon Territory, Canada. See FHL book 979.8 H2Lj.

1897-1940. *Lost and Found in Alaska: An Index of 40,000 Names of People in Alaska, the Klondike, and the Cassiar before 1940, Extracted From Northern Writings and Other Sources, and Where to Find Them* **[Printed Book],** by Marydith W. Beeman, published by the author, Chugiak, Alaska, 1997, 2 vols., 657 & 341 pages, FHL book 979.8 D42b.

1897-1964. *Alaska, Land Records* **[Digital Capture],** from originals at the National Archives, Seattle, WA. Records of the Bureau of Land Management, including Alaska Townsite Tract Books, Cadastral Survey Records, Homestead Relinquishments and Patent Registers. Digitized by FamilySearch International, 2017. The file folder contents include references to records from Anchorage, Cordova, Grael Hyder, Juneau, and Valdez. To access the FHL digital folder contents, and the digital images of each folder, see the online FHL catalog: www.familysearch.org/search/catalog/2835353.

- See also, *Alaska, Land and Property Records: Townsite Deed Books and Cadastral Survey Records, 1909-1979* [Digital Capture], from the originals held by the National Archives, Seattle, WA. Digitized by FamilySearch International, 2017. The file folder contents include references to records from Wrangel, Craig, Hyder, Tenakee, Ketchikan, Charcoal Pt, Juneau, Cordova, and Skagway. To access the FHL digital folder contents, and the digital images of each folder, see the online FHL catalog: www.familysearch.org/search/catalog/2835348.

1898-1934. *Alaska, State Archive (Juneau), Military Service Discharge Records* [Digital Capture], digitized by FamilySearch International, 2018. Includes discharge service records for Alaska servicemen in the Armed Forces from 1898-1934 (includes World War I records, 1917-1918). To access the digital images, see the online FHL catalog: www.familysearch.org/search/catalog/3159282.

- See also, *Alaska, State Archives (Juneau), Military Service Discharge Records, 1898-1934* [Online Database], digitized and indexed at FamilySearch.org. This database has 2,176 records, see www.familysearch.org/search/collection/3159282.

1898-1998. *A Century of Service in Alaska, 1898-1998: The Story of The Salvation Army in the Last Frontier* [Printed Book], by Henry Gariepy, published by Salvation Army USA Western Territory, Rancho Palos Verdes, CA, 1998, 145 pages. See FHL book 979.8 K2g.

1900. *Alaska, 1900 Federal Census: Soundex and Population Schedules* [Microfilm & Digital Capture], from the original records at the National Archives, Washington, DC, filmed by the National Archives, ca1970, 20 rolls (Soundex and schedules), beginning with FHL film #1241828 (Population schedules, Northern District, EDs 1-2, 4-5). The 1900 was Alaska's first full census. Although there had been statistics gathered in 1880 and 1890, no name lists were found. To access the digital images, see the online FHL catalog: www.familysearch.org/search/catalog/646973.

1900-1910. *Juneau, Alaska Naturalization Records* [Microfilm & Digital Capture], from original records located at the Alaska Section, National Archives Branch, Seattle, WA.. Includes surname indexes. Contains declarations of intention, U.S. District Court, Juneau. Declarations are filed with the United States District Court located in the election district covering the towns or villages where the applicants reside. Each declaration or application lists the name of the town or place of residence. Filmed by the Genealogical Society of Utah, 1988, 1 roll, FHL film #1492069. To access the digital images, see the online FHL catalog: www.familysearch.org/search/catalog/696709.

1900-1936. *Index to Baptisms, Marriages and Deaths in the Archives of the Russian Orthodox Greek Catholic Church in Alaska* [Microfilm & Digital Capture], filmed by the Library of Congress, Washington, DC. 1st filming: FHL film #l944197 (microfilm only). 2nd filming: FHL film #1445902 (linked to digital images). To access the digital images of this index, see the online FHL catalog page for this title: www.familysearch.org/search/catalog/16305.

1900-1959. Alaska, Juneau, United States District Court Records [Digital Capture], from originals at the AK State Archives, Juneau, AK. Digitized by FamilySearch International, 2014. To access the digital images, see the online FHL catalog: www.familysearch.org/search/catalog/2442316.

1900-1980s. *Obituaries from Alaska Weekly and Alaska Sportsman* [Typescript & Digital Capture], an index to deaths, with several formats Author and publisher not given. See FHL book 979.8 V42o. To access the digital images, see the online FHL catalog: www.familysearch.org/search/catalog/1854477.

1900-1991. *Alaska, State Archives (Juneau), Naturalization Records* [Online Database], from the originals at the AK State Archives, Juneau, AK. Digitized by FamilySearch International, 2014. The digital folder contents refers to records from Juneau, Nome, Skagway, Petersburg, Wrangell, and Ketchikan. The records include Petitions, Evidence, and Declarations of Intention; Orders of the Court, Naturalization Certificates; and Alaskan Indian Citizenship records. To access the FHL digital folder contents, and the digital images of each folder, see the online FHL catalog: This database has 8,931 records, see **www.familysearch.org/search/collection/3235391**.

1901. *Alaska Bar Association and Sketch of Judiciary* **[Microfilm & Digital Version],** from the original directory book published in 1901 by Sanborn, Vail & Co., San Francisco, 79 pages. This little directory has an interesting history of Alaska from a point of law viewpoint – with the many instances of lawlessness and Indian problems with whites. There are many photographs of Alaska's earliest judges, and brief biographical sketches of members of the bar. Filmed by the Genealogical Society of Utah, 1975, 1 roll, FHL film #908987. To access a digital version of this book, see the online FHL catalog page:
www.familysearch.org/search/catalog/214315.

1901-1917 Skagway Naturalization Records. See *Indexes to Naturalization Records of the U.S. District Court for the District, Territory & State of Alaska (Third Division), 1903-1991…* **[Microfilm & Digital Capture],** from records located at the National Archives. Includes surname indexes. Contains declarations of intention, U.S. District Court, Skagway. Declarations are filed with the United States District Court located in the election district covering the towns or villages where the applicants reside. Each declaration or application will list the name of the town or place of residence. Filmed by the Genealogical Society of Utah, 1988, 22 rolls, beginning with FHL film #2155623. To access the digital images, see the online FHL catalog:
www.familysearch.org/search/catalog/737908.

1901-1929. *Alaska, Mixed Vital Records* **[Digital Capture],** from the film entitled, *Births, Marriages, Deaths, 2nd Division Council, Nome, 1901-1913,* Alaska State Archives. Another series, 1907-1929, was not digitized. To access the digital images, see the online FHL catalog:
www.familysearch.org/search/catalog/2866637.

1902-1918. *Alaska-Yukon Directories* **[Microfilm],** from original records located in various libraries and societies. Filmed by Research Publications, Inc., Woodbridge, CT. FHL has 3 rolls, as follows:
- 1902 1903, 1905-1906 (2) Alaska-Yukon directories, FHL film #2308320.
- 1907, 1908, 1909-1910, 1911-1912 Alaska-Yukon directories, FHL film #2308321.
- 1915-1916, 1917-1918 Alaska-Yukon directories, FHL film #2308322. The directory is online, see the 1915-1916 entry.

1903-1905. See *Census of St. Paul Island, June 30, 1904; Births and Deaths of St. Paul Island, June 1903-May 1904; School Report, St. Paul Island, Alaska, April 29, 1904; Census of St. George Island, Alaska, June 30, 1904; Census of St. Paul Island, June 30, 1905; Census of St. George Island, June 30, 1905* **[Microfilm],** from a photocopy of original published by Government Printing Office, 1906, 25 pages. Reproduced from Letter from the Secretary of Commerce and Labor, Transmitting Copies of Certain Reports Relating to the Alaskan Seal Fisheries (Senate Document no. 98, 59th Congress, 1st session), published in the Serial Set of U.S. government documents, vol. 4911. Filmed by the Genealogical Society of Utah, 1976, 1 roll, FHL film #982047. To see if this microfilm was digitized yet, see the online FHL catalog:
www.familysearch.org/search/catalog/205721.

1903-1907. See *An Index to the Early History of Alaska as Reported in the 1903-1907 Fairbanks Newspapers* **[Printed Book],** compiled and edited by David A. Hales, published by the University of Alaska, 1980, 28 pages. FHL book 979.86 B32e.

1903-1991. *Indexes to Naturalization Records of the U.S. District Court for the District, Territory, and State of Alaska (Third Division-Anchorage)* **[Microfilm & Digital Capture],** introduction compiled by R. Bruce Parham and Tom Witsey, edited by Diana Kodiak. Lists name, address, petition number, date and place filed, birth date and place, certificate number, and remarks. Arranged in alphabetical order by surname. Filmed by the National Archives, Pacific Alaska Region, Seattle, WA, 1997, 22 rolls, beginning with FHL film #2155623 (Index, 1903-1991, Aadland, Hannes Nikolaisen – Bading, Willy Oscar Emil). To access the digital images, see the online FHL catalog:
www.familysearch.org/search/catalog/737908.

1903-1999. *Fairbanks, Alaska Cemetery Records* **[Online Database],** indexed at the Ancestry.com website. Source: book, same title, by Andrea Robb. One of the largest cities in Alaska, Fairbanks is located about two hundred miles north of Anchorage along the Tanana River. This database is a collection of records from the Clay Street Cemetery (since 1903) and Birch Hill Cemetery (since 1938) located in the city. Each record provides the decedent's name, death date, and location of headstone within the cemetery. Most entries also provide the individual's birth date. This database has 5,673 records. See https://search.ancestry.com/search/db.aspx?dbid=4044.

1904 and 1906-1907 Alaska Prospector [Online Database], a fully searchable text version of the Valdez, Alaska newspaper from 1904 and 1906-1907 is online at the Ancestry.com site. See http://search.ancestry.com/search/db.aspx?dbid=6568.

1904-1910. *Index to the Seward Gateway, a Newspaper* [Printed Book], by Mike Stallings, published by the Seward Community Library, 1983, FHL book 979.83 B32s.

1904-1959. *Alaska, Coroner's Inquests* [Digital Capture], from records of the Commissioner's Court, Alaska Territory, now at the Alaska State Archives, Juneau, AK. Digitized by the Genealogical Society of Utah, 2015. For access to the digital images, see the online FHL catalog: www.familysearch.org/search/catalog/2579352.

1905. See *Nome Telephone Directory for 1905* [Printed Book], facsimile reprint of original published for the Alaska Telephone and Telegraph Co., Nome, Alaska, Alaska Printing Co., 1905, 28 pages. Reprint by Shorey Publications, Seattle, 1971. FHL book 979.8 A1 No 5.

1905. *Fairbanks Evening News* [Online Database], a fully searchable digitized newspaper for 1905 is online at the Ancestry.com site. See http://search.ancestry.com/search/db.aspx?dbid=6509.

1906-1908 & 1911-1916. *Fairbanks Daily Times* [Online Database], a fully searchable digitized version of the newspaper from 1906-1908 and 1911-1916 is online at the Ancestry.com site. See http://search.ancestry.com/search/db.aspx?dbid=6508.

1906-1946. *Alphabetical Index of Alien Arrivals at Eagle, Hyder, Ketchikan, Nome, and Skagway, Alaska, June 1906-August 1946* [Microfilm & Digital Capture], from the original compiled by Claire Prechtel-Kluskens, published by the National Archives, 1997. May include name, age, nationality or citizenship, names of persons accompanying the individual, and port of entry. Arranged in reverse alphabetical order with some cards out of order. Filmed by the National Archives, series M2016, 1 roll, FHL film #2138428. To access the digital images, see the online FHL catalog: www.familysearch.org/search/catalog/738055.

1906-1954. *Index, Alaskan Churchman: Volumes 1-50* [Printed Book]. The Alaskan Churchman magazine was published by the Fairbanks Episcopal Church. See FHL book 979.8 K25a v. 1-50.

1906-1956. *Alaska Alien Arrivals* [Online Database], digitized and indexed at the Ancestry.com website. Source: National Archives microfilm A3434, M2016, M2017 & M2018. This database is an index to aliens (and a few returning U.S. citizens) arriving at various Alaskan ports, between 1906 and 1956. In addition, the names found in the index are linked to actual images of the records (some are index cards to long form manifests, and some are actual passenger arrival lists). Ports of arrival found in this database include: Eagle, Hyder, Ketchikan, Nome, and Skagway (White Pass). This database has 17,113 records. See https://search.ancestry.com/search/db.aspx?dbid=1056.

1906-1963. *Alaska, Passenger and Crew Manifests* [Online Database], digitized and indexed at the Ancestry.com website. Source: Selected Passenger and Crew Lists and Manifests, National Archives. These passenger and crew lists from both ships and aircraft were recorded on a variety of forms that were then turned over to the Immigration and Naturalization Service. Details requested on the forms varied, but they typically include the name of the vessel and arrival date, ports of departure and arrival (as well as future destinations on a ship's itinerary), dates of departure and arrival, shipmaster, full name, age, gender, physical description, military rank (if any), occupation, birthplace, citizen of what country, and residence. For military transports, you may find the next of kin, relationships, and address listed as well. Later manifests may include visa or passport numbers. This database has 315,606 records. See https://search.ancestry.com/search/db.aspx?dbid=9118.

1907. *Alaska Prospector* [Online Database], a fully searchable text version of the Valdez, Alaska newspaper for 1907 is online at the Ancestry.com site: http://search.ancestry.com/search/db.aspx?dbid=6567.

1907-1937. *Record of Funeral* **[Printed Book],** no author or publisher noted. FHL catalog notes: "Indexes records of a funeral home that is probably in Alaska. Many of those listed are from Yukon Territory in Canada." Manuscript, 115 pages, FHL book 979.86 V32r.

1908-1914. *Name Authority File for Fairbanks, Alaska Newspapers, 1908-February 1914* **[Printed Book],** published by Alaska Historical Commission, 1986, 52 pages. Contains an index to 2,500 names of individuals whose names appeared in the Fairbanks newspapers from 1908 to Feb. 19, 1914. FHL book 979.86 B32n.

1909-1910. *R.L. Polk & Co.'s 1909-10 Alaska-Yukon Gazetteer and Business Directory* **[Online Database],** digitized with an OCR index at Ancestry.com. This database has 732 pages, see www.ancestry.com/search/collections/27588.

1910. *Alaska, 1910 Federal Census: Population Schedules* **[Microfilm & Digital Capture],** from the original records at the National Archives, Washington, DC, filmed by the National Archives, ca1970, 3 rolls, as follow:
- Population schedules: First and Third Judicial Districts (EDs 1-4), FHL film #1375761.
- Population schedules: Third Judicial District (EDs 5-18); Fourth Judicial District, FHL film #1375762.
- Population schedules: Second Judicial District, FHL film #1375763.

To access the digital images, see the online FHL catalog: www.familysearch.org/search/catalog/652069.

1910-1929. **Fairbanks, Juneau, and Skagway Naturalization Records:** see *Declaration of Intention, 1910-1929; Naturalization Records, 1910-1929; Indexes, 1901-1929* **[Microfilm & Digital Capture],** from the originals now at the Seattle branch, National Archives. The Fairbanks naturalization records do not show an exact date for applying for citizenship. The date is from the stamp on the declaration of intention (when it was received). The records do not show if a person was accepted as a citizen of the United States in all the applications. The records also do not always show if or when a file was closed. Filmed by the Genealogical Society of Utah, 1988-1989, 6 rolls, as follows:
- Juneau & Skagway indexes to declarations of intention, 1900-1929, 1901-1917, FHL film #1605522.
- Juneau & Skagway indexes to declarations of intention 1900-1929, 1901-1917 (another filming), FHL film #1445999.
- Juneau declaration of intention, 1910-1929, FHL film #1492132.
- Fairbanks naturalization records No. 1-290, FHL film #1492133.
- Fairbanks naturalization records No. 290-550, FHL film #1492134.
- Fairbanks naturalization records no. 551-699, 1922-1924, FHL film #1492135.

To access the digital images, see the online FHL catalog: www.familysearch.org/search/catalog/364078.

1910-1956. *Alaska, Indexes and Manifests of Alien Arrivals at Anchorage, Juneau, Skagway, and Tok Junction* **[Digital Capture],** from the microfilm of the originals of the Immigration and Naturalization Service. Digitized by FamilySearch International. To access the digital images, see the online FHL catalog: www.familysearch.org/search/catalog/3160739.

1912-1915. See *Iditarod, Alaska Naturalization Records, Oct. 1912-July 1915* **[Microfilm & Digital Capture],** from the records at the National Archives, Seattle, WA. Contains declarations of intention and facts for petition for naturalization, U.S. District court, Iditarod. Includes surname index. Filmed by the Genealogical Society of Utah, 1988, 1 roll, FHL film #1492069. For access to the digital images, see the online FHL catalog page for this title: www.familysearch.org/search/catalog/696602.

1913-1916. *Index to the Petersburg Newspapers* **[Printed Book],** by Celia Forrest, published by the Alaska Historical Commission, 1984, 133 pages. Indexes the Petersburg Progressive (January 8, 1913-1915) and the Petersburg Weekly Report (1915). FHL book 979.82 B32f.

1913-1916 Fairbanks Sunday Times **[Online Database],** a fully searchable digitized version of the newspaper from 1913-1916 is online at the Ancestry.com site. See http://search.ancestry.com/search/db.aspx?dbid=6652.

1913-1935. *Alaska, Marriage Records* **[Microfilm & Digital Capture],** from the originals at the Alaska State Archives, Juneau, AK. The microfilm series of 5 rolls begins with FHL film #105128588, digitized 2018 by

FamilySearch International, 2018. To access the digital images, see the online FHL catalog: www.familysearch.org/search/catalog/2866635.

1913-1958. *Alaska, Pioneer Home Discharge Index* **[Digital Capture],** from originals at the Alaska State Archives, digitized from microfilm at the Granite Mountain Record Vault. Alaska's Pioneer Homes are assisted living homes operated by the Alaska Department of Health and Social Services, Division of Pioneer Homes. These records were digitized in 2018 by FamilySearch International. For access to the digital images, see the online FHL catalog page for this title: www.familysearch.org/search/catalog/2842080.
- See also, *Alaska, Pioneer Home Discharge Index, 1913-1958* **[Online Database],** this database has 3,973 records, see www.familysearch.org/search/collection/2842080.

1913-1958. *Alaska, State Archives (Juneau), Coroner's Inquests* **[Online Database],** digitized and indexed at FamilySearch.org. Commissioner's Court coroner's inquest records for various counties in Alaska from the Alaska State Archives. Digital images of the originals are held by the Alaska State Archives in Juneau. This database has 86 records, see www.familysearch.org/search/collection/3161312.

1915-1916. See *R.L. Polk & Co.'s 1915-16 Alaska-Yukon Gazetteer and Business Directory* **[Online Database],** digitized with an OCR index at Ancestry.com. This database has 948 pages, see www.ancestry.com/search/collections/27627.

1915-1923. *Fairbanks, Alaska Naturalization Records, Sept. 1915-Dec. 1923…* **[Microfilm & Digital Capture],** from records at the National Archives, Seattle, WA. Includes surname index. Contains declarations of intention, U.S. District Court, Fairbanks. Filmed by the Genealogical Society of Utah, 1 roll, FHL film #1492069. To access the digital images, see the online FHL catalog: www.familysearch.org/search/catalog/696670.

1915-1963. *Cemetery Records, Anchorage [Fort Richardson, Knik, Nome, Palmer] Alaska* **[Typescript],** typed by the Genealogical Society of Utah, author/publisher not noted, 1963, 133 pages. See FHL book 979.8 V22va. See also Cemetery Records of Alaska [Typescript] by the Genealogical Society of Utah, source unknown, 1962. Contents: Anchorage (Evergreen Memorial), Fairbanks (Birch Hill), Fairbanks City Cemetery, and Fort Richardson Cemetery. See FHL book 979.8 V22v.

1915-1980. *Anchorage Times Obituaries Index* **[Microfiche],** edited by Tohsook P. Change and Alden M. Rollins, published by the University of Alaska, Anchorage, AK, 1981, 8 microfiche, FHL fiche #6331408, 4 fiche and #6331409, 4 fiche.

1915-1991. *The Cemetery Book: Index Compilation of People Interred in Cemeteries Located in the Municipality of Anchorage, Alaska* **[Printed Book],** compiled and published by members of the Anchorage Genealogical Society, 1988, 202 pages. See FHL book 979.83/A1 V32a.

1915-1991. *Angelus Memorial Park, Anchorage, Alaska* **[Printed Book],** by Terry M. Schiller. First part contains cemetery inscriptions arranged in alphabetical order by surname. Second part is arranged by cemetery or "garden" sections also containing inscriptions arranged in alphabetical order by surname. Published by the author, Anchorage, AK, 1991, 208 pages. See FHL book 979.83/A1 V3s.

1915-1991. *Cemetery Database Tracking Report for Anchorage Memorial Park Cemetery, 1915-1991* **[Printed Book],** compiled and published by the Department of Public Works, Municipality of Anchorage, 1991, 136 pages. See FHL book 979.83/A1 V3c.

1916-1929. *Alaska, Mixed Vital Records* **[Digital Capture],** from the originals at the AK State Archives, Juneau, AK. Digitized by FamilySearch International, 2018. Includes Commissioner, Docket, Marriages, Probate, Inquest, and other records. To access the digital images, see the online FHL catalog: www.familysearch.org/search/catalog/2866901.

1917-1918. *Alaska, World War I Selective Service System Draft Registration Cards* **[Microfilm & Digital Capture],** from the original records at the National Archives branch in East Point, Georgia. The draft cards are arranged alphabetically by Alaskan city draft boards, and then alphabetically by surname of the registrants. Filmed by the National Archives, series M1509. FHL has 4 rolls, as follows:
- Anchorage City, A – Z; Cordova City, A – Z; Douglas City, A – Z; Eagle City, A – Z; Fairbanks City, A - Kalzer, Albert Maximilian, FHL film #1473296.

- Fairbanks City, Kaakinen, Alexander – Z; Haines City, A – Z; Iditarod City, A – Z; Juneau City, A – Z; Ketchikan City, A – Z, FHL film #1473297.
- McCarthy City, A – Z; Nenana City, A – Z; Nome City, A – Z; Petersburg City, A – Z; Ruby City, A – Z; Seward City, A – Z; Sitka City, A – Z; St. Michael, A – Z; Skagway, A – Z, FHL film #1473298.
- Tanana City, A – Z; Valdez City, A – Z; Wrangell, A – Z, FHL film #1473299.

To access the digital images, see the online FHL catalog: www.familysearch.org/search/catalog/746965.
- See also, *1917-1918 World War I Draft Registration Cards, State of Alaska* [Online Database], indexed at the USGenWeb site for Alaska. See http://files.usgwarchives.net/ak/military/wwi/a-am.txt.

1918. *Alaska, Information Sheets on Deaths From the Wreck of the Steamer Princes Sophia to Vancouver* [Digital Capture], from the original record at the AK State Archives, Juneau, AK. From Wikipedia: "On 25 October 1918, Princess Sophia sank with the loss of all aboard after grounding on Vanderbilt Reef in Lynn Canal near Juneau, Territory of Alaska. All 364 persons on the ship died, making the wreck of Princess Sophia the worst maritime accident in the history of British Columbia and Alaska. The circumstances of the wreck were controversial, as some felt that all aboard could have been saved." To access the digital images, see the online FHL catalog: www.familysearch.org/search/catalog/3460669.

1920. *Alaska, 1920 Federal Census: Soundex and Population Schedules* [Microfilm & Digital Capture], from the original records at the National Archives, Washington, DC, filmed by the National Archives, ca1970, 3 rolls, beginning with FHL film #1822039 (Population Schedules: 1st Judicial District, 4th Judicial District, and Town of Fairbanks). To access the digital images, see the online FHL catalog: www.familysearch.org/search/catalog/558342.

1919-1924. See *Ruby, Alaska Naturalization Records, Aug. 1919-May 1924* [Microfilm & Digital Capture], from records of the National Archives, Seattle, WA. Includes surname index. Contains declarations of intention and facts for petition for naturalization, U.S. District Court, Ruby. Filmed by the Genealogical Society of Utah, 1988, 1 roll, FHL film #1492069. To access the digital images, see the online FHL catalog: www.familysearch.org/search/catalog/696591.

1920. *Location Index Guide to the 1920 Federal Census of Alaska* [Printed Book], compiled by Robert E. King. From page 3: "…a guide to the 1,020 different headings used on all census pages for the 1920 Federal Census of Alaska. These headings generally conform to the various towns and regions where the Federal census was taken in 1920. This guide is useful in finding where records of a certain place are located in the census. It will save time and also help researchers realize that the census records for some locations are split and appear in 2 or more different places in the census." Published 1992 by the Bureau of Land Management, Anchorage, AK, 15 pages. FHL book 919.8 X22.

1920-1921 Fairbanks Weekly News-Miner [Online Database], a fully searchable digitized version of the newspaper from 1920-1921 is online at the Ancestry.com site. See http://search.ancestry.com/search/db.aspx?dbid=6565.

1923-1924 (Polk's) Alaska-Yukon Gazetteer and Business Directory: Containing Alphabetical Lists of Business Firms and Private Citizens of the Towns of Anchorage, Cordova, Dawson, Fairbanks, Juneau, Ketchikan, Mayo, Nenana, Nome, Petersburg, Seward, Skagway, and Valdez [Microfilm], from the original, publ. Seattle, 1923, R. L. Polk, 667 pages. Filmed by the W.C. Cox Co., Tucson, AZ, 1974, 1 roll, FHL film #934824. To see if this microfilm was digitized yet, see the online FHL catalog: www.familysearch.org/search/catalog/37553.
- See also *R.L. Polk & Co.'s 1923-24 Alaska-Yukon Gazetteer and Business Directory* [Online Database], digitized with an OCR index at Ancestry.com. This database has 664 pages, see www.ancestry.com/search/collections/27587.

1930. *Alaska, 1930 Federal Census: Population Schedules* [Microfilm & Digital Capture], from the original records at the National Archives, Washington, DC, filmed by the National Archives, ca1990, 3 rolls, as follow:
- Population schedules: First and Third Judicial Districts (EDs 1-1 to 1-43), FHL film #2342360.
- Population schedules: Second Judicial District (EDs 2-1 to 3-19), FHL film #2342361.
- Population schedules: Third Judicial District, FHL film #2342362.

To access the digital images, see the online FHL catalog: www.familysearch.org/search/catalog/1037564.

1934-1935. See *Alaska Directory and Gazetteer* **[Printed Book],** published by the Alaska Directory Co., Seattle, WA, 1934, see FHL book 979.8 E4a. Also on microfilm, FHL film #1321397.

1935-1953. *United Spanish War Veterans Death Announcements* **[Digital Capture],** from the original death notices from the Department of Washington and Alaska, 1935-1953. The United Spanish War Veterans includes veterans of the Spanish-American War, April 1898 to February 1899, the Philippine-American War, February 1899 to July 1902 and the Chinese Relief Expedition, 1900 to 1901. Digitized by the Genealogical Society of Utah, 2009. To access the digital images, see the online FHL catalog page for this title: www.familysearch.org/search/catalog/1614940.

1936-1968. *Alaska, Probate Records* **[Digital Capture],** from the originals at the AK State Archives, Juneau, AK. These probate records were digitized from 112 rolls of microfilm. digitized by FamilySearch International, 2017. The roll numbers are not given, but the FHL digital folder number shows the contents of each roll/folder, organized by year, and source of the probate. To access the digital images, see the online FHL catalog: www.familysearch.org/search/catalog/2839322.

1940. *Alaska, 1940 Federal Census: Population Schedules* **[Digital Capture],** digitized images from the microfilm of original records held by the Bureau of the Census in the 1940s. After microfilming, Congress allowed the Census Bureau to destroy the originals to free up space for WWII-related files. Digitizing of the 1940 census schedules microfilm images was done for the National Archives and made public in 2012. To access the digital images, see the online FHL catalog: www.familysearch.org/search/catalog/2052180.

1940 Federal Census Finding Aids **[Online Database]** The National Archives prepared a special website online with a detailed description of the 1940 federal census. Included are links to Enumeration District Maps, Geographic Descriptions of Census Enumeration Districts, and a list of 1940 City Directories available at the National Archives. The finding aids are all linked to other National Archives sites. The National Archives website also has a link to 1940 Search Engines using Stephen P. Morse's "One-Step" system for finding a 1940 E.D. or street address conversion. See www.archives.gov/research/census/1940/general-info.html#questions.

1940-1947. *Alaska, World War II Draft Registration Cards* **[Digital Capture],** Digital images of originals held by the National Personnel Records Center, St. Louis, MO. Includes Draft registration cards of men who registered during World War II, with the exception of the fourth registration. Images courtesy of Ancestry. place To access the digital images, see the online FHL catalog: www.familysearch.org/search/catalog/2684865.
- See also, another Digital Capture of this database: www.familysearch.org/search/catalog/2695953.
- See also, *Alaska, World War II Draft Registration Cards, 1940-1945* **[Online Database],** digitized and indexed at FamilySearch.org. This database has 22,410 records, see www.familysearch.org/search/collection/2684865.

1940-1997. Daily Sitka Sentinel [Online Database], a fully searchable digitized version of the newspaper from 1940-1997 is online at the Ancestry.com site. See http://search.ancestry.com/search/db.aspx?dbid=51289.

1941-1977. *Fairbanks Daily News-Miner* **[Online Database],** a fully searchable text version of the newspaper from 1941-1977 is online at the Ancestry.com site. See http://search.ancestry.com/search/db.aspx?dbid=51413.

1942. *Alaska, World War II 4th Draft Registration Cards* **[Digital Capture],** digital images of originals held at the National Personnel Records Center, St. Louis, MO. These cards represent older men, ages 45 to 65 in April 1942, that were registered for the draft. They had birth dates between 28 Apr 1877 and 16 Feb 1892. Includes name of individual, date and place of birth, address, age, telephone number, employer's name and address, name and address of person who would know where the individual can be located, signature, and physical description. To access the digital images, see the online FHL catalog: www.familysearch.org/search/catalog/2425783.

1947. *Tewkesbury's Who's Who in Alaska and Alaska Business Index: Containing a Biographical Index of Personal Sketches of Prominent Living Alaskans, an Alphabetical Directory of Business Concerns and Their Owners, a Complete Directory . .* **[Printed Book],** by William and David Tewkesbury, published by Tewkesbury Pub., Juneau, AK, 1947, 320 pages, FHL book 979.8 D3.

1947. *Juneau and Douglas Telephone Directory, July 1947* **[Microfilm],** from the original published by Juneau & Douglas Telephone Co., 1947. Filmed by the Genealogical Society of Utah, 1988, 1 roll, FHL film #1320749. To see if this microfilm was digitized yet, see the online FHL catalog:
www.familysearch.org/search/catalog/127017.

1950. *Sitka Telephone Directory* **[Microfilm],** from the original by Sitka Telephone. Filmed by the Genealogical Society of Utah, 1988, 1 roll, FHL film #1320749. To see if this microfilm was digitized yet, see the online FHL catalog:
www.familysearch.org/search/catalog/127013.

1956-1857. See *Historical Editions, Fairbanks, Alaska's Fairbanks Daily News-Miner, 1956-1957* **[Microfilm],** from original newspapers from Nov. 7, 1956 to Jul. 18, 1957, with the annual "Golden Days" celebration commemorating the original gold strike. Filmed by the Genealogical Society of Utah, 2006, 1 roll, FHL film #2401867. To see if this microfilm was digitized yet, see the online FHL catalog:
www.familysearch.org/search/catalog/1202252.

1959-1986. See *Fairbanks (Alaska) City Directory: Contains Buyers' Guide and a Complete Classified Business Directory* **[Printed Book],** published by R. L. Polk and Co., Kansas City, MO. FHL has directories for 1959, 1965, 1970, 1975, 1979, 1984, and 1986. FHL book 979.86 E4p 1959-1986.

1960-1985. *Anchorage (Alaska) City Directory: Including Advertising Section and a Complete Classified List* **[Printed Book],** published by R. L. Polk and Co., Kansas City, MO. FHL has directories for 1960, 1965, 1969-70, 1980, 1985. FHL book 979.83/A1 E4p 1960-1985.

1962-1984. *Ketchikan (Alaska) City Directory: Contains Buyers' Guide and a Complete Classified Business Directory* **[Printed Book],** published by R. L. Polk and Co., Kansas City, MO. FHL has directories for 1962, 1966, 1970, 1976, 1980, and 1984. FHL book 979.82/K1 E4p 1962-1984.

1965-1981. *Juneau (Alaska) City Directory: Including Auke Bay and Douglas, Contains Buyers' Guide, and a Complete Classified Business Directory* **[Printed Book],** published by R. L. Polk and Co., Kansas City, MO. FHL has directories for 1965, 1971, 1975, and 1981. FHL book 979.82 E4p 1965-1981.

1966-1970. See *The Anchorage Times Obituaries Index: 1966-1970, A Supplement* **[Printed Booklet]** Fairbanks, Juneau, Kenai, Kodiak, Sitka, and Wasilla.
- See also *Anchorage Times Obituaries Index* **[Microfiche],** compiled by Tohsook P. Change and Alden M. Rollins. Filmed by the University of Alaska, 1978-1981, FHL fiche #6331408 & 6331409. Both publications included in the GenealogyBank newspaper obituaries index. See
www.genealogybank.com/gbnk/obituaries/explore/USA/Alaska/.

1986. *Alaska Vital Statistics and Marriages986* **[Microfilm],** from newspaper clippings compiled by Wasilla Alaska Family History Center volunteers. Newspaper clippings taken from *The Frontiersman* (Mat-Su Valley, which includes Palmer, Wasilla, Big Lake, Sutton, Talkeetna), The *Anchorage Daily News* (Anchorage, Eagle River, Mat-Su Valley), *The Copper River County Journal* (Copper River Basin, Glen Allen, Copper River areas).Filmed by the Genealogical Society of Utah, 1996, 1 roll, FHL film #1597674. To see if this microfilm was digitized yet, see the online FHL catalog:
www.familysearch.org/search/catalog/540168.

1986-1988. *Alaska Obituaries* **[Microfilm],** compiled by the Wasilla Alaska Family History Center. Contains obituaries from The Frontiersman (Mat-Su Valley, which includes Palmer, Wasilla, Big Lake, Sutton, Talkeetna); The Anchorage Daily News (Anchorage, Eagle River, & Mat-Su Valley); The Copper River County Journal (Copper River basin, Glen Allen, and Copper River area); and The Anchorage Times. Filmed by the Genealogical Society of Utah, 1990, 1 roll, FHL film #1597674. To see if this microfilm was digitized yet, see the online FHL catalog:
www.familysearch.org/search/catalog/540127.

1987 Index, Weddings, Engagements, Anniversaries, Divorces and Dissolutions for Alaska: Anchorage Daily News; Anchorage Times; Frontiersman; Copper River News; Bristol Bay News **[Microfilm],** from the typescript publ. Wasilla Alaska Family History Center, 1988. Filmed by the Genealogical Society of Utah, 1996, 1 roll, FHL film #1698259. To see if this microfilm was digitized yet, see the online FHL catalog:
www.familysearch.org/search/catalog/623014.

***1988 Alaska Vital Records; Anniversary, Weddings & Engagements* [Microfilm],** from newspaper clippings compiled by Wasilla Alaska Family History Center volunteers. Filmed by the Genealogical Society of Utah, 1996, 1 roll, FHL film #1698259. To see if this microfilm was digitized yet, see the online FHL catalog: www.familysearch.org/search/catalog/623023.

***1988 Alaska Vital Records, Births* [Microfilm],** from newspaper clippings compiled by Wasilla Alaska Family History Center volunteers. Filmed by the Genealogical Society of Utah, 1996, 1 roll, FHL film #1698259.

***1988 Alaska Vital Records: Marriages, Divorces, Marriage Licenses* [Microfilm],** from newspaper clippings compiled by Wasilla Alaska Family History Center volunteers. Filmed by the Genealogical Society of Utah, 1996, 1 roll, FHL film #1698259. To see if this microfilm was digitized yet, see the online FHL catalog: www.familysearch.org/search/catalog/623006.

***1989 Alaska Marriages, Engagements* [Microfilm],** from newspaper clippings compiled by Wasilla Alaska Family History Center volunteers. Newspaper clippings taken from *The Frontiersman* (Mat-Su Valley, which includes Palmer, Wasilla, Big Lake, Sutton, Talkeetna), *The Anchorage Daily News* (Anchorage, Eagle River, Mat-Su Valley), *The Copper River County Journal* (Copper River Basin, Glen Allen, Copper River areas).Filmed by the Genealogical Society of Utah, 1996, 1 roll, FHL film #1598338. To see if this microfilm was digitized yet, see the online FHL catalog: www.familysearch.org/search/catalog/747342.

***1989 Anchorage Daily News Obituaries* [Microfilm],** compiled by Wasilla Alaska Family History Center. Includes surname index. Filmed by the Genealogical Society of Utah, 1996, 1 roll, FHL film #1698259. To see if this microfilm was digitized yet, see the online FHL catalog: www.familysearch.org/search/catalog/623019.

***1990 Alaska Marriages, Engagements* [Microfilm],** from newspaper clippings compiled by Wasilla Alaska Family History Center volunteers. Newspaper clippings taken from The Frontiersman (Mat-Su Valley, which includes Palmer, Wasilla, Big Lake, Sutton, Talkeetna), The Anchorage Daily News (Anchorage, Eagle River, Mat-Su Valley), The Copper River County Journal (Copper River Basin, Glen Allen, Copper River areas). Filmed by the Genealogical Society of Utah, 1996, 1 roll, FHL film #1598338. To see if this microfilm was digitized yet, see the online FHL catalog: www.familysearch.org/search/catalog/747343.

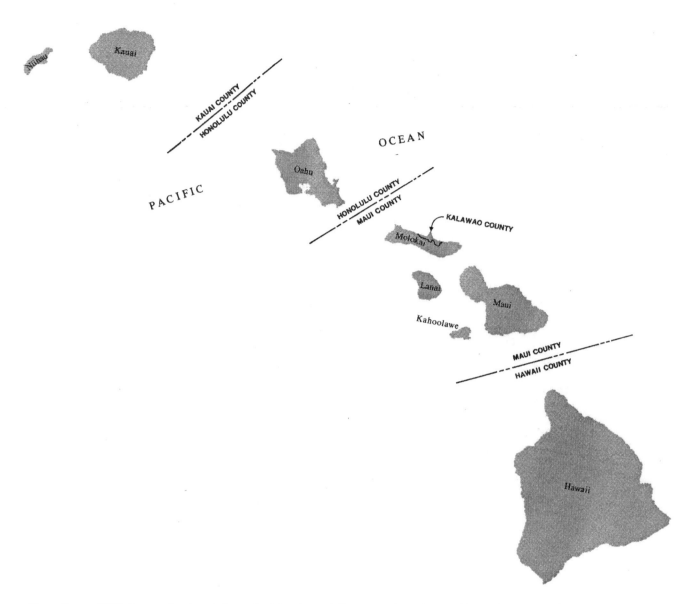

Hawaii • 1905-Current. The eight main islands and five counties of Hawaii are shown on the map above. There have been no county changes since they were first created in 1905. Kalawao County on Molokai Island is still a separate county, concurrent with the Kalaupapa National Historical Park. Kalaupapa is the site of the historical leper colony dating back to the 1860s. Northwest of Niihau lies a string of tiny islands belonging to Hawaii, such as Necker, French Frigate Shoals, and Laysan. The Hawaiian Archipelago comprises 132 islands, reefs, and shoals, stretching over 1,500 miles from the "Big Island" of Hawaii to Midway Atoll. Although Midway is part of the Hawaiian Archipelago, Midway was acquired by the U.S. in 1859 and has never been under Hawaii's jurisdiction. **Map source:** Page 92, *Map Guide to the U.S. Federal Censuses, 1790-1920*, by William Thorndale and William Dollarhide.

Hawaii
Censuses & Substitute Name Lists

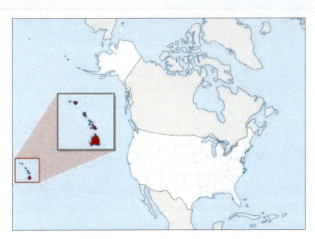

Historical Timeline for Hawaii, 1627-2019

1627. The first Europeans to see Hawaii were aboard Spanish sailing ships. In 1627, one Spanish ship captain described a volcanic eruption in his ship's log, the first known recorded mention of the islands. Polynesians had been there for centuries, with considerable evidence that the earliest Hawaiian villages date back to 300 A.D. and Polynesian folklore describes their earliest settlers coming by outrigger canoe from Tahiti.

1778. January. On an expedition to China, British explorer Captain James Cook discovered the present Hawaiian Islands. He named them the Sandwich Islands after the Earl of Sandwich, one of the expedition's sponsors. Cook went on to Alaska to look for the Northwest Passage and mapped the northern Pacific Ocean so accurately that his maps were used for 100 years. After his Alaska venture, Cook then returned to the Hawaiian Islands in November.

1779. February. Captain Cook visited the Big Island. After one of his ship's dinghies was stolen, Cook decided to kidnap the local chief to get it back – but his plan failed. He was killed in the resulting battle.

1785. The first French ships, the frigates *Boussole* and *Astrolabe* visited Hawaii, under the command of Jean-Francois de Galaup de La Pèrouse.

1789. The first American ship landed in Hawaii. Captain Robert Gray, in his ship *Columbia,* was on his first voyage to the south seas. Gray was hailed as the first American to circumnavigate the world, and for his discovery of the Columbia River in 1792, named after the same ship he had used to visit the Sandwich Islands.

1792-1794. British Captain George Vancouver, after meeting with American Captain Robert Gray, and learning the location of the newly discovered Columbia River, sent an expedition up the river for the first time. He also explored the present Oregon and Washington coasts, Puget Sound, and the largest island on the western side of North America, which he named after himself. Vancouver's visit with Gray also led to his decision to visit Hawaii. After his Pacific Northwest discoveries, Vancouver took his three ships to the Sandwich Islands. He became a personal advisor to Kamehameha, brought gifts, including the first longhorn cattle introduced to Hawaii. In 1794, Vancouver declared the Sandwich Islands as a protectorate of Great Britain.

1795-1854. Through conquest, King Kamehameha I (1795-1819) unified the Hawaiian Islands into one kingdom. A charismatic leader, he and his sons, Kamehameha II (1819-1824) and Kamehameha III (1825-1854) were to change the cultural rules of the Hawaiian society, such as eliminating Kapu restrictions on class distinctions and the subjugation of women. The kings also refused to worship the ancient Polynesian gods and told their people the gods were not real. For the first few generations under unified rule, the Hawaiian natives were open to just about any religious experience, and accepted the Europeans and Americans soon to arrive in great numbers to exploit the natural wonders and climate of the islands.

1821. Protestant missionaries arrived. Many Hawaiians were converted to Christianity. In just ten years, the New England Congregationalists dominated the religious scene, and were able to prevent other religious groups from getting a foothold in the Islands.

1831. Catholic missionaries from France that had arrived during the late 1820s were forced to leave or be imprisoned in 1831.

1835. The first sugar plantation was established on Kauai Island.

1839. Roman Catholics received religious freedom after the Islands were threatened by French warships. To avoid war, Kamehameha III paid reparations to France for the deportation of Catholic priests. But just a few years later, the French learned that their missionaries were still not being treated very well.

1840. Hawaii adopted its first constitution, moving from a Feudal Society to a Constitutional Monarchy. It gave religious freedom to subjects, and let commoners own their own land. The constitution called for all land to be divided between the King and Island Chiefs, which could then be sold to the people.

1842. A legislative and judiciary government was established within a limited monarchy. The first House of Representatives was called to order. Also in this year, the first class began at Punahou, the new private school. And Kamehameha III began sending emissaries to the U.S., France, and England to secure recognition of an independent and sovereign Hawaiian government. President John Tyler gave his assurance in writing in December 1842, and in March and April 1843. Hawaiian Independence was assured in writing by King Louis-Philippe of France and Queen Victoria of Great Britain.

1843. In February, two months before Queen Victoria's statement supporting the "Independence of the Sandwich Islands," Lord George Paulet moved the British warship HMS Carysfort into Honolulu Harbor and demanded that King Kamehameha III cede the islands to the British Crown. The King reluctantly agreed, but Paulet's action enraged the French and Americans, who were able to get Paulet's boss, Rear Admiral Richard Thomas to Honolulu in July. Thomas apologized for Paulet's actions, and restored Hawaiian sovereignty. In November 1843, at the Court of London, the British and French Governments formally recognized Hawaiian independence. John Tyler's 1843 statements of support were not formally confirmed by the U.S. Congress until 1849.

1849. In August, French forces arrived in Honolulu Harbor demanding full religious rights for their Catholic missionaries. They stormed the harbor fort, and did considerable damage, but left Honolulu a month later. King Kamehameha III basically ignored the French and their demands.

1852. January. The steamer *Constitution* from San Francisco arrived in Honolulu. One of the passengers on board was a Napa stockman, identified only as "Mr. Dollarhide." While in the Sandwich Islands, this ship made the first inter-island steamboat service: Honolulu to Lahaina and back (Jan 31 – Feb 2), then returned to San Francisco on Feb 18, 1852. (Rasmussen, *San Francisco Ship Passenger List,* Vol. III, p. 81).

1854-1863. The reign of King Kamehameha IV. He was a nephew and adopted son of Kamehameha I. He was not in favor of an American annexation of the Hawaiian Islands, being fonder of the British culture than that of the Americans.

1863-1872. King Kamehameha V reigned. He was an older brother of Kamehameha IV and was much respected by the Hawaiian people for his devotion to Hawaiian culture and restoration of Hawaiian medical practices. Mark Twain once spent four months in Hawaii in 1866 and wrote extensively about the islands. His comments about King Kamehameha V: "He was a wise sovereign; he had seen something of the world; he was educated and accomplished; he was popular, greatly respected, and even beloved."

1865. The first wave of immigrant plantation workers departed from Yokohama, Japan, for Hawaii.

1872-1874. After Kamehameha V died without an heir in 1872, his cousin was elected King Lunaliho in 1873, but died a year later.

1874-1891. During the reign of King Kalakua, many Hawaiian customs that had been discouraged by earlier rulers became popular again. He became known as the "Merry Monarch."

1875. King Kalakaua went to Washington, DC, visited President Ulysses S. Grant, and signed a treaty with the U.S. allowing Hawaiian sugar and rice to enter the U.S. tax-free.

1878. The first telephone was in operation, two years after Alexander Graham Bell's patent.

1879. The first steam locomotive pulled its first train load of sugarcane on Maui.

Hawaii • 39

1882. The Iolani Palace was first occupied by the Hawaiian royalty. Two monarchs governed from the Iolani Palace: King Kalakaua and Queen Liliuokalani. After the monarchy was overthrown in 1893, the building was used as the capitol building for the Provisional Government, Republic, Territory, and State of Hawaii until 1969. The palace was restored and opened to the public as a museum in 1978.

1883. Electricity arrived as five arc lamps were strung around Iolani Palace. This was also the year of the Great Chinatown Fire, with losses exceeding $1,455,000.

1887. To enhance trade with the United States, King Kalakaua allowed them exclusive use of Pearl Harbor as a naval base.

1890s. Several U.S. and European settlers had begun planting pineapples. Sugarcane planting also became an important industry. Thousands of workers were needed for these plantations; many came from China, Japan, and the Philippines.

1891. Upon the death of King Kalakaua, his sister, Lydia, became Hawaii's only ruling queen and last Hawaiian monarch. As Queen Liliuokalani, she tried to maintain Hawaii's culture against the large influx of Americans and Europeans who by now controlled the economy.

1893. In a trumped-up revolution, Queen Liliuokalani was overthrown, ending the 98-year-old Royal Kingdom of Hawaii. A Provisional Government was established, led by Sanford B. Dole and Lorrin A. Thurston. The Queen remained an important influence among the Hawaiian people. Over the next few years, she was successful in convincing President Grover Cleveland that an annexation of Hawaii to the United States should not take place without the approval of the Hawaiian native population. Those U.S. Congressmen in favor of Hawaii's annexation to the U.S. found that they would have to wait until Grover Cleveland was out of office.

1894. The revolution brought forth the American and British inspired Republic of Hawaii, sometimes called "Dole's Republic," which functioned as a recognized nation in the world community for four years. Sanford B. Dole served as the President of the republic.

1898. July. The Hawaiian Islands were annexed to the United States by means of a joint resolution of Congress, called the Newlands Resolution. Sanford B. Dole continued as the President of the Provisional Government until the Hawaiian Organic Act of 1900 established a permanent territorial government led by an appointed governor.

1900. Hawaii became a U.S. territory. Sanford B. Dole was appointed the Governor of Hawaii Territory by President William McKinley, taking office on 14 June 1900. The federal census of 1900 was taken with a census day of 1 June 1900, and Hawaii was included. Population: 154,001. No counties existed yet, and the census was divided into five districts for 1) Hawaii Island, 2) Kauai and Nihau Islands, 3) Maui, Kahoolawe, and Lanai Islands, 4) Molokai Island, and 5) Oahu Island.

1901. The Hawaiian Pineapple Company (now Dole) was established.

1905. Five counties were created by the territorial legislature: Hawaii, Honolulu, Kalawao, Kauai, and Maui. There have been no new counties or changes since 1905. Kalawao County comprised only the Kalaupapa Leper Colony on Molokai Island. The county stills exists, although the entire area is now a National Historical Park. The 90 (or so) permanent residents of Kalawao County do have one officer, a Sheriff, appointed by the U.S. National Park Service.

1910 Federal Census. Population of Hawaii Territory: 191,874

1920 Federal Census. Population of Hawaii Territory: 255,881.

1930 Federal Census. Population of Hawaii Territory: 368,300.

1934. President Roosevelt was the first U.S. President to visit Hawaii.

1940 Federal Census. Population of Hawaii Territory: 422,770.

1941. After the historic Japanese bombing of Pearl Harbor and Oahu on Dec. 7, 1941, the United States declared war on Japan and entered World War II.

1950 Federal Census. Population of Hawaii Territory: 499,794.

1959. August 21. Hawaii became the 50th state to enter the Union.

2020. The population of the State of Hawaii was estimated by the Census Bureau as 1.41 million people. Of that number, an estimated 953,200 people were living on the island of Oahu, also known as the City and County of Honolulu.

Bibliography
Hawaii Censuses & Substitutes

1795-1898. For centuries, the Hawaiian Islands were governed by tribal chiefs, generally one for each of the eight main islands. All of the island tribes were first unified under King Kamehameha I, beginning in 1795.
- Protestant missionaries had introduced a written Hawaiian language in the early 1820s which was enthusiastically adopted by the Hawaiians. By the 1850s, elementary education in Hawaii was universal, and virtually the entire native population was literate. And, it has always been a matter of pride in Hawaii to trace one's ancestry to early native beginnings.
- The Kingdom of Hawaii sponsored several census-like tabulations taken for all of the islands from as early as 1795, but only a few name lists, mostly school censuses from 1840, 1847, and 1866 have survived. The Kingdom of Hawaii also took three actual censuses for 1878, 1890, and 1896, the originals of which are located at the Archives of Hawaii. All are now digitized and indexed online.
- Vital records from all islands have been recorded in Hawaiian or English since the mid-1820s, at first by the missionaries that kept track of parish births and marriages, and by the 1840s, within the civil jurisdictions for each island. Included are births, christenings, marriages, divorces, deaths, burials, obituaries, and probates. They not only represent a large portion of the Hawaiian population, but they also provide genealogical links to parents and children, sometimes for several generations of families.
- Private land ownership has existed in Hawaii since the reign of Kamehameha III, who, at the urging of the growing number of Europeans in Hawaii, instituted a land system of Royal grants and private land sales in 1848. Most of the early land records still exist, and the records serve as good census substitutes, identifying a large portion of the head of households of Hawaii.

1898 – Current. In 1898, when Hawaii was annexed to the United States, virtually all of the arable land was in the hands of private ownership or held by the local governments. When Hawaii became a territory in 1900, it maintained ownership of its public land – the only U.S. territory to do that. Clear title to the land was another matter, however, and after decades of cross-claims and litigation, the Hawaiian royal lands confiscated by the Republic of Hawaii were finally returned to the Hawaiian state government. As a result, most island mountains, forests, and beaches are owned by the state of Hawaii today. In spite of the convoluted land claims from 1898 forward, tracing land sales in Hawaii is an important source for genealogical information, by using the records of the original land grants (patents) and subsequent land sales (deeds).
- The Territory/State of Hawaii has never taken a census separate from the federal censuses. However, in addition to the Federal Censuses taken in Hawaii, there are many valuable substitute name lists – listed below in chronological order.

♦ ♦ ♦ ♦ ♦

1790-1950. *Hawaii State Archives Digital Collections* **[Online Database],** these searchable databases are available online at the Hawaii State Archives website:
- Genealogy Index (separate search, see 1832-1929 Ulukau entry)
- Government Office Holders, 1843-1959
- Chinese Passenger Manifest Index, A-Z
- Japanese Passenger Manifests Index, A-L
- Japanese Passenger Manifests Index, M-Z
- Portuguese Passenger Manifests Index, A-Z
- Land Index - People Names, 1838-1918 (R-Z)
- Land Index - Place Names, 1838-1918 (A, E, U)
- Name Index, 1790-1950 (A-Bishop)

See the Digital Collections webpage:
https://digitalcollections.hawaii.gov/greenstone3/library.

1800s. *Hawaiian Genealogies in Bishop Museum* **[Microfilm],** from the original manuscripts at the Bernice P. Bishop Museum Archives in Honolulu, Hawaii. Text in Hawaiian and English. Most genealogies were recorded in the 1800s but deal with ancestors for hundreds of years before that time. Filmed by the Genealogical Society of Utah, 1978, 7 rolls,

beginning with FHL film #1025948 (genealogy of Hawaiian chiefs, Queen Liliuokalani, et al.). To locate contents, Hawaiian and European family names, types of collections, and film numbers, see the online FHL catalog page for this title:
www.familysearch.org/search/catalog/1177326.

1814-1917. See *Probate Records, 1845-1900; Indexes, 1814-1917* **[Microfilm & Digital Capture],** from the original records at the Archives of Hawaii, Honolulu, HI. Filmed by the Genealogical Society of Utah, 1977, 141 rolls, beginning with FHL #1010689 (First Circuit Court Index, et al). For a complete list of the roll numbers and contents of each roll, and access to the digital images of all 141 rolls, see the online FHL catalog page for this title:
www.familysearch.org/search/catalog/464929.

1822-1962. *Hawaii, Wills and Probate Records* **[Online Database],** digitized and indexed at the Ancestry.com website. Source: Ancestry extractions from Hawaii County, District, and Probate Courts. Probate records include Wills, Letters of Administration, Inventories, Distributions and Accounting, Bonds, and Guardianships. Each index record includes: Name, Probate place, Inferred death place, Case number, and Item description. A Table of Contents indicates the number images and category of papers. The document images have more information. This database has 9,572 records. See
https://search.ancestry.com/search/db.aspx?dbid=9046.

1826-1838. *Marriage Register of S. Whitney, Island of Oahu* **[Microfilm & Digital Capture],** from the originals at the Archives of Hawaii, Honolulu, HI. Text of the records are in Hawaiian. Filmed by the Genealogical Society of Utah, 1977, 1 roll, FHL film #1014414. To access the digital images, see the online FHL catalog:
www.familysearch.org/search/catalog/38048.

1826-1910. *Index to Archives of Hawaii Collection of Marriage Records* **[Microfilm & Digital Capture],** from an 814-page typescript. Includes the islands of Hawaii, 1832-1910; Maui, 1842-1910; Kauai, 1826-1910; and Molokai, 1850-1910. Filmed by the Genealogical Society of Utah, 1979, 1 roll, FHL film #1031145. To access the digital images, see the online FHL catalog:
www.familysearch.org/search/catalog/38175.

1826-1922. *Hawaii Marriages* **[Online Database],** digitized and indexed at the FamilySearch.org website, from microfilmed sources at the Family History Library in Salt Lake City, UT. This database has 101,136 records. See
www.familysearch.org/search/collection/1674811.

1826-1954. *Hawaii, Marriages* **[Online Database],** indexed at the FamilySearch.org website. This database has 52,852 records. Source: HI Dept of Health Services records on microfilm at the FHL in Salt Lake City. This database is an index to selected marriage records. Each index record includes: Name, Event type, Event date, Event place, Gender, Marital Status, Marriage place, Spouse's name, Spouse's gender, and FHL film number. See
www.familysearch.org/search/collection/2390844.

1826-2008. *Hawaii, USGenWeb Archives* **[Online Databases],** indexed at the usgwarchives.net site. Part of the USGenWeb Archives Project, The Aloha State's Table of Contents includes: Statewide Files, Island of Honolulu, Island of Kalawao (on Molokai Island), Island of Kauai (Kauai and Niihau); Island of Maui (Maui, Molokai, Lanai, & Kahoolawe); Hawaii USGenWeb (Honolulu; Hawaii (Hilo); Honolulu (Honolulu); Kalawao (Kalaupapa); Kauai (Lihue), and Maui (Wailuku). Typical county records include Bibles, Biographies, Cemeteries, Censuses, Court, Death, Deeds, Directories, Histories, Marriages, Military, Newspapers, Obituaries, Photos, Schools, Tax Lists, Wills, and more. See
www.usgwarchives.net/hi.

1832-1929. *Ulukau - Hawaiian Genealogy Indexes, Hawaii State Archives* **[Online Databases],** indexes prepared by the archives staff over the years include the book (volume), section, page, or case number of the original record. This information will allow a researcher to look up the original records available at the Hawaii State Archives and are briefly described as follows:

- **Marriage records, 1826-1929:** These records are primarily from individual ministers who conducted marriage ceremonies, or from marriage agents who issued licenses to marry. There are also a few early records from schoolteachers who were required by law to report marriages in their district. Records from 1896 onwards may provide more information such as parents of the bride/groom, race or ethnicity, age, and place of residence.
- **Divorce Records, 1848-1915:** These records often contain information about the couple, including the date of marriage, residence, circumstances, and reasons which led to filing for divorce, any children involved, and fees paid to the court.

- **Probate Records:** These cases document the disposition of a deceased person's estate according to the terms of the decedent's last will and testament.
- **Wills, 1852-1916:** These records contain names of heirs; appointed executor or guardians; and/or lists of possessions.
- **Naturalization Records, 1844-1894:** These records contain names of persons requesting to become naturalized citizens of the Kingdom of Hawaii, their country of origin, and their current place of residence.
- **Denizations, 1846-1898:** These records documented the admission of an alien to residence or conferred certain limited rights or privileges of citizenship. The records usually provide the applicant's name, nativity (birthplace), and place of residence.
- **Passports, 1845-1874:** These records were used for exit from and re-entry into Hawaii. They certified the identity and citizenship of the bearer. The records provide the applicant's name and signature, nativity (birthplace), place of residence, and name and destination of the vessel on which the applicant intended to travel. Records numbered from 959 may also contain the following information: age, business, height, hair, eyes, and complexion. Included are the following indexes:
  - Marriages - Hawaii Island - 1832-1910
  - Marriages - Hawaii Island - 1911-1929
  - Marriages - Kauai Island - 1826-1910
  - Marriages - Kauai Island - 1910-1929
  - Marriages - Maui Island - 1842-1910
  - Marriages - Maui Island - 1911-1929
  - Marriages - Molokai Island - 1850-1910
  - Marriages - Molokai Island - 1911-1929
  - Marriages - Oahu Island - 1832-1910 - Volume 1
  - Marriages - Oahu Island - 1832-1910 - Volume 2
  - Marriages - Oahu Island - 1911-1929 - Volume 1
  - Marriages - Oahu Island - 1911-1929 - Volume 2
  - Marriages - Niihau Island - 1849-1856
  - Divorces – 1st Circuit – 1851-1908
  - Divorces – 2nd Circuit – 1849-1917
  - Divorces – 3rd Circuit – 1854-1897
  - Divorces – 4th Circuit – 1890-1899
  - Divorces – 5th Circuit – 1852-1899
  - Deaths - Probates Index – 1st Circuit - 1845-1900
  - Deaths - Probates Index – 2nd Circuit - 849-1917
  - Deaths - Probates Index – 3rd Circuit - 1854-1897
  - Deaths - Probates Minute Books – 3rd and 4th Circuits – 1850-1915
  - Deaths - Probates Index – 4th Circuit - 1881-1904
  - Deaths - Probates Index – 5th Circuit – 1851-1914
  - Deaths - Probates Minute Books – 5th Circuit - 1853-1910
  - Deaths - Wills – 1st Circuit (no dates in index)
  - Deaths - Wills - Other Circuits (no dates in index)
  - Citizenship – Naturalization -18441894
  - Citizenship – Letters of Denizations – 1846-1898
  - Citizenship – Passports – 1874-1900

See **http://ulukau.org/gsdl2.7/cgi-bin/algene?a=d**.

1832-1866. *Marriage Register of Rev. O.P. Emerson, Island of Oahu* **[Microfilm & Digital Capture],** from the originals at the Archives of Hawaii, Honolulu, HI. Filmed by the Genealogical Society of Utah, 1977, 1 roll, FHL film #1014415. To access the digital images, see the online FHL catalog page for this title: **www.familysearch.org/search/catalog/38086**.

1836-1855. *Award Books* **[Microfilm & Digital Capture],** from the originals at the Department of Land and Natural Resources, Honolulu, HI. The Award Books are records of land transfers from the Hawaiian Royalty to private companies and individuals. Filmed by the Genealogical Society of Utah, 1964, 12 rolls, beginning with FHL film #571189 (Award book, vol. 1, 1836-1849). To access the digital images, see the online FHL catalog: **www.familysearch.org/search/catalog/153598**.

1836-1991. *Hawaii Newspaper Archives* **[Online Database],** digitized and indexed at the GenealogyBank.com website. One search screen for names and keywords for Hawaiian newspapers published in Honolulu, Pearl City, and Waialua. See **www.genealogybank.com/explore/newspapers/all/usa/hawaii**.

1837-1896. *Reports of Births, Marriages and Deaths, Island of Oahu* **[Microfilm & Digital Capture],** from the original records at the Archives of Hawaii, Honolulu, and the State Department of Health, Honolulu. Records in Hawaiian and English. Consists of lists submitted to the Hawaiian Government by local authorities. Filmed by the Hawaii State Archives, 1967, 5 rolls, beginning with FHL film #1014410 (Births and deaths, 1853-1858, includes Island of Hawaii). To access the digital images, see the online FHL catalog: **www.familysearch.org/search/catalog/221420**.

1838-1991. *Hawaii, Naturalization Records* **[Online Database],** digitized and indexed at FamilySearch.org. Records contain Petitions for Naturalization, Naturalization Certificates, Index to Overseas Military Petitions, Index to Petitions, and certificates of Identity. Each index record includes a name, event type, date and place of event, and birthplace of petitioner. The document image may have much more information. This database has 10,472 records, see **www.familysearch.org/search/collection/2842680**.

1840-1843. *Hawaii Territorial Census Records* **[Printed Index]**, edited by Ronald Vern Jackson, published by Accelerated Indexing Systems, North Salt Lake, UT, 1986. Mr. Jackson was famous for his creative titles – Hawaii did not become part of the U.S. until 1898 and a territory in 1900. The source of these "Territorial Census Records" are presumably from the original censuses of the Kingdom of Hawaii now located at the Archives of Hawaii and microfilmed by the Genealogical Society of Utah. Although there is a known 1840 list, there is no known 1843 list. See FHL book 996.9 X22j 1840.

1840-1866. *Census File* **[Microfilm & Digital Capture]**, from the originals at the HI State Archives, Honolulu, HI. Chronologically arranged. Earlier information consists largely of school census statistics, population census statistics, tax lists, and statistics of birth, marriage, and death. Later documents include the original schedules of the 1866 census of Hawaii. To access the digital images, see the online FHL catalog: www.familysearch.org/search/catalog/421789.

1841-1925. *Hawaii, Death Records and Death Registers* **[Online Database]**, indexed at FamilySearch.org. Each index record includes Name, Event type, Event date, Gender, Page number, and Record number. This database has 125,213 records, see www.familysearch.org/search/collection/2390846.

1841-1896. *Registers of Birth, Marriage and Death on the Island of Hawaii* **[Microfilm & Digital Capture]**, from the originals at the Dept of Health, Territory of Hawaii, and Daughters of the American Revolution, Honolulu. Filmed by the Genealogical Society of Utah, 1977-1979, 12 rolls, beginning with FHL film #1205690. To access the digital images, see the online FHL catalog: www.familysearch.org/search/catalog/221121.

1841-1896. *Births, Deaths and Marriages, City of Honolulu* **[Microfilm & Digital Capture]**, from the HI Kingdom Board of Health and DAR, Honolulu. Filmed by the Genealogical Society of Utah, 1978-1979, 15 rolls, beginning with FHL film #1205806. To access the digital images, see the online FHL catalog: www.familysearch.org/search/catalog/40113.

1843. *History of the Hawaiian or Sandwich Islands: Embracing Their Antiquities, Mythology, Legends, Discovery by Europeans Sixteenth Century, Rediscovery by Cook, With Their Civil, Religious and Political History, From the Earliest Traditionary Period to the Present Time* **[Printed Book]**, by James Jackson Jarves, microfilm of original book published by Tappan & Dennet, Boston, 1843. Filmed by the Genealogical Society of Utah, 1985, 1 roll, FHL film #1425609.

1843-1898. *Hawaii, Passenger Lists* **[Online Database]**, digitized and indexed at the Ancestry.com website. Original data: Collector General of Customs. Records of Passenger Arrivals and Departures. Series 82. Hawaii State Archives, Honolulu, Hawaii. This database consists of manifests (passenger lists) for ships arriving at and departing from ports in Hawaii between 1843 and 1898. Information contained in the index may include given and surname, age, gender, nationality or last place of residence, destination, ship name, and the date and place of departure or arrival. The names found in the index are linked to actual images of the manifests, digitized from originals at the Hawaii State Archives. This database has 165,630 records. See https://search.ancestry.com/search/db.aspx?dbid=61078.

1843-1909. *Hawaii, Births and Baptisms* **[Online Database]**, digitized and indexed at FamilySearch.org. Source: HI State Dept. of Health, Honolulu, HI. Some of the records are in Hawaiian and some are in English: www.familysearch.org/search/collection/2390841.

1844-1917. See *Deeds and Other Records (Hawaii), 1845-1900; Index, 1845-1917* **[Microfilm & Digital Capture]**, from the original records at the Dept. of Land and Natural Resources in Honolulu. Text in Hawaiian and English. Includes deeds for all islands. Filmed by the HI Dept. of Land and Natural Resources, 1975. FHL has 108 rolls, beginning with FHL film #986199 (Oahu grantee index, A-Z, 1845-1869). To access the digital images, see the online FHL catalog: www.familysearch.org/search/catalog/45575.

1845-1909. *Hawaii, Grantor and Grantee Index* **[Online Database]**. Digitized and indexed at the FamilySearch.org website. Index of Land Grantor and Grantee records for the islands of Oahu, Hawaii, Kauai, and Maui in the state of Hawaii from 1845-1909. Microfilm of the original records in the Department of Land and Natural Resources in Honolulu, Hawaii. The text in the collection is in English and Hawaiian. This database has 428,628 records, see www.familysearch.org/search/collection/2821304.

1846-1847. *Foreign Register* [Microfilm & Digital Capture], from a handwritten manuscript at the Department of Land and Natural Resources, Honolulu, HI. Filmed by the Genealogical Society of Utah, 1964, 1 roll, FHL film #571232. To access the digital images, see the online FHL catalog:
www.familysearch.org/search/catalog/153653.

1846-1848. *Native Registers* [Microfilm & Digital Capture], from a handwritten manuscript at the Department of Land and Natural Resources, Honolulu, HI. Filmed by the Genealogical Society of Utah, 1964, 4 rolls, beginning with FHL film #571220 (Native Register, 1846-1847). To access the digital images, see the online FHL catalog:
www.familysearch.org/search/catalog/153632.

1846-1862. *Foreign Testimony* [Microfilm & Digital Capture], from a handwritten manuscript at the Department of Land and Natural Resources, Honolulu, HI. Filmed by the Genealogical Society of Utah, 1964, 4 rolls, beginning with FHL film #571228 (Foreign Testimony, 1846-1854). To access the digital images, see the online FHL catalog:
www.familysearch.org/search/catalog/153646.

1846-1898. See *Hawaii, Denization Records, 1846-1849, 1883-1898* [Online Database], indexed at the Ancestry.com website. Source: Hawaii State Archives, Honolulu. This collection consists of denization records from the Kingdom of Hawaii. Applications were made by handwritten letter until 1895, when the use of pre-printed application forms began. Denization, a process used to grant status similar to permanent residency, gave rights to denizens that were normally only available to full citizens, such as the right to own land. Details available in these records vary, but may include the following: Name, Age, Occupation, Place of origin, Arrival date, and Record (residence) date, This database has 802 records. See
https://search.ancestry.com/search/db.aspx?dbid=61080.

1846-1900. *Marriage Certificates and Licenses, Island of Hawaii* [Microfilm & Digital Capture], filmed by the Genealogical Society of Utah, 1977, 2 rolls, FHL film #1014411 & #1014412. To access the digital images, see the online FHL catalog:
www.familysearch.org/search/catalog/38158.

1847-1896. *Census File* [Microfilm & Digital Capture], from the originals of the Hawaiian Bureau of Customs, now located at the Archives of Hawaii, Honolulu, HI. Chronologically arranged. Records consist of school census statistics, population census statistics, and summaries of births, marriages, and deaths. Includes four pages of the original 1866 census of Hawaii, and loose sheets of corrections to a later (apparently the 1896) census on Oahu. Filmed by the Genealogical Society of Utah, 1976, 1 roll, FHL film #1009896. To access the digital images, see the online FHL catalog:
www.familysearch.org/search/catalog/420332.

1847-1896. *Registers of Births, Marriages, and Deaths, Island of Oahu (Except Honolulu)* [Microfilm & Digital Capture], from the originals at the State Department of Health and the Daughters of the American Revolution Library, Honolulu. Indexes in English, records in Hawaiian. Marriage book 3 also known as Marriage register of Rev. A. Bishop. Book 1 contains births, Koolauloa District, 1867-1891; marriage certificates, Waianae, and Ewa Districts, 1847-1849; marriages, Ewa District, 1884-1891; deaths, Koolauloa District, 1865-1871; deaths, Ewa District, 1884-1894. Books 3, 5 and 6 contain marriages of Oahu, including Honolulu. Filmed by the Genealogical Society of Utah, 1978-1979, 11 rolls, beginning with FHL film #1205690 (Index to births in Book 1 by parents' names). To access the digital images, see the online FHL catalog:
www.familysearch.org/search/catalog/40025.

1847-1903. *Hawaii, Tax Assessment Lists* [Online Database], digitized and indexed at FamilySearch.org. The collection contains tax assessment rolls for the following districts: Honolulu, N. Kona, Niihau, Kauai, Waimae, Kaui, Koolau, Hanalei, Koloa, S. Kohala, N. Kohala, Koolauloa, Kau, Hilo, Puni, Lanai, Molokai, Maui, Waialua, Koolaupoko, Waianae, and Ewa. This database has 103,265 records, see
www.familysearch.org/search/collection/3159284.

1847-1961. *Patents Upon Confirmation of Land Commission* [Microfilm & Digital Capture], from the original records at the Hawaii Department of Land and Natural Resources, Honolulu. Filmed by the Genealogical Society of Utah, 1964, 19 rolls. The first roll in the series is a name index to all patent holders, FHL film #571219. (Index). To access the digital images, see the online FHL catalog:
www.familysearch.org/search/catalog/153605.

1848-1916. *Probate Records* [Microfilm & Digital Capture], from the original records at the Archives of Hawaii, Honolulu, HI. Filmed by the Genealogical

Society of Utah, 1976, 3 rolls, beginning with FHL film #1014408 (Probate packets 1-330). To access the digital images, see the online FHL catalog: www.familysearch.org/search/catalog/416869.

1849-1895. *Marriage Licenses and Certificates, Island of Oahu* **[Microfilm & Digital Capture],** from originals at the State Department of Health, and Archives of Hawaii, Honolulu, HI. Filmed by State of Hawaii (?) n.d., 3 rolls, beginning with FHL film # 1205811 (Index to Marriage Certificates, 1847-1849). To access the digital images, see the online FHL catalog: www.familysearch.org/search/catalog/38209.

1849-1900. *Hawaii, Passport Records* **[Online Database],** indexed at the Ancestry.com website. This collection consists of passport records from the former Kingdom of Hawaii. Details available in these records include: Name, Age, Occupation, Physical description, Country of origin, Residence in Hawaii, Departure date, Destination, and Signature. This database has 2,888 records. See
https://search.ancestry.com/search/db.aspx?dbid=61076.

1849-1915. *Divorce Records* **[Microfilm & Digital Capture],** from the originals at the Archives of Hawaii, Honolulu, HI. Filmed by the Genealogical Society of Utah, 1977, 34 rolls, beginning with FHL film #1015620 (First Circuit Court Divorce indexes, 1851-1908. To access the digital images, see the online FHL catalog: www.familysearch.org/search/catalog/382889.

1850-1853 *Sandwich Islands Marriages* **[Microfilm & Digital Capture],** from the originals at the Public Record Office, London. Part of the RG 33 *Series – Foreign Registers and Returns for British Nationals in Various Countries, 1809-1853,* filmed by the Public Record Office, London, 1992, 1 roll, FHL film #1818069. To access the digital images, see the FHL catalog:www.familysearch.org/search/catalog/621404.

1850s-1949. *Index to Births, Marriages, and Deaths in Hawaiian Newspapers Prior to 1950* **[Microfilm & Digital Capture],** from the originals at the Archives of Hawaii, Honolulu, HI. Filmed by the Genealogical Society of Utah, 1977, 6 rolls, beginning with FHL film #1002823 (Births, A-Z). For a complete list of roll numbers, roll contents, and access to the digital images of FHL film #1002823 (Births, A-Z)), see the FHL catalog: www.familysearch.org/search/catalog/433054.

1851-1896. *Reports of Births, Marriages, and Deaths, Island of Hawaii* **[Microfilm & Digital Capture],** from originals at the Archives of Hawaii. Filmed by the Archives of Hawaii, 1967, 6 rolls, beginning with FHL film #1014410. For a complete list of roll numbers, roll contents, and the digital images of the rolls, see the online FHL catalog page for this title: www.familysearch.org/search/catalog/221338.

1852-1953. *Hawaii, Births and Christenings* **[Online Database],** indexed at the FamilySearch.org website. Source: FamilySearch extractions from microfilm at the FHL in Salt Lake City. Name index to birth, baptism, and christening records from the state of Hawaii. This database has 145,570 records. Archived: https://web.archive.org/web/20200104185434/www.familysearch.org/search/collection/1674805.

1852-1853. *Marriage License Requests and Approvals for Remarriage, Island of Oahu* **[Microfilm & Digital Capture],** from the original at the Archives of Hawaii. Text in Hawaiian. Filmed by the Genealogical Society of Utah, 1977, 1 roll, FHL film #1014414. To access the digital images, see the online FHL catalog: www.familysearch.org/search/catalog/38363.

1852-1863. *Register of Marriages Performed on Oahu* **[Microfilm & Digital Capture],** from the originals at the Archives of Hawaii, Honolulu. Filmed by the Genealogical Society of Utah, 1978, 1 roll, FHL film #1014415. To access the digital images, see the online FHL catalog: www.familysearch.org/search/catalog/38250.

1852-1879. *Marriage Licenses of Foreigners, Island of Oahu* **[Microfilm & Digital Capture],** from the originals at the Archives of Hawaii, Honolulu. Records found in Folders 020 and 022, filmed with regular reports of marriages, island of Oahu. Filmed by the Genealogical Society of Utah, 1977, 1 roll, FHL film #1014414, items 22 & 24). To access the digital images, see the online FHL catalog: www.familysearch.org/search/catalog/221420.

1852-1933. *Hawaii Births and Christenings* **[Online Database],** digitized and indexed at the FamilySearch.org website, from various Family History Library sources. This database has 145,572 records. See
www.familysearch.org/search/collection/1674805.

1855-1877. *Register of Marriages Performed by Rev. Moses Kuaea, Island of Oahu* [Microfilm & Digital Capture], from the originals at the Archives of Hawaii, Honolulu. Also includes marriages performed on the island of Maui, 1870-1874, and Kauai, 1872. Filmed by Genealogical Society of Utah, 1977, 1 roll, FHL film #1014415. To access the digital images, see the online FHL catalog:
www.familysearch.org/search/catalog/38246.

1859-1879. *Registers of Births, Marriages, and Deaths on the Island of Molokai, Books 1-2* [Microfilm & Digital Capture], from the originals at the State Archives, Department of Health, and Daughters of the American Revolution Library, Honolulu. Index in English; registers in English or Hawaiian. Book 2 is also known as the marriage register of Rev. Samuel G. Dwight and is available in two manuscript copies. The first is not indexed; it covers the years 1857-1879 and is housed at the Hawaii State Archives under the call number M13. The second is indexed but covers only the years 1857-1877. It is housed at the State Department of Health. Both versions of Book 2 include a few marriages in the islands of Maui, Oahu, and Hawaii. Some index cards filed out of sequence; some Maui index cards filed in the Molokai indexes. Index to marriages on Oahu and Hawaii with: Index cards for other Oahu and Hawaii marriage registers. Filmed by the Genealogical Society of Utah, 1977-1979, 6 rolls, beginning with FHL film #1014413 (Archives of Hawaii collection: Marriage register of Rev. Samuel G. Dwight, 1859-1879). To access the digital images, see the online FHL catalog: www.familysearch.org/search/catalog/65951.

1859-1938. *Delayed Birth Registrations, ca.1859-1903; Index, ca.1859-ca.1938* [Microfilm & Digital Capture], from the originals at the State Department of Health, Honolulu, HI. Filmed by the Genealogical Society of Utah, 1978, 1979, 70 rolls, beginning with FHL film #1205949 (Index: Aarona – Hong Din). To access the digital images, see the online FHL catalog: www.familysearch.org/search/catalog/117211.

1861-1892. *Reports of Burials, Kingdom of Hawaii, 1861-1892* [Microfilm & Digital Capture], from the originals at the State Department of Health, Honolulu, HI. In Hawaiian or English. Arranged chronologically by island. Consists of lists burials covering primarily the years 1885-1886 and 1891-1892. Includes islands of Hawaii, Kauai, Maui, Molokai, and Oahu. Many districts missing. Filmed by the Genealogical Society of Utah, 1978, 1 roll, FHL film #295830. To access the digital images, see the online FHL catalog: www.familysearch.org/search/catalog/39069.

1862-1919. *Hawaii Deaths and Burials* [Online Database], digitized and indexed at the FamilySearch.org website, from microfilmed resources at the Family History Library in Salt Lake City, UT. This database has 105,070 records. See www.familysearch.org/search/collection/1674810.

1865-1896. *Kauai County, Hawaii Births, Marriages and Deaths* [Microfilm & Digital Capture], from microfilm now in storage at the Granite Mountain Vault. Digitized by the Genealogical Society of Utah, 2017, 8 rolls. For access to the digital images of each roll, see the online FHL catalog page for this title: www.familysearch.org/search/catalog/346485.

1866 Maui Census -Towns of Puaa, Kooka, Waianae, and Paunau [Online Database], indexed at the USGenWeb site for Maui Co HI. See http://www.usgwarchives.net/hi/maui.htm.

1874-1898. *Hawaii, Passport Records* [Online Database], digitized and indexed at FamilySearch.org. This project contains the following records from the state of Hawaii: Card Index to Chinese Passports, 1884-1898; Passports (cover pages) 1884-1888; Passport Registrations for Immigration, Madeira to Hawaii, 1878-1884. Card Index to Chinese Passports, 1884-1898: Author: Chinese Bureau. A card index to Chinese passports. Microfilm of original records at the Hawaii State Archives. This collection consists of two alphabetized card indexes. The first lists those people for whom the original passports were still on file at the time the index was compiled and includes some people whose passports were not on file. The second lists people whose passports were not on file and covers the years 1891-1893. It also includes a card file of unnamed Chinese arrivals in Hawaii, arranged by date, 1854-1898. Passports, 1884-1888: Author: Hawaii Minister of Foreign Affairs: Chinese passports granted by the Minister of Foreign Affairs in Hawaii. Microfilm of originals made at the Archives of Hawaii in Honolulu. Passport Registrations for Immigration from Madeira to Hawaii, 1878-1884: Author: Demello: Alphabetical extract to passport records with an index. The extracted records are in English, the actual documents are in Portuguese. Contains an alphabetized extract (several copies) an original passport registration documents and includes an index to passport records. This database has 6,575 records, see www.familysearch.org/search/collection/3021682.

1878-1896. *Census Records* **[Microfilm & Digital Capture],** from originals of the Hawaiian Bureau of Customs, now located at the Archives of Hawaii, Honolulu. Includes censuses taken in 1878, 1890, and 1896. Filmed by the Genealogical Society of Utah, 1977, 8 rolls, as follows:
- **1878** census records, island of Hawaii: town of Hilo, FHL film #1010681.
- **1878** census records, island of Hawaii: town of Hilo, FHL film #1010682.
- **1890** census records, island of Hawaii: town of Hilo, FHL film #1010683.
- **1890** census records, island of Hawaii: town of Hilo, FHL film #1010684.
- **1890** census records, island of Hawaii: town of Puna, No. Kohala, and So. Kohala; island of Kauai: town of Lihue, Koloa, and Waimea (Kekaha, Mana, Waimea, and Makaweli), FHL film #1010685.
- **1890** census records, island of Molokai and Maui; island of Oahu: towns of Koolaupoko and Waialua, FHL film #1010686.
- **1896** census records, island of Oahu: district of Kona (Honolulu), FHL film #1010687.
- **1896** census records, island of Oahu: district of Waikahalulu (Honolulu), FHL film #1010688.

To access the digital images for each roll, see the online FHL catalog page: **www.familysearch.org/search/catalog/421797**.

1879-1883. *Passport Registrations, Portuguese Immigrants from Azores to Sandwich Islands* **[Printed Book],** by Robert S. DeMello, Published by DeMello Publishing Co., 1982, 427 pages, FHL book 996.9 W2d.

1883 Marriage Register of H. Waterhouse, Island of Oahu **[Microfilm & Digital Capture],** from the original at the Archives of Hawaii, Honolulu, HI. Most marriages were performed in Honolulu. Filmed by the Genealogical Society of Utah, 1977, 1 roll, FHL film #1014415. To access the digital images, see the FHL catalog: **www.familysearch.org/search/catalog/38347**.

1884-1936 Honolulu and Hawaii Territory Directories **[Microfilm],** from the originals by various publishers in various libraries and societies, filmed by Research Publications, Woodbridge, CT, 1980-1995. FHL has 18 rolls, as follows:
- **1884** city directory of Honolulu and island of Oahu; **1890** directory, Kingdom of Hawaii; **1892** directory and hand-book of Honolulu and the Hawaiian Islands, FHL film #2156544.
- **1898** directory and hand-book of Honolulu and the Hawaiian Islands; **1900-1901** directory of Honolulu and Hawaii Territory, FHL film #2156545.
- **1902, 1903-1904** and **1904-1905** directories of Honolulu and the territory of Hawaii, FHL film #1759763.
- **1905-1906, 1907** and **1908** directories of Honolulu and the territory of Hawaii, FHL film #1759764.
- **1909** and **1910** directories of Honolulu and the territory of Hawaii, FHL film #1759765.
- **1911** and **1912** directories of Honolulu and the territory of Hawaii, FHL film #1759766.
- **1913** and **1914** directories of Honolulu and the territory of Hawaii, FHL film #1759767.
- **1915** and **1916** directories of Honolulu and the territory of Hawaii, FHL film #1759768.
- **1917** and **1918** directories of Honolulu and the territory of Hawaii, FHL film #1759769.
- **1919** and **1920** directories of Honolulu and the territory of Hawaii, FHL film #1759770.
- **1921** directory of Honolulu and the territory of Hawaii, FHL Film #1759771.
- **1922** directory of Honolulu and the territory of Hawaii, FHL film #1759772.
- **1923** and **1924** directories of Honolulu and the territory of Hawaii, FHL film #1759773.
- **1925** and **1926** directories of Honolulu and the territory of Hawaii, FHL film #1759774.
- **1927** and **1928-1929** directories of Honolulu and the territory of Hawaii, FHL film #1759775.
- **1929-1930** and **1930-1931** directories of and the territory of Hawaii, FHL film #1759776.
- **1931-1932** and **1932-1933** directories of the city and county of Honolulu and the territory of Hawaii, FHL film #1759777.
- **1934-1935** and **1935-1936** directories of the city and county of Honolulu and the territory of Hawaii, FHL film #1759778.

To access the digital images, see the online FHL catalog: **www.familysearch.org/search/catalog/620394**.

1884-1896. *Marriage Records for Districts on the Islands of Hawaii, Maui, Molokai, Oahu, and Kauai, 1884-1896* **[Microfilm & Digital Capture],** from the originals at the State Department of Health, Honolulu, HI. Filmed by the Genealogical Society of Utah, 1978, 2 rolls, beginning with FHL film #1205810 (Index), and FHL film #1026579 (Marriages, 1884-1896). To access the digital images, see the online FHL catalog: **www.familysearch.org/search/catalog/301068**.

1885. *An Account of the Polynesian Race, its Origin and Migrations and the Ancient History of the Hawaiian People to the Times of Kamehameha I* **[Printed Book],** by Abraham Fornander, original published 1885-1887, 3 vols. Reprint published by Tuttle, Rutland, VT, 1969, 3 vols. in 1 and includes *Index to The Polynesian Race,* by Abraham Fornander, FHL book 996 H6f.

1887-1888. *Register of Voters, Hawaiian Islands* **[Microfilm & Digital Capture],** from the original records of the Hawaiian Inspector of Elections, now located at the Archives of Hawaii in Honolulu. Contains a list of voters for all islands/districts. This register is a list of persons who took the oath to support the Constitution and laws and registered and voted at the General Election of September 12th, 1887 and (on the Island of Oahu) Special Election of August 22nd, 1888. Records arranged by island, district, ward, or precinct, then alphabetically by name of voter. Includes information on age, place of birth, occupation, local residence, registration date, entitled to vote for nobles (ownership of property required), and remarks. Includes Supplemental register of voters for nobles in wards of district of Honolulu. Filmed by Archives of Hawaii, 1992, 1 roll, FHL film #1674473. To access the digital images, see the online FHL catalog page: **www.familysearch.org/search/catalog/561458.**

1888-1898 Registers **[Microfilm & Digital Capture],** from the originals at the Hawaii State Archives, Honolulu, HI. Register of Hawaiian-born children of Chinese parents 1893-1898 (includes applications for certificates, nos. 1251-1300 1898). item 1 Register of naturalized Chinese leaving for China, 1893-1898 item 2 Permits for Chinese merchants and travelers, 1888-1894 item 3 Register of special residence bonds of merchants and travelers, 1892-1898 item 4 Register of special bonds, 1894-1895 item 5 Register of Chinese minors, with index, 1891-1898 item 6. Filmed by the Genealogical Society of Utah, 1977, 1 roll, FHL film #1017122. To access the digital images, see the FHL catalog: **www.familysearch.org/search/catalog/46999.**

1890. *Hawaiian Kingdom, 1890 Census* **[Microfilm],** from a photocopy made 1990 in Hawaii. Contains index (typescript) and extract (handwritten) of the 1890 Census of Hawaii for the districts or islands: Hilo – Kau – Hamakua – Kau, contains Bureau of Conveyance adoption index, 1847-1899; 3rd Circuit Court probate index, pkt. 1-522, approx. 1850-1899; 1910 census extract & index of Kau – Kohala (south & north) – Puna – Kauai – Maui – Molokai – Oahu. Includes index in each volume. Filmed by the Genealogical Society of Utah, 1990, 1 roll, FHL film #1675447. To see if this microfilm was digitized yet, see the online FHL catalog: **www.familysearch.org/search/catalog/637464.**

1890 Honolulu, Hawaii Directory **[Online Database],** indexed at the Ancestry.com website. See **www.ancestry.com/search/collections/5217.**

1893-1898. *Certifications of Hawaiian-born Children of Chinese Parentage* **[Microfilm & Digital Capture],** from the original records at the Hawaii State Archives, Honolulu, HI. Gives age of individual as of certification date; often gives parents names. The alphabetized entries include place of birth. Filmed by the Genealogical Society of Utah, 1977, 1 roll, FHL film #1002810. To access the digital images, see the online FHL catalog: **www.familysearch.org/search/catalog/432397.**

1894-1895. *Hawaii, Special Rights of Citizenship Certificates* **[Online Database],** indexed at the Ancestry.com website. Original data: Citizenship. Records, Hawaii State Archives, Honolulu. This collection consists of special rights of citizenship certificates stating that an individual "took active part or otherwise rendered substantial service in the formation of and has since supported the Provisional Government of Hawaii and is therefore entitled to all the privileges of Citizenship without thereby prejudicing his native Citizenship or allegiance." A record includes a Name, Age, Birthplace, and the Date and place a certificate was granted. This database has 4,462 records. See **https://search.ancestry.com/search/db.aspx?dbid=61095.**

1895-1898. *Hawaii, Certificates of Identification for Chinese Arrivals* **[Online Database],** indexed at the Ancestry.com website. Original data: Board of Immigration, Hawaii State Archives, Honolulu. This collection consists of certificates of identification for Chinese arrivals in the former Republic of Hawaii. Details available in these records include: Name, Date of arrival, Ship, Permit number, and Photograph locator. This database has 4,477 records. See **https://search.ancestry.com/search/db.aspx?dbid=61075.**

1896-1909. *See Birth Records, 1896; Indexes, 1896-1909* **[Microfilm & Digital Capture],** from the originals at the State Department of Health, Honolulu, HI. Filmed by the Genealogical Society of Utah, 1978, 11 rolls, beginning with FHL #1205691 (Child index, A-Keola (Hawaii Co), 1896-1909). To access the digital images, see the online FHL catalog: **www.familysearch.org/search/catalog/65681.**

1896-1909. See *Marriage Registers of the Island of Oahu, 1896-1903, and Indexes, 1896-1909* **[Microfilm & Digital Capture],** from the original records and index cards at the State Department of Health, Honolulu, HI. Filmed by the Genealogical Society of Utah, 1978, 3 rolls, beginning with FHL films #1205810 & 1205811 (Index 1896-1909) and FHL film #295835 (Marriage registers, 1896-1903). To access the digital images, see the online FHL catalog: www.familysearch.org/search/catalog/37799.

1896-1909. See *Death Registers (Hawaii), 1896-1903; Index, 1896-1909* **[Microfilm & Digital Capture],** from the originals at the State Department of Health, Honolulu, HI. Filmed by the Genealogical Society of Utah, 1978, 17 rolls, beginning with FHL film #1026581 (Index: A, Henry – Allen, Liliana). To access the digital images, see the online FHL catalog: www.familysearch.org/search/catalog/40184.

1898. *Directory and Handbook of the Kingdom of Hawaii* **[Digital Capture],** from *Husted's Directory of Honolulu and the Hawaiian Islands.* From the title page: "Giving the name, occupation, place of business, and residence of the adult population of the entire Hawaiian Kingdom. Also a complete classified business register of all the islands, with other valuable descriptive and statistical information." Digitized by the Genealogical Society of Utah, 2014. To access the digital images, see the online FHL catalog: www.familysearch.org/search/catalog/2382741.

1898-1902. *Death Certificates of Chinese Immigrants* **[Microfilm & Digital Capture],** from the originals at the Archives of Hawaii, Honolulu, HI. Filmed by the Genealogical Society of Utah, 1977, 1 roll, FHL film #1017113. To access the digital images, see the FHL catalog: www.familysearch.org/search/catalog/422254.

1900. *Hawaii Territory, 1900 Federal Census: Soundex and Population Schedules* **[Microfilm & Digital Capture],** from the original records held by the Bureau of the Census in the 1940s. After microfilming, Congress allowed the Census Bureau to destroy the originals to free up space for WWII-related files. Filmed on 35 rolls, beginning with FHL film #1242932 (Soundex, A000-A000 Rukichi), and FHL film #1241833 (Population schedules, Hawaii Island, EDs 39-56)). To access the digital images, see the FHL catalog: www.familysearch.org/search/catalog/649942.

1900. *Hawaii 1900: Pulama Na Kupuna (Cherish Our Ancestors)* **[Printed Index],** edited by Ronald Vern Jackson, et al, includes an index to the 1900 federal census for the Hawaiian Islands, published by Accelerated Indexing Systems, North Salt lake, UT, 1989, 692 pages, FHL book 996.9 X22h 1900.

1900. See *Honolulu County, Hawaii, Newspaper Obituaries, 1900 and Later* **[Microfilm & Digital Capture],** from index cards arranged alphabetically. Filmed by the Genealogical Society of Utah, 1990, 3 rolls, beginning with FHL film #1675446 (A-J). To access the digital images, see the online FHL catalog: www.familysearch.org/search/catalog/539193.

1900-1910. *Hawaii, Compiled Census Index* **[Online Database],** indexed at the Ancestry.com website. Source: Accelerated Indexing Systems, 1999. Contains the combined census indexes for the 1900 and 1910 federal censuses for Hawaii. This database has 373,089 records. See
https://search.ancestry.com/search/db.aspx?dbid=3543.

1900-1952. See *Index to Passengers, Not Including Filipinos, Arriving at Honolulu, Hawaii, ca. 1900-1952* **[Microfilm & Digital Capture],** from the original records at the National Archives, Washington, DC. Filmed by the National Archives, 1957, 37 rolls. After microfilming, the originals were destroyed. Includes a description of the records by Claire Prechtel-Kluskens (Genealogy Specialist at the National Archives). This collection contains 235,000 index cards of passengers (excluding Filipinos) arriving in Honolulu, Hawaii between 1900-1952. Each card lists a name, citizenship, age, sex, date and ship of arrival, book, page, and line number. Film rolls begin with FHL film #1878284 (Aada, Matsusuke – Ansuye, Tomoyashe). To access the digital images, see the online FHL catalog:
www.familysearch.org/search/catalog/1832398.
- See also, *Hawaii, Honolulu Index to Passengers, Not Including Filipinos, 1900-1952.* The online database has 255,042 images. See
www.familysearch.org/search/collection/1913398.

1900-1952. *Honolulu, Hawaii, Index to Passengers Arriving* **[Online Database],** digitized and indexed at the Ancestry.com website. Source: National Archives microfilm A3410 and A3407. This data collection contains index cards identifying passengers who arrived at Honolulu, Hawaii, by ship or air between 1900 and 1952. Besides American citizens, thousands of travelers from Japan, China, Australia, and other nations in Asia and the Pacific passed through the port at Honolulu. Each card lists the passenger's Name, Citizenship/Nationality, Age, Gender, Port of Arrival (Honolulu), Date of Arrival, Ship of Arrival, and the

Volume, page, and line number in the book where the passenger's arrival is recorded. This database has 393,367 records. See
https://search.ancestry.com/search/db.aspx?dbid=1914.

1900-1952. *Index to Filipino Passengers Arriving at Honolulu* **[Online Database],** digitized and indexed at the FamilySearch.org website. Source: National Archives microfilm A3407. This database is an indexed list of Filipino Passenger Arrivals from Index Cards. Each index record includes Name, Event type, Event date, Event place, Gender, Age, Birth year, and Birth Country. The digital image may have more information. This database has 127,926 records. See www.familysearch.org/search/collection/2141043.

1900-1953. *Hawaii, Honolulu Passenger Lists* **[Online Database],** digitized and indexed at the FamilySearch.org website. Source: National Archives microfilm A3422, *Passenger Lists of Vessels Arriving at Honolulu, Hawaii, 1900-1953*. Each index record includes: Name Event type, Event date, Event place, Gender, Age, Birth year, Birth country, and Ship name. The document image may have more information. This data base has 1,448,458 records. See
https://familysearch.org/search/collection/2141044.

1900-1959. *Honolulu, Hawaii, Passenger and Crew Lists* **[Online Database],** digitized and indexed at the Ancestry.com website. These databases derived from two microfilm publications of the National Archives, *Passenger Lists of Vessels Arriving or Departing Honolulu, Hawaii, 1900-1954*; and *Passenger and Crew Manifest of Airplanes Departing from Honolulu, Hawaii, 12/1957 – 9/1969*. Typical information recorded on a passenger list includes: 1) Name of passenger, 2) Age, 3) Gender, 4) Marital Status, 5) Occupation, 6) Citizenship (Nationality), 7) Last permanent residence, 8) Birthplace, 9) Ultimate destination, 10) Name and address of individual intended to join, 11) date of arrival, 12) Date and place of last arrival in U.S., and 13) Physical description. This database has 7,580,485 records. See
http://search.ancestry.com/search/db.aspx?dbid=1502.

1900-1976. *Index to Naturalizations [Petitions] in the U.S. District Court for the District of Hawaii* **[Microfilm & Digital Capture],** from the card index at the U.S. District Court in Honolulu. Each card may include name, dates of filing and admission, certificate number and date, and pertinent notes. The original petitions are located at the National Archives, Pacific Sierra Region, San Bruno, CA. Index cards filmed by the Genealogical Society of Utah, 1996, 23 rolls, beginning with FHL film #2048642 (Aakervik, Margit – Antonio, Jacinto). To access the digital images, see the online FHL catalog:
www.familysearch.org/search/catalog/782362.
- See also, *Overseas Military Naturalization Petitions Index (Hawaii)* **[Microfilm & Digital Capture],** from the original records at the National Archives, San Bruno, CA. There are no inclusive dates, but a check of the images shows many of the petitions are in the 1950s. This database is for aliens on active U.S. military duty in Hawaii applying for final naturalization status. A military version of the Petition for Naturalization form is included with the images, giving considerable information about the petitioner, name, home address, vitals, date, and place where first papers were files, and names and vitals of any children. To access the digital images, see the online FHL catalog:
www.familysearch.org/search/catalog/1906705.

1900-2000. *Obituary Clippings from the Honolulu Advertiser and the Honolulu Star-Bulletin* **[Microfilm & Digital Capture],** from the clippings collected and prepared by staff and volunteers of the Honolulu Hawaii West Stake Family History Center. Obituaries are for those who lived in Honolulu County and other parts of Hawaii. Most listings are after 1960. A few early (ca. 1900) obituaries are from the *Independent* newspaper. Filmed by the Genealogical Society of Utah, 1999, 33 rolls, beginning with FHL film #1145426 (A – Araki, 1900-1998). To access the digital images, see the online FHL catalog:
www.familysearch.org/search/catalog/826075.

1902 Medical Directory for the Island of Hawaii **[Online Database],** indexed at the USGenWeb site for Hawaii Co HI. Separate files for Hakalau, Hilo, Honokaa, Kailua, Kapoho, Kealakekua, Kolhala, Kkukaiau, Naalchu, Olaa, and Olaa Plantation. See www.usgwarchives.net/hi/hawaii.htm.

1902 Medical Directory for Honolulu **[Online Database],** indexed at the USGenWeb site for Honolulu. This same page has access to an array of databases for Honolulu, e.g., Cemeteries Index, Census Records, Court Records, Directories, Military Records/Civil War Rosters, Newspaper Articles Index, Obituaries Index, Queries, Photos of Tombstones, Birth Records, Death Records, and Marriage Records See **www.usgwarchives.net/hi/honolulu.htm.**

1902 Medical Directory for Kalawao **[Online Database],** indexed at the USGenWeb site for Kalawao. See
www.usgwarchives.net/hi/kalawao.htm.

1902 Medical Directory for Kauai **[Online Database],** indexed at the USGenWeb site for Kauai. See
www.usgwarchives.net/hi/kauai.htm.

1902 Medical Directory for Maui **[Online Database],** indexed at the USGenWeb site for Maui Co, HI. See
www.usgwarchives.net/hi/maui.htm.

1903-1944. *Hawaii, Index to Chinese Exclusion Case Files* **[Online Database],** digitized and indexed at the Ancestry.com website. This is an index to over 16,600 "Chinese Exclusion" case files, the immigration investigation files created by the Honolulu District Office of the Immigration and Naturalization Service, ca1903-1944. Most of the case files document the arrival into Hawaii from the U.S. mainland or foreign ports of Chinese aliens and the reentry of U.S. citizens of Chinese ancestry under the Chinese Exclusion Acts passed by Congress between 1882 and 1930 and repealed in 1943. There are also some case files relating to the arrival and departure of non-Chinese Asian immigrants and other foreign-born individuals. The index includes only names of individuals and case numbers. The case files are available from the National Archives, Pacific Region (San Francisco). Most case files include correspondence, lists of related cases, transcripts of interrogations, and witness statements. Some files include birth certificates, coaching documents, family history forms, and marriage licenses, and photographs of individuals and families. This database has 16,643 records. See
http://search.ancestry.com/search/db.aspx?dbid=3310.

1904-1909. *Birth Records* **[Microfilm & Digital Capture],** from the originals at the State Department of Health, Honolulu, HI. Filmed by the Genealogical Society of Utah, 1993-1994, 3 rolls, beginning with FHL film #1889021 (Births, Vol. 13-18, 1904-1909). To access the digital images, see the online FHL catalog: **www.familysearch.org/search/catalog/726369**.

1904-1909. *Death Records* **[Microfilm & Digital Capture],** from the originals at the State Department of Health, Honolulu, HI. Filmed by the Genealogical Society of Utah, 1994, 1 roll, FHL film #1955532. To access the digital images, see the online FHL catalog: **www.familysearch.org/search/catalog/727212**.

1904-1909. *Marriage Records, 1904-1909* **[Microfilm & Digital Capture],** from the originals at the State Department of Health, Honolulu, HI. Filmed by the Genealogical Society of Utah, 1994, 2 roll, FHL film #1955531 & #1955532. To access the digital images, see the online FHL catalog: **www.familysearch.org/search/catalog/727210**.

1909-1910. *Hawaii, Harbin File – Russian Immigrant Laborers Index A-Z* **[Online Database],** digitized and indexed at FamilySearch.org. from records at the HI State Archives, created in Harbin, Manchuria in 1909 listing the Russian recruits to work on the Hawaii plantations. This database has 2,314 records, see **www.familysearch.org/search/collection/**.

1909-1949. *Birth Records, 1909-1925; Index, 1909-1949* **[Microfilm & Digital Capture],** from the originals at the State Department of Health, Honolulu, HI. Index includes name of child and parents, birth date and place, sex, and register number, arranged by surname only. Filmed by the Genealogical Society of Utah, 1990-1991, 138 rolls, beginning with FHL film #1683770 (Index: Aala – Enade, 1909-1914). To access the digital images, see the online FHL catalog: **www.familysearch.org/search/catalog/482799**.

1904-1925. *Delayed Birth Records* **[Microfilm & Digital Capture],** from the originals at the State Department of Health, Honolulu, HI. Filmed by the Genealogical Society of Utah, 1993-1994, 132 rolls, beginning with FHL film #1853012 (Index: Aahn – Zukeran). To access the digital images, see the online FHL catalog: **www.familysearch.org/search/catalog/641908**.

1909-1949. See *Death Records, 1909-1925; Index, 1909-1949* **[Microfilm & Digital Capture],** from the originals at the State Department of Health, Honolulu, HI. Filmed by the Genealogical Society of Utah, 1991, 74 rolls, beginning with FHL film #1832091 (Index: Ah – Kagitani, 1909-1914). To access the digital images, see the online FHL catalog: **www.familysearch.org/search/catalog/483740**.

1909-1949. See *Marriage Records, 1909-1925; Indexes, 1909-1949* **[Microfilm & Digital Capture],** from the originals at the State Department of Health, Honolulu, HI. Filmed by the Genealogical Society of Utah, 1991, 61 rolls, beginning with FHL film #1851162 (Grooms: Aa – Kuba, Jul 1909-Jun 1914). To access the digital images, see the online FHL catalog: **www.familysearch.org/search/catalog/483723**.

1909-1989. *Hawaii, Board of Health, Marriage Record Indexes* **[Online Database],** digitized and indexed at FamilySearch.org. Includes marriage registers and indexes for various islands in Hawaii. Some cards are filed out of sequence. Each index record includes Name of groom, Name of bride, Age, Marriage date and place, and Name of parents. This database has 316,617 records, see www.familysearch.org/search/collection/3463469.

1910. *Hawaii Territory, 1910 Federal Census: Population Schedules* **[Microfilm & Digital Capture],** from the original records held by the Bureau of the Census in the 1940s. After microfilming, Congress allowed the Census Bureau to destroy the originals to free up space for WWII-related files. Filmed on 5 rolls, beginning with FHL film #1375764 (Hawaii County, EDs 101-134). To access the digital images, see the online FHL catalog: www.familysearch.org/search/catalog/648370.

1910. *Hawaii 1910 Census Index* **[Printed Index],** arranged alphabetically by surname., includes name, age, sex, birthplace, county of Hawaii, roll, and page number. Published by Heritage Quest, North Salt Lake, UT, 2002, 673 pages, FHL book 996.9 X22hc 1910.

1910. *Hawaii 1910: Pulama Na Kupuna (Cherish Our Ancestors)* **[Printed Index],** edited by Ronald Vern Jackson, et al, includes an index to the 1900 federal census for the Hawaiian Islands, published by Accelerated Indexing Systems, North Salt lake, UT, 1987, 756 pages, FHL book 996.9 X22h 1910.

1917-1918. *Hawaii, World War I Selective Service System Draft Registration Cards, 1917-1918* **[Microfilm & Digital Capture],** from the original records at the National Archives in East Point, Georgia. The draft cards are arranged by county or city draft board, and then alphabetically by surname of the registrants. Cards are in rough alphabetical order. Filmed by the National Archives, 1987-1988, 14 rolls, as follows:
- Hawaii County, No. 1, A - S, Kami, FHL film #1452025.
- Hawaii County, No. 1, T. Kamich – M. Seyas, FHL film #1452026.
- Hawaii County, No. 1, C. Shao – Z; Hawaii County, No. 2, A – M, FHL film #1452027.
- Hawaii County, No. 2, N - Z Honolulu City, No. 1, A – J, FHL film #1452095.
- Honolulu City, No. 1, K - P. Sampson, FHL film #1452096.
- Honolulu City, No. 1, P. San – Z; Honolulu City, No. 2, A – E. Contreras, FHL film #1452097.
- Honolulu City, No. 2, A. Cook - V. Kawai, FHL film #1452098.
- Honolulu City, No. 2, J. Kawaihea – N, FHL film #1452099.
- Honolulu City, No. 2, 0 - J. Texeira, FHL film #1452100.
- Honolulu City, No. 2, W. Thayer – Z; Kauai County, A - G, FHL film #1452101.
- Kauai County, H – V, FHL film #1452102; Kauai County, W – Z; Maui County, A – Z, Miazato, FHL film #1452103.
- Maui County, N. Michikawa – Z, FHL film #1452104.
- National Guard, A – Z, FHL film #1452105.

To access the digital images, see the online FHL catalog: www.familysearch.org/search/catalog/751145.

1917-1919. *Hawaii, World War I Service Records* **[Digital Capture],** from the original records at the HI State Archives, Honolulu, HI. The records consist of a card that contained information abstracted from the service record of each veteran. Clerks in the War Department and Navy Department executed the work. To access the digital images, see the online FHL catalog: www.familysearch.org/search/catalog/3019092.

1917-1979. *Directory of the City and County of Honolulu, Hawaii: Including Island of Oahu, Contains Buyers' Guide, and a Complete Classified Business Directory* **[Printed Books],** published by R. L. Polk and Company, Honolulu, HI. FHL has original directory books for 1917, 1938-39, 1940-41, 1959-60, 1961-62, 1977, 1978, and 1979. FHL book 996.93 E4p 1917-1979. Also on microfilm, FHL film #962960. To see if this microfilm was digitized yet, see the FHL catalog: www.familysearch.org/search/catalog/806292.

1920. *Hawaii Territory, Federal Census: Soundex and Population Schedules* **[Microfilm & Digital Capture],** from the original records held by the Bureau of the Census in the 1940s. After microfilming, Congress allowed the Census Bureau to destroy the originals to free up space for WWII-related files. Filmed on 31 rolls, beginning with FHL film #1831449 (Soundex, A000-A452)), and FHL film #1822033 (Population schedules, Hawaii County). To access the digital images, see the online FHL catalog: www.familysearch.org/search/catalog/558345.

1920-1966. *Affidavit on Application For Registration of Voters* **[Microfilm & Digital Capture],** from the original records of the city and county of Honolulu and stored at the Honolulu Hawaii West Stake Center. Records are arranged by the first two or more letters of the surname; therefore several different surnames may

appear to be misfiled. The first name is not considered in the arrangement. Name, address, age, birth date and place, and occupation are included in the information. Filmed by the Genealogical Society of Utah, 1990, 104 rolls, beginning with FHL film #1653824 (surnames Aa – Ahs). To access the digital images, see the online FHL catalog:
www.familysearch.org/search/catalog/559786.

1928-1947. *Hawaii, Hansen's Disease Records, Kalaupapa Vital Records Card Index* **[Online Database],** digitized and index at FamilySearch.org. This is the images of a card index of vital records for lepers received or admitted to the leper settlement at Molokai. (The modern name for leprosy is *Hansen's Disease*). The card index includes birth certificates of persons born at Kalaupapa, death records for the leper settlement at Molokai, and an index of marriages for patients with Hansen's Disease. This database has 7,850 records, see
www.familysearch.org/search/collection/3155903.

- See also, *Hawaii, Hansen's Disease Records, Kalaupapa Census Index, 1839-1970 [Online Database],* indexed at FamilySearch. Card index of census-type records for lepers received or admitted to the leper settlement at Molokai. Also called the Hansen's disease records. The card index includes patients admitted to the settlement; a census of individuals with Hansen's Disease; a census of names, index of parents of non-leprous children; an index of persons examined a Kakaako Hospital in Honolulu, and an index of persons apprehended and examined for leprosy. This database has 5,693 records, see
www.familysearch.org/search/collection/3155901.

1929. *Indices of Awards Made by the Board of Commissioners to Quiet Land Titles in the Hawaiian Islands* **[Microfilm & Digital Capture],** from the original published: Honolulu, Hawaii: Office of the Commissioner of Public Lands of the Territory of Hawaii, 1929. 1 vol. Filmed by the Genealogical Society of Utah, 1987, 1 roll, FHL film #1321397. To access the digital images, see the online FHL catalog:
www.familysearch.org/search/catalog/433790.

1930. *Hawaii (Territory), 1930 Federal Census: Population Schedules* **[Microfilm & Digital Capture],** from the original records held by the Bureau of the Census in the 1940s. After microfilming, Congress allowed the Census Bureau to destroy the originals to free up space for WWII-related files. Filmed on 7 rolls, beginning with FHL film #2342365 (Hawaii County, EDs 1-34). To access the digital images, see the online FHL catalog:
www.familysearch.org/search/catalog/1037576.

1938-1946 *Hawaii World War II Army Enlistment Records* **[Online Database].** indexed at the USGenWeb site for Hawaii. See
www.usgwarchives.net/hi/wwii-army.htm.

1940. *Hawaii Territory, 1840 Federal Census: Population Schedules* **[Digital Capture],** digitized images from the microfilm of original records originally held by the Bureau of the Census in the 1940s. After microfilming, Congress allowed the Census Bureau to destroy the originals to free up space for WWII-related files. Digitizing of the 1940 census images was done for the National Archives and opened to the public in 2012, see
www.familysearch.org/search/catalog/2057751.

1940 Federal Census Finding Aids **[Online Database].** The National Archives has prepared a special website online with a detailed description of the 1940 federal census. Included at the 1940 site are descriptions of finding aids, such as Enumeration District maps, Geographic Descriptions of Census Enumeration Districts, Instructions to Enumerators, Occupation and Industry Classifications, and a list of 1940 City Directories Available at the National Archives. The finding aids are all linked to other National Archives sites. The National Archives website also has a link to 1940 Search Engines using Stephen P. Morse's "One-Step" system for finding a 1940 E.D. or street address conversion. See
www.archives.gov/research/census/1940/general-info.html#questions.

1940-1945. *Hawaii, World War II Draft Registrations Cards* **[Digital Capture],** Draft registration cards of men who registered during World War II, with the exception of the fourth registration. Images courtesy of Ancestry. The event place is the residence of the registrant. To access the digital images, see the online FHL catalog:
www.familysearch.org/search/catalog/2709452.

- See also, *Hawaii, World War II Draft Registration Cards, 1840-1945* **[Online Database],** digitized and indexed at FamilySearch.org, see
www.familysearch.org/search/collection/2709452.

- See also, *Hawaii Selective Service System Registration Cards (World War II): Fourth Registration, 1942* **[Microfilm & Digital Capture],** from the original records at the National Archives, San Bruno, CA. These cards represent older men, ages 45 to 65 in April 1942, that were registered for the draft. They had birth dates between 28 Apr 1877 and 16 Feb

1892. Includes name of individual, date and place of birth, address, age, telephone number, employer's name and address, name and address of person who would know where the individual can be located, signature, and physical description. Arranged in alphabetical order by surname. Filmed by the Genealogical Society of Utah, 2008-2009, 21 rolls, beginning with FHL film #2435869 (A, John – Augustin, Feliciano). To access the digital images, see the online FHL catalog: www.familysearch.org/search/catalog/1566507.

1941. *Pearl Harbor Casualty List* **[Online Database],** indexed at the USGenWeb site for Hawaii. This is a comprehensive list of the names of all civilians and military personnel killed in the attack on Pearl Harbor, Dec. 7, 1941. See
http://files.usgwarchives.net/hi/military/pearl.txt.

1941-2011. *Honolulu, Hawaii, National Memorial Cemetery of the Pacific (Punchbowl)* **[Online Database],** indexed at the Ancestry.com website. Prior to the opening of the cemetery for the recently deceased, the remains of soldiers from locations around the Pacific Theater—including Wake Island and Japanese POW camps—were transported to Hawaii for final interment. The first interment was made Jan. 4, 1949. The cemetery opened to the public on July 19, 1949, with services for five war dead: an unknown serviceman, two Marines, an Army lieutenant and one civilian—noted war correspondent Ernie Pyle. Initially, the graves at National Memorial Cemetery of the Pacific were marked with white wooden crosses and Stars of David—like the American cemeteries abroad—in preparation for the dedication ceremony on the fourth anniversary of V-J Day. Eventually, over 13,000 soldiers and sailors who died during World War II would be laid to rest in the Punchbowl. See
http://search.ancestry.com/search/db.aspx?dbid=2462.

1941-1948. *Hawaii Passenger Lists* **[Online Database],** digitized and indexed at the Ancestry.com website. These databases were derived from two microfilm series of the National Archives, *Passenger Lists of Airplanes Departing from Honolulu, Hawaii, January 27, 1942-July 1, 1948,* and *Index to Filipino Contract Laborers and Their Wives and Children Arriving at Honolulu, Hawaii, 1946.* Each record may include: the name of the passenger, age, gender, marital status, occupation, citizenship, passport number, ultimate destination (city and state), date and place of last arrival in the U.S., date and airport of departure, date and airport of arrival, and aircraft ID. This database has 75,586 records. See
http://search.ancestry.com/search/db.aspx?dbid=1027.

- See also, *Hawaii, Passenger Lists of Airplanes Departing Honolulu, 1942-1948* [Online Database]. See www.familysearch.org/search/collection/2427245.

1945-1946 *Middle Pacific Stars and Stripes (Honolulu, Hawaii)* **[Online Database],** digitized and indexed at the Ancestry.com website. Middle Pacific Stars And Stripes newspaper was located in Honolulu, Hawaii. This database is a fully searchable text version of the newspaper for the following years: 1945-1946. The newspapers can be browsed or searched using a computer-generated index. See
http://search.ancestry.com/search/db.aspx?dbid=51698.

1945-1963 *Stars and Stripes Newspaper, Pacific Editions* **[Online Database],** digitized and indexed at the Ancestry.com website. This database contains issues from some Pacific editions of the 'Stars and Stripes' newspaper from 1945 to 1963. The 'Stars and Stripes' newspaper began during the Civil War. It appeared during World War I and was re-established during World War II by President Roosevelt to boost troop morale. The newspaper was printed specifically for the armed forces and reported on the progress of the war, activities of the U.S. troops, and news from the home front (including sports, comics, and editorials). Different editions of the paper were the editions began as weekly papers and later turned into dailies. By the end of the war, 30 different editions had been published in Europe, North Africa, and Asia. The first Pacific edition of the 'Stars and Stripes' was published in Honolulu, Hawaii in May 1945. Later that same year editions began being published in China and Japan as well. See
http://search.ancestry.com/search/db.aspx?dbid=1139.

1946. *Hawaii, Index to Filipino Arrivals to Honolulu* **[Online Database],** digitized and indexed at the FamilySearch.org website. Source: National Archives microfilm A3411. This collection contains an *Index to Filipino Contract Laborers and their wives and children arriving at Honolulu, Hawaii, 1946* The index cards in this collection are arranged alphabetically by surname then by first name. Each card contains the passengers name, age, gender, marital status, date, and ship arrival at Honolulu. This database has 7,397 records. See
www.familysearch.org/search/collection/2426310.

1947-1948. *California, Airplane Passenger Lists from Honolulu, Hawaii* **[Online Database],** digitized at the FamilySearch.org website. Source: National Archives microfilm A3374. This image-only database contains Passenger Lists of Airplanes Departing from Honolulu,

Hawaii, and Arriving at San Pedro and Los Angeles, California, The passenger lists are arranged chronologically by date of arrival. They primarily consist of Pan American Airways Passenger Manifests and the Immigration and Naturalization Service (INS) forms. Most of the passengers were U.S. citizens, but there are also Japanese citizens and people from other nations. Browse through the images, organized by roll number (Roll 1, 7 Mar 1946-23 Dec 1947; Roll 2, 23 Dec 1947-30 Jun 1948). This database has 3,802 images. See
www.familysearch.org/search/collection/2427229.

1848-1849. *Honolulu and Territory of Hawaii Telephone Directory* **[Microfilm],** Source: Mutual Telephone Company, Honolulu. Filmed by the Genealogical Society of Utah, 1 roll, FHL film #1320746. To see if this microfilm was digitized yet, see the online FHL catalog:
www.familysearch.org/search/catalog/2046970.

1951-1990. *Restricted: Divorce Records Index* **[Microfilm],** from the originals at the State Department of Health, Honolulu. Filmed by the Genealogical Society of Utah, 1996, 3 rolls, FHL film #2033897 (Divorce Index, wife A-I, 1985). No Printouts allowed while using this film at the FHL. To see if this microfilm was digitized yet, see the online FHL catalog: www.familysearch.org/search/catalog/781924.

1953-2011. *Overseas Military Naturalization Petitions Index (Hawaii)* **[Microfilm & Digital Capture],** from originals at the National Archives, Pacific Sierra Region, San Bruno, CA. Filmed by the National Archives, 2011, 1 roll, FHL film #2447581. To access the digital images, see the online FHL catalog: www.familysearch.org/search/catalog/1906705.

1960-1983. See *Directory of the islands of Hawaii, Maui, and Kauai (Hawaii): including Lanai and Molokai ;* **[Printed Book],** by R. L. Polk & Co. FHL has directory books for 1960, 1964, 1969, 1976, 1978, and 1983. See FHL book 996.9 E4p (year).

1967-1976. See *Index, The Hawaiian Journal of History, 1967-1976, Volumes 1-10* **[Printed Book],** complied by Lela Goodell, published by the Hawaiian Historical Society, 1980, 40 pages, FHL book 996.9 B2h v. 1-10 index.

1977-1986. See *Index, The Hawaiian Journal of History, 1977-1986, Volumes 11-20* **[Printed Book],** complied by Lela Goodell, published by the Hawaiian Historical Society, 1987, 40 pages, FHL book 996.9 B2h v. 11-20 index.

1980-Current. *Hawaii Obituaries Index* **[Online Database],** digitized and indexed at the FamilySearch.org website. Includes obituaries transcribed from *The Honolulu Advertiser, The Honolulu Star-Bulletin,* The *Kauai Garden Island News, The Maui News,* and *The Hawaii Tribune-Herald.* These obituaries were transcribed by volunteers from the Joseph F. Smith Library at Brigham Young University-Hawaii. Microfilm copies of some of the original newspapers are available at family history centers and at the Joseph F. Smith Library in Laie, Hawaii. This database has 93,702 records. See
www.familysearch.org/search/collection/2301762.

1982-2010. *Hawaii, Kauai County, Obituaries* **[Microfilm & Digital Capture],** from microfilm now in storage at the Granite Mountain Vault. Digitized by the Genealogical Society of Utah, 2017, 7 rolls. To access the digital images, see the online FHL catalog: www.familysearch.org/search/catalog/2495093.

1999-2014. *Hawaii Newspaper Obituaries* **[Online Database].** Digitized and indexed at the GenealogyBank.com website. One search screen for obituaries published in Hilo, Honolulu, Kailua-Kona, Kamuela, Kaunakakai, Laie, Lihue, Pearl Harbor Navy Base-Hickam AFB, and Schofield Barracks newspapers: See
www.genealogybank.com/gbnk/obituaries/explore/USA/Hawaii.

California Counties • 1850-1852. The above map shows California's Gold Rush counties at the time of the June 1850 Federal Census; Statehood in September 1850; and the June 1852 California State Census. The original 27 counties are shown in black; the modern 58 counties are shown in white. The 1850 Census tallied California's population at 92,597. The 1852 Census count came in at 260,949 and includes records from the three lost counties from the 1850 census - Contra Costa, San Francisco, and Santa Clara (shown as "lost" on the map). However, three counties are missing from the 1852 census records: Colusa, Sutter, and Marin. **Map source:** page 43, *Map Guide to the U.S. Federal Censuses, 1790-1920,* by William Thorndale and William Dollarhide.

California
Censuses & Substitute Name Lists

Historical Timeline of California, 1535-1860

1535-1542 Spanish Claims. The first European visitors to the Pacific Coast of North America were convinced that California was an island. In 1535, Hernando Cortes was the first to see California, and in 1539, Francisco de Uloa explored the gulf of California. The first claim came in 1542 when explorer Juan Rodriguez Cabrillo anchored his ship in San Diego Bay and claimed the entire "island" for Spain, which he named California. One explanation for the name was that Cabrillo had been reading Ordoez de Montalvo's romance of chivalry, *Las Sergas de Esplandian* (Madrid, 1510), in which is told of black Amazons ruling an island of the name California near the Indies. No one can find any other reference to the name California before 1542, and it has no other known Spanish origin.

1579. British Claim. Never one to cede anything to the Spanish, Sir Francis Drake sailed up the Pacific Coast beyond San Francisco Bay and claimed the entire region for England, naming the area New Albion. But the British claim was never reinforced by colonization.

1602. Spanish Claims Confirmed. Sebastian Vizca Níno charted the Pacific Coast and confirmed Spain's claim to the region, from the southern tip of present Baja California, Mexico to the northern tip of present Vancouver Island, British Columbia.

1603-1768. Spanish Presidios Established. For the next 165 years, Baja (lower) California and Alta (upper) California were part of **New Spain**, which was a description of all Spanish claims in North America. During this time, California was mostly ignored by Europeans, except as a re-supply point for Spanish ships sailing from Manila and other Pacific outposts before returning to Spain. During the late 1600s a few presidios (forts) were established as protection for the re-supply ports, such as the presidios at Monterey Bay and San Diego Bay. The Spanish were reacting to the intrusion of Russian and English trading posts established just north of San Francisco Bay, but both intruders left California after only a few years.

1769-1820. Spanish Colonial Era. The Spanish colonization of California did not really begin until the arrival of Junipero Serra in 1769. Serra was the Franciscan monk who founded the first nine California missions, ranging from San Diego Bay to San Francisco Bay. The Spanish were to establish a total of 21 missions, all connected with a wagon road called the El Camino Real (the Royal Road). For the most part, the Spanish missions were successful in converting the local Indians to Roman Catholicism, but a few California Indian tribes resisted by attacking and burning the missions. In response, the Spanish government provided military protection for the missions by establishing several more presidios, evenly distributed between the coastal missions. During the Spanish era, over 100 presidios were established.

Spanish pueblos (communal villages) were the first civilian towns in California. Mission workers were provided by the Catholic Church, while the presidios were manned by Spanish soldiers. But to provide civilian farmers and workers for the pueblos, incentives were required to get people to move there, and thus, a system of land grants, tax breaks, and other incentives was established. To attract settlers to the new towns, the Spanish government provided free land, livestock, farming equipment, and an annual allowance for the purchase of clothing and other supplies. In addition, the settlers were exempt from all taxes for five years. In return for this aid, the settlers were required to sell their surplus agricultural products to the presidios. The Spanish created three pueblos in California, the first was San José, founded in 1777. It was followed in 1781 with El Pueblo de Nuestra Señora la Reina de los Angeles (the Town of Our Lady Queen of the Angels). By 1790, the Los Angeles pueblo had 28 households and a population of 139. By 1800 Los Angeles had 70 households and a population of 315.

The villa de Branciforte near present Santa Cruz was another pueblo established in 1797, developed primarily as a place for discharged soldiers from the presidios, but the Branciforte pueblo was never able to attract many soldiers and was abandoned in 1802. The San José and Los Angeles pueblos were still active when California became an American possession in 1848.

1819. Adams-Onis Treaty. The treaty's initial agreement involved Spain's cession of Florida to the U.S., but also set the boundary between the U.S. and Spanish Mexico, from Louisiana to the Oregon Country. In this treaty, the line between the Oregon Country and Spanish California was set as the 42nd parallel, where it remains today. The treaty was named after John Quincy Adams, U.S. Secretary of State, and Luis de Onis, the Spanish Foreign Minister, the parties who signed the treaty at Washington on February 22, 1819.

John Quincy Adams was given credit for a brilliant piece of diplomacy by adding the western boundary settlements with Spain to the Florida Purchase. It was considered his crowning achievement, before, during, or after his presidency.

1821-1848. Mexican Era. Colonial Spanish rule in California ended when Mexico gained independence from Spain in February 1821, but the Californios never heard about it until the new Mexican governor arrived in November 1822. At first, the transition of power had no change to the California way of life. But within just a few years, the mission system in California came to an end.

As early as 1826, Americans began visiting California after establishing overland routes from the Rocky Mountains. After some initial resistance, the Californios accepted their intrusion into the area. As the most northern and western province of Mexico, California had few manufactured goods, and the Americans were welcomed for the items they brought for trade. By the early 1830s, the mission communities established by the Spanish were absorbed into the Mexican civilian government. The mission properties were distributed to soldiers in lieu of wages and to Mexican citizens in return for political favors. The local natives who remained were assimilated into the local society serving as laborers, household servants and vaqueros (cowboys).

The Mexican government did create more pueblos, mostly from converted missions (such as those in Sonoma and San Diego). But mainly, Mexico concentrated on the land grant process which the Spanish had initiated. With the demise of the Mission system, California evolved into an isolated province dominated by a series of large ranchos, some as large as 100,000 acres in size. By 1840, huge cattle ranches stretched from San Diego Bay to San Francisco Bay, including the greater Central Valley of California.

1840s. Manifest Destiny. In 1841, the first wagon train left Missouri for California, even though the area was not part of the United States, and the settlers had no guarantee they would be able to stay. During the 1840s, the American government was under the influence of an unofficial but practiced policy called "manifest destiny," meaning the U.S. believed they had the God-given right to take the entire continent by any means.

1845. Texas Annexation. Clearly, Americans began to covet the area of the southwest, and in fact, many historians feel that the annexation of Texas in 1845 led to a war that was as much to capture California and New Mexico from Mexico as it was to take the Rio Grande valley. After the 1845 annexation of Texas, the U.S. honored the Republic of Texas claim to the Rio Grande valley. This claim was the basis for the Mexican-American War, which began in December 1845 when U.S. forces invaded the Rio Grande valley and took possession of the area.

1846. Oregon Country. Since a treaty in 1818, the U.S. and Britain had agreed to joint occupancy of the Oregon Country, defined loosely as running from the Boundary (Siskiyou) Mountains of California to the Russian America boundary at about the 54th parallel and from the Pacific Ocean to the Continental Divide. In 1819, the Adams-Onis Treaty set the Oregon boundary with California as the 42nd parallel. Finally, in 1846, the U.S. settled with Britain its long-held claim to the Oregon Country, establishing the 49th parallel as the northern boundary with British territory, and confirming the southern boundary of Oregon with California as the 42nd parallel.

1848 Mexican Cession. As part of the 1848 Treaty of Guadalupe Hidalgo ending the war with Mexico, the U.S. obtained official ownership of the Texas Claim to the area east of the Rio Grande – an area the U.S. had already possessed by conquest in 1846. Also in the 1848 treaty, the U.S. acquired the *Mexican Cession* of the Mexican Provinces of California and New Mexico. (An area shown on the map above). As compensation for the Mexican Cession, the U.S. paid Mexico 18 million dollars for an area that was comparable in size to the Louisiana Purchase, and was over half of the Republic of Mexico. With the addition of the Oregon Country in 1846, the Mexican Cession made the United States a nation "from sea to shining sea," Map Source: Wikipedia.

1848-1860. Gold Rush, Statehood, and Population Surge. The combined ethnic populations of California in 1848 consisted of about 1,500 Anglos, 8,000 Latinos, and 100,000 Indians. Immediately after becoming an American possession in May 1848, gold was discovered, creating a stampede of prospectors from all over North America. In the 1850 Federal Census, the population rose to 92,597 people (no Indians counted).

California was never a territory, and after the State Constitutional Convention convened in Monterey, Congress declared California a state on 9 September 1850. Statehood led to the rapid organization of the entire state into counties, taxing districts, and voting precincts – units of government that quickly began recording name lists of its constituents. In the 1852 CA State Census, the population was at 260,949 people (no Indians counted).

The ethnic populations of California in 1860 consisted of about 380,000 Anglos, 5,000 Latinos, and 30,000 Indians. It is estimated that between 1848 and 1860, as many as 70,000 California Indians died from diseases introduced by the newcomers.

While the gold fields of Northern California and the first transcontinental railroad in 1869 contributed heavily to the growth of the state through the latter half of the 19th Century, the growth of Southern California in the early 20th Century was even greater. One explanation came from Buckminster Fuller, who observed that "the entire continent is tilted and everything loose slides into Southern California."

Bibliography
California Censuses & Substitutes

A review of the Spanish, Mexican, and American censuses taken in California:

1500s-1820. Spanish Era. The Mexican National Archives in Mexico City holds many original documents from the Spanish era, including some from the present-day areas of New Mexico, Arizona, and California. A microfilm collection of the documents is available which includes references to the missions, presidios, and pueblos of California. Mission registers also exist from several California missions from the mid-1700s to the end of the Spanish era in 1820.

1821-1848. Mexican Era. A Padron (census) was taken in areas of California in 1822, 1834, 1836, 1837, and 1844 by the Mexican government, and several of the name lists have survived. The Spanish land grant system was adopted by Mexico, and there still exists many records relating to land grants from the Spanish and Mexican eras. After a certain number of years of residency, land grants were offered to any Mexican citizen, whether Anglo or Hispanic. A "Spanish Archives" is maintained by the California State Archives in Sacramento, with land grants and other documents left over from the Spanish and Mexican eras of California. Mission registers that overlap the Spanish Era into the Mexican era are also available for several of the early California missions.

1848-Current. American Era. The 1850 federal census taken in California was considered flawed due to the loss of the schedules for some of the most populous counties. The state of California authorized its own census in 1852 as a means of rectifying the problem. The 1852 census was the only state census taken in California and has its own problems due to faded and often illegible pages. One of the questions asked on the CA 1852 was the residence of a person before coming to California. Thus, the valuable 1852 CA census identifies most of the gold rush pioneers by name, and also where they came from.

The California federal censuses are complete from 1850 to 1940, with the exception of the 1890, mostly destroyed for all states in a 1921 Washington, DC fire. The statewide substitute name lists identified in the bibliography are enhanced by including countywide name lists for California. In particular, the county Great Registers (voter lists) from 1866 forward are very useful genealogical resources. All of the county name lists were recently digitized and full-page images made available online. Added to the single county lists, there are also two large statewide compilations digitized online for the combined county Great Registers, from 1866-1898 and 1900-1968. These two major databases are identified in the bibliography that follows, each with a complete list of California counties, years of Great Registers available, and any missing years. It should be noted that the 1900-1968 database of Great Registers for California has over 67 million records, the largest name list for one state posted at the Ancestry.com website.

California's outstanding array of censuses and substitutes begins below:

♦ ♦ ♦ ♦ ♦

1700-1942. See *California, Collections of the California Genealogical Society* **[Online Database]**, digitized at the FamilySearch website. The genealogical collection is located at the California Genealogical Society in Oakland, consisting of cemetery records including the index of Philips-tombstone transcription, ca.1700-1900; IOOF Cemetery, 1866-1932; Griffin Allied Family Index, ca.1900; probate register of actions (San Francisco City and County; 1906-1942 Alta and other newspaper people index, 1860-1861. This database has 164,529 images. See
www.familysearch.org/search/collection/1385527.

1700s-1820 Spanish California. See *Ramo de Historia: 1522-1822* **[Microfilm & Digital Capture]**, from the original manuscripts, Archivo General de la Nación, México, documenting the official records of the colonial provinces of Spain and Mexico. The "Historia" collection in the National Archive of Mexico includes copies of early conquest chronicles, historical accounts from the Vice-regal period, and other documents of an ecclesiastical, civic, military, and geographical nature. There are many pages of documents relating to the missions, presidios, and pueblos of California. Most of the volumes include an index. Filmed by the Genealogical Society of Utah, 1993-1994, 81 rolls, beginning with FHL film #1857411 (Colección de memorias de Nueva Espana [Memories of New Spain]). To access the digital images, see the online FHL catalog:
www.familysearch.org/search/catalog/693641.

1700s-1800s. *Census Records for Latin America and the Hispanic United States* **[Printed Book]**, by Lyman D. Platt, published by Genealogical Publishing Co., Baltimore, 1998, 198 pages. Survey of census records for Latin America, including Mexico, Guatemala, Peru, and other Latin American countries, and the Hispanic United States (including California, Arizona, New Mexico, Texas, Louisiana, and Florida). Includes a listing of the archives and publications where census records are available, as well as Family History Library film numbers. FHL book 980 X23pc.

1752-1837. See *Early California and Nogales, Arizona Lists of Expeditionary Members, Soldiers and Residents, 1752, 1775, 1781-1837: Material Emphasizes Santa Barbara, California* **[Microfilm]**, from the original manuscripts at the Santa Barbara Historical Society, Santa Barbara, California. Text in English and Spanish. Includes Santa Barbara censuses taken in 1834 and 1837. Includes lists of military personnel and other areas of California. Filmed by the Genealogical Society of Utah, 1988, 1 roll, FHL film #1548299.

1769-1848. See *California, Pioneer Index, 1769-1848* **[Online Database]**, indexed at the Ancestry.com website. This compilation was extracted from the monumental seven-volume *History of California* by Hubert Bancroft. The information extracted was done with the genealogist in mind and includes lists of inhabitants, lists of pioneers, and a pioneer register. The first section is a list of all male inhabitants from 1769 through 1800 and the number following the name refers to the following dates (1) 1769-1773, (2) 1774-1780, (3) 1781-1790, and (4) 1791-1800. The second section is a list of pioneers with the date they arrived in the territory following the name. In the last section, biographies are given of selected settlers to the area. This database has 2,980 records. See https://search.ancestry.com/search/db.aspx?dbid=1040.
- See also, *California Pioneer Register and Index, 1542-1848: Including Inhabitants of California, 1769-1800, and List of Pioneers* **[Printed Book & Digital Version]**, by Hubert Howe Bancroft, reprint 1964, GPC, 392 pages, FHL book 979.4 D3. To access the digital version, see the online FHL catalog: www.familysearch.org/search/catalog/116498.

1781-1790. *California, Biographic Index Cards* **[Online Database]**, indexed at the Ancestry.com website. The records in this database come from the Biographical Card Index housed at the California State Library. According to the library, the cards in the file contain details "about or contributed by California artists, authors, actors, musicians, state officials, World War I soldiers, and other notables." There are several versions of cards in the file; the most detailed list (as applicable) includes: Name, Birthplace, Birth date, Father's name, Mother's name, Spouse's name, Place of marriage, Date of marriage, Place of death, State of death, Residence, and Years in California, In addition, you may find Profession, Education honors received, Clubs and societies, Party affiliation and/or offices held, and Publications or works. This database has 7,406 records. See https://search.ancestry.com/search/db.aspx?dbid=2412.

1770-1915 Mission Registers, Catholic Church, Mission San Carlos Burromeo de Carelo (Carmel, California) **[Microfilm & Digital Capture]**, from the original records in the Diocesan Pastoral Office, Monterey and in the CA State Archives, Sacramento, California. Includes baptisms, burials, marriages, confirmations, and miscellaneous business accounts. Filmed by the Genealogical Society of Utah, 1972, 10 rolls, beginning with FHL film #913159 (Index to baptisms and burials 1770-1885). A series of biographical sketches of clergy from 1817 is on FHL film #913167. To access the digital images, see the online FHL catalog: www.familysearch.org/search/catalog/304649.

1772-1906 Mission Registers, Catholic Church, Mission San Luis Obispo de Tolosa **[Microfilm & Digital Capture]**, from the original records in the Diocesan Pastoral Office, Monterey and in the CA State Archives, Sacramento, California. Includes baptisms, burial, marriages, confirmations, and miscellaneous business accounts. Filmed by the Genealogical Society of Utah, 1972, 4 rolls, beginning with FHL film #913300 (Baptisms 1772-1821). To access the digital images, see the online FHL catalog: www.familysearch.org/search/catalog/304645.

1775-1846. See *Ranchos of California, a List of Spanish Concessions, 1775-1822, and Mexican Grants, 1822-1846* **[Printed Book]**, Robert Granniss Cowan, published by Academy Library Guild, Fresno, CA, 1956, 151 pages. FHL book 979.4 R2cr.

1776-1912 Mission Registers, Catholic Church, Mission Santa Barbara **[Microfilm & Digital Capture]**, from the original records at the Mission Archives, Santa Barbara, California. Includes baptisms, burials, marriages, confirmations, and miscellaneous business accounts. Filmed by the Genealogical Society of Utah, 1972, 5 rolls, beginning with FHL film #913165 (Baptisms 1786-1858 Santa Barbara Indians). To access the digital images, see the online FHL catalog: www.familysearch.org/search/catalog/304637.

1784-1868. *California, Spanish Land Records* **[Online Database],** indexed at the Ancestry.com website. Source: CA State Archives, Spanish Archives. Before California came under U.S. rule the Spanish Crown, and later the Mexican government, made grants of land in California called ranchos. These records relate to those land grants which were acquired by the United States after it took possession of California. There are several records related to each grant. The main record for this database comes from a comprehensive index of the grantees. That record will have links to original land documents (in Spanish), English translations of some of these documents, and maps of the property (diseños). These maps show boundaries as of 1861. This database has 1,827 records: https://search.ancestry.com/search/db.aspx?dbid=8808.

"1790 Padron (Census) of California," **[Printed Article]**, a typescript (photocopy) copied from Las Familias de California section in Southern California Historical Society Quarterly. Includes index. FHL book 979.4 A1 no. 67, and FHL film #1036747.

1790. *California 1790 Census: Cities of Los Angeles, Monterey, San Diego, San Francisco, San Jose, and Santa Barbara* **[Printed Book]**, edited by Sue Powell Morgan. Contains transcripts of the 1790 censuses (padrones) of the pueblos, presidios, and missions for several colonial California cities and missions. The census information includes the name of the head of household, age, occupation, previous residence or nativity, marital status, name of spouse, names and number of children and their ages. The heads of households are listed in alphabetical order. Includes surname index. Published by Genealogical Services, West Jordan, UT, 1998, 63 pages. FHL book 979.4 X29m.

- See also, *1790 Spanish Census of California* **[Online Database]**, data taken from the Revillagigedo Census of 1793, which was originally collected in 1790. Included are Los Angeles, Missions, Monterey, San Diego, San Francisco, San Jose, and Santa Barbara. Archived at https://web.archive.org/web/20180118064726/www.sfgenealogy.com/spanish/cen1790.htm.

- See also, *1790 Spanish Census of California, San Francisco [Online Database]*, indexed at the SFGenealogy site. Archived at https://web.archive.org/web/20160415235947/www.sfgenealogy.com/sf/ca1790.htm.

1790-1890. *California, Compiled Census and Census Substitutes Index* **[Online Database]**, a collection of census indexes originally compiled by Ronald Jackson of Accelerated Indexing Systems. They are all treated as a single searchable database at the Ancestry.com website. Included are the following censuses/tax lists:
- 1790 Census Substitute
- 1850 Federal Census
- 1850 Federal Census Index
- 1870 Federal Census Index (excluding San Francisco)
- 1834 Census Index, Santa Barbara
- 1890 Veterans Schedule
- 1890 Naval Veterans Schedule

http://search.ancestry.com/search/db.aspx?dbid=3535.

1790-1950. *California, Pioneer, and Immigrant Files* **[Online Database]**, digitized and indexed at the Ancestry.com website. Some 10,000 records are contained in this database with biographical information about pioneers who arrived in California prior to 1860. The information is recorded on a series of index cards which were collected into the California Information File beginning in the early 1900s. Many of the facts were contributed by the pioneers themselves, their descendants, or other resources some of which are noted in the records. Available facts about individuals includes name, birth date and location, parents' names, spouse's name, marriage date and location, death date and location, and can include extensive personal details like, profession or occupation, residence before California, residence in California, political offices held, education, politics, participation in principle events of California history, and lists of descendants: This database has 6,975 records, see http://search.ancestry.com/search/db.aspx?dbid=2161.

1796-1798. *California Spanish Mission Censuses* **[Online Database]**, digitized and indexed at the Ancestry.com website. This database contains the following California mission censuses: San Antonio (1798); San Carlos (1796); San Luis Obispo (1797-1798); and Soledad (1798). Information available includes a Name, Age, and Enumeration date. See http://search.ancestry.com/search/db.aspx?dbid=1097.

- See also, *California, Census Records: Pre-Statehood Census, 1796-1798* **[Digital Capture]**, from the original records at the CA State Archives (Spanish Archives). To access the digital images, see the FHL catalog: www.familysearch.org/search/catalog/2818879.

1797-1937 *Mission Registers, Catholic Church, Mission San Miguel Arcangel (San Miguel, California)* **[Microfilm & Digital Capture],** from the original records in the Diocesan Pastoral Office, Monterey, California. Includes baptisms, burials, marriages, confirmations, and miscellaneous business accounts. Added to the San Miguel records are 1874 deeds and maps of San Luis Obispo, Santa Cruz, Soledad, Carmel, Rancho Laguna San Luis Obispo, and San Juan Bautista. Filmed by the Genealogical Society of Utah, 1972, 3 rolls, beginning with FHL film

#913312 (Baptisms 1797-1862 and includes some marriages). To access the digital images, see the online FHL catalog:
www.familysearch.org/search/catalog/304640.

1800-1994. *California, County Birth and Death Records* **[Online Database],** indexed at the FamilySearch.org website. Source: CA State Archives, Sacramento. Registers, records and certificates of county birth and death records acquired from county courthouses. This collection contains some delayed birth records, as well. Some city and towns records are also included. Records have not been acquired for Contra Costa, Imperial, Kern, Kings, Modoc, Napa, San Francisco, San Mateo, Siskiyou, Solano, Tulare and Ventura counties. The name index for death records covers Stockton, Lodi and Manteca cities and San Benito and San Joaquin counties. This database has 777,005 records. See
www.familysearch.org/search/collection/2001287.

1800s-1846. *California Ranchos: Patented Private Land Grants Listed by County* **[Printed Book],** edited by Michael & Mary Burgess, published by Borgo Press, San Bernardino, CA, 1988, 144 pages. Includes index. Lists name of rancho, and to whom the patent was granted, including date and description of the location. FHL book 979.4 R2s.

1801-1932. *California Mortuary and Cemetery Records* **[Online Database],** digitized and index at the Ancestry.com website. This is a collection of Northern California burial and death records from ca.1801-1932. The records come from four different books that cover both Northern California in general and San Francisco, El Dorado, and Tehama County cemeteries. The books contain index cards with vital records on them. They serve as a mini-biography of the deceased. Some cards have more information than others. Some cards simply have the name and years of birth and death while others contain specific dates, cause of death, attending physician, burial location and parents' names. These records may include a name, birthplace, age, birth date, death date, location of death, and location of burial. This database has 49,494 records. See
http://search.ancestry.com/search/db.aspx?dbid=2054.

1801. *Estadística del Censo,* **1801 [Microfilm & Digital Capture],** from the original manuscript at the Mission Archives, Santa Barbara, California, including census statistics of the mission and town of Laguna 1801. Filmed by the Genealogical Society of Utah, 1972, 1 roll, FHL film #913167. To access the digital images, see the online FHL catalog:
www.familysearch.org/search/catalog/218983.

1809-2011. *Western States Marriage Index* **[Online Database],** indexed at the FamilySearch.org website. All data was obtained from Brigham Young University-Idaho. A link to their website is at the Ancestry search screen. At the BYU-Idaho webpage, a list of each state/county/number of marriages is available. This database has 1,334,005 records. See
https://search.ancestry.com/search/db.aspx?dbid=70016.

1812-1988. *California, Births and Christening* **[Online Database],** indexed at the FamilySearch.org website, a name index to birth, baptism and christening records from the state of California. Microfilm copies of these records are available at the Family History Library. See
www.familysearch.org/search/collection/1674703.
- See also, *California, Select Births and Christening, 1812-1988* **[Online Database],** digitized and indexed at Ancestry.com, see
https://search.ancestry.com/search/db.aspx?dbid=60239.

1820-1846. *The History of San Diego County Ranchos: The Spanish, Mexican and American Occupation of San Diego County and the Story of the Ownership of Land Grants Therein* **[Printed Book],** by Robert W. Brackett, sponsored by the San Diego Historical Society, published by Union Title Insurance Co., 1960, 70 pages. FHL book 979.498 R2h.

1820s-1840s. *Index to the Spanish-Mexican Private Land Grant Records and Cases of California* **[Microfilm],** from the book by J.N. Bowman, published by the Bancroft Library, University of California, Berkeley, CA, 1958, filmed by the Genealogical Society of Utah, 1970, 1 roll, FHL film #833343. To see if this microfilm was digitized yet, see the online FHL catalog:
www.familysearch.org/search/catalog/28503.

1821-1846. *Spanish and Mexican Land Grants in California* **[Printed Book],** by Rose Hollenbaugh Aviña, includes lists of names. Published Arno Press, New York, 1976, 137 pages. FHL book 979.4 R2m.

1822. *Chihuahua, Mexico Padrones/Census 1822: Para/for Babanoyava, San Andres, Santa Ysabel, Santa Cruz Tapacolmes, Satevo, Villa de Chihuahua y Quartels 1, 2, 3, 4, Ciudad de Chihuahua* **[Printed Book],** by Patsy Mendoza Castro de Ludwig, published by the author, San Jose, CA, 1998, 473 pages. Extracts of microfilms #145 and #149, from the Bancroft Library, University of California at Berkeley, of the 1822 Padrones. Only legible entries were extracted. Text in Spanish and English. Includes index. FHL book 972.16 X22L.

1822-1844. *Index to the Padrones* **[Printed Index],** by Zoeth Skinner Eldredge, published by the Bancroft Library, University of California at Berkeley, Bancroft Library Series, Vol. III, 130 pages. This is an index to the Bancroft Library collection of 18th and 19th century padrones of residents of California. FHL book 979.4 X22e.

1822-1845. *Spanish Archives* **[Microfilm & Digital Capture],** from the original records at the California State Archives, Sacramento, CA. Additional indexes filmed with each volume. Years are mixed within each volume. Written in Spanish and English. Filmed by the Genealogical Society of Utah, 1975. 14 rolls, beginning with FHL film #978888 (Index to Spanish archives). To access the digital images, see the online FHL catalog: www.familysearch.org/search/catalog/209107.

1822-1920 *Vital Statistics Index* **[Microfilm & Digital Capture],** from the original card file located at the Special Collections Unit of the California State Library, Sacramento, CA. The card file is arranged in alphabetical order by surname, of responses to vital records inquiries. Information includes the name and event in question and applies to the state of California in general. Inquiries deal with births, marriages, deaths, naturalizations, etc., and responses include newspapers, county registers, California great register, and various other record sources throughout the state of California. Filmed by the Genealogical Society of Utah, 1991, 10 rolls, as follows:
- A - Brutt, J, FHL film #1711369.
- Brutt, J - Demont, A, FHL film #1711370.
- Demont, A - Gold, F, FHL film #1711371.
- Gold, F - Holman, N, FHL film #1711372.
- Holman, N - Landrum, R, FHL film #1711373.
- Landrum, R - Menne, A, FHL film #1711484.
- Menne, A - Peterson, A, FHL film #1711485.
- Peterson, A - Scott, C, FHL film #1711486.
- Scott, C - Vail, F, FHL film #1711487.
- Vail, F – Z, FHL film #1711488.

To access the digital images, see the online FHL catalog: www.familysearch.org/search/catalog/486201.

1822-1964. *California Biographical Collection: Responses to Vital Record Inquiries* **[Online Database],** indexed at the Ancestry.com website. Source: Original data: Miscellaneous Card Indexes; Vital Statistics Index (1900–1951). California State Library, California History Section, Sacramento. When responding to queries for details about births, marriages, divorces, deaths, and proof of citizenship, California State Library employees created these cards summarizing their answers. The library did not have access to the vital records themselves, so responses included references to city directories and obituaries and notices of marriages and births in California newspapers, transcribed entries from California voter registers (Great Registers), and other sources. Cards mention unsuccessful searches as well. The cards mention the request and may include names, places, dates, and sources for events such as births, marriages, divorces, deaths, and naturalizations. Most of the requests were made in the 1930s. This database has 18,326 records. See https://search.ancestry.com/search/db.aspx?dbid=2347.

1824-1997. *California, San Francisco County Records* **[Online Database],** digitized and indexed at the FamilySearch.org website. Includes an alphabetical newspaper clipping file of the *San Francisco Examiner*, death reports, general index, indexes to deeds, deeds, indexes to marriage certificates, marriage licenses, indexes to naturalizations, naturalization records, coroner's records, and alien registrations. This database has 195,049 records. See www.familysearch.org/search/collection/1402856.

1850-1985. See *California County Naturalizations, 1831-1985* **[Online Database],** digitized and indexed at FamilySearch.org. The 1831 date was for a birth year, not a naturalization year. This database includes county naturalization records for Alameda, Amador, Alpine, Butte, Calaveras, Calusa, El Dorado, Fresno, Glenn, Lake, Lassen, Los Angeles, Mendocino, Napa, Nevada, Orange, Placer, Sacramento, San Francisco, Sonoma, Santa Clara, Stanislaus, Santa Barbara, San Benito, San Diego, Solano, Sutter, Yolo, and Yuba counties. This database has 438,824 records, see www.familysearch.org/search/collection/2125028.

1833-1991. *California, Probate Estate Files* **[Online Database],** digitized at the FamilySearch.org website. Estate files of the Probate and Superior Courts in the counties of Alpine, Amador, Butte, Calaveras, Colusa, Glenn, Lassen, Napa, Sacramento, San Benito, and Solano. The date ranges of the files will vary. This database has 2,059,415 images. See www.familysearch.org/search/collection/1999181.

1835-1979. See *California, San Francisco Area Funeral Home Records, 1835-1931; Index 1896-1931* **[Online Database],** digitized and indexed at the FamilySearch website. This project was indexed in partnership with the California Genealogical Society and Library. Name index and images of funeral home records from the Halsted N. Gray - Carew & English Mortuary Collection, located at the San Francisco Public Library. Images for all years in collection can be browsed, but name index currently covers only years 1896-1931. Collection includes a number of different funeral homes acquired over time by the Halsted N. Gray - Carew & English Mortuary company, most from the San Francisco area, but also including some from Burlingame, Stockton, and Sacramento. The collection includes funeral register books, burial registers, account books, case books, etc. Indexes are at the beginning of some volumes. See www.familysearch.org/search/collection/1385518.

"1836 Mexican Census of Los Angeles and Orange County Area: Including the Rancho Santiago de Santa Ana After Which the Rancho Santiago Community Was Named" [Printed Article], prepared from the 1836 Los Angeles Padron published in the *Southern California Historical Society Quarterly* in 1936 by Nanci Cole, Leonard Johnson, and Carol Swanson as a class project for Wayne Dell Gibson. Published by Santa Ana College Foundation Press, 1976, 104 pages. FHL book 979.4. X2mx. Also on microfilm, filmed by the Genealogical Society of Utah, 1987, 1 roll, FHL film #1320513 (not digitized).

1836, 1844. *Padrones de la Ciudad de Los Angeles* **[Microfilm & Digital Capture],** from the original records by the Genealogical Society of Utah, 1972, 1 roll, FHL film #913156. To access the digital images, see the online FHL catalog: www.familysearch.org/search/catalog/42503.

1838-1851. *Pre-statehood Records, San Francisco County, California* **[Microfilm & Digital Capture],** from the original records at the San Francisco County courthouse. Indexes have been filmed at the end of some volumes. These are mostly land and property records; additional material may be found in the copies. Text in Spanish and English. Filmed by the Genealogical Society of Utah, 1975, 21 rolls, beginning with FHL film #974651 (Spanish blotters, 1839 & on). To access the digital images, see the online FHL catalog: www.familysearch.org/search/catalog/209194.

1838-1973. *California, Santa Clara County, San Jose, Oak Hill Cemetery Headstone Inscriptions* **[Online Database],** digitized and indexed at FamilySearch.org. The inscriptions were made by the Santa Clara Historical and Genealogical Society as a part of a cemetery project. The collection is a card index and arranged alphabetically. This database has 62,462 records, see www.familysearch.org/search/collection/3161103.

1840-1954. See *Alphabetical Index of Ships Arrival at the Port of San Francisco, California, from ca. 1840 to December 1954* **[Microfilm & Digital Capture],** from originals at the National Archives, Washington, DC. Filmed by the National Archives, Central Plains Region, 1987, 1 roll, FHL film #1380995. To access the digital images, see the online FHL catalog: www.familysearch.org/search/catalog/484340.

1841-1849. *Pueblo de Sonoma Court Records: Expedientes* **[Printed Abstracts],** Translated, edited, and abstracted by Camelia Domenech O'Connor, published by Sonoma County Genealogical Society, 2003, 30 pages. From intro: "Historically, these records involve some of the first land grants made to private individuals in the area north of San Francisco. The petitions in this project were submitted to the court to document proof of ownership of these grants and to verify title. They also contain two land sales. However, these are not a complete listing of all the land grants in the North Bay area." Includes bibliographical references and a surname index. FHL book 979.418 R29o.

1841-1906 *Naturalization Records, Sonoma County, California* **[Online Database],** indexed at the RootsWeb site for Sonoma Co CA. See www.rootsweb.ancestry.com/~cascgs/nat.htm.

1842 *Census, San Francisco* **[Online Database],** extracted in the same order as the original, at the SFGenealogy site. Archived at https://web.archive.org/web/20171210072907/www.sfgenealogy.com/sf/sf1842.htm.

1843-1918. *California County Marriages* **[Online Database],** indexed at the FamilySearch.org website. Source: CA State Archives; Sacramento. This is an index to selected marriage records, most from Napa County. This database has 9,629 records. Archived https://web.archive.org/web/20170816132257/www.familysearch.org/search/collection/2534488.

1843-1999. *California, Federal Naturalization Records* **[Online Database],** indexed at the Ancestry.com website. Source: National Archives Naturalization records. The records include mostly Petitions, Declarations, and Certificates. Each Petition index record may include: Name, Petition age, Record type, Birth date, Birthplace, Petition date, and Petition Number. The document image may have much more information about a person and relatives. This database has 3,095,732 records. See https://search.ancestry.com/search/db.aspx?dbid=3998.

1846 San Francisco City Directory **[Online Database]**, indexed at the SFGenealogy site. Archived https://web.archive.org/web/20161018061958/www.sfgenealogy.com/sf/sf1846.htm.

1846-1850 Land Grants, Sonoma County, California **[Online Database]**, indexed at the RootsWeb site for Sonoma Co CA. See www.rootsweb.ancestry.com/~cascgs/intro.htm.

1846-1890. *The Decline of the Californios, a Social History of the Spanish-Speaking Californians* **[Printed Book]**, by Leonard Pitt, published by the University of California Press, Berkeley, CA, 1965, 324 pages. FHL book 979.4 H2p.

1846-1850. *Early Sonoma County, California, Land Grants* **[Microfilm of Printed Extract]**, edited by Carmen J. Finley, projects director, Sonoma County Genealogical Society. Contains abstracts of original land grant records, arranged in alphabetical order by surname, showing name of grantee, description of property, acres, number of lots, cost, date of grant deed, authority, original deed book volume and page numbers. Also contains photocopies of original pages in grant deed books. Contents: Early history of the town of Sonoma (historical sketch) – Grants, vol. 2-A (includes alphabetical listing by surname of grantee, property description or lot number, acres, cost, date of grant deed, authority, book and page numbers), with photocopy of original record book -- Grants, book A, town lots (includes alphabetical listing of petitioners, giving lot numbers, cost, size in acres, date of petition and reference to volume and page numbers) – Grants, vol. B, town lots (includes alphabetical listing by surname of petitioners, giving lot nos. cost in dollars, size in acres, date of petition, and reference to volume and page number) with photocopy of original record book. Filmed by the Genealogical Society of Utah, 2002, 1 roll, FHL film #1440586. To see if this microfilm was digitized yet, see the online FHL catalog: www.familysearch.org/search/catalog/1019467.

1846-1900 Index to Militia Lists, Sonoma County, California **[Online Database]**, indexed at the RootsWeb site for Sonoma Co CA. See www.rootsweb.ancestry.com/~cascgs/militia.htm.

1846-1986. *California Information File, 1846-1986* **[Microfiche]**, from the index cards at the California State Library, Sacramento. Contains an index to the California Information File which has 717,000 cards bearing about 1.4 million citations to information in California periodicals, newspapers, manuscript collections, selected books, vertical file collections, county histories, government documents, theses, biographical encyclopedias, biographical files, etc. A User's Guide to the California Information File, is available under FHL call no. 979.4 A1 No. 127. Card file filmed by Commercial Microfilm Service, Bellevue, WA, 1986, 550 microfiche, beginning with FHL fiche #6333977. (A. – Adams, Charles). For a complete list of fiche numbers and the contents of each, see the online FHL catalog page for this title: www.familysearch.org/search/catalog/651525.

✓ **NOTE:** The *California Information File* is a huge card index at the CA State Library in Sacramento. It is one of the most important sources of genealogical information for California people. The California Information File is only available outside of the CA State Library as a microfiche publication. Unfortunately, this extremely valuable database will never be seen online as a searchable database anytime soon. Unless, that is, the State of California digitizes this file. But like all states, California depends heavily on the Family History Library in Salt Lake to undertake the work to digitize their databases. But the policies of FamilySearch International (the FHL digitizing group) places microfiche way down on their list of priorities for digitizing projects. To date, they have digitized exactly zero microfiche databases. They have several million rolls of microfilm to digitize, and that means several more years before they will tackle the thousands of microfiche in their collection, if at all. The FHL is set up with numerous automated reel microfilm digitizers, but nothing for microfiche.

1846-2016. *California Newspaper Archives* **[Online Database]**, digitized and indexed at the GenealogyBank.com website. One search screen for names and keywords in the following city newspapers: Benicia, Berkeley, Coachella, Coloma, Colton, Columbia, Darwin, Downieville, El Centro, Folsom, Fowler, Fresno, Glendale, Grass Valley, Idyllwild, Imperial, Jackson, Llano, Los Angeles, Manzanar, Mariposa, Marysville, Merced, Monterey, Newell, Oakland, Placerville, Quincy, Redding, Riverside, Sacramento, San Diego, San Francisco, San Jose, San Luis Obispo, Santa Anita, Santa Barbara, Santa Monica, Stanford, Stockton, Tanforan, Yankee Jim's, and Yreka www.genealogybank.com/gbnk/newspapers/explore/USA/California.

1847-1860. *California, Slave Era Insurance Polies Index* **[Online Database]**, indexed at the Ancestry.com website. Original data: Slavery Era Insurance Registry. California Department of Insurance. Each index record includes: Name,

Residence Date, Residence Place, Slaveholder, Slaveholder Residence, Submitted by, and a link to the CA Dept of Insurance website. This database has 688 records. See
https://search.ancestry.com/search/db.aspx?dbid=70760.

1849-1856 List of Emigrants who came to California via Rancho Santa Ana del Chino, San Bernardino County, California [Online Database], indexed at the USGenWeb site for San Bernardino Co, see http://files.usgwarchives.net/ca/sanbernardino/emigrants/chino.txt.

1849-1860. *The Argonauts of California: Being the Reminiscences of Scenes and Incidents that Occurred in California in Early Mining Days by a Pioneer* [Printed Book & Digital Version], by C. W. Haskins, publ., 1890, NY: Fords, Howard & Hubert, 501 pages, FHL book 979.4 H2. To access the digital images, see the online FHL catalog: www.familysearch.org/search/catalog/1857345.
- See also, *Index to The Argonauts of California, by Charles Warren Haskins* [Printed Book & Digital Version], by Libera Martina Spinazze, publ. 1975, New Orleans: Polyanthos, 514 pages, FHL book 979.4 H2. To access the digital version, see the online FHL catalog: www.familysearch.org/search/catalog/282435.

1849-1888. *List of Deaths Copied from Records in the California State Library* [Microfilm & Digital Capture], from original manuscripts at the California State Library, Sacramento, CA. Contains records of deaths compiled from various sources, such as the U.S. censuses [Mortality Schedules] of 1850-1870; deaths and interments in Sacramento during the years 1849, and 1885 copied from books of the Clark-Booth and Yardley Funeral Home; Book of the Dead compiled by H. B. Phillips and B. M. Newcomb, which contains records of N. Gray & Co. undertakers in San Francisco; and from entries copied from head stones in the old cemeteries at Coloma, Diamond Springs, and Red Bluff. Filmed by the Genealogical Society of Utah, 1975, 1 roll, FHL film #2631. Another filming, 1985, FHL film #1405497. To access the digital images, see the online FHL catalog:
www.familysearch.org/search/catalog/612629.

1849-1985. *California County Naturalizations* [Online Database], indexed at the FamilySearch.org website. Source: County courts of California. Includes county naturalization records for Alameda, Amador, Alpine, Butte, Calaveras, Colusa, El Dorado, Fresno, Glenn, Lake, Lassen, Los Angeles, Mendocino, Napa, Nevada, Orange, Placer, Sacramento, San Francisco, Sonoma, Santa Clara, Stanislaus, Santa Barbara, San Benito, San Diego, Solano, Sutter, Yolo, and Yuba counties. Coverage dates will vary by county. This database has 312,705 records. See www.familysearch.org/search/collection/2125028.

1849-1935. *California, Pioneer Migration Index, Compiled 1906-1935* [Online Database], digitized and indexed at FamilySearch.org, from microfilm of a card file located at the California State Library, Sacramento. This database is an index to persons who were California pioneers or migrated to California from other states. Includes name, place, and date of birth, parents, spouse, place, and date married, date of arrival in California, overland or by vessel, name of vessel, states lived in before coming to California, places of residence in California, profession or occupation, public offices held, politics, where educated, principal events in history of California, place, and date of death, signature, miscellaneous notes. See
www.familysearch.org/search/collection/2137266.
- See also, *California, Pioneer Migration Index, Compiled 1906-1935* [Microfilm & Digital Capture], from the card file at the California State Library. To access the digital images, see the online FHL catalog: www.familysearch.org/search/catalog/2137266.

1849-1960. *Mortuary (Burial) Records, Northern California* [Microfilm & Digital Capture], from a card file at the CA State Library, Sacramento. Filmed by the Genealogical Society of Utah, 1991, 13 rolls, beginning with FHL film #1683914 (A-Battly, J). This database is a card file arranged in alphabetical order by surname of burials in the northern California area ca. 1849-1900. Includes name of deceased, age and date of birth, date and cause of death, name of attending physician (if known), and place of burial: along with a listing of the various sources for burial information. The title "Mortuary records" was supplied by the Special Collections Section of the California State Library, Sacramento. The file actually indexes burial records from a variety of sources in the library's collection. To access the digital images, see the online FHL catalog:
www.familysearch.org/search/catalog/486002.
- See also, *List of Deaths Copied From Records in the California State Library* [Microfilm & Digital Capture], from a manuscript at the CA State Library. Contains records of deaths compiled from various sources, such as the U.S. censuses of 1850-1870; deaths and interments in Sacramento during the years 1849, and 1885 copied from books of the Clark-Booth and Yardley Funeral Home; Book of the Dead compiled by H. B. Phillips and B. M. Newcomb, which contains records of N. Gray & Co. undertakers in San Francisco; and from entries copied from head stones in the old cemeteries at Coloma, Diamond Springs, and Red

Bluff. Filmed by the Genealogical Society of Utah, c1975, 1 roll, FHL film #2631, another filming, 1985, FHL film #1405497. To access the digital images, see the online FHL catalog:
www.familysearch.org/search/catalog/612629.

1849-1980. *California, County Birth, Marriage, and Death Records* **[Online Database],** indexed at the Ancestry.com website. Source: CA Dept. of Public Health. Each marriage record includes: Name, Gender, Event type, Marriage date, Marriage place, and Spouse. Birth and death records are similar. This database has 3,028,466 records. See
https://search.ancestry.com/search/db.aspx?dbid=61460.

1849-1994. *California, County Birth and Death Records* **[Online Database],** digitized at the Ancestry.com website. Source: FamilySearch extractions. This is an image-only database, derived from a larger span of years at the FamilySearch.org website. Ancestry's page has a link to the FamilySearch information page. This database has 2,922,713 records:
https://search.ancestry.com/search/db.aspx?dbid=60240.

1849-1986. *Pioneers of California Index: Index to the Daughters of the American Revolution Collection of all 26 Volumes of California Pioneer Biographies* **[Printed Book & Digital Version],** indexed by Robert L. Davignon for the DAR (California), 1986, 57 pages, FHL book 079.4 D32. To access the digital version, see the online FHL catalog:
www.familysearch.org/search/catalog/210373.

1849-1988. *Index to American Biography and Genealogy: California Edition v. 1 & 2* **[Printed Book & Digital Version],** by the East Bay Genealogical Society, 1988, 112 pages. To access the digital images, see the online FHL catalog:
www.familysearch.org/search/catalog/2505993.

1850 San Francisco City Directory **[Online Database],** indexed at the SFGenealogy site. Archived: https://web.archive.org/web/20161018061952/www.sfgenealogy.com/sf/1850/hd850a.htm..

1850. *California, 1850 Federal Census: Population Schedules* **[Microfilm & Digital Capture],** from the originals at the National Archives, part of series M432, 4 rolls, FHL has the following:
- Butte and Calaveras Counties, FHL film #2490.
- El Dorado County & Colusa County, FHL film #2491.
- Los Angeles, Marin, Mariposa, Mendocino, Monterey, Napa, Sacramento, Santa Barbara, Santa Cruz, San Diego, San Joaquin, and San Luis Obispo Counties; Shasta County (part), Shasta City (part), FHL film #2492.
- Solano, Sonoma, Sutter, Colusa (part), Shasta County (part), Shasta City (part), Trinity, Tuolumne, Yolo, and Yuba Counties, FHL film #442879.

To access the digital images, see the online FHL catalog: www.familysearch.org/search/catalog/744471.

✓ **NOTE.** The 1850 CA census had three missing counties: Contra Costa, San Francisco, and Santa Clara. These three counties were included in the 1852 CA State Census, but three more counties are missing from the 1852 census records: Colusa, Sutter, and Marin. See the map on page 56 for more details.

1850. *Index to the 1850 Census of the State of California* **[Printed Index],** compiled by Alan P. Bowman, published by Genealogical Publishing Co., Inc., Baltimore, 1972, 605 pages. Includes all California counties except Contra Costa, San Francisco, and Santa Clara Counties. FHL book 979.4 X2p.

1850. See *California 1850 Census Index* **[Printed Index],** edited by Ronald Vern Jackson, et al, published by Accelerated Indexing Systems, Bountiful, UT, 1978, 144 pages. FHL book 979.4X2j.

1850. See *California 1850 Census Index, A-Z* **[Printed Index],** published by Heritage Quest, Bountiful, UT, 2001, 643 pages. FHL book 979.4 X22h.

1850. *Census of the City and County of Los Angeles, California For the Year 1850, Together With an Analysis and an Appendix* **[Printed Book],** by Maurice H. Newmark and Marco R. Newmark, published by the Los Angeles Times-Mirror Press, 1929, 139 pages. FHL book 979.493 X2p 1850.

1850 Census, San Joaquin County **[Online Database],** digitized and indexed at the Ancestry.com website. Original data prepared by the San Joaquin County Genealogical Society, 1959. See
http://search.ancestry.com/search/db.aspx?dbid=26638.

1850-1860. *Monterey, California Census* **[Online Database],** indexed at the FamilySearch.org website. Source: 1850, 1852, and 1860 Censuses for Monterey Co CA, databases created by Lorrain Escobar, 1999. This database has 12,094 records. See
https://search.ancestry.com/search/db.aspx?dbid=4141.

1850 and 1852. *San Diego Census, 1850 Federal, 1852 California* **[Printed Book],** compiled by the San Diego Genealogical Society, 1984, 64 pages. FHL book 979.498 X2s.

1850 and 1852. *San Diego Taxpayers* **[Printed Book]**, researched and typed by members of San Diego Genealogical Society, 1984, 48 pages. Contains various lists of assessments and tax rolls for San Diego City for the years 1850-1852. FHL book 979.498/S1 R4s.

1850, 1852, and 1860 Monterey, California Census, 1852 Census of San Diego County, and 1860 Census of Santa Cruz County **[Online Database]**, digitized and indexed at the Ancestry.com website. See http://search.ancestry.com/search/db.aspx?dbid=4141.

1850-1864. *San Francisco Ship Passenger Lists* **[Online Database]**, digitized and OCR indexed at the Ancestry.com website. Original data: Rasmussen, Louis J., *San Francisco Ship Passenger Lists,* 3 Vols., publ. Genealogical Publishing Co., Baltimore, 2003. In the absence of official port records - destroyed by fire in 1940 - this work attempts a reconstruction of passenger arrivals from newspapers and journals. Typically, each passenger list is preceded by the name of ship, type of ship, port of embarkation, date of arrival, name of captain, description of cargo, and notes concerning the passage, which include date of departure, ports of call, length of voyage, and names of passengers who died en route, with their places of residence and dates of death.
- For Vol. I (1850-1864), See
http://search.ancestry.com/search/db.aspx?dbid=49329.
- For Vol. II (1850-1851), see
http://search.ancestry.com/search/db.aspx?dbid=49066.
- For Vol. III (1851-1852), see
http://search.ancestry.com/search/db.aspx?dbid=49330.

1850-1865. *Marriage Records of San Joaquin County* **[Online Database]**, digitized and indexed at the Ancestry.com website. Original data prepared by the San Joaquin County Genealogical Society, 1969. See http://search.ancestry.com/search/db.aspx?dbid=26496.

1850-1877. *California Marriages* **[Online Database]**, digitized and indexed at the Ancestry.com website. This is a database compiled by the Upper Snake River Family History Center and BYU- Idaho, part of an ongoing project to extract and index original county marriage records from all states west of the Mississippi River. Not all CA counties are included. The records were extracted from marriage books located at county courthouses. See
http://search.ancestry.com/search/db.aspx?dbid=7848.

1850-1880. See *California Mortality Schedules, 1850, 1860,1870, 1880* **[Printed Index]**, extracted and published by the Roots Cellar-Sacramento Genealogical Society, Citrus Heights, CA, 1995, 237 pages, FHL book 979.4 X28c.

1850-1898 San Francisco County Index of Naturalized Voters **[Microfilm & Digital Capture]**, from the original index cards located in the San Francisco Archives. Cards contain name of voter and date when voter was naturalized. Also includes number of voter's precinct and ward. Filmed by the Genealogical Society of Utah, 1983, 6 rolls, as follows:
- Voters index, A – C, FHL film #1378779.
- Voters index, C – H, FHL film #1378780.
- Voters index, H - McLeod, D, FHL film #1378781.
- Voters index, McLeod, A – R, FHL film #1378782.
- Voters index, R – V, FHL film #1378783.
- Voters index, V – Z, FHL film #1378784.

To access the digital images, see the online FHL catalog: www.familysearch.org/search/catalog/106446.

1850-1900. *Index to Patents (Solano County, California)* **[Microfilm & Digital Capture]**, from original records at the County Register/Recorder Clerk's Office in Norwalk, CA. Patents are the original documents given to the first owner of land (land grants, homesteads, public land sales, etc.). Filmed by the Genealogical Society of Utah, 1998, 1 roll, FHL film #2115530. To access the digital images, see the online FHL catalog:
www.familysearch.org/search/catalog/1129614.

1850 to early 1900s. See *The Confirmation of Spanish and Mexican Land Grants in California* **[Printed Book]**, by Ivy Belle Ross, reprint of thesis done in 1928 for the University of California, published by R. & E. Research Associates, 1974, 59 pages. FHL book 979.4 A1 No. 46.

1850-1904. *Pre-1905 Death Index, El Dorado County, California* **[Online Database]**. indexed at the RootsWeb site for El Dorado Co CA. See
www.rootsweb.ancestry.com/~cabf1905/El-Dorado/ElDoradoCoIndx.htm.

1850-1930. *Index to Records of Supreme Court Cases* **[Microfilm & Digital Capture]**, from original records at the State Archives, Sacramento, CA. Filmed by the Genealogical Society of Utah, 1975, 2 rolls, FHL film #978908 (Plaintiff Index) and FHL film #978909 (Defendant Index). To access the digital images, see the online FHL catalog:
www.familysearch.org/search/catalog/208747.

1850-1931. *San Francisco Area, California, Funeral Home Records* **[Online Database]**, indexed at the Ancestry.com website. Source: FamilySearch extractions. This database has 115,845 records. See https://search.ancestry.com/search/db.aspx?dbid=60249.

1850-1941. *California, Marriage Records from Select Counties* **[Online Database],** indexed at the Ancestry.com website. Source: CA State Archives, Sacramento. This collection includes marriage records from two counties in California: Alameda County, licenses, certificates, and indexes, 1850-1941; and Marin County, affidavits for marriage licenses, 1919-1936. Indexes will include the names of the bride and groom (and in some cases the officiant). This database has 416,981 records. See **https://search.ancestry.com/search/db.aspx?dbid=8797.**

1850-1944 Index to Wills and Probate Records, Colusa County, California **[Online Database],** indexed at the USGenWeb site for Colusa Co CA. See **http://files.usgwarchives.net/ca/colusa/probate/willprob.txt**

1850-1945. *California County Marriages* **[Online Database],** from the original records housed in the clerks' offices of the district courts in various counties throughout California. digitized and indexed at the FamilySearch website, these marriage records come from the FamilySearch collection on microfilm, including licenses, certificates, applications, affidavits, stubs, etc. This database has 92,154 records, see **www.familysearch.org/search/collection/1674735.**
- This database is also available at Ancestry.com . See **https://search.ancestry.com/search/db.aspx?dbid=60241.**

1850-1952. *California, County Marriages* **[Online Database],** indexed at the FamilySearch.org website. Source: FamilySearch extractions from CA county courthouses. Index and images of marriage records. Includes licenses, certificates, registers, applications, affidavits, and stubs. This database has 1,986,899 records. See **www.familysearch.org/search/collection/1804002.**

1850-1953. *California, Wills and Probate Records* **[Online Database],** indexed at the Ancestry.com website. Original data: California County, District and Probate Courts. Records include Will, Letters of Administration, Inventories, Distributions and Accounting, Bonds, and Guardianships. Each index record includes: Name, Probate Date, Probate Place, Inferred Death Year, Inferred Death Place, and Item Description. Each record also displays a useful Table of Content with the number of images, and the page range for types of papers, such as Will Papers, Order Papers, Account Papers, Petition Papers, etc. This database has 199,138 records. See **https://search.ancestry.com/search/db.aspx?dbid=8639.**

1850-1960. *California, Cemetery Transcriptions* **[Online Database],** digitized and indexed at FamilySearch.org. Includes transcriptions from cemeteries in Amador, Fresno, Los Angeles, Mariposa, Merced, Napa, Riverside, Sacramento, San Joaquin, San Mateo, Santa Cruz, Siskiyou, Solano, Stanislaus, Sutter, Tulare, Yolo, and Yuba counties. See **www.familysearch.org/search/collection/1985807.**

1850-1970s. *Index to Transcripts of Court Cases in State Archives, Attorney General, State of California* **[Microfilm & Digital Capture],** from original records at the State Archives, Sacramento, CA. Filmed by the Genealogical Society of Utah, 1975, 1 roll, FHL film #978914. To access the digital images, see the online FHL catalog: **www.familysearch.org/search/catalog/208730.**

1850-1986. *California, State Court Naturalization Records* **[Online Database],** indexed at the Ancestry.com website. Source: CA State Archives, Sacramento. The records include mostly Petitions, Declarations, and Certificates. Each Declaration index record may include: Name, Declaration age, Record type, Birth date, Birthplace, Declaration date, and Declaration place. The document image may have much more information about a person and relatives. This database has 121,323 records. See **https://search.ancestry.com/search/db.aspx?dbid=8839.**

1850-1991. *California, San Joaquin, County Public Library Obituary Index* **[Online Database],** digitized at the FamilySearch.org website. Includes images of index cards located at the San Joaquin County Public Library, Stockton, CA. The index cards contain clippings from various county and city newspapers of obituaries. This database has 98,787 records. See **www.familysearch.org/search/collection/1929846.**
- This database is also at the Ancestry.com website. See **https://search.ancestry.com/search/db.aspx?dbid=60248.**

1850-Present. *Countywide Genealogical Name Lists* **[Online Databases],** indexed at the USGenWeb sites for most California counties. At the main CA Index, select a county, then review the list of genealogical databases available online for each. A typical county list includes biographies, cemeteries, histories, land records, military records, obituaries, photographs, vital records, see **http://files.usgwarchives.net/ca/.**

1850-Present. *Napa County Records* **[Online Database],** index to probates, deaths, censuses, early pioneers, and more, at the USGenWeb site for Napa Co CA, see **www.usgwarchives.net/ca/napa/napa.html.**

1850-Present. *Solano County Records* **[Online Database],** index to probates, deaths, censuses, early pioneers, and more, at the RootsWeb site for Solano Co CA, Archived at: **https://web.archive.org/web/20160417211817/http://www.rootsweb.ancestry.com/~cascgsi/**

1851-1891. *California, San Mateo County Records* **[Online Database],** indexed at the FamilySearch.org website. Source: Mateo County Clerk, Redwood City, CA. County records including marriage intentions, naturalizations, deeds, patents, homesteads, and military service discharges. The marriage intentions have been indexed. This database has 14,144 records. See **www.familysearch.org/search/collection/1878749.**

1851-1904. *Pre-1905 Death Index, Placer County, California* **[Online Database],** indexed at the RootsWeb site for Placer Co CA. See **www.rootsweb.ancestry.com/~cabf1905/Placer/PlacerCoIndx.htm.**

1851-1907. *Imperial County Grantor and Grantee Indexes to Deeds* **[Microfilm & Digital Capture],** from the records located at the Imperial County Recorder's Office, El Centro, CA. These name lists are shown for Imperial County because that county has no Great Registers available. Filmed by the Genealogical Society of Utah, 1985, 1 roll, FHL film #1433101. To access the digital images, see the online FHL catalog: **www.familysearch.org/search/catalog/499164.**

1851-1953. *California, Prison and Correctional Records* **[Online Database],** indexed at the Ancestry.com website. Source: CA State Archives, records from Folsom State Prison, San Quentin State Prison, and Dept of Corrections, Youth Authority Dept. Records. This collection includes a variety of records from state prisons and reform schools, including inmate registers, photo albums, photo identification cards, mug shots, and descriptive lists. Each index record may include: Date and number of commitment, Name, Nativity, Occupation, Crime, Sentence date and term, Conviction date, County sent from. Age, Physical description, Discharge dates, and Prison number. This database has 284,800 records. See **https://search.ancestry.com/search/db.aspx?dbid=8833.**

1851-1967. *California, San Mateo County Records* **[Online Database],** digitized at the FamilySearch website. County records including marriage intentions, naturalizations, deeds, patents, homesteads, and military service discharges. This collection is being published as images become available. The database has 414,624 images. See **www.familysearch.org/search/collection/1878749.**

1852 California State Census **[Microfilm & Digital Capture],** from the original schedules at the California State Archives, Sacramento. This was the only state census taken by the state of California. Filmed by the Genealogical Society of Utah, 1972, 6 rolls, as follows:
- Butte, Calaveras, Contra Costa, and El Dorado Counties, FHL film #909229.
- El Dorado, Los Angeles, Mariposa, Klamath Mendocino, Monterey, Napa, Nevada, and Placer (part) Counties, FHL film #909230.
- Placer (part), Sacramento, San Diego, San Francisco (part) Counties, FHL film #909231.
- San Francisco (part), and San Joaquin (part) Counties, FHL film #909232.
- San Joaquin, San Luis Obispo, Santa Barbara, Santa Clara, Santa Cruz, Shasta, Sierra, Siskiyou, Solano, Sonoma, Trinity, and Tulare Counties, FHL film #909233.
- Tuolumne, Yolo, and Yuba Counties, FHL film #909234.

To access the digital images, see the online FHL catalog: **www.familysearch.org/search/catalog/189335.**

1852 California State Census **[Online Database],** digitized and indexed at the Ancestry.com website. California's 1850 state constitution dictated that a census be taken in 1852, in 1855, and every 10 years after that. The 1852 census was the only one taken, but it proved to be an important count. The gold rush would bring about 300,000 people to California between 1848 and 1854. The CA 1852 State Census needs to be considered as an extension of the 1850 CA Federal Census. The accuracy of the 1850 census was called into some question because of the rapid growth and mobility of the population at the time as miners poured into the state. The 1850 U.S. Federal Census tallied California's population at 92,597. The 1852 California state census count came in at 260,949 (neither census include the Native American population, estimated at over 100,000 in 1848). Not only did the 1852 census provide a record of an additional 150,000 people but includes records from the three lost counties from the 1850 census - Contra Costa, San Francisco, and Santa Clara. However, three counties are missing from the 1852 census records: Colusa, Sutter, and Marin. Also, the images for 1852 Butte County are included, but due to the condition of the images no names could be captured from them. This database has 164,511 records. See **http://search.ancestry.com/search/db.aspx?dbid=1767.**

- See also, *1852 California State Census (and Index)* **[Microfilm & Digital Capture],** from a typed transcript compiled in 1935 by the Daughters of the American Revolution. Includes index. Filmed by the DAR, 3 rolls, as follows:
- Butte, Calaveras, Colusa, Contra Costa, Eldorado, Klamath, Los Angeles, Marin, Mariposa, Mendocino, Monterey, Napa, Nevada, Placer, San Diego, and Sacramento Counties, FHL film #558285.
- San Diego, San Francisco, San Joaquin, San Luis Obispo, Santa Barbara, Santa Clara, Santa Cruz, and Shasta Counties, FHL film #558286.

• Sierra, Siskiyou, Solano, Sutter, Trinity, Tulare, Tuolumne, Yolo, and Yuba Counties, FHL film #558287.

To access the digital images, see the online FHL catalog: www.familysearch.org/search/catalog/225297.

- See also, *Index to the Gold Rush Census, California, 1852: Every-Name Index of the 1852 California Census Microfilm and the Subsequent 1935 D.A.R. Transcription* [CD-ROM], prepared by the Southern California Genealogical Society, 2000, Burbank, CA, see FHL CD No. 1017.

- See also, *California, State Census, 1852* [Online Database], indexed at the FamilySearch.org website. Includes a complete name index of population schedules listing the inhabitants of the state of California in 1852. See www.familysearch.org/search/collection/1771089.

1852 California State Census, Klamath County, California [Online Database], page images of the original census pages at a RootsWeb Site. See http://freepages.genealogy.rootsweb.ancestry.com/~klamathcountycalif/census1852/census1852.htm.

1852 California State Census, Placer County, California [Online Database], page images of the original census pages at the BudLink. Site. See www.budlink.us/index_52.htm.

1852. *Solano County, California 1852 State Census Index* [Printed Index], compiled by Cordell Cowart, published by the Solano County Genealogical Society, Fairfield, CA, 1992, 60 pages. Index gives name of person, age, sex, occupation, birth state or country and page number in original census. FHL book 979.452 X22c.

1852 California State Census. See An Alphabetical Index and Reprint of the Schedules for the Residents of Sonoma County, California, June 21 - October 21, 1852 [Printed Extract & Index], edited by Dennis Harris, Redwood Empire Social History Project, Department of History, Sonoma State University. Published by the Sonoma County Historical Records Commission, Santa Rosa, CA, 1983, 146 pages. FHL book 979.418 X22h 1852.

1852 California State Census, Tulare County, California [Online Database], indexed at the USGenWeb site for Tulare Co CA. See http://files.usgwarchives.net/ca/tulare/census/tul1852.txt.

1852 San Francisco City Directory [Online Database], indexed at the SFGenealogy site. Archived: https://web.archive.org/web/20161018061954/www.sfgenealogy.com/sf/1852/52menu.htm.

1852-1853 San Francisco City Directory [Online Database], indexed at the SFGenealogy site. Archived: https://web.archive.org/web/20161018062005/http://www.sfgenealogy.com/sf/1853/53menu.htm.

1852-1989. *California, Northern U.S. District Court Naturalization Records Index* [Online Database], digitized and indexed at FamilySearch.org. Source: National Archives microfilm series M1744. This collection is a card index to naturalization records in the district and circuit courts of Northern California. Each court underwent jurisdictional and name changes over time. The circuit court(s) include: the Special Circuit Court, 1855-1863; the Tenth Circuit Court, 1863-1866; the Ninth Circuit Court for the District of California, 1866-1886; and the Circuit Court for the Northern District of California, 1886-1911. The District Courts included: the Northern District of California, 1852-1916; the Southern Division of the Northern District, 1917-1966; the Northern District, 1966-1973; and the Northern Division of the Northern District, 1973-1989. This database has 1,391,725 records, see www.familysearch.org/search/collection/1849982.

1852-1904. *Marriage Records of Shasta County, California* [Online Database], digitized and OCR indexed at the Ancestry.com website. Source: Book, same title, publ. Shasta Co Genealogical Society, Redding CA. This database has 93 pages. See https://search.ancestry.com/search/db.aspx?dbid=30202.

- See also *Shasta County, California Marriages, 1852-1904* [Online Database], indexed at the Ancestry.com website. Source: Shasta Genealogy Society, Redding, CA. Search by either the name of the bride or the name of the groom. This database has 3,249 records. See https://search.ancestry.com/search/db.aspx?dbid=3862.

1852-1910. *Private Land Grant Cases in the Circuit Court of the Northern District of California, 1852-1910* [Microfilm & Digital Capture], from the original records located in the National Archives, Washington, DC. The Circuit Court of the Northern District of California was abolished in 1911. The cases were given to the U.S. District Court for the Northern District of California in 1912. Courts are located in San Francisco. The land grants were originally made from 1769-1846 by the Spanish and the Mexican governments, and later confirmed by the U.S. government from 1852-1910 through the Board of California Land Commissioners. Title to more than 8.8 million acres, nearly 14,000 square miles, of California land was based on 588 grants that were originally made by Spanish or Mexican authorities from 1769 to 1846 and later confirmed by the U.S. Government. Litigation concerning the land titles began immediately after the

area was ceded by Mexico in 1848 and is continuing. Filmed by the National Archives, series T1207, 28 rolls, beginning with FHL film #940180 (General index to cases). To access the digital images, see the online FHL catalog:
www.familysearch.org/search/catalog/225508.
- See also, *California, Private Land Claim Dockets, 1852-1858* **[Online Database],** indexed at the Ancestry.com website. Source: National Archives microfilm T910. This series contains dockets (lists of case files) concerning private land claims in California. These claims were based on historical Spanish and Mexican land grants that took place before California became part of the United States. The primary purpose of the dockets in this series was to show the actions taken regarding the claims after they were confirmed as valid by the United States. Included are notices and evidence of claims, certificates and plats of survey, affidavits, deeds, abstracts of title, testimonies regarding claims, copies of decisions in contests in Federal Courts, appeals, and letters. The collection is organized by docket number. Each record in the index typically includes the name of the landowner, their docket number, and a record date for the docket. This database has 721 records. See
https://search.ancestry.com/search/db.aspx?dbid=61191.
- See also, *Index and Calendar to Private Land Grant Cases, U.S. District Court, Northern District of California, 1853-1904* **[Microfilm & Digital Capture],** from the original records located in the National Archives. Filmed by the National Archives, series T1214, 1 roll, FHL film #940151. Another filming: FHL film #1415714. To access the digital images, see the online FHL catalog:
www.familysearch.org/search/catalog/231761.

1852-1932. *Shasta County, California, Naturalization Records* **[Online Database],** indexed at the Ancestry.com website. Source: Database compiled. by the Shasta Co Genealogical Society. Each index record includes: Name, Country of Birth, Date Naturalized, and Court Record Book. This database has 1,804 records. See
https://search.ancestry.com/search/db.aspx?dbid=6099.

1852-1989. *California, Northern U.S. District Court Naturalization Index* **[Online Database],** digitized at the FamilySearch website. This collection is a card index to naturalization records in the district and circuit courts of Northern California. Each court underwent jurisdictional and name changes over time. The circuit court(s) include: the Special Circuit Court, 1855-1863; the Tenth Circuit Court, 1863-1866; the Ninth Circuit Court for the District of California, 1866-1886; and the Circuit Court for the Northern District of California, 1886-1911. The District Courts included the Northern District of California, 1852-1916; the Southern Division of the Northern District, 1917-1966; the Northern District, 1966-1973; and the Northern Division of the Northern District, 1973-1989. NARA publication M1744: Index to Naturalization in the U.S. District Court for the Northern District of California, 1852-ca. 1989. This database has 581,446 records. See
www.familysearch.org/search/collection/1849982.

1852-1999. *Merced County, California Deaths* **[Online Database],** indexed at the Ancestry.com website. Source: Vitalsearch, Inc. extractions from the county recorder's office in Merced, CA. This database has 51,816 records. See
https://search.ancestry.com/search/db.aspx?dbid=4390.

1853-1904. See *Pre-1905 Death Index, San Bernardino County, California* **[Online Database].** indexed at the RootsWeb site for San Bernardino Co CA. See www.rootsweb.ancestry.com/~cabf1905/San-Bernardino/SanBdnoColndx.htm.

1854 Assessment Roll, Marin County, California **[Online Database],** indexed at SFgenealogy.com site. Archived at
https://web.archive.org/web/20170810052454/www.sfgenealogy.com/marin/1850s/1854assess.htm.

1854-1878. *Index to Private Land Grant Cases, U.S. District Court, Southern District of California* **[Microfilm & Digital Capture],** from the original records located in the National Archives, Washington, DC. Contains index and dockets of land grant cases, arranged by docket number, for the years 1854-1878. Filmed by the National Archives, Series T1215, 1 roll, FHL film #940153. Another filming: FHL film #1415715. To access the digital images, see the online FHL catalog:
www.familysearch.org/search/catalog/231979.

1855 Naturalizations, Sacramento County, California **[Online Database],** extracted list of names and places of nativity by date, from the Sacramento Daily Union, Jan. 4, 1956. Extract at the RootsWeb site for Sacramento Co CA. See
http://freepages.genealogy.rootsweb.ancestry.com/~npmelton/nat55.htm.

1855-1991. *California, San Mateo County Records* **[Online Database],** digitized at the FamilySearch.org website. Includes marriage intentions, naturalizations, deeds, patents, homesteads, and military service discharges. This database has 1,594,496 records. See
www.familysearch.org/search/collection/1878749.
- This database is also at the Ancestry.com website. See
https://search.ancestry.com/search/db.aspx?dbid=60244.

1855, 1860-1861, 1861-1862, 1897, & 1898 Assessment Rolls, Shasta County, California **[Online Database],** transcribed from the original Assessment, Tax Roll, or Poll Tax books, at the RootsWeb site for Shasta Co CA. See http://freepages.genealogy.rootsweb.ancestry.com/~shastaca/taxrollindex.html.

1856-1995 California Land Patents Database **[Online Database],** indexed by county by the Bureau of Land Management (BLM). Separate websites can be accessed for most California counties, giving an alphabetized list of the name of the patent holder, date entered, and a complete property description, including Meridian, Township, Range, Section, and Document ID. For an index to the available California counties, see http://files.usgwarchives.net/ca/.

1856. *Personal Name Index to the 1856 City Directories of California* **[Printed Index],** compiled By Nathan C. Parker, published by Gale Research, Detroit, MI, 1980, 250 pages, FHL book 979.4 E42p.

1856-1923. *California, State Hospital Records* **[Online Database],** indexed at the Ancestry.com website. Source: CA State Archives records from state hospitals in Stockton, Sonoma, and Mendocino, CA. This collection contains case books and descriptions, commitment registers, and indexes for patients admitted to or discharged from mental hospitals in the state of California. Some indexes include: Name, Age, Birth date, Birthplace, Record date, Race, Gender. And Hospital location. This database has 40,822 records: https://search.ancestry.com/search/db.aspx?dbid=9206.

1856-1967. See *California, San Mateo County, Colma, Italian Cemetery Records* **[Online Database],** digitized at the FamilySearch website. Index cards and daily logbook of the Italian Cemetery in Colma. This collection is being published as images become available. This database has 30,857 images: www.familysearch.org/search/collection/1922526.

1856 County Directory, Nevada County, California **[Online Database],** indexed at the USGenWeb site for Nevada Co CA. See www.cagenweb.com/nevada/nc1856.html.

1857 Assessor's List, San Francisco, California **[Online Database],** indexed at the SFGenealogy site. See www.sfgenealogy.com/sf/list1857.htm.

1857-1973. *California, Oakland, Mountain View Cemetery Records* **[Online Database],** digitized and indexed at FamilySearch.org. This collection includes indexes to burials, internments, and funeral home records. This database has 129,202 records, see www.familysearch.org/search/collection/3161361.

1858-1923. *California, Military Registers* **[Online Database],** indexed at the Ancestry.com website. Source: CA State Archives, records of the Adjutant General. Details in the records can include soldier or sailor's name; regiment; company; rank; nativity; age; occupation; enlistment and discharge dates and places; injuries, illnesses or diseases; marital status and remarks. This database has 142,771 records. See https://search.ancestry.com/search/db.aspx?dbid=8807.

1859. *Sacramento California, "Sacramento Bee" Newspaper, Obituaries, Marriages, Births* **[Online Database],** indexed at the Ancestry.com website. Original data: Harris, Sandra, Sacramento Bee newspaper. Sacramento, CA: 1859. Located at the Sacramento State Library. This database has 6,092 records. See https://search.ancestry.com/search/db.aspx?dbid=5724.

1859-1920 Probate Case Index, Tulare County, California **[Online Database],** indexed at the USGenWeb site for Tulare Co CA. See http://files.usgwarchives.net/ca/tulare/probate/tcprbt20.txt.

1860. *California, 1860 Federal Census: Population Schedules* **[Microfilm & Digital Capture],** from the original records at the National Archives, Washington, DC. Filmed twice by the National Archives, 1950, 1967, 23 rolls total, beginning with FHL film #803055 (2nd filming, Alameda and Amador counties). To access the digital images, see the online FHL catalog: www.familysearch.org/search/catalog/704546.

1860. See *California, 1860* **[Printed Index],** compiled by Ronald Vern Jackson, et al, published by Accelerated Indexing Systems, Salt Lake City, UT, 1984, 726 pages, FHL book 979.4 X22.

1860. *See California 1860 Census Index* **[Printed Index],** compiled by Index Publishing, published by Heritage Quest, Bountiful, UT, 1999, 2 vols., FHL book 979.4 X22h 1860 v.1 & v. 2.

1860-1901 Probate Case Index, Tulare County, California **[Online Database],** indexed at the USGenWeb site for Tulare Co CA. Archived at https://web.archive.org/web/20110920034403/http://files.usgwarchives.net/ca/tulare/probate/tularprb.txt.

1861-1865. *Index to Compiled Service Records of Volunteer Union Soldiers Who Served in Organizations From the State of California* **[Microfilm],** from the original records at the National

Archives, Central Plains Branch, Kansas City, MO, Series M0533, filmed by the National Archives, FHL has 7 rolls, as follows:
- Surnames A-C, FHL film #881609.
- Surnames Co-Fos, FHL film #881610.
- Surnames Fot-I, FHL film #881611.
- Surnames J-McD, FHL film #881612.
- Surnames McE-P, FHL film #881613.
- Surnames Q-St, FHL film #881614.
- Surnames Su-Z, FHL film #881615.

To see if this microfilm was digitized yet, see the online FHL catalog: www.familysearch.org/search/catalog/313585.

1861-1865. *Index to Soldiers & Sailors of the Civil War* **[Online Database],** a searchable name index to 6.3 million Union and Confederate Civil War soldiers now available online at the National Park Service website. A search can be done by surname, first name, state, or unit. California supplied 21,405 men to the war (all Union). To search for one, go to the Soldiers and Sailors Database. See www.nps.gov/civilwar/soldiers-and-sailors-database.htm.

1861-1865. *Compiled Service Records, Union & Confederate Soldiers* **[Online Database].** This fully searchable database contains digitized images of the card abstracts of a soldier's Compiled Service Record, with information collected from original muster rolls, returns, rosters, payrolls, appointment books, hospital registers, prison registers and rolls, parole rolls, and inspection reports. This database is the images and includes a whole new index that can be compared with the earlier Soldiers and Sailors Database. See www.fold3.com/category_19.

1861-1867. *Records of California Men in the War of the Rebellion* **[Online Database],** digitized and OCR indexed at the Ancestry.com website. From the 883-page book at the State Office with the same title, published in 1890. See
http://search.ancestry.com/search/db.aspx?dbid=28258.

1861-1867. *A Personal Name Index to Orton's "Records of California Men in the War of the Rebellion, 1861-1867,"* compiled by Parker J. Carlyle, published by Gale Research, 1978, 153 pages, FHL book 979.4 M2.

1861-1923 San Francisco City Directories [Online Database], digitized and indexed at the Fold3 website. Years inclusive except 1866, 1870, 1872, and 1906 missing. This database has 97,359 images. See www.fold3.com/title_471/city_directories_san_francisco/.

1862-1866 Internal Revenue Assessment Lists for California **[Microfilm & Digital Capture],** from the original records located in the National Archives, Washington, DC. Lists are arranged alphabetically by surname of those being assessed for each period. Filmed by the National Archives, 1988. FHL has 33 rolls, beginning with FHL film #1534664 (Annual lists, 1863). To access the digital images, see the online FHL catalog: www.familysearch.org/search/catalog/577932.

1862-1880. See *Fresno County Assessment Rolls, 1872-1880* **[Microfilm & Digital Capture],** from the records located at the Fresno County Public Library, Fresno, CA. Rolls are arranged in alphabetical order by first initial of surname of owner. Contains record of assessments of real and secured personal property, showing name of owner, description of property, value, amount assessed, and date paid, etc. Filmed by the Genealogical Society of Utah, 1994, 2 rolls, FHL film #1955259 (1862, 1872-1873 Assessment rolls), and FHL film #1955260 (1872-1880 Assessment rolls). To access the digital images, see the online FHL catalog: www.familysearch.org/search/catalog/743805.

1862-1950. *California, Railroad Employment Records* **[Online Database],** indexed at the Ancestry.com website. Original data: California Railroad Employment Records, 1862-1950. 579 volumes. California State Railroad Museum Library, Sacramento, CA. This collection of employment records from railroad companies operating in California includes pay lists, blacklists, and seniority lists. Many of the employees on these lists were Asian immigrants who came to build the railroads. This collection contains payroll records for the Southern Pacific, its subsidiaries, and additional railroad companies. It also contains the San Joaquin Division Seniority List from 1878-1917 and the Blacklist Book from 1887-1892, which contains employees who had been blacklisted from working on the railroad, as well as records from the Sierra Railway Company of California from 1899-1937. The index of these records is searchable by name, date, and railroad, and the records contain: Name, Occupation, Pay date, and Roll date. This database has 5,689,563 records. See https://search.ancestry.com/search/db.aspx?dbid=2046.

1863 San Francisco City Directory **[Online Database],** indexed at the SFGenealogy site. Archived: https://web.archive.org/web/20160316193834/www.sfgenealogy.com/php/dbs/1863sfd.php.

1864 San Francisco City Directory **[Online Database],** indexed at the SFGenealogy site. Archived: https://web.archive.org/web/20160416000108/www.sfgenealogy.com/php/dbs/1864sfd.php.

1864-1985. *California, Church Records* **[Online Database],** digitized and indexed at FamilySearch.org. This collection contains church records from various denominations in California, for the years 1864 to 1985, including: St. Clement's Episcopal Church (Berkeley, California) and The Reorganized Church of Jesus Christ of Latter-day Saints (El Monte, Los Angeles County). The record content and time period varies by denomination and locality, see
www.familysearch.org/search/collection/2790461.

1865-1923 San Francisco Chronicle **[Online Database],** this newspaper was digitized, and OCR indexed at the Fold3.com website. See
www.fold3.com/title_246/san_francisco_chronicle/.

1865-1904. See *Pre-1905 California Death Index, San Francisco County, CA* **[Online Database],** listed by date of death at the RootsWeb site for San Francisco, CA. See
www.rootsweb.ancestry.com/~cabf1905/San-Francisco/SanFranCoIndx.htm.

1866-1898. *California Great Registers* **[Online Database],** digitized and indexed at the Ancestry.com website, taken from the microfilm of the originals at the California State Library, Sacramento, CA. The first voter registrations in California took place in 1866 following the Registry Act, an effort to prevent voter fraud that called for "the registration of the citizens of the State, and for the enrollment in the several election districts of all the legal voters thereof, and for the prevention and punishment of frauds affecting the elective franchise." An 1872 law required counties to publish an index or alphabetical listing of all registered voters every two years. These lists were kept by the county clerk and eventually were usually printed in even-numbered years, though a few counties, including San Francisco, published them yearly for a few years at a time. The voter lists produced are known as the Great Registers, and this database contains the printed copies of the registers produced by the county clerks. Only men over the age of 21 were eligible to vote until 1911, when women were granted the right. The state occasionally passed other exclusionary voting laws: an 1879 state constitutional amendment denied franchise to natives of China (it was repealed in 1926), and an 1894 law established a literacy requirement. Content in the registers varies some from county to county and year to year. Earlier registers may list only a name, age, nativity (state or country), occupation, local residence, and naturalization details. However, the lists grew more detailed as time went on, and in later registers you may find: name, occupation, age, height, complexion, color of eyes, color of hair, visible marks or scars, country of nativity, place of residence, date, place, and court of naturalization, date of voter registration, post office address, able to read Constitution, able to write name, able to mark ballot, nature of disability, or transferred from different voting precinct. Below is a list of counties and years for which records are included in this database. Even though this list sometimes indicates an inclusive year range of a decade or more, the records were typically published every other year. This database has 3,682,235 records. To search for a person in the 1866-1898 California Great Registers database:
http://search.ancestry.com/search/db.aspx?dbid=2221.
- See also, *California, Great Registers, 1866-1910* **[Online Database],** digitized and indexed at the FamilySearch.org website. County Clerk voting registers from most counties in California. The registers were created every other year. Time period varies by county. See
www.familysearch.org/search/collection/1935764.

1866-1898 California Great Registers, by county:
- Alameda (1867, 1872–1873, 1875–1898)
- Alpine (1873–1890)
- Amador (1867–1898)
- Butte (1867, 1872–1873, 1875, 1879–1882, 1886, 1890– 1898)
- Calaveras (1867–1898)
- Colusa (1871–1898)
- Contra Costa (1867–1898)
- Del Norte (1872–1898)
- El Dorado (1867–1898)
- Fresno (1867, 1871–1873, 1875–1877, 1879–1880, 1884–1886, 1890–1898)
- Glenn (1892–1898)
- Humboldt (1871–1873, 1875, 1879–1882, 1890–1898)
- Inyo (1871–1872, 1875, 1877, 1879–1898)
- Imperial (none in this database, see 1900-1968 series)
- Kern (1867, 1872–1873, 1877, 1879–1898)
- Kings (none in this database, see 1900-1968 series)
- Klamath (1869, 1873)
- Lake (1872–1873, 1875, 1879–1880, 1888–1898)
- Lassen (1868, 1873, 1877, 1879, 1886, 1890, 1898)
- Los Angeles (1873, 1875–1876, 1879–1894, 1896
- Madera (1898)
- Marin (1867–1868, 1873, 1875–1876, 1879–1898)
- Mariposa (1872–1873, 1875–1877, 1879–1898)
- Mendocino (1867, 1871–1898)
- Merced (1867–1872, 1875–1880, 1890–1898)
- Modoc (1875–1876, 1879–1880, 1888–1898)
- Mono (1872, 1875–1876, 1879–1898)
- Monterey (1867–1869, 1872, 1875–1876, 1879–1880, 1884–1898)
- Napa (1867–1898)
- Nevada (1867–1868, 1871, 1873, 1875–1877, 1879–1898)
- Orange (1892–1896)

- Placer (1867–1868, 1871–1873, 1876–1877, 1879–1898)
- Plumas (1867–1898)
- Riverside (none, see 1905-1935 city directories for substitutes)
- Sacramento (1867–1868, 1872–1873, 1875–1877, 1879–1892, 1896–1898)
- San Benito (1875–1898)
- San Bernardino (1872, 1876, 1879–1898)
- San Diego (1867, 1871–1873, 1875–1877, 1879–1880, 1884–1886, 1890–1898)
- San Francisco (1866–1867, 1869, 1871 supplement, 1872–1873, 1875, 1876–1877, 1878, 1880, 1882, 1886–1890) [Districts 29–48], 1892, 1896–1898)
- San Joaquin (1867–1869, 1871–1873, 1875–1877, 1880–1884, 1888–1898)
- San Luis Obispo (1867–1868, 1871–1873, 1875, 1877, 1879–1880, 1884–1892, 1898)
- San Mateo (1867–1869, 1871–1872, 1875–1877, 1879–1880–1886, 1890–1898)
- Santa Barbara (1873–1875, 1877, 1879, 1890–1898)
- Santa Clara (1867–1869, 1871–1873, 1875–1876, 1879, 1880–1884, 1888–1896)
- Santa Cruz (1868–1869, 1871–1873, 1880, 1886, 1890–1898)
- Shasta (1867–1869, 1871–1873, 1875–1877, 1880–1882, 1886–1896)
- Sierra (1872–1898)
- Siskiyou (1867–1898)
- Solano (1867, 1872–1873, 1875–1882, 1888–1898)
- Sonoma (1867, 1871–1873, 1875, 1879–1880, 1884, 1888–1896)
- Stanislaus (1867, 1869, 1871–1872, 1875, 1879–1880, 1886–1898)
- Sutter (1867–1898)
- Tehama (1875–1896)
- Trinity (1867–1868, 1871–1873, 1875, 1877, 1879, 1888–1896)
- Tulare (1869, 1872, 1879–1896)
- Tuolumne (1867, 1871, 1873, 1875, 1877, 1879–1898)
- Ventura (1875, 1877, 1879–1880, 1882, 1886–1890, 1898)
- Yolo (1867, 1871–1872, 1875, 1877–1882, 1886–1898)
- Yuba (1867–1896)

1866-1878 Butte County, California, Great Register **[Microfilm & Digital Capture], from** the typescripts located at the Paradise Genealogical Society Library, Paradise, California. Contains an extraction in chronological order, then alphabetical order by first letter only of surname of the great registers or voting registers of Butte County. Gives name, age, birthplace, occupation, residence and date registered. Filmed by the Genealogical Society of Utah, 1992, 1 roll, FHL film #1831809. To access the digital images, see the online FHL catalog: **www.familysearch.org/search/catalog/630973**.

1866-1909. Butte County Great Registers and Indexes **[Microfilm & Digital Capture], from** the original records located at the Meriam Library, California State University, Chico. Filmed by the Genealogical Society of Utah, 1990, 6 rolls, as follows:
- Index, Great registers, 1866-1878, A-Z, FHL film #1685570.
- Index, Great registers, 1884-1894, A-Z, FHL film #1685571.
- Great registers, 1896, FHL film #1685572.
- Great registers, 1900, FHL film #1685573.
- Great registers, 1902-1909, FHL film #1685574.
- Great registers, 1906-1907, FHL film #1685575.

To access the digital images, see the online FHL catalog: **www.familysearch.org/search/catalog/364443**.

1866-1908 Fresno County Great Registers **[Microfilm & Digital Capture], from** the records located at the Fresno County Public Library, Fresno, CA. Contains registers of legal voters giving name, age, occupation, country of nativity, post office address, naturalization court and place (if applicable), etc. Early registers from 1866 to 1895 are arranged alphabetically by surname. Registers from 1896 are arranged alphabetically by precinct name and then alphabetically by surname within the precinct. Filmed by the Genealogical Society of Utah, 1994, 16 rolls, as follows:
- 1866-1877, 1878-1887, 1887-1890, FHL film #1955187.
- 1887-1899, 1896-1899 Fresno City, FHL film #1955188.
- 1893-1895, 1873-1874, FHL film #1955717.
- 1896-1899, FHL film #1955189.
- 1896-1900, FHL film #1955190.
- 1900, FHL film #1955191.
- 1900-1902 , Fresno City, FHL film #1955193.
- 1902, FHL film #1955194.
- 1902, Fresno City, 1904 Precincts, FHL film #1955195.
- 1904 Precincts, FHL film #1955196.
- 1904 Precincts, 1904 Fresno City, FHL film #1955197.
- 1906 Precincts, FHL film #1955198.
- 1906 Precincts, FHL film #1955199.
- 1906 Fresno City, 1906 Precincts, 1908 Precincts, FHL film #1955257.
- 1908 Fresno County, FHL film #955258.
- 1908 Fresno Co., 1908 Fresno City, FHL film #1955259.

To access the digital images, see the online FHL catalog: **www.familysearch.org/search/catalog/703169**.

1866-1909 Colusa County Great Registers **[Microfilm & Digital Capture]**, from the original records at the Colusa County Clerk's Office, Colusa, CA. Each year is alphabetically arranged by first letter of surname. Filmed by the Genealogical Society of Utah, 1989, 4 rolls, as follows:
- 1866-1877, FHL film #1666711.
- 1866-1890, 1890, A-L, FHL film #1666712.
- 1890, A-Z; 1892, A-Z, 1896, FHL film #1666724.
- 1900-1902, A-Z, 1904-1909, A-Z, FHL film #1666725.

To access the digital images, see the online FHL catalog: **www.familysearch.org/search/catalog/571690**.

1866-1875. *County of Humboldt Great Registers* **[Printed Abstract & Index]**, compiled by Marilyn Keach Milota, published by Humboldt County Genealogical Society, Eureka, CA, 1996, 322 pages. Contains an abstract of the original great register, arranged in alphabetical order by surname and giving complete name, registration number, age, place of nativity, occupation, place of residence and date of registration. FHL book 979.412 N48m 1866-1875.

1866-1880. *Great Register: Containing the Names and Registration of the Domiciled Inhabitants of the County of Sacramento, Qualified Electors and Legal Voters Thereof* **[Microfilm & Digital Capture]**, from an apparent original volume, source and location unknown. Filmed by the Genealogical Society of Utah, c1975, 1 roll, FHL film #590424. To access the digital images, see the online FHL catalog: **www.familysearch.org/search/catalog/155344**.

1866-1890, 1892-1894, 1896-1901 Lassen County Great Registers **[Microfilm & Digital Capture]**, from the original records located at Lassen County Courthouse, Susanville, CA. Volumes arranged alphabetically by first letter of surname. Register includes name, age, occupation, county or state of nativity, local residence, naturalization (if applicable), etc. Filmed by the Genealogical Society of Utah, 1992, 1 roll, FHL film #1853495. To access the digital images, see the online FHL catalog: **www.familysearch.org/search/catalog/628981**.

1866-1873, 1866-1879 Mendocino, California Great Registers **[Microfilm & Digital Capture]**, from the registers located at Held Poage Memorial Home & Research Library, Mendocino County Historical Society, Ukiah, CA. Contains a register of voters, giving name, age, country of nativity, occupation, local residence, date, place and court when naturalized, and date of voter registration. Although the dates for both registers would seem to indicate duplicates; they are separate and not the same. The first register is missing surnames from A to D. Arranged in alphabetical order by surname initial. Filmed by the Genealogical Society of Utah, 1991, 1 roll, FHL film #1769135. To access the digital images, see the online FHL catalog: **www.familysearch.org/search/catalog/523306**.

1866-1892. *Napa and Butte Counties, Obituaries* **[Online Database]**, indexed at the FamilySearch.org website. Index and images of obituaries and news stories from Napa County and from the town of Paradise in Butte County. Indexed records may have connections to multiple images due to articles continuing on multiple pages. This database has 37,422 records. See **www.familysearch.org/search/collection/2284856**.

1866-1908 Marin County Great Registers **[Microfilm & Digital Capture]**, from the original records at the California State Archives, Sacramento, CA. Original register of printed copies in the State Library. Each year is alphabetically arranged by first letter of surname. Filmed by the Genealogical Society of Utah, 1975, 6 rolls, as follows:
- Great registers, 1866-1892, FHL film #980447.
- Great registers, 1892, 1894, FHL film #980448.
- Great registers, 1896, FHL film #980449.
- Great registers, 1900, FHL film #980450.
- Great registers, 1902, 1904, FHL film #980451.
- Great registers, 1906, 1908, FHL film #980452.

To access the digital images, see the online FHL catalog: **www.familysearch.org/search/catalog/212350**.

1866-1920 Alpine County Great Registers; Indexes **[Microfilm & Digital Capture]**, from the original records located at the Alpine County Historical Records Commission, Markleeville, CA. Registers list registration number, name, age, occupation residence, precinct, country or state of nativity, post office address, date, place and court of naturalization, date of registration. Indexes to great registers are arranged by precinct number and give registration number, name, address, occupation and sometimes political party. Filmed by the Genealogical Society of Utah, 1993, 1 roll, FHL film #1888010 (Great registers and indexes). To access the digital images, see the online FHL catalog: **www.familysearch.org/search/catalog/663187**.

1866-1873. *Great Register, San Diego County* **[Printed Extract]**, researched and compiled by Patricia Sewell, published by the San Diego Genealogical Society, 1984, 203 pages. Contains a list of voters of San Diego County for the years 1866-1873. FHL book 979.498 N4s.

1866-1884 Great Registers, Shasta County, California **[Online Database],** indexed at the RootsWeb site for Shasta Co CA. See http://freepages.genealogy.rootsweb.ancestry.com/~shastaca/voter.html.

1866-1904. *Great Registers, 1866-1898, Indexes, 1866, 1888-1904, San Francisco County, California* **[Microfilm & Digital Capture],** from the original records at the California State Library, Sacramento, CA. Filmed by the Genealogical Society of Utah, 1975, 184 rolls, beginning with FHL film #1001665 (Index, Abbe – Hamilton, C). To access the digital images, see the online FHL catalog: www.familysearch.org/search/catalog/313680.

1866-1884, & 1894 Great Registers, Shasta County, California **[Online Database],** indexed at the RootsWeb site for Shasta Co CA. See http://freepages.genealogy.rootsweb.ancestry.com/~shastaca/voter.html.

1866-1901. *Sacramento County Great Registers* **[Microfilm],** from the original records at the California State Archives, Sacramento, CA. Each year is alphabetically arranged by first letter of surname. Contains original volumes of the printed copies in the State Library. Filmed by the Genealogical Society of Utah, 1975, 19 rolls, as follows:
- Great registers, 1866, 1871, 1873, FHL film #978917.
- Great registers, 1874-1880, FHL film #978918.
- Great registers, 1880-1881, FHL film #978919.
- Great registers, 1881-1888, FHL film #978920.
- Great registers, 1882, 1884, 1886, FHL film #978921.
- Great registers, 1888, FHL film #978922.
- Great registers, 1890, FHL film #978923.
- Great registers, A-N 1890, FHL film #978924.
- Great registers, O-Z 1890, FHL film #978925.
- Great registers, 1892, FHL film #978926.
- Great registers, 1894, FHL film #978927.
- Great registers, 1895 (supplement), FHL film #978928.
- Great registers, A-K 1896, FHL film #978929.
- Great registers, L-Z 1896, FHL film #978930.
- Great registers 1897 (supplement), A-K 1898, FHL film #978931.
- Great registers, L-Z 1898, FHL film #978932.
- Great registers (supplement) 1898-1899, A-D 1900, FHL film #978933.
- Great registers, E-Q 1900, FHL film #978934.
- Great registers, R-Z 1900, 1900-1901 (supplement), FHL film #978935.

To access the digital images, see the online FHL catalog: www.familysearch.org/search/catalog/210199.

1867 San Francisco Delinquent Tax List **[Online Database],** indexed at the SFGenealogy site. Archived: https://web.archive.org/web/20171210070510/www.sfgenealogy.com/sf/tax1867.htm.

1867 and 1872 Index to Sacramento County Voter Registrations **[Microfilm & Digital Capture]** from the original card file located at the California State Library, Sacramento. Contains names of voters taken from the Great Register for Sacramento County, 1867 and 1872, arranged in alphabetical order by surname, giving name, age, nationality, occupation, location of residence, and date of registration. Filmed by the Genealogical Society of Utah, 1991, 7 rolls, as follows:
- 1867, A - Craw, A 1867, FHL film #1711488.
- 1867, Craw, A – Smith, A, FHL film #1711489.
- 1867, Smith, A - Z, FHL film #1711597.
- 1872, Clays - Hatch, C, FHL film #1711598.
- 1872, Hatch, C. - Mix, FHL film #1711599.
- 1872, Mix - Thomas, A, FHL film #1711600.
- 1872, Thomas, A - Z, FHL film #1711601.

To access the digital images, see the online FHL catalog: www.familysearch.org/search/catalog/486373.

1867-1872. See *Sacramento, California, California Biographical Great Books* **[Online Database],** indexed at the Ancestry.com website. Original data: California State Library, California Section, miscellaneous card indexes. This database contains an index and images of index cards with biographical data extracted from the Sacramento County Great Register of Voters for the years 1867 and 1872. Information on the cards making up this database was extracted from the 1867 and 1872 registers for Sacramento County. The cards may contain: Name, Age, Birthplace (nativity), Occupation, Local residence by city or township, Naturalization date or place, and Date of registration. This database has 14,493 records. See https://search.ancestry.com/search/db.aspx?dbid=2343.

1867-1892 Calaveras County Great Registers **[Microfilm & Digital Capture],** from the original records at the California State Library, Sacramento, CA. Includes the following years: 1867, 1871, 1872, 1873, 1875, 1876, 1877, 1879, 1880, 1882, 1884, 1886, 1888, 1890, and 1892. Filmed by the Genealogical Society of Utah, 1975, 1 roll. FHL film #976456. To access the digital images, see the online FHL catalog: www.familysearch.org/search/catalog/207211.

1867-1898 Sacramento County Great Registers **[Microfilm & Digital Capture],** from the original records at the California State Library, Sacramento, CA. Each year is alphabetically arranged by first letter of surname. Filmed by the Genealogical Society of Utah, 1975, 3 rolls, as follows:

- Great registers, 1867-1868, 1872-1873, 1875-1877, 1879, FHL film #977088.
- Great registers, 1880, 1882, 1884, 1886, 1888, 1890, FHL film #977089.
- Great registers, 1892, 1896, 1898, FHL film #977090.

To access the digital images, see the online FHL catalog: www.familysearch.org/search/catalog/208109,

***1867-1894 Alameda County Great Registers* [Microfilm & Digital Capture],** from the original records at the California State Library, Sacramento, CA. Each year is alphabetically arranged by first letter of surname. Filmed by the Genealogical Society of Utah, 1975, 7 rolls, as follows:
- 1867, 1872-1873, 1875-1878, FHL film #976446.
- 1879-1880, 1882, 1884, 1886, 1888, FHL film #976447.
- 1890, 1892, FHL film #976448.
- 1894, FHL film #976449.
- 1896, FHL film # 976450.
- 1898, FHL film #976451.
- 1898 (supplement), FHL film #976452.

To access the digital images, see the online FHL catalog: www.familysearch.org/search/catalog/206978.

***1867-1898 Amador County Great Registers* [Microfilm & Digital Capture],** from the original records at the California State Library, Sacramento. Includes the following years: 1867, 1868, 1871, 1872, 1873, 1875, 1876, 1877, 1879, 1880, 1884, 1886, 1888, 1890, 1892, 1894, 1896, 1898. Filmed by the Genealogical Society of Utah, 1975, 1 roll, FHL film #976453. To access the digital images, see the online FHL catalog: www.familysearch.org/search/catalog/207200.

***1867-1898 Butte County Great Registers* [Microfilm & Digital Capture],** from the original records at the California State Library, Sacramento, CA. Each year is alphabetically arranged by first letter of surname. Filmed by the Genealogical Society of Utah, 1975, 2 rolls, as follows:
- 1867, 1872-1873, 1875, 1879-1880, 1882, 1886, 1890, 1892, 1894, and 1896, FHL film #976454.
- 1898, FHL film #976455.

To access the digital images, see the online FHL catalog: www.familysearch.org/search/catalog/207301.

***1867-1908 Butte County, California, Great Register* [Microfilm & Digital Capture],** from the typescript located at the Paradise Genealogical Society Library, Paradise, California. Contains a listing by district and precinct of adult males over 21 years of age, giving name, age, state or country of nativity, occupation, local residence. Filmed by the Genealogical Society of Utah, 1992, 1 roll, FHL film #1831809. To access the digital images, see the online FHL catalog: www.familysearch.org/search/catalog/631040.

***1867-1898 San Diego County Great Registers* [Microfilm & Digital Capture],** from the original records at the California State Library, Sacramento, CA. Filmed by the Genealogical Society of Utah, 1975, 2 rolls, as follows:
- Great registers, 1867, 1871-1873, 1875-1877, 1879-1880, 1884, 1886, 1890, FHL film #977094.
- Great registers, 1892, 1894, 1896, 1898, FHL film #977095.

To access the digital images, see the online FHL catalog: www.familysearch.org/search/catalog/208148.

***1867-1898 Contra Costa County Great Registers* [Microfilm & Digital Capture],** from the original records at the California State Library, Sacramento, CA. Filmed by the Genealogical Society of Utah, 1975, 1 roll. Includes the following years: 1867, 1871, 1872, 1873, 1875, 1877, 1879, 1880, 1884, 1886, 1890, 1892, 1894, 1896, 1898, FHL film #976458. To access the digital images, see the online FHL catalog: www.familysearch.org/search/catalog/207312.

***1867-1898 El Dorado County Great Register* [Microfilm & Digital Capture],** from the original records at the California State Library, Sacramento, CA. Includes the following years: 1867, 1868, 1872, 1873, 1875, 1876, 1877, 1878, 1879, 1880, 1882, 1886, 1888, 1890, 1892, 1894, 1896, 1898. Filmed by the Genealogical Society of Utah, 1975, 1 roll, FHL film #976460. To access the digital images, see the online FHL catalog:
www.familysearch.org/search/catalog/207324.

***1867-1898 Fresno County Great Registers* [Microfilm & Digital Capture],** from the original records at the California State Library, Sacramento, CA. Filmed by the Genealogical Society of Utah, 1975, 2 rolls, as follows:
- Great registers 1867, 1871-1873, 1875-1877, 1879-1880, 1884, 1886, 1890, FHL film #976461.
- Great registers 1892, 1894, 1896, 1898, FHL film #976462.

www.familysearch.org/search/catalog/207042.

***1867-1898 Kern County Great Registers* [Microfilm & Digital Capture],** from the original records at the California State Library, Sacramento, CA. Filmed by the Genealogical Society of Utah, 1975, 2 rolls, as follows:
- Great registers 1867, 1872-1873, 1873, 1877, 1879-1880, 1882, 1884, 1886, 1888, 1890, FHL film #976467.

- Great registers 1892, 1894, 1896, 1898, FHL film #976468.

To access the digital images, see the online FHL catalog: www.familysearch.org/search/catalog/207005.

***1867-1898 Napa County Great Registers* [Microfilm & Digital Capture],** from the original records at the California State Library, Sacramento, CA. Includes the following years: 1867, 1872, 1875, 1880, 1888, 1890, 1892, 1894, 1896, 1898. Filmed by the Genealogical Society of Utah, 1975, 1 roll, FHL film #977081.
To access the digital images, see the online FHL catalog: www.familysearch.org/search/catalog/207611.

***1867, 1869, 1872, 1875-1876, 1879-1880, 1884, 1886, 1888, 1890, 1892, 1894, 1896, 1898 Monterey County Great Registers* [Microfilm & Digital Capture],** from the original records at the California State Library, Sacramento, CA. Each year is alphabetically arranged by first letter of surname. Filmed by the Genealogical Society of Utah, 1975, 1 roll, FHL film #977080. To access the digital images, see the online FHL catalog: www.familysearch.org/search/catalog/207637.

***1867-1898 Nevada County Great Registers* [Microfilm & Digital Capture],** from the original records at the California State Library, Sacramento, CA. Filmed by the Genealogical Society of Utah, 1975, 2 rolls, as follows:
- Great registers 1867-1868, 1871, 1873 1875-1877, FHL film #977082.
- Great registers 1879-1880, 1882, 1884, 1886, 1888, 1890, 1892, 1894, 1896, 1898, FHL film #977083.

To access the digital images, see the online FHL catalog: www.familysearch.org/search/catalog/207571.

***1867-1894 Lake County Great Registers* [Microfilm & Digital Capture],** from the records located at the Lake County Museum, Lakeport, CA. Contains registration information of voters, giving registration number, name, age, country of nativity, occupation, local residence, naturalization date, place, and court (if pertinent), date of registration, sworn, and cancellations. Names are arranged within alphabetical sequence (i.e., no strict order within each surname initial letter). Filmed by the Genealogical Society of Utah, 1991, 1 roll, FHL film #1750347. To access the digital images, see the online FHL catalog: www.familysearch.org/search/catalog/493007.

***1867-1868, 1873, 1875-1876, 1879-1888, 1886, 1888, 1890, 1892, 1894, 1896, 1898 Marin County Great Registers* [Microfilm & Digital Capture],** from the original records at the California State Library, Sacramento, CA. Each year is alphabetically arranged by first letter of surname. Filmed by the Genealogical Society of Utah, 1975, 1 roll, FHL film #976933. To access the digital images, see the online FHL catalog: www.familysearch.org/search/catalog/207944.

1867. *San Luis Obispo County 1867 Great Register* [Printed Book], reprint of 1867 original published by William B. Cook, San Francisco, CA, reprint by San Luis Obispo County Genealogical Society, 1994, 8 pages. Contains an alphabetical listing by surname of voters, showing name, age, occupation, citizenship status, residence and date of entry in register. FHL book 979.4 A1 No. 195.

***1867-1868, 1871-1873, 1875, 1877, 1879-1880, 1884, 1886, 1888, 1890, 1892, 1898, San Luis Obispo County Great Registers* [Microfilm & Digital Capture],** from the original records at the California State Library, Sacramento, CA. Each year is alphabetically arranged by first letter of surname. Filmed by the Genealogical Society of Utah, 1975, 1 roll, FHL film #977284. To access the digital images, see the online FHL catalog: www.familysearch.org/search/catalog/208204.

***1867, 1869, 1871-1872, 1875-1877, 1879-1880, 1890, 1892, 1894, 1896, 1898 Merced County Great Registers* [Microfilm & Digital Capture],** from the original records at the California State Library, Sacramento, CA. Each year is alphabetically arranged by first letter of surname. Filmed by the Genealogical Society of Utah, 1975, 1 roll, FHL film #976937. To access the digital images, see the online FHL catalog: www.familysearch.org/search/catalog/207936.

***1867-1898 Plumas County Great registers* [Microfilm & Digital Capture],** from original records at the California State Library, Sacramento, CA. Includes the following years: 1867-1869, 1871, 1872, 1875-1877, 1879-1880, 1884, 1886, 1888, 1890, 1892, 1894, 1896 & 1898. Filmed by the Genealogical Society of Utah, 1975, 1 roll, FHL film #977087. To access the digital images, see the online FHL catalog: www.familysearch.org/search/catalog/208086.

***1867-1898 Placer County Great Registers* [Microfilm & Digital Capture],** from the original records at the California State Library, Sacramento, CA. Each year is arranged alphabetically by the first letter of surname. Filmed by the Genealogical Society of Utah, 1975, 2 rolls, as follows:
- Great registers, 1867-1868, 1871-1873, 1876-1877, 1879-1880, 1882, FHL film #977085.
- Great registers, 1884, 1886, 1888, 1890, 1892, 1894, 1896, 1898, FHL film #977086.

To access the digital images, see the online FHL catalog: www.familysearch.org/search/catalog/208067.

1867-1898 Solano County Great Registers **[Microfilm & Digital Capture],** from the original records at the California State Library, Sacramento, CA. Each year is alphabetically arranged by first letter of surname. Filmed by the Genealogical Society of Utah, 1975, 2 rolls, as follows:
- Great registers, 1867, 1872-1873, 1875-1880 1882, 1886, 1888, 1890, FHL film #978585.
- Great registers, 1892, 1894, 1896, 1898, FHL film #978586.

To access the digital images, see the online FHL catalog: **www.familysearch.org/search/catalog/210056.**

1867-1898 Sonoma County Great Registers **[Microfilm & Digital Capture],** from the original records at the California State Library, Sacramento, CA. Each year is alphabetically arranged by first letter of surname. Filmed by the Genealogical Society of Utah, 1975, 3 rolls, as follows:
- Great registers, 1867, 1871-1873, 1875, 1879-1880, 1884, 1888, 1890, FHL film #978587.
- Great registers, 1892, 1894, 1896, FHL film #978588.
- Great register, 1898, FHL film #978589.

To access the digital images, see the online FHL catalog: **www.familysearch.org/search/catalog/209628.**

1867-1898. *San Mateo County Great Registers, 1867-1869, 1871-1872, 1875-1877, 1879-1880, 1882, 1884, 1886, 1890, 1892, 1894, 1896, 1898* **[Microfilm & Digital Capture],** from the original records at the California State Library, Sacramento, CA. Each year is alphabetically arranged by first letter of surname. Filmed by the Genealogical Society of Utah, 1975, 1 roll, FHL film #977285. To access the digital images, see the online FHL catalog: **www.familysearch.org/search/catalog/208196.**

1867, 1869, 1871-1872, 1875, 1879-1880, 1886, 1888, 1890, 1892, 1894, 1896, 1898 Stanislaus County Great Registers **[Microfilm & Digital Capture],** from the original records at the California State Library, Sacramento, CA. Each year is alphabetically arranged by first letter of surname. Filmed by the Genealogical Society of Utah, 1975, 1 roll, FHL film #978590. To access the digital images, see the online FHL catalog: **www.familysearch.org/search/catalog/209621.**

1867-1898 Yolo County Great Registers **[Microfilm & Digital Capture],** from the original records at the California State Library, Sacramento, CA. Each year is alphabetically arranged by first letter of surname. Filmed by the Genealogical Society of Utah, 1975, 2 rolls, as follows:
- Great registers, 1867, 1871-1872, 1875, 1877-1880, 1882, 1886, 1888, 1890, FHL film #978597.
- Great registers 1892, 1894, 1896, 1898, FHL film #978598.

To access the digital images, see the online FHL catalog: **www.familysearch.org/search/catalog/208287.**

1867-1896 Yuba County Great Registers **[Microfilm & Digital Capture],** from the original records at the California State Library, Sacramento, CA. Each year is alphabetically arranged by first letter of surname. Includes the following years: 1867-1869, 1871-1873, 1875-1877, 1879-1880, 1882, 1884, 1888, 1890, 1892, 1894, 1896. Filmed by the Genealogical Society of Utah, 1975, 1 roll, FHL film #978599. To access the digital images, see the online FHL catalog: **www.familysearch.org/search/catalog/208261.**

1867, 1871, 1873, 1875, 1877, 1879-1888, 1882, 1884, 1886, 1888, 1890, 1892, 1894, 1896, 1898, Tuolumne County Great Registers **[Microfilm & Digital Capture],** from the original records at the California State Library, Sacramento, CA. Each year is alphabetically arranged by first letter of surname. Filmed by the Genealogical Society of Utah, 1975, 1 roll, FHL film #978595. To access the digital images, see the online FHL catalog: **www.familysearch.org/search/catalog/208347.**

1867-1898 Sutter County Great Registers **[Microfilm & Digital Capture],** from the original records at the California State Library, Sacramento, CA. Each year is alphabetically arranged by first letter of surname. Includes the following years: 1867, 1869, 1872-1873, 1875-1877, 1879-1880, 1882, 1886, 1888, 1890, 1892, 1894, 1896, 1898. Filmed by the Genealogical Society of Utah, 1975, 1 roll, FHL film #978591. To access the digital images, see the online FHL catalog: **www.familysearch.org/search/catalog/209619.**

1867-1868, 1871-1873, 1875, 1877, 1879, 1888, 1890, 1892, 1894, 1896 Trinity County Great Registers **[Microfilm & Digital Capture],** from the original records at the California State Library, Sacramento, CA. Each year is alphabetically arranged by first letter of surname. Filmed by the Genealogical Society of Utah, 1975, 1 roll, FHL film #978593. To access the digital images, see the online FHL catalog: **www.familysearch.org/search/catalog/208482.**

1867-1898 Siskiyou County Great Registers **[Microfilm & Digital Capture],** from the original records at the State Library, Sacramento, CA. Each year is alphabetically arranged by the first letter of a surname. Includes the following years: 1867-1868, 1872, 1875, 1877, 1879-1880, 1886, 1890, 1892, 1894, 1896, 1898. Filmed by the Genealogical Society of Utah, 1975, 1 roll, FHL film #978584, see www.familysearch.org/search/catalog/210065.

- See Also, *The 1867 Great Register for Siskiyou County, California* **[Printed Book],** compiled by John A. Dye and Judy K. Dye, published by the authors, Kent, WA, 1988, 24 pages. Includes surname index. FHL book 979.421 X2d 1867.

- See *Klamath County Great Registers, 1869-1873*, for the area of western Siskiyou County before 1874.

1867-1869, 1871-1873, 1875-1877, 1880, 1882, 1886, 1888, 1890, 1892, 1894, 1896 Shasta County Great Registers **[Microfilm & Digital Capture],** from the original records at the California State Library, Sacramento, CA. Each year is alphabetically arranged by first letter of surname. Filmed by the Genealogical Society of Utah, 1975, 1 roll, FHL film # 978582. To access the digital images, see the online FHL catalog:
www.familysearch.org/search/catalog/210151.

1867-1896, Santa Clara County Great Registers **[Microfilm & Digital Capture],** from the original records at the California State Library, Sacramento, CA. Each year is alphabetically arranged by first letter of surname. Filmed by the Genealogical Society of Utah, 1975, 4 rolls, as follows:
- Great registers, 1867-1869, 1871- 1873, 1875-1876, 1879, FHL film #977287.
- Great registers, 1880, 1882, 1884, 1888, 1890, FHL film #977288.
- Great registers, 1892, 1894 (A-Bailey), FHL film #977289.
- Great registers, 1894 (B-Z), 1896, FHL film #977290.

To access the digital images, see the online FHL catalog: **www.familysearch.org/search/catalog/208253.**

1867-1898 San Joaquin County Great Registers **[Microfilm & Digital Capture],** from the original records at the California State Library, Sacramento, CA. Each year is alphabetically arranged by first letter of surname. Filmed by the Genealogical Society of Utah, 1975, 3 rolls, as follows:
- Great registers, 1867-1869, 1871-1873, 1875-1877, 1880, 1882, 1884, 1888, 1890, FHL film #977281.
- Great registers, 1892, 1894, 1896, FHL film #977282.
- Great registers 1898 - FHL film #977283.

To access the digital images, see the online FHL catalog: **www.familysearch.org/search/catalog/208177.**

1868-1905 Abstract of Napa County Great Registers **[Microfilm & Digital Capture],** from the original records located at the Napa Valley Genealogical and Biographical Society, Napa, California. Copied by members of the society and arranged in alphabetical order for all Great Register years. Each entry contains name, age, nativity, date of registration, occupation, date of naturalization, residence and physical description of persons who registered to vote. Filmed by the Genealogical Society of Utah, 1997, 8 rolls, as follows:
- Great register, A to Buc, 1868-1905, FHL film #2074324.
- Great register, Buc to Far, 1868-1905, FHL film #2074354.
- Great register, Far to His, 1868-1905, FHL film #2074355.
- Great register, His to Mcc, 1868-1905, FHL film #2074356.
- Great register, Mcc to Ped, 1868-1905, FHL film #2074357.
- Great register, Ped to Ros, 1868-1905, FHL film #2074358.
- Great register, Ros to Vet, 1868-1905, FHL film #2074432.
- Great register, Vet to Zol, 1868-1905, FHL film #2074433.

To access the digital images, see the online FHL catalog: **www.familysearch.org/search/catalog/693940.**

1868-1869, 1871-1873, 1880, 1886, 1890, 1892, 1894, 1896, 1898 Santa Cruz County Great Registers **[Microfilm & Digital Capture],** from the original records at the California State Library, Sacramento, CA. Each year is alphabetically arranged by first letter of surname. Filmed by the Genealogical Society of Utah, 1975, 1 roll, FHL film #978581. To access the digital images, see the online FHL catalog: **www.familysearch.org/search/catalog/210163.**

1868. See *Certified Copies of All Poll Lists For Trinity County: As Transmitted to the County Clerk, for the General Election, to be Holden Tuesday, the Third Day of November, A.D. 1868* **[Microfilm],** from the original published by Gorden Printers, Weaverville, CA, 1868, 17 pages. Alphabetically arranged. Filmed by the Genealogical Society of Utah, 1960, 1 roll, FHL film #207673. To see if this microfilm was digitized yet, see the online FHL catalog:
www.familysearch.org/search/catalog/176708.

1868, 1873, 1877, 1879, 1886, 1890, 1898 Lassen County Great registers **[Microfilm & Digital Capture],** from the original records at the California State Library, Sacramento, CA. Each year is arranged

arranged by first letter of surname. Filmed by the Genealogical Society of Utah, 1975, 1 roll, FHL film #976470. To access the digital images, see the online FHL catalog:
www.familysearch.org/search/catalog/206749.

1868-1958. *California, San Diego Naturalization Index* **[Online Database],** digitized and indexed at the FamilySearch website, this is an index to Naturalized Citizens from the Superior Court of San Diego, California, 1868-1958. These index cards include the petitioner's name and file number, and often include residence and date of birth. Index courtesy of Fold3.com. See
www.familysearch.org/search/collection/1840471.

1868-1958 Naturalization Indexes, San Diego, California **[Online Database],** digitized and indexed at the Fold3 website. Each index card lists a petitioner's name, address, age or date of birth, and petition number. The "complete and true signature of holder" is also included, but not country of origin. The reverse of some cards may include a maiden name, names of children, and cross-referenced information (including name changes) from related files. This title contains over 23,000 cards. Look for wives and mothers on separate cards after 1922, as women were naturalized separately from men beginning in this time period. See
www.fold3.com/title_97/naturalization_index_ca_san_diego/.

1869 Great Register, Tulare County, California **[Online Database],** indexed at the USGenWeb site for Tulare Co CA. See
http://files.usgwarchives.net/ca/tulare/greatregister/gr1869.txt

1869, 1872, 1879-1880, 1882, 1884, 1886, 1888, 1890, 1892, 1894, 1896 Tulare County Great Registers **[Microfilm & Digital Capture],** from the original records at the California State Library, Sacramento, CA. Each year is alphabetically arranged by first letter of surname. Filmed by the Genealogical Society of Utah, 1975, 1 roll, FHL film #978594. To access the digital images, see the online FHL catalog:
www.familysearch.org/search/catalog/208459.

1869-1873 Klamath County Great Registers **[Microfilm & Digital Capture],** from the original records at the California State Library, Sacramento, CA. Each year is alphabetically arranged by first letter of surname. Klamath County was abolished in 1874, its area now in Del Norte County, northern Humboldt County, and western Siskiyou County. Filmed by the Genealogical Society of Utah, 1975, 1 roll, FHL film #976469. To access the digital images, see the online FHL catalog:
www.familysearch.org/search/catalog/206697.

1869-1911 Great Registers of the County of Santa Barbara, California **[Microfilm & Digital Capture],** from the original published by Santa Barbara Press, 1869. Includes Great Registers for the years 1866-1869; 1867; 1875; 1877; 1879; 1880; 1882; 1882 & 1884; 1886; 1886 with supplement of 1888; 1892; 1896; supplement to 1898 register; index to supplement to precinct, 1911. Names are in alphabetical order. Filmed by the Genealogical Society of Utah, 1988, 1 roll, FHL film #1548299. Another filming of 1879 vol., 1988, FHL film #1571207. To access the digital images, see the online FHL catalog:
www.familysearch.org/search/catalog/609766.

1870 California Federal Census: Population Schedules **[Microfilm & Digital Capture],** from the original records at the National Archives, Washington, DC. Filmed twice by the National Archives, 1962, 1968, 35 rolls total, beginning with FHL film #545567 (2nd filming, Alameda County). To access the digital images, see the online FHL catalog:
www.familysearch.org/search/catalog/698886.

1870. See *California 1870 census Index* **[Printed Index],** edited by Raeone Christensen Steuart, published by Heritage Quest, Bountiful, UT, 2000, 2 vols., FHL book 979.4 X22s v.1- v.2.

1870. See *California Census, 1870, Schedules of Products of Agriculture and Mortality Schedules* **[Microfilm],** from the original records at the California State Library, Sacramento, CA, Agriculture: gives name of agent, owner or manager, acres of land, present cash value, livestock, crops, value, etc.; Mortality: gives name of person who died, description, place of birth, month of death, cause of death, profession, etc. Filmed by the Genealogical Society of Utah, 1988, 1 roll, FHL film #1549970. To see if this microfilm was digitized yet, see the online FHL catalog:
www.familysearch.org/search/catalog/510082.

1870-1933. *California, Mortuary Records of Chinese Decedents* **[Online Database],** indexed at the Ancestry.com website. Source: National Archives microfilm A4040. These records were compiled by the San Francisco, California Immigration Office. The records consist of six volumes of registers (chronological lists) of mortuary records. Volumes 1 through 5 contain records of both native and foreign-born Chinese decedents. Volume 6 contains records only of native-born Chinese. Each volume is arranged in rough chronological order by the date the death

occurred or was recorded or reported. This database has 28,834 records. See
https://search.ancestry.com/search/db.aspx?dbid=2453.

1871 Great Register of Fresno County (Madera Precincts) [Online Database], indexed at the USGenWeb site for Madera Co CA. Archived at https://web.archive.org/web/20161229072603/http://www.cagenweb.com/madera/FresnoGreatR1871.htm.

1871-1872, 1875, 1877, 1879-1880, 1882, 1884, 1886, 1890, 1892, 1894, 1896, 1898 Inyo County Great Registers [Microfilm & Digital Capture], from the original records at the California State Library, Sacramento, CA. Each year is alphabetically arranged by first letter of surname. Filmed by the Genealogical Society of Utah, 1975, 1 roll, FHL film #976466. To access the digital images, see the online FHL catalog: www.familysearch.org/search/catalog/207019.

1871-1898 Colusa County Great Registers [Microfilm & Digital Capture], from the original records at the California State Library, Sacramento, CA. Filmed by the Genealogical Society of Utah, 1975. Includes the following years: 1871, 1872, 1873, 1875, 1876, 1880, 1886, 1890, 1892, 1894, 1896, 1898. FHL film #976457. To access the digital images, see the online FHL catalog: www.familysearch.org/search/catalog/207208.

1871-1898 Humboldt County Great Registers [Microfilm & Digital Capture], from the original records at the California State Library, Sacramento, CA. Each year is alphabetically arranged by first letter of surname. Filmed by the Genealogical Society of Utah, 1975, 2 rolls, as follows:
- Great registers, 1871-1873, 1875, 1879-1880, 1882, and 1890, FHL film #976464.
- Great registers, 1892, 1894, 1896, and 1898, FHL film #976465.

To access the digital images, see the online FHL catalog: www.familysearch.org/search/catalog/207027.

1871. See *Published by Authority, General List of Citizens of the United States Resident in the County of San Luis Obispo and Registered in the Great Register of Said County, August, 1871* [Printed Book], reprint of original printed by A. L. Bancroft & Company, San Francisco, reprinted by San Luis Obispo County Genealogical Society, Atascadero, CA, 1977, 25 pages. Contains name of resident, age, occupation, citizenship status, place of residence, date of entry in register. FHL book 979.478 N4p. Another copy: FHL book 979.478 N4Ge.

1872. See *The Foreign-born Voters of California in 1872: Including Naturalization Dates, Places, and Courts of Record* [Microfiche], compiled by Jim W. Faulkinbury, published by the author, Sacramento, 1994. Arranged in two sections: the first containing nativity demographics for each county, listing the number persons from various countries; and the second containing an alphabetical listing by surname, showing name, age, nativity, date and place naturalized, name of court, remarks, year registered and county where registered. Information taken from the great registers for 1872 of each county entered by the county clerks. FHL has 6 microfiche, beginning with FHL fiche #6334778. For a complete list of fiche numbers and contents of each, see the online FHL catalog page: www.familysearch.org/search/catalog/744409.

1872 Foreign-Born Voters of California [Online Database], taken from the publication by Jim W. Faulkinbury, indexed at the jwfresearch.com site. See www.jwfgenresearch.com/GR1872Home.htm.

1872 Great Register, Mariposa County, California [Online Database], indexed at the Mariposa Research.net site. See www.mariposaresearch.net/GR.html.

1872-1898 Del Norte County Great Registers [Microfilm & Digital Capture], from the original records at the California State Library, Sacramento, CA. Del Norte County absorbed part of old Klamath County in 1874. Includes the following years: 1872, 1875, 1876, 1878, 1886, 1890, 1892, 1894, 1896, 1898. Filmed by the Genealogical Society of Utah, 1975, 1 roll. FHL film #976459. To access the digital images, see the online FHL catalog: www.familysearch.org/search/catalog/207320.

1872-1905 Death Index, Ventura County, California [Online Database], originally indexed at the Ventura Co Gen Society site. Archived at http://web.archive.org/web/20120315235923/http://www.venturacogensoc.org/Obituaries.html.

1872-1873, 1875, 1879-1880, 1888, 1890, 1892, 1894, 1896, 1898 Lake County Great Registers [Microfilm], from the original records at the California State Library, Sacramento, CA. Each year is alphabetically arranged by first letter of surname. Filmed by the Genealogical Society of Utah, 1975, 1 roll, FHL film #976469. To access the digital images, see the online FHL catalog: www.familysearch.org/search/catalog/206989.

1872-1898 San Bernardino County Great Registers **[Microfilm & Digital Capture],** from the original records at the California State Library, Sacramento, CA. Each year is alphabetically arranged by first letter of surname. Filmed by the Genealogical Society of Utah, 1975, 2 rolls, as follows:
- Great registers, 1872, 1876, 1879-1880, 1882, 1884, 1886, 1888, 1890, 1892, 1894, 1896, FHL film #977092.
- Great registers, 1898, FHL film #977093.

To access the digital images, see the online FHL catalog: **www.familysearch.org/search/catalog/208136.**

1872-1873, 1875-1877, 1879-1880, 1882, 1884, 1886, 1888, 1890, 1892, 1894, 1896, 1898 Mariposa County Great Registers **[Microfilm],** from the original records at the California State Library, Sacramento, CA. Each year is alphabetically arranged by first letter of surname. Filmed by the Genealogical Society of Utah, 1975, 1 roll, FHL film #976934.

1872, 1875-1876, 1879-1880, 1882, 1884, 1886, 1888, 1890, 1892, 1894, 1896, 1898 Mono County Great Registers **[Microfilm & Digital Capture],** from the original records at the California State Library, Sacramento, CA. Each year is alphabetically arranged by first letter of surname. Filmed by the Genealogical Society of Utah, 1975, 1 roll, FHL film #976939. To access the digital images, see the online FHL catalog: **www.familysearch.org/search/catalog/208033.**

1872-1898 Sierra County Great Registers **[Microfilm & Digital Capture],** from the original records at the California State Library, Sacramento, CA. Each year is alphabetically arranged by first letter of surname. Includes the following years: 1872-1873, 1875-1877, 1879-1880, 1884, 1886, 1890, 1892, 1894, 1896, 1898. Filmed by the Genealogical Society of Utah, 1975, 1 roll, FHL film #978583. To access the digital images, see the online FHL catalog: **www.familysearch.org/search/catalog/210122.**

1872-1987. *California, Birth Records from Select Counties* **[Online Database],** indexed at the Ancestry.com website. Source: CA State Archives, Sacramento. This collection has birth records from six counties in California: Butte County, certificates, returns and indexes (1872–1918); El Dorado County, delayed certificates (1872-1936), registers (1903–1922) and indexes (1904-1987); Fresno County, registers (1889-1905) and indexes (1882–1950); Stanislaus County, certificates (1872–1905); Sutter County, registers (1904–1926); and Yolo County, unbound birth returns (1878–1897).Note: Images for the El Dorado county indexes are not available in this collection. This database has 131,563 records. See **https://search.ancestry.com/search/db.aspx?dbid=8834.**

1873-1890 Alpine County Great Registers **[Microfilm & Digital Capture],** from the microfilm of original records at the Alpine County courthouse, Markleeville, CA. Includes the following years: 1873, 1875, 1876, 1877, 1879, 1886, 1888, 1890. Filmed by the Genealogical Society of Utah, 1975, 1 roll, FHL #976453. To access the digital images, see the online FHL catalog: **www.familysearch.org/search/catalog/206926.**

1873-1896 Los Angeles County Great Registers **[Microfilm & Digital Capture],** from the original records at the California State Library, Sacramento, CA. Each year is alphabetically arranged by first letter of surname. Filmed by the Genealogical Society of Utah, 1975, 6 rolls, as follows:
- Great registers 1873, 1875-1876, 1879-1880, 1882, 1884, 1886, FHL film #976928.
- Great registers 1888, 1890, FHL film #977994.
- Great registers 1892, 1894, FHL film #976929.
- Great registers, Los Angeles precincts 1-47, 1896, FHL film #976930.
- Great registers, Los Angeles precincts 48-74, 1896; precincts Acton – Pomona, 1-2, 1896, FHL film #976931.
- Great registers, Precincts, Pomona 3-4 – Wilmington, 1896, FHL film #976932.

To access the digital images, see the online FHL catalog: **www.familysearch.org/search/catalog/207184.**

1873-1905 Death Records, Sonoma County, California **[Online Database],** indexed at the RootsWeb site for Sonoma Co CA. See **www.rootsweb.ancestry.com/~cascgs/dr.htm.**

1873-1935 *Los Angeles City Directories* **[Microfilm],** from the originals published by various publishers. Filmed by Research Publications, Woodbridge, CT, 1980-1984, FHL has 49 rolls, beginning with FHL film #1376980 (1873). To see if this microfilm was digitized yet, see the online FHL catalog: **www.familysearch.org/search/catalog/530837.**

1873-1888; 1890-1924 *Los Angeles City Directories* **[Online Database],** digitized and indexed at the Fold3 website. 1873-1888 for selected years; 1890-1924: one for each year in the range. This database has 74,184 images. See **www.fold3.com/title_87/city_directories_los_angeles/**

1873-1875, 1877, 1879, 1890, 1892, 1894, 1896, 1898 Santa Barbara County Great Registers **[Microfilm]**, from the original records at the California State Library, Sacramento, CA. Each year is alphabetically arranged by first letter of surname. Filmed by the Genealogical Society of Utah, 1975, 1 roll, FHL film #977286. To access the digital images, see the online FHL catalog:
www.familysearch.org/search/catalog/208189.

1874-1963. See *Tulare County, California, Sheriff's Office and Jail Records* **[Online Database]**, indexed at the Ancestry.com website. Source: Tulare County Sheriff's Office, Visalia, CA. This collection includes jail registers, registers of actions, descriptions of criminals, coroner's register, cash books, records of meals, warrants of arrest, and other books. Photos are included for several of the books, and there are some wanted posters and newspaper clippings. Registers of prisoner descriptions (with photos) from the California state prisons at Folsom and San Quentin are included as well. Note: Some of the people listed in this database were not arrests, but people who were served with a court summons by the Sheriff's Office. The types of arrests range from victimless crimes, such as intoxication; to serious crimes, such as assault with a deadly weapon, or murder. This database has 236,339 records. See
https://search.ancestry.com/search/db.aspx?dbid=5330.

1873-1987. *California, Death and Burial Records from Select Counties* **[Online Database]**, indexed at the Ancestry.com website. Source: CA State Archives, Sacramento. This collection includes a variety of records from the counties of Butte, Colusa, El Dorado, Fresno, Santa Clara, Stanislaus, Sutter, and Yolo, as well as the Portuguese Union of California. Included are death certificates, returns, and registers; burial permits; indexes to death records and obituaries; and death benefit claim registers (Portuguese Union of California). Each record may include: Date of death, Place of death, Age at the time of death, Cause of death, Occupation, Dates and locations of obituaries, Date and place of birth, Location of interment, Marital status, Parents' names and birthplaces, and Names of beneficiaries (in benefit claims). This database has 130,157 records. See
https://search.ancestry.com/search/db.aspx?dbid=8835.

1874, 1877, 1882, 1883 Delinquent Tax Rolls, Mariposa County, California **[Online Database]**, indexed at the MariposaResearch.net site. See
www.mariposaresearch.net/TAXINDEX.html.

1875 County Directory, Monterey County, California **[Online Database],** indexed at the RootsWeb site for Monterey Co CA. See
www.rootsweb.ancestry.com/~camonter/

1875-1876, 1879-1880, 1888, 1890, 1892, 1894, 1896, 1898 Modoc County Great Registers **[Microfilm & Digital Capture],** from the original records at the California State Library, Sacramento, CA. Includes a separate index for 1876-1879. Each year is alphabetically arranged by first letter of surname. Filmed by the Genealogical Society of Utah, 1975, 1 roll, FHL film #976938. To access the digital images, see the online FHL catalog:
www.familysearch.org/search/catalog/207932.

1875, 1877, 1879-1880, 1882, 1886, 1888, 1890, 1898 Ventura County Great Registers **[Microfilm & Digital Capture],** from the original records at the State Library, Sacramento, CA. Each year is alphabetically arranged by first letter of surname. Filmed by the Genealogical Society of Utah, 1975, 1 roll, FHL film #978596. To access the digital images, see the online FHL catalog:
www.familysearch.org/search/catalog/208327.

1875-1896 Tehama County Great Registers **[Microfilm & Digital Capture],** from the original records at the California State Library, Sacramento, CA. Each year is alphabetically arranged by first letter of surname. Includes the following years: 1875, 1877, 1880, 1884, 1886, 1888, 1890, 1892, 1894, 1896. Filmed by the Genealogical Society of Utah, 1975, 1 roll, FHL film #978592. To access the digital images, see the online FHL catalog:
www.familysearch.org/search/catalog/209556.

1875-1898 San Benito County Great Registers **[Microfilm & Digital Capture],** from the original records at the California State Library, Sacramento, CA. Includes the following years: 1875-1877, 1879-1880, 1882, 1884, 1886, 1890, 1892, 1894, 1896, 1898. Filmed by the Genealogical Society of Utah, 1975, 1 roll, FHL film #977091. To access the digital images, see the online FHL catalog:
www.familysearch.org/search/catalog/208120.

1876-1915 Naturalization Records of the Superior Court of Los Angeles, California **[Online Database],** digitized and indexed at the Fold3 website. This database has 36,861 images. See
www.fold3.com/title_108/naturalizations_ca_los_angeles/.

1876-1969. *California, Occupational Licenses, Registers, and Directories* **[Online Database],** indexed at the Ancestry.com website. Source: Occupational Records, CA State Archives, Sacramento. This collection contains occupational licenses, registers, exam applications, directories, and similar documents issued in California for various occupations, including attorneys, cosmeticians, dental hygienists, dentists, hairdressers, manicurists, medical examiners, nurses, pharmacists, physicians, and surgeons. Details vary widely depending on the document but might include name, residence, birth date and place or age, record date, photo, school, graduation or licensing date, or other information. Note: In some cases, individuals who were licensed or registered in California are listed as residing out-of-state. This database has 848,561 records. See https://search.ancestry.com/search/db.aspx?dbid=9207.

1877 Delinquent Tax List, Mariposa County, California **[Online Database],** indexed at the MariposaResearch.net site. See www.mariposaresearch.net/1877.html.

1878-1905 Births, Madera County, California **[Online Database],** indexed at the USGenWeb site for Madera Co CA. See www.cagenweb.com/madera/MadBirths.htm.

1878 County Directory, Marin County, California **[Online Database],** indexed at the SFGenealogy.com site. Archived at https://web.archive.org/web/20160602023227/http://www.sfgenealogy.com/php/dbs/1878mcd.php.

1878 San Francisco Phone Directory **[Online Database],** index of the American Speaking Telephone Company's first subscribers, listed at the SFGenealogy site, archived at: https://web.archive.org/web/20190315234204/http://www.sfgenealogy.org/sf/hgtel.htm.

1879. *Certified Copy of the Great Register of Monterey County, California, September 3, 1879* **[Microfilm],** from the original published by Monterey Democrat Book and Job Printing Office, Salinas City, CA, 1879, 31 pages. Contains registration information for 1866. Filmed by the Genealogical Society of Utah, 1976, 1 roll, FHL film #982110. To see if this microfilm was digitized yet, see the online FHL catalog: www.familysearch.org/search/catalog/78211.

1879-1880 Amador County Directory **[Online Database],** indexed at the USGenWeb site for Amador Co CA. Archived: https://web.archive.org/web/20161103231141/http://www.cagenweb.com/lr/amador/directory.html.

1880. *California, 1880 Federal Census: Soundex and Population Schedules* **[Microfilm & Digital Capture],** from the original records at the National Archives, Washington, DC (in 1970), now located at the California State Archives, Sacramento, CA. Filmed by the National Archives, 1970, 60 rolls, beginning with FHL film #1254061 (Population Schedules: Alameda Co., part). To access the digital images, see the online FHL catalog: www.familysearch.org/search/catalog/670368.

1880 Colusa County Great Register **[Microfilm],** from the original volume loaned for filming by Virginia Lee Stinchfield McKay, published by Addington & Green, county printers in 1880. Filmed by the Genealogical Society of Utah, 1981, 1 roll, FHL film #1035840. To see if this microfilm was digitized yet, see the online FHL catalog: www.familysearch.org/search/catalog/251587.

1880 Great Register of Fresno County (Madera Precincts) **[Online Database],** indexed at the USGenWeb site for Madera Co CA. Archived at https://web.archive.org/web/20160328230425/http://www.cagenweb.com/madera/FresnoGreatR1880.htm.

1880 Great Register, Marin County, California **[Online Database],** indexed at the SFGenealogy.com Archived at https://web.archive.org/web/20200128005920/https://www.sfgenealogy.org/marin/1880gr/grtreg.htm.

1881 County Directory, Shasta County, California **[Online Database],** indexed at the RootsWeb site for Shasta Co CA. See http://freepages.genealogy.rootsweb.ancestry.com/~shastaca/directory1881.html.

1882. See *Great Register of the County of Mendocino, California For the Year 1882* **[Microfilm],** from the original published: Ukiah, Calif.: Mendocino Dispatch and Democrat, 1882, 49 pages. Filmed by the Genealogical Society of Utah, 1960, 1 roll, FHL film #207670. To see if this microfilm was digitized yet, see the online FHL catalog: www.familysearch.org/search/catalog/176668.

1882 Delinquent Tax List, Mariposa County, California **[Online Database],** indexed at the MariposaResearch.net site. See www.mariposaresearch.net/1882TAX.html.

1882. See *Supplement to the Great Register of the County of Sacramento for the Year 1882* **[Microfilm & Digital Capture],** from the original published by H.S. Crocker & Co., 1882, 12 pages. Alphabetically arranged. Filmed by the Genealogical Society of Utah, 1960, 1 roll, FHL film #207672. To access the digital images, see the online FHL catalog: www.familysearch.org/search/catalog/176680.

1882. See *Great Register of the County of San Bernardino, State of California: Un-canceled Entries Existing on Said Register the Ninth Day of October, A.D. 1882; Made and Done Pursuant of the Provisions of the Political Code* **[Microfilm]**, from the original published by Times Print House, San Bernardino, CA, 1882, 16 pages. Filmed by the Genealogical Society of Utah, 1960, 1 roll, FHL film #207671. To see if this microfilm was digitized yet, see the online FHL catalog: www.familysearch.org/search/catalog/176701.

1882 Veterans of the Mexican War, Plumas County, California **[Online Database],** indexed at the USGenWeb site for Plumas Co CA. See http://files.usgwarchives.net/ca/plumas/military/mexican/other/veterans234mt.txt.

1882-1888. *San Francisco, California, Registers of Chinese Laborers Returning to the U.S.* **[Online Database],** indexed at the Ancestry.com website. Source: National Archives microfilm M1413. Although the Chinese Exclusion Act of 1882 halted the immigration of laborers from China, Chinese immigrants who had been in the U.S. prior to 17 November 1880 were allowed to stay, and if they traveled abroad, they were allowed reentry. This collection includes the arrival records of Chinese laborers reentering the U.S. through the port of San Francisco for the years 1882–1888. Details found in these records can include the following: Immigrant's name, Age, Occupation, Physical description and identifying marks or characteristics, Year of original arrival in the U.S., and date and name of the ships of departure and return. This database has 69,741 records: https://search.ancestry.com/search/db.aspx?dbid=5418.

1882-1959. *California, Passenger and Crew Lists* **[Online Database],** digitized and indexed at the Ancestry.com website. Information contained in the index includes name of passenger, the ship name, port of arrival, and arrival date, and may also include their age, gender, ethnicity, nationality or last country of permanent residence, birth date, birthplace, or port of departure. If a name of a friend or relative whom the passenger was going to join with, or place of nativity was provided, that information is included as well. The names found in the index are linked to actual images of the passenger and crew lists, forms/cards which may have much more information about a person and relatives. This database has 5,871,015 records. See http://search.ancestry.com/search/db.aspx?dbid=7949.

1883 Delinquent Tax List, Mariposa County, California **[Online Database],** indexed at the MariposaResearch.net site. See. www.mariposaresearch.net/1883tax.html

1883-1924. *California, San Francisco, Register of Chinese Immigrant Court Cases and Foreign Seamen Tax Cards* **[Online Database],** indexed at the FamilySearch.org website. Source: National Archives microfilm A3381. This collection contains Register of Court Cases related to Chinese Immigrants arriving at or departing from San Francisco, California, 1883-1916. It also contains tax cards of foreign crew members examined at San Francisco, California, 1921-1924. The court case index cards are arranged numerically by court case number and usually list the name of the petitioner, claimant, or defendant. The tax cards are arranged numerically by ship arrival number and may contain person's name, sex, age, marital status, head tax status, citizenship, race, place of last permanent residence, destination, port and date of arrival, destination, and purpose for entering the U.S. This database has 9,914 records. See www.familysearch.org/search/collection/2443318.

1883-1958 Naturalization Records of the Superior Court of San Diego, California **[Online Database],** digitized and indexed at the Fold3 website. This database has 22,575 images. See www.fold3.com/title_109/naturalizations_ca_san_diego/.

1884. *List of the Names and Registration of the Domiciled Inhabitants of the County of Humboldt: Copied From the Great Register of Humboldt County, October 7th, 1884* **[Photocopy of Original],** by Louis T. Kinsey, County Clerk, original published by L.T. Kinsey, County Clerk, 1884; reprinted by Redwood Genealogical Society, Fortuna, CA, 1991, 68 pages. FHL book 979.412 N4L.

1884 (1885). See *List of the Names and Registration of the Domiciled Inhabitants of the County of Humboldt, Copied From the Great Register of Humboldt County, October 7th, 1884* **[Printed Abstract & Index],** compiled by Marilyn Keach Milota, published by Humboldt County Genealogical Society, Eureka, CA, 1997, 267 pages. Contains an abstract of the 1885 great register of voters, arranged in alphabetical order by surname and giving full name, age, place of birth, occupation, residence, date when sworn, number in register. FHL book 979.412 N48m.

1884-1940. *California, Chinese Arrival Case Files Index* **[Online Database],** indexed at the Ancestry.com website. This database consists of an index to Chinese immigrants to America who arrived between 1884 and 1940. The index is the result of work done by The National Archives at San Francisco in San Bruno; Bob Barde, and Judy Yung, with the assistance of the Angel Island Immigration Station Foundation and other volunteers. It was compiled from information found in the original immigration case files that reside at National Archives branch in San Bruno, CA. The following details, when available, are included in the index: Name, Age. Gender, Birth Date and Place, Arrival Date, Ship Name, Case Number, and Box Number. This database has 90,734 records. See https://search.ancestry.com/search/db.aspx?dbid=61228.

1885 County Directory, Del Norte County, California **[Online Database],** indexed at the RootsWeb site for Del Norte Co CA. See http://freepages.genealogy.rootsweb.ancestry.com/~shastaca/a1885delnort.html.

1885 County Directory, Lassen County, California **[Online Database],** indexed at the RootsWeb site for Lassen Co CA. See http://freepages.genealogy.rootsweb.ancestry.com/~shastaca/a1885lassen.html.

1885 County Directory, Modoc County, California **[Online Database],** originally indexed at the ModocCountyGenealogy.com site. For an archived database, see https://web.archive.org/web/20101224202127/www.modoccountygenealogy.com/1885_directory.htm.

1885 County Directory, Plumas County, California **[Online Database],** indexed at the RootsWeb site for Plumas Co CA. See http://freepages.genealogy.rootsweb.ancestry.com/~shastaca/a1885plumas.html.

1885 County Directory, Shasta County, California **[Online Database],** indexed at the RootsWeb site for Shasta Co CA. See http://freepages.genealogy.rootsweb.ancestry.com/~shastaca/a1885shasta.html.

1885 County Directory, Sierra County, California **[Online Database],** indexed at the RootsWeb site for Sierra Co CA. See http://freepages.genealogy.rootsweb.ancestry.com/~shastaca/a1885sierra.html.

1885 County Directory, Siskiyou County, California **[Online Database],** indexed at the RootsWeb site for Siskiyou Co CA. See http://freepages.genealogy.rootsweb.ancestry.com/~shastaca/a1885siskiyou.html.

1885 County Directory, Tehama County, California **[Online Database],** indexed at the RootsWeb site for Tehama Co CA. See http://freepages.genealogy.rootsweb.ancestry.com/~shastaca/a1885tehama.html.

1885 County Directory, Trinity County, California **[Online Database],** indexed at the RootsWeb site for Trinity Co CA. See http://freepages.genealogy.rootsweb.ancestry.com/~shastaca/a1885trinity.html.

1885 Directories, Yuba, Sutter, Colusa, Butte, and Tehama Counties, California **[Online Database],** indexed at the Ancestry.com website. Source: McKenney & Co., Oroville, CA, 1885. Each index record includes: Name, City, State, Occupation, and Year. This database has 13,118 records. See https://search.ancestry.com/search/db.aspx?dbid=5384.

1886-1900 Alameda County Great Registers **[Microfilm & Digital Capture],** from the original records at the Alameda County Clerk's office, Oakland, CA. Registers of voters alphabetically arranged by first letter of surname within each precinct. Filmed by the Genealogical Society of Utah, 1957, 1974, 3 rolls, as follows:
- 1896 Great register, FHL film #2502.
- 1892-1894 Great registers, FHL film #1000101.
- 1900 Great register, FHL film #1000102.

To access the digital images, see the online FHL catalog: www.familysearch.org/search/catalog/311682.

1886-1909 Notaries Public from California Blue Books & Governmental Rosters **[Online Database],** indexed by county and year(s). Listing gives a name, place of residence, and expiration of term. See http://freepages.genealogy.rootsweb.ancestry.com/~npmelton/np.html.

1887 Great Register, Trinity County, California **[Online Database],** indexed at the USGenWeb: http://files.usgwarchives.net/ca/trinity/greatregister/ac1887reg.txt.

1887-1949 Naturalizations – California Southern **[Online Database],** digitized and indexed at the Fold3 website. This database has 386,118 images. See www.fold3.com/title_110/naturalizations_ca_southern/.

1887-1919. See *San Diego, California, Compiled Records from San Diego Genealogical Society, 1887, 1913-1919* **[Online Database],** digitized and indexed at Ancestry.com. This database includes: 1) Admissions to St Joseph's Hospital. 2) Permits for burial. 3) The San Diego City and County Directory, 1904, 4) The San Diego Genealogical Society City Directory. 5) Cruise books for the USS Yorktown and USS Truett, 6) The Anchor (1965 Version). a yearbook for the United States Naval Training Center, 7) The Schaal Family Bible, 8) The San Diego Great Register of Voters, and 9) Hannifan's New Map and Gazetteer of Massachusetts, 1896. The Permits for burial, the San Diego City and County Directory, and the San Diego Great Register of Voters comprise most of the records. This database has 12,749 records, see
www.ancestry.com/search/collections/61353.

1888 Great Register, San Mateo County, California [Online Database], indexed at the SFGenealogy site. Archived at
https://web.archive.org/web/20150626223838/http://www.sfgenealogy.com/php/dbs/1888smgr.php.

1888-1890. *Los Angeles, California City Directories* **[Online Database],** indexed at the Ancestry.com website. Each index record includes: Name, Location 1, Business Name, Occupation, Year, City, and State. This database has 59,396 records. See
https://search.ancestry.com/search/db.aspx?dbid=4415.

1889. *California State Roster, Government and Military Records* **[Online Database],** indexed at the Ancestry.com website. Original data: California Blue Book or State Roster 1899. Sacramento, CA, USA: State Printing Office. Each index record includes: Given name, Surname, Residence, Page No., Office, and Location. This database has 13,527 records. See
https://search.ancestry.com/search/db.aspx?dbid=5733.

1889. *Sacramento, California Bee Newspaper, Vital Records* **[Online Database],** indexed at the Ancestry.com website. Original data: Sacramento Bee newspaper. Sacramento, CA, USA: 1889. Located at the Sacramento State Library. This database has 999 records. See
https://search.ancestry.com/search/db.aspx?dbid=6857.

1889-1890. *Sacramento California, Sacramento Bee Newspaper, Vital Records* **[Online Database],** indexed at the Ancestry.com website. Original data: Sacramento Bee newspaper. Sacramento, CA, USA: 1889-1890. This database has 2,320 records. See
https://search.ancestry.com/search/db.aspx?dbid=6098.

1889-1891. *San Francisco, California Directories* **[Online Database],** indexed at the FamilySearch.org website. Source: 1889-1890, W.H.L. Corran; 1890-1891, Painter and Co. Each index record includes: Name, Location 1, Location 2, Business Name, Occupation, Year, City, and State. This database has 252,944 records. See
https://search.ancestry.com/search/db.aspx?dbid=4436.

1890. See *The California 1890 Great Register of Voters Index* **[Printed Index & CD-ROM],** compiled by volunteers of various California genealogical societies as part of a project for the California State Genealogical Alliance, Janice G. Cloud, editor, Margaret Goodwin, database manager, published by Heritage Quest, North Salt Lake, UT, 2001, 3 vols. Includes name of voter, age, birth place, current residence, county, registration date, naturalized, and page in original register. This work indexes 311,028 men living in California in 1890 and includes significant personal information useful to historians and genealogists. It goes far to replace lost 1890 federal census information. A citizen registering to vote in 1890 provided significant data: Name, Age, Birthplace, Occupation, Home address, and Naturalization information for immigrants. Given that approximately one third of the voters of California were immigrants, it is obvious that this information may be particularly useful. FHL book 979.4 N4c v.1-3. A CD-ROM version of the 3-vol. index was published by Heritage Quest.

1890. *Great Register and Supplement of the County of Humboldt, State of California, 1890: A Full, True, and Correct Transcript of the Registered Voters of Humboldt County, on the Sixth Day of October, A.D. 1890* **[Microfilm],** from the original register in possession of the Redwood Genealogical Society, Fortuna, California. Filmed by the Genealogical Society of Utah, c1995, FHL film #1750861. Book reprinted by the society, 130 pages, FHL book 979.412 N4h 1890. To see if this microfilm was digitized yet, see the online FHL catalog:
www.familysearch.org/search/catalog/725017.

1890. *The Great Register (Voter Registration), Kern County, California: A Partial Substitute for 1890 Census* **[Printed Index],** data input and compilation by J. Hoyle Mayfield, published by Kern County Genealogical Society, Bakersfield, CA, 1995, 72 pages. Contains an alphabetical listing by surname of voters, showing name, age, state where born, occupation, residence, registration date, naturalization date, and remarks. FHL book 979.488 N4m.

1890. *Index to the 1890 Los Angeles County Great Register, State of California* **[Printed Index],** compiled by Whittier Area Genealogical Society, 1993, 335 pages. Index includes register page, surname, given name, age, date of birth, residence, registration date. FHL book 979.493 N42w.

1890. *Great Register of Marin County, 1890* **[Printed Index],** compiled by the Marin County Genealogical Society, Novato, CA, 1992, 52 pages. Indexed by John E. Hale. Indexed first in alphabetical order by surname, giving name, age, state where last resided, occupation, current residence, and if naturalized; indexed second by town of residence, occupation, where born, and name. FHL book 979.462 N42h 1890.

1890. *Abstract From the 1890 Great Register of the State of California, County of Mendocino* **[Printed Index],** by the Santa Barbara County Genealogical Society, 1998, 102 pages. Contains an alphabetical listing by surname, giving names, page no. in register, age, birthplace, current residence, registration date, naturalization remarks (by code) if applicable. FHL book 979.415 N48a.

1890. *The Great Register of Mariposa County, California, 1890: Registered Voters of Mariposa County* **[Printed Index],** compiled and edited by Fresno Genealogical Society, Fresno, CA, 1992, 30 pages. Contains an alphabetical listing of registered voters, giving full name, age, birthplace, residence, registration date, naturalization date, and occupation. FHL book 979.446 N4m.

1890. *Merced County, California 1890 Great Register of Voters* **[Printed Index],** compiled by members of the Merced County Genealogical Society, published Merced, CA, 1993, 59 pages. Includes alphabetized by surname voter registration for each precinct and a general index to voters. FHL book 979.458 N4m.

1890. *Great Register of the County of Mono, for the Year 1890* **[Printed Index],** reprint of original volume, published by the Santa Barbara County Genealogical Society, 1991, 16 pages. Contains an alphabetical register (by first letter of surname only) of voters, giving voting number, name of voter, age, place of nativity, occupation, local residence, naturalized date, place and court, date of registration and if sworn. FHL book #979.4 A1 no. 220.

1890 Great Register of Monterey County, California **[Printed Index],** data extracted by volunteers from the Monterey County Genealogy Society, project coordinator, Karen Clifford; quality control editor, Bettyann Hedegard, published 1993, 114 pages. Arranged in alphabetical order by surname. From intro: "The following entries were extracted from the Great Register of Monterey County, a voter registration listing that can be used as a substitute of the missing 1890 federal census." Contains page number of original register, last and given names, age, where born, occupation, residence, naturalized plus date, place and court, and date registered. FHL book 979.476 N4g.

1890 Great Register of Nevada County, California Voter Registration List **[Printed Index],** compiled by Emma Lee Price, published by Conejo Valley Genealogical Society, Thousand Oaks, CA, 1994, 96 pages. Shows page number in original register, an alphabetical listing by surname of voter, age, birthplace, precinct, date of registration and naturalization status. FHL book 979.437 N4p.
- See also, an online version:
http://files.usgwarchives.net/ca/nevada/voters/1890/vote-ab.txt.

1890. *The Great Register of Orange County, California, 1890* **[Printed Index],** compiled by Orange County California Genealogical Society, Orange, CA, 1996, 48 pages. Contains a transcript of the original registers arranged in alphabetical order by surname, showing page and registration number, surname, given name, age, birthplace (state or country), occupation, residence, date, place and court where naturalized, and registration date. FHL book 979.496 N4o.

1890. See *Great Register of Yolo County, 1890: Yolo County Index for the 1890 Great Register Project* **[Printed Abstract &Index],** compiled by J. E. Hale, published by the author, Kentfield, CA, 1992, 1 vol., various paging. The register has been abstracted and indexed in alphabetical order by surname in section one; by town in section two; and by precinct in section three of this compilation. From intro: "The 1890 great register project is designed to recreate a census of sorts to replace the U.S. census of 1890 that was lost in a fire. Since the great registers record only those eligible to vote it is not as broad a coverage as the U.S. census." FHL book 979.451 N48h.

1890. *Great Register of Voters, Sonoma County, California* **[Printed Index],** compiled by members of the Sonoma County Genealogical Society, published by the society, Santa Rosa, CA, 1989, 206 pages. FHL book 979.418 N4g.

1890. *Great Register of the County of Stanislaus, State of California* **[Printed Index],** compiled by Mileta Farr Kilroy and Bette Locke, published by the Genealogical Society of Stanislaus County, 1992. Transcript gives name, age, birthplace, residence and date of voter registration, occupation, and date of naturalization. FHL book 979.457 N4k.

1890 Great Register of Trinity County, California: (Voter Registration List) **[Printed Index],** compiled and edited by Delores V. Pederson, published by the Conejo Valley Genealogical Society, Thousand Oaks, CA, 1993, 30 pages. Shows page number in original register, name of voter (in alphabetical order by surname), age, birthplace, local residence, date of registration, and naturalization status. FHL book 979.414 N4p.

1890 Great Register, Tulare County, California **[Online Database],** indexed at the USGenWeb site for Tulare Co CA. See http://files.usgwarchives.net/ca/tulare/greatregister/gr1890.txt.

1890 Tuolumne County Great Register of Voters **[Printed Index],** excerpted by Viola McRae, Nell Holloway, and Dythe-Mary Egleston, published by the Tuolumne County Genealogical Society, Sonora, CA, 1993, 44 pages. Contains an alphabetical listing of voters copied from the original register, showing surname, given name, age, nativity, residence, date registered. FHL book 979.4 A1 No. 234.

1890 Shasta County Great Register **[Printed Index],** compiled and published by Joe Mazzini, Montgomery Creek, CA, 1996, 82 pages. Contains an abstract from the great register (voting registration) giving surname, given name, age, state where born, occupation, residence (town), date registered, if naturalized citizen, comments, register and page numbers. Arranged in alphabetical order by surname. FHL book 979.424 N49m.

1890. See *Index to the 1890 Great Register of Solano County, California* **[Printed Index],** compiled by Cordell Coward, published by the Solano County Genealogical Society, Fairfield, CA, 1994, 97 pages. Contains an alphabetical listing by surname of persons, giving page number in original register, surname and first/middle names, age, birthplace (state or country), current town of residence, date when registered, and if naturalized. FHL book 979.452 N42c.

1890. See *Index to The Great Register of San Mateo County, 1890, California* **[Printed Index],** compiled by The San Mateo County Genealogical Society, 1991, 37 pages. Includes person's name, age, birthplace, residence, if naturalized, and date of registration. FHL book 979.469 N4i.

1890. *The Great Register of the County of Santa Barbara, California* **[Photocopy of Original],** by Santa Barbara County Genealogical Society, 1991, 67 pages. Contains a register in alphabetical order by surname, giving voting no., register no., name, age, country of nativity, occupation, local residence, if naturalized and date, place, by what court, date of registration and if sworn. FHL book 979.4 A1 No. 219.

1890. See *Santa Clara County, California 1890 Great Register* **[Printed Index],** published by the Santa Clara County Historical and Genealogical Society, Santa Clara, CA, 1999, 151 pages. Contains a transcription of the original register, arranged in alphabetical order by surname, giving registration number, name, age, country of nativity, occupation, local residence, naturalization date, place, court, and date of voting registration. FHL book 979.473 N4s.

1890 Great Register With Index for San Luis Obispo County **[Printed Index],** compiled from originals in the possession of San Luis Obispo County Historical Society, San Luis Obispo, CA, by the San Luis Obispo County Genealogical Society, 1993, 60 pages. Includes surname index. Contains a register of voters showing name, age, country of nativity, occupation, local residence (town), naturalization date, place and court, date of registration. FHL book 979.478 N4e.

1890 Sacramento County Great Register Index **[Microfilm & Digital Capture],** from the original manuscript at the Sacramento County Clerk's Office. An alphabetical register of voters, by precinct, showing names and addresses of voters, with name and number of precinct, and may include name of court, with date and place of naturalization if foreign born. Filmed by the Genealogical Society of Utah, 2000, 1 roll, FHL film #2200427. To access the digital images, see the online FHL catalog: www.familysearch.org/search/catalog/1003704.

1890 Great Register, Sacramento County, California **[Microfiche],** transcribed & edited by Verna L. Benedict, published by the Genealogical Association of Sacramento, 1995. Includes district number, precinct number, surname, given names, age, birthplace, address of residence, registration date, naturalization

date and location if applicable. Arranged in alphabetical order for voters. FHL has 6 microfiche:
- Aagaard – Chatterton, FHL fiche #6334616, fiche 1.
- Chenu – Gannon, FHL fiche #6334616, fiche 2.
- Garbarino – Kelly, FHL fiche #6334616, fiche 3.
- Kelly, T – Neubauer, FHL fiche #6334616, fiche 4.
- Neuhaus – Skelton, FHL fiche #6334616, fiche 5.
- Skidmore – Zora, FHL fiche #6334616, fiche 6.

1890 San Francisco City Directory [Online Database], indexed at the SFGenealogy site. Archived: https://web.archive.org/web/20160322062218/http://www.sfgenealogy.com/php/dbs/1890sfd.php.

1890. *San Francisco, California, 1890 Great Register of Voters* [Transcript], edited by Jane Billings Steiner, published by Heritage Quest, North Salt Lake, 2001, 950 pages. Contains a transcript of the 1890 register, giving name of voter, age, birthplace, occupation, address of residence, naturalization details, date registered, district and precinct numbers. FHL book 979.461 N4s. Also on CD-ROM.

1890 Great Register of Voters, Solano County, California [Online Database], indexed at the RootsWeb site for Solano Co CA. Archived at https://web.archive.org/web/20150912032139/http://www.rootsweb.ancestry.com/~cascgsi/greatregister1890introduction.htm.

1890 Great Register of Voters, Sonoma County, California [Online Database], indexed at the RootsWeb site for Sonoma Co CA. See www.rootsweb.ancestry.com/~cascgs/gr_intro.htm.

1890 Great Register of Ventura County, California: (Voter Registration List) [Printed Book], compiled and edited by Dolores V. Pederson, published by the Conejo Valley Genealogical Society, Thousand Oaks, CA, 1993, 69 pages. Shows page number in original register, names of voters (in alphabetical order by surname), age, birthplace, precinct, date of registration, naturalization status. FHL book 979.492 N4p.

1890-1950. *Biography Card Index, California State Library, Sacramento, CA* [Microfilm & Digital Capture], an index to biographies in various books and articles held by the CA State Library. Filmed by the Genealogical Society of Utah, 1991, 6 rolls, beginning with FHL film #1711668 (A – rook). Each card includes a name, profession, positions held, notes, etc. To access the digital images, see the online FHL catalog: www.familysearch.org/search/catalog/486460.

1891. *Sacramento, California Bee Newspaper, Vital Records* [Online Database], indexed at the Ancestry.com website. Original data: Sacramento Bee newspaper. Sacramento, CA, USA: 1891. Located at the Sacramento State Library. This database has 1,106 records. See https://search.ancestry.com/search/db.aspx?dbid=6841.

1892. *Sacramento California, Sacramento Bee Newspaper, Vital Records* [Online Database], indexed at the Ancestry.com website. Original data: Sacramento Bee newspaper. Sacramento, CA, USA: 1889-1890. This database has 2,299 records. See https://search.ancestry.com/search/db.aspx?dbid=7152.

1892. *San Luis Obispo County, CA, 1892 Great Register* [Printed Extraction], compiled by Buelah Heidom and Helen Keller, published by the San Luis County Genealogical Society, Atascadero, CA, 1990, 2 vols. Contents, vol. 1: A-K; vol. 2: K-Z. Gives name, age, height, complexion, color of eyes, color of hair, visible marks or scars (and location); occupation; country of nativity; place of residence; precinct; post office address; naturalized date, place, court; date registered in 1892. FHL book 979.478 N4g v. 1-2.
- See also, *Great Register, San Luis Obispo County, California, 1892* [Printed Extraction], extracted by the California Central Coast Genealogical Society, San Luis Obispo, c1975, 186 pages. FHL book 979.478 N43c.

1892 Social Directory, San Mateo County, California [Online Database], extracted from the 1892 San Francisco Blue Book & Pacific Coast Elite Directory, listed at the SFGenealogy site. Archived at https://web.archive.org/web/20150626221000/http://www.sfgenealogy.com/sanmateo/smb92.htm.

1892 Santa Clara County Great Register [Microfilm & Digital Capture], from the original records, filmed by the Genealogical Society of Utah, 1957, 1 roll, FHL film #2502. To access the digital images, see the online FHL catalog: www.familysearch.org/search/catalog/341509.

1892 Great Register for Siskiyou County, California [Printed Extract & Index], compiled by John A. Dye and Judy K. Dye, published by the authors, Spokane, WA, 1986, 60 pages. Includes surname index. Register gives name of person, age, height, complexion, color of eyes, color of hair, visible marks, country of birth, precinct, P.O. address, occupation, date, place and court of naturalization, and date of registration. FHL book 979.421 X2d 1892.

1892, 1894, 1896 Orange County Great Registers **[Microfilm],** from the original records at the California State Library, Sacramento, CA. Filmed by the Genealogical Society of Utah, 1975, 1 roll, FHL film #977084.

1892, 1894, 1896, 1898 Glen County Great Registers **[Microfilm & Digital Capture],** from the original records at the California State Library, Sacramento, CA. Filmed by the Genealogical Society of Utah, 1975, 1 roll, FHL film #976463. To access the digital images, see the online FHL catalog: www.familysearch.org/search/catalog/207039.

1892. *Great Register of Marin County, California, 1892* **[Printed Book],** facsimile reproduction of original published 1892, published by the Marin County Genealogical Society, Novato, CA, 2002, 39 pages. FHL book 979.462 N4g 1892.

1892-1898 Mendocino County Great Registers **[Microfilm & Digital Capture],** from the original records at the California State Library, Sacramento, CA. Filmed by the Genealogical Society of Utah, 1960-1975, 2 rolls, as follows:
- Great registers for 1892, 1894, 1896, 1898, FHL film #976936.
- Great registers for 1867, 1871, 1873, 1875-1877, 1879-1889, 1882, 1884, 1886, 1888, 1890, FHL film #976935.

To access the digital images, see the online FHL catalog: www.familysearch.org/search/catalog/291474.

1892-1908 Nevada County Great Registers **[Microfilm & Digital Capture],** from the records located at the Searls Historical Library, Nevada City, CA. Contains voting registers, showing voter's registration number, name, age, distinguishing physical marks or characteristics, occupation, country of nativity, place of residence, precinct, post office address, date, place and court of naturalization, date of registration. Filmed by the Genealogical Society of Utah, 1998, 3 rolls, as follows:
- Great registers, 1892-1894, FHL film #2132607.
- Great registers, 1900-1902, FHL film #2132608.
- Great registers, 1906-1908, FHL film #2132609.

To access the digital images, see the online FHL catalog: www.familysearch.org/search/catalog/1041809.

1893-1943. *California, Chinese Partnerships and Departures from San Francisco* **[Online Database],** indexed at the FamilySearch.org website. Source: National Archives microfilm A3362. Includes lists of Chinese firms in San Francisco, and an index of Chinese departing from San Francisco. This database has 54,617 records. See www.familysearch.org/search/collection/2427227.

1893-1953. *California, San Francisco Passenger Lists* **[Online Database],** digitized at the FamilySearch website. Passenger list of those arriving in San Francisco, California, corresponds to NARA Publication M1410. Passenger List of Vessels Arriving at San Francisco, CA 1893-1953. This database has 1,188,641 records. See www.familysearch.org/search/collection/1916078.

1894-1979. *California, Berkeley Public Library Obituary Index* **[Online Database],** indexed at the Ancestry.com website. This database is also available at the Berkeley Public Library. This database has 33,090 records. See https://search.ancestry.com/search/db.aspx?dbid=9266.

1895. *Nevada County, California Directory* **[Online Database],** indexed at the Ancestry.com website. Source: 1895 Directory, Pacific Press Publ. Co. Each index record includes: Name, City, State, Occupation, and Year. This database has 4,645 records. See https://search.ancestry.com/search/db.aspx?dbid=5269.

1895-1964. *Border Crossings: From Mexico to U.S.* **[Online Database],** digitized and indexed at the Ancestry.com website. Source: National Archives microfilm series, including those for the California ports of Calexico, series A3467; San Ysidro/Tia Juana, series M1767, and Andrade and Campo/Tecate, series M2030. This database contains an index of aliens and some citizens crossing into the U.S. from Mexico via various ports of entry along the U.S.-Mexican border between 1895 and 1964; covering records for ports in Arizona, California, New Mexico, and Texas. The index record usually includes: Name, Age, Birth date, Birthplace, Gender, Ethnicity/Nationality, Names of individuals accompanied by, Port of arrival, and Arrival date. View the image of the immigration-manifest forms or cards for more possible information. This database has 5,878,615 records. See https://search.ancestry.com/search/db.aspx?dbid=1082.

1895-1985 San Francisco California Area Funeral Home Records **[Online Database],** digitized and indexed at the Ancestry.com website. These records are from funeral homes within the San Francisco area from 1895 to 1985. Recorded on the forms are most of the information that would be found on a death certificate about the deceased such as first name, surname, death date, place of death, place of burial, and possibly other information like gender, age, parents' names, birth dates and places, etc. The data in the race field is as seen on the record; examples include Black and Caucasian. A death certificate is attached to some of the

forms along with a copy of the newspaper obituary which could list the names of children, grandchildren, brothers, and sisters. See
http://search.ancestry.com/search/db.aspx?dbid=2118.

1896-1897. *Pomona, California Directory* **[Online Database],** indexed at the Ancestry.com website. Source: 1896, R.L. Polk Co. Each index record includes: Name, Location, City, State, and Occupation. This database has 1,753 records. See
https://search.ancestry.com/search/db.aspx?dbid=5303.

1896, 1900 *Great Registers of Voters of Yuba County* **[Microfilm & Digital Capture],** from the records located at the John Q. Packard Library, Marysville, CA. Filmed by the Genealogical Society of Utah, 1991, 2 rolls, as follows:
- Great register, 1896, FHL film #1738594.
- Great register, 1900, FHL film #1738595.

To access the digital images, see the online FHL catalog: **www.familysearch.org/search/catalog/457564.**

1896. *County of Humboldt Great Register* **[Printed Abstract & Index],** compiled by Marilyn Keach Milota, published by Humboldt County Genealogical Society, Eureka, CA, 1996, 441 pages. Contains an abstract of the original great register, arranged in alphabetical order by surname and giving complete name, registration number, age, place of nativity, occupation, place of residence and date of registration. FHL book 979.412 N48m 1896.

1896. *Certified Copy of the Precinct Registers of Monterey County, California, 1896: Includes Information Transcribed From Other Sources and Submitted in Place of Missing Pages by the Staff Members of the Monterey, California Stake Branch Genealogical Library of the Church of Jesus Christ of L.D.S.* **[Microfilm & Digital Version],** Transcript filmed by the Genealogical Society of Utah, 1976, 1 roll, FHL film #982110. To access the digital version, see the online FHL catalog:
www.familysearch.org/search/catalog/223043.

1896-1921. See *Alien Crew Manifests of Vessels Arriving at San Francisco, California, 1896-1921: NARA Publication M1437* **[Microfilm & Digital Capture],** from originals at the National Archives, Washington, DC. Arranged chronologically by date of arrival. These passenger manifest forms list alien seamen admitted to the United States, filmed by the National Archives, 1988, 8 rolls, beginning with FHL film #1578399 (Vol. 1 1896-1917). To access the digital images, see the online FHL catalog:
www.familysearch.org/search/catalog/573422.

1898 Tulare County Voters Register, Book One and Book Two **[Printed Book & Online Database],** copied by Jack and Alfreda Gilliam, published by the authors, c1995, 164 pages. Divided into three sections: index, transfers/cancellations, and corrections. Each section is in alphabetical order by name. Index gives name, number, precinct, age, and birthplace (state or country). Transfers-cancellations gives name, whether cancelled or transferred, from what precinct transferred, and to what precinct transferred. Corrections give name, corrected name, and precinct. Includes list of post offices listed in precincts. FHL book 979.486 N42g.
- Also online, see
http://files.usgwarchives.net/ca/tulare/greatregister/gr1898.txt.

1898. *Illustrated Roster of California Volunteer Soldiers in the War with Spain: Enlisted Under the President's Proclamations of April 23rd and May 25th 1898* **[Microfilm & Digital Capture],** filmed by the Library of Congress, 1988, 1 roll, FHL film 1550665. To access the digital images, see the online FHL catalog: **www.familysearch.org/search/catalog/666713.**
- See also, *1st California Regiment of U.S. Volunteers, 1898* **[Online Database],** list of the Spanish American War volunteers from California, listed at the SFGenealogy site. Archived at:
https://web.archive.org/web/20160306184612/http://www.sfgenealogy.com/sf/history/hgcal.htm.

1898 Madera County Great Register **[Microfilm & Digital Capture],** from the original records at the California State Library, Sacramento, CA. Alphabetically arranged by first letter of surname. Filmed by the Genealogical Society of Utah, 1975, 1 roll, FHL film #976933. To access the digital images, see the online FHL catalog:
www.familysearch.org/search/catalog/207940.

1898 Butte County Great Register Index **[Microfilm & Digital Capture],** from the card index located at the Paradise Genealogical Society Library, Paradise, California. Index gives name, place of residence, occupation, age, height, state of nativity or last residence. Filmed by the Genealogical Society of Utah, 1992, 2 rolls, FHL Film #1819679 (Index, A-M), and FHL film #1819680 (Index, Mc – Z). To access the digital images, see the online FHL catalog:
www.familysearch.org/search/catalog/629181.

1898. *Great Register of Mendocino County, State of California* **[Printed Book],** reprint of 1898 original by Pomo Chapter, Daughters of the American Revolution, 1979, 96 pages. FHL book 979.415 N4m.

1898 Telephone Directory, San Francisco, California **[Online Database],** indexed at the SFGenealogy site. Archived at
https://web.archive.org/web/20150318120124/http://www.sfgenealogy.com/sf/1898t/t98t.htm.

1898. *Shasta County, California Register* **[Online Database],** indexed at the Ancestry.com website. Source: Shasta Co Genealogy Society, Redding, CA, 2001. Each index record includes: Name, Occupation, Age, Nativity, and PO Address. This database has 5,244 records. See
https://search.ancestry.com/search/db.aspx?dbid=3819.

1899-1910. *San Francisco, California, Immigration Office Minutes* **[Online Database],** indexed at the Ancestry.com website. Source: National Archives microfilm M1387. This database contains minutes of INS hearings in San Francisco dealing with appeals from individuals who had been denied entry into the United States. Each index record includes: Name, Age at arrival, Nationality, Arrival date, Arrival place, and Ship name. View the image of the documents for more possible information. This database has 4,038 records:
https://search.ancestry.com/search/db.aspx?dbid=2974.

1899. *California State Roster, Government and Military Records* **[Online Database],** This is the "California Blue Book, or State Roster, 1899" compiled by Charles Forrest Curry, Secretary of State, Printed at the State Printing office, Sacramento, (no date given). This book contains a listing of over 13,000 state and municipal employees of the State of California for the year 1899. This database has 13,527 records, see
www.ancestry.com/search/collections/5733.

1899-2011. *California, San Mateo County, Colma, Italian Cemetery* **[Online Database],** digitized at the FamilySearch.org website. Includes index cards and daily logbook of the Italian Cemetery in Colma, California. See
www.familysearch.org/search/collection/1922526.

1900. *California, 1900 Federal Census: Soundex and Population Schedules* **[Microfilm & Digital Capture],** from the original records at the National Archives, Washington, DC. Filmed by the National Archives, c1970, 234 rolls, beginning with FHL film #1242202 (Soundex: A000-A000 Soy); and FHL film #1240081 (Population schedules: Alameda Co.). To access the digital images, see the online FHL catalog:
www.familysearch.org/search/catalog/647555.

1900-1930. *Index to Records of Appellate Court Cases* **[Microfilm & Digital Capture],** from original records at the State Archives, Sacramento, CA. Filmed by the Genealogical Society of Utah, 1975, 2 rolls, FHL film #978910 (Plaintiff Index) and FHL film #978911 (Defendant Index). To access the digital images, see the online FHL catalog:
www.familysearch.org/search/catalog/208701.

1900-1968. *California Voter Registrations* **[Online Database],** digitized and indexed at the Ancestry.com website, taken from the records at the California State Library, Sacramento, CA. This database consists primarily of the county voter registers published every two years, plus any indexes to the Great Registers, to affidavits for registration, and to precinct registers. An 1872 law required that counties publish an index or alphabetical listing of all registered voters every two years. This usually happened on the even numbered years. In California, women were granted the right to vote in late 1911 and women first appear in the registers in early 1912. Voter registrations were kept at each county by the county clerk. Indexes to these records are organized according to county and voting wards and/or precincts. Within each precinct voters are listed alphabetically by surname. Information listed about each voter may include: Name, Age, Address, Occupation, and Political Affiliation. Below is a list of the counties and years for which records are included in this database. All California counties are listed, those without Great Registers during this period are noted. Even though this list sometimes indicates an inclusive year range of a decade or more, the records were typically published every other year. This database has 67,318,901 records. To search for a person in the 1900-1968 California Voter Registrations database, see
https://search.ancestry.com/search/db.aspx?dbid=61066.

1900-1968 California Voter Registrations, by county:
- Alameda (1900-1944)
- Alpine (1902-1944, missing 1904, and 1908)
- Amador (1900-1944)
- Butte (1900-1944)
- Calaveras (1900-1944)
- Colusa (none in this series, see 1866-1898 series)
- Contra Costa (1942-1944)
- Del Norte (1900-1944, missing 1900, 1906, 1908, and 1910)
- El Dorado (1900-1944)
- Fresno (1900-1944)
- Glenn (1900-1944)
- Humboldt (1900-1948)
- Imperial (1900-1960, missing 1900, 1902, 1904, and 1906)
- Inyo (1900-1944, missing 1910, 1912, and 1914)
- Kern (1910-1960)
- Kings (1900-1944)
- Klamath (none in this series. Klamath Co was abolished in 1874. See the 1866-1898 series)
- Lake (1900-1944, missing 1908)

- Lassen (1900-1944)
- Los Angeles (1916-1962, missing 1918, 1920, 1932, 1960, and 1962)
- Madera (1900-1944)
- Marin (1900-1944)
- Mariposa (1900-1944)
- Mendocino (none in this series, see 1866-1898 series)
- Merced (none in this series, see 1866-1898 series)
- Modoc (none in this series, see 1866-1898 series)
- Mono (1900-1944)
- Monterey (1900-1944, missing 1904)
- Napa (1900-1944, missing 1902)
- Nevada (1902-1928)
- Orange (1900-1968)
- Placer (none in this series, see 1866-1898 series)
- Plumas (none in this series, see 1866-1898 series)
- Riverside (none, see 1905-1934 city directories substitutes)
- Sacramento (1900-1944, missing 1904)
- San Benito (1928-1944)
- San Bernardino (1902-1964)
- San Diego (1902-1944, missing 1908)
- San Francisco (1900-1944, missing 1933, 1942)
- San Joaquin (1900-1944)
- San Luis Obispo (1900-1944)
- San Mateo (1900-1944)
- Santa Barbara (1900-1944)
- Santa Clara (1902-1942)
- Santa Cruz (1900-1944)
- Shasta (1900-1944)
- Sierra (1900-1944, missing 1914)
- Siskiyou (1900-1944, missing 1906)
- Solano (1900-1944)
- Sonoma (1900-1944, missing 1904 and 1916)
- Stanislaus (1900-1944)
- Sutter (1900-1916; 1938-1944, missing 1906)
- Tehama (1900-1944)
- Trinity (1900-1944, missing 1930)
- Tulare (1900-1944, missing 1908)
- Tuolumne (1900-1944)
- Ventura (1902-1944)
- Yolo (1902-1944)
- Yuba (1900-1944, missing 1906)

1900-1910 San Joaquin County Great Registers **[Microfilm & Digital Capture],** from the original records located at the Stockton-San Joaquin County Public Library, Stockton, CA. Includes name, age, nativity, place of residence, date and place of naturalization etc. Filmed by the Genealogical Society of Utah, 1992, 8 rolls, as follows:]
- Great registers, 1900, A-S, FHL film #1838363.
- Great registers, 1900, S-Z; 1902, A-M, FHL film #1838465.
- Great registers, 1902, M-Z; 1904, A-H, FHL film #1838466.
- Great registers, 1904, H-Z; 1906, A-C, FHL film #1838467.
- Great registers, 1906, C-Y, FHL film #1838468.
- Great registers, 1906, Y-Z: 1908, A-Q, FHL film #1838584.
- Great registers, 1908, R-Z; 1910, A-K, FHL film #1838585.
- Great registers, 1910, L-Z, FHL film #1838675.

To access the digital images, see the online FHL catalog: **www.familysearch.org/search/catalog/659060.**

1902 Index to Great Register, San Luis Obispo County **[Microfilm & Digital Capture],** from the original published 1902. Filmed by the Genealogical Society of Utah, 1988, 1 roll, FHL film #1571207. To access the digital images, see the online FHL catalog: **www.familysearch.org/search/catalog/612289.**

1903 San Francisco Telephone Directory **[Online database],** indexed at the SFGenealogy site. Archived: **https://web.archive.org/web/20150318100315/http://www.sfgenealogy.com/sf/1903t/images/t3d.htm.**

1903-1944. *California, Index to Chinese Exclusion Cas Files* **[Online Database],** indexed at the Ancestry.com website. Source: National Archives records, *Chinese Exclusion Case Files of the San Francisco District Office of the U.S. Immigration and Naturalization Service.* Most of the case files document the arrival into San Francisco from the U.S. mainland or foreign ports of Chinese aliens and the reentry of U.S. citizens of Chinese ancestry under the Chinese Exclusion Acts passed by Congress between 1882 and 1930 and repealed in 1943. There are also some case files relating to the arrival and departure of non-Chinese Asian immigrants and other foreign-born individuals. This database has 5,034 records. See **https://search.ancestry.com/search/db.aspx?dbid=3378.**

1903-1947. *San Francisco, California, Chinese Passenger Arrivals and Disposition* **[Online Database],** indexed at the Ancestry.com website. Source: National Archives microfilm M1476. This database contains descriptive lists of Chinese immigrants arriving at the port of San Francisco, California between 1903 and 1947. Information recorded in these documents includes: Ship or vessel name, Sate of arrival, Name, Age, Gender, Marital status, Occupation, Nationality, Last place of residence, and Final destination. This database has 136,214 records. See **https://search.ancestry.com/search/db.aspx?dbid=2232.**

1904, 1908, Precinct Index Great Register of San Joaquin County **[Microfilm & Digital Capture],** from the original records located at the Stockton-San

Joaquin County Public Library, Stockton, CA. Contains alphabetical listing of names for all precincts in San Joaquin County for 1904 and 1908. Filmed by the Genealogical Society of Utah, 1992, 1 roll, FHL film #1838362. To access the digital images, see the online FHL catalog:
www.familysearch.org/search/catalog/659048.

1904-1949 San Francisco Newspapers Index **[Microfiche],** from the original index cards located at the California State Library in Sacramento. The San Francisco Newspapers index is made up of three interfiled indexes covering the San Francisco Call, Jan. 1, 1904-Aug. 31, 1913, the San Francisco Examiner, Sept. 1, 1913-Sept. 23, 1928, and the San Francisco Chronicle, Sept. 1, 1913-Dec. 31, 1959. Includes an index which also has cross references to the subject headings or topics in the newspaper index. Includes a user's guide, compiled by Richard Terry, and published by the California State Library, Sacramento. FHL microfiche series contains 703 fiche, beginning with FHL fiche #6333980. For a complete list of fiche numbers and contents of each, see the online FHL catalog page for this title:
www.familysearch.org/search/catalog/651530.

1904-1952. *California, San Diego Passenger Lists* **[Online Database],** indexed at the FamilySearch.org website. Source: National Archives microfilm A3471. This collection contains Passenger Lists of Vessels Arriving at San Diego, California, 1904-1952. The records usually includes full name, age, gender, marital status, occupation, citizenship, race, last permanent residence, birthplace, and final destination. This database has 70,546 records. See
www.familysearch.org/search/collection/2442742.

1905-1923. *California, San Diego, Chinese Passenger and Crew Lists* **[Online Database],** indexed at the FamilySearch.org website. Source: National Archives microfilm A3470. The records usually includes full name, age, gender, occupation, citizenship, race, last permanent residence, birthplace, birth date and final destination. This database has 1,807 records. See
www.familysearch.org/search/collection/2443335.

1905-1934. See *1905-1934 Riverside City/County Directories* **[Microfilm],** from the original records located in various libraries and societies. Filmed by Research Publications, Inc., Woodbridge, CT, 1995, 6 rolls. FHL has the following:
- 1905, 1906, 1907, 1908 & 1910 Riverside City directories, FHL film #2308395.
- 1911, 1912, 1913 & 1914 Riverside city and county directories, FHL film #2308396.
- 1915, 1916, 1917 & 1918-1919 Riverside city and county directories. FHL film #2308397.
- 1921, 1923, 1925 & 1928 Riverside city directories, FHL film #2308398.
- 1927, 1929 & 1930 Riverside city directories, FHL film #2308399.
- 1931-1932 & 1934 Riverside city directories, FHL film #2308400.

1905-1939. *California, Death Index* **[Online Database],** digitized and indexed at the FamilySearch.org website. Death index located at the Office of the State Register, Sacramento, and the Butte County Courthouse, Oroville. The index is arranged alphabetically by the name of the deceased, initials of spouse, age, and date of death. Place of death or county of death is coded. This database has 1,894,973 records: www.familysearch.org/search/collection/1932433.
- This database is also at the Ancestry.com website, see https://search.ancestry.com/search/db.aspx?dbid=5187.

1905-1995. *California Birth Index* **[Online Database],** digitized and indexed at FamilySearch.org. Source: CA Dept of Health, Vital Statistics, Sacramento. Includes surnames, first names, middle names/initials, birthdates, gender, the county of birth (in California), and the mother's maiden name. This database has over 24 million names, see
www.familysearch.org/search/collection/2001879.
- This database is also at the Ancestry.com website, see https://search.ancestry.com/search/db.aspx?dbid=5247.

1905 Births, Butte County, California **[Online Database],** indexed at the USGenWeb site for Butte Co CA. Archived at
https://web.archive.org/web/20150314040227/http://www.cagenweb.com/butte/bir-dea.1905.htm.

1906 Deaths in the San Francisco Earthquake **[Online Database],** index at the SFMuseum site. See www.sfmuseum.org/perished/index.html.
- See also, *California, San Francisco, Earthquake Cards, 1906* **[Digital Capture],** from a card file at the Museum of the City of San Francisco. The card file indexes the titles, subject, or author of news articles related to the 1906 San Francisco earthquake. To access the digital images, see the online FHL catalog:
www.familysearch.org/search/catalog/2304002.

1906 San Francisco City Directory **[Online Database],** indexed at the SFGenealogy site. See www.sfgenealogy.com/sf/1906t/may06.htm.

1906-1908 Death Index, Ventura County, California **[Online Database],** originally indexed at the Ventura Co Gen Society website. For an archived database, see
https://web.archive.org/web/20120625104519/www.venturacogensoc.org/DeathIn2.htm.

1906-1930 Naturalization Records, Sonoma County, California **[Online Database],** indexed at the RootsWeb site for Sonoma Co CA. See www.rootsweb.ancestry.com/~cascgs/nat2.htm.

1906-1946. *San Francisco, California, Surrendered Alien Certificates* **[Online Database],** digitized and indexed at the Ancestry.com website. Source: National Archives microfilm A3975. This database contains images of certificates provided to aliens entering the United States after leaving from Hawaii. Before Hawaii became a state, it and other territories and insular possessions of the United States (such as Puerto Rico and the Philippines) created a peculiar situation for immigration officials. U.S. immigration law did not require the typical immigration documents for aliens coming from ports in these areas to the United States. The issue was addressed by creating Form 546, an Alien Certificate—Insular Territory. These were issued to aliens who left from Hawaii and other ports and surrendered when the individual arrived on the U.S. mainland. The forms vary some, but they may include the following details: Name, Native country, Port of arrival, Arrival date (both in Honolulu and continental U.S.), Age at arrival, Vessel, Height, Weight, Hair color, Eye color, and Final destination. This database has 23,004 records. See https://search.ancestry.com/search/db.aspx?dbid=2980.

1907 San Francisco City Directory **[Online Database],** indexed at the SFGenealogy site. Archived: https://web.archive.org/web/20150308114938/http://www.sfgenealogy.com/php/dbs/1907sfd.php.

1907-1948 California, Los Angeles Passenger Lists **[Online Database],** digitized and indexed at the FamilySearch.org website. Passenger lists for those arriving at San Pedro, Wilmington, or Los Angeles, California, 1907-1948. Corresponds to NARA Publication M1764: Passenger Lists of Vessels Arriving at San Pedro/Wilmington/Los Angeles, California, June 29, 1907 - June 30, 1948. See www.familysearch.org/search/collection/1916084.

1909. *California State Roster, Government and Military Records* **[Online Database],** indexed at the Ancestry.com website. Original data: California Blue Book or State Roster 1909. Sacramento, CA, USA: State Printing Office. Each index record includes: Given name, Surname, Birth Date, Position, and Page No. This database has 25,712 records. See https://search.ancestry.com/search/db.aspx?dbid=6290.

1910. *California, 1910 Federal Census: Soundex and Population Schedules* **[Microfilm & Digital Capture],** from the original records at the National Archives, Washington, DC. Filmed by the National Archives, c1970, 315 rolls, beginning with FHL film #1369280 (Soundex: A000-A200 Joe); and FHL film #1374082 (Population schedules: Alameda Co.). To access the digital images, see the online FHL catalog: www.familysearch.org/search/catalog/646949.

1910. *California 1910 U.S. Federal Census Index* **[CD-ROM],** compiled and published by Heritage Quest, Bountiful, UT, 2003, FHL CD No. 1177.

1910. *California Special Indian Census* **[Printed Book],** edited and indexed by Larry S. Watson. Census is arranged by name of Indian Band, giving most precise location and name of tribe, with Indian name, English name, sex, family relationship and age. Published by Histree, Yuma, AZ, 1993, 211 pages, FHL book 979.4 X29w.

1910-1941. *California, San Francisco, Immigration Office Special Inquiry Records* **[Online Database],** indexed at the FamilySearch.org website. Source: National Archives microfilm M1388. Registers of persons held for Boards of Special Inquiry. This database has 66,304 records. See www.familysearch.org/search/collection/2299374.

1911. *California State Roster, Government and Military Records* **[Online Database],** indexed at the Ancestry.com website. Original data: California Blue Book or State Roster 1899. Sacramento, CA, USA: State Printing Office. Each index record includes: Given name, Surname, Position, Birthplace, Birth Date, and Page No. This database has 12,898 records. See https://search.ancestry.com/search/db.aspx?dbid=6321.

1912 Great Register, Mariposa County, California **[Online Database],** indexed at the Mariposa-Footprints.com site. See www.mariposafootprints.org/voters/.

1912 Great Register, Ventura County, California **[Online Database],** originally indexed at the Ventura Co Gen Society website. For an archived database, see https://web.archive.org/web/20121123200417/www.venturacogensoc.org/1912GRCam.htm.

1914-1918. *World War I Draft Report: List of California Men Who Enlisted or Were Inducted into the Army, Navy, or Marine Corps* **[Microfilm],** from the originals at the Adjutant General's Office, Sacramento, CA. Arranged alphabetically. Filmed by the Genealogical Society of Utah, 1957, 1 roll, FHL film #2496.

1915-1976. *California, Southern District Court (Central) Naturalization Index* **[Online Database],** digitized at the FamilySearch website. Collection of approximately 273,000 naturalization index cards of the U.S. District Court for the Southern District of California, Central Division (Los Angeles) in two alphabetic sequences. The first sequence represents naturalizations 1915-1930, the second naturalization from 1931 to 1976. The cards include the person's name, the petition number, date of petition, volume and page number of the petition. Some cards also include the declaration number, the date of declaration, volume and page number of the declaration, certification number, and date of issuance. This corresponds to NARA publication M1525: Naturalization Index Cards of the U.S. District Court for the Southern District of California, Central Division (Los Angeles), 1915-1976. See www.familysearch.org/search/collection/1849628.

1916-1996. *Ventura County, California, Obituary Index* **[Online Database],** indexed at the Ancestry.com website. Source: Ventura County Genealogical Society. Each record includes: Name, Death Date, Death Place, Publication, Publication Date, and a link to the VCGS website. This database has 9,560 records. See https://search.ancestry.com/search/db.aspx?dbid=9750.

1917-1918. *California World War I Selective Service System Draft Registration Cards* **[Microfilm & Digital Capture],** from the original records at the National Archives branch, East Point, GA. Filmed by the National Archives, 1988, 158 rolls, beginning with FHL film #1530652 (California: Alameda Co. No. 1, A – Stowell, Seth M.). To access the digital images, see the online FHL catalog: www.familysearch.org/search/catalog/746968.

1917-1918. *California WWI Soldier Service Cards and Photos* **[Online Database],** digitized and indexed at the Ancestry.com website. Service records document an individual's involvement with the military. This database contains the soldier service records for California citizens. A large amount of information pertinent to genealogical research can be found within these records like birth date and place, spouse's name, next of kin, etc. Considerable biographical information can be found such as residence, date of service entry, place or camp the individual was sent to, marital status, age, educational background and work experience. This database has 9,983 records. See http://search.ancestry.com/search/db.aspx?dbid=1701.

1917-1918. *California, WWI Soldier Photographs* **[Online Database],** indexed at the Ancestry.com website. Source: CA State Library, Sacramento. Photographs of California soldiers who fought in WWI are in this database. This collection of over 4,800 records is held by the California State Library and was created by the War History Committee, which was formed by the California State Council of Defense in 1918 to assemble historical material pertaining to California's participation in WWI. See https://search.ancestry.com/search/db.aspx?dbid=1784.

1917-1918. *Information from the World War I Draft Registration Cards* **[Online Database],** indexed at the USGenWeb sites for several California counties. At the main directory list, select a county, then review the list of genealogical databases available online for each. See the Military category to find the 1917-1918 database. WWI databases included for Alpine, Del Norte, Mariposa, Modoc, Mono, Nevada, Sierra, Trinity, Yuba, see http://files.usgwarchives.net/ca/.

1918. *California, San Francisco, World War I Enemy Alien Registration Affidavits* **[Online Database],** digitized and indexed at the FamilySearch.org website. Includes registration affidavits of people from counties at war with the United States. The records were acquired from the San Francisco Public Library. See www.familysearch.org/search/collection/1878523.

1918-1921. *California World War I Death Announcements* **[Online Database],** digitized and indexed at the Ancestry.com website. This database is primarily a collection of newspaper clippings reporting the deaths of California men and women serving in the military in World War I. They cover the years 1918–1922 and were taken from both local newspapers and clipping services. The clippings vary in length and detail but can provide the types of information typically found in obituaries—name; family members; date, place, and cause of death; residence; a life sketch; and military and other details. This database has 5,695 records. See http://search.ancestry.com/search/db.aspx?dbid=2245.

1918-1921. *California, World War I Soldier Citations* **[Online Database],** indexed at the FamilySearch.org website. Source: Records of the War History Committee, CA State Library. This database is primarily a collection of newspaper clippings announcing awards and citations received by Californians serving in the military during World War I. They cover the years 1918–1922 and were taken from both local newspapers and clipping services. They list names and details such as hometowns, names of family members, and a description of the action the award was given for. This database has 3,341 records. See https://search.ancestry.com/search/db.aspx?dbid=2244

1920. *California, 1920 Federal Census: Soundex and Population Schedules* **[Microfilm & Digital Capture],** from the originals at the National Archives. Filmed by the National Archives, c1970, 395 rolls, beginning with FHL film #1823396 (Soundex: A000-A165 Myrtle); and FHL film #1820087 (Population schedules: Alameda Co.). To access the digital images, see the online FHL catalog:
www.familysearch.org/search/catalog/555684.

1920s–1990s. See *California Name Lists at My Heritage.com* **[Online Database].** 117 collections with 89,616,378 records for California. Databases include city directories, county histories, and yearbooks from California high schools, colleges, and private academies. One search screen for the entire collection can be accessed at:
www.myheritage.com/records/California/all-records.

1921-1952. *California, Alien Land Ownership records* **[Online Database],** indexed at the Ancestry.com website. Source: CA State Archives, from records of the Office of the Secretary of State. In the early 20th century, Japanese immigrants were coming to California in large numbers, spurring anti-Japanese and Asian sentiment throughout the state. Because many of these immigrants took up farming and owned land, restricting land ownership was seen as a way to stem the tide of immigration. The records in this collection represent individuals who attempted to circumvent these laws by means such as having their American-born children become the owners of the estate. In 1920 an amendment to an earlier 1913 proposition required guardians to be appointed to minor citizens whose parents could not own real property and were therefore ineligible for citizenship. This collection includes land reports filed by guardians, as well as a card index for part of the collection. This database has 39,170 records. See
https://search.ancestry.com/search/db.aspx?dbid=8804.

1926-1970s. *California City Directories* **[Online Database],** digitized and OCR indexed at the Ancestry.com website. This database is a collection of city directories for various years and cities in California. Generally a city directory will contain an alphabetical list of its citizens, listing the names of the heads of households, their addresses, and occupational information. Sometimes the wife's name will be listed in parentheses or italics following the husband's name. Search the entire collection by name, location, keyword, and more. Also, a search for a certain city and year is available. This database has 31,666 records. See
https://search.ancestry.com/search/db.aspx?dbid=8856.

1928-1933. *California, Index to Census Roll of Indians* **[Online Database],** indexed at the Ancestry.com website. Source: National Archives microfilm M1853. Information contained in the index typically includes the following: Name (Indian and/or English), Gender, Age, Birth date, Census date, Relationship to head of family, Marital status, and Tribe name. This database has 26,744 records. See
https://search.ancestry.com/search/db.aspx?dbid=61006.

1928-1942. *California Immigration Registers of Japanese, Filipinos, and Hawaiians at San Francisco* **[Online Database],** indexed at the FamilySearch.org website. Source: National Archives microfilm A3408. This collection contains Registers of Japanese, Filipinos, and Hawaiians Held for Boards of Special Inquiry at San Francisco, California, September 1928-February 1942. The records are a chronological listing of people detained for boards of special inquiry. The records are arranged by date of arrival then by vessel. This database has 6,994 records. See
www.familysearch.org/search/collection/2427230.

1928-1960. *California, Order Sons of Italy in America, Lodge Records* **[Online Database],** indexed at the Ancestry.com website. Source: OSIA California Grand Lodge Documents. This database contains a number of different document types from the Grand Lodge of California, including membership applications, transfer cards, hospital fund applications, member file cards, and other miscellaneous documents. Information included in the records varies widely by document type, but you may find details such as Residence, Age, Name, Birth date, Birth country, Father's name, Mother's name, Marital status, Spouse's name and age, Number of children, and Occupation. This database has 2,671 records. See
https://search.ancestry.com/search/db.aspx?dbid=1931.

1929-1954. *California, San Diego, Airplane Passenger and Crew Lists* **[Online Database],** indexed at the FamilySearch.org website. Source: National Archives microfilm A3472. The records may include airports of arrival, date of arrival, and the following information about each passenger: name, age, date and place of birth or date and court of naturalization, and U.S. address. This database has 40,536 records. See
www.familysearch.org/search/collection/2465054.
- This database is also at the Ancestry.com website, see
https://search.ancestry.com/search/db.aspx?dbid=2249.

1930. *California, 1930 Federal Census: Population Schedules* **[Microfilm & Digital Capture],** from the originals at the National Archives, Washington, DC. Filmed by the National Archives, c1990, 129 rolls,

beginning with FHL film #2339835 (Population schedules: Alameda Co.). To access the digital images, see the online FHL catalog:
www.familysearch.org/search/catalog/1034478.

1930-1936. *California, San Pedro, Immigration Office Special Inquiry Records* **[Online Database],** indexed at the FamilySearch.org website. Source: National Archives microfilm M1852. Record of persons held for Boards of Special Inquiry at the San Pedro, California, Immigration Office; November 3, 1930 - September 27, 1936. This database has 2,722 records. See
www.familysearch.org/search/collection/2299394.

1931 Mariposa Telephone Exchange **[Online Database],** indexed at the MariposaResearch.net site. See www.mariposaresearch.net/1931phndir.html.

1932 Social Directory, San Francisco, California **[Online Database],** extracted from the 1932 San Francisco social register at the SFGenealogy site. Archived at
https://web.archive.org/web/20160307174933/http://www.sfgenealogy.com/sf/1932b/sr32toc.htm.

1934-1963. *Alcatraz, California, U.S. Penitentiary, Prison Index* **[Online Database],** indexed at the FamilySearch.org website. Source: National Archives Microfilm Publication 458. After locating the inmate identification number in this index, the inmate's case files can then be requested from the National Archives Pacific Regional Office in San Bruno, CA. The listing includes "Scarface" Al Capone and Robert Franklin Stroud, the "Birdman of Alcatraz." The inmate files are meant to document the prisoner's time while in the penitentiary and can include biographies, family histories, medical and psychiatric information, mail sent and received, number of visitors, legal documents, conduct records, mug shots, and rap sheets. This database has 1,575 records. See
https://search.ancestry.com/search/db.aspx?dbid=34666.

1936-1949. *San Francisco Airplane Arrival Card Index* **[Online Database],** indexed at the FamilySearch.org website. Source: National Archives microfilm A3361. The index cards are arranged by series then chronologically by date of arrival and contains: Name, Date of Birth, Place of Birth, Age, Sex, Occupation, Nationality, Address, Date of Arrival, Airport of Arrival and Airplane Number. This database has 11,356 records. See
www.familysearch.org/search/collection/2442743.

1939. *Index by County to Private Land Grant Cases, U.S. District Court, Northern and Southern districts of California* **[Microfilm & Digital Capture],** from the original records located in the National Archives. Contains Spanish and Mexican land grants for ranchos listed by counties as the counties existed on Jan. 1, 1939. Arranged by county, rancho name, and includes name of claimant. Filmed by the National Archives, series T1216, 1 roll, FHL film #940152. Another filming: FHL film #1415716. To access the digital images, see the online FHL catalog:
www.familysearch.org/search/catalog/231778.

1940. *California, Federal Census: Population Schedules* **[Digital Capture],** digitized images from the microfilm of original records held by the Bureau of the Census in the 1940s. After microfilming, Congress allowed the Census Bureau to destroy the originals to free up space for WWII-related files. Digitizing of the 1940 census schedules microfilm images was done for the National Archives and made public on April 2, 2012. To access the digital images, see the online FHL catalog: www.familysearch.org/search/catalog/2057743.

1940 Federal Census, Finding Aids **[Online Database].** The National Archives prepared a special website online with a detailed description of the 1940 federal census. Included at the site are descriptions of location finding aids, such as Enumeration District Maps, Geographic Descriptions of Census Enumeration Districts, and a list of 1940 City Directories available at the National Archives. The finding aids are all linked to other National Archives sites. The National Archives website also has a link to 1940 Search Engines using Stephen P. Morse's "One-Step" system for finding a 1940 E.D. or street address conversion. See
www.archives.gov/research/census/1940/general-info.html#questions.

1940-1947. *California, World War II Draft Registration Cards* **[Digital Capture},** from the originals at the National Personnel Center, St. Louis, MO. Digitized by FamilySearch International, 2016. Draft registration cards of men who registered during World War II, with the exception of the fourth registration. The event place is the residence of the registrant. To access the digital images, see the online FHL catalog:
www.familysearch.org/search/catalog/2786603.
- See also, *California, World War II Draft Registration Cards, 1940-1945* **[Online Database],** digitized and indexed at FamilySearch.org. This database has 2,083,000 records, see
www.familysearch.org/search/collection/2786603.

1940-1997. *California Death Index* **[Online Database],** digitized and indexed at FamilySearch.org. The records are indexed by the last name, first name, middle name or initial, death date, and the father's

Surname. The records include an individual's Social Security Number. The database has 9,356,990 records. See **www.familysearch.org/search/collection/2015582**.
- This database is also at the Ancestry.com website, see **https://search.ancestry.com/search/db.aspx?dbid=5180**.

1941-1945 WWII Army Enlistees, California Counties **[Online Database],** indexed at the USGenWeb site for each California county. At the main directory list, select a county, then review the list of genealogical databases available online for each. See the Military category to find the 1941-1945 WWII database, archived at
https://web.archive.org/web/20200918143412/http://files.usgwarchives.net/ca/

1942. *California Selective Service System Registrations Cards, World War II: Fourth Registration* **[Microfilm & Digital Capture],** from the originals at the National Archives, Pacific Region, San Francisco. Includes name of individual, date and place of birth, address, age, telephone number, employer's name and address, name and address of person who would know where the individual can be located, signature, and physical description. Arranged in alphabetical order by surname, the registration cards cover several counties of California for the letter A. From B-Z the cards are in alphabetical order within each draft board. Filmed by the Genealogical Society of Utah, 2006, 632 rolls, beginning with FHL film #1307999 (Aaby – Adams, Charles Wesley). To access the digital images, see the online FHL catalog: **www.familysearch.org/search/catalog/1211846**.

1943-1980. *California, Los Angeles County, North Hollywood, Piece Brothers Memorial Park Cemetery, Memorial Tablets* **[Online Database],** digitized and indexed at FamilySearch.org. This collection gives name and address of lot owner, deed number and description and location of lot and section of the cemetery, as well as name or names of those already interred. Microfilm of cemetery records located at Pierce Brothers Valhalla Memorial Park and Cemetery, North Hollywood, California. Other cemetery sections, gardens, mausoleum crypts, etc., as well as acquired cemeteries, includes dates of deeds, the name of the section, contract numbers, name of deceased and contract or lot owner, and often the dates of burial or cremation, and method of disposal of cremains. This database has 52,721 records, see
www.familysearch.org/search/collection/3235392.

1947-1948. *California, Airplane Passenger Lists from Honolulu, Hawaii* **[Online Database],** digitized at the FamilySearch.org website. Source: National Archives microfilm A3374. This is an image-only database with Passenger Lists of Airplanes Departing from Honolulu, Hawaii, and Arriving at San Pedro and Los Angeles, California compiled 03/07/1946 - 06/30/1948. The passenger lists are arranged chronologically by date of arrival. They primarily consist of Pan American Airways Passenger Manifest and the Immigration and Naturalization Service (INS) forms. Most of the passengers were U.S. citizens, but there are also Japanese citizens and people from other nations. Browse through 3,802 images from 2 rolls of microfilm, records listed in chronological order. See **www.familysearch.org/search/collection/2427229**.

1949-1959. *California, Marriage Index* **[Online Database],** indexed at the Ancestry.com website. Source: CA Dept of Health, Vital Records, Sacramento. Details in the index include: Groom's Name, Bride's Name, Bride and Groom's Ages, Marriage Date, Marriage County, and State File Number. This database has 2,339,344 records. See **https://search.ancestry.com/search/db.aspx?dbid=5186**.

1960. *The California Register: The Only Statewide Directory for California Listing Prominent Citizens; Their Addresses; Telephone Numbers; Social, Cultural, and Philanthropic Affiliations, and Family Members…* **[Printed Book & Digital Version],** publ. 1960, Social Blue Book of California, FHL book 979.4 E4. To access the digital images, see the online FHL catalog: **www.familysearch.org/search/catalog/2281251**.

1954-1957. *California, San Francisco Passenger and Crew Lists of Vessels Arriving* **[Online Database],** digitized and indexed at the FamilySearch.org website. Source: National Archives microfilm M1411. The passenger lists are form 1-415 (manifest of inbound passengers, alien) and form 1-416 (manifest of inbound passengers, US citizens or nationals). This database has 366,640 records. See
www.familysearch.org/search/collection/2299683.

1960-1985. *California Marriage Index* **[Online Database],** digitized and indexed at the Ancestry.com website. From the original data at the Center for Health Statistics, California Department of Health Services, Sacramento, CA. Information includes the name of the bride and groom, their ages, county, and date of marriage. Each entry is linked to an index image, with additional information, such as the registrar number and state file number. With the information in this index, marriage records can be obtained from the county office (County Clerk or County Recorder) from where the record was issued. The original marriage record may list the bride's and groom's birthplaces, and their parent's names and birthplaces. This database has 9,800,967 records. See
http://search.ancestry.com/search/db.aspx?dbid=1144.
- This database is also available at FamilySearch.org: **www.familysearch.org/search/collection/1949339**.

California • 105

1966-1984. *California Divorce Index* **[Online Database],** digitized and indexed at the Ancestry.com website. From the original data at the Center for Health Statistics, California Department of Health Services, Sacramento, CA. The database has over five million divorces that were filed between 1960 and 1985. Information may include the husband's name, wife's name, date divorce was filed, and county divorce was filed in. With the information in this index, divorce records can be obtained from the Clerk of the Superior Court in the County were the proceedings took place: http://search.ancestry.com/search/db.aspx?dbid=1141.
- This database is also located at the FamilySearch.org website. See www.familysearch.org/search/collection/2015584.

1974-1997. *California, Fresno and Napa Counties, Obituaries* **[Online Database],** digitized and indexed at the FamilySearch.org website. Source: Card indexes compiled by the Napa Valley Genealogical and Biographical Society, Napa, and Fresno County Public Library, Fresno. This database has 65,850 records. See www.familysearch.org/search/collection/2282846.

1982-1987. *Fresno Bee Obituary Index for California* **[Microfilm & Digital Capture],** from the original card index at the Fresno County Public Library, Fresno, CA. Contains obituaries clipped from the Fresno Bee newspaper and pertain to much of the state of California. Filmed by the Genealogical Society of Utah, 1994, 5 rolls, beginning with FHL film #1954983 (Aaron, R. – Cella, E.). To access the digital images, see the online FHL catalog: www.familysearch.org/search/catalog/702835.

1983-Current. *California Newspaper Obituaries* **[Online Database].** Digitized and indexed at the GenealogyBank.com website. One search screen for obituaries published in all of the following city newspapers: Agoura Hills, Alameda, Alturas, Anaheim, Anderson, Antioch, Arroyo Grande, Auburn, Avenal, Bakersfield, Berkeley, Beverly Hills, Big Bear Lake, Bishop, Burbank, Camarillo, Cambria, Ceres, Chico, Chino, Coalinga, Colfax, Compton, Concord, Crescent City, Culver City, Danville, Davis, Eureka, Folsom, Fort Bragg, Fountain Valley, Fresno, Garberville, Glendale, Gridley, Half Moon Bay, Hanford, Hayward, Hermosa Beach, Huntington Beach, Kingsburg, La Cañada Flintridge, Laguna Woods, Lake Arrowhead, Lake Forest, Lake Isabella, Lakeport, Lodi, Lompoc, Long Beach, Los Angeles, Los Banos, Los Gatos, Madera, Manhattan Beach, Manteca, Marina Del Rey, Marysville, Mendocino, Merced, Milpitas, Modesto, Monrovia, Montclair Village, Monterey, Moorpark, Morro Bay, Mount Shasta, Needles, Newport Beach, Costa Mesa, Novato, Oakdale, Oakhurst, Oakland, Ojai, Ontario, Oroville, Pacific Palisades, Pacifica, Palm Springs, Palo Alto, Paradise, Pasadena, Piedmont, Placerville, Pleasanton, Porterville, Red Bluff, Redding, Redlands, Rialto, Richmond, Ridgecrest, Riverdale, Rocklin, Rolling Hills Estates, Roseville, Sacramento, Salinas, San Bernardino, San Clemente, San Diego, San Fernando San Francisco, San Jose, San Luis Obispo, San Mateo San Ramon, Santa Ana, Santa Clarita, Santa Maria, Santa Monica, Santa Rosa, Saratoga, Scotts Valley, Selma, Sonoma, Sonora, Taft, Torrance, Turlock, Twenty-Nine Palms, Ukiah, Vacaville, Vallejo, Ventura, Walnut, Walnut Creek, West Covina, Whittier, Willits, Woodland, Woodland Hills, Yreka, and Yucca Valley. See www.genealogybank.com/gbnk/obituaries/explore/USA/California/.

1985-2011. See *California, Oakland, Alameda County, Newspaper Record Collection* **[Online Database],** digitized and indexed at the FamilySearch.org website. This database contains card file indexes created from local newspapers. The card files for 1985-2002, 2003-2006 and 1986-2011 are located at the Oakland Family History Center. The collection includes obituaries, wedding, anniversaries, and birth announcements. The obituaries are mixed with biographical news stories. This database has 68,934 records. See www.familysearch.org/search/collection/2303048.

1992-2016. *Los Angeles, California, Coroner's Inquest Index* **[Online Database],** indexed at the Ancestry.com website. Source: LA County Coroner. Each record includes: Name, Gender, Ethnicity, Age, Birth Date, Death Date, Death Site, Death Place, Case Number, Investigator, Medical Examiner, a link to the lacounty.gov website. This database has 101,702 records. See https://search.ancestry.com/search/db.aspx?dbid=70833.

1993-1994 Obituaries, San Diego Union-Tribune **[Online Database],** digitized and indexed at the Ancestry.com website. The Sa Diego Union-Tribune is the oldest business in the county and one of the oldest newspapers in the state. Each record provides the individual's name, birthplace, birth date, death date, death location, name of spouse and children, if any. This database has 11,548 records. See http://search.ancestry.com/search/db.aspx?dbid=4109.

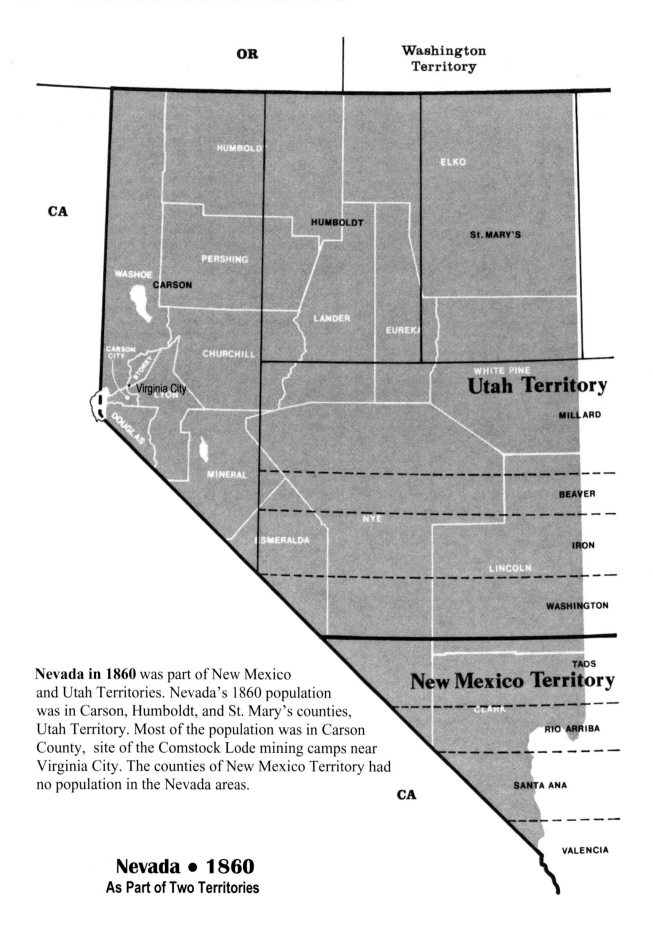

Nevada in 1860 was part of New Mexico and Utah Territories. Nevada's 1860 population was in Carson, Humboldt, and St. Mary's counties, Utah Territory. Most of the population was in Carson County, site of the Comstock Lode mining camps near Virginia City. The counties of New Mexico Territory had no population in the Nevada areas.

Nevada • 1860
As Part of Two Territories

Nevada
Censuses & Substitute Name Lists

Nevada History to Statehood in 1864

The first Spanish exploration of the area took place in 1540 when Melchi Diaz and party traveled through the southern part of present Nevada. Like most Spanish explorers for the first 200 years of New Spain, Diaz was looking for the "seven cities of gold," which the clever natives had continually insisted were real and kept the Spanish from staying in one place long enough to cause anyone harm. All the Indians had to do was tell the Spaniards that the cities of gold were just a few miles further on, and off they would go again. Had Diaz considered moving his expedition a bit further north, and changed his thinking to "mountains of silver," he might have had much more success in Nevada.

- No further activity was recorded in Nevada until 1776, when Spanish Padre Garces, on a search for mission sites along the Old Spanish Trail to California, crossed the Colorado River into southern Nevada. Apparently, Nevada was just a bit too dry and too far away from Mexico or California to attempt colonization – the Spanish never founded a single pueblo, mission, or presidio in Nevada. In fact, the first white settlements in the area came from the Americans, well after the Spanish and Mexican eras.

- After independence from Spain in 1821, Mexico developed a little more interest in Nevada, but only as a means of getting to California. Like the Spanish, Mexico made no attempts to colonize the area.

- In 1826, mountain man Jedediah Smith was the first American to cross Nevada's northern mountains, blazing a major section of a route that would become the primary California Trail.

- In 1828, Peter Ogden was the first to discover the Humboldt River, and immediately saw it as a route for traveling further west. A dozen explorers over the next several years tried to find the destination of the Humboldt, which as it turned out, ran out of water (by evaporation in the desert), ending at the Humboldt Sink, some 60 miles east of present Reno.

- One notable Mexican trader, Antonio Armijo, led a party from Santa Fe to Los Angeles in 1829. He was traveling on what was to become known as the Old Spanish Trail. Passing through the southern desert of Nevada, his party found an abundance of artesian spring water that allowed travelers to cut directly through the vast desert to Los Angeles. The traders named the desert oasis Las Vegas, Spanish for "The Meadows."

- Captain John C. Fremont, leader of several map-making expeditions for the U.S. Army, was very influential in the early discoveries of Nevada, particularly for the immigrant routes that would follow. In 1833, Fremont's expedition of about 25 men discovered a large fresh-water lake, some 30 miles north of present Reno, which he named Lake Pyramid. John Fremont and his guide, Kit Carson, were the first Americans to see Lake Tahoe, and together they used their Pyramid Lake camp as a mustering point for later expeditions across the Sierra-Nevada Mountains into northern California and southern Oregon. Moving on to California, Fremont became a player in the events leading up to the war with Mexico and was a leader of the first attempt to declare California and Nevada as part of the United States.

- In 1841, the first wagon train to California passed along the Humboldt River route through Nevada. This was the Bartleson-Bidwell party departing from Independence, Missouri. They crossed Nevada by way of the Humboldt, Carson Sink, and Walker River. Nevada and California were still part of Mexico – but Americans began to see the area as theirs, based on the "manifest destiny" attitude of the time. As it turned out, the war with Mexico, 1846-1848, was to be Nevada's admission ticket to become part of the United States.

- The Mormons played a big role in early Nevada history, and contributed to the success of the American takeover of the Southwest. In 1847, the Mormons took possession of the Great Salt Lake Valley of

Utah. At the time, they were in Mexican territory. But, before leaving Iowa in 1846, Brigham Young had made a special arrangement with the United States government to supply a battalion of soldiers to march from Iowa to San Diego during the Mexican-American war, keeping them in alliance with the United States.

- In 1848, discharged soldiers of the Mormon Battalion in California had to find all new trails to rejoin their families, now in Utah. In doing so, they established some of the first routes through the Sierra-Nevada Mountains into the Carson Valley of Nevada.

- The treaty of Guadalupe Hidalgo ended the war with Mexico in 1848. As part of the Mexican Cession, the area of Utah, which included present Nevada, was added to the United States; along with all or parts of present California, Arizona, New Mexico, and Colorado.

- The California gold rush brought thousands of prospectors through Nevada. One estimate was that in 1849, 24,000 people crossed the Sierra-Nevada mountains via the Carson Valley of Nevada. In 1850, some 45,000 people made the trek; and up to 52,000 in 1852. Yet, Nevada gained none of these folks – Nevada was seen only as a mustering point to cross the mountains and get to the gold fields of California. But, many of the same people who had ignored Nevada were to find themselves clamoring to get back there within just a few years.

- Meanwhile, Brigham Young decided the Mormons should take advantage of the business opportunities from the thousands of prospectors crossing into Nevada. In June 1851, Mormon settlers from Salt Lake began a trading post in the Carson Valley, which was called Mormon Station (later the town of Genoa), the first white settlement in Nevada.

- In 1855, Brigham Young repeated the exercise and sent a party of 30 men who founded Mormon Fort, which became the town of Las Vegas, Nevada.

- The first real interest in Nevada as a destination began with the discovery of silver deposits. In 1859, the largest known deposit of silver in the world was discovered – the Comstock Lode – an extremely rich four-mile-long lode near present Virginia City, Nevada. The frenzy to mine the Comstock Lode essentially ended the California Gold Rush, because many of the California miners hurried back to Nevada to get in on the bonanza. The population of the Carson Valley exploded with thousands of prospectors arriving in a matter of a few weeks, and the rush continued for several more years.

- As a direct result of the new population attracted to the Comstock Lode, Nevada was organized as a territory in 1861, with Genoa as the first territorial capital. Nevada Territory's population was recorded at 14,404 persons, of which about 4,581 persons resided in and around Virginia City, site of the Comstock Lode mines.

- At the height of the Civil War, the Comstock Lode exercised a far-ranging political and economic influence. Seeking to bolster the Union with another free state, and to ensure his reelection, President Lincoln encouraged Nevada to seek statehood at such a rapid pace that the proposed state constitution had to be telegraphed to Washington.

- The territory became the 36th state in October 1864, a matter of days before the presidential election. Nevada's added voters may have provided the winning margin for Abraham Lincoln's 2nd term.

Bibliography
Nevada Censuses & Substitutes

Nevada Territory, State, & Federal Censuses: Although present Nevada was included in the area of Utah Territory at the time of the 1850 federal census (Taken in April 1851), there was no white population there until June 1851 (at Mormon Station/Genoa).

- The **1860** federal census for Utah Territory included five counties extended into the Nevada country. Of these, three Utah counties had enumerated settlements in the Nevada area: St. Mary's, Humboldt, and Carson Counties. Most of the Nevada area population was in Carson County, the scene of the Comstock Lode and associated mining camps. Carson County was established by Utah Territory in 1854 and encompassed all of what subsequently became the counties of Douglas, Lyon, Ormsby (now Carson City), Storey and portions of Washoe, Pershing, Churchill, Mineral, Esmeralda, and Nye in Nevada.

- In **1861**, the new territorial legislature authorized the first census. The Nevada State Archives in Carson City has all original territorial censuses with dates of **1861** (statewide tally, no names); **1862** (all counties, all white inhabitants, their residences, ages, and sex), **1863** (Lander, Lyon, and Churchill counties only), and **1864** (Nye and Churchill counties only).

- In the **1870** federal census of Nevada, a few anomalies for southern Nevada exist. Several communities of Washington County, Utah Territory were enumerated, but actually lay in Lincoln County, Nevada. Old Pah-Ute County, Arizona Territory was also in Nevada, but enumerated as part of Arizona and Nevada.

- In **1875**, the state of Nevada took its only state census, which also survives.

- NV Federal Censuses, **1880-1940** are complete for all Nevada counties, with the exception of the 1890, lost for all states.

- Census Substitutes outnumber censuses in Nevada by a ratio of 10 to 1. The substitutes are identified below in chronological order:

◆ ◆ ◆ ◆ ◆

1855-1861. *An Inventory & Index to the Records of Carson County, Utah & Nevada Territories* **[Printed Book]**, compiled by Marion Ellison for the Carson Valley Historical Society in cooperation with the Nevada State Division of Archives & Records. Published by the Grace Dangberg Foundation, 1984, 438 pages. Includes index. Includes history of early Utah and Nevada Territories. Consists chiefly of land records. Contains probate records. FHL book 979.3 R2e.

1855-1985. *Carson City, Nevada, Marriage Index* **[Online Database]**, indexed at the Ancestry.com website. Source: Carson City Recorder's Office, Carson City, NV. Each index record includes: Name, Gender, Marriage date, Marriage place, Spouse, Marriage description, and Marriage record number. This database has 600,296 records. See http://search.ancestry.com/search/db.aspx?dbid=60954.

1856-1864. *Early Nevada Records* **[Microfilm]**, from a typescript by J. S. Thompson. Contents: *Records of the Mormon Battalion*; *Records of Early Nevada Military Units and Personnel*; *Early Nevada Records: Certificates of Survey, Carson Valley, 1856*; *1862 Census of Churchill County*; *1864 Census of Nye County*; *Lander County, Nevada 1863 Census*; and *An Alphabetical Listing of the First Directory of Nevada Territory*; Filmed by the Genealogical Society of Utah, 1995, 1 roll, FHL film #1598348. To see if this microfilm was digitized yet, see the online FHL catalog: www.familysearch.org/search/catalog/751445.

1860. *Utah Territory, 1860 Federal Census: Population Schedules* **[Microfilm & Digital Capture]**, filmed by the National Archives, 1967, 3 rolls, beginning with FHL film #805313 (Great Salt Lake, Tooele, Green River, Summit, Davis, Weber, and Box Elder counties); and FHL film #805314 (including St. Mary's, Humboldt, and Carson counties – now Nevada counties). To access the digital images, see the online FHL catalog:
www.familysearch.org/search/catalog/707067.

1860-1987. *Western States Marriage Index* **[Online Database]**, indexed at the Ancestry.com website. This 2011 database is also accessible at the BYU-Idaho website. This database has marriages from several western states, including Nevada, Utah, Idaho, Colorado, Wyoming, Washington, Oregon, California, Arizona, and New Mexico. Each index record includes: Name, Spouse, Marriage date, Marriage place, and a link to the BYU-Idaho website for more information. This database has 1,334,009 records. See http://search.ancestry.com/search/db.aspx?dbid=70016.
- See also, An earlier *Western States Marriage Index* for just Nevada was published in 2004, see *Nevada Marriages, 1860-1987* **[Online Database]**, indexed at the Ancestry.com website. This database has 18,004 records. See
http://search.ancestry.com/search/db.aspx?dbid=7850.

1860-1910. *Nevada, Compiled Census Index* **[Online Database]**, indexed at the Ancestry.com website. Source: Accelerated Indexing Systems, Salt Lake City, UT, acquired 1999. This collection contains the following indexes: 1860 Territorial Census Index; 1870 Territorial Census Index; 1880 Federal Census Index; 1890 Veterans Schedules; 1900 Federal Census Index; 1910 Federal Census Index. This database has 114,240 records. See
http://search.ancestry.com/search/db.aspx?dbid=3560.

1860s-2000s. *Nevada State Library, Archives and Public Records – Digital Collections* **[Online Database]**, see the Historical Nevada Collections, digital copies of original manuscripts, photos, and records, including the following databases:
- Adjutant General of Nevada Reports 1865-1931.
- First Constitutional Convention – 1863.
- Indigent Insane & Hospital for Mental Disease 1871-1931.
- Nevada Historical Society Quarterly.
- Nevada Mining Reports 1893-1931.
- Nevada Orphanages & Reformatories 1871-1930.
- Nevada State Land Patents.
- Nevada State Prison & State Police Reports 1866-1931.
- Nevada Territorial Auditor.
- Nevada Territorial Governor James Warren Nye.
- Nevada Territorial Secretary Orion Clemens.
- Nevada Territorial Supreme Court Cases.
- Nevada Territorial Treasurer John H. Kinkead.
- Nevada Territory Censuses.
- Nevada Territory Oaths, Bonds and Seals.
- Nevada's Sesquicentennial.
- Sarah Winnemucca.
- Secretary of State Biennial Reports 1866-1931.

- State Nevada Election Returns 1904-1930.
- State of Nevada Engineer Biennial Reports 1903-1931.
- State of Nevada Governor Messages 1867-1931.
- Superintendent of Public Instruction Reports 1865-1930.
- Weather & Meteorological Observations 1885-1904

See the Nevada Library Cooperative Search Screen: https://nvlibrarycoop.contentdm.oclc.org/digital/search/advanced.

1860s-2000s. *Nevada US GenWeb Archives* **[Online Databases],** name lists are available for all counties. Typical county records include Bibles, Biographies, Cemeteries, Censuses, Court, Death, Deeds, Directories, Histories, Marriages, Military, Newspapers, Obituaries, Photos, Schools, Tax Lists, Wills, and more. Links to all Nevada counties and projects are located at the USGenWeb home page for Nevada. See **http://usgwarchives.net/nv/nvfiles.htm**.

1860s-2000s. *Linkpendium – Nevada: Family History & Genealogy, Census, Birth, Marriage, Death, Vital Records & More* **[Online Databases].** Linkpendium is a genealogical portal site with links to state, county, town, and local databases. Currently listed are selected sites for Nevada statewide resources (317), Renamed/Discontinued Counties (5), Churchill County (123) Clark County (314), Douglas County (125), Elko County (226), Esmeralda County (152), Eureka County (126), Humboldt County (135), Lander County (131), Lincoln County (145), Lyon County (137), Mineral County (96), Nye County (439), Ormsby County/Carson City (157), Pershing County (108), Storey County (218), Washoe County (301), and White Pine County (157). See **www.linkpendium.com/nv-genealogy**.

1860s – Current. *Carson City Marriage Inquiry* **[Online Database],** searchable database at the Carson City Recorder's website. Archived at https://web.archive.org/web/20190313222722/www.ccapps.org/cgi-bin/dmw200.

1861-1864, 1875. See *Nevada Territory Manuscript Census, 1861-1864; and Nevada State Manuscript Census for Washoe County, 1875* **[Microfilm & Digital Capture],** from the original records located at the Nevada State Archives, Carson City, NV. Includes partial index to 1862 census for Storey and Ormsby Counties, Nevada Territory; census report of Henry DeGroot, 1861 (summaries only); Churchill County census report, 1862 (summaries only); Douglas County, 1862; Humboldt County, Buena Vista, 1862; Humboldt County, Echo township, 1862; Humboldt County, Humboldt township, 1862; Humboldt County, Prince Royal township, 1862; Humboldt County, Santa Clara township, 1862; Humboldt County, Star township, 1862; Lander County, 1863; Lyon County, Dayton, El Dorado Canyon, Palmyra, 1862; Lyon County, Silver City, 1862; Lyon and Churchill Counties, census report, 1863 (summaries only); Ormsby County, 1862; Storey County, Flowery District, 1862; Storey County, Gold Hill, 1862; Storey County, Virginia City, 1862; Washoe County, 1862; Washoe County, 1875. Filmed by the Nevada Division of Printing and Micrographics, 1991, FHL has 1 roll, FHL film #1689341. To access the digital images, see the online FHL catalog: **www.familysearch.org/search/catalog/615923**.

1861-1865. *Index to Compiled Service Records of Volunteer Union Soldiers Who Served in Organizations from the State of Nevada* **[Microfilm],** from the original records at the National Archives, Washington, DC. Nevada supplied 1,684 men to the war (all Union). Filmed by the National Archives, series M0548, 1 roll, FHL film #821939. To see if this microfilm was digitized yet, see the online FHL catalog: **www.familysearch.org/search/catalog/316897**.
- See also, *Nevada, Civil War Service Records of Union Soldiers, 1861-1865* **[Online Database],** indexed at the FamilySearch.org website. Source: National Archives microfilm series M1789, Records of the Adjutant General's Office. This database is an index to the Union service records of soldiers who served in organizations from the Territory and State of Nevada. The records include a jacket-envelope for each soldier, labeled with his name, his rank, and the unit in which he served. The jacket-envelope typically contains card abstracts of entries relating to the soldier as found in original muster rolls, returns, rosters, payrolls, appointment books, hospital registers, prison registers and rolls, parole rolls, inspection reports; and the originals of any papers relating solely to the particular soldier. Each index record includes: Name, Event type, Event year, Age, and Military unit note. The image is viewable at the fold3.com subscription site. This database has 25,709 records. See https://familysearch.org/search/collection/1932420.

1861-1908 Naturalization Records, Washoe County, Nevada [Microfilm & Digital Capture], from the original records at the San Bruno branch, National Archives. Includes partial index. Filmed by the Genealogical Society of Utah, 1975, 2 rolls, FHL film #977771 (Declarations of Intention, 1861-1906), and FHL film #977772 (Declaration of Intention, 1880-1906; 1906-1908; 1877-1906). To access the digital images, see the online FHL catalog: **www.familysearch.org/search/catalog/210942**.

1862 Territorial Census, Churchill County, Nevada Territory **[Online Database],** indexed at the USGenWeb site for Churchill Co NV. See **http://us-census.org/pub/usgenweb/census/nv/churchill/1862/territorial.txt**.

1862 Territorial Census, Ormsby County, Nevada Territory **[Online Database],** indexed at the USGenWeb site for Ormsby Co NV. See **http://us-census.org/pub/usgenweb/census/nv/ormsby/1862**.

1862 Territorial Census, Storey County, Nevada Territory **[Online Database],** indexed at the USGenWeb site for Storey Co NV. See **http://us-census.org/pub/usgenweb/census/nv/storey/1862**.

1862 Territorial Census, Washoe County, Nevada Territory **[Online Database],** indexed at the USGenWeb site for Washoe Co NV. See **http://us-census.org/pub/usgenweb/census/nv/washoe/1862/territory.txt**.

1863 Territorial Census, Lander County, Nevada Territory **[Online Database],** indexed at the USGenWeb site for Lander Co NV. See **http://us-census.org/pub/usgenweb/census/nv/lander/1863/territorial.txt**.

1862 Territorial Census, Douglas County, Nevada Territory **[Online Database],** indexed at the USGenWeb site for Douglas Co NV. See **http://us-census.org/pub/usgenweb/census/nv/douglas/1862/territorial.txt**.

1862 Territorial Census, Humboldt County, Nevada Territory **[Online Database],** indexed at the USGenWeb site for Humboldt Co NV. **See http://us-census.org/pub/usgenweb/census/nv/humboldt/1862/territorial.txt**.

1862 Territorial Census, Lyon County, Nevada Territory **[Online Database],** indexed at the USGenWeb site for Lyon Co NV. See **http://us-census.org/pub/usgenweb/census/nv/lyon/1862/territorial.txt**.

1862 Census of Washoe County, Territory of Nevada **[Microfilm & Digital Capture],** from the original records at the Nevada State Archives, Carson City, NV. Filmed 1983, 1 roll, FHL film #1705177. To access the digital images, see the online FHL catalog: **www.familysearch.org/search/catalog/490029**.

1862. *First Directory of Nevada Territory: Containing the Names of Residents in the Principal Towns* **[Printed Book]** compiled by J. Wells Kelly, published by Valentine, San Francisco, 1862. FHL book 979.3 E4v 1862.

1862. *An Alphabetical Listing of the First Directory of Nevada Territory: Directory* **[Microfilm],** from a typescript compiled by J. Wells Kelly, 1861-1862, for the Towns of Aurora, Carson City, Dayton, Empire, Genoa, Gold Hill, Jack's Valley, Silver City, Virginia City, Washoe, microfilm of typescript, dated 1995, 120 pages. Filmed by the Genealogical Society of Utah, 1995, 1 roll, FHL film #1598348. To see if this microfilm was digitized yet, see the online FHL catalog: **www.familysearch.org/search/catalog/751437**.

"1862 **Nevada Territorial Census**" **[Printed Articles],** name lists by towns, published in *Name Tracer,* a periodical of the Las Vegas Branch Library, Las Vegas, NV. For Empire City, Genoa, and Washoe, see Vol. 1, No. 1 (Jul 1997); Aurora, see Vol. 1, No. 3 (Sep 1967) and Vol. 1, No. 4 (Nov 1967); Dayton, see Vol. 1, No. 2 (Jul 1967) and Vol. 1, No. 3 (Sep 1967); Virginia City, see Vol. 2, No. 2 (Mar 1968) and Vol. 2, No. 3 (May 1968).

1862-1882 Nevada Territory & State Directories **[Microfilm],** from the originals published by various publishers. Filmed by Research Publications, Inc., Woodbridge, CT, 1980-1984. FHL has 4 rolls, as follows:
- 1862 First directory of Nevada Territory; 1863 Second Directory of Nevada Territory; 1864-1865 Mercantile guide and directory for Virginia City, Gold Hill, Silver City and American City; 1866 Harrington's directory of the city of Austin; 1868-1869 The Nevada directory, FHL film #1377106.
- 1871-1872 Storey, Ormsby, Washoe and Lyon Counties directory; 1871-1873 The Pacific Coast business Directory; 1872 Wells, Fargo & Co.'s express directory; 1872 McKennys' gazetteer and directory of the Central Pacific Railroad and its branches; FHL film #1377107.
- 1873-1874 The Virginia City and Truckee railroad directory, 1875 A general business and mining directory of Storey, Lyon, Ormsby, and Washoe Counties, Nevada; Business directory of San Francisco and principal towns of California and Nevada; 1878 Business directory of the Pacific States and Territories; FHL film #1377108.
- 1878-1879 Bishop's directory of Virginia City, Gold Hill, Silver City, Carson City and Reno; 1880-1881 Pacific Coast directory, FHL film #1377109.

1862-1929. *Storey County Records* **[Microfilm & Digital Capture],** from a typescript compiled by Nona Parkin in the Nona Parkin collection of the Reno, Nevada Stake Family History Center, Reno, Nevada. Contents: vol. 1: Birth records/notices: Storey County records 1869-1912; Cemetery census: American Flat and Gold Hill with index, City of Gold Hill Cemetery record, Virginia City Cemetery with index; vol. 2: Death records/notices: Newspaper notices 1862-1912, Storey County death records 1887-1991 with index, Storey County records from 1875, Virginia City death records 1879-1890, Newspaper obituaries, Storey County 1922-1983, Storey County Coroner's records 1879-1887; vol. 3: Funeral home records: Register of funerals, Virginia City 1879-1914, Old mortuary records 1891-1918, Virginia City mortuary records 1879-1883 with index; City directories: American City, Gold Hill and Silver City 1864-1865; vol. 4: Marriage records/notices: Storey County marriage records 1862-1929 with index, Newspaper notices 1875-1912; vol. 5: Newspaper "scats," Pioneer families, Union membership rolls; vol. 6: Church records: Gold Hill Catholic Church, St. Paul's Episcopal Parish, Virginia City; vol. 7: Church records: Virginia City Catholic Church, St. Paul Episcopal Church. Includes some indexing. Filmed by the Genealogical Society of Utah, 1997, 2 rolls, FHL film #1598459 (Vols. 1-3); and FHL film #1598460 (Vols. 4-7). To access the digital images, see the online FHL catalog: www.familysearch.org/search/catalog/780379.

1862-1993. *Nevada County Marriages* **[Online Database],** digitized at the FamilySearch.org website. Source: FamilySearch images from county records on microfilm at the Family History Library, Salt Lake City, UT. This is an image only database with images of marriages from Carson City, Clark, Douglas, Elko, Esmeralda, Eureka, Humboldt, Lander, Lincoln, Lyon, Mineral, Nye, Pershing, Storey, and White Pine counties. Browse through the images, organized by County, then Record Type, Year Range, and Volume Number. This database has 123,409 records. See https://familysearch.org/search/collection/1943751.

1862-1903. *Storey County Nevada Death & Birth records* **[Online Database],** indexed at the Ancestry.com website. Source: database, same title, compiled by Doreen Robinson, 2001. Starting in the early 1860's, Virginia City and Gold Hill, the two primary towns of Storey County, grew rapidly into boomtowns, their populations swelling with miners, merchants and their families. This database contains birth, death and burial records for Virginia City, Gold Hill and the surrounding area including: Lousetown, Divide, American City, Devil's Gate and Six Mile Canyon - all within few miles of Gold Hill and Virginia City. This database has 6,483 records. See http://search.ancestry.com/search/db.aspx?dbid=6084.

1862-1923. *Douglas County, Nevada Vital Records* **[Online Database],** indexed at the Ancestry.com website. Source: database, same title, compiled by Doreen Robinson, 2000. This database contains birth records from 1885-1900, marriage records from 1862-1919, and death records from 1887-1923. This database has 4,273 records. See http://search.ancestry.com/search/db.aspx?dbid=5013.

1862-1993. *Nevada, County Marriages* **[Online Database],** indexed at the Ancestry.com website. Source: FamilySearch extractions from records on microfilm at the Family History Library, Salt Lake City, UT. This is an image only database. Browse the images, organized by County, Record Type, Year Range, and Volume Number. This database has 123,409 records. See http://search.ancestry.com/search/db.aspx?dbid=60081.

1863. *Lander County, Nevada 1863 Census* **[Microfilm],** from a typescript compiled by J.S. Thompson, 62 pages. Contents: part 1: Every-name index giving age (when known) and town; part 2 Alphabetical listing by surname in each town. Filmed by the Genealogical Society of Utah, 1995, 1 roll, FHL film #1598348. To see if this microfilm was digitized yet, see the online FHL catalog: www.familysearch.org/search/catalog/751441.

1863. *Early Tax Lists For Nevada Territory* **[Online Database],** indexed at the USGenWeb site for Nevada. The 1863 tax list is arranged alphabetically and gives a location, occupation, and date. Archived at https://web.archive.org/web/20170325033748/http://www.nvgenweb.org/nvtax.txt.

1863-1866. *Nevada Civil War Volunteers* **[Online Database],** indexed at the Ancestry.com website. Source: database compiled by Doreen Robinson from *Muster Roll Indexes for the 1st Nevada Volunteer Cavalry, 1863*. This database consists of muster rolls indexes for this unit from its creation in 1863 through 1866. Each index record includes: Name, Birth date, Nativity, Date joined, Place joined, Age, Date mustered in, Place mustered in, Rank, Battalion, Arm of service, and Company. This database has 868 pages. See http://search.ancestry.com/search/db.aspx?dbid=3349.

***1863-1866 Internal Revenue Assessment Lists for the Territory and State of Nevada* [Microfilm & Digital Capture],** from the original records at the National

Archives, Washington, DC. Filmed by the National Archives, 1980, series M779, 2 rolls, FHL film #1578506 (District 1 Feb. 1863 - Nov. 1865), and FHL film #1578506 (District 1 Jan. - Dec. 1866). To access the digital images, see the online FHL catalog: www.familysearch.org/search/catalog/578001.

1864-1922. *Nevada Newspaper Archives* **[Online Databases],** digitized and indexed newspapers at the GenealogyBank website, for Austin, Carson City, Elko, Eureka, Hamilton, Pioche, Reno, Treasure City, Unionville, and Virginia City, Nevada. See www.genealogybank.com/explore/newspapers/all/usa/nevada.

1864-1964. *Master Index to Pioneer Families, Information Collected in 1964 to Celebrate Nevada's Centennial: Pioneer Families Are Included in Each Nevada County History* **[Microfilm & Digital Capture],** from a 94-page manuscript prepared by Nona Parkin, in the Nona Parkin collection, Nevada Stake Family History Center, Reno, NV. Filmed by the Genealogical Society of Utah, 1997, 1 roll, FHL film #1598462. To access the digital images, see the online FHL catalog: www.familysearch.org/search/catalog/781051.

1864-1983. See *Esmeralda County Records* **[Microfilm & Digital Capture],** from a typescript compiled by Nona Parkin, in the Nona Parkin collection of the Reno, Nevada Stake Family History Center, Reno, NV. Contents: vol. 1: Cemetery census: Index to Goldfield Cemetery; Goldfield Cemetery; vol. 2: Death records/obituaries: Esmeralda County death notices from newspapers 1864-1920, Goldfield newspaper obituaries 1922-1983, Newspaper notices 1864-1920; Marriage records/notices: Newspaper notices 1875-1916; Tax assessment records: Esmeralda County assessment roll 1864. Includes index. Filmed by the Genealogical Society of Utah, 1997, 1 roll, FHL film #1598448. To access the digital images, see the online FHL catalog: www.familysearch.org/search/catalog/780259.

1866-1867. *Territorial Enterprise Birth, Marriage, & Death Notices (Virginia City, Nevada)* **[Online Database],** indexed at the Ancestry.com website. Source: database, same title, compiled by Doreen Robinson, 1998. The *Territorial Enterprise* was published in Virginia City, Nevada and perhaps its greatest claim to fame is the young journalist, Samuel Clemens, who worked for the paper early in his career as a writer. This database is a collection of notices of births, marriages, voter registrations, and deaths from the newspaper in the years 1866 and 1867. With over 10,200 records, this collection includes information regarding the type of event, date of occurrence, issue of newspaper in which it appeared and in the case of marriages, the name of spouse. Covering the territory of Nevada and parts of northern California, it was extracted from microfilm of the original newspaper. This database has 10,224 records. See http://search.ancestry.com/search/db.aspx?dbid=3515.

1867-1957. *Carson City, Nevada, Birth Index* **[Online Database],** indexed at the Ancestry.com website. This database is also accessible at the Carson City Recorder's website. Each index record includes: Name, Birth date, Birthplace, Father, Mother, and a link to the Carson City Recorder's website. This database has 3,113 records. See http://search.ancestry.com/search/db.aspx?dbid=9264

1867-Current. *Carson City Recorder – Genealogy* **[Online Database],** the Browse our Files pages shows searchable databases for Birth Records, 1867-1957; Death Records, 1887-1957; Public Health Office Reports, 1911-1941; Citizenship Records, 1868-1926; and Cemetery Indexing, to Present. Archived at https://web.archive.org/web/20180131011403/http://www.carson.org/government/departments-a-f/clerk-recorder/genealogy.

1868-1869. *Nevada Directory* **[Online Database],** indexed at the Ancestry.com website. Source: The Nevada Directory for 1868-1869, by William R Gillis, publ. 1868. Each index record includes: Given name, Surname, Location (Place in Nevada, includes "boards with"), and Occupation. This database has 4,223 records. See http://search.ancestry.com/search/db.aspx?dbid=4741.

1869-1904 Election and Court Records of Humboldt County, Nevada **[Printed Book],** 12-page typescript, dated 1979, author, publisher not noted.. Includes election registers, 1869-1904 and justice court records. FHL book 979.3 A1 No. 27.

1870. *Nevada, 1870 Federal Census: Population Schedules* **[Microfilm & Digital Capture],** filmed by the National Archives, 1968, 3 rolls, beginning with FHL film #552333 (Churchill, Douglas, Elko, Esmeralda, Humboldt, Lander, Lincoln, Lyon, Nye, Ormsby, Pah Ute, and Roop (Subdivision of Ormsby) counties. To access the digital images, see the online FHL catalog: www.familysearch.org/search/catalog/698909.

- See also, *1870 Federal Census, Panaca and Clover Valley, Washington County, Utah Territory; and Pah-Ute County, Arizona Territory* [Online Database]. In 1870, the boundaries between Utah, Arizona and Nevada Territories were not surveyed and misunderstood – causing the communities of Clover Valley and Panaca in Lincoln County, Nevada Territory to be enumerated with Washington Co UT Territory. The abolished Arizona county of Pah-Ute continued to function as part of Arizona Territory, but was actually entirely within Nevada Territory. To search the 1870 federal census, use Residence Place: Panaca, Clover Valley, or Pah-Ute to locate the names of inhabitants there. For the FamilySearch digitized and indexed version of the 1870 federal census. See https://familysearch.org/search/collection/1438024.
- See also, The *1870 Pah Ute Census* was indexed at the USGenWeb site for Nevada. See www.us-census.org/pub/usgenweb/census/nv/pahute/1870/indx-a-z.txt.
- See also, *1870 Federal Census, Rio Virgin and Washington County, Utah* [Microfilm & Digital Capture], from the original schedules by the National Archives. Rio Virgin County was created in 1869 to gather outlying Mormon communities under Utah government. But the area of Rio Virgin County was actually in Nevada. The area should have been enumerated as part of Lincoln County, Nevada, but the Nevadans were less aware of the precise boundary with Utah, as were the Utahans with their boundary with Nevada or Arizona. In fact the Nevadans still thought of the area as "Pah-Ute" County, left over from Arizona. The settlers in Panaca and Clover Valley within Lincoln County, Nevada were enumerated as part of Washington County, Utah Territory. Names of residents of Rio Virgin communities can be found on FHL film #553110. (1870 Federal Census of Kane, Millard, Morgan, Piute, Rich, Rio Virgin, and Salt Lake Counties, Utah Territory). The Panaca and Clover Valley people were listed on FHL film #553112 (1870 Federal Census of Wasatch, Washington, and Weber Counties, Utah Territory). To access the digital images, see the online FHL catalog:
www.familysearch.org/search/catalog/698909.

1870-1920. *Nevada, Orphan's Home Records* [Online Database], indexed at the Ancestry.com website. Source: database, same title, compiled by Doreen Robinson, 1998. In Carson City, Nevada stands the building which housed the State Orphans Home from 1870 until 1992. This database contains admissions records for the home from October 1870 until 1920. Requirements for admission were an orphaned child under 14 years of age deemed "worthy" by the County Board of Commissioners. The records in this database contain name of the child, age and place of birth, the dates of admission and discharge. This database has 996 records. See
http://search.ancestry.com/search/db.aspx?dbid=3347.

1871-1872. *State of Nevada Directory* [Printed Book], copied from the original by Nona Parkin. Original published Reno, NV, 1872. FHL book 979.3 E4pn and FHL film #1425608.

1871-1930. *Lincoln County Records* [Microfilm & Digital Capture], from a typescript compiled by Nona Parkin, in the Nona Parkin collection of the Reno, Nevada Stake Family History Center, Reno, NV. Contents: vol. 1: Birth notices: Newspaper notices 1906-1912; Cemetery census: Caliente, Logandale, Panaca, Pioche; Death records/obituaries Newspaper notices 1871-1909, Panaca 1928-1978, Pioche 1922-1974, Pioche Daily Record 1906-1926; Jurors called for duty: Lincoln County 1876 & 1893; Marriage records/notices: Lincoln County records 1872-1915, Newspaper notices 1883-1900; Newspaper "scats;" vol. 2: Pioneer families; Registered voters: Buillionville 1876, Small precincts 1876 & 1890, Panaca 1890, Pioche 1876, 1886, 1888, 1890 & 1892; Tax assessment records: Lincoln County 1886, 1887, 1889, 1892; Pioche 1886, 1889-1893; Church records: Moapa Epiphany Mission 1930 (became St. Matthew's in 1931). Filmed by the Genealogical Society of Utah, 1997, 1 roll, FHL film #1598462. To access the digital images, see the online FHL catalog:
www.familysearch.org/search/catalog/780378.

1871-1992. *Nevada County Birth and Death Records* [Online Database], digitized at the FamilySearch.org website. Source: FamilySearch images from county records on microfilm at the Family History Library, Salt Lake City, UT. This is an image only database with images of birth and death registers of Nevada counties (does not include Carson, Carson City, Churchill, Clark, Elko, Lake, Lincoln, Mineral, Pershing, and Washoe counties). This database has 14,425 records. See
https://familysearch.org/search/collection/2053817.

1874-1885. *Storey County Nevada Marriage Records* [Online Database], indexed at the Ancestry.com website. Source: database, same title, compiled by Doreen Robinson, 2001. Taken from the Storey County Clerk's Marriage License book, these records contain information on those requesting a marriage license. These are not Marriage Certificates, but Marriage License applications, required as they are today to be filled out prior to the ceremony. Always keep in mind, an application does not necessarily mean a marriage took place. Information contained in these records: Groom's name, Residence, Bride's name, Residence, Age, Date of Application, Volume and Page No. from the License book, and Remarks. Remarks include such information as who authorized the marriage of a minor and any other additional information on the record considered pertinent. This database has 2,659 records: http://search.ancestry.com/search/db.aspx?dbid=5829.

1875 Nevada State Census [Online Database], indexed at the Ancestry.com website. Source: Report publ. by the state in 1876, Carson City, NV. In 1875, the state legislature of Nevada ordered a state census. It was the only state census ever taken in Nevada. Counties included: Churchill, Douglas, Elko, Esmeralda, Eureka, Landon, Lincoln, Lyon, Nye, Ormsby, Storey, Washoe, and White Pine counties. For each index entry, the Person's given name, Surname, Age, Sex, Race, Occupation, Place of birth, Status as head of household, and Place of residence is given. This database has 51,506 records:
http://search.ancestry.com/search/db.aspx?dbid=4873.

1875 Nevada State Census. See *Census of the Inhabitants of the State of Nevada, 1875* **[Microfiche],** from the original printed report published Carson City, Nevada: John J. Hill, State Printers, 1877, 2 vols. Filmed by Kraus-Thomson, Millwood, NY, 1985, 18 microfiche, as follows:
- Churchill, Douglas & Esmeralda Counties, FHL fiche #6016536.
- Elko (part), FHL fiche #6016537.
- Elko (part) & Eureka (part), FHL fiche # 6016538.
- Eureka (part), FHL fiche #6016539.
- Eureka (part), Humboldt & Lander (part), FHL fiche #6016540.
- Lander (part) & Lincoln (part), FHL fiche #6016541.
- Lincoln (part) & Lyon (part), FHL fiche #6016542.
- Ormsby (part) & Storey (part), FHL fiche #6016544
- Storey (part), FHL fiche #6016545-6016550.
- Washoe (part), FHL fiche #6016551.
- Washoe (part) & White Pine (part), FHL fiche #6016552.
- White Pine (part), FHL fiche #6016553.

1875 Nevada State Census - Name Index [Microfiche], compiled by the Nevada State Library, Each county is separately indexed. White Pine County (film #6332701) is mislabeled as Hite County. Provides years, sex, race, occupation, vol. and page where complete census information for each name can be found. Filmed by the Nevada State Library, 14 fiche. FHL has the following:

- Churchill County, FHL fiche #6332696.
- Douglas County, FHL fiche #6332697.
- Elko County, FHL fiche #6332698.
- Esmeralda County, FHL fiche #6332699.
- Eureka County, FHL fiche #6332700.
- Humboldt County, FHL fiche #6332702.
- Lander County, FHL fiche #6332703.
- Lincoln County, FHL fiche #6332704.
- Lyon County, FHL fiche #6332705.
- Nye County, FHL fiche #6332706.
- Ormsby County, FHL fiche #6332707.
- Storey County, FHL fiche #6332708.
- Washoe County, FHL fiche #6332709.
- Hite (White Pine) County, FHL fiche #6332701.

1875 Nevada State Census by County [Microfilm & Digital Capture], from a typescript (2 volumes) in the Nona Parkin collection of the Reno, Nevada Stake Family History Center, Reno, NV. Contents: vol. 1: Churchill, Douglas, Esmeralda, Elko, Eureka, Lyon, Lincoln, Humboldt, Ormsby, Nye, and Lander counties; vol. 2: Storey, Washoe, and White Pine counties. Includes surname, age, sex, profession (for head of household) and birthplace arranged by household as abstracted from census. Filmed by the Genealogical Society of Utah, 1977, 1 roll, FHL film #1598455. To access the digital images, see the online FHL catalog:
www.familysearch.org/search/catalog/780383.

1875. *Persons Living in Nevada Who Were Born in New Jersey, Extracted From Nevada State Census, 1875* **[Microfilm & Digital Version],** from a 10-page extract by Genevieve S. Jensen; a project of the Las Vegas, Nevada Multi-Regional Family History Center. Surnames are in alphabetical order. Includes Name, Age, Sex, Color, Occupation, Value of real estate, Value of personal estate, Place of birth, Father of foreign birth, Mother of foreign birth, County, Volume and Page. Filmed by the Genealogical Society of Utah, 1994, 1 roll, FHL film #1598226. To access the digital version, see the online FHL catalog:
www.familysearch.org/search/catalog/700994.

"1879-1916 Bunkerville Residents, Clark County, Nevada" [Printed Article], name list published in *Name Tracer*, a periodical of the Las Vegas Branch Library, Las Vegas, NV, Vol. 6, No. 4 (Oct 1972) through Vol. 7, No. 2 (Apr 1973).
- See also **"1890 Bunkerville Residents,"** in Vol. 6, No. 3 (Jul 1972).

1880. *Nevada, 1880 Federal Census: Soundex and Population Schedules* **[Microfilm & Digital Capture],** filmed by the National Archives, c1970, 5 rolls, beginning with FHL film #1254758 (Churchill, Douglas, Elko, Esmerelda, Eureka, Humboldt, Lander, Lincoln, and Lyon Counties). To access the digital images, see the online FHL catalog: www.familysearch.org/search/catalog/676488.

1881 History. *Reproduction of Thompson and West's "History of Nevada, 1881" With Illustrations and Biographical Sketches of its Prominent Men and Pioneers"* **[Printed Book],** with introduction by David F. Myrick. Includes history of Nevada and biographical sketches of some of the prominent men and pioneers and a patron directory. Original published by Thompson & West, Oakland, CA, 1881, 680 pages. Reprint published by Howell-North, Berkeley, CA, 1958. FHL book 979.3 H2t. Indexed in *Index to History of Nevada*, by Helen J. Poulton and Myron Angel, published by the University of Nevada Press, Reno, NV, 1966, 148 pages. This index can be used with the original 1881 edition published by Thompson and West, and the 1958 reprint. See FHL book 979.3 B4u v. 6.

1881. *Nevada History* **[Online Database],** digitized and indexed at the Ancestry.com website. Source: *History of Nevada with Illustrations and Biographical Sketches of its Prominent Men and Pioneers*, publ. Thompson and West, Oakland, CA, 1881. Includes the full text page images and an OCR index. This database has 839 pages. See http://search.ancestry.com/search/db.aspx?dbid=7924.

1882 Lists of Registered Voters in Nevada, Various Precincts **[Printed Book],** typescript of extract of voter lists taken from the *Reno Evening Gazette* and *Nevada State Journal* of Reno. The places involved are Wadsworth, Verdi Precinct, Franktown Districts, Buffalo Springs Precinct, Brown's Precinct, Glendale Precinct. FHL book 979.3 A1 No. 6.

1886-1892. *Territorial Enterprise (Virginia City, Nevada)* **[Online Database],** indexed at the Ancestry.com website. Source: database, same title, compiled by Doreen Robinson, 1998. This database is a collection of notices of births, marriages, and deaths from the newspaper between 1886 and 1892. This collection includes information regarding parents, date of event, place of birth and death, county in which the event took place, and residence. This database has 3,956 records. See http://search.ancestry.com/search/db.aspx?dbid=3457.

"1888-1892 Tax Lists, Eureka County, Nevada" [Printed Article], name lists to identify former Cornwall miners working Nevada mines, from an article published in *Cornwall Family Historical Society Journal* (Falmouth, Cornwall County, England), No. 71 (Mar 1994).

1890-1926. *Nevada Records of Marriages, Wills, and Miscellaneous Data* **[Microfilm],** from a transcript copied by the Daughters of the American Colonists (Nevada). Includes marriage records 1890-1896, First Presbyterian Church, Carson City, Nevada; abstracts of Wills 1906-1926, Fallon, Nevada; report of Stanton Post, No. 29, located at Carson City, County of Ormsby, Department of California, G.A.R. for third quarter of 1870; tax list of Lyon County, Nevada, for the year 1897. Includes a partial index. Filmed by the Genealogical Society of Utah, 1959, 1 roll, FHL film #176646. To see if this microfilm was digitized yet, see the online FHL catalog: www.familysearch.org/search/catalog/175168.

1900. *Nevada, 1900 Federal Census: Soundex and Population Schedules* **[Microfilm & Digital Capture],** filmed by the National Archives, c1970, 8 rolls, beginning with FHL film #1240943. To access the digital images, see the online FHL catalog: www.familysearch.org/search/catalog/638247.

1900-Current. *Marriage Search – Clark County Recorder's Office* **[Online Database],** searchable database at the Clark Co NV Recorder's website. See http://recorder.co.clark.nv.us/RecorderEcommerce.

1904-1919. *Ross-Burke Funeral Records, Reno, Nevada* **[Online Database],** indexed at the Ancestry.com website. Source: database, same title, compiled by Doreen Robinson, 1999. This database is a collection of funeral home records from one of the oldest and most respected undertakers in the state. This collection includes information on persons who died between 1904 and 1919 in and around Reno, including Carson City. In addition to giving the Name of deceased, Place of birth, Death date, and Age at time of death can be found here. This database has 2,261 records. See http://search.ancestry.com/search/db.aspx?dbid=3625.

1906-1968. *Index to Marriage Licenses and Marriage Notices in Miscellaneous Nevada Newspapers, 1906-1968* **[Microfilm & Digital Version],** from a manuscript by Edna E. Ostrander; typed by Thelma

Denton; project of the Las Vegas Branch Genealogical Library, Las Vegas, NV. Filmed by the Genealogical Society of Utah, 1986, 1 roll, FHL film #1421646. To access the digital version, see the online FHL catalog: https://familysearch.org/search/catalog/455151.

1910. *Nevada, 1910 Federal Census: Population Schedules* **[Microfilm & Digital Capture],** filmed by the National Archives, c1970, 2 rolls, FHL film #1374871 (Churchill, Clark, Douglas, Elko, Lincoln, Esmeralda, Eureka, Humboldt, and Lander Co), and FHL film #1384972 (Lyon, Nye, Ormsby, White Pine, Storey, and Washoe Co). To access the digital images, see the online FHL catalog: www.familysearch.org/search/catalog/638155.

1911-1965. *Nevada, Death Records* **[Online Database],** digitized and indexed at the Ancestry.com website. Source: NV Dept of Health. This database includes the images of death certificates with an index. Each index record includes: Name, Gender, Birth date, Birthplace, Death date, Death place, Age, Father, Mother, and Certificate number. The certificate image has much more information. This database has 227,903 records. See
http://search.ancestry.com/search/db.aspx?dbid=60974.

1913-1918. *Nevada, Car Registration Records* **[Online Database],** indexed at the Ancestry.com website. NV State Library, Carson City, NV. This database is a collection of registration records for cars registered between 1913 and 1918 in the state. Each record provides the automobile owner's name and town of residence. The registration date is also included. This database has 24,671 records. See
http://search.ancestry.com/search/db.aspx?dbid=4328.

1913-1935 *Reno City Directories* **[Microfilm],** from the original records located in various libraries and societies. Filmed by Research Publications, Inc., Woodbridge, CT, 1995, 3 rolls, as follows:
- 1913-1914; 1917; 1920-1921; 1923 R.L. Polk & Co.'s Reno, Sparks and Washoe County directory, FHL film #2309382.
- 1925-1926, 1927-1928; 1930-1931 R.L. Polk & Co. of California, publishers, FHL film #2309383.
- 1932; 1933; 1935 Polk's Reno city directory, including Washoe County and Carson City, FHL film #2309384.

1915-1981 *Reno, Sparks, Washoe County, and Carson City Directory* **[Printed Book],** published by R. L. Polk and Company, Kansas City, MO. FHL has Library has: 1915 (photocopy), 1917, 1923, 1970, 1973, and 1981. See FHL book 979.35 E4pr 1915-1981.

1917-1918 *World War I Selective Service System Draft Registration Cards, Nevada* **[Microfilm & Digital Capture],** from the original records at the National Archives in East Point, Georgia. The draft cards are arranged alphabetically by state, then alphabetically by county or city, and then alphabetically by surname of registrants. Cards are in rough alphabetical order. Filmed by the National Archives, 1987-1988, 7 rolls, as follows:
- Churchill County; Clark County; Douglas County; Elko County, A-N; FHL film #1711534.
- Elko County, O-Z; Esmeralda County, Eureka County, Humboldt County, FHL film #1711535.
- Lander County; Lincoln County; Lyon County; Mineral County; Nye County, A-O; FHL film #1711536.
- Nye County, P-Z; Ormsby County; Storey County; Washoe County, A-M; FHL film #1711537.
- Washoe County, N-Z; White Pine County, A-J; FHL film #1711538.
- White Pine County, K-Z; FHL film #1711539.
- Indians, Prisoners, Insane, In Hospitals, Late Registrants, FHL film #2022391.

To access the digital images, see the online FHL catalog: www.familysearch.org/search/catalog/746986.

1917-1919. *Nevada, World War I American Expeditionary Forces, Deaths* **[Digital Capture],** digitized by FamilySearch International, 2018. To access the digital images, see the online FHL catalog: www.familysearch.org/search/catalog/3023938.

1918. *Official List of Primary Voting Registration in Lyon County, Nevada: Taken from the Yerington Times, Yerington, Nevada, 1918* **[Printed Book],** copied by Nona Parkin, published by the author, 1964, 14 pages, FHL book 979.3 A1 No. 5.

1920. *Nevada, 1920 Federal Census: Soundex and Population Schedules* **[Microfilm & Digital Capture],** filmed by the National Archives, c1970, 11 rolls, beginning with FHL film #1821004 (Churchill, Douglas, Elko, Eureka, Lander, Clark, Esmeralda, and Humboldt counties). To access the digital images, see the online FHL catalog:
www.familysearch.org/search/catalog/576377.

1930. *Nevada. 1930 Federal Census: Population Schedules* **[Microfilm & Digital Capture],** filmed by the National Archives, 2 rolls, FHL film #2441031 (Churchill, Clark, Elko, Douglas, Esmeralda, Eureka, Humboldt, Lander, Lincoln, Lyon, Mineral, and

Ormsby Counties; and FHL film #2341032 (Nye, Pershing, Storey, White Pine, and Washoe Counties. To access the digital images, see the online FHL catalog: www.familysearch.org/search/catalog/1037454.

1940. *Nevada, Federal Census: Population Schedules* **[Digital Capture],** digitized images from the microfilm of original records held by the Bureau of the Census in the 1940s. After microfilming, Congress allowed the Census Bureau to destroy the originals to free up space for WWII-related files. Digitizing of the 1940 census schedules microfilm images was done for the National Archives and made public on April 2, 2012. To access the digital images, see the online FHL catalog: www.familysearch.org/search/catalog/2057770.

1840 Federal Census, Finding Aids **[Online Database].** The National Archives prepared a special website online with a detailed description of the 1940 federal census. Included at the site are descriptions of location finding aids, such as Enumeration District Maps, Geographic Descriptions of Census Enumeration Districts, and a list of 1940 City Directories available at the National Archives. The finding aids are all linked to other National Archives sites. The National Archives website also has a link to 1940 Search Engines using Stephen P. Morse's "One-Step" system for finding a 1940 E.D. or street address conversion. See www.archives.gov/research/census/1940/general-info.html#questions.

1940-1945. Nevada, World War II Draft Registration Cards **[Digital Capture],** digitized by Ancestry.com. Draft registration cards of men who registered during World War II, with the exception of the fourth registration. Images courtesy of Ancestry. The event place is the residence of the registrant. To access the digital images, see the online FHL catalog: www.familysearch.org/search/catalog/2729393.

1942. *Nevada, Military Records: World War II 4th Draft Registration Cards* **[Digital Capture],** from the original records at the National Personnel Center, St. Louis, MO. digitized by Genealogical Society of Utah, 2015. These cards represent older men, ages 45 to 65 in April 1942, that were registered for the draft. They had birth dates between 28 Apr 1877 and 16 Feb 1892. Includes name of individual, date and place of birth, address, age, telephone number, employer's name and address, name and address of person who would know where the individual can be located, signature, and physical description. To access the digital images, see the online FHL catalog: www.familysearch.org/search/catalog/2624863.

1956-1991. *Nevada, Naturalization Petitions* **[Online Database],** indexed at the Ancestry.com website. Source: National Archives records of district courts. This database is limited to Petitions for Naturalizations from Las Vegas, Nevada. Each index record includes: Name, Gender, Birth date, Birthplace, Even, Petition date, Petition age, Petition place, and Petition number. The image of the Petition document has more information about a person. This database has 16,706 records. See http://search.ancestry.com/search/db.aspx?dbid=60615.

1956-2005. *Nevada Marriage Index* **[Online Database],** indexed at the FamilySearch.org website. Source: NV Dept of Health. Each index record includes: Name, Event type, Event place, Residence place, Registration place, Gender, Spouse's name, Spouse's residence place, Type of officiator, Page, Instrument number, and Registrations year. This database has 5,069,680 records. See https://familysearch.org/search/collection/1949338.

- See also, *Nevada, Marriage Index, 1956-2005* **[Online Database],** digitized and indexed at the Ancestry.com website. Source: NV Dept of Health & Clark Co NV Marriage Bureau. This database contains an index to marriages for Clark County, Nevada (including Las Vegas) from 1956-1966 (with a few marriages from earlier and later years). The database also contains a statewide index to marriages from 1966-2005. Information available in this database includes: Names of bride and groom, Marriage date, City or county of marriage, Officiant, Date marriage was recorded, City or county of recording, County book and page number. All of the above information may not be available for every marriage. Records from Clark County for 1956-1966 also contain an image of a computer print-out register. Some information for these records, such as the county book and page number, may only be obtained by viewing the image. Records that indicate a place of residence for the parties confirms that Nevada is a marriage capital, with many out-of-state people coming to Nevada to get married – but not all of the records include the residence information. This database has 9,501,782 records. See http://search.ancestry.com/search/db.aspx?dbid=1100.

1961-Current. *Index to Marriages, Douglas County, Nevada* **[Online Database],** indexed at the Douglas Co Recorder's website. An index is available and copies of marriage records can be ordered: https://recorder-search.douglasnv.us/DigitalResearchRoom/RecordType.

1968-2015. *Nevada, Divorce Records, 1968-2015* **[Online Database],** indexed at the Ancestry.com website. Source: NV State Dept of Health. Each index record includes: Name, Record type, Divorce date, Spouse, Control certificate number, Court code, and County file number. This database has 1,028,546 records. See http://search.ancestry.com/search/db.aspx?dbid=1090.

1970s-Current. *Washoe County Marriage Records* **[Online Database],** searchable database at the Washoe Co NV Recorder's website. See www.washoecounty.us/clerks/mlb/search_marriage_records.php.

1975-2012. *Nevada, Birth Index* **[Online Database],** indexed at the Ancestry.com website. Source: NV State Dept of Health. Each index record includes: Name, Birth date, and Birthplace. This database has 894,478 records. See http://search.ancestry.com/search/db.aspx?dbid=8998.

1980-2012. See *Nevada, Death Index, 1980-2012* **[Online Database],** indexed at the Ancestry.com website. Source: NV Dept of Health. Each index record includes: Name, Birth date, Birthplace, Death date, and Death place. This database has 443,479 records. See http://search.ancestry.com/search/db.aspx?dbid=8997.

1996-Current. *Nevada Recent Newspaper Obituaries* **[Online Database],** digitized and indexed at the GenealogyBank.com website. Search Nevada newspaper obituaries for Battle Mountain, Boulder, City, Caliente, Carson City, Elko, Ely, Eureka, Hawthorne, Henderson, Las Vegas, Lovelock, Mesquite, North Las Vegas, Pahrump, Sparks, Virginia City, and Winnemucca, Nevada. See www.genealogybank.com/explore/obituaries/all/usa/nevada.

2002-2015. *Nevada, Marriage Certificates* **[Online Database],** digitized and indexed at the Ancestry.com website. Source: NV Dept of Health. Each index record includes: Name, Marriage date, Marriage place, Recorded date, Spouse, and File number. The marriage certificates have more information, including the place of residence of the couple. This database has 19,559 records. See http://search.ancestry.com/search/db.aspx?dbid=61108.

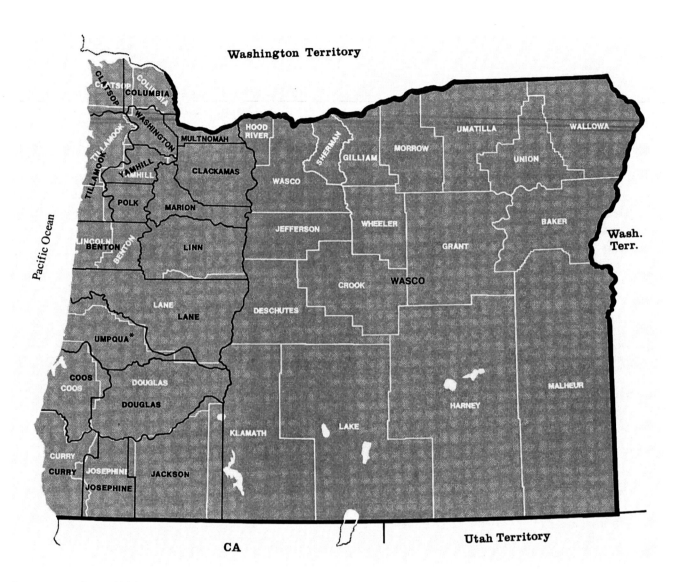

Oregon • June 1860. Oregon became a state in 1859. The 19 counties of Oregon at the time of the 1860 Federal Census are shown in black. The current 36 counties of Oregon are shown in white. * Umpqua County was annexed to Douglas County in 1862. **Map Source:** Page 282, *Map Guide to the U.S. Federal Censuses, 1790-1920*, by William Thorndale and William Dollarhide.

Oregon
Censuses & Substitute Name Lists

Historical Timeline for Oregon, 1775-1860

1775. British Capt. James Cook, fresh from Hawaii, explored and charted the Northwest Coast. He was intent on finding a "northwest passage" that would allow a ship to sail from the Pacific to Hudson Bay. En route, he looked for the mouth of an exceptionally large river in the area reported by the Spanish, but never found it. Based on the latitude-longitudes noted in his ship's log, he passed by the mouth of the Columbia River within a couple of miles.

1783. The United States Of America was recognized at the Treaty of Paris. From day one, the new government asserted a plan to inhabit the entire continent; with plans for explorations in the west, including the Pacific coast, by land or sea.

1784. The North West Fur Company was formed in Montreal. It became a rival of the Hudson's Bay Company for dominance of the fur trade in British North America. Although both companies were British-owned, the North West Fur Company was manned mostly by French-Canadians, while the Hudson's Bay Company was mostly Scottish-Canadians. For nearly forty years, the NW Fur Co fought furiously for fur trading rights, attacking Hudson's Bay forts, burning their ships, etc., until the two companies were forced to end their differences by the British Crown.

1792. American Capt. Robert Gray entered and named the Columbia River after his ship, the same ship he used to become the first American to circumnavigate the globe. Gray and party were in the area at the same time as British Capt. George Vancouver's party, who he met with and revealed the location of the Columbia River. Vancouver then sent Lieutenant William Broughton to confirm the existence of the Columbia River. Broughton not only confirmed it, but he also took his ship well into the river, landing at a point 100 miles from the mouth on the Washington side, built a temporary shelter, and named it Point Vancouver.

1803. William Clark and Meriwether Lewis led the Corps of Discovery, the first transcontinental expedition of the land west of the Missouri River. Their trek to the Pacific was mostly via river routes, beginning at St. Louis on the Mississippi, up the Missouri River to its source in Montana, then by foot across the Mountains, picking up Idaho's Clear River, to the Snake River of Idaho, Oregon, and Washington, and finally, the Columbia River all the way to its mouth at present Astoria, Oregon.

1805. Lewis and Clark explored the Washington side of the Columbia River, including Point Vancouver, the site of the future Fort Vancouver, but built their own Fort Clatsop on the Oregon side near the mouth of the Columbia River, where they spent the Winter of 1805-1806.

1806. John Jacob Astor had amassed a fortune in the trading of furs to European markets. He was America's first multi-millionaire. Astor had established a strong business relationship with the North West Fur Company of Montreal, a British-owned company of French-Canadians in competition with the London based Hudson's Bay Company. Immediately after the 1806 return of Meriwether Lewis and William Clark from their historic expedition to the Oregon Country, Astor began planning for a repeat of the Lewis and Clark journey. Lewis and Clark had recorded the numbers of deer, elk, bears, and beavers they encountered as part of their explorations. Astor's motive was to gain profits from the untapped fur trading locations he had learned about from Lewis and Clark's journals.

1807-1810. British fur trader and mapmaker David Thompson, with the North West Fur Company, began looking for routes from the Rocky Mountains to the Pacific Ocean. He led a crew of French-Canadian fur trappers, established fur trading opportunities with any Indian Tribes he encountered, and charted detailed maps of the Columbia River. Back in Montreal, Thompson had been given instructions to join up with Astor's American fur trappers if they should be found near the Columbia River.

1810. John Jacob Astor formed the Pacific Fur Company to expand his trading empire to the Pacific coast.

1811. Astor's American fur traders erected Fort Astoria near the mouth of the Columbia River as headquarters for the Pacific Fur Company. Manned by two shiploads of men and supplies, it was the first American settlement on the Pacific Coast of North America.
- A Pacific Fur Company expedition called the *Overland Astorians* traveled to the Oregon Country with the intent of arriving at Fort Astoria at the same time as Astor's ships. They followed the same path as Lewis and Clark to get there, arriving a few weeks after the ships.
- Astor had convinced the North West Fur Company to participate in his expedition to the Oregon Country. David Thompson and his party of French-Canadian trappers connected with the Astorians at the Columbia River and followed them down river to Fort Astoria. Thompson then set up a fur trading operation for the North West Fur Company next door to Fort Astoria.

1813. After war was declared in 1812, British warships blockaded Fort Astoria. The Astorians decided it was better to get out before shots were fired, and the entire Fort Astoria operation was taken over by the British-owned North West Fur Company, who renamed it Fort George. The Astorians returned overland to St. Louis, and in doing so, became the first to cross South Pass, the route through the Rocky Mountains that would be followed by thousands of Oregon Trail travelers.

1814. Dec. The **Treaty of Ghent** ended the War of 1812 and restored all boundaries between the U.S. and Britain to the lines before the war. Invoking the Treaty of Ghent, John Jacob Astor used the provisions for returning all occupied lands by the British back to the Americans and got the American government to allow his Pacific Fur Company to take possession of Fort Astoria again. Although the fort changed hands again, the North West Fur Company continued to use Fort Astoria as their base of operations for many more years, and with continued good relations with the Americans

1818. Anglo-American Convention. The United States and Great Britain agreed to a joint occupation of the Oregon Country/Columbia District. Both parties accepted the area as extending from the Continental Divide to the Pacific Ocean, and from the Russian America boundary at about Latitude 54° in present British Columbia, to the Boundary Mountains (now Siskiyou Mountains) at about Latitude 42°. In 1827 a provision was added to the treaty that allowed either party to invoke a conclusion of ownership, by giving 12 months' notice to the other. Notice was not given until 1845, when President James K. Polk sought resolution, leading to a new treaty in 1846.
- Also in the 1818 treaty, Britain and the U.S. agreed to the 49th parallel as the international boundary from the Lake of the Woods (now Minnesota) to the Continental Divide.

1821. After being ordered to end their differences by the British Crown, the Hudson's Bay Company and the North West Fur Company merged into one British company, retaining the name Hudson's Bay. The company now had a monopoly on fur trading activity in British North America and were intent on monopolizing the Oregon Country as well.

1825. The British-owned Hudson's Bay Company established Fort Vancouver as a center for their fur trading operations in the *Columbia District*, the British name for the Oregon Country. Most of the employees of the Hudson's Bay Company in the Oregon Country were French-Canadians left over from their days with the North West Fur Company. In defiance of their orders, the Hudson's Bay Company leaders in the Oregon Country continued to cooperate with the American fur traders.

1841. The Western Emigration Society, a group of about 70 settlers set off on the Oregon Trail, beginning at Independence, Missouri. This was the first organized wagon train to head for California and Oregon. It is usually called the "Bartleson-Bidwell party" named for the two leaders. The group included a small party of Jesuit Missionaries led by Father Pierre-Jean de Smet, who left the main group at Soda Springs (now ID) and headed to the Oregon Country. Bartleson & Bidwell continued with the main body via the California Trail to the Sacramento Valley.

- Also in 1841, a group of Willamette Valley settlers met to organize a provisional government under the protection of the United States. However, the Americans were outnumbered by left-over French-Canadians formerly employed by the North West Fur Co/Hudson's Bay Co, and no action was taken.

1842. Dr. Elijah White, a Doctor, Missionary, and Indian Agent, took a census of settlers in the Oregon Country. It included the numbers of men, women, and children and a summary of their crops for the 1841-1842 year. White intended to show that it was possible to farm the Oregon region and to have something to show the U.S. Congress in support of an American government in the Oregon Country.

1843. A group of 50 Americans and 52 French-Canadians met again in 1843. This time they took a vote to determine who should govern the Oregon Country. A vote of 52-50 favored keeping Oregon as American territory (two Canadians switched their votes). From that meeting, a Provisional Territory of Oregon was established.
- The Oregon Country was just three votes away from being part of Canada. But, over the next five years, the Provisional Territory of Oregon elected a governor, created counties, established a court system, and continued to operate with the consent of the local population. They promoted the territory as a place where Americans were welcome, and actively petitioned the U.S. Congress to make the Provisional Oregon Territory part of the United States.
- Also in 1843, the largest wagon train to date left the Missouri River near Independence and headed out on the Oregon Trail. Destination: the Willamette Valley of Oregon. There were over 120 wagons, a large herd of livestock, and nearly 1,000 pioneers. This wagon train became the model for the thousands of wagon trains that would follow. For a list of the 1843 wagon train members, see
http://freepages.history.rootsweb.ancestry.com/~mransom/pioneers.html.
NOTE: Many descendants of Oregon Pioneers claim that when wagon trains reached a place in present southwest Wyoming called *Parting of the Ways*, there was a sign-post, (← **California | Oregon** →), and those who could read went to Oregon.

1844-1846. In the 1844 presidential election, James K. Polk, Democrat, defeated Henry Clay, Whig, to become President of the United States. The two burning political issues of the day were the annexation of Texas and the acquisition of the Oregon Country. James K. Polk, as the "Manifest Destiny" candidate, was elected with campaign slogans of *Annex Texas!* and *Fifty-four forty or fight!* In 1845, Texas was annexed to the U.S. and war with Mexico began soon after. But in 1846, Polk settled for the 49th parallel as the northern boundary of the Oregon Country. Polk had no intention of fighting a war with Mexico and Great Britain at the same time. The treaty of 1846 brought the Oregon Country into the United States.

1848. James K. Polk signed a bill that created Oregon Territory. It encompassed the area between the 42nd and 49th parallels, from the Pacific Ocean to the Continental Divide. The first capital was Oregon City. Virtually all of the political structures established by the Provisional Oregon Government were adopted by the official Territory of Oregon, including the counties in place at that time, most of the laws, and most of the court system was retained. Polk became the President who brought more territory (12 modern states) into the United States than any other. During his administration, the Oregon Country, Texas, and the Mexican Annexation were added to the U.S., and for the first time, America became a nation "from sea to shining sea." (Manifest Destiny fulfilled).

1850. June. A **Federal Census** was taken in Oregon Territory, which included the area of present Oregon, Washington, and Idaho; and Montana and Wyoming areas west of the Continental Divide. The population was revealed as 12,093 people. The population was limited in the present Washington area to a few residents of Clarke and Lewis counties, all south of Puget Sound and west of the Cascade Mountains. No population was recorded in the present Idaho, Montana, or Wyoming areas.
- Sept. 27th, Congress passed the Donation Land Claim Act. The forerunner of the 1862 Homestead Act, the Donation Land Claim Act was aimed entirely as an incentive to get settlers to move to Oregon Territory. From 1850 to 1862, land records for the areas that became Oregon and Washington provide detailed genealogical sources, revealing names, birthdates, birthplaces, marriage information, citizenship, and more.

1852-1854. The height of the Oregon Trail migrations was in 1852. In this year, it was estimated that about 67,000 people traveled the Oregon/California Trail to Oregon and California. In Dec 1854, the *Oregon Statesman* newspaper at Portland published a list of person who died on the trail in that year, as reported by the immigrants arriving in Oregon. The list of names, with their former residence, is at the USGenWeb site for Oregon. See
http://files.usgwarchives.net/or/vitals/tradeath.txt.

1853. Washington Territory created. It encompassed the present area of Washington, but extended east to the Rocky Mountains, incorporating areas that today are in northern Idaho and western Montana. As a result, the original Oregon Territory was split in half. Oregon Territory now had lands on the same line as its present northern border stretching to the Continental Divide, and included the southern half of present Idaho, and a portion of present western Montana and Wyoming.

1859. Oregon joined the Union as the 33rd state, a Free State with the same boundaries as present. The population of the new state was about 45,000 people. The eastern remnants of Oregon Territory, 1853-1859, were added to Washington Territory.

1860. June. Federal Census. The State of Oregon population was at 52,465. Refer to the map on page 120 to see the counties in place in 1860, compared with the counties of today.

Online Resources at the Oregon State Archives

The Oregon Historical Records Index (OHRI) includes entries compiled by archives staff and numerous volunteers from original records held by the Oregon State Archives. At the About Page, a very impressive list of Oregon original records included in the OHRI are identified under an alpha list of counties, cities, and other entities. For example, the entry for **Oregon Health Division** reveals these records in the OHRI:
- Delayed Birth Evidences (statewide), 1845-1903, 16,998 records indexed.
- Delayed Birth Records (statewide), 1842-1903, 74,374 records indexed.
- Marriage Returns (statewide), 1906-1910, 22,196 records indexed.

Another example is the entry for **Washington County**, with these records included in the index:
- Coroner's Reports, 1869-1919, 51
- Delayed Births, 1857-1910, 1,680
- Divorces, 1850-1899, 1917-1939, 1,030
- Insane Commitments, 1895-1927, 569
- Naturalizations, 1844-1956, 4,228
- Old Age Pensions, 1933-1936, 420
- Probates, 1842-1921, 2,599
- Women's Property Register, 1881-1882, 22

- Nearly all of Oregon's 36 counties are listed as having records indexed in the OHRI, as well as the Oregon State Defense Council, Hawthorne Asylum, Oregon Health Division, Oregon State Hospital, Oregon Military Department, Oregon State Penitentiary, City of Portland, Provisional and Territorial Government, and Provisional Government. The complete list can be reviewed at the *About* webpage. See http://sos.oregon.gov/archives/Pages/records/genealogy/about-historical-records.aspx.

- Although a huge database, the records included in the OHRI index represent only a fraction of the total archival holdings of the Oregon State Archives. At the About Page, make note of **More Guides:**
- Oregon Historical County Records Guide.
- Oregon Historical Record Types.
- State Agency Records Guides.
- Topical Research Aids.

Early Oregonian Search. This database is a project that attempts to document all individuals who lived in Oregon prior to statehood through 1860. There are approximately 103,000 Early Oregonians represented in the database. After searching for a name, clicking on the hyperlinked name takes you to the **Person Profile**, which represents all the information the State Archives has on this particular Early Oregonian. The Person Profile can be a genealogical goldmine, with birth, marriage, and death details, all listed with their sources. Additional information, such as associated records, federal census records, and territorial/state census records are also possible. A name tied to an early Oregon location can also be used in searching. The list includes all 36 current Oregon counties plus counties now defunct or renamed, such as Champoeg, Tuality; and Vancouver; and counties formed in Oregon Territory, now in Washington. See https://secure.sos.state.or.us/prs/personProfileSearch.do?earlyOregonian=true&searchReset=true.

Bibliography
Oregon Censuses & Substitutes

Oregon Territorial and State Censuses: All of the surviving original territorial and state censuses are located at the Oregon State Archives in Salem. They include these censuses taken by:
- Dr. Elijah White: census of 1842.
- Provisional Government of Oregon: 1845, 1845-1846, and 1847.
- Oregon Territory: 1849, 1853, 1854, 1855, 1856, 1857, 1858, and 1859.
- State of Oregon: 1865, 1875, 1885, 1895, and 1905.

None of the territorial and state censuses are complete for the entire territory or state. A list of these censuses and the counties included in each can be found at the State Archives Census Records webpage. See http://sos.oregon.gov/archives/Pages/records/aids-census_osa.aspx.

Federal Censuses for Oregon: Complete for 1850-1880; and 1900-1940 (1890 census lost for all states).

Census Substitutes: In addition to Oregon's Territorial, State, and Federal Censuses, there are numerous census substitutes available: name lists derived from Court Records, Tax Lists, Voter Lists, Military Lists, Vital Records, et al. Descriptions begin below in chronological order:

♦ ♦ ♦ ♦ ♦

1836-1838. See *Settlers on French Prairie, Oregon Territory, in 1836-1838* **[Online Database],** The French Canadians of French Prairie sent petitions to the Bishop of Juliopolis (at Red River, now Winnipeg, Manitoba, Canada). They requested priests to be sent to minister to their religious needs. The second and third of their petitions are presented here. Source: Letters to the Bishop of Juliopolis, Red River from the Willamette Settlement, March 22, 1836 and March 8, 1837. Mss. 83, Catholic Church in Oregon, Oregon Historical Society, Oregon, Portland, Oregon. Compiled at the LenzenResearch.com site. Archived: https://web.archive.org/web/20120402182323/www.lenzenresearch.com/STPaulpages/spfrprairie.html.

"Canadian Settlement in Willamette Valley" [Printed Article], in *Forebears*, (Clatsop County Genealogical Society, Astoria, OR),Vol. 6, No. 3 (Aug 1991),

1837-1850. See *Genealogical Research in Oregon – Oregon's First Settlers* **[Online Database],** an online essay with links to several name lists, compiled by Connie Lenzen, CG, and posted at her website. Archived at https://web.archive.org/web/20160126044751/http://www.lenzenresearch.com/STPaulpages/firstsettlers.html.

- See also, *The Oregon Territory and its Pioneers* **[Online Database],** a website devoted to the early history of Oregon. See www.oregonpioneers.com/ortrail.htm.

Pre-1838. *Names Index: By Year of Arrival in Oregon* **[Online Database],** a list of names of Mountain Men, Ship's Captains, Fur Traders, and anyone else who was ever recorded as being in the Oregon Country. Compiled by the USGenWeb site for Clackamas Co OR. See www.usgennet.org/alhnorus/ahorclak/list38.html.

1838-2006. *Willamette Valley, Oregon, Death Records* **[Online Database],** digitized and indexed at the Ancestry.com website. Source: Willamette Valley OR Gen. Society, Salem. Each index record includes: Name, Gender, Birthplace, Death age, and Spouse. The document/obituary image may have more information about a person. This database has 86,174 records. See http://search.ancestry.com/search/db.aspx?dbid=2468.

1840s-1860. *Oregon, Early Oregonians Index* **[Online Database],** indexed at the Ancestry.com website. This database is also accessible at the OR State Archives website. Each index record includes: Name, Birth date, Birthplace, and a link to the OR State Archives webpage. This database has 102,546 records: http://search.ancestry.com/search/db.aspx?dbid=60545.

1840s-1900s. *Oregon, Biographical and Other Index Card File* **[Online Database],** digitized and indexed at the FamilySearch.org website. Source: Oregon Historical Society, Portland, OR. Each index record includes: Name, Event date, Event place, and Other name/spouse. The index card image may have much more information about a person. This database has 207,751 records. See http://search.ancestry.com/search/db.aspx?dbid=9056.

1840s-1900. *Oregon Pioneers Card Index at the Multnomah County Library, Portland, Oregon.* (not the official title, but the library staff will know what you are talking about). Contains thousands of references to people of early Oregon from newspaper articles, books, and various public records. For more information, visit the library's genealogy webpage at: **www.multcolib.org/ref/gene.html#oregon**.

1840s-1900. *The Lockley Files: Voices of the Oregon Territory; Conversations With Bull-whackers, Muleskinners, Pioneers, Prospectors, '49ers, Indian Fighters, Trappers, Ex-barkeepers, Authors, Preachers, Poets and Near Poets, and All Sorts and Conditions of Men* **[Printed Book],** by Fred Lockley; compiled and edited by Mike Helm, published by Rainy Day Press, Eugene, OR, 1981, 358 pages. FHL book 979.5 D2L. Fred Lockley (1871-1958), wrote a newspaper column for Portland's *Oregon Journal* for over 30 years. The main topics of his columns were interviews with Oregon Pioneers. His subjects represent the "Who's Who" of the history of Oregon. This book is an extraction of some of the more interesting subjects of his interviews. It should be noted that all of the names mentioned in Lockley's newspaper articles have been indexed and are part of the Oregon Pioneers Card Index at the Multnomah County Library.

1840s-1933 *Oregon State Archives Combined Military Alphabetical Index* **[Microfilm & Digital Capture],** from the original computer-generated index at the Oregon State Archives in Salem, Oregon. This 12,000-page index was compiled by the State Archives staff and includes Oregon military and other names

extracted from 1) Provisional and Territorial Government Documents, 1837-1859; 2) Supreme Court Case Files, 1855-1904; 3) Oregon Soldiers Home Patient Histories, 1894-1933; 4) State Treasurer Quarterly Reports of Estates, 1903-1913; and 5) Defense Council Personal Military Service Records, 1917-1918. Includes name, state archives number, and description of record. Arranged in alphabetical order by surname. Filmed by the Genealogical Society of Utah, 2000, 37 rolls, beginning with FHL film #2194727 (Aandahl to Austin, Henry R.). To access the digital images, see the online FHL catalog:
www.familysearch.org/search/catalog/987519.

1840s-1965. *Oregon, Church and Cemetery Records* **[Online Database],** digitized and indexed at the Ancestry.com website. Source: OR State Library. Each index record includes: Name, Gender, Birth date, Birthplace, Event type, Baptism date, Baptism place, Father, and Mother. The register image may have more information about a person. This database has 77,910 records. See
http://search.ancestry.com/search/db.aspx?dbid=2527.

1840s-2000s. *Linkpendium – Oregon: Family History & Genealogy, Census, Birth, Marriage, Death, Vital Records & More* **[Online Databases].** Linkpendium is a genealogical portal site with links to state, county, town, and local databases. Currently listed are selected sites for Oregon statewide resources (498), Renamed/Discontinued Counties (3), Baker County (515), Benton County (363), Clackamas County (509), Clatsop County (379), Columbia County (192), Coos County (732), Crook County (125), and 30 more counties. See
www.linkpendium.com/or-genealogy

1840s-2000s. *Oregon US GenWeb Archives* **[Online Databases],** name lists are available for all Oregon counties. Typical county records include Bibles, Biographies, Cemeteries, Censuses, Court, Death, Deeds, Directories, Histories, Marriages, Military, Newspapers, Obituaries, Photos, Schools, Tax Lists, Wills, and more. Links to all Oregon counties and projects are at the USGenWeb site for Oregon. See
http://usgwarchives.net/or/orfiles.htm.

1842. *List of Settlers West of the Rockies, 1842, By Elijah White, Indian Agent* **[Online Database].** In 1842, Dr. Elijah White, the first Oregon Indian Agent, led a wagon train of pioneers from "the States" into the Willamette Valley. One of the first things White did was to take a census of settlers in the Oregon Country. It included the numbers of men, women, and children and a summary of their crops for the 1841-1842 year.

White intended to show that it was possible to farm the Territory and that the British had a foothold. Unless American settlers moved in, the Canadians (British) would be in the majority. The Territory was under a "joint occupancy" agreement, but an overwhelming number of British settlers could tip the balance of power, and Oregon could go British. At that time, Oregon extended from the Rocky Mountains to the Pacific Ocean and from Canada to northern California. The people named in this census, however, were living in the Willamette Valley and at Wailatpu near present day Walla Walla, Washington. Most were in the area called French Prairie, north of present-day Salem, Oregon. They were a diverse mix of retired Northwest Fur/Hudson's Bay employees (mostly French-Canadians), American Mountain Men, Methodist Ministers, and Catholic priests. The list of settlers is at the RootsWeb site for Oregon. See
www.rootsweb.ancestry.com/~orspmhs/18421st.html.

"1842 Census of Willamette Valley" [Printed Article], in *Trackers*, (Mount Hood Genealogical Forum, Oregon City, OR), Vol. 15, No. 1 (1975).

1842-1859 Provisional and Territorial Census Records of Oregon **[Microfilm & Digital Capture],** from the original typescripts and manuscripts at the Oregon State Archives, Salem, OR. Includes alphabetical index of old and new counties at the beginning of the film. Filmed by the Oregon State Archives, 1970, 1 roll. FHL's copy is FHL film #899786. To access the digital images, see the online FHL catalog:
www.familysearch.org/search/catalog/91051.
- See also: The list of years and counties included are shown at the OR State Archives website. See
http://sos.oregon.gov/archives/Pages/records/aids-census_osa.aspx.
- See also, *Oregon Census Records 1841-1849*, compiled by Ronald Vern Jackson, et al, published by Accelerated Indexing Systems, North Salt Lake, UT, 1984, 79 pages. FHL book 979.5 X22o.
-See also, *Oregon Census Records, 1851-1859*, compiled by Ronald Vern Jackson, et al., published by Accelerated Indexing Systems, North Salt Lake, UT, 1984, FHL book 979.5 X22o.

1842-1880 Oregon Census Records **[Original Manuscripts, Photostatic copies, and Typescript Transcriptions],** from the original records, located at the Oregon Historical Society in Portland, Oregon. Census records include Photostat of original copy of Joseph Meek's *1845 Census of Oregon*; and Elijah White's *1842 Oregon census*; original hand script *1849* *census* of males over the age of 21; typescript of *1854 Benton County census*; *1856 Washington County census*; *Jackson County census rolls (ca. 1854-1855, 1858)*; typescript copy of *United States Census roll for Coos County (1860)*; partial typescript of *1880 United States Census for Wasco County*; and a typescript report of *1850 census for Butte and Calaveras Counties in California*. Oregon Historical Society Call Number: Mss. 1.

1842-1890. *Oregon, Compiled Census Index* **[Online Database],** indexed at the Ancestry.com website. Source: Accelerated Indexing Systems, Salt Lake City, UT, 1999. Each index record includes: Name, State, County, Township, Year, and Database (census year, etc.) This database has 55,286 records. See http://search.ancestry.com/search/db.aspx?dbid=3569.

1842-1902. *Oregon Statewide Delayed Filings of Births* **[Microfilm & Digital Capture],** from the original records at the Oregon State Archives in Salem, Oregon. Arranged in chronological order by the year of birth (of the person filing a delayed birth record) and then alphabetical by county wherein the delayed birth was filed. (The place of birth could be anywhere, including out-of-state locations). The first two rolls in the series contain an alpha index to the names of persons filing a delayed birth record, which includes the name, date of birth, and place of filing; allowing a researcher to find the roll of film containing the microfilmed image of the delayed birth record. The delayed birth record itself is more revealing than a standard birth certificate because it includes affidavits of relatives and acquaintances, and supporting documents such as Bible pages, identification papers, etc. The films are not in strict numerical order, but following the 2-roll index are 72 rolls of birth records, filmed by the Genealogical Society of Utah, 2001, 2003, beginning with FHL film #2363225 (State wide delayed birth index, Aamold, Walter – Hood, Helen Owsley) and FHL film #2363226 (State wide delayed birth index, Holzmeyer, Selma Elsie Johanna – Zysett, Lawrence Albert); followed by FHL film #2230783 (Delayed birth filings, 1842 - 1868, Deschutes County). To access the digital images, see the online FHL catalog: www.familysearch.org/search/catalog/1002406.

1842-1914. See *Oregon Deaths, 1842-1952 and Delayed Births, 1844-1914* **[Online Database],** digitized and indexed at FamilySearch.org. Index and images of selected death and delayed birth records from Oregon. A few marriage and christening records may also be found in this collection. This database has 113,499 images, see
www.familysearch.org/search/collection/2352707.

1843. See *Oregon Memorial of Citizens of the U.S. and Miscellaneous Information: Census Records for 1843, Tax Rolls, Newspaper Clippings of Oregon Pioneers, Government Document on the Boundary Line Between the British and United States Territories in Northwestern America* **[Microfilm],** of an original Ms. (1 v.), filmed by the Genealogical Society of Utah, 1966, 1 roll, FHL film #430055. To see if this microfilm was digitized yet, see the online FHL catalog:
www.familysearch.org/search/catalog/306395.

1843. *Oregon Pioneers Already in Oregon by 1843* **[Online Database],** a list of people from wagon trains to Oregon Country. Compiled at the RootsWeb site for Oregon. See
http://freepages.history.rootsweb.ancestry.com/~mransom/already.html.

"1843 Census of the Oregon Country" [Printed Article], in *Beaver Briefs*, (Willamette Valley Genealogical Society, Salem, OR), Vol. 18, No. 3 (Jul 1986).

1844-1942. *Land Records (Oregon)* **[Microfilm & Digital Capture],** from the original plat books and tract books from the land offices located in Oregon: Oregon City, LaGrande, The Dalles, Lakeview, Burns, Portland, Vale, Winchester, Roseburg, Linkville-Klamath Falls and Harney, Oregon. These land records include Donation Land Claims, Homestead Claims, Cash Sales, and Credit Sales of public land. If you know your ancestor came to Oregon and acquired land, his name will be in this database, plus an exact legal description of the land. The plat books will even give you the names of his neighbors. A Range/Township land description can lead you to detailed modern maps such as the USGS Topographic Maps. To access the digital images, see the online FHL catalog:
www.familysearch.org/search/catalog/453173.
- See also, *Genealogical Material in Oregon Provisional Land Claims, Abstracted vols. I-VIII, 1845-1849* **[Printed Book],** compiled by Lottie LeGett Gurley, published by Genealogical Forum of Portland, 1982, 300 pages. FHL book 979.5 R2gL; and see Index to Oregon Donation Land Claims, 2nd edition, 1987, compiled by members of the Genealogical Forum of Oregon, Portland, OR, 1987, 172 pages. FHL book 979.5 R2g.

1845 Census of the Territory South of the Columbia and West of the Cascade Mountains [Printed Book], abstracted by Julie Kidd, published by the Oregon Territorial Press, Portland, OR, 1997, 27 pages.

Includes Champoeg, Clackamas, Clatsop, Tualatin, and Yamhill Counties. Copy at the Oregon Historical Society Library, Portland, OR (REF 312 O66t 1845).

1845. *Champoeg County (now Marion Co), Oregon Territory 1845 Territorial Census* **[Online Database],** indexed at the USGenWeb site for Oregon. Includes names of "single men keeping house" and Heads of Families, indicating age grouping for males and females, under 12, 12-18, 18-45, and 45 & over, with total males/females, and total all together. See http://files.usgwarchives.net/or/census/1845/1845champoeg.txt.

1845. *Tualatin County (now Washington Co), Oregon Territory 1845 Territorial Census* **[Online Database],** indexed at the USGenWeb site for Oregon. Includes names of "single men keeping house" and Heads of Families, indicating age grouping for males and females, under 12, 12-18, 18-45, and 45 & over, with total males/females, and total all together. See http://files.usgwarchives.net/or/census/1845/1845tuality.txt

"1845 Census, Clackamas County, Provisional Oregon Territory" [Printed Article], in *Trackers*, (Mount Hood Genealogical Forum, Oregon City, OR). Vol. 12, No. 4 (Summer 1972).
- See also **"Territorial Census, 1845, Clackamas County" [Printed Article],** in *Oregon End of Trail Researchers*, (Salem, OR), Vol. 7, No. 2 (Fall 1976).

***1845-1846 Census of Twality County, Oregon, (now Washington County)* [Microfilm & Digital Capture],** from the original records at the Oregon State Archives in Salem, Oregon. Tualaly or Twallity County changed to Washington County in 1849. Filmed with the Washington County delinquent tax records. Filmed by the Genealogical Society of Utah, 2001, 1 roll, FHL film #2257683. To access the digital images, see the online FHL catalog: www.familysearch.org/search/catalog/1050115.

1845-1849. See *History of the Willamette Valley: Being a Description of the Valley and Resources, With an Account of its Discovery and Settlement by White Men, and its Subsequent History; Together with Personal Reminiscences of its Early Pioneers* **[Printed Book],** edited by Herbert O. Lang, published by Himes & Lang, Portland, OR, 1885, 902 pages. Includes *Census Returns of Oregon in 1845*, for the five counties of the Willamette Valley; plus an extraction of the *1849 Territorial Census* for 10 Oregon counties. FHL book 979.53 H2L. Also on microfilm, FHL film #1321001.

1846-1851. *Oregon Newspaper Abstracts Volume 1* **[Printed Book & Digital Version],** by Julie Kidd, publ. Portland, OR, 2001, 258 pages. There is an index. Dated information tells of what is occurring in the area, people, products, arrivals, marriages, claims and travel. It appears to be almost like a log of events. To access the digital images, see the online FHL catalog: www.familysearch.org/search/catalog/2280828.

1848-1987. See *Oregon Newspaper Archives* **[Online Databases],** digitized and indexed newspapers at the GenealogyBank website, for Astoria, Corvallis, Eugene, Lakeview, Monmouth, Oregon City, Portland, Salem, and St. Benedict, Oregon. See www.genealogybank.com/explore/newspapers/all/usa/oregon.

1848-1959. *Territorial Papers of the United States for the Territory of Oregon* **[Microfilm & Digital Capture],** from the originals at the National Archives in Washington, D.C. Includes papers from the U.S. Senate, U.S. House of Representatives, U.S. Supreme Court, Department of Justice, Department of State, Bureau of Census, U.S. Post Office, Secretary of the Interior, Bureau of Indian Affairs, and the Department of the Treasury. Some pages wanting, faded, torn, etc. For complete explanation of information contained herein see beginning of each film for note. Filmed by National Archives, series M1049, 1977-1978, 12 rolls, beginning with FHL film #1695681 (Records of the 30th-35th Congress Senate and House). To access the digital images, see the online FHL catalog: www.familysearch.org/search/catalog/479414.

1849 Territorial Census, Lewis County, Oregon (now Washington State) **[Online Database],** indexed at the USGenWeb site for Oregon. See http://files.usgwarchives.net/or/census/1849/1849censlewisa.txt.

1849 Territorial Census, Clackamas County, Oregon **[Online Database],** indexed at the USGenWeb site for Clackamas Co OR. See http://files.usgwarchives.net/or/clackamas/census/1849/1849censclacka.txt.

"1849 Census, Clackamas County, Provisional Oregon Territory" [Printed Article], in *Trackers,* (Mount Hood Genealogical Forum, Oregon City, Oregon), Vol. 13, No. 1 (Winter 1973),

"1849 Census of Foreigners, Linn County, Oregon Territory" [Printed Article], in *Oregon End of Trail Researchers* (Salem, OR), Vol. 7, No. 1 (Spring 1976).

1849-1900. *Marion County, Oregon, Marriage Records* **[Online Database],** digitized and indexed at the Ancestry.com website. Source: Book, same title, publ. Willamette Valley Gen. Society, Salem. Each index record includes: Name, Gender, Event type, Event date, Spouse, and Spouse gender. The textual page image may have more information about a person. This database has 11,796 records. See http://search.ancestry.com/search/db.aspx?dbid=2466.

1849-1952. *Oregon Marriage Records* **[Online Database],** digitized and indexed at FamilySearch.org. This database has 5,598 images, see www.familysearch.org/search/collection/2352706.

1849-1963. *Oregon, Wills and Probate Records* **[Online Database],** digitized and indexed at the Ancestry.com website. Source: OR County, District, and Probate Courts. Each index record includes: Name, Probate date, Probate place, Death year, Death place, and Item description. A table of contents may list the papers included. The textual record book images may have much more information about a person. This database has 60,000 records. See http://search.ancestry.com/search/db.aspx?dbid=9078.

1849-1976. *Oregon, Marion County Records* **[Online Database],** digitized at the FamilySearch.org website. This is an image only database with marriage, birth, land and property, probate, naturalization, tax and old age pension records from the Marion County Clerk's office, Salem, OR. Browse the images, organized by Record Category, Record Type, Year Range, and Volume. This database has 406,225 images. See https://familysearch.org/search/collection/2071970.

1850. *Oregon, 1850 Federal Census: Population Schedules* **[Microfilm & Digital Capture],** population: 12,093. Filmed by the National Archives, 1964, 1 roll, FHL film #20298. To access the digital images, see the online FHL catalog: www.familysearch.org/search/catalog/744495.

1850-1853. *Linn County, Oregon Early 1850 Records* **[Printed Book],** edited by Lois M. Boyce, published by Boyce-Wheeler Publishing, Portland, OR, 1983, 59 pages. Includes corrected 1850 Linn Co. census, lists of judges, clerks, recorders, sheriffs, etc., 1851 to 1853 assessment rolls. FHL book 979.535 X28L.

1850-1862. *Oregon and Washington Donation Land Files* **[Microfilm & Digital Capture],** from the original land records at the National Archives, Washington, DC. Contains records from the La Grande Land Office, Oregon City Land Office, Winchester-Roseburg Land Office, The Dalles Land Office, Olympia Land Office, Colfax-Spokane Falls Land Office, Walla Walla Land Office, and Vancouver Land Office. From the Pamphlet Finding Aid: "The donation claims files are arranged alphabetically by name of State and thereunder by name of land office. For each office there is a main series for approved claims, arranged by final certificate number. There are some variations in the arrangement of records for several offices… Documents within the files are arranged as nearly as possible in the order in which they were maintained by the clerks in the land offices. ... The records for a typical donation claim are filmed as follows: the endorsement on the outer page, followed by the final certificate, the notification, and the other documents in chronological order. For the files not having final certificates, the notations on the outer page have been filmed first, followed by the notification and other documents. For canceled or rejected claims some documents may not be present, especially the final certificate." For more detailed information see explanation at front of films. Filmed by the National Archives, 1970, 108 rolls, beginning with FHL film #1028543 (Oregon City office). To access the digital images, see the online FHL catalog: www.familysearch.org/search/catalog/18339.

- See also, *Genealogical Material in Oregon Donation Land Claims, 1850-1862* **[Online Database],** indexed at the Ancestry.com website. Source: 3-vol. publ. of the Genealogical Forum of Oregon, 1957. This is a complete digitized textual version of the book, which abstracted vital information from the original Donation Land Claims at the Bureau of Land Management Office in Portland, OR. An OCR index includes all names of land patentees, witnesses, and any other associated names. Because the DLC applicants received double acreage if they were married, the names of wives, dates of marriage, etc., are also included. This database has 806 pages. See http://search.ancestry.com/search/db.aspx?dbid=25452.

- See also, *Index to Oregon Donation Land Claims* **[Microfiche & Digital Version],** compiled by the OR State Archives, filmed by the Genealogical Society of Utah, 1985, 3 microfiches. To access the digital version, see the online FHL catalog: www.familysearch.org/search/catalog/217794.

- See also, *Index to Oregon Donation Land Claim Files in the National Archives* **[Online Database],** indexed at the Ancestry.com website. Source: Book, same title, publ. Genealogical Forum of Oregon, 1953. This volume indexes the patent holders of the Oregon Donation Land Claims. See http://search.ancestry.com/search/db.aspx?dbid=25541.

- See also, ***Donation Land Claims by Orphans in Oregon and Washington, 1867-1873*** **[Microfilm & Digital Capture],** from the originals at the National Archives, Seattle, WA. Filmed by the Genealogical Society of Utah, 1989, 1 roll, FHL film #1367767. To access the digital images, see the online FHL catalog: www.familysearch.org/search/catalog/521818.

1850-1870. ***Genealogical Notes on the Oregon Territory and State of Oregon*** **[Microfilm & Digital Capture],** by Sherman Lee Pompey, an unpublished manuscript. Includes some indexes. Contains miscellaneous genealogical notes compiled from census, marriage, territorial, military, and business directory records of Oregon Territory and State. Also includes information copied from the 1850, 1860, and 1870 census records of Oregon Territory and State, and an index to the 1865 state census. Filmed by the Genealogical Society of Utah, 1986, 1 roll, FHL film #1421678. To access the digital images, see the online FHL catalog:
www.familysearch.org/search/catalog/470605.

1850-1983. ***Oregon, Douglas County Records*** **[Online Database],** digitized at the FamilySearch.org website. This is an image only database with deed records and indexes, 1852-1920. It also includes marriage records and indexes from 1913-1952. Browse the images, organized by Record Category, Record Type, Year Range, and Volume. This database has 515,750 images. See https://familysearch.org/search/collection/1972896

1851-1940. ***Portland Death Records, Portland, Multnomah Co., Oregon*** **[Printed Book],** compiled by J.C. Westergaard, publ. Genealogical Society of Utah, 1940, 3 vols. Includes name of deceased, dates of birth and death, cemetery, and names of parents and/or spouse. See FHL book, 979.549/P1 V23w v.1-3. Also on microfilm, FHL film #1321454.

1851-1975. ***Oregon, County Marriages*** **[Online Database],** digitized and indexed at the FamilySearch.org website. Source: FamilySearch extractions from county courthouses in Oregon. Each index record includes: Name, Event type, Event date, Event place, Gender, Birthplace, Spouse's gender, Spouse's age, Spouse's marital status, Spouse's birth year, and Spouse's birthplace. The images of certificates and licenses have much more information about the couple. This database has 163,484
https://familysearch.org/search/collection/1803968.

1852-1921. ***Oregon, Lane County, Marriage Records*** **[Online Database],** digitized and indexed at FamilySearch.org. This collection contains digital images for three books. Each book holds an index as well as affidavits (license) and certificates of marriage. Digital images of the original records are held by the Lane County Historical Museum located in Eugene, Oregon. This database has 1,462 records, see www.familysearch.org/search/collection/2848497.

1851-1992. ***Oregon, Grant County Records*** **[Online Database],** digitized at the FamilySearch.org website. This is an image only database with land, vital, probate and naturalization records and available indexes from the Grant County Clerk's Office, Canyon City, OR. Browse the images, organized by Record Category, Record Type, Year Range, and Volume. This database has 234,517 images. See
https://familysearch.org/search/collection/2135625.

"1853 Census, Marion County, Oregon Territory" [Printed Article], in *Coos Genealogical Forum Bulletin,* (North Bend, Oregon), Vol. 20, No. 2A (Spring 1985),

1853-1859. See ***Pioneer People of Jackson County, Oregon: DLC Surveyor's Record, Census 1853, 1854, 1855, 1856, 1857, 1858, 1859, Hospital Outpatients, 1855-56, Militia Muster Rolls*** **[Printed Book],** compiled by Ruby Lacy and Lida Childers, published R. Lacy, Ashland, OR, 1990, 301 pages. FHL book 979.527 X28L.

1853-1935. ***Oregon Marriages*** **[Online Database],** indexed at the FamilySearch.org website. Source: FamilySearch extractions from records on microfilm at the Family History Library, Salt Lake City, UT. Each index record includes: Name, Spouse's name, Event date, and Event place. This database has 27,780 records. See
https://familysearch.org/search/collection/1675533

1853-1874. ***Oregon, Church Records*** **[Online Database],** digitized and indexed at FamilySearch.org. This collection contains the church records for the following church: First Presbyterian Church (Corvallis). The records include session minutes for the years 1853 to 1874 and includes some baptisms. See www.familysearch.org/search/collection/2790272.

1854. ***Enumeration of the Inhabitants of Benton County, Oregon Territory, as Taken by Charles Wells, Assessor for the Year 1854*** **[Printed Book],** copied from the original by Mrs. James C. Moore, published 1947. Includes index. Includes name of the legal voter, number of males and number of females in house. FHL book 979.5 A1 No. 151. Also on microfilm, FHL film #1321058.

- See also **"1854 Census, Benton County, Oregon Territory," [Printed Article]**, in Genealogical Forum of Portland Bulletin, Vol. 19, No. 3 (Nov 1969) through Vol. 19, No. 6 (Feb 1970).
- See also, *1854 Census of Benton County, Oregon Territory* **[Online Database]**, indexed at the RootsWeb site for Benton Co OR. See www.rootsweb.ancestry.com/~orbenton/1854bent.txt. Another list, see http://files.usgwarchives.net/or/benton/census/1854/1854bent.txt.

1854 Lane County Agricultural Census **[Printed Book]**, compiled by Wilma Stahl from an original book held at the Lane County Public Service Building, Surveyors and Road Department, published by the Oregon Genealogical Society, Eugene, OR, 1990, 95 pages, FHL book 979.531 X2s.

1854-1855, 1857 Clackamas County, Oregon Census Rolls **[Microfilm & Digital Capture]**, from the original records at the Oregon State Archives in Salem, Oregon. Includes names of individuals and age categories. No names are listed for 1854. Also includes undated census. Filmed by the Genealogical Society of Utah, 1999, 1 roll, FHL film #2168754. To access the digital images, see the online FHL catalog: www.familysearch.org/search/catalog/832669.
- See also *Census of Clackamas County, Oregon Territory and Territorial Road Petition* **[Printed Book]**, compiled by Eloise C. Mabee, published Mount Hood Genealogical Forum, Oregon City, OR, 1974, 28 pages. Includes the following years: 1845, 1849, 1856-1857, and road petition circulated in 1851 or 1852. Also lists sheriffs, 1841-1973. FHL book 979.5 A1 N. 21.

1854, 1857-1858 Census Records, Tillamook County, Oregon Territory **[Microfilm & Digital Capture]**, from the original records at the Oregon State Archives, Salem, OR. Filmed by the Genealogical Society of Utah, 2001, 1 roll, FHL film #2313400. To access the digital images, see the online FHL catalog: www.familysearch.org/search/catalog/1053528.
- See also, *Oregon, Tillamook County Records, 1854-1967* **[Online Database]**, digitized at the FamilySearch.org website. This is an image only database with marriage records, and land and property records. Browse the images, organized by Record Category, Record Type, Year Range, and Volume. This database has 64,546 images. See https://familysearch.org/search/collection/2115693.

1854-1900 Tax Lists, Election Records, and Censuses, Columbia County, Oregon **[Microfilm & Digital Capture]**, from the original records of the County Recorder and County Clerk, St. Helens, Columbia County, Oregon, now located at the Oregon State Archives. Includes tax lists, delinquent tax lists, delinquent road tax, list of taxable property for 1874, precinct register for 1900, poll books for 1884 and 1887, abstract of votes 1854-1888, tax assessments and county census. Film by the Genealogical Society of Utah, 2002, 10 rolls, beginning with FHL film #2293501 (Tax and election records, 1854-1900). To access the digital images, see the online FHL catalog: www.familysearch.org/search/catalog/1151055.

1854-1958. *Oregon, Columbia County Records* **[Online Database]**, digitized at the FamilySearch.org website. This is an image only database with land and property, marriage, and other miscellaneous records and indexes digitally captured at the Columbia County Courthouse in St. Helens, Oregon. Browse the images, organized by Record Category, Record Type, Year Range, and Volume. This database has 91,013 images: https://familysearch.org/search/collection/1923992.

1854-1960. *Oregon, Wasco County Records* **[Online Database]**, digitized at the FamilySearch.org website. This is an image only database with digital images of land and marriage records filmed at the office of the Wasco County Clerk in The Dalles, Oregon. Browse the images, organized by Record Category, Record Type, Year Range, and Volume. This database has 129,959 images. See https://familysearch.org/search/collection/1927592.

"1855 Census, Coos County, Oregon Territory" [Printed Article], in *Coos Genealogical Forum Bulletin*, (North Bend, Oregon), Vol. 21, No. 2 (Spring 1986),

"1855, 1856, 1857 Census, Jackson County, Oregon Territory" [Printed Article], in *Rogue Digger,* Rouge Valley Genealogical Society, Phoenix, OR), Vol. 3, No. 2 (Summer 1968) through Vol. 5, No. 2 (Summer 1970).

1855-1865. *Multnomah County, Oregon Marriage Records* **[Digital Capture]**, from the 98-page book, no compiler or publisher noted. Marriages are from Record Book I – Jan 1855 to Aug 1865. Taken from a book at the New York City Family History Center. Digitized by the Genealogical Society of Utah. (FHL 979.549 V2). To access the digital version of this book, see the online FHL catalog page: https://familysearch.org/search/catalog/2527307.

1855-1911. *Multnomah County, Oregon Marriage Index* **[Online Database]**, indexed at the Ancestry.com website. This database is also accessible

at the Genealogical Forum of Oregon website. Each index record includes: Name, Marriage year, Marriage place, Spouse, Volume, Page, and a link to the Gen. Forum of Oregon website. This database has 79,438 records. See
http://search.ancestry.com/search/db.aspx?dbid=70762.

"1856 Census, Clackamas County, Oregon Territory" [Printed Article], in *Trackers*, (Mount Hood Genealogical Forum, Oregon City, OR), Vol. 13, No. 3 (Summer 1973).

1856 Census, Columbia County, Oregon Territory **[Microfilm],** from the original records at the Oregon State Archives, Salem, OR. Arranged in alphabetical order by surname. Filmed by the Genealogical Society of Utah, 2002, 1 roll, FHL film #2293501. To see if this microfilm was digitized yet, see the online FHL catalog: **www.familysearch.org/search/catalog/1151045**.

1856. *Copy of Census Roll for Polk County for the Year 1856* **[Printed Book],** compiled and published by Adelina S. Dyal, Salem, OR, 1976, 27 pages. Cover title: "Oregon; Copy of Census Roll for Polk County for the year 1856: A Facsimile of Territorial Document No. 6912, Oregon State Archives, Salem, Oregon." Includes index. FHL book 979.5 A1 No. 37.

1856-1939. See *Probate Case Files, Multnomah County, Oregon, 1856-1900; Index, 1856-1939* **[Microfilm & Digital Capture],** from the originals at the OR State Archives, Salem, OR. Includes original papers in probate cases in County Court, 1856-1919, and Circuit Court, 1920 pertaining to settlement of estates, title of paper, signatures of persons involved, and date filed. Arranged chronologically by filing date. Some files are missing. Filmed by the Genealogical Society of Utah, 1995, 208 rolls, beginning with FHL film #1913326 (Indexes to probates 1856-1939). To access the digital images, see the online FHL catalog: **https://familysearch.org/search/catalog/730160**.

1856-1984. *Oregon, Benton County Records* **[Online Database],** digitized at the FamilySearch.org website. This is an image only database with land and property records, old age pensions, naturalization records, military records, and a few probate records from the county clerk's office in Corvallis, OR. Browse the images, organized by Record Category, Record Type, Year Range, and Volume. This database has 75,599 images. See
https://familysearch.org/search/collection/1929994.

"1857 Census, Clackamas County, Oregon Territory" [Printed Article], in *Trackers*, (Mount Hood Genealogical Forum, Oregon City, OR), Vol. 14, No. 1 (1974),

1857-1963. *Oregon, Yamhill County Records* **[Online Database],** digitized at the FamilySearch.org website. This is an image only database with images of deeds, mortgages, and military service records from the Yamhill County Courthouse, McMinnville, OR. It also includes 6 volumes of "Miscellaneous Records" dated 1899-1957. The miscellaneous records include some land transactions, licensing records and other items. Browse the images, organized by Record Category, Record Type, Year Range, and Volume. This database has 96,736 images. See
https://familysearch.org/search/collection/1930095.

1857-1972. *Oregon, Polk County Records* **[Online Database],** digitized at the FamilySearch.org website. This is an image only database with digital images of land and property records, pension records, and probate records from the Polk County Courthouse in Dallas, OR. Browse the images, organized by Record Category, Record Type, Year Range, and Volume. This database has 34,823 images. See
https://familysearch.org/search/collection/1453591.

1859-1956. *Indexes to Naturalization Records of the U.S. Circuit and District Courts for the District of Oregon* **[Microfilm & Digital Capture],** filmed by the National Archives, series M1242, 3 rolls, beginning with FHL film # 1433979 (Index to declarations, 1859-1907; Index to admission to citizenship 1859-1906; and Index to declarations and petitions 1906-1935). To access the digital images, see the online FHL catalog: **www.familysearch.org/search/catalog/544534**.

1860. *Oregon, 1860 Federal Census: Population Schedules* **[Microfilm & Digital Capture],** population: 52,465. Filmed by the National Archives, 1967, 3 rolls, beginning with FHL film #805055. To access the digital images, see the online FHL catalog: **www.familysearch.org/search/catalog/706371**.

1860-1952. *Oregon Births* **[Online Database],** indexed at the FamilySearch.org website. Source: FamilySearch extractions. Each index record includes: Name, Event type, Event date, Event place, Gender, Race, Father's name, Father's age, Father birth year, Mother's name, Mother's birthplace, Mother's age, Mother birth year, and FHL film number. This database has 12,923 records. See
https://familysearch.org/search/collection/2351853.

1861-1865. *Index to Soldiers & Sailors of the Civil War* **[Online Database],** a searchable name index to 6.3 million Union and Confederate Civil War soldiers now available online at the National Park Service website. A search can be done by surname, first name, state, or unit. Oregon supplied 2,754 men to the war (all Union). To search for one, go to the Soldiers and Sailors Database. See
www.nps.gov/civilwar/soldiers-and-sailors-database.htm.

1861-1865. *Oregon, Civil War Service Records of Union Soldiers* **[Online Database],** indexed at the FamilySearch.org website. Source: National Archives microfilm series M1816. This database contains records of soldiers who served in organizations from Oregon. The records include a jacket-envelope for each soldier, labeled with his name, his rank, and the unit in which he served. Each index record includes: Name, Event type, Event year, Age, and Military unit note. A link to the images is the Fold3 subscription site. This database has 53,945 records. See
https://familysearch.org/search/collection/1932421.

1861-1890. *Morning Oregonian (Portland, Oregon)* **[Online Database],** digitized and OCR indexed at Ancestry.com. The *Morning Oregonian* newspaper was located in Portland, Oregon (*Oregonian* today). This database is a fully searchable text version of the newspaper for the years 1861-1890. The newspapers can be browsed or searched using an OCR-generated index. The accuracy of the index varies according to the quality of the original images. The images for this newspaper can be browsed sequentially, or via links to specific images, which may be obtained through the search results. Over time, the name of a newspaper may have changed, and the time span it covered may not always be consistent. The date range represented in this database is not necessarily the complete published set available. See
www.ancestry.com/search/collections/7362.

1861-1917. *Organization Index to Pension Files of Veterans Who Served Between 1861 and 1917* **[Microfilm & Digital Capture],** from the original manuscripts for all states at the National Archives, Washington, DC. Filmed by the National Archives, series T0289, 1949, 765 rolls (16mm). Use the online index to civil war soldiers to locate an Oregon soldier/sailor, which will give the exact unit in which the person served. The index to Oregon pension records is contained on 1 roll, FHL film #1725944. To access the digital images on that roll, see the online FHL catalog: **www.familysearch.org/search/catalog/573022.**

1862-1950. *Oregon, Baker County Records* **[Online Database],** digitized and indexed at the FamilySearch.org website. This is an image only database with naturalization, military, deed, and mortgage records from the county clerk's office in Baker City, OR. Browse the images, organized by Record Category, Record Type, Year Range, and Volume. This database has 66,538 images: **https://familysearch.org/search/collection/1384963.**

1863-1935 *City Directories, Portland, Oregon* **[Microfilm],** from the originals published by various publishers. Filmed by Research Publications, Inc., Woodbridge, CT, 1980-1984. FHL has 34 rolls, with a complete run of directories, 1863-1935, beginning with FHL film #1377327 (1863 Portland Directory) through FHL film #1611935 (1935 Portland Directory).

1864-1902. *Oregon Newspaper Death Notices, 1864-1902: An Index to Death Notices Published in Eugene, Lane County, Oregon Newspapers* **[Printed Book],** by Gregory Toftdahl, publ. Springfield, OR, 1995, 139 pages. Arranged alphabetically by surname as published in Eugene, Lane County, newspapers, and other areas of Oregon, as well as out of state accounts of a relative of an Oregon resident. Includes name, newspaper issue date, page number and place from *Oregon State Journal*, *Eugene City Guard*, *Daily City Guard* and *Eugene Weekly Guard*. See FHL book 979.531/E1 V42t.

1865. *Poll Tax Book, Multnomah County, Oregon* **[Microfilm],** from the original records at the Portland Oregon East Stake Family History Center. Filmed by the Genealogical Society of Utah, 1981, 1 roll, FHL film #1421988. To see if this microfilm was digitized yet, see the online FHL catalog:
www.familysearch.org/search/catalog/378059.

1865, 1870, 1875, and 1885 Agricultural and Property Assessment and Census for Umatilla County, Oregon **[Microfilm & Digital Capture],** from the original records at the Oregon State Archives in Salem, Oregon. Includes name, number of acres, lots, and blocks, value of land, amount of state and county taxes, number of females and males and age groups, number of bushels of various products, amount of various farm animals, amount of seafood, and remarks from the state 1865 and 1875 census. Filmed by the Genealogical Society of Utah, 2002, 2 rolls, FHL film #2319765 (Oregon state census 1865; 1870 Federal census; Oregon state census 1875 (p. 1-30); and FHL film #2319766 (Oregon state census 1875 (p. 31-end); Oregon state

census 1885). To access the digital images, see the online FHL catalog:
www.familysearch.org/search/catalog/1125331.

1867-1873 Internal Revenue Assessment Lists, Oregon **[Microfilm & Digital Capture],** from the originals at the National Archives Branch in Seattle, Washington. Some years missing. There are no volume numbers on books. Filmed by the Genealogical Society of Utah, 1989, 2 rolls, FHL film #1639854 (Assessment lists 1867-1870) and FHL film #1639855 (Assessment lists 1871-1873). To access the digital images, see the online FHL catalog:
www.familysearch.org/search/catalog/521391.

1865-1991. *Oregon, Naturalization Records* **[Online Database],** digitized and indexed at Ancestry.com. Source: National Archives, Records of the District Courts of the United States, RG21. The records includes Petitions, Declarations of Intention to become a citizen, and Naturalization certificates. This database has 178,080 records, see
www.ancestry.com/search/collections/2530.

1868-1929. *Oregon Births and Christenings* **[Online Database],** indexed at the FamilySearch.org website. Source: FamilySearch extractions. Each index record includes: Name, Event type, Event date, Event place, Gender, Marital status, Father's name, Mother's name, and Reference ID. This database has 1,239 records. See **https://familysearch.org/search/collection/1675468.**

1868-1929. *Oregon, Select Births and Christenings* **[Online Database],** indexed at the Ancestry.com website. Source: FamilySearch extractions from records on microfilm at the Family History Library, Salt Lake City, UT. Each index record includes: Name, Gender, Birth date, Birthplace, Father, Mother, and FHL film number. This database has 182,745 records:
http://search.ancestry.com/search/db.aspx?dbid=60106.

1870. *Oregon, 1870 Federal Census: Population Schedules* **[Microfilm & Digital Capture],** population: 90,923. Filmed by the National Archives, 1968, 8 rolls, beginning with FHL film #552784. To access the digital images, see the online FHL catalog:
www.familysearch.org/search/catalog/698916.

1870-1930. *Oregon Grand Army of the Republic Membership Records* **[Online Database],** digitized and indexed at the FamilySearch.org website. Source: OR Historical Society, manuscript 1378. Includes images of membership records of the Union Civil War veterans. The Descriptive books are arranged by Post name and number. Each index record includes: Name, Event type, Event date, Event place, Residence place, and Age. The register image may have more information about a person. This database has 3,044 records. See
https://familysearch.org/search/collection/2239231.

1870-1991. *Oregon, Harney County Records* **[Online Database],** digitized at the FamilySearch.org website. This is an image only database with probates, naturalizations, vital records, and land records from the county courthouse in Burns, OR. Browse the images, organized by Record Category, Record Type, Year Range, and Volume. This database has 111,750 images, see **https://familysearch.org/search/collection/2120716.**

1871-1985. *Oregon, Deschutes County Records* **[Online Database],** digitized at the FamilySearch.org website. This is an image only database with marriages, probates, and land records at the county courthouse in Bend, OR. Browse the images, organized by Record Category, Record Type, Year Range, and Volume. This database has 110,521 images. See **https://familysearch.org/search/collection/2284387.**

1875 Enumeration of the Inhabitants and Industrial Products of the County of Lake, State of Oregon for Year 1875 **[Microfilm & Digital Capture],** from the original records at the Oregon State Archives in Salem, Oregon. Filmed by the Genealogical Society of Utah, 2001, 1 roll, FHL film #2260282. To access the digital images, see the online FHL catalog:
www.familysearch.org/search/catalog/1021726.
- See also **"1875 Census, Lake County, Oregon" [Printed Article],** in *Oregon Genealogical Bulletin,* (Oregon Genealogical Society, Eugene, OR), Vol. 34, No. 5 (Summer 1996).

1876-1908 Birth and Death Record, Congregation Beth Israel, Portland, Oregon **[Microfilm & Digital Capture],** from the originals held by the Congregation. Filmed by the Genealogical Society of Utah, 1977, 1 roll, FHL film #1013426. To access the digital images, see the online FHL catalog:
www.familysearch.org/search/catalog/455577.

1876-1918. *Oregon, Adoptions and Name Changes* **[Online Database],** digitized and indexed at the Ancestry.com website. Source: publ. Laws of the State of Oregon at the OR State Library. Each index record includes: Name (another name in brackets), Civil date, Civil place, Father, and Mother. The textual page images of the Law Books have detailed information, including names of adopted children and their birth names. This database has 2,425 records. See
http://search.ancestry.com/search/db.aspx?dbid=2524.

1877-1952. *Oregon Deaths* **[Online Database],** indexed at the FamilySearch.org website. Source: Various archives. Each index record includes: Name, Event type, Event date, Event place, Gender, Marital status, Birth year, Father's name, Mother's name, Spouse's name, Spouse's gender, Reference ID, and FHL film number. This database has 90,302 records: https://familysearch.org/search/collection/2352707.

1880. *Oregon, 1880 Federal Census: Soundex and Population Schedules* **[Microfilm & Digital Capture],** population: 174,768. Filmed by the National Archives, c1970, 11 rolls, beginning with FHL film #1255080. To access the digital images, see the online FHL catalog: www.familysearch.org/search/catalog/676507.

1881-1883. *Alphabetical Index to Deaths Found in the City of Portland, Oregon, Chronologic Index to Deaths, Vol. 1, March 1881-December 1883* **[Printed Book],** compiled by Janice M. Healy, publ. by the author, Aloha, OR, 1994, 27 pages, FHL book 979.549/P1 V22h.

1885 Oregon State Census, Linn County, Oregon **[Microfilm & Digital Capture],** from the original records at the Oregon State Archives, Salem, Oregon. FHL title: *Enumeration of the Inhabitants and Industrial Products of the County of Linn, State of Oregon, for the year 1885.* Arranged in alphabetical order by first letter of surname. Filmed by the Genealogical Society of Utah, 1998, 1 roll, FHL film #2109932. To access the digital images, see the FHL catalog: www.familysearch.org/search/catalog/730779.

"1885 Oregon State Census, Umatilla County, Oregon" [Printed Article], in *Oregon End of Trail Researchers,* (Salem, OR), Vol. 4, No. 4 (Winter 1973).

1888-1963. *Oregon, Passenger and Crew Lists* **[Online Database],** digitized and indexed at the Ancestry.com website. Source: National Archives, *Selected Passenger and Crew Lists and Manifests*. Each index record includes: Name, Gender, Nationality, Age at arrival, Birth date, Birthplace, Arrival date, Arrival place, Departure place, and Vessel. The manifest/document image has more information about a person. This database has 555,959 records. See http://search.ancestry.com/search/db.aspx?dbid=1042.

1889-1900. *Election Voter Register, Multnomah County, Oregon* **[Microfilm & Digital Capture],** from a typescript of the original at the OR State Archives, Salem, OR. Names are arranged alphabetically in each precinct. Filmed by the Genealogical Society of Utah, 1995, 1 roll, FHL film #2026897. To access the digital images, see the online FHL catalog: www.familysearch.org/search/catalog/758749.

1893 History. See *An illustrated History of the State of Oregon: Containing a History of Oregon From the Earliest Period of its Discovery to the Present Time, Together With Glimpses of its Auspicious Future; Illustrations and Full-page Portraits of Some of its Eminent Men and Biographical Mention of Many of its Pioneers and Prominent Citizens of Today* **[Printed Book],** by Harvey K. Hines, published by Lewis Publishing Co., Chicago, 1893, 1,300 pages. FHL book 979.5 H2hh. Also on microfilm, FHL film #1000358.
- See also *Abstract of Biographies Appearing in "An Illustrated History of the State of Oregon,"* by Rev. H. K. Hines, compiled by Susan N. Bell, publ. Willamette Valley Genealogical Society, Salem, OR, 1996, 138 pages. Includes index. Contains abstracts of biographies submitted by the individuals listed for publication in 1893. FHL book 979.5 D38b.

1895 Oregon State Census, Linn County, Oregon **[Microfilm],** from the original records at the Oregon State Archives, Salem, Oregon. FHL title: *Enumeration of the Inhabitants and Industrial Products of the County of Linn, State of Oregon, for the year 1895.* Arranged in alphabetical order by first letter of surname. Filmed by the Genealogical Society of Utah, 1998, 1 roll, FHL film #2109932. To see if this microfilm was digitized yet, see the online FHL catalog: www.familysearch.org/search/catalog/730789.

1895. *Oregon, Marion County, 1895 Census* **[Printed Book],** abstracted by Jean Custer, et al., publ. Willamette Valley Genealogical Society, Salem, Oregon, 1993, 2001, 2 vols. Contents: vol. 1. City of Salem, suburbs, Oregon state penitentiary, and Oregon state insane asylum; vol. 2. Ale, Aumsville, Aurora, Brooks, Butteville Champoeg, Chemawa, Detroit, Gates, Gervais, Hubbard, Jefferson, Macleay, Marion, Mehama, Mill City, Minto, Mt. Angel, Niagara, Rural, Scotts Mills, Shaw, Silverton, St. Paul, Stayton, Sublimity, Turner, and Woodburn. Includes alphabetical list by surname of Name, Place of birth, Height, Weight, Complexion (light or dark), Occupation, Ailment, Religion, Voter status, Sex and Age. FHL book 979.537 X28c v. 1-2.
- See also **"1895 Aumsville Census" [Printed Article],** in *Beaver Briefs,* (Willamette Valley Genealogical Society, Salem, Oregon) ,Vol. 17, No. 2 (Apr 1985).

1895. *Marion County, Oregon, Census* **[Online Database],** digitized and indexed at the Ancestry.com website. Source: Typescript, by Willamette Valley Genealogical Society, Salem, OR. Each index record includes: Name, Birthplace, Birth year, Residence place, Occupation, Gender, Age, and Enumeration year. The typescript image may have more information about a person. This database has 29,677 records. See http://search.ancestry.com/search/db.aspx?dbid=2467.

1895. *Duplicate Census Roll for 1895, Morrow County, Oregon* **[Microfilm & Digital Capture],** from the original records at the Oregon State Archives, Salem, Oregon, 2 volumes. Includes Names, Gender, and Age range, whether a Voter, and Agricultural census. Filmed by the Genealogical Society of Utah, 1995, 1 roll, FHL film #2027031. To access the digital images, see the online FHL catalog: www.familysearch.org/search/catalog/758793.

1895 Oregon State Census, Multnomah County, Oregon **[Microfilm & Digital Capture],** from the original records at the Oregon State Archives, Salem, Oregon. Includes names of all persons in family with Age, Sex, Color, Profession, Place of birth, and Marital status, as well as a list of persons who died during the year. Filmed by the Genealogical Society of Utah, 1995, 3 rolls, as follows:
- 1895 state census, vol. 1-16 precincts (some missing) Vol. 3-4 precincts 25-30, FHL film #2026697.
- 1895 state census, vol. 4-6 precincts 31-46 Vol. 7 precincts 47-54 (some missing); Vol. 8 precincts 55-64, FHL film #2026895.
- 1895 state census, Vol. 8 precincts 65-77, FHL film #2026896.

To access the digital images, see the online FHL catalog: www.familysearch.org/search/catalog/758649.

1895-1999. *Oregon, Naturalization Records* **[Online Database],** digitized and indexed at the Ancestry.com website. Source: National Archives microfilm, Idaho, Oregon, and Washington Petitions for Naturalizations. Each index record includes: Name, Birth date, Birth place, Gender, Court state, Court district, Naturalization date, Naturalization record type, Petition number, Residence place, and Photograph (y/n). The document image has more information about a person. This database has 45,202 records. See http://search.ancestry.com/search/db.aspx?dbid=2530.

1898-1903. *Oregon Volunteers, Spanish American War and Philippine Insurrection* **[Online Database],** indexed at the Ancestry.com website. Source: *Official Record*, Adjutant General's report, database compiled by Debra Graden for Ancestry. Each index record includes: Given name, Surname, Unit, Company, Rank, Age, Birthplace, Occupation, Muster-in place, and Page number. This database has 1,581 records. See http://search.ancestry.com/search/db.aspx?dbid=4830.

1898-2008. *Oregon, Death Index* **[Online Database],** digitized and indexed at the Ancestry.com website. Source: OR State Archives. Each index record includes: Name, Age, Birth date, Death date, Death place, and Spouse. The computer print-out image may have more information about a person. This database has 1,903,430 records. See http://search.ancestry.com/search/db.aspx?dbid=5254.

1900. *Oregon, 1900 Federal Census: Soundex and Population Schedules* **[Microfilm & Digital Capture],** population: 413,536. Filmed by the National Archives, c1970, 63 rolls, beginning with FHL film #1241345. To access the digital images, see the online FHL catalog: www.familysearch.org/search/catalog/641584.

1900 Malheur County, Oregon Census **[Printed Book],** by Oregon Genealogical Society, Inc., and Louise Hill, published by Oregon Genealogical Society, Eugene, OR, 1998, 95 pages. Includes photocopy of the 1900 census for Malheur County, Oregon, and an index for that census. FHL book 979.597 X2o.

1900-1962. *Oregon, Multnomah County, Poor Farm Admissions Records* **[Online Database],** digitized and indexed at FamilySearch, from records at the Multnomah County Archives, Portland, OR. This collection may contain the following: Name, Birthplace, Former residence, Marital status, Occupation, and Address of relative. This database has 18,060 records, see www.familysearch.org/search/collection/2759503.

1900-1986. *Oregon, Biographical Index Card File* **[Online Database],** digitized at the Ancestry.com website. This is an image only database of a major card index file at the Oregon State Library in Salem, OR. Browse the images of each card, organized in alpha groups. See http://search.ancestry.com/search/db.aspx?dbid=1874.

1903-1947. *Oregon Deaths and Burials* **[Online Database],** indexed at the FamilySearch.org website. Source: FamilySearch extractions from records on

microfilm at the Family History Library, Salt Lake City, UT. Each index record includes: Name, Gender, Death date, Death place, Age, Birth date, Birthplace, Occupation, Race, Marital status, Father's birthplace, and Mother's birthplace. This database has 29,035 records. See
https://familysearch.org/search/collection/1675532.

1903-1970 Oregon Death Records Index [Microfilm & Digital Capture], from a transcript at the Oregon State Archives, Salem, OR. Each record includes name of deceased, spouse, county of death, date of death, certificate number, age. Filmed by the Oregon State Archives and Records Center, ca1975, FHL has 12 rolls, beginning with FHL film #1373869. To access the digital images, see the online FHL catalog: www.familysearch.org/search/catalog/32718.

1903-1998. *Oregon Death Index* [Online Database], indexed at the FamilySearch.org website. Source: OR State Archives. Each index record includes: Name, Event type, Event date, Event place, Birth date, Spouse's name, and Certificate number. This database has 1,447,641 records. See
https://familysearch.org/search/collection/1946790.

1905. *Oregon, Marion County, 1905 Census* [Printed Book], an extract and index copied and compiled by Harriett Gaylord, publ. Willamette Valley Genealogical Society, Salem, OR, 1998, 2 vols. Includes index. FHL has bound book 1 & 2 together. FHL book 979.537 X28g v. 1-2. The 1905 Marion County census names were originally published serially in the society's periodical, *Oregon End of Trail Researchers,* Vol. 2, No. 4 (Winter 1971) through Vol. 7, No. 2 (Fall 1976).

1906-2008. See *Oregon, Marriage Indexes, 1906-1924, 1946-2008* [Online Database], indexed at the Ancestry.com website. Source: OR State Library. Each index record includes: Name, Marriage date, County, and Spouse's name. The computer print-out image may have more information about a person. This database has 1,581,783 records. See
http://search.ancestry.com/search/db.aspx?dbid=5193.

1908-1958. *Oregon, Multnomah County, Voting Registration Records* [Online Database], digitized and indexed at FamilySearch.org. Each index record includes Name, Event type (residence), Event date, and Event place (Multnomah Co OR). The image of the registration card has much more information: e.g., name of spouse, place of birth, names of parents, naturalization information; and the card also gives the political party and has the person's signature as well. This database has 988,549 records, see
www.familysearch.org/search/collection/2759505.

1910. *Oregon, 1910 Federal Census: Population Schedules* [Microfilm & Digital Capture], Population: 672,765. Filmed by the National Archives, c1970, 14 rolls, beginning with FHL film #1375291. To access the digital images, see the online FHL catalog: www.familysearch.org/search/catalog/640355.

1911. *Soldier Home Roster* [Online Database], Oregon State Soldier's Home, Roseburg, OR, indexed at the GenealogyTrails site for Douglas Co OR. See www.genealogytrails.com/ore/douglas/military/soldierhome_roster1911.html.

1911-1946. Oregon, Motor Vehicle Registrations [Online Database], digitized and indexed at the Ancestry.com website. Source: OR State Library. Each index record includes: Name, Residence date, and Residence place. For some years, the textual image includes a street address, others may include the make of the vehicle, license numbers. This database has 3,588,120 records. See
http://search.ancestry.com/search/db.aspx?dbid=1852.

1915-1924. *Portland, Oregon Deaths* [Online Database], indexed at the Ancestry.com website. Source: OR Vital Statistics Dept. Each index record includes: Given name, Surname, Month, Day, Year, and Certificate number. This database has 29,586 records. See
http://search.ancestry.com/search/db.aspx?dbid=4479.

1917-1918. World War I Era Databases:
- See, *Oregon, World War I Selective Service System Draft Registration Cards, 1917-1918* [Microfilm & Digital Capture]. The draft cards are arranged alphabetically by state, then alphabetically by county or city, and then alphabetically by surname of registrants. Filmed by the National Archives, 34 rolls, beginning with FHL #1851979 (Baker County, A-Z; Benton County, A-B). To access the digital images, see the online FHL catalog:
www.familysearch.org/search/catalog/746996.
- See also, *World War I Veterans Who Were Residents of Oregon* [Microfilm & Digital Capture], from the original records compiled by John Lockran and Spencer Leonard for the Genealogical Forum of Oregon, Arranged in alphabetical order by surname. Filmed by the Genealogical Society of Utah, 2003, 4 rolls, beginning with FHL #2367765 (Abalos, Angel -

Adkins, Louis C). To access the digital images, see the online FHL catalog:
www.familysearch.org/search/catalog/1152597.

- See also, *Oregon, World War I County Military Service Records, 1919-1920* **[Online Database],** digitized and indexed at FamilySearch.org. The records are arranged alphabetically by county name, then numerical by the school district and alphabetical by surname. This series documents an individual's military service in Oregon during WWI and used as a basis for medal distribution. This database has 15,228 records, see www.familysearch.org/search/collection/3010088.

- See also, *Oregon, World War I, Veteran State Aid Applications, 1921-1938* **[Online Database],** digitized and indexed at FamilySearch.org. Card index includes, name, place of enlistment, place, and date of birth, name, and address of nearest relative, date, and place of first enlistment and date and place of discharge, military serial number, aid or bonus desired and dates approved or rejected, address where correspondence should be sent, and other miscellaneous information. Microfilm of original records located at the Oregon State Archives in Salem, OR. This database has 37,195 records, see
www.familysearch.org/search/collection/3007580.

- See also, *Oregon's Honor Roll: Names of Officers and Enlisted Men from Oregon Who Lost Their Lives While Serving in the Armed Forces During the World War* **[Digital Capture],** from the original records of the State of Oregon, Adjutant-General's Office, Salem, publ. State Printing Dept., 1922, 15 pages, digitized by FamilySearch International, 2012. To access the digital version, see the online FHL catalog:
www.familysearch.org/search/catalog/1987039.

1920. *Oregon, 1920 Federal Census: Soundex and Population Schedules* **[Microfilm & Digital Capture],** population: 783,389. Filmed by the National Archives, c1970, 85 rolls, beginning with FHL film #1821491. To access the digital images, see the online FHL catalog:
www.familysearch.org/search/catalog/555227.

1930. *Oregon, 1930 Federal Census: Population Schedules* **[Microfilm & Digital Capture],** population: 953,786. Filmed by the National Archives, c1970, 20 rolls, beginning with FHL film #2341673. To access the digital images, see the online FHL catalog:
www.familysearch.org/search/catalog/1037509.

1940. *Oregon, Federal Census: Population Schedules* **[Digital Capture],** digitized images from the microfilm of original records held by the Bureau of the Census in the 1940s. After microfilming, Congress allowed the Census Bureau to destroy the originals to free up space for WWII-related files. Digitizing of the 1940 census schedules microfilm images was done for the National Archives and made public on April 2, 2012. Oregon's population in 1940 was 1,089,684 people. To access the digital images, see the online FHL catalog:
www.familysearch.org/search/catalog/2057782.

1940-1947. *Oregon, World War II Draft Registration Cards (Young Men)* **[Digital Capture],** from the original records at the National Personnel Center, St. Louis, MO. Digitized by FamilySearch International, 2017, from 126 rolls of microfilm (now in storage), beginning with the 1st digital file folder: Draft Registration Cards, Anderson, Jack – Arnup, James, 1940-1947). To access the digital images, see the online FHL catalog:
www.familysearch.org/search/catalog/4114748.

1942. *Oregon, Military Records: World War II 4th Draft Registration Cards* **[Digital Capture],** from the original records at the National Personnel Center, St. Louis, MO. These cards represent older men, ages 45 to 65 in April 1942, that were registered for the draft. Digitized by FamilySearch International, 2017, from 136 rolls of microfilm (now in storage), beginning with the 1st digital file folder: Draft registration cards, Aadland, Nels J. - Albrecht, John William, 1942. To access the digital images, see the online FHL catalog:
www.familysearch.org/search/catalog/2425784.

1949-1955. *Oregon, Portland, Index and Register of Vessels* **[Online Database],** digitized at the FamilySearch.org website. Source: National Archives microfilm series A4001. This is an image only database with an Index and Register of Vessels, Portland, Oregon, August 1949-September 1955. The register indicates the vessel name, country in which registered, date of arrival, last port of departure, date of departure from Portland and port for which destined. Browse the images, organized by roll number (the handwritten index begins on image page 5) This database has 88 images. See
https://familysearch.org/search/collection/2443351.

1961-1985. See *Oregon, Divorce Records* **[Online Database],** indexed at the Ancestry.com website. Source: OR Dept of Health. Each index record includes: Name, Gender, Divorce date, Divorce place, Spouse, Spouse gender, and Certificate number. This database has 611,397 records. See
http://search.ancestry.com/search/db.aspx?dbid=60966.

1971-1980 and **1991-2000 Oregon Death Records Index [Microfiche],** from the original records of the Oregon Board of Health, Division of Vital Statistics. Includes index of deaths from 1971-1980 created 07/01/96 and index of deaths from 1991-2000 created 06/21/01. (1981-1990 status unknown). Lists Name of deceased, Name of spouse, Death county number, Death date, Certificate number, and Birth date or year if known. Arranged in alphabetical order by surname of deceased. The county code number is given at the beginning of the series. FHL has 66 microfiche:
- **1971-1980** Oregon death index, (28 fiche), FHL fiche #6201552.
- **1991-2000** Oregon death indexes, (38 fiche), FHL Fiche #6201553.

- See also, *Oregon, Death Index, 1971-2008* **[Digital Capture],** digitized by FamilySearch International, 2019.The images are arranged in alphabetical order, beginning with Digital File Folder #106851102 (Oregon Death Index, A, 2007). To access the digital images, see the online FHL catalog: **www.familysearch.org/search/catalog/1030662.**

1971-1988. *Oregon City Directories (Salem and Pendleton)* **[Online Database],** digitized and OCR indexed at Ancestry.com. This collection is for City Directories from Pendleton, 1974-1981; and Salem, 1971-1988. A global search for name, keyword, title is available, or browse the collection to select the city, then the range of years to search specific time periods. See **www.ancestry.com/search/collections/8855.**

1988-Current. *Oregon Recent Newspaper Obituaries* **[Online Database],** digitized and indexed newspaper obituaries at the GenealogyBank website, including newspapers for Albany, Ashland, Astoria, Baker City, Beaverton, Bend, Brookings, Canby, Cannon Beach, Clackamas, Coos Bay, Corvallis, Enterprise, Estacada, Eugene, Forest Grove, Gresham, Hermiston, Hillsboro, Hood River, John Day, Keizer, Klamath Falls, La Grande, Lake Oswego, Lakeview, Lebanon, Madras, Medford, Molalla, Newberg, Ontario, Pendleton, Portland, Prineville, Redmond, Salem, Sandy, Scappoose, Seaside, Sherwood, The Dalles, Tigard, Wilsonville, and Woodburn, OR. See **www.genealogybank.com/explore/obituaries/all/usa/oregon**.

1991-2005. *Oregon, Marriage Index* **[Digital Capture],** from microfilmed records at the Willamette Valley Genealogical Society, Salem, OR. Digitized by FamilySearch International. To access the digital images, see the online FHL catalog: **www.familysearch.org/search/catalog/3500591.**

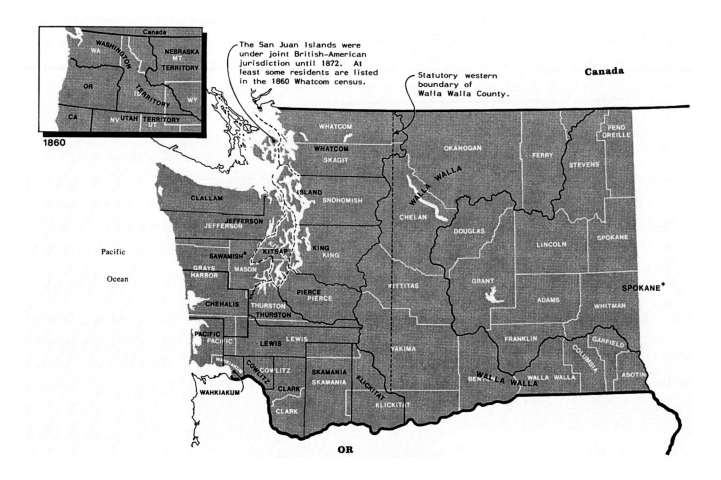

Washington Territory • June 1860. This map shows, in black, the 19 counties of Washington Territory at the time of the 1860 Federal Census. The current 39 counties of the state of Washington are shown in white. * **Notes:** Washington Territory was created in 1853. When the state of Oregon was established in 1859, the eastern parts of old Oregon Territory were added to Washington Territory. *In 1860, Old Spokane County encompassed an area from the Columbia River through the present-day Idaho panhandle and into northwestern Montana. The first Spokane County was abolished in 1864, then the same area resurrected as Stevens County. The current Spokane County was created in 1879. Sawamish was renamed Mason in 1864. **Map Source:** Page 361, *Map Guide to the U.S. Federal Censuses, 1790-1920*, by William Thorndale and William Dollarhide.

Washington
Censuses & Substitute Name Lists

Historic Timeline for Washington, 1775-1889

1775. British Capt. James Cook, fresh from Hawaii, explored and charted the Northwest Coast. He was intent on finding a "northwest passage" that would allow a ship to sail from the Pacific to Hudson Bay. En route, he looked for the mouth of an exceptionally large river in the area reported by the Spanish, but never found it. Based on the latitude-longitude noted in his ship's log, he passed by the mouth of the Columbia River within a couple of miles.

1783. The United States Of America was recognized at the Treaty of Paris. From day one, the new government asserted a plan to inhabit the entire continent; with plans for explorations in the west, including the Pacific coast, by land or sea.

1784. The North West Fur Company was formed in Montreal. It became a rival of the Hudson's Bay Company for dominance of the fur trade in British North America. Although both companies were British-owned, the North West Fur Company was manned mostly by French-Canadians, who fought furiously for fur trading rights, attacking Hudson's Bay forts, burning their ships, etc., until the two companies were forced to end their differences by the British Crown.

1792. American Capt. Robert Gray entered and named the Columbia River after his ship, the same ship he used to become the first American to circumnavigate the globe. Gray and party were in the area at the same time as British Capt. George Vancouver's party, who he met with and revealed the location of the Columbia River. Vancouver then sent Lieutenant William Broughton to confirm the existence of the Columbia River. Broughton not only confirmed it, he took his ship well into the river, landing at a point 100 miles from the mouth on the Washington side, built a temporary shelter, and named it Point Vancouver.

1803. William Clark and Meriwether Lewis led the Corps of Discovery, the first transcontinental expedition of the land west of the Missouri River. Their trek to the Pacific was mostly via river routes, beginning at St. Louis on the Mississippi, up the Missouri River to its source in Montana, then by foot across the Mountains, picking up Idaho's Clear River, to the Snake River of Idaho, Oregon, and Washington, and finally, the Columbia River all the way to its mouth at present Astoria, Oregon.

1805. Lewis and Clark explored the Washington side of the Columbia River, including Point Vancouver, the site of the future Fort Vancouver, but built their own Fort Clatsop on the Oregon side near the mouth of the Columbia River, where they spent the Winter of 1805-1806.

1806. John Jacob Astor had amassed a fortune in the trading of furs to European markets. He was America's first multi-millionaire. Astor had established a strong business relationship with the North West Fur Company of Montreal, a British-owned company of French-Canadians in competition with the London based Hudson's Bay Company. Immediately after the 1806 return of Meriwether Lewis and William Clark from their historic expedition to the Oregon Country, Astor began planning for a repeat of the Lewis and Clark journey. Lewis and Clark had recorded the numbers of deer, elk, bear, and beaver they encountered as part of their explorations. Astor's motive was to gain profits from the untapped fur trading locations he had learned about from Lewis and Clark's journals.

1807-1810. British fur-trader and map-maker David Thompson, with the North West Fur Company, began looking for routes from the Rocky Mountains to the

Pacific Ocean. He led a crew of French-Canadian fur trappers, established fur trading opportunities with any Indian Tribes he encountered, and charted detailed maps of the Columbia River. Back in Montreal, Thompson had been given instructions to join up with Astor's American fur trappers if they should be found near the Columbia River.

1810. John Jacob Astor formed the Pacific Fur Company to expand his trading empire to the Pacific coast

1811. Astor's American fur-traders built Fort Astoria near the mouth of the Columbia River as part of the Pacific Fur Company. Manned by two shiploads of men and supplies, it was the first American settlement on the Pacific Coast of North America.
- A Pacific Fur Company expedition called the *Astorians* traveled overland to the Oregon Country with the intent of arriving at Fort Astoria at the same time as Astor's ships. They followed the same path as Lewis and Clark to get there, arriving a few weeks after the ships.
- Astor had convinced the North West Fur Company to participate in his expedition to the Oregon Country. David Thompson and his party of French-Canadian trappers contacted the Astorians and followed them down river to Fort Astoria. Thompson then set up a fur trading post for the North West Fur Company next door to Fort Astoria.

1813. After war was declared in 1812, British warships blockaded Fort Astoria. The Astorians decided it was better to get out before shots were fired, and the entire Fort Astoria operation was sold to the British-owned North West Fur Company, who renamed it Fort George. The Astorians returned overland to St. Louis, and in doing so, became the first to cross South Pass, the route through the Rocky Mountains that would be followed by thousands of Oregon Trail travelers.

1814. The **Treaty of Ghent** ended the War of 1812 and restored all boundaries between the U.S. and Britain to the lines before the war. Invoking the Treaty of Ghent, John Jacob Astor used the provisions for returning all occupied lands by the British back to the Americans and got the American government to allow his Pacific Fur Company to take possession of Fort Astoria again. Although the fort changed hands in ownership, the North West Fur Company continued to use it for their operations for several more years.

1818. Anglo-American Convention. The United States and Great Britain agreed to a joint occupation of the Oregon Country/Columbia District. Both parties accepted the area as extending from the Continental Divide to the Pacific Ocean, and from about Latitude $54°$ in present British Columbia, to the Boundary Mountains (now Siskiyou Mountains) at about Latitude $42°$). In 1827 a provision was added to the treaty that allowed either party to invoke a conclusion of ownership, by giving 12 months' notice to the other. Notice was not given until 1845, when President James K. Polk sought resolution, leading to a new treaty in 1846.
- Also in the 1818 treaty, Britain and the U.S. agreed to the 49th parallel as the international boundary from the Lake of the Woods (now Minnesota) to the Continental Divide.

1821. The Hudson's Bay Company and the North West Fur Company merged, retaining the name Hudson's Bay. The company now had a monopoly on fur trading activity in British North America and were intent on monopolizing the Oregon Country as well.

1825. The British-owned Hudson's Bay Company established Fort Vancouver as a center for their fur trading operations in the *Columbia District*, the British name for the Oregon Country. Most of the employees of the Hudson's Bay Company in the Oregon Country were French-Canadians left over from their days with the North West Fur Company. In defiance of their orders, the Hudson's Bay Company leaders in the Oregon Country continued to cooperate with the American fur traders.

1834. The Whitman Party, including Dr. Marcus Whitman and his wife Narcissa and also Reverend Henry H. Spalding and his wife Eliza set up a protestant mission at the junction of the Columbia and Snake Rivers. The travel route they followed to get there would become known as the Oregon Trail and used by thousands of future settlers.

1839. Fr. Pierre-Jean DeSmet arrived among the Flatheads in the Bitterroot Valley. He and his staff would set up a number of Jesuit missions in the present states of Montana, Idaho, and Washington.

1841. The Western Emigration Society, a group of about 70 settlers bound for California and the Oregon Country set off on the Oregon Trail, beginning at Independence, Missouri. This was the first organized wagon train to head for California and Oregon. The Oregon-bound part of the group was a small party of

Jesuit Missionaries led by Fr. Pierre-Jean de Smet, who left the main group at Soda Springs (now ID) to return to their missions in the Spokane and Bitterroot valleys of present Washington, Idaho, and Montana. Bartleson & Bidwell led the California-bound group via the California Trail to the Sacramento Valley.

1842. John C. Fremont led an Army Topographical Corps' Expedition to the Oregon Country. He witnessed an eruption of Mt. St. Helens. His maps of this expedition and one the following year were printed by the government and were widely used by pioneers heading west.

1843. A group of 50 Americans and 52 French-Canadians met in the Willamette Valley of Oregon and took a vote to determine who should govern the Oregon Country. A vote of 52-50 favored keeping Oregon as American territory (two Canadians switched their votes). From that meeting, a Provisional Territory of Oregon was established.

1844-1846. In the 1844 presidential election, James K. Polk, Democrat, defeated Henry Clay, Whig, to become President of the United States. The two burning political issues of the day were the annexation of Texas and the acquisition of the Oregon Country. James K. Polk, as the "Manifest Destiny" candidate, was elected with campaign slogans of *Annex Texas!* and *Fifty-four forty or fight!* In 1845, Texas was annexed to the U.S. and war with Mexico began soon after. But in 1846, Polk settled for the 49th parallel as the northern boundary of the Oregon Country. Polk had no intention of fighting a war with Mexico and Great Britain at the same time. The treaty of 1846 brought the Oregon Country into the United States.

1848. President James K. Polk signed a bill that created Oregon Territory. It encompassed the area between the 42nd and 49th parallels, from the Pacific Ocean to the Continental Divide. The first capital was Oregon City. Virtually all of the political structures established by the Provisional Oregon Government were adopted by the official Territory of Oregon, including the counties in place at that time, most of the laws, and most of the court system was retained. Polk became the President who brought more territory (12 modern States) into the United States than any other. During his administration, the Oregon Country, Texas, and the Mexican Annexation were added to the U.S., and for the first time, America became a nation "from sea to shining sea."

1850. June. A **Federal Census** was taken in Oregon Territory, which included the area of present Oregon, Washington, and Idaho; and Montana and Wyoming areas west of the Continental Divide. The population was revealed as 12,093 people. The population was limited in the present Washington area to a few residents of Clarke and Lewis counties, all south of Puget Sound and west of the Cascade Mountains. No population was recorded in the present Idaho, Montana, or Wyoming areas.

– Sept. 27th, Congress passed the Donation Land Claim Act. The forerunner of the 1862 Homestead Act, the Donation Land Claim Act was aimed entirely as an incentive to get settlers to move to Oregon Territory. From 1850 to 1862, land records for the areas that became Oregon and Washington provide detailed genealogical sources, revealing names, birthdates, birthplaces, marriage information, and citizenship. Note: a searchable database for DLC grants is available at the WA Digital Archives.

1853. Washington Territory was created. It encompassed the present area of Washington, but extended east to the Rocky Mountains, incorporating areas that today are in northern Idaho and western Montana. As a result, the original Oregon Territory was split in half. Oregon Territory now had lands on the same line as its present northern border stretching to the Continental Divide, and included the southern half of present Idaho, and a portion of present western Montana and Wyoming.

1859. Oregon joined the Union as the 33rd state, a Free State with the same boundaries as present. The population of the new state was about 45,000 people. The eastern remnants of Oregon Territory, 1853-1859, were added to Washington Territory.

1860. June. **Federal Census, Washington Territory.** The population of Washington Territory was at 11,594 people. Refer to the map on page 140 to see the counties in place in 1860, compared with the counties today.

1863. Idaho Territory was created, reducing Washington Territory to its present size and shape.

1883. The Northern Pacific Railroad was completed to Tacoma WA, becoming the third Transcontinental Railroad in America..

1889. Nov 11th. **Washington** became the 42nd state in the Union. Olympia was the state capital.

Washington State Library, State Archives, Regional Branches & Digital Archives

The Washington Secretary of State oversees the State Library, State Archives, Regional Branches, and the Digital Archives.

Washington State Library. The main library is located in Olympia, WA. Visit the special webpage, *Genealogy at the Washington State Library*, with a list of resources of interest to genealogists. See www.sos.wa.gov/library/Genealogy.aspx.

Washington State Archives. The main State Archives is located in Olympia. WA. Materials maintained here are statewide in nature, documents created by various state institutions, statewide functions, past governors, and past legislatures. Visit the special webpage at the State Archives website, *Genealogical Resources*. See www.sos.wa.gov/legacy/genealogy.aspx.

Washington State Archives - Regional Branches. In addition to the main State Archives, there are five regional archives, each holding original county records for a number of counties within their region of coverage. The various countywide archival records from Washington's 39 counties have been dispersed to the regional branches.
- Of primary interest to genealogists, Washington's surviving territorial and state censuses have all been microfilmed and digitized, and each of the regional archives has both the originals and microfilmed copies for the counties within their coverage area. Other original county records maintained at the regional archives may include birth, marriage, and death records; court records, including naturalizations, dockets, and civil, criminal, and probate case files; land records, including general indices to recordings, deeds, and patents; county council and county commissioner proceedings, county ordinances and resolutions; real and personal property tax records; school district and education district records, including school censuses; and many others.
- The five regional branches of the state archives each have their own website, where a researcher can review the types of original records available for the counties under their coverage:

Northwest Regional Branch. Located next to the campus of Western Washington University in Bellingham, WA, this archives maintains original records from Clallam, Island, Jefferson, San Juan, Skagit, Snohomish, and Whatcom counties. See www.secstate.wa.gov/archives/archives_northwest.aspx.

Southwest Regional Branch. Located in Olympia, WA, this archives maintains original records from Clark, Cowlitz, Grays Harbor, Lewis, Mason, Pacific, Skamania, Thurston, and Wahkiakum counties. See www.secstate.wa.gov/archives/archives_southwest.aspx.

Central Regional Branch. Located next to the campus of Central Washington University in Ellensburg, WA, this archives maintains records from Benton, Chelan, Douglas, Franklin, Grant, Kittitas, Klickitat, Okanogan, and Yakima counties. See www.secstate.wa.gov/archives/archives_central.aspx.

Eastern Regional Branch located on the campus of Eastern Washington University in Cheney, WA, this archives maintains records from Adams, Asotin, Columbia, Ferry, Garfield, Lincoln, Pend Oreille, Spokane, Stevens, Walla Walla, and Whitman counties. See www.secstate.wa.gov/archives/archives_eastern.aspx.

Puget Sound Regional Branch located in Bellevue, WA, maintains records from King, Pierce, and Kitsap counties. See www.secstate.wa.gov/archives/archives_puget.aspx.

Washington State Archives – Digital Archives. Created in 2004, located on the campus of Eastern Washington University, Cheney, WA, the Washington Digital Archives was the nation's first archives dedicated specifically to the preservation of electronic records of historic value; and has become the model for several other states' digital archives. As of May 2021, the number of records preserved (digitized) stands at 233 million records, while searchable (indexed) records stand at 80 million records. In any given month, over two million records are added to the Digital Archives total. To see an extensive list of the Current Collections, see www.digitalarchives.wa.gov/Collections#RSID:5.

- A program to digitize the images of all of Washington's Territorial Censuses is complete, and name indexes to the censuses as well as many other resources are combined in one Digital Archives search system. In addition to census records, the other state and county records indexed include Marriage Records, Naturalization Records, Death Records, Birth Records, Military Records, Institution Records, Physician Records, Oaths of Office, and all Washington Territory Donation Land Claims. Visit the search screen for the Digital Archives, see **www.digitalarchives.wa.gov**.

Bibliography
Washington Censuses & Substitutes

WA Territorial Censuses. Washington Territory, created from Oregon Territory in 1853, had territory-wide censuses conducted every few years until statehood in 1889. There is good coverage for virtually all Washington Territory counties, some borrowed from Oregon Territory from as early as 1847-1851; and WT counties from 1856-1889.

- To cover the earliest possible censuses for the area of present Washington, one needs to look at Oregon Territory first. For example, the 1850 federal census of Oregon Territory included Lewis County (west of the Cascade Mountains), and Clarke County (east of the mountains), covering all of the populated areas of what became Washington Territory.
- Between the time of the 1850 federal census and the formation of Washington Territory in 1853, the Oregon Territory legislature created six more counties in the area of present Washington. As a result, the area that became Washington Territory in 1853 began with eight counties inherited from Oregon Territory, all of which need to be reviewed for possible censuses. The eight counties and their Oregon creation dates, and parent counties were as follows:
  - Clarke County, 1844, as the original "Vancouver District" by the Provisional Oregon Government. The name Clarke came in 1849, the 'e' was dropped in the 1920s.
  - Lewis County, 1845, an original county created by the Provisional Oregon Government.
  - Pacific County, 1851, from Lewis.
  - Jefferson County, 1852, from Lewis.
  - Thurston County, 1852, from Lewis.
  - King County, 1852, from Thurston.
  - Pierce County, 1852, from Lewis.
  - Island County, 1853, from Lewis.

At its first legislative session in 1854, Washington Territory recognized the eight Oregon-born counties; then created eight more on its own:
  - Clallam County, from Jefferson.
  - Cowlitz County, from Lewis.
  - Chehalis County, from Thurston. (Chehalis was renamed Grays Harbor County in 1915).
  - Sawamish County, from Thurston. (Sawamish was renamed Mason in 1864).
  - Skamania County, from Clarke.
  - Wahkiakum County, from Lewis.
  - Walla Walla County, from Clarke.
  - Whatcom County, from Island.

- The above sixteen counties represent the "original" counties of Washington Territory. The federal organic act creating Washington Territory in 1853 dictated that a census be taken "previous to the first election." This was a territorial census conducted in 1854 for the purpose of apportionment of the first elected territorial legislature. (Of the sixteen counties, only the 1854 Pierce County census name list appears to have survived).
- After the first territorial census of 1854, several more territorial censuses were authorized for the purpose of apportionment of the territorial legislature. Surviving census manuscripts exist for at least one county for the years 1856, 1857, 1858, 1859, 1861, 1871, 1879, 1881, 1883, 1885, 1887, and the last one in 1889, the same year in which Washington became a state. Those censuses taken in the 1880s are fairly complete for all of the counties in place during the territorial era.

WA State Censuses. After joining the Union as a state in 1889, Washington took at least two state-sponsored censuses, perhaps more – since censuses exist for a few counties dated 1891, 1892; and a few more dated 1894; and one county dated 1898.

WA Federal Censuses. As part of Oregon Territory, the first federal census for Washington areas was complete for all counties in 1850; Washington Territory in 1860, 1870, and 1880; and Washington State, 1900 through 1940. The 1890 was lost, like all states.

Census Substitutes: In addition to Washington's Territorial, State, and Federal Censuses, there are numerous census substitutes available: name lists derived from Court Records, Tax Lists, Voter Lists, Military Lists, Vital Records, et al. Descriptions begin below in chronological order:

❖ ❖ ❖ ❖ ❖

1850. *Oregon Territory, 1850 Federal Census: Population Schedules* **[Microfilm & Digital Capture],** filmed by the National Archives, 1964, 1 roll, FHL film #20298. To access the digital images, see the online FHL catalog:
www.familysearch.org/search/catalog/744495.

- NOTE: The 1850 Federal Census taken in Oregon Territory included the areas of present Oregon, Washington, and Idaho; and Montana and Wyoming areas west of the Continental Divide. The population was revealed as 12,093 people. The population was limited in the present Washington area to a few residents of Clarke and Lewis counties, all south of Puget Sound and west of the Cascade Mountains. No population was recorded in the present Idaho, Montana, or Wyoming areas.

1850-1890. *Washington, Compiled Census Index* **[Online Database],** indexed at the Ancestry.com website. Source: Accelerated Indexing Systems, Salt Lake City, UT, 1999. This collection contains the following indexes: 1850 (Oregon) Territorial Census Index; 1857-1861 Territorial Census Index; 1860 Federal Census Index; 1870 Federal Census Index; 1880 Federal Census Index; and 1890 Veterans Schedule. This database has 9,546 records. See
http://search.ancestry.com/search/db.aspx?dbid=3579.

1850-1903. *Oregon and Washington Donation Land Files* **[Microfilm & Digital Capture],** from the original land records at the National Archives, Washington, DC. Contains records from the La Grande Land Office, Oregon City Land Office, Winchester-Roseburg Land Office, The Dalles Land Office, Olympia Land Office, Colfax-Spokane Falls Land Office, Walla Walla Land Office, and Vancouver Land Office. From the Pamphlet Finding Aid: "The donation claims files are arranged alphabetically by name of State and thereunder by name of land office. For each office there is a main series for approved claims, arranged by final certificate number. There are some variations in the arrangement of records for several offices... Documents within the files are arranged as nearly as possible in the order in which they were maintained by the clerks in the land offices... The records for a typical donation claim are filmed as follows: the endorsement on the outer page, followed by the final certificate, the notification, and the other documents in chronological order. For the files not having final certificates, the notations on the outer page have been filmed first, followed by the notification and other documents. For canceled or rejected claims some documents may not be present, especially the final certificate." For more detailed information see explanation at front of films. Filmed by the National Archives, 1970, 108 rolls, beginning with FHL film #1028543 (Oregon City office). To access the digital images, see the online FHL catalog:
www.familysearch.org/search/catalog/18339.
- See also, *Abstracts of Washington Donation Land Claims, 1855-1902* **[Microfilm & Digital Capture],** filmed by the National Archives, 1951, 1 roll, FHL film #1024457. Another filming: FHL film #418160. To access the digital images, see the online FHL catalog:
www.familysearch.org/search/catalog/47803.

1850-1954. *Washington, County Land Records* **[Online Database],** digitized at the FamilySearch.org website. Source: WA State Archives. This is an image only database with land and property records (with Direct/Grantor & Indirect/Grantee indexes), from Clark, Grays Harbor, King, Kitsap, Lewis, Mason, Pacific, Pierce, Thurston, and Wahkiakum counties. Browse the images, organized by County, then Record Type, Date Range, and Volume. This database has 884,953 records. See
https://familysearch.org/search/collection/1762885.
- See also, *Washington, County Land Records, 1850-1954* **[Online Database],** indexed at the Ancestry.com website. Source: FamilySearch image database. This database has 884,953 records. See
http://search.ancestry.com/search/db.aspx?dbid=60225.

1850-1982. *Washington, County Naturalization Records* **[Online Database],** digitized at the FamilySearch.org website. Source: WA State Archives. This is an image only database with records of naturalization proceedings from Clark, Cowlitz, Grays Harbor, King, Kitsap, Lewis, Mason, Pacific, Pierce, Skamania, Thurston, and Wahkiakum Counties. The records include petitions, declarations of intention, certificates, depositions, and final papers. Browse the images, organized by County, Record Type, Date Range, and Volume. This database has 170,192 records. See
https://familysearch.org/search/collection/1932554.
- See also, *Washington, County Naturalization Records, 1850-1982* **[Online Database],** indexed at the Ancestry.com website. Source: FamilySearch. See
http://search.ancestry.com/search/db.aspx?dbid=60227.

1850s-1960. See *Washington Deaths and Burials, 1810-1960* **[Online Database],** digitized and indexed at FamilySearch.org. From records on microfilm at the Family History Library in Salt Lake City, Utah. The 1810 date is a typo. The source of the extra names appears to be other people listed on a death certificate, i.e., spouse, parents, informant, et al. This database has 650,057 records, see
www.familysearch.org/search/collection/3518729.

1850s-2000s. *Linkpendium – Washington: Family History & Genealogy, Census, Birth, Marriage, Death, Vital Records & More* **[Online Databases].** Linkpendium is a genealogical portal site with links to state, county, town, and local databases. Currently listed are selected sites for Washington statewide resources (420), Renamed/Discontinued Counties (3), Adams County (411), Asotin County (147), Benton County (235), Chelan County (385), Clallam County

(234), Clark County (370), Columbia County (177), Cowlitz County (263, and 30 more counties. See **www.linkpendium.com/wa-genealogy**.

1850s-2000s. *Washington USGenWeb Archives* **[Online Databases],** name lists are available for all 39 Washington counties. Typical county records include Bibles, Biographies, Cemeteries, Censuses, Court, Death, Deeds, Directories, Histories, Marriages, Military, Newspapers, Obituaries, Photos, Schools, Tax Lists, Wills, and more. Links to all Washington counties and projects are at the USGenWeb site for Washington. See **http://usgwarchives.net/wa/wafiles.htm**.

1851-1889 Territorial Censuses. See *Transcribed and Printed Copies of Various Territorial Census Rolls, Done by Various Genealogical Organizations* **[Printed Books],** copies at the Washington State Archives, Olympia, WA. Includes Adams County (1889), Asotin County (1889), Chehalis County (1885), Clarke County (1850, 1860, 1871), Columbia County (1889), Douglas County (1887), Franklin County (1885, 1887), Island County (1889), Lewis County (1851), Lincoln County (1889), Mason County (1889), San Juan County (1889), Snohomish County (1889), and Walla Walla County (1887). Visit the search screen for the WA Digital Archives, see **www.digitalarchives.wa.gov**.

1851-1970. *Washington, Wills and Probate Records* **[Online Database],** digitized and indexed at the Ancestry.com website. Source: Ancestry database, records extracted from Washington county, district, and probate courts. Each index record includes: Name, Probate date, Probate place, Death place, Case number, and Item description (case files numbers, dates, etc.). A table of contents gives number and type of images. The document images have much more information about a person. This database has 124,056 records. See **http://search.ancestry.com/search/db.aspx?dbid=9086**.

- See also, **Washington, County Probate Case Files, 1832-1950 [Online Database],** digitized at FamilySearch.org. This is an image-only database of probate records created in the county courts of King, Lewis, and Pacific counties. Other counties will be added as they become available. This database has 247,040 images, see **www.familysearch.org/search/collection/1454946**.

1852-1950. *Washington, County Divorce Records* **[Online Database],** digitized at the FamilySearch.org website. Source: WA State Archives. This is an image only database with digital images of divorce records from the civil courts in Clark, Cowlitz, Grays Harbor, Lewis, Mason, Pacific, Thurston, and Wahkiakum counties. It also includes divorce records from Washington Territory from the years 1854-1871. Browse the images, organized by County, then Case Number Range. This database has 127,147 records. See **https://familysearch.org/search/collection/1930340**.
- See also, *Washington Territorial Divorces Extracted From Territorial Laws, 1854-1871* **[Digital Capture],** digitized by the Genealogical Society of Utah, 2008, from microfilm (now in storage). This collection of images is included in the 1852-1950 set online. To access the digital images of just the 1854-1871 set, see the online FHL catalog: **www.familysearch.org/search/catalog/2002600**.

1852-1906. See *The Ox Team, or, the Old Oregon Trail, 1852-1906: An Account of the Author's Trip Across the Plains, From the Missouri River to Puget Sound, at the age of Twenty-two, with an Ox and Cow Team in 1852, and of his Return with an Ox Team in the year 1906, at the Age of Seventy-six, with Copious Excerpts from his Journal and Other Reliable Sources of Information; a Narrative of Events and Descriptive of Present and Past Conditions* **[Printed Book & Digital Version],** by Ezra Meeker, publ. 1907, New York, 248 pages, digitized by FamilySearch International, 2013. To access the digital version, see the online FHL catalog: **www.familysearch.org/search/catalog/1050793**.

1852-1950. *Washington, County Divorce Records* **[Online Database],** digitized at the Ancestry.com website. Source: FamilySearch image database. This is an image only database with divorce records from the civil courts in the following counties: Clark, Cowlitz, Grays Harbor, Lewis, Mason, Pacific, Thurston, and Wahkiakum counties. Browse the images, organized by county, then Case File Number Range. This database has 127,147 records. See **http://search.ancestry.com/search/db.aspx?dbid=60224**.

1853-1929. *Washington, County Probate Records* **[Online Database],** digitized at the FamilySearch.org website. Source: WA State Archives. This is an image only database with county probate records from the Washington State Archives Northwest Regional Branch in Bellingham. They include records from Jefferson, Skagit, Island, Whatcom, San Juan, Clallam, and Snohomish counties. This collection is being published as images become available. Browse the images, organized by County, then Record Type, Date Range, and Volume. This database has 587,055 images. See **https://familysearch.org/search/collection/1979435**.

1853-1957. *Washington, Western District, Naturalization Records* [Online Database], digitized at the FamilySearch.org website. Source: National Archives microfilm series M1542. This is an image only database with records of the U.S. District Court for the Western District of Washington. The records includes Indexes, Declarations of Intentions, Petitions for Naturalization, Petitions Evidence, and other Naturalization Papers. Browse the images, organized by Record Type, Year Range, and Volume Number. This database has 141,968 records. See https://familysearch.org/search/collection/2296985.

1853-1980. *Washington, Naturalizations* [Online Database], digitized and indexed at the Ancestry.com website. Source: Extractions by the WA State Digital Archives, Cheney, WA. Each index record includes: Name, Record type, Arrival date, Declaration date, Declaration place, and Spouse. The naturalization document image may have much more information about a person. This database has 112,323 records. See http://search.ancestry.com/search/db.aspx?dbid=2379.

"1854 Territorial Census, Pierce County, Washington Territory" [Printed Article], in *American Monthly Magazine*, Vo. 78, No. 6 (Jun 1944), a publication of the National DAR, Washington, DC.
- See also, **"Census, 1854,"** in *Researcher,* (Tacoma-Pierce County Genealogical Society, Tacoma, WA), Vol. 1, No. 1 (Nov 1969) and Vol. 13, No. 3 (Mar 1982).

1854-1892. *Wahkiakum County, Census* [Printed Book], compiled and indexed by Evelyn Morris Heurd for Lower Columbia Genealogical Society, Longview, WA, 1994, 227 pages. FHL book 9791,l.791 X29h.

1854-1902. *Washington Marriages* [Online Database], indexed at the Ancestry.com website. Source: Liahona Research, Orem, UT (Liahona starting dates are impossible). Each index record includes: Name, Gender, Spouse name, County, and Source (includes FHL film number). This database has 12,884 records. See http://search.ancestry.com/search/db.aspx?dbid=7874.

1854-1917. *Index of Probate Court Records, King County, Washington* [Printed Book], compiled and edited by Sue Fleming Dolliver, publ. Eastside Genealogical Society, 1993, 221 pages, FHL book 979.777 P22d.

1854-1927. *Washington, King County Probate Records* [Online Database], digitized at the FamilySearch.org website. Source: WA State Archives. This is an image only database with probate records from King County. Browse the images, organized by Volume, Title, and Year. This database has 33,530 records. See https://familysearch.org/search/collection/1878788.

1854-1950. *Washington, County Probate Case Files* [Online Database], digitized and indexed at the FamilySearch.org website. Source: WA State Archives. This collection currently includes digital images of probate records created in the county courts in King, Lewis, and Pacific counties. Other counties will be added as they become available. Each index record includes: Name, Event place, Event year, Number of images, First image number, and Last image number. The document images may have much more information about a person. This database has 4,310 records. See https://familysearch.org/search/collection/1454946.

1854-1955. *Western States Marriage Index, 1809-2011* [Online Database], indexed at the Ancestry.com website. This database is also accessible at the BYU-Idaho website. Each index record includes: Name, Spouse, Marriage date, Marriage place, and a link to the BYU-Idaho website. This database has 6,334 WA records. See http://search.ancestry.com/search/db.aspx?dbid=70016.

1854-1965. *Washington Postmaster Indexes, Prior to 1965* [Online Database], digitized at the FamilySearch.org website. Source: WA State Archives: Postmaster General records. This is an image only database with index cards of postal workers in the state of Washington prior to 1965. Cards include the name of the individual, location, and years of activity. Some cards also contain maiden names of spouses. Browse the images, organized by County, then Surname Range. This database has 15,381 records. See https://familysearch.org/search/collection/1404287.

1854-1984. *Washington Newspaper Archives* [Online Databases], digitized and indexed newspapers at the GenealogyBank website, for Bellingham, Olympia, Pasco, Port Townsend, Puyallup, Seattle, Steilacoom, and Tacoma. See www.genealogybank.com/explore/newspapers/all/usa/washington.

1854-2010. *Washington, County Records* [Online Database], digitized at the FamilySearch.org website. Source: WA State Archives. This is an image only database with vital records, probate records, school records, tax records, naturalization records, and other records. All 39 counties of Washington are included. Browse the images, organized by County, Record Type, Date Range, and Volume. This database has 6,880,104 records. See
https://familysearch.org/search/collection/1910364.

1854-2013. *Washington, Marriage Records* [Online Database], digitized and indexed at the Ancestry.com website. Source: WA State Archives. Each index record includes: Name, Marriage date, Marriage place, Date recorded, Spouse, and Reference number. The certificate image has much more information about the couple. This database has 13,315,117 records. See
http://search.ancestry.com/search/db.aspx?dbid=2378.

1855-1979. *Washington, Supreme Court Naturalization Records* [Digital Capture], from the originals at the WA State Archives, Olympia, WA. Digitized by FamilySearch International, 2010. To access the digital images, see the online FHL catalog:
www.familysearch.org/search/catalog/1878877.

1855-2008. *Washington, County Marriages* [Online Database], digitized and indexed at the FamilySearch.org website. Source: WA State Archives. This database includes images and partial index of marriage records from Washington counties. The index includes marriage records for Clallam, Lewis, Pacific, Snohomish, Thurston, and Wahkiakum Counties. Images for both indexed and non-indexed counties are available in the browse. Additional records from other counties will be added to this collection as they become available. This database has 4,324,117 records. See
https://familysearch.org/search/collection/1534448.

1855-2008. *Washington, County Marriages* [Online Database], digitized and indexed at the Ancestry.com website. Source: FamilySearch extractions from county records on microfilm at the Family History Library, Salt Lake City, UT. Each index record includes: Name, Gender, Marriage date, Marriage place, and Spouse. The auto-linked FamilySearch image of the marriage certificate will give more information about the couple, witnesses, minister, address of place of marriage, etc. This database has 826,920 records. See
http://search.ancestry.com/search/db.aspx?dbid=60226.

1856-2009. *Washington, County Records* [Online Database], digitized at FamilySearch.org. Source: WA State Archives, Puget Sound Branch. This is an image-only database, a collection of various records including vital, probate, school, tax, naturalization, and other records. The following counties are available with records: Adams, Asotin, Benton, Chelan, Columbia, Douglas, Franklin, Grant, Kittitas, Klickitat, Lincoln, Okanogan, Pend Oreille, Pierce, Spokane, Stevens, Walla Walla, Whitman, and Yakima. Browse the images, organized by County, then Record Type, Date Range, and Volume. This database has 6,879,890 records. See
www.familysearch.org/search/collection/1910364.
- This database is also located at Ancestry.com:
http://search.ancestry.com/search/db.aspx?dbid=60228.

1856-2009. See *Washington, County Records* [Online Database], digitized at the FamilySearch.org website. Source: database acquired from the WA State Archives, various regional branches. This is an image only database including vital, probate, school, tax, naturalization, and other records. The records are from all 39 counties in Washington State, 1856-2009. Browse the images, organized by County, Record Type, Date Range, and Volume. This database has 6,880,104 images. See
https://familysearch.org/search/collection/1910364.
- **NOTE:** This database has several county copies of federal census originals that can be compared with the federal set.

"1857 Census, Clallam County, Washington Territory" [Printed Article], in *Clallam County Genealogical Society Bulletin*, (Port Angeles, WA), Vol. 4, No. 2 (Jun 1984).

1857-1860. *An Index to Early King County Pioneers: Includes Seattle* [Printed Book], by M. C. Rhodes, published by the University of Washington, 1984, 76 pages. This index was compiled from the 1857 and 1860 census records. Includes photocopies of 1860 enumeration schedules for Seattle, King County. FHL book 979.777 X22r.

1857-1892. *Washington State and Territorial Censuses* [Online Database], digitized and indexed at the Ancestry.com website. Source: WA State Archives, 1987 microfilm edition, 20 rolls. Washington became a territory in 1853 and a state in 1889. Many territorial

but few state censuses were taken for Washington. This database is an index and images to most of the censuses known at the time of the microfilm project in 1987. This set does not include all of the microfilm series by the WA State Archives in 2003. This edition includes the following counties and years: **Adams:** 1885, 1887, 1889. **Asotin:** 1885, 1887, 1889. **Chehalis:** 1860, 1871, 1885. **Clallam:** 1857, 1860*, 1871, 1883, 1885, 1887. **Clark:** 1860*, 1871, 1883, 1885, 1887. **Columbia:** 1883, 1885, 1887, 1889. **Cowlitz:** 1871, 1883, 1885, 1887. **Douglas:** 1885, 1887. **Franklin:** 1885, 1887. **Garfield:** 1883, 1885, 1887, 1889, 1892, 1898. **Island:** 1860*, 1871, 1883, 1885, 1887. **Jefferson:** 1860*, 1871, 1875, 1877, 1878, 1879, 1880, 1881, 1883, 1885, 1887, 1889, 1891. **King:** 1856, 1871, 1879, 1880, 1881, 1883, 1885, 1887, 1889, 1892. **Kitsap:** 1857 (county then called Slaughter), 1860*, 1871, 1883, 1885, 1887, 1889. **Kittitas:** 1885, 1887, 1889. **Klickitat:** 1871, 1883, 1885, 1887, 1889, 1892. **Lewis:** 1857, 1860*, 1871, 1883, 1885, 1887. **Lincoln:** 1885, 1887, 1889. **Mason:** 1860 (county then called Sawamish), 1871, 1879, 1880, 1881, 1883, 1885, 1887, 1889, 1892. **Pacific:** 1883, 1885, 1887. **Pierce:** 1857, 1871, 1878, 1879, 1883, 1885, 1887, 1889, 1892. **San Juan:** 1885, 1887, 1889. **Skagit:** 1885, 1887. **Skamania:** 1871, 1885, 1887. **Snohomish:** 1871, 1883, 1885, 1887, 1889. **Spokane:** 1885, 1887. Stevens: 1871, 1878, 1885, 1887, 1892. **Thurston:** 1871, 1873, 1875, 1877, 1878, 1879, 1880, 1881, 1883, 1885, 1887, 1889, 1892. **Wahkiakum:** 1871, 1885, 1887. **Walla Walla:** 1885, 1887, 1892. **Whatcom:** 1860*, 1871, 1885, 1887, 1889. **Whitman:** 1883, 1885, 1887, 1889, and **Yakima:** 1883, 1885, 1887. Each index record includes: Name, Census date, Residence county, Residence state, Locality, Birth location, Gender, Birth year, Race, Line, and Roll. The census page image may have more information about a person. This database has 772,246 records. See
http://search.ancestry.com/search/db.aspx?dbid=1018.
- This series includes 1860 censuses for Clallam, Clarke, Island, Jefferson, Kitsap, Lewis, and Whatcom counties. These unique records are original county copies of a federal census retained by the county (a copy went to Washington, DC). Comparing these original local censuses with the 1860 federal copies (also digitized at Ancestry) will reveal that they often do not agree with spellings of names, birthplaces, etc. Also, the county copies have the population schedules of the 1860 federal censuses followed by the agriculture and mortality schedules. (The microfilmed/digitized federal set separated all special schedules from the population schedules).

- See also, *Washington Territory Census Rolls, 1857-1892* **[Printed Booklet & Digital Version]**, a pamphlet with a list of Washington Territorial Census Rolls, 1857-1892, publ. WA Secretary of State, 1987, 11 pages. To access the digital version, see the online FHL catalog:
www.familysearch.org/search/catalog/543867.
- See also, *Washington, Census Records: Territorial Census, 1857-1892* **[Digital Capture],** digitized by FamilySearch International, 2017, from originals held by the Washington State Archives, Olympia, WA. The microfilm is now in storage, but the contents list of 62 rolls begins with Digital file folder #101447649 (Adams to Clark, 1885-1889). To access the digital images, see the online FHL catalog:
www.familysearch.org/search/catalog/2821867.

1860. *Washington Territory, 1860 Federal Census: Population Schedules* **[Microfilm & Digital Capture],** filmed twice by the National Archives, 1950, 1967, 2 rolls total, FHL film #805398 (2nd filming: Island, Whatcom, Clallam, Kitsap, Jefferson, Klickitat, Pacific, Wahkiakum, Chehalis, Clark, Cowlitz, Skamania, Spokane, Sawamish, Thurston, Lewis, Pierce, King, and Walla Walla Counties). To access the digital images, see the online FHL catalog:
www.familysearch.org/search/catalog/708784.
- See also, *Index to 1860 Washington Territory Census: With Mortality and Production of Agriculture Schedules* **[Printed Book],** transcribed by members of the Jefferson County Genealogical Society, Port Townsend, WA, 1997, 13 pages. This was taken from the county's original copy of the 1860 federal census. FHL book 979.798 X2j.

1860-1887. *Skamania Washington, Census Records* **[Printed Book],** compiled by Daphne Hon Ramsay, published by Clark County Genealogical Society, Vancouver, WA, 1987, 101 pages. Include index. FHL book 979.784 X2r.

1860-1991. *Washington, Petitions for Naturalization* **[Online Database],** digitized and indexed at Ancestry.com. Source: National Archives, Records of the District Courts of the United States. Each index record includes a Name, Record type (Petition), Birthdate, Birthplace, Petition date, Petition place, and Petition number. The document image may have more information. This database has 245,300 records, see
www.ancestry.com/search/collections/2531.

"**1861 Washington Territorial Census, Snohomish County**" **[Printed Article]**, in *Washington Heritage*, (Heritage Quest, Orting, WA), Vol. 1, No. 4 (Fall 1983),
- See also, "**1861 Census, Snohomish County**" **[Printed Article]**, in *Star*, (Stillaguamish Valley Genealogical Society, Arlington, WA); Vol. 5, No. 4 (Jan 1992), and in *The Sounder,* (Sno-Isle Genealogical Society, Edmonds, WA), Vol. 8, No. 4 (1994).

1861-1865. *Index to Compiled Service Records of Volunteer Union Soldiers Who Served in Organizations From the Territory of Washington* **[Microfilm]**, filmed by the National Archives, 1964, 1 roll, FHL film #821948.
- See also, *Index to Soldiers & Sailors of the Civil War* **[Online Database]**, a searchable name index to 6.3 million Union and Confederate Civil War soldiers now available online at the National Park Service website. A search can be done by surname, first name, state, or unit. Washington Territory supplied 1,524 men to the war (all Union). See www.nps.gov/civilwar/soldiers-and-sailors-database.htm.

"**1862 Washington Territorial Census, Snohomish County**" **[Printed Article]**, in *The Sounder,* (Sno-Isle Genealogical Society, Edmonds, WA), Vol. 5, No. 4 (1991) and Vol. 5, No. 3 (Fall 1987);
- See also, "**1862 Snohomish City Census,**" Vol. 1, No. 3 (Fall 1987).

1864-1990. *Washington, King County, Naturalization Records* **[Digital Capture]**, from the originals at the Washington State Archives, Puget Sound Branch, Bellevue, WA. Digitized by the Genealogical Society of Utah, 2008. To access the digital images, see the online FHL catalog:
www.familysearch.org/search/catalog/1876623.

1867-1873. *Oregon Internal Revenue Assessment Lists* **[Microfilm & Digital Capture]**, from originals at the National Archives, Seattle, WA. Filmed by the Genealogical Society of Utah, 1989, 2 rolls, FHL film #1639854 (Assessment lists, 1867-1870); and FHL film #1639855 (Assessment lists, 1871-1873). To access the digital images, see the online FHL catalog:
www.familysearch.org/search/catalog/521391.

1869-1950. *Washington Birth Records* **[Online Database]**, digitized and indexed at the FamilySearch.org website. Source: WA State Archives. Each index record includes: Name, Event type, Even date, Event place, Gender, Father's name, and Mother's name. The document image has more information. This database has 159,323 records. See https://familysearch.org/search/collection/1463676.

1869-1950. *Washington, King County Delayed Births* **[Online Database]**, indexed at Ancestry.com. Source: FamilySearch extractions from microfilm at the Family History Library, Salt Lake City, UT. Each index record includes a Name, Gender, Birthdate, Birthplace, Father, Mother, and FHL film number. This database has 438,830 records, see
www.ancestry.com/search/collections/60230/.

1870. *Washington Territory, 1870 Federal Census: Population Schedules* **[Microfilm & Digital Capture]**, filmed twice by the National Archives, 1962, 1968, series M593, 2 rolls, FHL Film #553182 (2nd Filming: Chehalis, Clallam, Clark, Cowlitz, Island, Jefferson, King, Kitsap, Klickitat, Lewis, Mason, Pacific, Pierce, Skamania, Snohomish, Stevens, Thurston, Wahkiakum, Walla Walla, Whatcom, and Yakima Counties). To access the digital images, see the online FHL catalog:
www.familysearch.org/search/catalog/698925.

1870s-1880. *King County Tax Rolls Prior to 1880: King County, Washington Territory* **[Printed Book]**, compiled by M.C. Rhodes, publ. 1986, Seattle, 77 pages, FHL book 979.777 R4r.

1870-1935. *Washington, Birth Records* **[Online Database]**, digitized and indexed at the Ancestry.com website. Source: WA State Archives. Each index record includes: Name, Date of birth, Gender, Birthplace, Father, and Mother. The digitized register image may have more information about a person, parents, etc. This database has 1,566,547 records:
http://search.ancestry.com/search/db.aspx?dbid=1209.

1871 Territorial Census, Jefferson County, Washington **[Printed Book]**, extracted by members of the Jefferson County Genealogical Society, Port Townsend, WA, 1990. FHL book 979.798 X2j.

1871 Lewis County, Washington Census **[Printed Book],** compiled by Darlene Stone and Linda Patton, published by Lewis County Genealogical Society, Chehalis, WA, 1979, 2001, 28 pages. FHL book 979.782 X2s.

1871-1887. See *Whatcom County, Washington, 1871-1885-1887 Territorial Auditor's Census* **[Printed Book],** compiled and published by Whatcom Genealogical Society, Bellingham, WA, ca1985, FHL book 979.773 X2w.

1871, 1883, 1885, 1887, 1889 Census, Klickitat County, Washington Territory **[Printed Book],** Indexed, abstracted, and compiled by Jack M. Lines, published by Yakima Valley Genealogical Society, Yakima, WA, 1983, 367 pages. FHL book 979.753 X2k.

1871-1887. *1871, 1883, 1885, and 1887 Cowlitz County, Washington Territory, Auditor's Census With Surname Index* **[Printed Book],** compiled and published by Lower Columbia Genealogical Society and Longview Public Library, Longview, WA, 1985. Includes territorial census years 1871, 1883, 1885, 1887. FHL book 979.788 X2c.

1871-1892. *Washington Territorial County Censuses (2003 Edition)* **[Microfilm],** from the original territorial censuses now located at one of five regional branches of the Washington State Archives. Filmed by the Archives' Imaging and Preservation Services, for the Washington State Library, Office of the Secretary of State, 2003, 35 rolls, State Library call number: 929.3797(roll #). There are county years unique to this series (not included in the 1987 microfilming). And, there are county years repeated in this series from the earlier one. The county/census years on each roll are as follows:
- Roll 1: Adams, 1885, 1887, 1889.
- Roll 2: Asotin, 1885, 1887, 1889.
- Roll 3: Clallam, 1871, 1883, 1885.
- Roll 4: Clarke, 1871, 1883, 1885, 1887.
- Roll 5: Columbia, 1883, 1885, 1887, 1889.
- Roll 6: Cowlitz, 1871, 1883, 1885, 1887.
- Roll 7: Douglas, 1885, 1887.
- Roll 8: Franklin, 1885, 1887.
- Roll 9: Garfield, 1883.
- Roll 10: Grays Harbor (nee Chehalis), 1871, 1885.
- Roll 11: Island, 1871, 1883, 1885, 1887.
- Roll 12: Jefferson, 1871, 1885, 1887.
- Roll 13: King, 1871, 1883, 1885, 1887.
- Roll 14: Kitsap, 1871, 1883, 1885, 1887, 1889.
- Roll 15: Kittitas, 1885, 1887, 1889.
- Roll 16: Klickitat, 1871, 1883, 1885, 1887, 1889, 1892.
- Roll 17: Lewis, 1871, 1883, 1885, 1887.
- Roll 18: Lincoln, 1885, 1887, 1889.
- Roll 19: Mason (nee Sawamish), 1871, 1883, 1885, 1887, 1889, 1892.
- Roll 20: Pacific, 1883, 1885, 1887.
- Roll 21: Pierce, 1871, 1885, 1887, A-K; 1889.
- Roll 21A: Pierce, L-Y 1889, recapitulation 1889.
- Roll 22: San Juan, 1885, 1887, 1889.
- Roll 23: Skagit, 1885, 1887.
- Roll 24: Skamania, 1871, 1885, 1887; & Snohomish, 1871.
- Roll 25: Snohomish, 1883, 1885, 1887, 1889.
- Roll 26: Spokane, 1885, 1887.
- Roll 27: Stevens, 1871, 1878, 1885, 1887, 1892.
- Roll 28: Thurston, 1871, 1873, 1877, 1878, 1881, 1883, 1885, 1887, 1889.
- Roll 29: Wahkiakum, 1885, 1887.
- Roll 30: Walla Walla, 1885, 1887, 1892.
- Roll 31: Whatcom, 1871, 1885, 1887, 1889.
- Roll 32: Whitman, 1883, 1885, 1887.
- Roll 32A: Whitman, 1889.
- Roll 33: Yakima, 1871, 1883, 1885, 1887.

- NOTE: Many of the above county censuses were digitized and indexed. Visit the search screen for the Washington Digital Archives, see **www.digitalarchives.wa.gov**.

1871-1899. See *Yakima County Territorial Census, 1871, 1883, 1885, 1887: Including Benton County (formed in 1905), Including 1871-1883 for Kittitas & Chelan Counties, (Kittitas County formed in 1883, Chelan in 1899)* **[Printed Book],** abstracted and compiled by Jack M. Lines, published by Yakima Valley Genealogical Society, Yakima, WA, 1983, 199 pages. FHL book 979.755 X2y. Also on microfiche, FHL fiche #6088898.

1876-1951. *Washington, Cowlitz County Civil Court Dockets* **[Online Database],** digitized at the FamilySearch.org website. Source: WA State Archives. This is an image only database with docket books from the Cowlitz County Superior Court and from the Territory of Washington, Second Judicial District Court. The dockets are a calendar of court actions in civil cases including primarily divorces and disputed estates. The page numbers refer to pages in the docket book, the file number range refers to the cases included in the docket book. Browse the images, organized by Record Type, Year, Volume/File number. This database has 14,203 records. See **https://familysearch.org/search/collection/2002293**.

1878-1879. *Pierce County, Washington Territory, Auditor's Census Extractions for 1878 and 1879* **[Printed Book],** by the Tacoma-Pierce County Genealogical Society, Tacoma, WA, 1997, 103 pages. FHL book 979.778 X2p.

1879 Territorial Census for King County, Washington [Printed Book], transcribed and indexed by M.C. Rhodes, publ. 1988, 110 pages, FHL book 979.777 X2r.

1879-1907. See *Declaration of Intention, 1890-1972; Petition for Naturalization, 1907-1950; Repatriations, 1940-1942; Application for Citizenship, 1879-1906; Indexes, 1890-1947 (U.S. District Court, Eastern District, Washington)* [Microfilm & Digital Capture], from the originals at the National Archives, Seattle, WA. The records all appear to be from courts in Yakima and Walla Walla. Filmed by the Genealogical Society of Utah, 1988, 26 rolls, beginning with FHL film #1536438 (Declarations of Intentions). To access the digital images, see the online FHL catalog:
www.familysearch.org/search/catalog/654919.

1880. *Washington Territory, 1880 Federal Census: Soundex and Population Schedules* [Microfilm & Digital Capture], filmed by the National Archives, c1970, 7 rolls, beginning with FHL Film #1255396 (Chehalis, Clallam, Clark, Columbia, Cowlitz, Island, Jefferson, and King Co-part). To access the digital images, see the online FHL catalog:
www.familysearch.org/search/catalog/676535.

1881 Census of Jefferson County, Washington County: With Index [Printed Book], by the Jefferson County Genealogical Society, Port Townsend, WA, 1997, 49 pages. FHL book 979.798 X2j. Also on microfiche, FHL fiche #6067417.

1881-2015. *Tacoma, Washington, Obituary Index* [Online Database], indexed at the Ancestry.com website. This database is also accessible at the Tacoma Public Library's website. Each index record includes: Name, Death date, Publication place, and a link to the Tacoma Public Library's website. This database has 431,407 records. See
http://search.ancestry.com/search/db.aspx?dbid=70049.

1882-1965. *Washington, Passenger and Crew Lists* [Online Database], digitized and indexed at the Ancestry.com website. Source: National Archives microfilm: *Selected Passenger and Crew Lists and Manifests*. the amount of information available for an individual in this database will vary according to the form used and the questions asked on it. The type of information that is generally contained in this database includes: Name, Age, Birth date, Birthplace, Gender, Ethnicity/nationality, Last residence, Vessel or airline name, Port of departure, Port of arrival, and Date of arrival. The manifest image may have more information about a person.
This database has 3,577,120 records. See
http://search.ancestry.com/search/db.aspx?dbid=8945.

"1883 Washington Territorial Census, Snohomish County" [Printed Article], published serially in *The Sounder*, (Sno-Isle Genealogical Society, Edmonds, WA), Vol. 6, No. 1 (1992) through Vol. 7, No. 2 (1993).

1883-1960. *Washington, Death Records* [Online Database], indexed at the Ancestry.com website. Source: WA State Archives. Each index record includes: Name, Gender, Birth date, Age at death, Death location, Father, Mother, and Record source: (WA State Archives). This database has 1,035,372 records. See
http://search.ancestry.com/search/db.aspx?dbid=1208.

"1885 Grant County Census" [Printed Article], in *Big Bend Register*, (Grant County Genealogical Society, Ephrata, WA), Vol. 19, No. 3 (Sep 1999).
- NOTE: Grant County was still part of Douglas Co WT in 1885. This name list was most likely extracted from the 1885 Douglas Co WT list based on known precincts, districts, etc. after Grant was created in 1909.

1885 Census of Jefferson County, Washington Territory: With Index [Printed Book], by the Jefferson County Genealogical Society, Port Townsend, WA, 1997. FHL book 979.798 X2j. Also on microfiche, FHL fiche #6067419.

1885. *Census, Chehalis (Grays Harbor) County, Washington Territory* [Printed Book], transcribed and indexed by Dolores Dunn Ackerman, published by Stack Enterprises, Bellingham, WA, 1986. Includes index. Chehalis County was renamed Grays Harbor County in 1915. FHL book 979.795 X2c. Also on microfilm, FHL film #1698053.

1885 Census of Skagit County, Washington Territory [Printed Book], compiled and published by Whatcom Genealogical Society, Bellingham, WA, 1986, 60 pages. Includes index. See FHL book 979.772 X2s. Also on microfiche, FHL fiche #6100573.

1885. *Skagit County, Washington 1885 Territorial Census* [Printed Book], transcribed by Hazel Rasar, published by Skagit Valley Genealogical Society, Conway, WA, 2001, 52 pages. From title page: "The information contained herein has been transcribed from the original census books located at the Skagit County Courthouse, Mount Vernon, Washington." Names are listed in alphabetical order. FHL book 979.772 X2s.

1885, 1887, 1889 Washington Territorial Censuses, Kittitas County [Printed Book], abstracted and published by the Yakima Valley Genealogical Society, Yakima, WA, 1982, 295 pages. Includes surname index. FHL book 979.757 X28k. See Yakima County for Kittitas before 1885.

1885 & 1887 Censuses, Franklin County, Washington Territory [Printed Book], transcribed by Dolores Dunn Ackerman, published by Stack Enterprises, Bellingham, WA, 1986. Includes index. FHL book 979.733 X2c.

1887. See *Census, Washington Territory, Pacific County* [Printed Book], abstracted and compiled by Dolores Dunn Ackerman, published by Stack Enterprises, Bellingham, WA 1989, 60 pages. FHL book 979.792 X2c. Also on microfilm, FHL film #1425057.

1887. *Census, Douglas County, Washington Territory* [Printed Book], transcribed by Dolores Dunn Ackerman, published by Stack Enterprises, Bellingham, WA 1986. Includes index. FHL book 979.731 X2c. Also on microfilm, FHL film #1697961.

"1887 Census Index, Spokane County, Washington Territory" [Printed Article], in *Eastern Washington Genealogical Society Bulletin* (Spokane, WA), beginning with Vol. 38, No. 2 (Jun 2001).

"1887 San Juan County, Washington Territorial Census" [Printed Article], name list published in *Whatcom Genealogical Society Bulletin* (Bellingham, WA), Vol. 6, No. 2 (Dec 1975) and Vol. 6, No. 3 (Mar 1976).

1887 Census, Walla Walla County, Washington Territory [Printed Book], compiled by Dolores Dunn Ackerman; indexed by Zelda Harlan Stout, published by Stack Enterprises, Bellingham, WA, 1986, FHL book 979.748 X2c.

1887. *Whitman County, Washington Territory, 1887 Military Census* [Printed Book], compiled and published by Twin Rivers Genealogy Society, Lewiston, Idaho, 1997, 57 pages. FHL book 979.739 M2wh. Also on microfilm, FHL film #1750865.

1887. *Skagit County, Washington Territorial Census* [Printed Book], transcribed by Hazel Rasar and Diane Partington, published by Skagit Valley Genealogical Society, 2001, 69 pages. FHL book 979.772 X2s.

"1887, 1889, 1898, and 1902 Censuses, Garfield County, Washington Territory" [Printed Article], in *Washington Heritage* (Orting, WA), Vol. 3, No. 3 (Fall 1986).

1887-1939. *McNeil Island, Washington, U.S. Penitentiary, Photos and Records of Prisoners Received* [Online Database], digitized and indexed at the FamilySearch.org website. Source: National Archives: Bureau of Prisons records. Each index record includes: Name, Birth date, Received date, Age when received, Facility (McNeil Island Penitentiary), Prison location (McNeil Island, Washington). The prison register image may have much more information about a prisoner. This database has 18,784 records. See http://search.ancestry.com/search/db.aspx?dbid=1253.

1888-2009. *Wenatchee, Washington, Obituary Index* [Online Database], indexed at the Ancestry.com website. This database is also accessible at the Wenatchee Area Genealogical Society's website. Each index record includes: Name, Publication place, and a link to the Wenatchee Area GS website. This database has 97,481 records. See http://search.ancestry.com/search/db.aspx?dbid=70155.

1889. *Census, Adams County, Washington Territory* [Printed Book], transcribed and indexed by Dolores Dunn Ackerman, published by Stack Enterprises, Bellingham, WA, 1986, 1 vol., various paging. FHL book 979.734 X2c. Also on microfilm, FHL film #1697959.

1889. *Census, Washington Territory, Asotin County* [Printed Book], transcribed and indexed by Dolores Dunn Ackerman, published by Stack Enterprises, Bellingham, WA, 1986, 35 pages. FHL book 979.742 X2a. Also on microfilm, FHL film #1698010.

1889. *Clallam County, Washington Census* [Microfilm & Digital Capture], from the originals at the Clallam County Genealogical Society Library in Port Angeles, WA. Filmed by the Genealogical Society of Utah, 1994, 1 roll, FHL film #1940023. To access the digital images, see the online FHL catalog: www.familysearch.org/search/catalog/696810.

Washington • 155

- See also, *Census of the Inhabitants in the County of Clallam, Territory of Washington, 1889: Washington State Centennial Project* [Printed Book], compiled and published by the Clallam County Genealogical Society, Port Angeles, WA, ca1989, 118 pages. FHL book 979.799 X2c.

1889 Columbia County, Washington Territory Census [Printed Book], compiled and published by Ruby Simonson McNeill, Spokane, WA, c1980, 117 pages. Includes index. FHL book 979.746 X29mc. Also on 2 microfiche, FHL fiche #6051025.

1889. *Island County, Washington Territory* [Printed Book], transcribed and indexed by Dolores Dunn Ackerman, published by Stack Enterprises, Bellingham, WA, 1987, FHL book 979.775 X2c. Also on microfilm, FHL film #1697959.

1889 Territorial Census, Jefferson County, Washington [Printed Book], extracted and compiled by Illma Mund and Harlean Hamilton of the Jefferson County Genealogical Society, Port Townsend, WA, 1989, FHL book 979.798 X2t.

1889. *Census, Washington Territory, Lincoln County* [Printed Book], transcribed and indexed by Dolores Dunn Ackerman, published by Stack Enterprises, Bellingham, WA 1987, 300 pages. FHL book 979.735 X2c. Also on microfiche, FHL fiche #6004530.

1889. *Census, Mason County, Washington Territory* [Printed Book], transcribed and indexed by Dolores Dunn Ackerman, published by Stack Enterprises, Bellingham, WA, 1986, FHL book 979.797 X2c. Also on microfilm, FHL film #1697959.

1889 Auditor's Census of Pierce County, Washington [Printed Book], by the Tacoma-Pierce County Genealogical Society, Tacoma, WA, 1987, 2 vols. Contents: vol. 1: A-L; vol. 2: M-Z. FHL book 979.778 X2a. v. 1-2.

1889. *Census, Washington Territory, Skagit County* [Printed Book], compiled by Dolores Dunn Ackerman, published by Stack Enterprises, Bellingham, WA, 1989, 153 pages. FHL book 979.772 X2c. Also on microfiche, FHL fiche #6002701.

1889. *Census, San Juan County, Washington Territory* [Printed Book], compiled by Dolores Dunn Ackerman; indexed by Zelda Harlan Stout, published by Stack Enterprises, Bellingham, WA, 1986. FHL book 979.774 X2c.

1889. *Skagit County, Washington, 1889: Census Taken Prior to Washington Territory Being Granted Statehood* [Printed Book], compiled and published by Skagit Valley Genealogical Society, Conway, WA, 2001, FHL book 979.772 X2s.

1889. *Census, Snohomish County, Washington Territory* [Printed Book], compiled by Dolores Dunn Ackerman; indexed by Zelda Harlan Stout, published by Stack Enterprises, Bellingham, WA, 1986. FHL book 979.771 X2c.

1889. *Spokane Falls City Directory* [Microfilm], from the original publ. R. L. Polk & Co., 1889. Filmed by the Eastern Washington Genealogical Society, 1982, 1 rolls, FHL film #1914912.

1889 Census, Thurston County, Washington Territory [Printed Book], compiled and published by Olympia Genealogical Society, 1987, 57 pages. FHL book 979.779 X2c.

1889 Territorial Auditor's Census, Whatcom County, Washington Territory [Printed Book], compiled and published by Whatcom Genealogical Society, Bellingham, WA, ca1985, 126 pages. FHL book 979.773 X2wg.

1889-1935. Tacoma (Washington) City Directories [Microfilm], from the originals filmed by Research Publications, Woodbridge, CT, 1995, 20 rolls, beginning with FHL film #2194099 (Tacoma City Directory, 1889, plus Orting, Puyallup, Steilacoom, Sumner, and Pierce County). For a complete list of roll numbers and contents of each roll, see the online FHL catalog page:
https://familysearch.org/search/catalog/602871.

1890 Census Substitute [Online Database], indexed at the Ancestry.com website. This is Ancestry's collection of city directories (and other name lists) from all over the U.S. for the time of the lost 1890 federal census. Included are Washington databases, *1888-1890 Seattle City Directories*; *1889-1893 Spokane City Directories*; and *Tacoma City Directories, 1889-1891*. Go to *View All Collections Included in this Search* for a complete list of databases, alphabetically by place (county, city, state, etc.), and year. See
http://search.ancestry.com/search/group/1890census#databases.

1890. *Ballard Census of 1890* [Printed Book], compiled and published by the Seattle Genealogical Society, 1989, 28 pages. From the intro, page 1:

"December 1890. Ordered taken by the Council of the Town of Ballard for the purpose of ascertaining whether said town had the requisite population to advance to a city of the third class. Total number of inhabitants – 1,636. Filed December 19th, 1890." Note: By 1905, Ballard was the second largest city in King County (after Seattle), but an inadequate water supply forced them to join Seattle via annexation in 1907. See FHL book 979.777/B1 X2b.

1890-1953. *Indexes to Naturalization Records of the U.S. District Court, Western District of Washington, Southern District (Tacoma)* **[Microfilm & Digital Capture],** from the original records at the National Archives, Seattle, WA. Filmed by the Genealogical Society of Utah, 1984, 2 rolls, FHL film #1433975-1433976. To access the digital images, see the online FHL catalog:
www.familysearch.org/search/catalog/331138.

1890-1957. *Washington, Seattle, Passenger Lists* **[Online Database],** digitized and indexed at the FamilySearch.org website. Source: National Archives microfilm series M1383. Each index record includes: Name, Event type, Event date, Event place, Gender, Age, Birthplace, Ship name, and Birth year. The manifest image may have more information about a person. This database has 709,727 records. See https://familysearch.org/search/collection/1916081.

1891 Census of Jefferson County, Washington Territory: With Index **[Printed Book],** by the Jefferson County Genealogical Society, Port Townsend, WA, 75 pages. FHL book 979.798 X2j.

1891-1907. *Washington, County Deaths* **[Online Database],** digitized and indexed at the FamilySearch.org website. Source: WA State Archives. This collection includes an index and images of deaths recorded at the county level before the state records were kept. The counties included in this collection are Wahkiakum; Grays Harbor, including the city of Aberdeen; Clark; Lewis and Mason. Each index record includes: Name, Even type, Event date, Even place, Gender, Age, Birth year, and Certificate number. The document image has more information about a person. This database has 2,734 records. See https://familysearch.org/search/collection/1389738.

1891-1904. *Washington, Pierce County, Index to Birth Returns* **[Digital Capture],** from the FHL's microfilm of the originals at the Washington State Archives, Puget Sound Region, Bellevue, WA. After digitizing, the microfilm was archived at the Granite Mountain Record Vault. Digitized by the Genealogical Society of Utah, 2010, from 4 rolls of microfilm, as follows:
- Index to birth returns, Book 3, 1891-1904, DGS #5033841.
- Pierce County births index, 1891-1904, DGS #033846.
- Index to birth returns, v. 2, 1905-1907. DGS #5033845.
- Birth register, 1891-1907, DGS #5033844.

To access the digital images, see the online FHL catalog:
https://familysearch.org/search/catalog/1920797.

1891-1907. *Washington, County Deaths* **[Online Database],** digitized and indexed at the Ancestry.com website. Source: FamilySearch extractions from county records on microfilm at the Family History Library, Salt Lake City, UT. This database is an index and images of deaths recorded at the county level before the state records were kept. The counties included in this collection: Clark and Grays Harbor (including the city of Aberdeen), Lewis, Mason, and Wahkiakum. Each index record includes: Name, Gender, Birth year, Death place, Age, and Digital folder number. The Death Return image has more information about the deceased person. This database has 6,823 records. See http://search.ancestry.com/search/db.aspx?dbid=60223.

1891-1938. *Washington, Pierce County Marriage Returns* **[Online Database],** digitized and indexed at FamilySearch.org. This database has 13,476 records, see www.familysearch.org/search/collection/1924073.

1891-1945. *Washington, Soldier Home Records* **[Online Database],** digitized at the FamilySearch.org website. Source: WA State Archives. This is an image only database with records from the State Soldiers' Home in Orting, WA; the State Soldiers' Colony in Orting, WA; and the Washington Veterans' Home in Retsil, WA (near Port Orchard). These records are arranged by file number. Includes application for admission to home, lists military service, unit, date and place of enlistment and date and place of discharge, cause of discharge, name, and address of nearest

relative or friend, and other miscellaneous information. Browse the images, organized by Soldier Home, then an alphabetical list solders. This database has 13,061 records. See
https://familysearch.org/search/collection/2143178.

1891-1950. *Washington, Pierce County Marriage Returns* **[Online Database],** digitized at the FamilySearch.org website. Source: WA State Archives. This is an image only database with marriage records from Pierce County. Browse the images, organized by Record Type, Date Range, and Volume. This database has 13,521 records. See
https://familysearch.org/search/collection/1924073.
- See also, *Pierce County, Washington, Marriage Returns, 1891-1950* **[Online Database],** digitized at the Ancestry.com website, see
http://search.ancestry.com/search/db.aspx?dbid=60231.

1891-1969. See *Washington State Birth & Death Registers & Returns; 1891-1907, 1938-1969* **[Microfilm & Digital Capture],** from the original records at the WA State Archives, Olympia, WA. Registers and returns were created by the county auditor in each county. Includes index in some volumes. Birth records list name of child, date of birth, place of birth, sex, race, status of birth, name of mother, her age and race, name of father, and his age, race, occupation, and state of birth, date of return and name of person returning information. Death records lists name of deceased, date of death, age, sex, race, marital status, place of death, cause of death, birthplace, residence, occupation, name of father and mother and their birthplace, and name of person giving death information. Also includes delayed birth certificates and justification. Filmed by the Washington State Archives, 76 rolls, beginning with FHL film #1307853 (Asotin County register of births, 1891-1907). To access the digital images, see the online FHL catalog:
www.familysearch.org/search/catalog/1216442.

1892. *Skagit County Washington: First Washington State Census* **[Printed Book],** transcribed by Mary Handstad, et al., published by Skagit Valley Genealogical Society, Conway, WA, 2001, 163 pages. FHL book 979.772 X2s.

"1892 King County Census, Washington Territory" [Printed Article], in the *Seattle Genealogical Society Bulletin*, (Seattle, WA), Vol. 41, No. 3 (Spring 1992).

"1892 Washington State Census, Pacific County" [Printed Article], name lists for various county locations, in *Sou'wester* (Pacific County Historical Society & Museum, South Bend, WA), beginning in Vol. 9, No. 2 (Summer 1974) intermittently through Vol. 16, No. 1 (Spring 1981).

"1892 Washington State Census, Pierce County, Washington" [Printed Article], name list published serially in *Researcher* (Tacoma-Pierce County Genealogical Society, Tacoma, WA), beginning with vol. 10, No. 2 (Nov 1978) through Vol. 13, No. 3 (Mar 1982).

1898-1953. *United Spanish War Veterans Death Announcements* **[Digital Capture],** from the Department of Washington and Alaska chapter. This organization includes veterans of the Spanish-American War, April 1898 to February 1899; the Philippine–American War, February 1899 to July 1902 and the Chinese Relief Expedition, 1900 to 1901. Digitized by FamilySearch International, 2009. To access the digital version, see the online FHL catalog:
www.familysearch.org/search/catalog/1614940.

1898-2008. *Washington, Cemetery Records* **[Digital Capture],** digitized by FamilySearch International, 2017, from original records at the Washington State Archives, Olympia, WA. The is a collection of cemetery registers, covering the period 1898-2008. An index is in the works and both the images and index will go online in the near future. In the meantime, to access the digital images, see the online FHL catalog:
www.familysearch.org/search/catalog/2841924.

1900. *Washington, 1900 Federal Census: Soundex and Population Schedules* **[Microfilm & Digital Capture],** filmed by the National Archives, c1970, 83 rolls, beginning with FHL film #1241741 (Adams, Asotin, and Chehalis Counties). To access the digital images, see the online FHL catalog:
www.familysearch.org/search/catalog/654978.

1904-1991. *Washington, Petitions for Naturalization* **[Online Database],** digitized and indexed at the Ancestry.com website. Source: National Archives microfilm: *Idaho, Oregon, and Washington Petitions for Naturalization, 1932-1991.* Each index record includes: Name, Birth date, Birthplace, Gender, Court

state: (Washington), Court District, Naturalization date, Naturalization record type, Petition number, and Residence place. The naturalization document image may have more information about a person. This database has 114,640 records. See
http://search.ancestry.com/search/db.aspx?dbid=2531.

1906-1927. *Washington, King County, School Census* [Digital Capture], digital images from the originals at the WA State Regional Archives, Bellevue, WA. Digital capture by the Genealogical Society of Utah, 2009, 37 databases, beginning with FHL DGS #5541886 (School census, box 1, Krummer, district No. 123 – district 50-80). To browse the images of all 37 databases, see the online FHL catalog page for this title. See
https://familysearch.org/search/catalog/1878789.

1907-1919. *Washington Births* [Online Database], indexed at the Ancestry.com website. Source: WA Dept of Health. Each index record includes: Name, Birth date, Location, Sex, Race, Father's name, Mother's name, and Image filename. This database has 386,910 records. See
http://search.ancestry.com/search/db.aspx?dbid=6493.
- See also, ***Washington, Birth Registers, 1907-1929 [Digital Capture],*** from the originals at the WA State Archives, Olympia, WA. Digitized by FamilySearch International, 2017, from 7 rolls of microfilm (now in storage), beginning with Register of Births, Ah thru Zoring, 1907-1909; ending with Register of Births, Quay thru Zermantz, 1920-1929. To access the digital images, see the online FHL catalog:
www.familysearch.org/search/catalog/2831244.

1907-1960. *Washington Death Certificates* [Online Database], indexed at the FamilySearch.org website. Source: WA Dept of Health. Each index record includes: Name, Event date, Event place, Gender, Age, Birth year, Marital status, Spouse's name, Father's name, and Mother's name. This database has 975,866 records. See
https://familysearch.org/search/collection/1454923.
- See also, ***Washington, Select Death Certificates, 1907-1960* [Online Database],** indexed at the Ancestry.com website. Source: WA Dept of Health microfilm indexed by FamilySearch. The index records vary in content for certain years, but usually have at least: Name, Gender, Age, Birth year, Death date, Death place, Father, Mother, FHL film number, and Reference File. This database has 2,995,462 records:
http://search.ancestry.com/search/db.aspx?dbid=60229.

- See also ***Death Certificates (Washington State), 1907-1960; Index to Death Certificates, 1907-1979* [Microfilm & Digital Capture],** 988 rolls of film, digitized by FamilySearch. To access the digital images, see the online FHL catalog:
www.familysearch.org/search/catalog/179363.
- See also, ***Washington, Death Records, 1907-1979* [Digital Capture],** from the original records at the WA State Archives, Olympia, WA. Digitized by FamilySearch, 2017. To access the digital images, see the online FHL catalog:
www.familysearch.org/search/catalog/2831245.

1909-1914. *Directories of Stevens, Pend Oreille, and Ferry Counties, Washington* [Microfilm], by R. L. Polk and Co., filmed by Primary Source Microfilm, Woodbridge, CT, ca1997, 1 roll, FHL film #2310409 (includes Pend Oreille County for 1909-1910; 1911-1912; and 1913-1914).

1910. *Washington, 1910 Federal Census: Population Schedules* [Microfilm & Digital Capture], filmed by the National Archives, c1970, 23 rolls, beginning with FHL film #1375666 (Adams, Asotin, Benton, and Chehalis Counties). To access the digital images, see the online FHL catalog:
www.familysearch.org/search/catalog/646884.

1917-1918. *Washington, World War I Selective Service System Draft Registration Cards* [Microfilm & Digital Capture]. From the National Archives info pamphlet: "During World War I there were three registrations. The first, on June 5, 1917, was for all men between the ages of 21 and 31. The second, on June 5, 1918, registered those who attained age 21 after June 5, 1917. (A supplemental registration was held on August 24, 1918 for those becoming 21 years old after June 5, 1918. This was included in the second registration). The third registration was held on September 12, 1918 for men age 18 through 45." Filmed by the National Archives, 1988, 62 rolls, beginning with FHL film #1991532 (Adams and Asotin Counties, A-Z; Bellingham City, A-G). To access the digital images, see the online FHL catalog:
www.familysearch.org/search/catalog/754901.
- See also, ***Washington, World War I American Expeditionary Forces, Deaths, 1917-1919* [Digital Capture],** from the originals of the U.S. Adjutant General's Office, now at the National Archives. Digitized by FamilySearch International, 2018. To access the digital images, see the online FHL catalog:
www.familysearch.org/search/catalog/3023957.

- See also, ***Washington, World War I Veteran's Compensation Fund Application Records, 1921-1925 [Digital Capture],*** digitized by FamilySearch International, 2010, from the originals at the Washington State Archives, Olympia, WA. This database contains applications for the World War I "Bonus," which was officially called the "World War I Adjusted Compensation Act." The act awarded veterans additional pay, based on time served during 1917-1919 ($1.00 per day of service; $1.25 for service overseas, up to $500.00 maximum). The state form (Application for Equalized Compensation – State of Washington), has details about the applying veteran, including Name, Address, Place of birth, Date of birth, Resident of Washington in years and months, present occupation, business address, Name and address of employer; Name of nearest relative and relationship, Name and address of veteran's father and mother at the time of enlistment, and other details. To access the digital images, see the online FHL catalog:
www.familysearch.org/search/catalog/1878898.

1920. ***Washington, 1900 Federal Census: Soundex and Population Schedules*** **[Microfilm & Digital Capture],** filmed by the National Archives, c1970, 145 rolls, beginning with FHL film #1821920 (Adams, Benton, Garfield, Asotin, Cowlitz, and Franklin Counties). To access the digital images, see the online FHL catalog:
www.familysearch.org/search/catalog/558333.

1926-1932. ***Washington, Pierce County, Census Records*** **[Digital Capture],** from the FHL's microfilm of the originals at the Washington State Archives, Puget Sound Region, Bellevue, WA. After digitizing, the microfilm was archived at the Granite Mountain Record Vault. Digital capture by the Genealogical Society of Utah, 2010, from 4 rolls of microfilm, as follows:
- Census Records, Box 1, Folders 1-10, 1926-1932, DGS #5715266.
- Census Records, Box 1, Folders 11-31, 1926-1932, DGS #5715267.
- Census Records, Box 2, Folders 33-43, 1926-1932, . DGS #5715268.
- Census Records, Box 2, Folders 47-120, DGS #5715269.

To access the digital images, see the online FHL catalog: https://familysearch.org/search/catalog/1920804.

1930. ***Washington, 1930 Federal Census: Population Schedules*** **[Microfilm & Digital Capture],** filmed by the National Archives, c1970, 42 rolls, beginning with FHL film #2342218 (Adams, Asotin, Benton, and Chelan Counties). To access the digital images, see the online FHL catalog:
www.familysearch.org/search/catalog/1037534.

1940. ***Washington, Federal Census: Population Schedules*** **[Digital Capture],** digitized images from the microfilm of original records held by the Bureau of the Census in the 1940s. After microfilming, Congress allowed the Census Bureau to destroy the originals to free up space for WWII-related files. Digitizing of the 1940 census schedules microfilm images was done for the National Archives and made public on April 2, 2012. To access the digital images, see the online FHL catalog: www.familysearch.org/search/catalog/2057797.

1940 Federal Census, Finding Aids **[Online Database].** The National Archives prepared a special website online with a detailed description of the 1940 federal census. Included at the site are descriptions of location finding aids, such as Enumeration District Maps, Geographic Descriptions of Census Enumeration Districts, and a list of 1940 City Directories available at the National Archives. The finding aids are all linked to other National Archives sites. The National Archives website also has a link to 1940 Search Engines using Stephen P. Morse's "One-Step" system for finding a 1940 E.D. or street address conversion. See
www.archives.gov/research/census/1940/general-info.html#questions.

1940-1947. ***Washington, World War II Draft Registration Cards*** **[Digital Capture],** from the originals at the National Personnel Center, St. Louis, MO. Digitized by FamilySearch International. The card images are organized in general alphabetical order. Use the list of Digital File Folders to find an alpha group of interest. To access the digital images, see the online FHL catalog:
www.familysearch.org/search/catalog/4114751.

- See also, ***Washington, Military Records: World War II 4th Draft Registration Cards, 1942*** **[Digital Capture],** from the original records at the National Personnel Center, St. Louis, MO. These cards represent older men, ages 45 to 65 in April 1942, that were registered for the draft. They had birth dates between

28 Apr 1877 and 16 Feb 1892. Includes name of individual, date and place of birth, address, age, telephone number, employer's name and address, name and address of person who would know where the individual can be located, signature, and physical description. To access the digital images, see the online FHL catalog:
www.familysearch.org/search/catalog/2425782.

1940-1959. *Washington, Marriage Records (Licenses)* **[Digital Capture],** from the originals at the WA State Archives, Olympia, WA. The forms all start with "To any person legally authorized to solemnize marriage: Greetings…" Minimum information: the name of male and female with their place of residence, and the date. Digitized by FamilySearch International, 2012. To access the digital images, see the online FHL catalog: **www.familysearch.org/search/catalog/2109636.**

1940-2017. *Washington, Death Index* **[Online Database],** indexed at the Ancestry.com website. Source: WA Dept of Health. Each index record includes: Name, Gender, Age, Birth year, Death date, Death place, and Certificate number. Later records include the deceased's social security number. A copy of a death certificate can be ordered from a link at the record site. This database has 5,357,095 records. See
http://search.ancestry.com/search/db.aspx?dbid=6716.

1941-1942. *Washington, King County Delayed Births* **[Online Database],** indexed at the Ancestry.com website. Source: FamilySearch extractions from records on microfilm at the Family History Library, Salt Lake City, UT. Each index record includes: Name, Gender, Birth date, Birthplace, Father's name, Mother's name, Reference ID, and FHL film number. The auto-linked FamilySearch image of the birth certificate will give more information. This database has 16,855 records. See
http://search.ancestry.com/search/db.aspx?dbid=60230.
- See also, *Washington, Various Counties, Birth Records, 1942-1943* **[Digital Capture],** from records of the Dept. of Health, now WA State Archives, Olympia, WA. Digitized by FamilySearch International, 2013, from 1 roll of microfilm (now in storage), titled, *Delayed Birth Certificates, 1942-1943.* To access the digital images, see the FHL catalog: **www.familysearch.org/search/catalog/2204322.**

1947-1954. *Washington, Seattle, Passenger and Crew Lists of Airplanes* **[Online Database],** digitized and indexed at the FamilySearch.org website. Source: National Archives microfilm series M1386. Each index record includes: Name, Event type, Event date, Event place, Gender, and Ship/airline. The manifest image may have more information about a person. This database has 43,835 records. See
https://familysearch.org/search/collection/2299373.

1947-1957. *Seattle and Tacoma, Washington, Passenger and Crew Lists of Airplane Departures* **[Online Database],** digitized and indexed at the Ancestry.com website. Source: National Archives microfilm series A3376. Each index record includes: Name, Gender, Age, Birth year, Birthplace, Arrival port, Departure port, and Ship/airline. The manifest image may have more information about a person. This database has 134,871 records. See
http://search.ancestry.com/search/db.aspx?dbid=2250.

1959-1968. See *Puyallup (Pierce County, Wash.) City Directory: Including Graham, North Puyallup, Orting, Sumner and Rurals, Also the Yellow Pages With a Special Advertising Sections and a Complete Classified List* **[Printed Book],** publ. R. L. Polk & Co., Los Angeles, CA. The Family History Library has copies of the 1959, 1961, 1962, and 1968 directories. See FHL book 979.778 E4pp 1959-1968. For a digital version of the directories, click on the year at the FHL catalog page for this title. See
https://familysearch.org/search/catalog/86784.

1965-2014. *Washington, Death Index* **[Online Database],** indexed at FamilySearch.org. Source: WA Dept. of Health index at the WA State Archives. The index includes the decedent's Name, Date of death, Place of death, Place of Residence, Sex, Age, and Year of Birth. This database has 1,891,273 records, see **www.familysearch.org/search/collection/2761117.**

1969-2014. *Washington, Marriage Index* **[Online Database],** indexed at FamilySearch.org. Source: WA Dept. of Health index at the WA State Archives. Each index record includes Name, Spouse's name, Event type, Event date, Event place, and Marriage license place. This database has 3,988,953 records, see **www.familysearch.org/search/collection/2761120.**

1969-2017. *Washington, Divorce Index* **[Online Database],** indexed at FamilySearch.org. Source: WA Dept. of Health index at the WA State Archives. The index includes the names of both parties, date of divorce, and in some records, number of minor children. This database has 2,606,871 records, see www.familysearch.org/search/collection/2759158.

1985-Current. See *Washington Recent Newspaper Obituaries* **[Online Database],** digitized and indexed newspaper obituaries at the GenealogyBank website, including newspapers for Aberdeen, Anacortes, Arlington, Auburn, Bainbridge Island, Bellevue, Bellingham, Bonney Lake, Bothell, Kenmore, Bremerton, Brewster, Camas, Cashmere, Centralia, Chelan, Colville, Coupeville, Deer Park, Eastsound, Edmonds, Ellensburg, Enumclaw, Everett, Federal Way, Forks, Friday Harbor, Gig Harbor, Issaquah, Kennewick, Kent, Kingston, Kirkland, Leavenworth, Long Beach, Longview, Lopez Island, Lynnwood, Maple Valley/Covington, Marysville, Mercer Island, Montesano, Moses Lake, Mount Vernon, Mountlake Terrace, Naval Base Kitsap, Ocean Shores, Olympia, Oroville, Port Angeles, Port Orchard, Poulsbo, Puyallup, Quincy, Redmond Renton, Sammamish, Seattle, Sequim, Silverdale, Snoqualmie, Spokane, Stanwood, Tacoma, Tukwila, Vancouver, Vashon, Wenatchee, Westport, Whidbey Island Naval Base, and Yakima. See www.genealogybank.com/explore/obituaries/all/usa/washington.

1986-2010. *Kitsap County, Washington, Marriage Index* **[Online Database],** indexed at the Ancestry.com website. This database is also accessible at the Kitsap County Auditor's website. Each index record includes: Name, Spouse, Marriage date, Marriage place, and a link to the Kitsap County Auditor's website. This database has 134,792 records: http://search.ancestry.com/search/db.aspx?dbid=70354.

162 • *Census Substitutes & State Census Records*

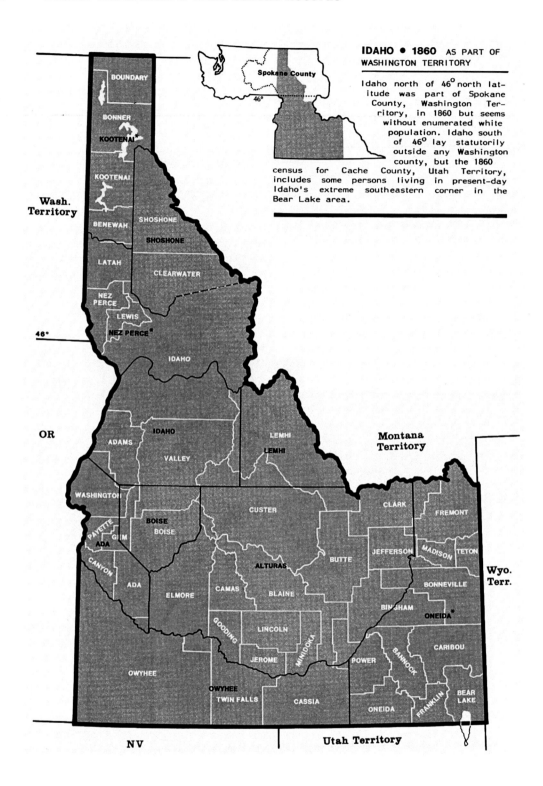

Idaho Territory in 1870. The modern footprint of Idaho is shown in the 1860 inset map, when present-day Idaho was entirely within the area of Washington Territory. Created in 1863, the original Idaho Territory included all of present-day Idaho and Montana, and most of Wyoming until Montana Territory was created in 1864, and Wyoming Territory in 1868. The main map above is for 1870, as the territory appeared at the time of Idaho's first federal census. Idaho's 44 current counties are in white, the 1870 counties are in black. **Map Source:** Page 93, **Map Guide to the U.S. Federal Censuses, 1790-1920**, by William Thorndale and William Dollarhide.

Idaho
Censuses & Substitute Name Lists

Historical Timeline for Idaho, 1670-1890

1670. The Hudson's Bay Company was formed in London, with the intent of establishing fur trading posts in North America. The company was granted the right to exploit huge tracts of land by the British Crown and became the dominate force in the settlement of British North America from the Atlantic to the Pacific. The first governor of the Hudson's Bay Company was Prince Rupert of the Rhine, a nephew of Charles I, and the territory of the Hudson's Bay Company was first known as "Rupert's Land." Manned mostly by Scots-Canadians, the company extended its influence from the drainage of Hudson's Bay to all of western Canada and parts of southeast Alaska. At one time, the company's claims extended into the present areas of Minnesota, North Dakota, Montana, Idaho, Washington, and Oregon.

1784. The North West Fur Company was formed in Montreal. It became a rival of the Hudson's Bay Company for dominance of the fur trade in British North America. Although both companies were British-owned, the North West Fur Company was manned mostly be French-Canadians, who fought furiously for fur trading rights, attacking Hudson's Bay forts, burning their ships, etc., until the two companies were forced to end their differences by the British Crown.

1803. Captains Meriwether Lewis and William Clark led the Corps of Discovery, the first expedition to explore the lands west of the Mississippi River. Their trek to the Pacific was mostly via river routes, beginning at St. Louis on the Mississippi, up the Missouri River to its source in Montana, then by foot and horseback across the mountains, picking up Idaho's Clearwater River, to the Snake River of Idaho, Oregon, and Washington, and finally, the Columbia River all the way to its mouth at present Astoria, Oregon.

1805. August. The first whites to see present-day Idaho, the Lewis and Clark expedition left the Missouri Breaks in present-day Montana on horseback and crossed the Continental Divide at what is now called Lemhi Pass, moving into present-day Idaho. At that point they had entered into the land of the Shoshone Indians, the same tribe from which their guide, Sacajawea, was native.

1807. British fur-trader and map-maker David Thompson, former employee of the Hudson's Bay Company, now with the North West Fur Company, began looking for routes from the Rocky Mountains to the Pacific Ocean. He established fur trading opportunities with any Indian tribes he encountered, and charted detailed maps of the Columbia River. From 1807 to 1809, Thompson established the first trading post in present Montana at Kootenai Falls, near Libby; the first in present Idaho, Kullyspell House, on Pend Oreille Lake; and the first trading post in present Washington, now Bonner's Ferry, on the Columbia River.

1808. John Jacob Astor formed the American Fur Company to work alongside the North West Fur Company in the northern Plains. The two companies supported each other in the pursuit of furs.

1810. Fort Henry, the first American fur post west of the Rocky Mountains was established near present St. Anthony, Idaho. That same year, John Jacob Astor formed the Pacific Fur Company, intent on establishing a fur trade west of the Rockies.

1811. March. American fur-traders built Fort Astoria near the mouth of the Columbia River as part of Astor's Pacific Fur Company. Manned by two

163

shiploads of men and supplies, it was the first American settlement on the Pacific Coast of North America. Meanwhile, an expedition of the Pacific Fur Company led by Astor's second-in-command, Wilson P. Hunt, headed overland from St. Louis to meet up with the Astoria crew, hoping to arrive there at the same time as Astor's ships. They were called the "Overland Astorians." En route from St. Louis to Astoria, they discovered the Boise Valley, and explored the Snake River Valley on their way to the Columbia River. The Astorians had hard times in present Idaho and decided to divide into two groups, one led by Wilson Hunt, the other led by Donald MacKenzie, a Scotsman-Canadian Astor had hired away from the North West Fur Company in 1810. MacKenzie's group eventually found the Salmon River leading to the Clearwater, Snake, and Columbia rivers. They marked a trail for Hunt to follow. MacKenzie also made note of a location for a fur trading post on the Clearwater River and vowed to return to Idaho.

1812. In January, MacKenzie's group of Astorians arrived at Fort Astoria. A month later, Wilson Hunt's group arrived. On the Columbia, Wilson's group had joined with David Thompson, who had just finished his maps of the river. Thompson then followed Hunt's party for the remainder of their trip to Fort Astoria. Soon after arriving, Thompson set up a rival fur trading post next door to Fort Astoria. Although competitors, the two companies supported each other and often sent teams of trappers out together to find and retrieve the animal hides they both coveted.
- Later in 1812, Donald MacKenzie, formerly of the North West Fur Company, now working for Astor's Pacific Fur Company, accompanied his friend David Thompson back to the Clearwater River near present-day Lewiston, Idaho, where they established a new trading fort for the Pacific Fur Company called MacKenzie's Post.

1813. After war was declared in 1812, British warships blockaded Fort Astoria. The Astorians decided it was better to get out before shots were fired, and the entire Fort Astoria operation was given to the British-owned North West Fur Company, who renamed it Fort George. The North West Fur Company also took over all of Astor's fur trading posts, including MacKenzie's Post in Idaho. All of the Astorians, including MacKenzie, then returned overland to St. Louis, and followed a more southern route through present-day Wyoming than was used to get there. In doing so, the returning Astorians became the first to cross South Pass, the Wyoming route through the Rocky Mountains that would be followed by thousands of Oregon Trail travelers.

1814. The Treaty of Ghent officially ended the War of 1812. In 1814, John Jacob Astor used the treaty's provision for returning all occupied lands by the British back to the Americans and took possession of Fort Astoria again. Although the fort changed hands, the North West Fur Company continued to use it for their operations for several more years.

1818. Anglo-American Convention. The United States and Great Britain agreed to a joint occupation of the Oregon Country/Columbia District. Both parties accepted the area as extending from the Continental Divide to the Pacific Ocean, and from about Latitude 54° in present British Columbia, to the Boundary Mountains (now Siskiyou Mountains) at about Latitude 42°). In 1827 a provision was added to the treaty that allowed either party to invoke a conclusion of ownership, by giving 12 months' notice to the other. Notice was not given until 1845, when President James K. Polk sought resolution, leading to a new treaty in 1846.
- Also in the 1818 treaty, Britain and the U.S. agreed to the 49th parallel as the international boundary from the Lake of the Woods (now Minnesota) to the Continental Divide.

1821. The Hudson's Bay Company and the North West Fur Company merged, retaining the name Hudson's Bay. The company now had a monopoly on fur trading in British North America. Their presence continued in the Oregon Country as well, including their fur trading operations in present-day Montana, Idaho, Oregon, and Washington. Today, the Hudson's Bay Company continues: "Shop the Bay!" is the slogan of Canada's largest retailer.

1822. The Rocky Mountain Fur Company was formed by General William Ashley. He placed an ad in a St. Louis newspaper to recruit able-bodied men for his new fur-trading enterprise. There was no shortage of willing young men. Ashley did not build a chain of forts to manage his fur trading operation. Instead, he sent his men out alone and planned to meet them all at a central place a year later. At the predetermined time, Ashley loaded up his wagons with supplies and headed out to meet his crew of mountain men.

1825. The British-owned Hudson's Bay Company established Fort Vancouver as a center for their fur trading operations on the Pacific Coast. Fort Vancouver was located about 100 miles upriver from Fort Astoria, the center for the American-owned Pacific Fur Company. The Columbia River now became a highway to Canada, leading to routes for the fur trade that extended to the Great Lakes and beyond.
– William Ashley's Rocky Mountain Fur Company wagons were the first vehicles to penetrate into the west, blazing a wagon road for the Oregon Trail settlers who would follow years later. When Ashley finally reached his men each year, it was cause for celebration – a wild party they called "the rendezvous." Many of the rendezvous took place in present-day Idaho, usually along the Snake River Valley. In 1826, William Ashley retired a wealthy man, and began a life of politics. He sold his interest in the Rocky Mountain Fur Company to his employees.

1830. Jedediah Smith and William Sublette, now partners in the successor to William Ashley's trading company, led the first wagon train across the Rocky Mountains at South Pass and on to the Upper Wind River. The 500-mile journey through Indian country took about six weeks and proved that even heavily loaded wagons and livestock – the prerequisites for settlement – could travel overland to the Pacific.

1834. Fort Hall was established as a fur trading post on the Snake River in present-day southeastern Idaho by Nathaniel Jarvis Wyeth, a Boston entrepreneur. Three years later, Wyeth gave up and sold the fort to the Hudson's Bay Company. In the 1840s and 1850s, Fort Hall became the most important rest and re-supply point for all Oregon Trail wagon trains.
- Also in 1834, Fort Boise was established by the Hudson's Bay Company, at the mouth of the Boise River.

1836. Dr. Marcus Whitman and his wife Narcissa and also Rev. Henry H. Spalding and his wife Eliza crossed the mountains into the Oregon Country. Their travel route would become known as the Oregon Trail and would be used by thousands of future settlers. Narcissa and Eliza were the first white women to make that trip. Dr. Whiman immediately set up a Protestant Mission near the junction of the Columbia and Snake Rivers.

- Also in 1836, Rev. Henry H. Spalding established an Indian mission near present Lapwai, Idaho, where he printed Idaho's first book, established Idaho's first school, developed Idaho's first irrigation system, and grew Idaho's first potatoes. The Spauldings stayed in Idaho until 1847, leaving after the massacre of Dr. Whiman, Narcissa, and 12 members of the Whitman mission at Wailatpu (near present Walla Walla, WA).

1841. The Western Emigration Society, a group of about 70 settlers bound for California and the Oregon Country set off on the Oregon Trail, beginning at Independence, Missouri. This was the first organized wagon train to head for California and Oregon. It is usually called the "Bartleson-Bidwell party" named for the two leaders. The group included a small party of Jesuit Missionaries led by Fr. Pierre-Jean de Smet, who left the main group at Soda Springs (now ID) and headed to the Oregon Country. Bartleson & Bidwell continued with the main body via the California Trail to the Sacramento Valley.

1843. The Great Migration begins. A wagon train with over 120 wagons, a large herd of livestock, and nearly 1,000 pioneers headed out on the Oregon Trail. Once they reached Fort Hall (now ID), they were guided by Dr. Marcus Whitman, returning to his mission on the Snake River. For an online narrative and biographies of pioneers of the 1843 Wagon Train, see **www.oregonpioneers.com/1843.htm**.

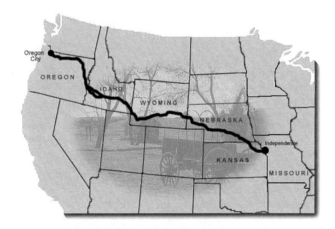

The Oregon Trail. The 2,000-mile-long wagon road began at Independence, Missouri and ended at Oregon City, Oregon. Visit the Oregon National Historic Trail website for details, photos, and maps, see **www.nps.gov/oreg/planyourvisit/maps.htm**.

1843. May 2nd, a group of 50 Americans and 52 French Canadians met in the Willamette Valley to take a vote to determine who should govern the Oregon Country. A vote of 52-50 favored aligning Oregon as American territory (two Canadians switched their votes). The group then proceeded to form a provisional territorial government with Champoeg as its capital, established on July 5, 1843. The Provisional Territory of Oregon elected a governor, established courts, created several counties, and functioned with the consent of the local population. In 1843, the Provisional Territory of Oregon was not part of the U.S., but its organization was a key element in the resolution of the U.S. - British Joint Occupation in favor of the U.S.

1844-1848. In the 1844 presidential election, James K. Polk, Democrat, defeated Henry Clay, Whig, to become President of the United States. The two burning political issues of the day were the annexation of Texas and the acquisition of the Oregon Country. James K. Polk, as the "Manifest Destiny" candidate, was elected with campaign slogans of *Annex Texas!* and *Fifty-four Forty or fight!* In 1845, Texas was annexed to the U.S. and war with Mexico began soon after. But in 1846, Polk settled for the 49th parallel as the northern boundary of the Oregon Country. The treaty of 1846 brought the Provisional Oregon Territory into the United States. And, in 1848, President Polk signed a bill that created an official U.S. Oregon Territory. The new territory included all of present-day Oregon, Washington, and Idaho, plus lands in Montana and Wyoming west of the Continental Divide.

✓ **NOTE:** The presidential campaign slogans for James K. Polk were somewhat different from what really took place. His first slogan should have been, *"Annex Texas and Fight!"* and his second should have been *"Fifty-four Forty or Whatever!"* In fact, the reason for Polk's willingness to settle the Oregon Country question with the 49th parallel was simply that he did not want to go to war with Mexico and Britain at the same time.

1849. Over 30,000 emigrants who joined the California gold rush came over the Oregon Trail into Idaho to Fort Hall, and from there to the California Trail. The following year, it is estimated that as many as 55,000 made the trip. In 1849, a U.S. Military post, Cantonment Loring, was established near present Fort Hall, Idaho.

1850 Federal Census. June 1st. The first federal census was taken in Oregon Territory, which included the area of present-day Oregon, Washington, and Idaho; and Montana and Wyoming areas west of the Continental Divide. The population was revealed as 12,093 people. No population was recorded in the present-day Idaho, Montana, or Wyoming areas.

1852. In this year, it was estimated that over 67,000 people traveled the Oregon Trail across Wyoming's South Pass into Idaho, and on to Oregon or California. Recommended reading: *Route of the Oregon Trail in Idaho: From Thomas Fork Valley at the Wyoming State Line Westward to Fort Boise at the Oregon State Line,* published by the Idaho Department of Highways and Idaho Historical Society, Boise, ID, 1963, 32 pages, FHL book 979.6 E76. To access the digital version of this book, see the online FHL catalog: **www.familysearch.org/search/catalog/199741**.

1853. Washington Territory was created by Congress, taken from the Oregon Territory area. The original Oregon Territory was divided on a line following the Columbia River to the point of intersection with Latitude 46° North, then following that parallel to the Continental Divide. Thus, Washington Territory included the northern panhandle of present-day Idaho, while the southern portion of Idaho remained in Oregon Territory.

1858. Washington Territory created Spokane County, extending from the Columbia River to the Continental Divide, from Latitude 46° North to 49° North. The present-day panhandle of Idaho was included in the first Spokane County.

1859. Oregon became a state with its present boundaries. The eastern remnant of Oregon Territory to the Continental Divide was given to Washington Territory, which now included all of present-day Idaho.

1860. April. The town of Franklin was established by a few Mormon families sent to the Cache Valley by Brigham Young. They were included in the 1860 Utah Territory Federal Census, but in 1872, a new survey of the boundary between Utah and Idaho Territories revealed that Franklin was actually in Idaho.

1860 Federal Census. June 1st. The census returns reported "no population" for the area of Spokane County, Washington Territory (including the panhandle of present Idaho). The non-county area of Washington Territory south of Latitude 46° also showed no population. See the 1860 Inset Map on page 162.

1860-1863. Birth of Idaho. A few weeks after the federal census enumerators had returned their reports of "no population," gold was discovered on the Clearwater River in late 1860. After the demise of MacKenzie's Post, the same location gave birth to the gold rush town of Lewiston, established near the junction of the Clearwater and Snake Rivers in 1861. Lewiston became the entry point to Idaho's gold rush. Lewiston also became (and still is) the most inland American seaport of the Pacific Ocean. More gold was discovered on the Salmon River in 1861, and the Boise River Basin in 1862; and gold and silver were found in the Owyhee River country in 1863.

Most of the settlements are only ghost towns now, but the many settlers who poured in during the gold rush in just three years increased the population of the Idaho areas dramatically, in fact, much larger than the rest of Washington Territory.

In late 1862, the mining communities began proposing plans for the creation of a new territory, at first suggesting Walla Walla as its capital. But the main Washington Territory population around Puget Sound did not want to lose its farming communities in the Columbia Basin area. The Olympia-based Puget Sounders were already outnumbered, and with the increased voting population in the Idaho mining areas, they would soon be outnumbered in the territorial legislature as well. In order to preserve as much of Washington Territory as possible, they proposed a compromise Idaho Territory division line beginning near Lewiston on the Snake River The compromise plan was passed in Congress in February 1863.

1860-1863 Washington Territory Counties Created in Gold Rush Idaho: As a direct result of the gold rush settlements, five counties were created in Idaho areas by Washington Territory between 1860 and 1863:
- **Missoula County,** December 1860, taken from Spokane Co WT.
- **Shoshone County**, January 1861, taken from Spokane Co WT.
- **Idaho County**, December 1861, taken from Shoshone Co WT.
- **Nez Perce County**, December 1861, taken from Missoula Co WT.
- **Boise County**, January 1863, taken from Idaho Co WT .

The first Idaho Territory, March 1863.

1863. March 4th. President Lincoln signed into law an act creating **Idaho Territory**. The first territorial capital was at Lewiston, and the original area included all of present-day Idaho and Montana, and most of Wyoming. The recent Washington Territory counties of Boise, Idaho, Missoula, Nez Perce, and Shoshone became the first Idaho Territory counties. In addition, large non-county areas extended across the mountainous expanse to the Dakota Territory line.

Idaho Territory (with a panhandle) after the creation of Montana Territory, and the expansion of Dakota Territory in 1864.

1864. The Panhandle. Right after the formation of Idaho Territory in 1863, Congress realized they had created an ungovernable political mammoth. The first Idaho Territory was larger than Texas. In the congressional hearings for creating a new Montana Territory from oversized Idaho, Congress began discussing a rearrangement of Washington Territory back to its 1853 boundaries (from the Pacific to the Continental Divide). But that proposal was overruled by a new plan to balance the Idaho territorial population by leaving a northern panhandle in Idaho Territory. It was no coincidence that the proposed panhandle happened to have a greater number of non-Mormons in its northern mining communities than there were Mormons in the southern Snake River Valley farming communities. The Idaho Panhandle was created when Montana Territory was formed in 1864, but at the same time, a large part of the southern part of Idaho Territory was given to Dakota Territory.

1865. The territorial capital was moved from Lewiston to Boise.

1868. Congress created Wyoming Territory, reducing Idaho Territory to its present size and shape.

1890. July 3rd. Idaho became the 43rd state, with Boise as the state capital. The population was 88,548 people.

Online Indexes Accessible at the Idaho Historical Society Website

In Idaho, the State Museum, State Library and State Archives are part of the Idaho Historical Society (IHS), located at the Idaho History Center in Boise. There are a number of extremely useful IHS indexes, separate from the State Library or the State Archives websites. See the **Search Our Collections** webpage: https://history.idaho.gov/searchable-indexes.

This web page describes the following databases, shown with underlined webpages (repeated in the bibliography):

Biographical Index. The Idaho Biographical Index (IBI) is an index of persons named in state, county and community histories, regional periodicals, and selected newspaper articles from around the state and throughout its history.

Census 1890: Reconstructed Idaho Information. Most of the 1890 US Federal Census was destroyed by fire in 1921. The Idaho State Historical Society created the Reconstructed 1890 Idaho Census with the goal to fill that gap for researchers.

Census Schedules: 1870 and 1880 Agricultural, Industrial, Mortality. Index of "non-population" schedules including 1870 and 1880 agricultural, industrial, mortality, and other schedules compiled between 1850 and 1910.

Civil War Veterans. Over two thousand Civil War veterans who lived or died in Idaho have been identified from a variety of records. Records are indexed alphabetically by surname and wherever possible dates of births and deaths, the states from which they served, and the Idaho counties where they resided are included.

Inmate Catalog. This chronological and indexed catalog provides a comprehensive list of Idaho territorial and state penitentiary prisoners: men, women, and children, between the years 1864 and 1947.

Naturalization Records. In Idaho, beginning in 1863, the process of naturalization generally began when the applicant filed a declaration of intention with the local court of record (federal, state, or local), followed by a naturalization petition, and ended when a certificate or record of naturalization was issued. Selected records from Ada, Alturas, Bingham, Boise, Canyon, Clearwater, Elmore, Idaho, Nez Perce, Oneida, Teton, and Twin Falls counties, and the Idaho Supreme Court have been indexed where the Idaho State Archives holds the original record.

Mothers' Pension Records. In 1913, the State of Idaho approved a program to provide a small monthly payment to mothers and orphans under certain circumstances. The Mothers' Pension Records includes material transferred from Ada, Bannock, Bear Lake, Bingham, Blaine, Caribou, Clearwater, Minidoka, Oneida, Power, Teton, and Twin Falls counties

Old Age Pension Records. The Old Age Pension Act became official in the legislative session of February 1931. The act provided a monthly payment of up to $25 to qualified residents of Idaho. Recipients were required to be over 65 years of age, a county resident for the three years immediately prior to the date of application, and a resident of the state for fifteen years, five of which had to be immediately preceding the application. Old Age Pension Records includes information on over 1,400 program applications from Ada, Kootenai, Twin Falls, Jerome, Clearwater, Bannock, Boundary, and Teton counties, ranging from 1931 to 1936.

Research Requests. The IHS staff is available to help with research questions. Special fees may apply.

Idaho State Archives Collections

The **State Archives** online programs are mostly aimed at indexing major collections and creating useful guides to finding manuscript records, rather than digitally imaging the records online. Most of the original records are still in archival manuscript form, and a researcher needs to identify and locate the records first, as in any archives.

The IHS participates in the national interlibrary loan program, and except for original archival manuscripts, all published materials and microfilm are available through interlibrary loan to another participating library/archives anywhere in the U.S.

For access to the State Archives Collections, see http://history.idaho.gov/archives-collections. This web page describes the following categories (with hyperlinks to specific webpages):

Manuscripts and Archival Materials. 123,000 cubic feet of manuscript (non-governmental records) and state government material, includes:
- Personal papers of Senator William E. Borah
- Records of the Territorial government
- Gubernatorial papers from George Shoup through James E. Risch
- Records of the Idaho Soldiers' Home
- Carey Act materials dealing with water rights and irrigation

Maps. 32,000 maps, includes:
- Hand-drawn and hand-colored maps prepared by Lafayette Cartee, Idaho's first Surveyor General
- State highway maps
- Fire insurance maps for a variety of towns and businesses
- Blueprints and architectural plans from the state's premier architectural firms including Tourtellotte and Hummel, Sundberg and Sundberg and Edgar Jensen

Newspapers and Records. 40,000 rolls of microfilm, includes:
- Idaho newspapers dating from 1863 to present
- County-level records (land and property, citizenship, court, vital and tax) dating from 1863
- Sanborn fire insurance maps for many Idaho cities
- Idaho death certificates (1911-1937), federal census schedules (1790-1930), and a variety of materials related to Idaho history and purchased from the National Archives.

Oral Histories. 3,100 individual interviews (audio and video formats), documenting topics such as:
- African-Americans in Southeast Idaho
- Czechoslovakian culture in the Buhl-Castleford area
- Women and political activism in Idaho 1945-1980

Photographs and Motion Pictures. Over 500,000 photographic images (prints, negatives, slides, and transparencies), includes:
- Images taken by Jane E. Gay during the allotment of lands for the Nez Perce Indians
- The life work of Boise photographer R. Harold Sigler
- Images from the Sherwood family, pioneer settlers of the Henry's Lake area of Idaho
- Inmate 'mug shots' from the Idaho Territorial/State Prison
- Photographs are also available for purchase. 5,000 motion picture films and videos, includes:
- 16mm copy of a 1916 film celebrating the 10th anniversary of the town of Buhl
- Footage of a 1935 National Geographic Society expedition on the Salmon River
- Promotional films produced by the Idaho Department of Commerce (1960's-1990's)

And More
- Idaho yearbooks from 1909-2006
- Open-stack reference collection of book and periodical titles for the study of regional, state, community and family history
- Comprehensive list of Idaho Territorial and State Penitentiary Inmates including men, women and children between 1864-1947.

Bibliography
Idaho Censuses & Substitutes

The only census report of Idaho Territory, dated September 1863, was produced to determine the population figures for its first election, leading to the apportionment of the first territorial legislature. Without names, the 1863 statistical census report gives only the number of voters, nonvoters, females, and children in each county and its subdivisions. However, a published *1863 Idaho Territorial Voters Poll List* exits, and this name list can be used as a substitute to the territorial census of 1863.

No subsequent censuses were taken during the territorial period, 1863-1890, and the state of Idaho has never taken a state census. Idaho population figures and apportionment from 1870 forward have been taken from the federal censuses.

Without census records other than the federal censuses, substitute name lists at the state level and county level need to be identified. The first place to do this is at the website for the Idaho Historical Society / Idaho State Archives, where several statewide name lists are online, and a comprehensive list of microfilmed county records for every Idaho county was posted.

The Genealogical Society of Utah, the microfilming arm of the Family History Library (FHL) in Salt Lake City, has visited every Idaho county courthouse, filming many of the county records of interest to family historians. In addition, the Idaho Historical Society (IHS) has microfilmed more records since the FHL films were first made available. Together, the microfilmed Idaho county records include vital records, probates, naturalizations, tax lists, deeds and deed indexes, civil court, criminal court, military lists, and more. Many of these records on microfilm were recently digitized online, now accessible via the Family History Library's online catalog. There are other online databases, printed books, or printed articles available. Descriptions of the Idaho resources begin below in chronological order:

♦ ♦ ♦ ♦ ♦

1860-1914. *History of Idaho* **[Online Database],** digitized and indexed at the Ancestry.com website. This is a large, printed history of Idaho by Hiram T. French, published in 3 vols. by the Lewis Publishing Co. in 1914. Includes many biographical sketches of Idaho's prominent men. See
http://search.ancestry.com/search/db.aspx?dbid=7174.

1860-1920. *History of Idaho The Gem of the Mountains* **[Online Database],** digitized and indexed at the Ancestry.com website. This is the definitive printed history of Idaho by James H. Hawley, published in 3 vols. by the S.J. Clarke Publishing Co. in 1920. Includes many biographical sketches of Idaho's prominent men. See
http://search.ancestry.com/search/db.aspx?dbid=7303.

1860-1930. *The Trail Blazer: History of the Development of Southeastern Idaho* **[Online Database],** digitized and indexed at the Ancestry.com website. This history book was produced by the Idaho Daughters of the Pioneers in 1930 and describes the first settlements in Franklin and other early towns of Idaho in the Bear Lake region, and areas that were mistakenly thought to be in Utah from 1860-1872. See
http://search.ancestry.com/search/db.aspx?dbid=28781.

1860-1965. *Idaho Births and Christenings* **[Online Database],** indexed at the FamilySearch.org website. This is a name index to births, baptisms, and christening records from the state of Idaho, from microfilm copies at the Family History Library in Salt Lake City, UT. This database has 75,881 records. See www.familysearch.org/search/collection/1674809.
- This database is also available at Ancestry.com:
https://search.ancestry.com/search/db.aspx?dbid=60265.

1860-1980s. *Idaho State Archives County Records on Microfilm* **[Online Database],** indexed at the Idaho Historical Society website. For searching Idaho's county records, the IHS has produced a source list of over 4,000 items of Idaho county records on microfilm, all in one database. The list gives the IHS and/or FHL film number for every roll of film. This database was produced in *Microsoft Excel* format, which can be downloaded to a personal computer for printing, sorting, etc. See
https://docs.google.com/spreadsheets/d/1OsooSAaiX3Neee qPXWStuKuWOgQAg7hTC1rBZ0xujqQ/edit#gid=819075912.

1860-1980s. *Idaho – Collection Catalog, MyHeritage.com* **[Online Database],** 8 collections with 924,584 records can be searched for free at the MyHeritage.com website. Collections include censuses, vital records, histories, and college and high school yearbooks. A search can be done for a name, place, year, or keyword. See
www.myheritage.com/records/Idaho/all-records.

1860-1980s. *Idaho Surname Index* **[Printed Index],** compiled by Judy Schmick. Source of the names not noted. Published by the Idaho Historical Society, 1989, 114 pages, FHL book 979.6 D2s.

1860-1980s. *Upper Snake River Valley, Idaho, Newspaper Obituary Index* **[Microfilm & Digital Capture],** from original published by Ricks College, Rexburg, ID, 1984. Filmed by the Genealogical Society of Utah, 1985, 1 roll, FHL film #1402498. To access the digital images, see the online FHL catalog: www.familysearch.org/search/catalog/292971.

1860-1989. *Idaho, Wills and Probate Records* **[Online Database],** digitized and indexed at the Ancestry.com website. Original data: Idaho County, District and Probate Courts. Probate records include Wills, Letters of Administration, Inventories, Distributions and Accounting, Bonds, and Guardianships. Each index record includes: Name, Probate place, and Inferred death place. For cases files with multiple pages, a Table of Contents list the type of papers and number of images. The document images have much more information. This database has 32,574 records. See
https://search.ancestry.com/search/db.aspx?dbid=9047.

1861-1911. *Idaho, Birth Index* **[Online Database],** indexed at the FamilySearch.org website. Source: Idaho Bureau of Vital Records and Health Statistics. Each index record includes: Name, Event type, Event date, Event place, Father's name, Father's birthplace, Father's age, Mother's name, Mother's birthplace, Mother's age, Certificate number, and Mother's birth year. This database has 59,852 records. See
www.familysearch.org/search/collection/2110744.

1861-1970. *Idaho Genealogical Records* **[Microfilm & Digital Capture],** collected from various DAR chapters in Idaho. Microfilm of original records in the DAR Library in Washington, DC. Includes index and table of contents. **Contents:** Booher family bible, Brown family records, Kinley family records, Tillotson family records, Acton/Kunkel family records, Boyer family bible record, Babbitt family bible, The McHenry family, Ramsey family, Mackley family, Landon family, Talbot and Moore family, Turley family, Copied from the bible of Lizzie B. Elliott of July 1892, Robert Dickey family record, Family bible of the Rev. Barnes Irwin, Record of the Fellows family, [Andrews] family bible, Emily Finch bible, Preston family bible record, Rowland, Bowen, Pease, Davis, Fish, and Husted [bible and other records], Bible records and newspaper clippings, Family bible of William J. Hayes, French family records, Pratt [bible records], Obituaries taken from Lewiston (Idaho) Morning Times, Jordan Cemetery, Orbisonia, Huntington [i.e. Huntingdon] County, Penn., Bonanza Cemetery (Clayton, Idaho), Cemetery above Custer, Boot Hill Cemetery at Bonanza (Clayton, Idaho), Silver City Cemetery, Owyhee County, Idaho, Idaho City, Idaho, Cemetery, Court records-Elmore County, Idaho [1874-1899], Taken from the Idaho Daily Statesman, Boise Idaho: Idaho Pioneers, 1852-1864, and Idaho Pioneers, 1904. Note: Silver City in Owyhee County is now a ghost town. Filmed by the Genealogical Society of Utah, 1970, 1 roll, FHL film #849914. To access the digital images, see the online FHL catalog: www.familysearch.org/search/catalog/222354.

1861-1990s. *Idaho State Archives Newspaper Inventory* **[Online Database],** indexed by the Idaho State Archives. This is an index to Idaho newspaper titles available at the IHS Library & Archives. The IHS is a lead agency for the United States Newspaper Program (USNP) to catalog and microfilm Idaho newspapers. To date, over 300,000 pages from 672 separate newspaper titles have been microfilmed. This database was produced in *Microsoft Excel* format, which can be downloaded to a personal computer for printing, sorting, etc. See
https://docs.google.com/spreadsheets/d/1lCSVNfcaYj6o6RP-b4RAesgbDsDy42f9mwlTLOdAXkY/edit#gid=637690559.

1861-1990s. *Idaho State Archives Biographical Index* **[Online Database],** indexed by the Idaho State Archives This is an index of persons named in state, county and community histories, regional periodicals, and selected newspaper articles from around the state and throughout its history. The index is a downloadable *Excel* file containing over 33,000 entries. See
https://docs.google.com/spreadsheets/d/1zX-X7C53WZremB3_m8HAEJH1l_TjUiMf_K0RNMntkKQ/edit#gid=1704927322.

1861-2001. *Roman Catholic Diocese of Boise, Catholic Chancery Records of Idaho, Master Index* **[Printed book],** compiled by the Idaho Genealogical Society, from the original records (FHL copies of originals found under the Locality file under the Idaho county, town, city, or parish). There are 26 volumes of printed index pages. See FHL book 979.628 K2i v. 1-26.

1861-Present. *Linkpendium – Idaho: Family History & Genealogy, Census, Birth, Marriage, Death Vital Records & More* **[Online Database],** Linkpendium is a portal to websites with genealogical information. The Idaho section is organized by Location (Number of Sites), as follows: Statewide Resources Selected sites (288), Independent Cities, Renamed Counties, Discontinued Counties (3), Ada County (976), Adams County (88), Bannock County (197), Bear Lake County (143), Benewah County (83), Bingham County (187), Blaine County (220), Boise County (148), Bonner County (125), Bonneville County (194), Boundary County (102), Butte County (80), Camas County (77), Canyon County (543), Caribou County (111), Cassia County (216), Clark County (101), Clearwater County (93), Custer County (106), Elmore County (130), Franklin County (104), Fremont County (190), Gem County (257), Gooding County (96), Idaho County (136), Jefferson County (158), Jerome County (83), Kootenai County (164), Latah County (184), Lemhi County (142), Lewis County (83), Lincoln County (103), Madison County (140), Minidoka County (95), Nez Perce County (162), Oneida County (140), Owyhee County (146), Payette County (250), Power County (97), Shoshone County (164), Teton County (105), Twin Falls County (222), Valley County (86), and Washington County (134). See
www.linkpendium.com/id-genealogy.

1861-Present. *USGenWeb Archives, Idaho* **[Online Database},** data files of Bibles, Biographies, Cemeteries, Deaths, Histories, Obituaries, Photos, Tombstones, Military Records, and more, submitted by volunteers. Databases are organized by Idaho counties. For the ID index, see
http://usgwarchives.net/id.

- **NOTE: 1861-1865 Civil War Era.** At the onset of the Civil War in April 1861, Idaho was still part of Washington Territory. There were possibly some Union soldiers recruited from the mining communities of the present Idaho panhandle, who would have served with Washington Territory units; and possibly some from the Bear Lake region, who would have served with Utah Territory units. After Idaho Territory was established in March 1863, no Civil War militia units were formed there. But conveniently, the Idaho State Archives compiled a list of Civil War soldiers who lived or died in Idaho, all of whom served with units outside of Idaho:

1861-1865. *Idaho State Archives Civil War Veterans Index* **[Online Database],** This is an alphabetized list of over 2,000 Civil War veterans who lived or died in Idaho, identified from a variety of records. The index is a downloadable Excel database. See
https://docs.google.com/spreadsheets/d/1o8bD9ylu0XJplK9MGfrIaTrOqg_QjWEUH8CCORqXJ_E/edit#gid=737730942.

1861-1865. *Index to Compiled Service Records of Volunteer Union Soldiers Who Served in Organizations From the Territory of Washington* **[Microfilm],** from the originals at the National Archives, Washington, DC. Filmed by the National Archives, 1964, series M558, 1 roll, FHL film #821948.

1861-1865. *Index to Compiled Service Records of Volunteer Union Soldiers Who Served in Organizations From the Territory of Utah* **[Microfilm],** from the originals at the National Archives, Washington, DC. Includes records from Captain Smith's Company, Utah Calvary. Each index card gives name, rank, and unit in which he served. Filmed by the National Archives, 1964, series M556, 1 roll, FHL film #1292645.

- **NOTE:** Both of Indexes for WA and UT above are included in the national database, *United States Civil War Soldiers Index, 1861-1865* **[Online Database],** see www.familysearch.org/search/collection/1910717.

1861-1952. *We Served in the Military, Civil War to World War II* **[Microfilm],** from the original book by James Lafayette Holloway. Includes names of all veterans living or buried in Twin Falls County, Idaho, from the Civil War to the Korean War. Filmed by the Genealogical Society of Utah, 1998, 1 roll, FHL film #2056000. To see if this microfilm was digitized yet, see the online FHL catalog:
www.familysearch.org/search/catalog/691069.

1861-1956. See *Cemetery Records, Ada County, Idaho* **[Microfilm & Digital Capture],** from the manuscript created by the Genealogical Committee of Provo, LDS Church. Filmed by the Genealogical Society of Utah, 1956, 1 roll, FHL film #2107 Item 1. To access the digital images of this roll, see the online FHL catalog page:
www.familysearch.org/search/catalog/122203.

1861-1963. See *Idaho Vital Statistics: Cemetery Records* **[Printed Book & Digital Capture],** Volume I comprises all the cemetery records which have been compiled to date within the following three counties: Bingham, Bonneville, Madison. compiled and published by the Idaho Genealogical Society, Boise, ID, 1963, 243 pages, FHL book 979.6 V3ig v.1. To access a digital version of this book, see the online FHL catalog page:
www.familysearch.org/search/catalog/201016.

1861-1967. See *Idaho, Birth Index, 1861-1917, Stillbirth Index, 1905-1967* **[Online Database],** indexed at the Ancestry.com website. Source: 1861-1910: various counties, compiled lists, etc. 1911-1967: Idaho Bureau of Vital Records, Boise. Each index record includes: Name, Death age (if applicable), Birth date, Birthplace, Father, Mother, Certificate year and number. This database has 411,368 records. See
https://search.ancestry.com/search/db.aspx?dbid=8973.

1861-1974. *Idaho, County Naturalizations* **[Online Database],** digitized at the FamilySearch.org website. This is an image-only database of county district court naturalization records from Alturas, Bannock, Bear Lake, Benewah, Bingham, Blaine, Bonner, Bonneville, Butte, Canyon, Cassia, Clark, Clearwater, Custer, Elmore, Franklin, Fremont, Gooding, Idaho, Jefferson, Kootenai, Latah, Lemhi, Lewis, Lincoln, Logan, Madison, Minidoka, Nez Perce, Oneida, Owyhee, Power, Shoshone, Teton, Valley and Washington counties. Alturas and Logan counties were abolished in 1895 at the creation of Blaine and Lincoln. Naturalization records include Declarations Petitions, and Certificates. This database has 32,807 images. Browse through the images, organized by County, Record Type, Year Range, and Volume. See
www.familysearch.org/search/collection/2078306.

1862-1876 *Mortgage Index, Idaho County, Idaho* **[Online Database],** indexed at the USGenWeb site for Idaho Co ID. See
http://idaho.idgenweb.org/Land%20Records/mortgage_index.htm.

1863. See *Idaho Territorial Voters Poll Lists, 1863* **[Printed Book, Microfilm & Digital Version],** transcribed, edited, and indexed by Gene F. Williams, published by Williams Printing, Boise, ID, 1996, 52 pages. Includes index. Contains description of towns, voting districts, and a list by name of the voters for 1863, arranged in alphabetical order by surname. FHL book 979.6 N4w. Also on microfilm, FHL film #2055552. To access a digital version of this book, see the online FHL catalog page for this title:
www.familysearch.org/search/catalog/653670.

1863. "First Census Report, 1863" **[Printed Article],** statistics published in *Idaho Genealogical Society Quarterly* (Idaho Genealogical Society, Boise, ID), Vol. 2, No. 1 (Mar 1959).

***1863 Census of Some Prominent Men in the Idaho Territory* [Microfilm & Digital Capture],** part of a manuscript, Pompey S. L. Papers, by Sherman Lee Pompey, 1970, pp 295-310. Source of name list not noted. Filmed by the Genealogical Society of Utah, 1970, 1 roll, FHL film #823651. To access the digital images of this roll, see the online FHL catalog page for this title
www.familysearch.org/search/catalog/83719.

1863-1964. *Idaho, County Marriage Records* **[Online Database],** indexed at the Ancestry.com website. Source: Idaho State Archives, Boise. There are a variety of marriage forms, including: Marriage Certificates, Marriage Licenses, Marriage Affidavits, and Marriage Applications. Each index record may include: Name of groom, Age and race of groom, Groom's birth date and place, Groom's parents' names, Marriage date, License date, Engagement date, Name of bride, Age and race of bride, Bride's birth date and place, and Bride's parents' names. This database has 144,439 records. See
https://search.ancestry.com/search/db.aspx?dbid=61480.

1863-1967. *Idaho, Marriage Records* **[Online Database],** indexed at the Ancestry.com website. Source: ID Dept of Health & Welfare, Vital Records, et al. Each index record includes: Name, Gender, Marriage date, Marriage place, and Spouse. This database has 687,419 records. See
https://search.ancestry.com/search/db.aspx?dbid=7849.

1863-1970. *Idaho, County Births and Death Records* **[Online Database],** digitized and indexed at the Ancestry.com website. Source: Idaho State Archives. Each index record includes: Name, Gender, Race, Event type, Birthplace, Death date, Death place, Father, and Mother. The document image may have more information. This database has 73,006 records. See
https://search.ancestry.com/search/db.aspx?dbid=61443.

1863-1984. *Western States Marriage Index, 1809-2011* **[Online Database],** indexed at the Ancestry.com website. This is a project of the Special Collections & Family History department of BYU-Idaho, Rexburg, ID. The Idaho portion of the index has a large number of marriages for most counties. To access the list, do a search at the Ancestry.com website database, and go to the link to the BYU-Idaho website, where more details about the county list and number of marriages is available. This database has 184,116 Idaho records. See
https://search.ancestry.com/search/db.aspx?dbid=70016.

1864-1882. *Idaho Tri-Weekly Statesman (Boise City, Idaho)* **[Online Database],** digitized and indexed at the Ancestry.com website, a fully searchable text of the newspaper for the years 1864-1866, 1872, 1875-1878, and 1881-1882. See
http://search.ancestry.com/search/db.aspx?dbid=7212.

1864-1897. *Idaho Statesman (Boise City, Idaho)* **[Online Database],** digitized and indexed at the Ancestry.com website, a fully searchable text of the newspaper for the years 1864-1874; 1877-1882; 1888-1891; and 1897. See
http://search.ancestry.com/search/db.aspx?dbid=7197.

1864-1911. See *Deeds, Ada County, Idaho, 1865-1911; Index, 1864-1902* **[Microfilm & Digital Capture],** from the originals of the Ada County Court, Probate Court, and District Court, now located at the ID State Archives. Includes general index with some volumes individually indexed. Filmed by the Genealogical Society of Utah, 1987, 17 rolls, beginning with FHL film #1509724 (Index v.A 1864-1878). To access the digital images, see the online FHL catalog:
www.familysearch.org/search/catalog/389173.

1864-1969. *Idaho Newspaper Archives* **[Online Database],** digitized and indexed at the GenealogyBank.com website. Search for names or keywords in newspapers for the following cities: Ashton, Blackfoot, Boise, Hunt, Idaho Falls, Lewiston, Nampa, Rathdrum, Ruby City, Salmon City, Silver City, and Twin Falls, See
www.genealogybank.com/explore/newspapers/all/usa/idaho

1864-1950. *Idaho, County Marriages* **[Online Database],** digitized and indexed at the FamilySearch.org website. Currently the collection includes the following counties: Ada, Adams, Benewah, Blaine, Bonner, Bonneville, Butte, Camas, Canyon, Caribou, Cassia, Clark, Custer, Elmore, Franklin, Fremont, Gem, Gooding, Idaho, Jefferson, Jerome, Kootenai, Latah, Lemhi, Lewis, Lincoln, Madison, Minidoka, Nez Perce, Oneida, Payette, Power, Shoshone, Teton, Twin Falls, Valley, and Washington. This database has 297,704 records. See **www.familysearch.org/search/collection/1662500.**
- See also, *Idaho, County Marriages, 1864-1950* **[Online Database],** digitized and indexed at Ancestry.com. This database has 297,704 records, see **https://search.ancestry.com/search/db.aspx?dbid=60269.**
- See also, *Idaho, County Marriage Records, 1864-1967* **[Online Database],** digitized and indexed at Ancestry.com. This database has 317,712 records, see **www.ancestry.com/search/collections/61480.**

1864-1971. *Idaho, Kootenai County, Cemeteries* **[Printed Book & Digital Version],** compiled by Dean and Iola Stocking, publ. 1971, 250 pages. Includes the following cemeteries: Athol Cemetery; Sacred Heart Cemetery; Garwood Cemetery; Harrison Cemetery; Hope Cemetery; Lane Cemetery; Medimont Cemetery; Pine Grove Cemetery; Rimrock Cemetery; Rose Lake Cemetery and St. Thomas Catholic Cemetery; and Worley Cemetery. To access a digital version of this book, see the online FHL catalog page for this title: **www.familysearch.org/search/catalog/2623824.**

1864-1975. Inmate Records [Online Database], indexed at the Idaho Historical Society website. This chronological and indexed catalog provides a comprehensive list of Idaho territorial and state penitentiary prisoners, including men, women, and children, between the years 1864 and 1975. The catalog provides access to inmate files in the custody of the Idaho State Historical Society by names, aliases, register number, crime, county or jurisdiction, age, year of birth, and year of incarceration. The catalog database is organized into 1) All inmates 1864-1947; 2) Women 1864-1947; 3) Miners 1865-1910; and 4) Index to inmates 1948-1975. This database was produced in *Microsoft Excel* format, which can be downloaded to a personal computer for printing, sorting, etc. See **www.history.idaho.gov/old-idaho-penitentiary-inmates-catalog.**

1864-1976. *Idaho Church Marriages* **[Online Database],** indexed at the FamilySearch.org website. Index to selected marriages, mostly from the Catholic Church. Many of the records are for Boise. Each index record includes: Name, Event type, Event date, Event place, Gender, Marital status, Father's name, Mother's name, Spouse's name, Spouse's gender, Spouse's father's name, and Spouse's mother's name. This database has 11,561 records. See **www.familysearch.org/search/collection/2549611.**

1864-2007. *Idaho, Southeast Counties Obituaries* **[Online Database],** digitized and indexed at the FamilySearch.org website. Digital images of originals collected and housed by the Idaho Falls Regional Family History Center. The obituaries are from various Idaho newspapers printed up to 2007. The images are organized by these Idaho places: Aberdeen to Ammon, Annis to Archer, Arco to Atlanta, Bancroft to Boise, Bonanza to Burton, Caldwell to Custer, Darby to Dubois, Eagle to Emmett, Fairfield to Franklin, Geneva to Groveland, Haden to Humphrey, Idaho City to Iversons, Idaho Falls, Fielding to Rose Hill, Jackson to Juniper, Kamiah to Kuna, Lago to Lund, MacKay to Milo, Mink Creek to Mountain Home, Nampa to Nounan, Oakley to Ozone, Palisades to Prospect, Pocatello, Franciscan to Mountain View, Pocatello, Restlawn, Rapid River, Rigby, Retakes, Riggins-Rupert, Saint Anthony, Riverview to Sharon, Shelley to Swan Valley, Taylor to Turner, Twin Falls, and Ucon to Yellowjacket. This database has 313,571 records. See **www.familysearch.org/search/collection/1876879.**

1865-1874 Internal Revenue Assessment Lists For the Territory of Idaho **[Microfilm & Digital Capture],** from the originals at the National Archives in Washington, DC and Central Plains regional branch, Kansas City, MO. Contains annual, monthly, and special tax lists. FHL has the following:
- Internal Revenue Assessment Lists for the Territory of Idaho, 1865-1866, FHL film #1578503. Another film copy, FHL film #1024432.
- Internal Revenue Assessment Lists for the Territory of Idaho, 1867- 1874, FHL film #1578504.

To access the digital images, see the online FHL catalog: **www.familysearch.org/search/catalog/577985.**

1865-1872 Birth Records, Owyhee County, Idaho **[Online Database],** indexed at the USGenWeb site for Owyhee Co ID. See **http://files.usgwarchives.net/id/owyhee/vitals/births/b186572.txt.**

1865-1890. See *Assessment Rolls, Ada County, Idaho, 1865-1890; Delinquent Tax Lists, 1878-1886* **[Microfilm & Digital Capture]**, from the originals at the Idaho State Archives, Boise. Filmed by the Genealogical Society of Utah, 1987, 7 rolls, beginning with FHL film #1513377. To access the digital images, see the online FHL catalog:
www.familysearch.org/search/catalog/390364.

1865-1902. *Deeds, Canyon County, Idaho, 1865-1902; Index, 1865-1902* **[Microfilm & Digital Capture]**, from the originals at the Canyon County Courthouse in Caldwell, Idaho. Filmed by the Genealogical Society of Utah, 1986, 10 rolls, beginning with FHL film #1255619 (Index, Grantors). To access the digital images, see the online FHL catalog:
www.familysearch.org/search/catalog/366589.

1865-1905. *Milleman Newspaper Clippings, Annotated Index* **[Printed Book]**, by Joyln Rae Lockhart-Lawson, from Theodore Milleman's scrapbook of newspaper clippings. The newspapers were all from Southwestern Idaho. Published by the Idaho Genealogical Society, Boise, ID, 2001, 237 pages, FHL book 979.6 B32L.

1865-1911. See *Homestead Records, Ada County, Idaho, 1865-1911; Indexes, 1865-1911* **[Microfilm & Digital Capture]**, from the originals at the Idaho State Archives, Boise. Filmed by the Genealogical Society of Utah, 1987, 2 rolls, FHL film #1509774 & #1509775. To access the digital images, see the online FHL catalog:
www.familysearch.org/search/catalog/389479.

1865-1996. *Idaho Marriages* **[Online Database]**, indexed at the Ancestry.com website, from Idaho county courthouse records. Information that may be found in this database for each individual includes their name, spouse's name, spouse's gender, marriage date and location, county, and state in which the marriage was recorded, residence of the bride and groom, and source information. This database has 253,015 records. Ancestry's database title has the date range of 1842-1996. There is one marriage with the date 1842 from Bonneville County, ID. But checking other marriages from the same source (Bonneville marriage book, vol. 7), all other marriages in that book were performed in 1942, not 1842. A check for the earliest dates of marriages for all counties of Idaho revealed the earliest in this database were in Ada County in 1865. See
http://search.ancestry.com/search/db.aspx?dbid=7849.

1867-1874. *Internal Revenue Assessment Lists for the Territory of Idaho* **[Microfilm & Digital Capture]**, from the original records at the National Archives, Washington, DC. Filmed by the National Archives, 1977, series T1209, 1 roll, FHL film #1578504. To access the digital images, see the online FHL catalog:
www.familysearch.org/search/catalog/577988.

1867-2012. *Idaho, Bonneville County Records* **[Online Database]**, digitized at the FamilySearch.org website. Source: County Recorder, Idaho Falls, ID. This is an image-only database with marriages, military discharges, and land and property records. This database has 123,122 images. Browse through the images, organized by Record Categories (Land and Property, Military, Mining, and Vital Records), then by Record Type, Date Range, and Volume. See
www.familysearch.org/search/collection/2135572.

1868-1913. *Land Records (Idaho Land Offices)* **[Microfilm & Digital Capture]**, from the original records at the National Archives, Seattle, WA. Land offices were located in Boise, Blackfoot, Hailey, Lewiston, Coeur d'Alene, and Oxford (later known as Blackfoot). Includes tract books, mining records, timber records and other miscellaneous records pertaining to land. Filmed by the Genealogical Society of Utah, 1989, 23 rolls, beginning with FHL film #1617970 (Boise Land Office, 1874-1888). To access the digital images, see the online FHL catalog:
www.familysearch.org/search/catalog/453022.

1868-1949. See *Miscellaneous Records, Canyon County, Idaho, 1868-1927; Index, 1868-1949* **[Microfilm & Digital Capture]**, from the original records at the Courthouse in Caldwell, Idaho. Filmed by the Genealogical Society of Utah, 1986, 5 rolls, beginning with FHL film #1255614 (Index, 1868-1949). For a complete list of roll numbers, roll contents, and the digital images of each roll, see the online FHL catalog page for this title:
www.familysearch.org/search/catalog/366524.

1868-1964. *Idaho, Lemhi County Records* **[Online Database]**, digitized at the FamilySearch.org website. This is an image-only database. Includes marriage, coroners, deeds, declarations of intention, discharges, estate files, school census and student records from the county courthouse in Salmon, ID. This database has 129,909 images. Browse through images, organized by Record Categories (Land and Property, Military, Naturalization, Probate, School, and Vital Records). See
www.familysearch.org/search/collection/1983169.

- This database is also available at the Ancestry.com website. See
https://search.ancestry.com/search/db.aspx?dbid=60272.

1868-1977. See *Declaration of Homesteads, Canyon County, Idaho, 1868-1919; Index, 1868-1977* **[Microfilm & Digital Capture],** from the originals at the Canyon County Courthouse in Caldwell, Idaho. Filmed by the Genealogical Society of Utah, 1986, 1 roll, FHL film #1255609. To access the digital images, see the online FHL catalog:
www.familysearch.org/search/catalog/366414.

1868-1985. *Idaho State Archives Naturalization Records* **[Online Database].** The Idaho State Archives holds a good collection of Naturalization Records, primarily from various counties, although some state-level records can be found as well. Selected records from Ada, Alturas, Bingham, Boise, Canyon, Clearwater, Elmore, Idaho, Nez Perce, Oneida, Teton, and Twin Falls counties, and the Idaho Supreme Court records have been indexed where the Idaho State Archives holds the original paper record. This database was produced in *Microsoft Excel* format, which can be downloaded to a personal computer for printing, sorting, etc. See
https://docs.google.com/spreadsheets/d/1UpMPcO8Jr3FLIFvy27a5xNMcCPqF20wur8YtOjH8tw0/edit#gid=1474309575.

1868-1985. *Idaho, Naturalization Records* **[Online Database],** indexed at the Ancestry.com website. These records are from *Records of the District Courts of the United States,* originals at the National Archives, Seattle, WA, and include Declarations of Intentions, Petitions, and Certificates of Arrival. The records all include a name, age, date of birth, nationality, sex, and many other items of identification. This database has 10,790 records. See
http://search.ancestry.com/search/db.aspx?dbid=2032.

1868-2013. *Idaho, Obituary Collection* **[Online Database],** digitized and indexed at the Ancestry.com website. Source: Pocatello Family History Center. This is an indexed collection of newspaper clippings of obituaries. This database has 51,747 records. See
https://search.ancestry.com/search/db.aspx?dbid=61354.

1869. *Ada County, Idaho, Index to Separate Property of Married Women* **[Microfilm & Digital Capture],** from the originals at the ID State Archives, Boise, ID. Includes general index with some volumes individually indexed. Filmed by the Genealogical Society of Utah, 1987, 1 roll, FHL film 1509724. To access the digital images, see the online FHL catalog:
www.familysearch.org/search/catalog/389207.

1870. *Idaho Territory, 1870 Federal Census: Population Schedules* **[Microfilm & Digital Capture],** from the originals at the National Archives, Washington, DC. Filmed twice by the National Archives, 1962 & 1968, 2 rolls total, FHL film #545684 (2nd filming: Ada, Alturas, Boise, Idaho, Lemhi, Nez Perce, Oneida, Owyhee, and Shoshone counties); and FHL film #7156 (1st filming: Ada, Alturas, Boise, Idaho, Lemhi, Nez Perce, Oneida, Owyhee, and Shoshone counties). To access the digital images, see the online FHL catalog:
www.familysearch.org/search/catalog/699190.

1870. *Idaho Territory Federal Population Schedules and Mortality Schedules* **[Printed Index],** compiled by the Idaho Genealogical Society, includes index. Printed by Williams Print Co., Boise, ID, 1973, 218 pages, FHL book 979.6 X2pa 1870.

1870. *Idaho 1870 Census Index, A-Z* **[Printed Index],** edited by Raeone Christensen Steuart, published by Heritage Quest, 2000, 82 pages, FHL book 979.6 X22s 1870.

1870. *Idaho 1870 Mortality Schedule* **[Printed Index],** edited by Ronald Vern Jackson, et al, published by Accelerated Indexing Systems, Bountiful, UT, 1980, 14 pages, FHL book 979.6 X2i 1870.

1870 Tax List, Idaho County, Idaho **[Online Database],** indexed at the USGenWeb site for Idaho Co ID. See
http://idaho.idgenweb.org/TAX/1870_idaho_county_tax_list.htm.

1870 and 1880 Agricultural, Industrial, Mortality and Other Special Census Schedules for Idaho **[Online Database],** indexed at the Idaho Historical Society website. These are names list from the special schedules, downloadable from the IHS website as two *Excel* files, containing over 2,700 entries. Archived at
https://web.archive.org/web/20160330211141/www.history.idaho.gov/1870-and-1880-census-schedules-idaho.

1870-1995. *Prairie View Cemetery Inscriptions, Grangeville, Idaho* **[Online Database],** indexed at the Ancestry.com website. The data comes from tombstone inscriptions and sexton's records compiled and published in a book by the Idaho County Genealogical Society, Grangeville, ID. This database has over 4,500 records. See
http://search.ancestry.com/search/db.aspx?dbid=4212.

1871-1881 Idaho Directories [Microfilm & Digital Capture]. See *McKenney's Pacific Coast Directory,* or under the title, *The Pacific Coast Directory: Giving Name, Business, and Address of Business and Professional Men of California, Oregon, Washington, British Columbia, Alaska, Nevada, Utah, Idaho, Montana, Arizona, and New Mexico Together with Sketches of the Different Towns, Giving Location, Population, etc.,* from the original published by L.M. McKenney, San Francisco, 1871-1884. Filmed by the Genealogical Society of Utah, 1975, 1994, 5 rolls, as follows:
- 1871-1873, FHL film #1004513.
- 1878, FHL film #1004515.
- 1880-1881, FHL film #1004517.
- 1883-1884, FHL film #1697991.
- 1883-1884, FHL film #1004519.

To access the digital images of the rolls, see the online FHL catalog page (1871-1873):
www.familysearch.org/search/catalog/1356852.

1874 Tax List, Idaho County, Idaho **[Online Database],** indexed at the USGenWeb site for Idaho Co ID. See
http://idaho.idgenweb.org/TAX/1874Poll.htm.

1877-1962. *Idaho, Gem County Records* **[Online Database],** digitized at the FamilySearch.org website. This is an image-only database. Includes homestead patents, deeds, marriage licenses, naturalizations and probate records from the county clerk and recorder's office in Emmett, Idaho. This database has 45,542 images. Browse through the images, organized by Record Categories (Land and Property, Naturalization, and Vital Records). See
www.familysearch.org/search/collection/2181357.

1878-1885 Homestead Receipts, Idaho County, Idaho [Online Database], indexed at the USGenWeb site for Idaho Co ID. See
http://idaho.idgenweb.org/Land%20Records/homestead_final.htm.

1878-1942. See *Idaho Marriages, 1878-1898; 1903-1942* **[Online Database],** indexed at the FamilySearch.org website, from microfilm at the Family History Library, Salt Lake City. This database has 75,179 records. See
www.familysearch.org/search/collection/1674817.
- See also, *Idaho, Select Marriages, 1878-1898; 1903-1942* **[Online Database],** indexed at the Ancestry.com website. This database has 211,115 records. See
https://search.ancestry.com/search/db.aspx?dbid=60274.

1879-1962. *Idaho, Gooding County Records* **[Online Database],** digitized at the FamilySearch.org website. This is an image-only database. Records include land, naturalization, marriage, military, school, and probate records from the Clerk of the District Court in Gooding. This database has 52,108 images. Browse through the images, organized by Record Categories, Record Type, Record Description, and Year Range. See
https://familysearch.org/search/collection/2117003.

1879-1989. *Idaho, Cassia County Records* **[Online Database],** digitized and indexed at the FamilySearch.org website. Records include marriages, probates, soldier discharges, school censuses, deeds, patents, homesteads, mining locations, coroners, and mothers pension records, located at the county courthouse in Burley, Idaho. This database has 14,323 records, see
www.familysearch.org/search/collection/1921818.

1880. *Idaho Territory, 1880 Federal Census: Soundex and Population Schedules* **[Microfilm & Digital Capture],** from the originals at the National Archives, Washington, DC. After microfilming the National Archives transferred the original 1880 population schedules to local repositories. The 1880 was the only census handled in this way. Idaho Territory's original 1880 population schedules, contained in one bound volume, were donated to the Idaho Historical Society in Boise, ID. Filmed by the National Archives, 3 rolls, FHL film #378006 (Soundex: A000-A655); FHL film #378007 (Soundex: N000 – Institutions); and FHL film #1254173 (Population Schedules: Entire territory).
To access the digital images, see the online FHL catalog: www.familysearch.org/search/catalog/670390.

1880. See *Idaho Territory Federal Population Schedules and Mortality Schedules, 1880* **[Printed Index],** compiled by the Idaho Genealogical Society, includes index. Printed by Williams Print Co., Boise, ID, 1976, 983 pages, FHL book 979.6 X2p.

1880. *Idaho 1880 Territorial Census Index* **[Printed Index],** edited by Ronald Vern Jackson, published by Accelerated Indexing Systems, Salt Lake City, UT, 1979, 400 pages, FHL book 979.6 X22i 1880.

1880. *Mortality Schedule, Idaho* **[Typescript],** photocopy of typescript, arranged by enumeration district, published by the Genealogical Society of

Utah, Salt Lake City, UT, 2001, 24 pages, FHL book 979.6 X28m.

1880s-1906. See *Territorial Vital Records: Births, Divorces, Guardianship, Marriages, Naturalization, Wills; 1800's Thru 1906 Utah Territory, AZ, CO, ID, NV, WY, Indian Terr.; LDS Branches, Wards; Deseret News Vital Recs.; J.P. Marriages; Meth. Marriages* [CD-ROM], a publication by Genealogical CD Publishing, St. George, UT, 1995, 1 disc, FHL CD-ROM No. 15.

1880s-1907. *Homestead Patents, Kootenai County, Idaho* [Online Database], indexed at the USGenWeb for Kootenai Co ID. See
http://files.usgwarchives.net/id/kootenai/land/hp181907.txt.

1880-1910. *Deeds, Bonner County, Idaho* [Online Database], indexed at the USGenWeb site for Bonner Co ID. See
http://files.usgwarchives.net/id/bonner/deeds/18001910.txt.

1880-2007. *Idaho, Cemeteries Burial Index* [Digital Capture], from originals at the Idaho Falls Family History Center, Idaho Falls, ID. Digitized by the Genealogical Society of Utah, 2007. To see the list of cemetery locations and access the digital images, see the online FHL catalog:
www.familysearch.org/search/catalog/1385728.
- See also, *Index of Idaho Cemetery Records* [Printed Book & Digital Version], book located at the Pocatello Family History Center - includes Idaho cemetery records from the following cemeteries: Almo, Atlanta, Bancroft, Black Pine, Chesterfield, Grand View, Riverside, Ivins, Juniper, Kuna, Marion, Meridian, Moulton, Pella, Island, Sublett, Malta, Wendell, Wilford, Indian Valley, Fash Haven, Placerville, Pioneer, Grant, St. Michals, Pine Grove, Slickpoo, Broncheau Burial Ground (Indian), Darby, and Salubra cemeteries, located in various counties in Idaho. To access the digital version, see the online FHL catalog:
www.familysearch.org/search/catalog/2525181.

1881-1905. See *Deeds, Kootenai County, Idaho, 1881-1905; Index, 1882-1905* [Microfilm & Digital Capture], from the originals at the Kootenai County Courthouse, Coeur D'Alene, Idaho. Filmed by the Genealogical Society of Utah, 1988, 10 rolls, beginning with FHL film #1548231 (Index, v.A 1882-1887). To access the digital images, see the online FHL catalog:
www.familysearch.org/search/catalog/384976.

1882-1955 Probate Record Index, Oneida County, Idaho [Online Database], indexed at the RootsWeb site for Oneida Co ID. Archived at
https://web.archive.org/web/20150915012035/www.rootsweb.ancestry.com/~idoneida/Estates_in_probate.htm.

1882-1961. *Idaho, Old Penitentiary Prison Records* [Online Database], indexed at the Ancestry.com website. Source: Idaho State Archives. The prison documents may contain the following information: Name of inmate, Age and race of inmate, Birth date and place, Marriage date, and place, Date of trial, Date of pardon, Date of conviction, Spouse of inmate, Other miscellaneous information such as physical attributes and the crime committed. This database has 24,546 records. See
https://search.ancestry.com/search/db.aspx?dbid=61475.
- See also, *Old Idaho Penitentiary Glass-Plate Negative Collection Catalogue* [Printed Book & Digital Version], compiled by Jody Hawley, publ. ID State Hist. Soc, 1985, 191 pages. To access the digital version, see the online FHL catalog:
www.familysearch.org/search/catalog/2564899.

1882-1970. *Idaho, Butte County Records* [Online Database], digitized at the FamilySearch.org website. This is an image-only database. Includes land, marriage, and probate records from the county courthouse in Arco, ID. This database has 23,226 images. Browse through the images, organized by Record Category, Record Type, and Year Range. See
www.familysearch.org/search/collection/2103492.

1883-1929. *Idaho, County Birth and Death Records* [Online Database], digitized and indexed at the FamilySearch.org website. County birth and death registers acquired for the following counties: Ada, Bannock, Bingham, Blaine, Bonner, Bonneville, Boundary, Canyon, Cassia, Clearwater, Elmore, Fremont, Kootenai, Latah, Nez Perce, Owyhee, Shoshone, Twin Falls and Washington counties. Each index record includes: Name, Event type, Event date, Event place, Gender, Father Name, Mother's name, and Page number. The document image may have more information. This database has 17,583 records. See www.familysearch.org/search/collection/1951759.

1883-1957. See *Deeds, Bannock County, Idaho, 1883-1957; Index, 1880-1927* [Microfilm & Digital Capture], from the original records at the Bannock County Courthouse, Pocatello, Idaho. Filmed by the Genealogical Society of Utah, 1974-1975, 69 rolls, beginning with FHL film #1527211. For a complete

list of roll numbers, roll contents, and the digital images for certain rolls, see the online FHL catalog page for this title:
www.familysearch.org/search/catalog/653223.

1884 Election Data, Alturas County, Idaho [Online Database], indexed at the USGenWeb site for Alturas Co ID. The data is limited to voting precincts, polling places, registry agents, and judges. Alturas County was created in 1864 but disappeared after it was combined with Logan to form Blaine County in 1895:
http://files.usgwarchives.net/id/alturas/history/1884vote.txt.

1884-1998. *Idaho, Clark County Records* [Online Database], digitized at the FamilySearch.org website. This is an image-only database. Records include marriage affidavits, naturalization records, declarations of intentions, deeds, patents, brands and marks, mining records, probate records, and estate files located at the Clark County courthouse, Dubois, ID. This database has 19,976 images. Browse through the images, organized by Record Category, Record Type, Volume, and Date Range. See
www.familysearch.org/search/collection/1920125.

1885-1920. *Idaho, Bingham County Historical Society, Bigham County Records* [Online Database], digitized and indexed at FamilySearch.org. Records include the following: Abstract Land Dept Idaho, 1893-1909; Assessment Roll, 1890; Tax Collectors Register and ledger 4, 1898-1899; and Jail Vol 1, 1885-1907. This database has 7,197 records, see
www.familysearch.org/search/collection/2841010.

1886 Taxpayers, Idaho County, Idaho [Online Database], indexed at the USGenWeb site for Idaho Co ID. See
http://idaho.idgenweb.org/TAX/1886_tax.htm.

1886-1903. *Idaho County Free Press, Vital Records* [Online Database], indexed at the Ancestry.com website. The data was compiled by Carol Sams Anglen for the Idaho County Genealogical Society, Grangeville, ID. The database has 3,030 records. See
http://search.ancestry.com/search/db.aspx?dbid=3631.

1886-1893. *Idaho County, Idaho Newspaper Tax Lists* [Online Database], indexed at the Ancestry.com website. The data was compiled by Carol Sams Anglen for the Idaho County Genealogical Society, Grangeville, ID. The database has over 7,600 records. See
http://search.ancestry.com/search/db.aspx?dbid=3816.

1886-1972. *Idaho, Lincoln County Records* [Online Database], digitized at the FamilySearch.org website. This is an image-only database. Includes vital records, coroner's inquests, military discharges, deeds, patents, probate case files and registers of cases located at the Clerk of the District Court, Clerk and Recorder Offices in Shoshone, ID. This database has 168,580 images. Browse through the images, organized by Record Category, Record Type, and Date Range. See
www.familysearch.org/search/collection/2058671.
- This database is also available at the Ancestry.com website. See
https://search.ancestry.com/search/db.aspx?dbid=60273.

1887 Land Patents, Idaho County, Idaho [Online Database], indexed at the USGenWeb site for Idaho Co ID. See
http://idaho.idgenweb.org/Land%20Records/1887patents.htm.

1888 Delinquent Tax List, Idaho County, Idaho [Online Database], indexed at the USGenWeb site for Idaho Co ID. See
http://idaho.idgenweb.org/TAX/1888_Delinq_Tax.htm.

1888-1891 and **1897-1902.** *Idaho Daily Statesman (Boise City, Idaho)* [Online Database], a fully searchable text version of the newspaper, digitized and indexed at the Ancestry.com website:
http://search.ancestry.com/search/db.aspx?dbid=7211.

1888-1914. *Wills, Bonneville County, Idaho* [Microfilm & Digital Capture], from the originals at the Bonneville County Courthouse, Idaho Falls, Idaho. Filmed by the Genealogical Society of Utah, 1986, 1 roll, FHL film #1450810. To access the digital images, see the online FHL catalog:
www.familysearch.org/search/catalog/366354.

1888-1955. *Wills, Bannock County, Idaho* [Microfilm & Digital Capture], from the original records at the Bannock County Courthouse, Pocatello, Idaho. Filmed by the Genealogical Society of Utah, 1974-1975, 1 roll, FHL film #1527298. To access the digital images, see the online FHL catalog:
www.familysearch.org/search/catalog/654193.

1889 Delinquent Tax List, Idaho County, Idaho [Online Database], indexed at the USGenWeb site for Idaho Co ID. See
http://idaho.idgenweb.org/TAX/1889_tax.htm.

1889-1972. *Idaho, Elmore County Records* **[Online Database],** indexed at the FamilySearch.org website. This is an image-only database. Includes images of court, land, naturalization, marriage, and probate records from the county clerk's office in Mountain Home, ID. This database has 26,811 images. Browse through the images, organized by Record Category, Record Type, Record Description, and Year Range. See **www.familysearch.org/search/collection/2135633.**

1890. See *Idaho State Archives Reconstructed 1890 Census* **[Online Database],** indexed by the Idaho State Archives. Using federal, state, local government records, and local newspapers; and materials published in nationally distributed genealogical publications; the IHS has attempted to identify as many persons residing in Idaho during the period, 1885-1894, as possible. An alphabetical surname index is contained in an *Excel* database that can be downloaded. See **https://docs.google.com/spreadsheets/d/1WlRwmFcbYtd drDZCmyvGvTbhHmZLM3W14BA3zJD7qO4/edit#gid=676 905024.**

1890-1967. *Idaho, Death Records* **[Online Database],** digitized and indexed at the Ancestry.com website. Source: 1890-1910: various counties, churches, mortuaries, physicians. (Registers, compiled lists, etc.). 1911-1967: Idaho Bureau of Vital Records, Boise (Death Certificates). Each index record includes: Name, Birth date, Birthplace, Death date, Death place, Father, Mother, and Certificate number. The document image may have much more information. This database has 674,817 records. See **https://search.ancestry.com/search/db.aspx?dbid=60566.**

1890-1964. *Idaho, Death Index, 1890-1964* **[Online Database],** indexed at the Ancestry.com website. Source: Idaho Bureau of Vital Statistics. Each index record includes: Name, Birthplace, Birth date, Death place, Death date, Father, Father's birthplace, Mother, Certificate year, and Certificate number. This database has 258,840 records. See **https://search.ancestry.com/search/db.aspx?dbid=6856.**

1891. *Boise City, Idaho Directory* **[Online Database],** indexed at the Ancestry.com website. This database has 2,248 records. See **http://search.ancestry.com/search/db.aspx?dbid=4417.**

1891-1929 Naturalization Records, Oneida County, Idaho **[Online Database],** indexed at the RootsWeb site for Oneida Co ID. Archived at **https://web.archive.org/web/20170131162403/www.roots web.ancestry.com/~idoneida/naturalization_records.htm.**

1891-1934 Naturalization Records, Southern District, Boise, Idaho **[Microfilm & Digital Capture],** from the original records at the federal courthouse, Boise, ID. Includes admission to citizenship records, petitions, declarations, and naturalization certificates. Filmed by the Genealogical Society of Utah, 1987, 4 rolls, beginning with FHL film #1513549. To access the digital images, see the online FHL catalog: **www.familysearch.org/search/catalog/662282.**

1892-1935. *Naturalization Records, Central District, Moscow, Idaho* **[Microfilm & Digital Capture],** from the original records at the federal courthouse, Boise, ID. Includes admission to citizenship records, petitions, declarations, and naturalization certificates. Filmed by the Genealogical Society of Utah, 1987, 1 roll, FHL film #1513554. To access the digital images, see the online FHL catalog:
www.familysearch.org/search/catalog/570774.
- See also, **Idaho Naturalization *Records, 1892-1990* [Online Database],** digitized and indexed at FamilySearch.org. Source: National Archives, records of the federal district courts of Idaho. This database has 15,751 records, see
www.familysearch.org/search/collection/3241358.

1893-1939. See *Wills, Canyon County, Idaho, 1893-1939; Index, 1900-1936* **[Microfilm & Digital Capture],** from the originals at the Canyon County Courthouse in Caldwell, Idaho. Filmed by the Genealogical Society of Utah, 1986, 2 rolls, FHL film #1255612 and #1255628. To access the digital images, see the online FHL catalog:
www.familysearch.org/search/catalog/366506.

1893-1945. *Naturalization Records, Eastern District, Pocatello, Idaho* **[Microfilm & Digital Capture],** from the original records at the federal courthouse, Boise, ID. Includes admission to citizenship records, petitions, declarations, and naturalization certificates. Filmed by the Genealogical Society of Utah, 1987, 4 rolls, beginning with FHL film #1513554. To access the digital images, see the online FHL catalog:
www.familysearch.org/search/catalog/570776.

1893-1977. *Idaho, Bannock County, Index to Estates and Guardianships* **[Digital Capture],** from the original records at the Bannock County Courthouse, Pocatello, Idaho. Digitized by the

Genealogical Society of Utah, 2010. To access the digital images, see the online FHL catalog: www.familysearch.org/search/catalog/2200481.

1897-1945 Directories, Payette County, Idaho [Online Database], indexed at the Payette County Info site. See
http://payettecounty.info/directories/intro.html.

1898-1910. *School Census, Kootenai County, Idaho* [Microfilm & Digital Capture], from the originals at the Kootenai County Courthouse, Coeur D'Alene, Idaho. Filmed by the Genealogical Society of Utah, 1988, 3 rolls, FHL film #1548249, #1548250, & #1548251. To access the digital images of these rolls, see the online FHL catalog page for this title: www.familysearch.org/search/catalog/387228.

1899. See *An Illustrated History of the State of Idaho: Containing a History of the State of Idaho from the Earliest Period of its Discovery to the Present Time, Together with Glimpses of its Auspicious Futures; Illustrations… and Biographical Mention of Many Pioneers and Prominent Citizens of Today* [Printed Book, Microfilm & Digital Capture], by Lewis Pub. Co., Chicago, IL, 1899, 2 vols., FHL book 979.6 H2ih v.1-2. Also on microfilm, FHL film #1000164. To access the digital images of this book, see the online FHL catalog page for this title:
www.familysearch.org/search/catalog/200849.

1899-1903 School Census, Kootenai County, Idaho [Online Database], indexed at the USGenWeb site for Bonner Co ID. See
http://files.usgwarchives.net/id/bonner/history/schools/18991903.txt.

1899-1903 School Census, Bonner County, Idaho [Online Database], indexed at the USGenWeb site for Bonner Co ID. See
http://files.usgwarchives.net/id/bonner/history/schools/18991903.txt.

1900. *Idaho, 1900 Federal Census: Soundex and Population Schedules* [Microfilm & Digital Capture], from the original records held by the Bureau of the Census in the 1940s. After microfilming, Congress allowed the Census Bureau to destroy the originals to free up space for WWII-related files. Filmed on 23 rolls, beginning with FHL film #1242913 (Soundex, A000-B400), and FHL film #1240231 (Population schedules, Ada, Bannock, Bear Lake, and Bingham counties). To access the digital images, see the online FHL catalog:
www.familysearch.org/search/catalog/650116.

1900-1969 Idaho Directories, as part of *U.S. City Directories, 1822-1995* [Online Database], digitized and OCR indexed at the Ancestry.com website. See each directory title page image for the full title and publication information. This collection is one of the largest single databases on the Internet. All states are represented (except Alaska) with a total of 1.56 billion names, all indexed from scanned images of the city directory book pages. Idaho directories are listed here for an **Idaho City/County** (No. of years), and Date-Range: **Blackfoot** (1) 1939, **Boise** (35) 1900-1960, **Canyon Co** (8) 1945-1960, **Clearwater Co** (4) 1909-1916, **Coeur d'Alene** (11) 1911-1954, **Grangeville** (1) 1913, **Idaho Falls** (23) 1911-1969, **Kootenai Co** (2) 1914-1916, **Lewiston** (2) 1903-1908, **Nampa** (7) 1945-1960, **Pocatello** (31) 1901-1960, **Rexburg** (1) 1939, **Sandpoint** (1) 1910, **Twin Falls** (6) 1920-1932, **Wallace** (1) 1910, and **Weiser** (2) 1913-1915. Use Ancestry's *Browse this Collection* feature to choose a state, choose a city, and choose a directory year available for that city. This database has 1,560,284,702 U.S. records. See https://search.ancestry.com/search/db.aspx?dbid=2469.

1900-1988. *Idaho, Teton County Records* [Online Database], digitized and indexed at the FamilySearch.org website. Records include marriage, land, and property records at the county courthouse in Driggs, ID. This database has 778 records, see www.familysearch.org/search/collection/1921129.

1902-1984. *Boise City and Ada County Directory* [Microfilm], the R.L. Polk directories from 1902 to 1984, with some years missing. Filmed by the Genealogical Society of Utah, 1973-1989, 11 rolls, beginning with FHL film 1036517 (1902-1903). For a complete list of roll numbers and contents of each roll, see the online FHL catalog page for this title. See www.familysearch.org/search/catalog/79258.

1903-1904. *The Idanha Chieftain (Soda Springs, Idaho)* [Online Database], newspaper digitized and indexed at the Ancestry.com website:
http://search.ancestry.com/search/db.aspx?dbid=6877.

1903-1932. *Lewiston and Nez Perce County (Idaho) Directories* [Microfilm], from the originals located at various libraries, for the 1903-1904, 1908-1909, 1910-1911, and 1931-1932 directories. Filmed by Primary Source Microfilm, Woodbridge, CT, 1995, 1 roll, FHL film #2310374.

1903-1982. *Idaho, Naturalization Records* **[Online Database],** digitized and indexed at the Ancestry.com website. Source: U.S. District courts in Idaho. Naturalization records include Declarations, Petitions, and Certificates. Each index record includes: Name, Gender, Record type, Birth date, Birthplace, Petition date, Petition place, Spouse, Court district, and Petition number. The document image may have more information. This database has 16,130 records. See
https://search.ancestry.com/search/db.aspx?dbid=2032.

1904-1931. *Soda Springs Chieftain (Soda Springs, Idaho)* **[Online Database],** digitized and indexed at the Ancestry.com website, a fully searchable text version of the newspaper from 1904-1907, 1911-1914, 1916-1921, 1924, and 1928-1931. This database has 5,130 records. See
http://search.ancestry.com/search/db.aspx?dbid=6875.

1906-1968. *Idaho, Twin Falls County Records* **[Online Database],** digitized at the FamilySearch.org website. This is an image-only database. Includes death index, probate index, marriages, deeds, homesteads, patents discharges, and coroner's records from the Clerk of District Court, Clerk and Recorder offices in Twin Falls, ID. This database has 180,915 images. See
www.familysearch.org/search/collection/2023222.
- This database is also available at the Ancestry.cm website. See
https://search.ancestry.com/search/db.aspx?dbid=60278.

1907-1911 Death Register, Lincoln County, Idaho **[Online Database],** indexed at the USGenWeb site for Lincoln Co ID. See
http://files.usgwarchives.net/id/lincoln/vitals/deaths/death-register.txt.

1907-1965. *Idaho, Deaths and Burials* **[Online Database],** digitized and indexed at the FamilySearch.org website, from microfilm at the Family History Library in Salt Lake City, UT. This database has 28,352 records. See
www.familysearch.org/search/collection/1674815.
- This database is also available at the Ancestry.com website, see
https://search.ancestry.com/search/db.aspx?dbid=60271.

1907-1920. *Idaho, County Birth and Death Records* **[Online Database],** indexed at the Ancestry.com website. Source: FamilySearch. This database has 2,426 records. See
https://search.ancestry.com/search/db.aspx?dbid=60268.

1908. See **Index to 1908 Idaho County Tax List** **[Online Database],** indexed at the USGenWeb site for Idaho Co ID. See
http://idaho.idgenweb.org/TAX/tax1908.htm.

1908-1911. *Inheritance Tax Records, Kootenai County, Idaho* **[Microfilm & Digital Capture],** from the original records at the Kootenai County Courthouse, Coeur D'Alene, Idaho. Filmed by the Genealogical Society of Utah, 1988, 1 roll, FHL film #1548121. To access the digital images, see the online FHL catalog:
www.familysearch.org/search/catalog/384810.

1909-1929. *Naturalization Records, Northern District, Coeur d'Alene, Idaho* **[Microfilm & Digital Capture],** from the original records at the federal courthouse, Boise, ID. Includes admission to citizenship records, petitions, declarations, and naturalization certificates. Filmed by the Genealogical Society of Utah, 1987, 3 rolls, beginning with FHL film #1513552. For a complete list of roll numbers, roll contents, and the digital images of each roll, see the online FHL catalog page for this title. See
www.familysearch.org/search/catalog/570768.

1909-1917. *Carey Act Final Certificates and Patents, Lincoln County, Idaho* **[Online Database],** indexed at the USGenWeb site for Jerome Co ID. Includes now Gooding and Jerome counties. The Carey Act was also called the Federal Desert Land Act. It allowed private companies in the western semi-arid states to construct irrigation systems for profit. See
http://files.usgwarchives.net/id/gooding/land/careyact.

1910. Idaho, 1910 Federal Census: Population Schedules **[Microfilm & Digital Capture],** from the original records held by the Bureau of the Census in the 1940s. After microfilming, Congress allowed the Census Bureau to destroy the originals to free up space for WWII-related files. Filmed on 8 rolls, beginning with FHL film #1374234 (Ada and Bannock counties). To access the digital images, see the online FHL catalog:
www.familysearch.org/search/catalog/648372.

1910 Idaho Census Index **[Printed Index],** compiled by Upper Snake River Valley Family History Center volunteers and McKay Library employees at Ricks College; edited by Blaine R. Bake, published by Precision Indexing, Bountiful, UT, 1993, 1,245 pages, FHL book 979.6 X22u. Reprinted by Heritage Quest, North Salt Lake, UT, 2001, 2 vols., FHL book 979.6 X22b v.1-2.

1910. *Idaho State Federal Census Index, 1910* **[Printed Index],** compiled by the Idaho Genealogical Society, printed by Northwest Printing, Boise, ID, 1991, 941 pages, FHL book 979.6 X22i.

1911-1937. See **Idaho Death Certificates, 1911-1937; Index, 1911-1932 [Microfilm & Digital Capture],** from the originals at the Department of Health and Welfare in Boise, Idaho (1988). Death certificates are arranged by filing order number. Some certificates are out of order or are missing. Some are filmed at the end of the film. Certificates are arranged somewhat chronologically. Includes index. Filmed by the Genealogical Society of Utah, 1988, 63 rolls, beginning with FHL film #1543485 (Index, Aakre, Ingeborg Saaveson – Bailan, Alex). To access the digital images, see the online FHL catalog:
www.familysearch.org/search/catalog/644787.

1911-1937. *Idaho Death Certificates* **[Online Database],** this series was digitized and indexed at the FamilySearch.org website. This database has 106,484 records. See
www.familysearch.org/search/collection/1546448.

1911-1950. See *Idaho Death Index For Years 1911 thru 1950.* CD-ROM publication of the Department of Health & Welfare, Bureau of Vital Records & Health Statistics, Boise, ID. Includes name of deceased, year and certificate number, city of death, date of death and birth. FHL CD-ROM No. 661.
- See also, *Idaho Death Index, 1911-1950* **[Online Database],** indexed at the Ancestry.com website, from data of the Idaho Bureau of Health Policy and Vital Statistics, Boise, ID. This database has 175,722 records. See
http://search.ancestry.com/search/db.aspx?dbid=6856.
- See also, *Idaho State Death Index, 1911-1956* **[Online Database],** indexed at the BYU-Idaho Special Collections website. Search screen:
http://abish.byui.edu/specialCollections/famhist/Death/searchForm.cfm.

1913. *Index to the 1913 Stockman's Guide (Southeastern Idaho)* **[Microfilm],** from the original published by J. Burrup, West Valley City, UT, 1992 filmed by the Genealogical Society of Utah, 1992, 1 roll, FHL film #1597930.

1913-1920s. *Idaho State Archives Mothers' Pensions Index* **[Online Database],** indexed by the Idaho State Archives. In 1913, the State of Idaho approved a program to provide a small monthly payment to mothers and orphans under certain circumstances. Originally maintained by each county, the Mothers' Pension Records includes materials transferred from Ada, Bannock, Bear Lake, Bingham, Blaine, Caribou, Clearwater, Minidoka, Oneida, Power, Teton, and Twin Falls counties. The records continue through the 1920s and are valuable genealogical sources. This database was produced in *Microsoft Excel* format, which can be downloaded for printing, sorting, etc. See
https://docs.google.com/spreadsheets/d/1HV79MBtYtk_9rF4qxallzbggyXCnugnHzsUTotzZjq0/edit#gid=836656701.

1913-1928 *Declaration of Intention Index, Franklin County, Idaho* **[Online Database],** indexed at the RootsWeb site for Franklin Co ID:. Archived at
https://web.archive.org/web/20160615225939/www.rootsweb.ancestry.com/~idfrankl/declaration_of_intention.htm.

1913-1961. *Idaho, Minidoka County Records* **[Online Database],** digitized at the FamilySearch.org website. This is an image-only database. Records include marriages, naturalizations, land and property, probates, school, and military records located at the courthouse in Rupert, ID. This database has 42,995 images. Browse through the images, organized by Record Category, Record Type, Volume, and Date Range. See
www.familysearch.org/search/collection/1928861.

1915-1916. *Kelly's Farm Directory; Bonneville, Jefferson and Madison Counties, Idaho* **[Printed Book & Digital Capture],** by T. Leo Kelly, publ. Caxton Printers, Boise, ID, 1916, 320 pages, FHL book 979.6 E4. For access to the digital version of this book, see the online FHL catalog page:
www.familysearch.org/search/catalog/2172634.

1915-1954. *Soda Springs Sun (Soda Springs, Idaho)* **[Online Database],** digitized and indexed at the Ancestry.com website. A fully searchable text version of the newspaper from 1915-1916, 1932-1935, and 1938-1954. This database has 8,637 records. See
http://search.ancestry.com/search/db.aspx?dbid=6878.

1917-1918. *Idaho, World War I Selective Service System Draft Registration Cards, 1917-1918* **[Microfilm & Digital Capture],** from the originals at the National Archives, East Point, GA. The draft cards are arranged by county or city, then by surname

of the registrants. Filmed by the National Archives, Series M1509, 20 rolls, beginning with FHL film #1452106 (Ada, Adams, Bannock Counties). To access the digital images, see the online FHL catalog: www.familysearch.org/search/catalog/746974.
- See also, *Idaho, World War I American Expeditionary Forces, Deaths* [Digital Capture], from records of the Adjutant General's Office, National Archives, Washington, DC., title, World War I Dead. To access the digital images, see the online FHL catalog: www.familysearch.org/search/catalog/3023922.

1917-1918 Civilian Draft Registrations, Idaho [Online Database], indexed at the USGenWeb site for each Idaho county. Go to the ID Index, find a county of interest, then go to "Military." For the ID index, see http://files.usgwarchives.net/id/.

1920. *Idaho, 1920 Federal Census: Soundex and Population Schedules* [Microfilm & Digital Capture], from the original records held by the Bureau of the Census in the 1940s. After microfilming, Congress allowed the Census Bureau to destroy the originals to free up space for WWII-related files. Filmed on 41 rolls, beginning with FHL film #1824257 (Soundex, A000-A616), and FHL film #1820289 (Population schedules, Ada, Adams, Bear Lake, and Boise counties). To access the digital images, see the online FHL catalog: www.familysearch.org/search/catalog/568135.

1924-1956. *Idaho, Eastport, Arrival Manifests* [Online Database], digitized and indexed at the FamilySearch.org website. Source: National Archives microfilm A3460. This collection contains arrival and departure manifests at Eastport, Idaho from 1924-1956. This database has 217,016 records. See www.familysearch.org/search/collection/2072140.

1927. *Boise City and Ada County, Idaho Directory* [Online Database], indexed at the Ancestry.com website. This database contains the 1927 directory for Boise City and Ada County, Idaho. This directory includes a street and avenue guide for Boise, an alphabetical listing of names of residents of Boise (including their addresses and occupational information), a farmers and landowners listing for Ada County, a householder's directory, and a business directory. There is also miscellaneous information on the following towns in Ada County: Barber, Eagle, Kuna, Mayfield, Meridian, Mora, Orchard, Owyhee, Star, and Ustick: http://search.ancestry.com/search/db.aspx?dbid=7324.

1930. *Idaho, 1930 Federal Census: Population Schedules* [Microfilm & Digital Capture], from the original records held by the Bureau of the Census in the 1940s. After microfilming, Congress allowed the Census Bureau to destroy the originals to free up space for WWII-related files. Filmed on 10 rolls, beginning with FHL film #2340130 (Ada, Adams, and Bear Lake counties). To access the digital images, see the online FHL catalog: www.familysearch.org/search/catalog/1035336.

1930. *Idaho Gazetteer and Business Directory: And Buyers' Guide* [Printed Book], published by R. L. Polk & Co., Chicago, 1930. FHL book 979.E4p.

1930 Naturalizations, Payette County, Idaho [Online Database], indexed at the Payette County.info site. See http://payettecounty.info/sub/natural.html.

1931-1936. *Idaho State Archives Old Age Pension Index* [Online Database]. Indexed by the Idaho State Archives. In 1931, the State of Idaho introduced an Old Age Pension Act, which provided a monthly payment of $25.00 to qualified residents of Idaho. The state old age pensions were continued until replaced by the national pension system (Social Security), which began in 1935. These records are for applications for an old age pension from Ada, Kootenai, Twin Falls, Jerome, Clearwater, Bannock, Boundary, and Teton counties, ranging from 1931 to 1936. The records provide the applicant's first and last name, date and place of birth, nationality, occupation, and residence at time of application, total property holdings, and previous yearly income. In addition, many records provide the names, residences, occupations, and estimated yearly incomes of the applicant's relatives, including siblings and children. This database was produced in Microsoft Excel format, which can be downloaded for printing, sorting, etc. See
https://docs.google.com/spreadsheets/d/1Hvg8mmA4WOuZjgRUl0BoVXzB6DL55WWOE9H-kejFq7k/edit#gid=1572461861.

1936-1964. *Idaho, Madison County Records* [Online Database], digitized and indexed at FamilySearch.org. Includes marriage license records, 1936-1946; 1946-1951; and marriage records, 1952-1962; and 1962-1964. This database has 2,352 records, see
www.familysearch.org/search/collection/1916167.

1938-1961. *Idaho Death Certificates* [Online Database], indexed at the FamilySearch.org website. Source: Idaho Dept of Health and Welfare, Boise, ID. Each index record includes: Name, Event type, Event

date, Event place, Birthdate, Birthplace, Father's name, Father's birthplace, Mother's name, Mother's birthplace, and Certificate number. This database has 115,804 records. See
www.familysearch.org/search/collection/2612577.

1938-1948. *The North Gem Herald (Bancroft, Idaho)* **[Online Database]**, indexed at the Ancestry.com website for 1938 and 1947-1948:
http://search.ancestry.com/search/db.aspx?dbid=6874.

1940. *Idaho, 1940 Federal Census: Population Schedules* **[Digital Capture]**, digitized images from microfilm of original records held by the Bureau of the Census in the 1940s. After microfilming, Congress allowed the Census Bureau to destroy the originals to free up space for WWII-related files. Digitizing of the 1940 census schedules microfilm images was done for the National Archives and made public in 2012. To access the digital images, see the online FHL catalog:
www.familysearch.org/search/catalog/2057752.

1940 Federal Census Finding Aids **[Online Database]**. The National Archives prepared a special website online with a detailed description of the 1940 federal census. Included at the site are descriptions of location finding aids, such as Enumeration District Maps, Geographic Descriptions of Census Enumeration Districts, and a list of 1940 City Directories available at the National Archives. The finding aids are all linked to other National Archives sites. The National Archives website also has a link to 1940 Search Engines using Stephen P. Morse's "One-Step" system for finding a 1940 E.D. or street address conversion. See
www.archives.gov/research/census/1940/general-info.html#questions.

1940-1945. *Idaho, World War II Draft Registration Cards* **[Online Database]**, digitized and indexed at FamilySearch.org. Draft registration cards of men who registered during World War II, with the exception of the fourth registration. Images courtesy of Ancestry. At the database search page, click on "Learn More" for a review of the World War II drafts, conducted seven times between 1940 and 1943. This database has 138,954 records, see
www.familysearch.org/search/collection/2709446.
- See also, *Idaho, World War II Draft Registration Cards, 1940-1945* **[Digital Capture]**, digitized from the National Archive microfilm by Ancestry.com. The registration cards are organized in alpha order for the name of the registrants. To view the list of Digital File Folders with contents, and to access the digital images, see the online FHL catalog:
www.familysearch.org/search/catalog/2709446.

1942. *Idaho Military Records: World War II 4th Draft Registration Cards, 1942* **[Microfilm & Digital Capture]**, from the original records at the National Personnel Records Center, St. Louis, MO. Digitized from FHL microfilm, 2014, 52 rolls, beginning with FHL film #100770112. (Draft Registrations, Abbot, Charles – Anderson, Edward, 1942). To access the digital images, see the online FHL catalog:
www.familysearch.org/search/catalog/2425785.

1941-1945. *World War II Casualty & Prisoner List, Utah & Idaho* **[Typescript & Digital Version]**, from a 300-page typescript at the Family History Library in Salt Lake City. To access the digital version, see the online FHL catalog:
www.familysearch.org/search/catalog/2696321.

1942-1945. *Idaho, Jerome County Historical Society, Minidoka Japanese Relocation Center Military Records* **[Online Database]**, indexed at the FamilySearch.org website. This collection is an index to military record index cards of those interned at the Minidoka Japanese Relocation Center (also known as Camp Hunt) located in Jerome County, Idaho from 1942-1945. It reached its' maximum population of 9,397 in March 1943. Most of the internees came from the Seattle, Washington and Portland, Oregon areas with a few (200) also coming from Alaska. This database has 1,469 records. See
www.familysearch.org/search/collection/2821287.

1942-1945. *Idaho, Jerome County Historical Society, Minidoka Japanese Relocation Center Mixed Vital Records* **[Online Database]**, indexed at the FamilySearch.org website. The mixed vital records included in this index are deaths, engagements, and weddings. The index card images reference the date and page of the Minidoka Irrigator, a weekly newspaper published in and for the camp, in which the records can be found as well as the record type, name, and any other pertinent information for the record. This database has 398 records. See
www.familysearch.org/search/collection/2821288.

1943-2013. *Idaho, Southern Counties Obituaries* **[Online Database]**, indexed at the FamilySearch.org website. Source: Blackfoot Idaho Family History Center. Obituaries from a variety of Idaho newspapers and housed at different LDS Family

History Centers throughout the state. This database has 169,412 records. See
www.familysearch.org/search/collection/2290243.

1947-1948. *Gem Valley Chronicle (Grace, Idaho)* **[Online Database],** newspaper indexed at the Ancestry.com website. See
http://search.ancestry.com/search/db.aspx?dbid=6873.

1947-1961. *Idaho, Marriage Index* **[Online Database],** indexed at the FamilySearch.org website, an index to marriages created by the Bureau of Vital Records and Health Statistics, covering marriages filed between May 1, 1947 and December 31, 1961. This database has 131,597 records. See
www.familysearch.org/search/collection/2106101.

1947-1963. *Idaho, Divorce Index* **[Online Database],** indexed at the FamilySearch.org website, an index to divorces created by the Bureau of Vital Records and Health Statistics, covering divorces filed between May 1, 1947 and December 31,1961. This database has 43,956 records. See
www.familysearch.org/search/collection/2106102.

1947-1967. *Idaho, Divorce Records* **[Online Database],** digitized and indexed at the Ancestry.com website. Source: Idaho Bureau of Vital Records. Each index record includes: Name, Divorce date, Divorce place, Spouse, Certificate year, Certificate number. The document image has more information. This database has 112,056 records. See
https://search.ancestry.com/search/db.aspx?dbid=8989.

1948 Village Census, Fruitland, Idaho **[Online Database],** indexed at the PayetteCounty.info site:
http://payettecounty.info/census/fruitland.html.

1949-1977. *Idaho State Journal (Pocatello, Idaho)* **[Online Database],** digitized and indexed at the Ancestry.com website, a fully searchable text version of the newspaper for the years 1949-1977:
http://search.ancestry.com/search/db.aspx?dbid=51536.

1950-1977. *Post-Register (Idaho Falls, Idaho)* **[Online Database],** digitized and indexed at the Ancestry.com website, a fully searchable text version of the newspaper for the years 1950-1977:
http://search.ancestry.com/search/db.aspx?dbid=51890.

1950s-1920s. See *Utah and Idaho Cemetery Records* **[Online Database],** indexed at the Ancestry.com website, this database was taken from a 2-volume book of cemetery extractions published by the Genealogical Society of Utah. A check of the earliest dates of birth for persons interred in the various cemeteries revealed some in the 1820s, and most were before 1920. The source of the cemetery record will be known after a surname search. The contents page of the book is listed at the Ancestry.com site with an alphabetical list of the names of cemeteries involved:
http://search.ancestry.com/search/db.aspx?dbid=28786.

1959-1962. *Caribou County Sun (Soda Springs, Idaho)* **[Online Database],** digitized and indexed at the Ancestry.com website, a fully searchable text version of the newspaper from 1959, and 1961-1962. This database has 1,017 records. See
http://search.ancestry.com/search/db.aspx?dbid=6876.

1965-1976. *Idaho Free Press (Nampa, Idaho)* **[Online Database],** digitized and indexed at the Ancestry.com website, a fully searchable text version of the newspaper for the years 1965-1976:
http://search.ancestry.com/search/db.aspx?dbid=51534.

1969 Directory, Idaho Falls, Idaho **[Online Database],** indexed at the Ancestry.com website. The database title is *Idaho City Directories*, and indicates there are several cities represented, but a search of the database for years and cities revealed only the Idaho Falls directory for 1969 is included:
http://search.ancestry.com/search/db.aspx?dbid=8983.
- Digital images of a 1969 Directory is also available at the FHL catalog page (with the title ***Bonneville County Farm Directory).*** See
www.familysearch.org/search/catalog/2137593.

1977-1991. *Eastern Idaho Anniversaries, 1977-1991* **[Microfilm & Digital Capture],** from newspaper clippings at the Bonneville County Family History Center, Idaho Falls, ID. Includes newspaper clippings of wedding anniversaries of 50 or more years. Includes index at beginning of each year. Filmed by the Genealogical Society of Utah, 1994, 1 roll, FHL film #1954303. To access the digital images, see the online FHL catalog:
www.familysearch.org/search/catalog/702042.

1977-1882. Eastern Idaho Births [Microfilm & Digital Capture], from records at the Bonneville County Family History Center, Idaho Falls, Idaho. Includes yearly index by parents' names, arranged by hospital where birth occurred. To access the digital images, see the online FHL catalog:
www.familysearch.org/search/catalog/702026.

1981-1985. *Eastern Idaho Marriage Licenses* **[Microfilm & Digital Capture],** from records at the Bonneville County Family History Center, Idaho Falls, ID. Arranged chronologically. Filmed by the Genealogical Society of Utah, 1994, 1 roll, FHL film #1954302. To access the digital images, see the online FHL catalog:
www.familysearch.org/search/catalog/702040.

1982-1992. *Eastern Idaho Weddings* **[Microfilm & Digital Capture],** from records at the Bonneville County Family History Center, Idaho Falls, ID. Includes newspaper clippings of weddings. Includes index at beginning of each year. Filmed by the Genealogical Society of Utah, 1994, 2 rolls, FHL film #1954302 (1982-1989) and FHL film #1954303 (1990-1992). To access the digital images, see the online FHL catalog:
www.familysearch.org/search/catalog/702042.

1989-Current. *Idaho Newspaper Obituaries* **[Online Database].** Digitized and indexed at the GenealogyBank.com website. Search for obituaries published in city newspapers for Blackfoot, Boise, Bonners Ferry, Challis, Coeur d'Alene, Emmett, Idaho Falls, Kellogg, Kuna, Lewiston, Meridian, Montpelier, Moscow, Nampa, Payette, Pocatello, Preston, Priest River, Rigby, Sandpoint, Shelley, and Twin Falls. See
www.genealogybank.com/gbnk/obituaries/explore/USA/Idaho.

1990-2007. *Idaho, Obituaries, 2007* **[Online Database],** digitized and indexed at the FamilySearch.org website, from originals collected and housed at the Idaho Falls FamilySearch Center. Obituaries are from various Idaho newspapers printed in 2007. This collection has multiple arrangements by Idaho city or town, mixed cities, and name, and by out-of-state deaths of Idaho natives. This database has 9,165 images. See
www.familysearch.org/search/collection/1876879.

- See also, *Idaho, Miscellaneous Funeral Home Obituaries, 1990-2007* **[Digital Capture],** located at the Idaho Falls FamilySearch Center. To access the digital images, see the online FHL catalog:
www.familysearch.org/search/catalog/3477938.

188 • *Census Substitutes & State Census Records*

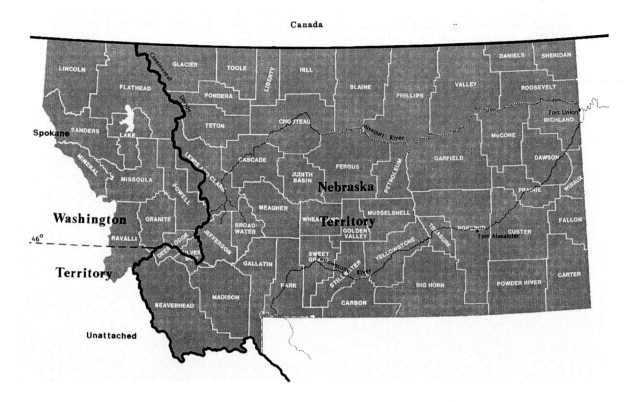

Montana Area in the 1860 Federal Census. The western population was in the Bitterroot Valley, Spokane County, Washington Territory. For convenience, the eastern population at Fort Union and Fort Alexander were both enumerated as part of Unorganized Dakota. Fort Benton was missed.

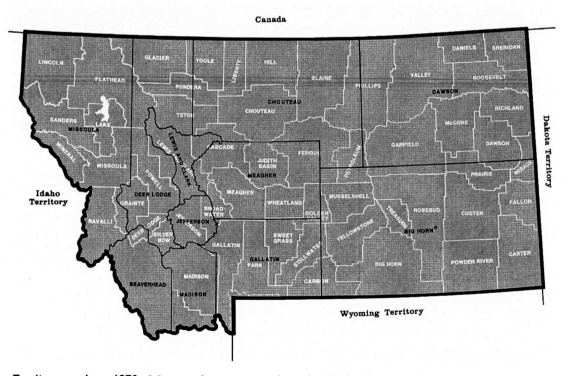

Montana Territory • June 1870. Montana became a territory in 1864. The map shows, in black, the 11 counties of Montana Territory as the time of the 1870 federal census. Montana's 56 current counties are shown in white.

Montana
Censuses & Substitute Name Lists

Historical Timeline for Montana, 1803-1864

1803. Captains William Clark and Meriwether Lewis led the Corps of Discovery, the first transcontinental expedition of the land west of the Missouri River. Their trek to the Pacific was mostly via river routes, beginning at St. Louis on the Mississippi, up the Missouri River to its source in Montana, then by foot across the Mountains, picking up Idaho's Clearwater River, to the Snake River of Idaho, Oregon, and Washington, and finally, the Columbia River all the way to its mouth at present Astoria, Oregon.

1807. British Canadian fur trader and mapmaker David Thompson, with the Montreal-based North West Fur Company, began looking for routes from the Rocky Mountains to the Pacific Ocean. He led a crew of French-Canadian fur trappers, established fur trading opportunities with any Indian tribes encountered, and charted detailed maps of the Columbia River. From 1807 to 1809, Thompson established the first trading post in present Montana at Kootenai Falls near Libby; the first in present Idaho, Kullyspell House, on Pend Oreille Lake; and the first trading post in present Washington, now Bonner's Ferry, on the Columbia River.

1807. Fur trader Manuel Lisa established Fort Raymond, a fur trading post in present day Montana, at the mouth of the Bighorn River on the Yellowstone River.

1807. John Colter, recent member of the Lewis and Clark expedition, now a mountain man, fur trapper, and explorer, was the first to describe a place where "hot water shoots straight into the air, the earth bubbles as if it were boiling, and almost extinct geysers thunder as if possessed by angry spirits." He referred to the area in his written report as *Colter's Hell*. Most easterners believed he was lying or exaggerating – it was hard to believe such a place could really exist. Colter's Hell is now called Yellowstone National Park.

1818. Anglo-American Convention. Britain and the U.S. agreed to the 49th parallel as the international boundary from the Lake of the Woods (now Minnesota) to the Continental Divide (in present Montana).
- Also in the 1818 treaty, The United States and Great Britain agreed to a joint occupation of the Oregon Country/Columbia District. Both parties accepted the area as extending from the Continental Divide to the Pacific Ocean, and from about Latitude 54° in present British Columbia, to the Boundary Mountains (now Siskiyou Mountains) at about Latitude 42°).
- In 1827 a provision was added to the treaty that allowed either party to invoke a conclusion of ownership, by giving 12 months' notice to the other. Notice was not given until 1845, when President James K. Polk sought resolution, leading to a new treaty in 1846.

1828. Fort Union. At the mouth of the Yellowstone River on the Missouri River (near the present Montana-North Dakota line), an earlier Fort Henry was taken over by the American Fur Company in 1828 and renamed Fort Union. It became the center for John Jacob Astor's fur trading empire in the northern Plains.

1832. The first steamboat into Montana was the *Yellowstone*, which began annual trips from St. Louis up the Missouri River to Fort Union. Similar to the annual rendezvous system used in Wyoming and Idaho, the early fur traders of Montana converged on Fort Union every Fall to trade their furs for supplies, weapons, and cash.

1839. Fr. Pierre-Jean DeSmet arrived among the Flatheads in the Bitterroot Valley of present Montana. He and his staff would set up a number of Jesuit missions in the present states of Montana, Washington, and Idaho.

1841. St. Mary's Mission, the first permanent settlement by Europeans in the Montana area was established by Jesuit missionaries led by Fr. DeSmet.

1847. Fort Benton was established on the Missouri River as a military and trading post. It soon became the "Head of Navigation" to the west, and the world's furthest inland port. Steamboats brought gold seekers, fur traders, settlers, and supplies, making Fort Benton the "Birthplace of Montana." Of all the forts on the Missouri and Yellowstone rivers, Fort Benton is the only one that continues as a town today. It is located in north central Montana, about 30 miles northeast of Great Falls.

1848. On February 2nd, the Treaty of Hidalgo Guadalupe was signed, ending the war with Mexico. As part of the treaty, the Mexican provinces of California and Santa Fe de Nuevo Mexico were annexed to the U.S., which included all or part of the present states of California, Nevada, Arizona, New Mexico, Utah, and western Colorado.
– On August 14th, **Oregon Territory** was created by Congress. It encompassed the area between the 42nd and 49th parallels, from the Pacific to the Continental Divide. The first capital was Oregon City.

1850. June. A **Federal Census** was taken in Oregon Territory, which included the area of present Oregon, Washington, and Idaho; and Montana and Wyoming areas west of the Continental Divide. The population was revealed as 12,093 people. No population was recorded in the present Idaho, Montana, or Wyoming areas.

1853. Washington Territory was created by Congress. It encompassed the present area of Washington, but extended east to the Rocky Mountains, incorporating areas that today are in northern Idaho and western Montana. As a result, the original Oregon Territory was split in half. Oregon Territory now had lands on the same line as its present northern border stretching to the Continental Divide, and included the southern half of present Idaho, and a portion of present western Montana and Wyoming.

1859. Oregon joined the Union as the 33rd state, a Free State with the same boundaries as present. The population of the new state was about 45,000 people. The eastern remnants of Oregon Territory, 1853-1859, were added to Washington Territory.

1860. June. **Federal Census.** Washington Territory population was at 11,594. The area included present Washington and Idaho; and areas west of the Continental Divide in present Montana and Wyoming. The only recorded population outside of the present Washington bounds was for the residents of the Bitterroot Valley and Ponderay Mountain areas of present Montana; and a few farmers in Idaho's Bear Lake area taken as part of Cache County, Utah Territory.
– Present Montana east of the Continental Divide was part of Nebraska Territory, but for convenience the trading posts of Fort Union on the Missouri River and Fort Alexander on the Yellowstone River were enumerated in 1860 as part of Unorganized Dakota. Fort Benton and a couple of other outposts in Montana were missed. See the 1860 map on page 188.

1861. Dakota Territory was created, with boundaries that included all of Montana and Wyoming east of the Continental Divide; and the areas of present North Dakota and South Dakota.

1863. Idaho Territory was created, with boundaries that included all of present Idaho, Montana, and Wyoming areas. This large area was short-lived, however, as Montana Territory was taken from the Idaho area a year later.

1864. Montana Territory was formed, taken from the obese Idaho Territory. From its beginning, Montana Territory had the same boundaries as the present state. The original area proposed for Montana Territory included what is now Idaho's northern panhandle, but Congress decided to keep that area as part of Idaho to offset the Mormon population in southern Idaho. The first territorial capital of Montana was established at Bannack, followed by Virginia City in 1865, and Helena in 1875.

1870. June. **Federal Census.** Montana Territory population at 20,595. The first eleven counties of Montana Territory, 1864-1867, are shown on the 1870 map on page 188.

1880. June. **Federal Census.** Montana Territory population at 39,159.

1889. Nov. 8th. **Montana** became the 41st state, with the state capital at Helena.

Bibliography
Montana Censuses & Substitutes

As Montana Territory, 1864-1889, no actual territory-wide census was ever taken. The only possible exception was a "Poll List of Voters" compiled in October 1864, which names the qualified voters for the entire territory. (Males 21 and over). An alphabetized extraction was published in 1987 with the tile, *Poll Lists for the Election of October 24, 1864*. but the sub-title and Introduction incorrectly states that the reason for the Poll List was "to establish Montana as a Territory." Montana had already become a Territory in May of 1864, and the reason for the Poll List was for the election of the first delegate to the U.S. House of Representatives.

As a guide to the territorial era, refer to the 1870 map of Montana (page 188) for the names and location of the first counties of the territory. The county courthouses, record centers, and local archives for these early counties were used as a source for identifying the earliest censuses and substitutes in this bibliography.

Upon statehood in 1889, Montana's state constitution provided that an enumeration of the population be taken in the year 1895 and each succeeding tenth year. Although authorized, no actual state-wide censuses were ever taken in Montana.

Statewide databases include online resources at Ancestry.com, FamilySearch.org, and several other Internet sites. The online databases, published books, articles, and microfilms are integrated in the bibliography, organized below in chronological order:

♦ ♦ ♦ ♦ ♦

1860 Census; Bitter Root Valley and Ponderay Mountains Area of Washington Territory, Now in the State of Montana **[Printed Book],** extracted & indexed by Margery H. Bell, Katherine Schaffer, Dennis Richards, no publication data noted. Includes index. The Bitterroot Valley extends through Ravalli and Missoula counties. From intro: "Includes an enumeration of the men attached to the American Boundary Commission (49 Degrees North). These men, surveying the northern boundary of the United States, could have been in present Montana, Idaho, or Washington." FHL book 978.6 X2b. Also on microfiche, FHL fiche #6049013.
- See also, *Montana 1860 Territorial Census Index* **[Printed Book],** by Accelerated Indexing Systems, Salt Lake City, UT, 1982, 6 pages. FHL book 978.6 X22m.

1860-2007. Montana Death Index **[Online Database],** indexed at the FamilySearch.org website. Source: MT Dept of Health, index by Ancestry.com. Each index record includes: Name, Event type, Event date, Gender, Age, Marital status, Birth year, Registration year, and Index number. This database has 663,371 records. See
https://familysearch.org/search/collection/1941331.

1860s-2000s. *Linkpendium – Montana: Family History & Genealogy, Census, Birth, Marriage, Death, Vital Records & More* **[Online Database].** Linkpendium is a genealogical portal site with links to state, county, town, and local databases. Currently listed are selected sites for Montana statewide resources (323), Renamed Counties, Discontinued Counties (1), Beaverhead County (327), Big Horn

County (115), Blaine County (110), Broadwater County (163), Carbon County (263), Carter County (73), Cascade County (568), Chouteau County (330), Custer County (201), Daniels County (74), Dawson County (147), Deer Lodge County (333), Fallon County (151), Fergus County (371), Flathead County (267), Gallatin County (519), Garfield County (84), Glacier County (107), Golden Valley County (75), Granite County (334), Hill County (159), Jefferson County (260), Judith Basin County (97), Lake County (117), Lewis and Clark County (785), Liberty County (92), Lincoln County (119), Madison County (329), McCone County (74), Meagher County (207), Mineral County (90), Missoula County (562), Musselshell County (113), Park County (297), Petroleum County (73), Phillips County (102), Pondera County (90), Powder River County (77), Powell County (204), Prairie County (77), Ravalli County (268), Richland County (106), Roosevelt County (107), Rosebud County (168), Sanders County (115), Sheridan County (99), Silver Bow County (767), Stillwater County (137), Sweet Grass County (176), Teton County (236), Toole County (89), Treasure County (80), Valley County (156), Wheatland County (105), Wibaux County (81), and Yellowstone County (483). See **www.linkpendium.com/mt-genealogy**.

1860s-2000s. *Montana USGenWeb Archives* **[Online Database].** The MTGenWeb site offers free genealogical databases with searchable statewide name lists and for all Montana counties. Databases may include Bibles, Biographies, Cemeteries, Censuses, Court Records, Deaths, Deeds, Directories, Histories, Marriages, Military, Newspapers, Obituaries, Photos, Schools, Tax Lists, Wills, and more. See **http://usgwarchives.net/mt/mtfiles.htm**.

1862-1890. See *1870-1900 Benton Area Census; 1890 Montana Census Schedules of Union Veterans and Widows of Civil War; 1862-1880 Record of French/Canadian Inhabitants of Chouteau County* **[Printed Book & Digital Version]**, no author, no publisher noted. To access the digital images, see the online FHL catalog:
www.familysearch.org/search/catalog/2848959.

1862-2009. *Montana, Beaverhead County Records* **[Online Database]**, digitized and indexed at the FamilySearch.org website. Source: FamilySearch extractions from the county courthouse, Dillon, MT. Each index record includes: Name, Event type, Event date, Event place, Gender, Age, Birth year, and Father's name. The original document image may have more information about a person. This database has 12,073 records. See
https://familysearch.org/search/collection/2075129.

1864. *Poll Lists for the Election of October 24, 1864* **[Printed Book & Digital Version].** Incorrect information from the Introduction: "This is a complete list of voters for the election on 24 October 1864. The election was held to determine if Montana was to become a Territory." Montana had already become a Territory in May of 1864, and the reason for the Poll List was to record the names of the voters participating in the election of Montana Territory's first delegate to the U.S. House of Representatives. The names were extracted and indexed, taken from the original published by the Montana Historical Society, Helena, MT, 1987. 139 pages. To access the digital images, see the online FHL catalog:
www.familysearch.org/search/catalog/3464827.

1864-1929. *First Families of Montana and Early Settlers* **[Printed Book]**, a project of the Montana State Genealogical Society to collect profiles of early pioneers, called the First Families of Montana, published by the society, 2000. The profiles were submitted by descendants. Al Stoner, project chairman. Includes lists of submitters. Contents: Part 1: To MT before 8 Nov 1889; and part 2: Early settlers of Montana 9 Nov 1889-31 Dec 1929. FHL book 978.6 D2s.

1864-1872 *Internal Revenue Assessments for the Territory of Montana* **[Microfilm & Digital Capture],** from the originals at the National Archives in Washington, DC. Includes annually, monthly and special lists of assessments for 1864-1872. Filmed by the National Archives, 1980 Series M0777, 1 roll, FHL film #1578505. To access the digital images, see the online FHL catalog:
www.familysearch.org/search/catalog/577995.

1864-1979. *Montana, County Naturalizations* **[Online Database],** digitized at the FamilySearch.org website. This is an image only database with county naturalization records for Beaverhead, Broadwater, Daniels, Dawson, Deer Lodge, Garfield, Granite, Jefferson, Lewis and Clark, Madison, McCone, Phillips, Powell, Ravalli, Richland, Roosevelt, Sheridan, Treasure, Valley, and Wibaux counties. Coverage dates vary by county. Browse the images, organized by County, then by Record Type, Year Range, and Volume Number. This database has 46,602 records. See
https://familysearch.org/search/collection/2091705.

1864-1985. *Gallatin County, Montana, Birth Index* **[Online Database],** indexed at the Ancestry.com website. This database is also accessible at the Gallatin County Genealogical Society website. Each index record includes: Name, Gender, Birth date, Birthplace, Father, Publication title, Publication date, Page, Repository, Notes, and a link to Gallatin Co GS website. This database has 6,590 records. See http://search.ancestry.com/search/db.aspx?dbid=9749.

1864-1993. See *Marriage Records, 1856-1952; Index, 1856-1993, Beaverhead County, Montana* **[Microfilm & Digital Capture]**, from the original records at the Beaverhead County Courthouse, Dillon, MT. Filmed by the Genealogical Society of Utah, 1993, 6 rolls, beginning with FHL film #1905608 (Index to marriages 1876-1910, Index to marriages (men) 1887-1946, Index to marriages (women) 1887-1946). To access the digital images, see the online FHL catalog: www.familysearch.org/search/catalog/682834.

1864-2004. *Montana, County Births and Deaths* **[Online Database]**, digitized and indexed at the FamilySearch.org website. This database includes county birth and death records acquired from county courthouses. (The 1840 date is a typo). The collections consist of registers and certificates from Broadwater, Deer Lodge, Jefferson, Lewis and Clark, Powell and Silver Bow counties. Each index record includes: Name, Event type, Event date, Event place, Gender, Age, Birth year, Father's name, and Mother's name. The document image may have more information about a person. This database has 417,427 records. See https://familysearch.org/search/collection/1930397.
- This database is also available at the Ancestry.com website, see http://search.ancestry.com/search/db.aspx?dbid=60061.

1864-2010. *Montana, Lake County Records* **[Online Database]**, digitized and indexed at the FamilySearch.org website. Source: FamilySearch extractions. Includes images of deeds, school census, mining, vital records, probate, and divorce records located at the county courthouse in Polson, MT. This collection is being published as images become available. The death and birth records have been indexed. Each index record includes: Name, Event type, Event date, Event place, Gender, Age, Birth year, Father's name, Mother's name, and Certificate number. The document image may have more information about a person. This database has 35,202 records. See https://familysearch.org/search/collection/1986787.
- See also, *Montana, Lake County Records, 1857-2010* **[Online Database]**, an image-only database digitized at Ancestry.com with 94,699 images, see http://search.ancestry.com/search/db.aspx?dbid=60064.

1864-2014. *Gallatin County, Montana, Death Index* **[Online Database]**, indexed at the Ancestry.com website. This database is also accessible at the Gallatin County Genealogical Society website. Each index record includes: Name, Death year, Record type, Publication place, Publication title, Publication date, and a link to Gallatin Co GS website. This database has 14,969 records. See http://search.ancestry.com/search/db.aspx?dbid=70786.

1865-1890s. *Society of Montana Pioneers, Missoula County* **[Online Database]**, index and biographies compiled by members of the Western Montana Genealogical Society. See http://files.usgwarchives.net/mt/missoula/books/mtpioneers.txt.

1865-1950. *Montana, County Divorce Records* **[Online Database]**, digitized and indexed at Ancestry.com. Original data: Montana State Historical Society, Helena, MT. Each index record includes a Name, Marriage date, Divorce date, Divorce place, Spouse, and Case number. The document image has much more information (these divorces, long before the "no fault" era, often have court documents with juicy details about who did what to who – it makes for some good reading about ancestors you thought were just nice people. Turns out, some of them were scoundrels! This database has 11,158 records, see www.ancestry.com/search/collections/61254.

1865-1950. *Montana, County Marriages* **[Online Database]**, digitized and indexed at the FamilySearch.org website. Source: FamilySearch extractions. This database is an index and images of Montana county marriage records acquired from local courthouses. Each index record includes: Name, Event type, Event date, Event place, Age, Birth year, Father's name, Mother's name, Spouse's name, Spouse's age, Spouse's birth year, Spouse's father's name, and spouse's mother's name. The document image may have more information about a person. This database has 338,104 records: https://familysearch.org/search/collection/1609797.

1865-1987. *Montana, County Marriages* **[Online Database]**, digitized and indexed at the Ancestry.com website. Original data: Montana State Historical Society, Helena, MT. These marriage records will typically include the Name of Groom, Name of bride, Marriage date, Age and race of groom, Age and race of bride, Birth date of groom, Birthplace of groom, Birth date of bride, Birthplace of bride, Parents of the groom,

and Parents of the bride. This database has 2,559,706 records, see
www.ancestry.com/search/collections/61578.
- See also, *Montana, County Marriage Records, 1865-1993 [Online Database],* indexed at Ancestry.com. Original data: Ancestry.com extractions of marriage records from Montana county courthouses. Each index record include the following information for both the bride and groom: Name, Age at marriage, Marriage date, Marriage place, and Parents' names. This database has 1,922,643 records, see
www.ancestry.com/search/collections/61375.

1865-2009. *Montana, Granite County Records* **[Online Database],** digitized and indexed at the FamilySearch.org website. Source: FamilySearch extractions. This database includes images of probate, land and property, naturalization, divorce and vital records from the County Clerk's Office in Philipsburg, MT. Each index record includes: Name, Event type, Event date, Event place, Gender, Age, and Birth year. The document image may have more information about a person. This database has 2,826 records. See
https://familysearch.org/search/collection/2029197.

1866-1886. *Episcopal Register, Protestant Episcopal Church, Idaho and Montana Missions* **[Digital Capture],** from a typescript prepared by Daniel Tuttle, digitized by FamilySearch International, 2012. To access the digital version, see the online FHL catalog:
www.familysearch.org/search/catalog/2000373.

1866-1922. *Montana Newspaper Archives* **[Online Databases],** digitized and indexed newspapers at the GenealogyBank website, for Anaconda, Butte, Deer Lodge, Fort Benton, Great Falls, Helena, and White Sulphur Springs, MT. See
www.genealogybank.com/explore/newspapers/all/usa/montana.

1866-1953. *Broadwater (and other Montana Counties), Deeds Index and Deed Records* **[Microfilm & Digital Capture],** from the originals at the Broadwater County Clerk/Recorder Office in Townsend, MT. Includes the Montana Territory counties of Flathead, Lake, Missoula, Madison, Gallatin, Jefferson, Lewis and Clark, Broadwater and many more. Some deed records include mining claims, quit claim, sheriff deeds under execution, administrative, estates, taxes, etc. Filmed by the Genealogical Society of Utah, 2002, 17 rolls, beginning with FHL film #2296808 (Deed Index, Grantor, 1866-1906). To access the digital images, see the online FHL catalog: www.familysearch.org/search/catalog/1115583.

1866-1965. *Montana, Wills and Probate Records* **[Online Database],** digitized and indexed at the Ancestry.com website. Source: Ancestry extractions from county, district, and probate courts. Each index record includes: Name, Probate place, Death place, Case number, and Item description. A table of contents lists the content and number of pages in the case file. The document image may have more information about a person. This database has 28,371 records. See
http://search.ancestry.com/search/db.aspx?dbid=9072.

1866-2010. *Montana, Sanders County Records* **[Online Database],** digitized and indexed at the FamilySearch.org website. Source: FamilySearch extractions. Includes images of county birth, death, marriage, veteran burials, voter, naturalization, land and probate records located in the county courthouse in Thompson Falls, MT. This collection is being published as images become available. The death certificates have been indexed. Each index record includes: Name, Event type, Event date, Event place, Gender, Age, Birth year, Father's name, Mother's name, and Spouse's name. The document image may have more information about a person. This database has 16,155 records. See
https://familysearch.org/search/collection/2109937.

1866-2012. *Montana, Meagher County Records* **[Online Database],** digitized and indexed at the FamilySearch.org website. Source: FamilySearch extractions. Includes images of deeds, homestead, cemetery, birth and death, naturalization and probate records from the Clerk/Recorder's Office; and probate and naturalization records from the Clerk of Court's Office located in White Sulphur Springs, MT. This collection is being published as images become available. The birth and death records are being indexed first. Each index record includes: Name, Event type, Event dater, Event place, Gender, Father's name, Mother's name, Page, and Volume. The document image may have more information about a person. This database has 3,259 records. See
https://familysearch.org/search/collection/2228169.

1867-1970. *Montana, County Naturalization Records* **[Online Database],** digitized and indexed at Ancestry.com. Source: MT State Historical Society, Helena, MT. The records are for every county of Montana. Use the *Browse this Collection* feature to choose a county and choose the type of records available for that county. The records include Declarations of Intention to Become a Citizen; and other Naturalization documents. Each index record (declarations) includes Name, Declaration age, Record type, Birthdate, Birthplace, Arrival date, Arrival place, Declaration date, Declaration place, Court, and

Declaration number. The image document may have much more information about a person. This database has 134,878 records, see
www.ancestry.com/search/collections/61420.

1868-1999. *Montana Naturalization Records* **[Online Database],** digitized at the FamilySearch.org website. This is an image only database with Naturalization Records from the U.S. Circuit Court for the District of Montana. Includes Declarations of Intentions, Petitions for Naturalization, Orders of the court, and other Naturalization papers. Browse the images, organized by County, then Record Type, Year Range, and Volume Number. This database has 54,964 records: https://familysearch.org/search/collection/2173973.

1868-1869 Montana Histories and Directories. See *Montana (Territory) Directories,* **[Microfilm],** from the originals published by various publishers, by Research Publications, Woodbridge, CT, 1980-1984, 1 roll, FHL film #1377090, including the following:
- 1868-1869 Historical Sketch and Essay on the Resources of Montana... by Herald Book and Job Printing Office,
- 1879-1880 Montana Territory History and Business Directory... by Fisk Brothers, Printers and Binders.

1868-1929 Indexes to Naturalization Records of the Montana Territorial and Federal Courts **[Microfilm & Digital Capture],** from the originals at the National Archives in Washington, DC and Central Plains Regional Branch, Kansas City, MO. Filmed by the National Archives, 1987, 1 roll, FHL film #1490886, including the following items:
- Items 1-8: Prefatory indexes to journals of proceedings: 1st district, 1878-1889; 2nd district, 1871-1880, 1888-1889; 3rd district, 1868-1888; 4th district, 1886-1887.
- Items 9-10: U.S. District Court (Helena): General index to naturalizations, 1891-1898; prefatory index to naturalizations, 1891-1893.
- Items 11-17: Butte U.S. District Court: General index to naturalizations, 1894-1906; prefatory indexes to declarations, 1892-1929; prefatory indexes to petitions, 1907-1927.
- Items 18-25: Great Falls U.S. District Court: General index to declarations, 1894-1902; general index to record of citizenship, 1894-1903; prefatory indexes to petition and record books.

To access the digital images, see the online FHL catalog: www.familysearch.org/search/catalog/484318.

1868-2011. *Montana, Death Index* **[Online Database],** indexed at the Ancestry.com website. Source: MT Dept of Health. This database is an index to deaths that took place within the territory or state between 1868 and 2011. Details in this index may include the full name of the deceased and the date and place of death. A copy of the actual death certificate may be ordered from the Office of Vital Statistics. This database has 682,209 records. See
http://search.ancestry.com/search/db.aspx?dbid=5437.

1870. *Montana, 1870 Federal Census: Population Schedules* **[Microfilm & Digital Capture],** from the original records at the National Archives, Washington, DC. The 1870 census was filmed twice. The second filming is listed first and is usually easier to read. However, since some of the records were faded or lost between the first and second filming, search the first filming whenever the material on the second filming is too light to read. FHL has 2 rolls, as follows:
- 1870 Montana (2nd filming): Beaverhead, Big Horn, Chouteau, Dawson, Deer Lodge, Gallatin, Jefferson, Lewis and Clark, Madison, Meagher, and Missoula Counties, FHL film #552326.
- 1870 Montana (1st filming): Beaverhead, Big Horn, Chouteau, Dawson, Deer Lodge, Gallatin, Jefferson, Lewis and Clark, Madison, Meagher, and Missoula Counties, FHL film #14886.

To access the digital images (2nd filming), see the online FHL catalog: www.familysearch.org/search/catalog/698907.

1870 Montana Territorial Census Index **[Printed Book],** edited by Ronald Vern Jackson, publ. Accelerated Indexing Systems, 1979, 241 pages. FHL book 978.6 X22m.

- See also, *Montana 1870 Census Index, A-Z* **[Printed Book],** edited by Raeone Christensen Steuart, published by Heritage Quest, Bountiful, UT, 2000, 109 pages. FHL book 978.6 X22s.

1870-1880. *Non–Population Census Schedules for Montana, 1870 and 1880* **[Microfilm],** from the original records held by the Montana Historical Society, Helena, MT. Includes non-population schedules for mortality, social statistics, products of agriculture, products of industry for 1870 and the schedules for mortality, defective, dependent, and delinquent classes, and products of industry for 1880. Arranged by schedule and then by county. Filmed by the National Archives, 1997, series M-1806, 1 roll. See FHL film #2155438. To see if this microfilm was digitized yet, see the online FHL catalog: www.familysearch.org/search/catalog/738381.

1870. *Montana 1870 Mortality Schedule* **[Printed Book],** edited by Ronald Vern Jackson, et al., publ. Accelerated Indexing Systems, Bountiful, UT, 1981, 18 pages, FHL book 978.6 X2m.

1870-1957. Montana Territory, Miscellaneous Records, and Index (Lewis and Clark County & Beaverhead County) **[Microfilm & Digital Capture]**, from the originals housed in the Treasurer/Clerk Recorder, Lewis and Clark County, Helena, MT. These miscellaneous records contain power of attorney, oaths, bonds, wills, rental of land and property, notary public assigned by the governor, mining claims, quit claims deed, loans, mortgages and etc. for the counties of Beaverhead and Lewis and Clark. Filmed by the Genealogical Society of Utah, 2002, 14 rolls, beginning with FHL film #2317890. To access the digital images, see the online FHL catalog:
www.familysearch.org/search/catalog/1120938.

1870-1986. *Montana, Birth Index* **[Online Database]**, indexed at Ancestry.com. Original data: Montana Dept. of Public Health and Human Services, Helena, MT. Each index record includes Name, Birthdate, Birthplace, and Certificate number. This database has 951,966 records, see
www.ancestry.com/search/collections/61471.

1870-1999. *Montana, Federal Naturalization Records* **[Online Database]**, digitized and indexed at Ancestry.com. This database includes Naturalization records that originated in U.S. District Courts located in Montana. Each index record includes Name, Record type, Birthplace, Naturalization date, and Naturalization place. Names of relatives are indicated for each person, if applicable. The document image has more information, including the names and addresses of witnesses. This database has 73,267 records, see
www.ancestry.com/search/collections/61204.

1870-2010. *Montana, Mineral County Obituaries* **[Online Database]**, digitized and indexed at the FamilySearch.org website. Source: Private collection of Kay Strombo from local and area newspapers. Each index record includes: Name, Event type, Event date, Event place, Gender, Age, Relationship to deceased, Birth date, Birth year, Birthplace, and Volume. The obituary image may have more information about a person. This database has 5,266 records. See
https://familysearch.org/search/collection/1921314.

1871-1981. *Montana, Flathead County Records* **[Online Database]**, digitized and indexed at FamilySearch.org. Includes coroner's records, deed records, divorce records, jail records, and probate records located at Flathead County courthouse, Kalispell, MT. This collection is being published as images and indexes become available. This database has 73,187 records. See
https://familysearch.org/search/collection/1387035.

1871-1982. See *Web: Gallatin, Montana, Marriage Index, 1871-1982* **[Online Database]**, indexed at the Ancestry.com website. Source: Gallatin Co Gen. Society. Each index record includes: Name, Gender, Race, Age, Birth date, Birthplace, Marriage date, Marriage place, Father, Mother, Spouse, FHL film number, and Reference ID number. This database has 18,759 records. See
http://search.ancestry.com/search/db.aspx?dbid=60065.

1872-1900. See *VanDersal & Conner's Stockgrowers' Directory of Marks and Brands for the State of Montana, 1872 to 1900: Comprising an Alphabetical List of Names of all Livestock Companies and... Also a Complete Classified Directory of Sheep and Wool Growers* **[Printed Book]**, originally publ. VanDersal & Conner, Helena, MT, 1900; Reprinted by Review Printing Co., Glendive, MT, 1974, 446 pages. Arranged by county and alphabetical by brand owner within the county. Includes brand index. See FHL book 978.6 R2v.

1872-1929. *Index to Registers of Birth and Death (Missoula County, Montana)* **[Microfilm & Digital Capture]**, from the original records at the Missoula County courthouse in Missoula, MT. Filmed by the Genealogical Society of Utah, 1993, 1 roll, FHL film #1902082 (Index to births, 1872-1929; index to deaths, 1895-1929). To access the digital images, see the online FHL catalog:
www.familysearch.org/search/catalog/679179.

1875-1954. See *Helena Independent, The (Helena, Montana), 1875-1884, 1894, 1924-1942, & 1954* **[Online Database]**, indexed at the Ancestry.com website. This database is a fully searchable text version of the newspaper. The newspapers can be browsed or searched using a computer-generated index. This database has 80,885 records. See
http://search.ancestry.com/search/db.aspx?dbid=6638.

1876-2011. *Montana, Chouteau County Records* **[Online Database]**, digitized and indexed at the FamilySearch.org website. Includes images of Chouteau County records held at various repositories. Records located in the **Museum of the Northern Plains** (River and Plains Society) include voter registers, school district records, St. Paul's Episcopal Church records, Riverside Cemetery records and newspapers clippings of births, marriages and deaths. Records held by the **Chouteau County Courthouse** include birth, death, probate, naturalization, deeds and

school census records. Only the birth and death records have been indexed and are searchable in this collection. This database has 9,505 records. See
https://familysearch.org/search/collection/2028318.
- See also, *Montana, Chouteau County Records, 1876-2011* [Online Database], digitized at the Ancestry.com website. Source: FamilySearch. This is an image only database with images of Chouteau County records held at various repositories. This database has 241,430 images. Archived at
https://web.archive.org/web/20150907070020/http://search.ancestry.com/search/db.aspx?dbid=60065.

1877-1907. *Church Death Records (Catholic Church, Missoula Mission (Montana)* [Microfilm & Digital Capture], filmed by the Genealogical Society of Utah, c1976, 1 roll, FHL film #1011812. To access the digital images, see the online FHL catalog:
www.familysearch.org/search/catalog/72338.

1878. *3rd Annual Western Montana Fair, Names From Booklet* [Online Database], indexed at the RootsWeb site for Missoula Co MT. See
www.rootsweb.ancestry.com/~mtmissou/1878fair.htm.

1878-2005. *Montana, Deer Lodge County, Anaconda, Cemetery Records* [Online Database], digitized and indexed at FamilySearch.org. Each index records includes a Name, Event type, Event place, Death date, and Cemetery. The image of the card may have more information about a person. This database has 5,768 records, see
www.familysearch.org/search/collection/1386115.

1878-2011. *Montana, Rosebud County Records* [Online Database], digitized and indexed at the FamilySearch.org website. This is an image only database with land records, vital records, voter lists and probate case files located at the Rosebud County courthouse, Forsyth, MT. This database has 10,568 records, see
https://familysearch.org/search/collection/1908714.
- See also, *Montana, Rosebud County Records, 1878-2011* [Online Database], digitized at the Ancestry.com website. Source: FamilySearch extractions. This is an image only database with records from the Rosebud County courthouse, Forsyth, Montana: Browse the images, organized by Record Type, Date Range, and Volume. This database has 97,864 images:
http://search.ancestry.com/search/db.aspx?dbid=60066.

1880 Montana Federal Census: Soundex and Population Schedules [Microfilm & Digital Capture], from the original records at the National Archives, Washington, DC. Filmed by the National Archives, 3 rolls, as follows:
- 1880 Soundex: A000 thru N666, FHL film #287767.
- 1880 Soundex: O100 thru Institutions, FHL film #287768.
- 1880 Population Schedules: Entire Territory, FHL film #1254742.

To access the digital images (Population Schedules), see the online FHL catalog:
www.familysearch.org/search/catalog/676483.

1880 Montana Territory Census Index [Printed Book], Dorothy Shammel, project chairman, publ. Lewistown Genealogy Society, Lewistown, MT, 1987, 365 pages. From intro: "This index covers Montana Territory, which in 1880 consisted of eleven counties: Beaverhead, Chouteau, Custer, Dawson, Deer Lodge, Gallatin, Jefferson, Lewis & Clark, Madison, Meagher, and Missoula." FHL book 978.6 X2mt.
- See also *Montana 1880 Census Index* [Printed Book], edited by Ronald Vern Jackson, et al., publ. Accelerated Indexing Systems, North Salt Lake, UT, 1984, FHL book 978.6 X2M. Copy 1: Contents: vol. 1. A-Lablano; vol. 2. Krunley-Z. Copy 2: vols. 1 & 2 bound together.

1880. See *Montana 1880 Mortality Schedule* [Printed Book], edited by Ronald Vern Jackson, et al., publ. Accelerated Indexing Systems, Bountiful, UT, 1981, 20 pages. FHL book 978.6 X2ms.

1880-2009. *Montana, Cascade County Records* [Online Database], digitized and indexed at the FamilySearch.org website. Includes county record collections from the following record custodians. **History Museum in Great Falls:** Probate, voter registers, naturalization and immigration records. **Great Falls Genealogy Society:** Probate case files, #535-3165, 1903-1926; court orders for dependent children, 1903-1937; old age applications, naturalization records, pre-1945. **County Clerk's Office:** Deeds from 1880-1941 and index to 1995. Each index record includes: Name, Event type, Event date, Event place, Gender, Birth date, Birthplace, Death place, Spouse's name, Newspaper, Volume note, and Volume date range. The document image may have more information about a person. This database has 527,617 records. See
https://familysearch.org/search/collection/1926700.
- See also, *Montana, Cascade County Records, 1880-2009* [Online Database], digitized at the Ancestry.com website. This is an image only database with various county records Browse the images, organized by Record Category, Record Type, Volume, and Year Range. This database has 614,563 images, see
http://search.ancestry.com/search/db.aspx?dbid=60059.

1881-1928. *General Land Office of the United States, Montana Territory* **[Microfilm & Digital Capture]**, from the original records in State Treasurer, Clerk, Recorder Office in Helena Montana. These records include land and mining records intermixed in Montana Territory. Filmed by the Genealogical Society of Utah, 2002, 4 rolls, beginning with FHL film #2317967 (Land Registrations Records, vol. 1, 1881-1901). To access the digital images, see the online FHL catalog: www.familysearch.org/search/catalog/1120919.

1891-1929. See *Montana: Southern District Declaration of Intent, 1891-1929; Petition for Naturalization, 1891- 1929; Citizenship Records, 1894-1906; Certificates, 1907-1927* **[Microfilm & Digital Capture]**, from the originals at the National Archives Branch, Seattle, WA. Includes general index with some volumes individually indexed. Filmed by the Genealogical Society of Utah, 1988, 3 rolls, as follows:
- District Court, Butte: Index to Declaration of intent, vol. 85, 1894-1902; Declaration of intent, vol. 86, 1894-1902; Petitions for naturalization, vol. 1-2, 1910-1923, FHL film #1492066.
- District Court, Butte: Petitions for naturalization, vol. 3-5, 1923-1929, FHL film #1492067.
- District Court, Butte: Index to citizenship, 1894-1903. District Court, Great Falls: Declaration of intent, 1924; Petitions for naturalization, 1926. District Court, Helena: Index to citizenship, 1894-1906; Citizenship records, 1894-1906; Index to naturalization, 1891-1906; Declaration of intent, 1891-1893; Records of citizenship, 1891-1898; Declaration of intent, 1896-1917. Certificate stubs, no. 21871-1541970, 1907-1927; Declaration of intent, 1917-1929, FHL film #1492068.

To access the digital images, see the online FHL catalog: www.familysearch.org/search/catalog/654213.

1881-2000. See *Index of Obituaries from Dillon Tribune, April 1881 - December 2000; Dillon, Montana* **[Printed Book]**, compiled and publ. Beaver Head Hunters Genealogical Society, Dillon, MT, 2001, 92 pages. FHL book 978.669/D1 V42b. Also on microfiche, FHL fiche #6005381.

1881-2011. *Montana, Yellowstone County Records* **[Online Database]**, digitized and indexed at the FamilySearch.org website. This database includes vital, probate, deeds and discharge records from the county courthouse in Billings, MT. This database has 5,827 records:
https://familysearch.org/search/collection/2013531.
- See also *Montana, Yellowstone County Records, 1881-2011* **[Online Database]**, digitized at the Ancestry.com website. Source: FamilySearch. This is an image only database with images of vital records, probate records, deeds, and discharge records from the county courthouse in Billings, MT. Browse the images, organized by Record Category, Record Type, Volume, and Year Range, see
http://search.ancestry.com/search/db.aspx?dbid=60067.

1881-2012. *Montana, Teton County Records* **[Online Database]**, digitized and indexed at the FamilySearch.org website. Source: FamilySearch extractions. Includes images of vital records, naturalization index, land index and probate records from the clerk of court, clerk and recorder offices, Choteau, MT. Each index record includes: Name, Event type, Event date, Event place, Gender, Age, Birth year, Father's name, Mother's name, and Spouse's name. The document image may have more information about a person. This database has 12,770 records. See
https://familysearch.org/search/collection/2170641.

1882-1915 *Election Registers, Lewis and Clark County, Meadow Creek, Madison County, Chouteau County, and Richland County, Montana* **[Microfilm]**, from the originals located at the Montana Historical Society, Helena, MT. Filmed by the Genealogical Society of Utah, 2002, 1 roll, FHL film #2318557. To see if this microfilm was digitized yet, see the online FHL catalog:
www.familysearch.org/search/catalog/1122391.

1883. *List of Pensioners, Montana Territory* **[Online Database]**, indexed at the RootsWeb site for Montana: www.rootsweb.ancestry.com/~mtteton/1883pensioners.html.

1883 *City Directory for Billings, Montana* **[Online Database]**, indexed at the GenealogyTrails website for Yellowstone Co MT. See
http://genealogytrails.com/mon/yellowstone/1883billingscitydirectory.html.

1884-2011. *Montana, Big Horn County Records* **[Online Database]**, digitized and indexed at the FamilySearch.org website. Source: FamilySearch extractions from the county clerk/recorder offices, Hardin, MT. Each index record includes: Name, Event type, Event date, Event place, Gender, Age, Birth year, Mother's name, and Volume number. The document image may have more information about a person. This database has 59,997 records. See
https://familysearch.org/search/collection/2117001.

1887-2011. *Montana, Sweet Grass County Records* **[Online Database]**, digitized and indexed at the FamilySearch.org website. Source: FamilySearch extractions. Includes images of birth, death, coroner, naturalization, probate (including estate files) and deed

records from the Clerk of the District Court, County Clerk, and Recorder's Offices, Big Timber, MT. This collection is being published as images and indexes become available. The birth and death records have been indexed. Each index record includes: Name, Event type, Event date, Event place, Gender, Age, Birth year, Father's name, Mother's name, Spouse's name, Spouse's gender, and Volume number. The document image may have more information about a person. This database has 7,731 records. See
https://familysearch.org/search/collection/2036960.

1887-2012. *Montana, Judith Basin County Records* **[Online Database],** digitized and indexed at the FamilySearch.org website. Source: FamilySearch extractions. Includes images of birth, death, marriage, naturalization, and probate records from the county clerk/recorder's and clerk of court offices in Stanford, MT. This collection is being published as images become available. The birth and death certificates are being indexed first. Each index record includes: Name, Event type, Event date, Event place, Gender, Age, Birth year, Father's name, Mother's name, and Volume number. The document image may have more information about a person. This database has 2,491 records. See
https://familysearch.org/search/collection/2110919.

1889-1891. *Helena, Montana Directories* **[Online Database],** indexed at the Ancestry.com website. Source: A.W. Ide, Helena, 1889-1891. Each index record includes: Name, City, State, Year, and Location (address). This database has 23,034 records:
http://search.ancestry.com/search/db.aspx?dbid=4975.

1889-1947. *Montana Marriages* **[Online Database],** indexed at the FamilySearch.org website. Source: FamilySearch extractions from records on microfilm at the Family History Library, Salt Lake City, UT. Each index record includes: Name, Birth date, Birthplace, Age, Spouse's name, Spouse's birthplace, Spouse's age, Event date, Event place, Father's name, Mother's name, Spouse's father's name, Spouse's mother's name, Batch number, and FHL film number. This database has 20,784 records. See
https://familysearch.org/search/collection/1675397.

1889-1947. *Montana, Select Marriages* **[Online Database],** indexed at the Ancestry.com website. Source: FamilySearch extractions. Each index record includes: Name, Gender, Race, Age, Birth date, Birthplace, Marriage date, Marriage place, Father, Mother, Spouse, FHL film number, and Reference ID Number. This database has 110,132 records. Archived
https://web.archive.org/web/20160706054631/http://search.ancestry.com/search/db.aspx?dbid=60065.

1890-1996. *Miscellaneous Death Records, Kalispell, Montana* **[Online Database],** indexed at the USGenWeb site for Flathead Co MT. For Surnames A thru K, see
http://files.usgwarchives.net/mt/flathead/vitals/miscd1.txt.
For surnames L thru Z, see
http://files.usgwarchives.net/mt/flathead/vitals/miscd2.txt.

1890s-1999. *Stevensville, Ravalli County, Montana Cemeteries* **[Online Database],** indexed at the Ancestry.com website. Source: Book, same title, by Patricia Sewell, 2000. This database is a listing of people interred in four local cemeteries in the nineteenth and twentieth centuries. It provides the decedent's name, birth date, death date and cemetery name. Additional notes are provided for many records and often include the name of spouse or record of military service. This database has 3,091 records. See
http://search.ancestry.com/search/db.aspx?dbid=4354.

1890s-1999. *Missoula and Ravalli County, Montana Cemeteries* **[Online Database],** indexed at the Ancestry.com website. Source: Book, same title, by Patricia Sewell, 2001. All three of the cemeteries transcribed in this database are located in the Bitterroot Valley, south of Missoula. Victor Cemetery, in Ravalli County, Montana, lies on a sloping hill about a mile and a half northwest of the city. St. Joseph Catholic Cemetery, also in Ravalli County, Montana, lies in the center of Florence, across the street from the St. Joseph Church. Florence Carlton Cemetery, in Missoula County, Montana, lies barely over the Ravalli County border, although it serves the community of Florence. Each record lists a person's last name, first name, birth date, death date, and other miscellaneous notes, which may include military and/or family information. This database has 3,033 records. See
http://search.ancestry.com/search/db.aspx?dbid=5449.

1891-1892. *Butte, Silver Bow County, Montana Directory* **[Online Database],** indexed at the Ancestry.com website. Source: R. L. Polk et al. During the 1890s, Butte, Montana was a copper mining boom town. This directory attempted to list the name of every adult male living or doing business in the city in 1891-92, along with the occupation, business location, and residence of each. Also listed are numerous women and names of deceased husbands. This database has 8,190 records:
http://search.ancestry.com/search/db.aspx?dbid=5296.

1894 History. *An Illustrated History of the State of Montana* **[Printed Book],** by Joaquin Miller, original publ. Lewis Publishing Co., 1894. Includes index. Reprint by Higginson Book Co., Salem, MA, 2000. FHL book 978.6 H2mj.

1894 City Directory for Billings, Montana **[Online Database],** indexed at the USGenWeb site for Yellowstone Co MT. See
http://files.usgwarchives.net/mt/yellowstone/history/billings1894.txt.

1897-1919. *Montana, Birth Records* **[Online Database],** digitized and indexed at Anestry.com. Original data: Montana Dept. Public Health and Human Services, Helena, MT. Each index record includes Name, Gender, Race, Birthdate, Birthplace, Certificate Number, Father, and Mother. The Certificate image has more information about a person. This database has 350,319 records, see
www.ancestry.com/search/collections/61591.

1900. *Montana, 1900 Federal Census: Soundex and Population Schedules* **[Microfilm & Digital Capture],** from the originals at the National Archives, Washington, DC. Filmed by the National Archives, 1970, 47 rolls, beginning with FHL film #1240909 (Population Schedules: Beaverhead, Broadwater, Carbon, and Cascade counties). To access the digital images, see the online FHL catalog:
www.familysearch.org/search/catalog/637337.

1900-1901 City Directory for Billings, Montana **[Online Database],** indexed at the GenealogyTrails website for Yellowstone Co MT. See
http://genealogytrails.com/mon/yellowstone/1900billingscitydirectory.html.

1902. *Butte, Silver Bow County, Montana, Directory, 1902* **[Online Database],** indexed at the Ancestry.com website. Source: R. L. Polk Directory, 1902. Each index record includes: Given name, Surname, Occupation or business, and Address. This database has 29,901 records. See
http://search.ancestry.com/search/db.aspx?dbid=5711.

1904-1918. *Montana, Military Records* **[Online Database],** digitized and indexed at FamilySearch.org. Military records from Montana, mostly containing WWI records, however, there may be records from the Spanish American War and World War II as well. See
www.familysearch.org/search/collection/3010075.

1905-1906. *Flathead County, MT, 1905-1906 Kalispell City Directory and Flathead County Directory* **[Online Database],** indexed at the Ancestry.com website. This database has 7,510 records. See
http://search.ancestry.com/search/db.aspx?dbid=6113.

1906-1917 Dillon (Montana) City and Beaverhead County Directories **[Microfilm],** from the original records located in various libraries and societies. Records by various publishers, microfilm by Research Publications, Woodbridge, CT, ca1995, 1 roll, FHL film #2309340 (1906, 1907-1908, 1909-1910, 1912-1913, 1916-1917 Dillon City and Beaverhead County Directories).

1907-2016. *Montana, State Deaths* **[Online Database],** digitized and indexed at Ancestry.com. Original data: State of Montana, Office of Vital Statistics, Helena, MT. In 1907, the state of Montana began requiring clergy, doctors, undertakers and those in similar professions to registers deaths, with statewide death registration. This database is an index to deaths that took place between 1907 and 2016. Occasionally, older death records may be found, dating back to 1868. Details in this index may include the full name of the deceased and the date and place of death. A copy of the actual death certificate may be ordered from the Office of Vital Statistics. This database has 3,096,239 records, see
www.ancestry.com/search/collections/5437.

1909-1910. *Dillon City and Beaverhead County Directory: Embracing a Complete Alphabetical List of Business Firms and Private Citizens* **[Microfilm],** from the original published by R. L. Polk, Helena, MT, 1909-1910, 235 pages. Filmed by the Genealogical Society of Utah, 1967, 1 roll, FHL film #528764. To see if this microfilm was digitized yet, see the online FHL catalog:
www.familysearch.org/search/catalog/2046900.

1910. *Montana, 1910 Federal Census: Population Schedules* **[Microfilm & Digital Capture],** from the originals at the National Archives, Washington, DC. Filmed by the National Archives, 1970, 9 rolls, beginning with FHL film #1374842 (Population schedules: Beaverhead, Carbon, Broadwater, and Custer Co). To access the digital images, see the online FHL catalog:
www.familysearch.org/search/catalog/638150.

1910-1977. *Billings Gazette (Billings, Montana)* **[Online Database],** digitized and indexed at the Ancestry.com website. This database is a fully searchable text version of the newspaper for the years 1910-1977. The newspapers can be browsed or searched using a computer-generated index. This database has 466,310 records. See
http://search.ancestry.com/search/db.aspx?dbid=51110.

1910-2012. *Montana, Pondera County Records* **[Online Database],** digitized and indexed at the FamilySearch.org website. Source: FamilySearch extractions. Includes images of birth, death and land records from the Clerk/Recorder's Office; probate and naturalization records from the Clerk of Court in Conrad, MT. This collection is being published as images become available. The birth and death records have been indexed. Each index record includes: Name, Event type, Event date, Event place, Gender, Age, Birth year, Page, and Volume number. The document image may have more information about a person. This database has 29,864 records. See
https://familysearch.org/search/collection/2127321.

1911-1977. *Daily Inter Lake (Kalispell, Montana)* **[Online Database],** indexed at the Ancestry.com website. This database is a fully searchable text version of the newspaper for the years 1911-1977. The newspapers can be browsed or searched using a computer-generated index. This database has 168,957 records. See
http://search.ancestry.com/search/db.aspx?dbid=51259.

1913 History. See *A History of Montana* **[Printed Book & Digital Version],** by Helen Fitzgerald Sanders, publ. Lewis Publishing Co., Chicago, IL, 1913, 3 vols. Includes index. FHL Library has volumes 2 and 3 in book form only. FHL book 978.6 D3s v.1-2. Also on microfilm (3 vols.) FHL film #1000174. To access the digital version of all 3 volumes, see the online FHL catalog:
www.familysearch.org/search/catalog/186979.

1913-1960. *Montana, Toole County Records, 1913-1960* **[Online Database],** digitized and indexed at the FamilySearch.org website. This database includes probate, naturalization and marriage records from the county courthouse in Shelby, MT. This database has 79,300 records. See
https://familysearch.org/search/collection/2138517.

1917-1918 *World War I Selective Service System Draft Registration Cards, Montana* **[Microfilm & Digital Capture],** from the original records at the Regional National Archives, East Point, Georgia. The draft cards are arranged by state, then by county or city, and then by surname of registrants. Cards are in rough alphabetical order. Filmed by the National Archives, 1987, 37 rolls, beginning with FHL film #1684099. (Beaverhead County, A–Z; Big Horn County, A–Z; Blaine County, A–D). To access the digital images, see the online FHL catalog:
www.familysearch.org/search/catalog/746985.

1918-1919 Spanish Flu Death Index, Cascade County, Montana **[Online Database],** indexed at the RootsWeb site for Cascade Co MT. See
www.rootsweb.ancestry.com/~mtcascad/1918-1919deaths.html.

1920. *Montana, 1920 Federal Census: Soundex and Population Schedules* **[Microfilm],** from the originals at the National Archives, Washington, DC. Filmed by the National Archives, 58 rolls, beginning with FHL film #1820967 (Population Schedules: Beaverhead, Big Horn, Broadwater, Carbon, and Carter Counties). To access the digital images, see the online FHL catalog: www.familysearch.org/search/catalog/576294.

1920-1925 Death Records, Lewis and Clark County, Montana **[Online Database],** indexed at the GenealogyTrails website for Lewis and Clark Co MT: http://genealogytrails.com/mon/lewisandclark/deaths.html.

1921 History. See *Montana, its Story and Biography: A History of Aboriginal and Territorial Montana and Three Decades of Statehood* **[Printed Book & Digital Version],** edited by Tom Stout, publ. American Historical Society, Chicago, IL, 1921, 3 vols. (Biographies in Vol. 2 & 3). FHL book 978.6 H2s. To access the digital images, see the online FHL catalog: www.familysearch.org/search/catalog/187493.
- Indexed in *Every-Name Index to Stout's Montana: Its Story and Biography* **[Printed Book & Digital Version],** by Hamilton Computer Service, Park City, UT, ca1985, 433 pages. Index includes names, birthdates, and birthplaces. FHL book 978.6 H2s index. To access the digital version, see the online FHL catalog: www.familysearch.org/search/catalog/161036.

1923-1956. *Montana Manifests of Immigrant Arrivals and Departures* **[Online Database],** digitized and indexed at the FamilySearch.org website. Source: National Archives microfilm series A3447. This database has manifests of vessels arriving at Chief Mountain, Cut Bank, Del Bonita, Gateway, Great Falls, and Roosvile, MT 1923-1956, and of departures from Great Falls, Montana, 1944-1945. The records usually include the person's Name, Gender, Age, Marital status, Citizenship, Race, Place of last permanent residence, and Destination, how long they intend to remain in the U.S., and whether they intend to become a U.S. citizen. Browse the images, organized by Roll number (begins with a table of contents). This database has 38,373 records. See
https://familysearch.org/search/collection/2479258.

- See also, *Manifests of Alien Arrivals at Havre, Loring, Opheim, Raymond, Turner, Westby, and White Tail, Montana, 1924-1956* **[Digital Capture]**, digitized by FamilySearch International, from the National Archives microfilm. To access the digital images, see the online FHL catalog: www.familysearch.org/search/catalog/2526183.

1928-1977. *Montana Standard (Butte, Montana)* **[Online Database]**, indexed at the Ancestry.com website. This database is a fully searchable text version of the newspaper for the years 1928-1977. The newspapers can be browsed or searched using a computer-generated index. This database has 141,691 records. See http://search.ancestry.com/search/db.aspx?dbid=6739.

1930. *Montana, 1930 Federal Census: Population Schedule* **[Microfilm & Digital Capture]**, from the originals at the National Archives, Washington. Filmed by the National Archives, 13 rolls, beginning with FHL film #2340987 (Population schedules: Beaverhead, Big Horn, Blaine, Broadwater, and Carbon counties). To access the digital images, see the online FHL catalog: www.familysearch.org/search/catalog/1037443.

1930-1975 Newspaper Index. See *Date and Source Information For the Biography Files in the Montana Room at the Parmly Billings Library* **[Microfilm & Digital Capture]**, compiled by the Yellowstone Genealogical Forum; editor Patricia K. Miller, microfilm of original card index (ca. 10,000 cards). Collection of cards indexing individuals who appeared in issues of several Montana newspapers between 1930 and 1975. Filmed by the Genealogical Society of Utah, 1994, 1 roll, FHL film #1307685. To access the digital images, see the online FHL catalog: www.familysearch.org/search/catalog/701536.

1930-1989. See *Billings (Yellowstone County, Mont.) City Directory: Contains Buyers' Guide and Complete Classified Business Directory* **[Printed Books,** from the original directories publ. R.L. Polk & Co., 1930-1989. Directories are available for 1930, 1933-1834, 1935, 1937, 1940, 1942, 1949-1950, 1955, 1958, 1960, 1961, 1962, 1963, 1964, 1968, 1971, 1975, 1980, 1984, 1986, 1987-1988, 1989, and 1990. See FHL book 978.639 E4p. .Also filmed by the Genealogical Society of Utah, 1988, beginning with FHL film #1320721.

1940. *Montana, 1940 Federal Census: Population Schedules* **[Digital Capture].** After microfilming, Congress allowed the Census Bureau to destroy the originals to free up space for WWII-related files. Digitizing of the 1940 census schedules microfilm images was done for the National Archives and made public on April 2, 2012. To access the digital images, see the online FHL catalog: www.familysearch.org/search/catalog/2057768.

1940 Federal Census Finding Aids **[Online Database].** The National Archives prepared a special website online with a detailed description of the 1940 federal census. Included at the site are descriptions of location finding aids, such as Enumeration District Maps, Geographic Descriptions of Census Enumeration Districts, and a list of 1940 City Directories available at the National Archives. The finding aids are all linked to other National Archives sites. The National Archives website also has a link to 1940 Search Engines using Stephen P. Morse's "One-Step" system for finding a 1940 E.D. or street address conversion. See **www.archives.gov/research/census/1940/general-info.html#questions**.

1940-1945. *Montana, World War II Draft Registration Cards* **[Online Database],** Draft registration cards of men who registered during World War II, with the exception of the fourth registration. Images courtesy of Ancestry. The event place is the residence of the registrant. This database has 144,392 records, see www.familysearch.org/search/collection/2796752.
- See also, *Montana, World War II Draft Registration Cards, 1940-1947* **[Digital Capture],** from the originals at the National Personnel Center, St. Louis, MO. Digitized by FamilySearch International, 2017, beginning with DGS File Folder #104074328 (Cook, Adell – Cupper, Homer). To access the digital images, see the online FHL catalog: www.familysearch.org/search/catalog/4114747.

1943-1955. *The Independent Record (Helena, Montana)* **[Online Database],** indexed at the Ancestry.com website. This database is a fully searchable text version of the newspaper for the years 1943-1955. The newspapers can be browsed or searched using a computer-generated index. This database has 43,886 records. See http://search.ancestry.com/search/db.aspx?dbid=6563.

1943-1986. *Montana, Marriage Records* **[Online Database],** digitized and indexed at Ancestry.com. Original data: Department of Public Health and Human Services, Helena, MT. Each index record includes Name, Gender, Race, Age, Birthdate, Birthplace, Marriage date, Marriage place, Father, Mother, Spouse, and Certificate number. The document image may have much more information. This database has 1,783,927 records, see
www.ancestry.com/search/collections/61478.

1947-1982. *Cemetery Records of Montana* **[Microfilm],** copied by members of the LDS Church; typed by the Genealogical Society, Salt Lake City, Utah. Typescript. Contents: vol. 1. (1947) Granite County: Drummond, Valley Cemetery; Lake County: Arlee, Ronan, St. Ignatius; Missoula County: Missoula; Sanders County: Dixon; vol. 2. (1959) Deer Lodge County: Anaconda, Lower Hill and New Hill Cemeteries, Warm Springs; Gallatin County: Willow Creek, Williams Family Cemetery; Silver Bow County: Butte, Mount Moriah and Mountain View Cemeteries, Sunset Memorial Gardens; vol. 3. (1961) Gallatin County: Willow Creek; Silver Bow County: Butte, Mount Moriah and Mountain View Cemeteries. FHL book 978.6 V3c v. 1-3. Also on microfilm, FHL film #873694; and microfiche, FHL fiche #6051445. To see if this microfilm was digitized yet, see the online FHL catalog:
www.familysearch.org/search/catalog/187583.

1974-1975. See *The Daily Independent (Helena, Montana)* **[Online Database],** digitized and indexed at the Ancestry.com website. A full image page of the newspaper, with an OCR index. This database has 1,202 records. See
http://search.ancestry.com/search/db.aspx?dbid=8089.

1996-Current. *Montana Recent Newspaper Obituaries* **[Online Database],** digitized and indexed newspaper obituaries at the GenealogyBank website, including newspapers for Belgrade, Bigfork, Billings, Bozeman, Columbia Falls, Helena, Kalispell, Libby, Missoula, Plains, Polson, Sidney, West Yellowstone, and Whitefish, Montana. See
www.genealogybank.com/explore/obituaries/all/usa/montana.

204 • *Census Substitutes & State Census Records*

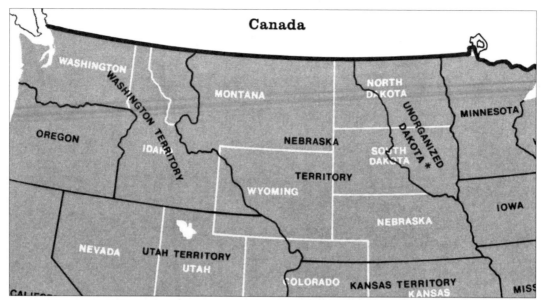

Western States • June 1860 (Wyoming as part of three territories). This map shows the area of Wyoming at the time of the 1860 federal census. Population was recorded at Fort Bridger, Green River County, Utah Territory; and Fort Laramie in Nebraska Territory.

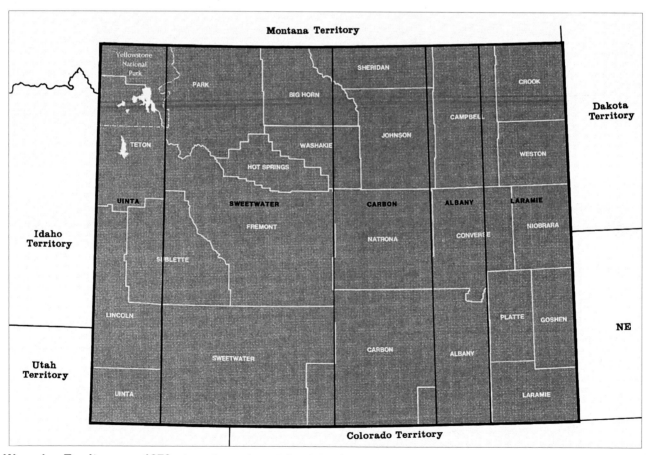

Wyoming Territory • 1870. A territory since July 1868, the above map shows in black the five original counties at the time of the 1870 Federal Census. The 23 current Wyoming counties are shown in white. **Map Source:** Page 388, *Map Guide to the U.S. Federal Censuses, 1790-1920,* by William Thorndale and William Dollarhide.

Wyoming
Censuses & Substitute Name Lists

Historical Timeline For Wyoming, 1742-1890

1742. The first non-Indian to visit the area of Wyoming was probably Francois Louis Vérendrye, a French-Canadian trapper and fur trader from the Red River Settlement of the Dakota Country.

1807. John Colter, recent member of the Lewis and Clark expedition, now a mountain man and explorer, was the first to describe a place where "hot water shoots straight into the air, the earth bubbles as if it were boiling, and almost extinct geysers thunder as if possessed by angry spirits." He referred to the area in his written report as *Colter"s Hell*. Most easterners believed he was lying or exaggerating – it was hard to believe such a place could really exist. Colter's Hell is now called Yellowstone National Park.

1811. Wilson Hunt led a party of "Astorians," an organized expedition for John Jacob Astor's Pacific Fur Company. The Astorians passed through present Wyoming, crossed the area on their way to Astoria in the Oregon Country. Hunt's route across the Rocky Mountains, later known as South Pass, was to become the primary crossing point for thousands of covered wagons traveling the Oregon Trail.

1812. Robert Stuart and returning Astorians crossed the Continental Divide in the vicinity of South Pass and built the first known cabin on the North Platte River at Bessemer Bend, a few miles southwest of present Casper, Wyoming.

1822. General William Ashley placed an ad in a St. Louis newspaper to recruit able-bodied men for his new fur-trading enterprise. There was no shortage of willing young men. Ashley would not build a chain of forts to manage his fur trading operation. Instead, he sent his men out alone and planned to meet them all at a central place a year later. At the predetermined time, Ashley would load up his wagons with supplies and head out to meet his Mountain Men.

1824. William Ashley's men rediscovered South Pass. The Rocky Mountain Fur Company trappers and traders, including Indians and mountain men, begin holding most of their annual meetings along the Green River.

1825. William Ashley's wagons were the first vehicles to penetrate into the west, blazing a wagon road for the Oregon Trail settlers who would follow twenty years later. When Ashley finally reaches his men each year, it was cause for celebration – a wild party they called "the rendezvous."

1832. Capt. B. L. E. Bonneville took the first wagons through South Pass, then built Fort Bonneville (the Green River Rendezvous) near present Daniel, Wyoming.

1834. Fort Laramie, a private trading post, was the first permanent settlement in Wyoming, established by William Sublette and Robert Campbell.

1836. Narcissa Whitman, wife of Dr. Marcus Whitman; and Eliza Spalding, wife of Rev. Henry H. Spalding; were the first white women to pass over the Oregon Trail to the Far West.

1837. A rendezvous on the Green River of Wyoming was attended by more than 2,000 trappers, traders and Indians. Styles had already begun to change, and top money was not received for the furs.

1842. The great migration began on the Oregon Trail. Also in this year, gold was discovered in the South Pass district, but the major gold rush would be delayed by the coming Civil War and would not start in earnest until the late 1860s.

1843. Fort Bridger, the second permanent settlement in Wyoming was established by Jim Bridger and Louis Vasquez.

1846. The Mormon migration to Utah began. In 1847, Mormon Ferry was established on the North Platte River.

1849. U.S. Government purchased Ft. Laramie, turning it into a military post. Many of the great treaties with the Indians were concluded here over the next thirty years.

1850. Present Wyoming was now part of Utah and Oregon Territories west of the Continental Divide; and in "Unorganized Territory," east of the divide. In the 1850 federal census, the only population in present Wyoming was that of Fort Bridger, taken as the "Green River Precinct" of Weber County, Utah Territory. The Federal Census was taken in Utah Territory with a census day of April 1, 1851.

1852. This was the peak year for emigration on the Oregon Trail. Over 55,000 people passed through Wyoming en route to Oregon or California.

1853. Washington Territory was created, taken from the area of Oregon Territory. The southwest corner of present Wyoming (west of the Continental Divide) was now part of Washington and Utah Territories; the area east of the divide was in "Unorganized Territory."
- Also in 1853, Fort Supply, an agricultural settlement in present Wyoming was established as a re-supply station by the Mormons.

1854. Nebraska Territory was established, extending from the Missouri River to the Continental Divide. The area of modern Wyoming was now within Nebraska Territory east of the Continental Divide; the area west of the divide, within Washington and Utah Territories.

1860. Present Wyoming was in three U.S. Territories for the federal census taken in 1860. Population was recorded at Fort Bridger, Green River County, Utah Territory; and Fort Laramie in Nebraska Territory. See the 1860 map on page 204.
- Also in 1860, the Pony Express was started, a mail route from St. Joseph, MO to Sacramento, CA which followed the same path as the original Oregon-California Trail through present Wyoming.

1861. Dakota Territory was created by Congress. Present Wyoming east of the Continental Divide was now part of Dakota and Nebraska Territories; and Washington and Utah Territories west of the divide.
- Also in 1861, the first transcontinental telegraph was completed, and soon after, the Pony Express was discontinued.

1862. The Overland Stage Line changed its route from the Oregon Trail to the Overland Trail. From Denver, the Overland Trail went north to Ft. Collins via what is now Interstate 25, then from Ft. Collins into Wyoming to the Laramie River via what is now U.S. Highway 287; then west to Ft. Bridger along the same general route of today's Interstate 80.

1863. Idaho Territory was created by Congress, with an area that included all of present Idaho, Montana, and Wyoming.
- Bozeman Trail established. The portion of the route from present Cheyenne, Wyoming to Billings, Montana followed the same general path as Interstate 25; and from Billings to Bozeman, Montana via what is now Interstate 90.

1866. Nelson Story drove the first herd of cattle through present Wyoming, going north to Montana, essentially along the route of the Bozeman Trail. (This cattle drive was the historical setting for Larry McMurtry's *Lonesome Dove*).

1867. The Union Pacific Railroad entered present Wyoming, still part of Dakota Territory. Railroad workers founded the city of Cheyenne in this year; and Laramie County was created by the Dakota Territory Legislature.

1868. July 25th. **Wyoming Territory** was created by Congress with the same boundaries as the present state. Cheyenne was named the territorial capital.

1869. A territorial census was taken for Wyoming Territory. This is the only census that survives for all Wyoming counties.
- Also in this year, John A. Campbell, first territorial governor, signed the Female Suffrage Bill giving women the right to vote. Wyoming was the first territory or state in the United States to do so.

1870. Federal census. Wyoming Territory's population was at 9,118. See the map on page 204.

1872. Yellowstone National Park was created, the first national park in America. A northern strip of the park is in Montana; a western strip is in Idaho; but most of the park is within Wyoming.

1880. Federal census. Wyoming's population was at 20,789.

1889. The state constitution submitted to Congress for admission as a state included an article that provided: "Elections shall be open, free and equal, and no power, civil or military, shall at any time interfere to prevent an untrammeled exercise of the right of suffrage," allowing Wyoming to become the first state to extend voting rights to women.

1890. The 1890 federal census was conducted nationwide from the 1st of June to the 30th of June 1890. 10 days later, Wyoming was admitted into the Union as the 44th state on July 10th with Cheyenne as the state capital. The population was at 62,555.

Bibliography
Wyoming Censuses & Substitutes

The 1850 federal census was the first to include inhabitants of the area of present Wyoming: Fort Bridger was enumerated as the "Green River Precinct" of Weber County, Utah Territory. The 1850 Federal Census was taken in Utah Territory with a census day of April 1, 1851.
- The 1860 federal census included Fort Bridger, Green River County, Utah Territory; and Fort Laramie in Nebraska Territory.
- Federal censuses for Wyoming are complete for all counties, 1870-1940 (with the exception of the 1890, lost for all states).
- There were several territorial/state censuses taken 1869 to 1905, but only the 1869 (entire territory) and 1885 (Ft. Laramie only), survive with names. The others have statistical reports only. There are no surviving state censuses for the State of Wyoming.
- Statewide resources include online databases at Ancestry.com, FamilySearch.org, and several other Internet sites. The online databases, published books, articles, and microfilms are integrated in the bibliography, organized below in chronological order:

◆ ◆ ◆ ◆ ◆

1850. *Utah Territory, 1850 Federal Census: Population Schedules* **[Microfilm & Digital Capture],** from the original records at the National Archives in Washington, DC. Wyoming people were enumerated as the "Green River Precinct" of Weber County, Utah. See FHL film #25540. To access the digital images, see the online FHL catalog: www.familysearch.org/search/catalog/744501.

1860. *Utah Territory, 1860 Federal Census: Population Schedules* **[Microfilm & Digital Capture],** from the original records at the National Archives, Washington, DC. Two filmings by the National Archives, 1950, 1967. The Utah Territory census included Wyoming people enumerated in Green River County, Utah Territory, which can be found on FHL film #805313 (2nd filming). To access the digital images, see the online FHL catalog: www.familysearch.org/search/catalog/707067.

1860. *Nebraska Territory, 1860 Federal Census: Population Schedules* **[Microfilm & Digital Capture],** from the original records at the National Archives, Washington, DC. Includes Fort Laramie, now Wyoming. The 1860 census was filmed twice. The second filming is listed first and is usually easier to read. Filmed by the National Archives, 1950, 1967. FHL has 2 rolls, as follows:
- Nebraska: (2nd filming) Entire territory, FHL film #803665.
- Nebraska: (1st filming) Entire territory, FHL film #14889.

To access the digital images, see the online FHL catalog: www.familysearch.org/search/catalog/705444.
- See also, *Wyoming 1860 Territorial Census Index* **[Printed Book],** edited by Ronald Vern Jackson, et al., published by Accelerated Indexing Systems, Bountiful, UT, 1984, 30 pages (front matter), 5 pages (names). Despite the title, Wyoming Territory was not created until 1868, this index is for the residents of Fort Laramie, as part of the Nebraska Territory census. It does not include the Fort Bridger residents who were part of Utah Territory in 1860. See FHL book 978.7 X22w.
- See also, **"1860 Census, Fort Laramie" [Printed Article],** in *The Colorado Genealogist,* (Colorado Genealogical Society, Denver, CO), Vol. 30 (Sep 1969) thru Vol. 31, No. 2 (Jun 1970)

1860-1910. *Wyoming, Compiled Census Index* **[Online Database],** indexed at the Ancestry.com website. Source: Accelerated Indexing Systems, Salt Lake City, UT, 1999. This collection contains the following indexes: 1860 Federal Census Index; 1870 Federal Census Index; 1880 Federal Census Index; 1890 Veterans Schedule; 1910 Federal Census Index. This database has 68,285 records. See http://search.ancestry.com/search/db.aspx?dbid=3582.

1861-1865. *Index to Compiled Service Records of Volunteer Union Soldiers Who Served in Organizations From the Territory of Dakota* **[Microfilm & Digital Capture],** from the original records at the National Archives, Washington, DC. Includes soldiers who served from Wyoming areas, part of Dakota Territory until 1867. Filmed by the National Archives, 1 roll, Series M0536. FHL film #881616. To access the digital images, see the online FHL catalog:
www.familysearch.org/search/catalog/313567.

1861-1865. *Index to Compiled Service Records of Volunteer Union Soldiers Who Served in Organizations From the Territory of Nebraska* **[Microfilm],** from the original records at the National Archives, Washington, DC. Includes the soldiers from the part of Wyoming Territory taken from Dakota Territory in 1867. Filmed by the National Archives, Series M547, 1964, 2 rolls, as follows:
- Index, A-La, 1861-1865, FHL film #821905.
- Index, Le-Z, 1861-1865, FHL film #821906.

1861-1865. See *Index to Soldiers & Sailors of the Civil War* **[Online Database],** a searchable name index to 6.3 million Union and Confederate Civil War soldiers now available online at the National Park Service Web site. A search can be done by surname, first name, and/or a unit from Dakota Territory, which supplied 269 men; or Nebraska Territory, which supplied 5,275 men to the war (all Union). See www.nps.gov/civilwar/search-soldiers.htm.

1864-1915. *Wyoming, Wills and Probate Records* **[Online Database],** digitized and indexed at the Ancestry.com website. Source: Ancestry database from County, District, and Probate Courts. The contents of a probate file can vary from case to case, but certain details are found in most probates, most importantly, the names and residences of beneficiaries and their relationship to the decedent. An inventory of the estate assets can reveal personal details about the deceased's occupation and lifestyle. There may also be references to debts, deeds, and other documents related to the settling of the estate. Each index record includes: Name, Probate date, Probate place, Inferred death year, Inferred death place, Case number, and Item description. The document image may have more information about a person. This database has 462 records. See
http://search.ancestry.com/search/db.aspx?dbid=60497.

1865-1866. *Internal Revenue Assessment Lists for the Territory of Idaho* **[Microfilm & Digital Capture],** from the originals at the National Archives, Kansas City branch. During the time of these assessments, Idaho Territory encompassed all of present Idaho, Montana, and Wyoming. Filmed by the National Archives, 1968, 1 roll, FHL film #1578503. To access the digital images, see the online FHL catalog:
www.familysearch.org/search/catalog/577985.

1867-1945. *Wyoming Newspaper Archives* **[Online Databases],** digitized and indexed newspapers at the GenealogyBank website, for Cheyenne, Evanston, Heart Mountain, and Laramie:
www.genealogybank.com/explore/newspapers/all/usa/wyoming.

1867-1920. *Laramie County, Wyoming, Naturalization Records* **[Online Database],** indexed at the Ancestry.com website. Source: WY State Archives. The records include Declarations of Intention to become a citizen, Oaths of Allegiance, and Naturalization Papers. Each index record includes: Name, Record type, Origin Place, Civil date, Court, Volume, and Page number. This database has 2,776 records. See
http://search.ancestry.com/search/db.aspx?dbid=4360.

1867-1920. *First Marriage Records of Laramie County at Court House* **[Digital Capture],** from the original records at the Laramie County Courthouse, Cheyenne, WY. Digitized by the Genealogical Society of Utah, 2013. To access the digital images, see the online FHL catalog:
https://familysearch.org/search/catalog/2227847.

1867-2000. *Western States Marriage Index* **[Online Database],** indexed at the Ancestry.com website. This database is also accessible at the BYU-Idaho website. Each index record includes: Name, Spouse, Marriage date and place, and a link to the BYU-Idaho website. This database has 23,890 WY marriages. See
http://search.ancestry.com/search/db.aspx?dbid=70016.

1868-1940. *Albany County Obituary Data* **[Printed Book],** compiled by Elnora Frye, et al, publ. Albany County Genealogical Society, Laramie, WY. The following is an index of accounts of deaths compiled by Elnora L. Frye from notices in the Laramie newspapers for the years of 1868 to 1899. The accounts abstracted are those involving deaths occurring in Albany county, deaths of former residents of Albany County, or individuals who were buried in Albany County. Some of these were taken from *Laramie Daily*

Sentinel newspaper accounts. "Laramie, Wyoming Burials 1867-1882." The date (year-month-day) of the newspaper issue is given as reference. The accounts listed are from the *Laramie Daily Sentinel (LDS)*, or *Weekly edition (LSW), Laramie Daily Boomerang (LDB)*, and *Laramie Semi-Weekly Boomerang (LSWB)*. These accounts were transcribed by Leroy R. Maki, April 1996, preliminary page, each work. Information for 1868-1899 is from *Laramie Daily Sentinel, Laramie Weekly Sentinel, Laramie Daily Boomerang, Semi-weekly Boomerang, and Laramie, Wyoming Burials, 1867-1882* by Ellen (Crago) Mueller. 1900-1940 information is from *Weekly or Semi-Weekly Boomerang* (1900), *Laramie Daily Boomerang* (1901-June 1906), *Laramie Republican* (daily) (1906-Jun 1926) and *Laramie Republican-Boomerang* (Jul 1926-May 1957). See FHL book 978.795 V42a.

1868-1961. See *Land and Miscellaneous Records, 1868-1925; Index, 1867-1961 (Laramie County, Wyoming)* **[Microfilm & Digital Capture]**, from the originals at the WY State Archives. Filmed by the WY State Archives, 1970, 75 rolls, beginning with FHL film #973775 (General index to deeds, 1867-1883). To access the digital images, see the online FHL catalog: **https://familysearch.org/search/catalog/85962**.

1868-1970. *The Historical Encyclopedia of Wyoming* **[Printed Book],** edited by Thomas S. Chamblin, publ. Wyoming Historical Institute, Cheyenne, WY, 1970, 1,669 pages (2 vols.). Contains "representative citizens who have had an integral part in the growth and development of Wyoming and historical sketches of leading cities, counties and tabulated principal facts of interest regarding every city, town, county, and district of the state." 1,425 pages of biography. FHL book 978.7 D3h v.1-2.

1868-1991. *Wyoming Blue Book* **[Printed Book]**, edited by Virginia Cole Trenhold, Loren Jost, Jim Donahue, et al., published by the Wyoming State Archives and Historical Department, Cheyenne, WY, 1974, 1991, 5 vols. Reprint of *Wyoming Historical Blue Book* by Marie Erwin, who prepared the original 1,471-page book in 1943. In 1974 Virginia Cole Trenhold edited Erwin's work into 2 volumes and added vol. 3 as a supplement, bringing the blue book up to 1974. Loren Jost edited vol. 4 to bring the series up to 1990. Jim Donahue edited vol. 5, *Guide to the County Archives of Wyoming*. Each volume is indexed. Contents: Vol. 1: acquisition of land through territorial days; creation, organization, and government of the territory; history of territorial counties; territorial and federal officers; events leading to statehood; constitution; territorial data; bibliography of biographies; historical highlights to 1890; Vol. 2: statehood until 1943; constitution with amendments to 1943; organization of state government; federal government in Wyoming; history of counties; election statistic; bibliography of biographies; chronology 1890-1943; Vol. 3: government of Wyoming; branches of government and functions; constitutional amendments, natural resources, counties and municipalities, tourism, Wind River Reservation; chronology 1943-1974; Vol. 4: state government, Congressional representatives, education, economic and cultural resources, the counties, Wind River Indian Reservation, events from 1974-1990; Vol. 5, pt. 1 is the *Guide to the County Archives of Wyoming*; Vol. 5, pt. 2 is the *Guide to the State Government and Municipal Archives of Wyoming*. FHL book 978.7 N2b vol. 1-5.

1868-1991. *Wyoming Biographies* **[Printed Book],** by Lawrence M. Woods, publ. High Plains Pub. Co., Worland, WY, 1991, 224 pages. Includes index. FHL book 978.7 D3w.

1868-2000s. *Wyoming USGenWeb Archives* **[Online Database].** This WYGenWeb site offers free genealogical databases with searchable statewide name lists and for all Wyoming counties. Databases may include Bibles, Biographies, Cemeteries, Censuses, Court Records, Deaths, Deeds, Directories, Histories, Marriages, Military, Newspapers, Obituaries, Photos, Schools, Tax Lists, Wills, and more. See **http://usgwarchives.net/wy/wyfiles.htm**.

1868-2000s. *Linkpendium – Wyoming: Family History & Genealogy, Census, Birth, Marriage, Death, Vital Records & More* **[Online Databases].** Linkpendium is a genealogical portal site with links to state, county, town, and local databases. Currently listed are selected sites for Wyoming statewide resources (265), Renamed Counties, Discontinued Counties (3), Albany County (195), Big Horn County (180), Campbell County (102), Carbon County (250), Converse County (139), Crook County (124), Fremont County (173), Goshen County (111), Hot Springs County (97), Johnson County (129), Laramie County (270), Lincoln County (141), Natrona County (177), Niobrara County (107), Park County (166), Platte County (100), Sheridan County (165), Sublette County (110), Sweetwater County (194), Teton County (116), Uinta County (191), Washakie County (93), and Weston County (130). See **www.linkpendium.com/wy-genealogy**.

1869. *Wyoming Territory 1869 Census* [Microfilm], from the originals at the WY State Archives, Cheyenne, WY. Several territorial & state censuses were conducted in Wyoming, but this 1869 territory-wide census is the only one to survive. (See 1885 for a Ft. Kearny census). Filmed by the WY State Archives, 1970, 1 roll, FHL film #2261365. To see if this microfilm was digitized yet, see the online FHL catalog: www.familysearch.org/search/catalog/958477.

1869-1920. *Marriage Records, Albany County, Wyoming* [Microfilm & Digital Capture], from the originals at the Albany County Courthouse, Laramie, WY. Filmed by the WY State Archives, 6 rolls, beginning with FHL film #968059 (Marriage records, 1869-1880, 1887-1891). To access the digital images, see the online FHL catalog: www.familysearch.org/search/catalog/84693.

1869-1923. *Wyoming Marriages* [Online Database], indexed at FamilySearch.org. This is an index to a few selected records from Albany, Natrona, Sheridan and Uinta counties. This database has 83 records, see www.familysearch.org/search/collection/2334596.

1870. *Wyoming Territory, 1870 Federal Census: Population Schedules* [Microfilm & Digital Capture], from the original records at the National Archives, Washington, DC. The 1870 census was filmed twice. The second filming is listed first and is usually easier to read. However, since some of the records were faded or lost between the first and second filmings, search the first filming whenever the material on the second filming is too light to read. Filmed by the National Archives, 1962, 1968. FHL has 2 rolls, as follows:
- Wyoming: (2nd filming) Albany, Carbon, Laramie, Sweetwater, and Uintah Counties, FHL film #553247.
- Wyoming: (1st filming) Albany, Carbon, Laramie, Sweetwater, and Uintah Counties, FHL film #34519.

To access the digital images (2nd filming), see the online FHL catalog: www.familysearch.org/search/catalog/698929.

- See also, *1870 Wyoming Territory Census* **[Photocopy],** of the original manuscript, 142 pages. Copy at the Family History Library in Salt Lake City. FHL book 978.7 X2p.

- See also, *1870 Wyoming Census Index, A-Z* **[Printed Book],** edited by Raeone Christensen Steuart, publ. Heritage Quest, Bountiful, UT, 2000, 55 pages, an every-name index. FHL book 978.7 X22s.

- See also, **"1870 Census, Fort Laramie, Wyoming Territory"** [Printed Article], name list in the *Colorado Genealogist,* (Colorado Genealogical Society, Denver, CO), Vol. 24, No. 1 (Jan 1963) thru Vol. 24, No. 4 (Oct 1963),

1872-1901. *Miscellaneous Records, Albany County, Wyoming* [Microfilm & Digital Capture], from the originals at the Albany County Courthouse, Laramie, WY. Includes indexes at beginning of volumes. Includes agreements, diplomas, deeds, leases, certificates of incorporation, statements of claim, school district records, declarations of trust, etc. Filmed by the WY State Archives, 1970, 2 rolls, FHL film #968064 (Misc. Records, Vol. B-C, 1872-1887); and FHL film #968065 (Misc. Records, Vol. D-E (1887-1901). To access the digital images, see the online FHL catalog: www.familysearch.org/search/catalog/84697.

1874-1908. *Wyoming, Laramie County, Homestead Records* [Digital Capture], from the originals at the National Archives, Denver Branch. Digital capture by the Genealogical Society of Utah, 2015. The original Homestead Act of 1862 was amended in 1873 and again in 1877, to create an incentive to restore timber lands, and plant trees in desert areas of the western U.S. This database is record of the homesteads issued in Wyoming during that period. The microfilm series begins with FHL Digital capture #101274218. To access the digital images, see the online FHL catalog: https://familysearch.org/search/catalog/2526478.

1875. *History and Directory of Laramie City, Wyoming Territory* [Printed Book], by J. H. Triggs, facsimile reproduction of original published by the Daily Sentinel Print, Laramie, WY, 1875, 91 pages. Contains a brief history of Laramie City from its first settlement to the present time, together with sketches of the characteristics and resources of the surrounding country; including a minute description of a portion of the mining region of the Black Hills.

- See also, *A General and Business Directory of Laramie City* **(Printed Book],** publ. 1875. FHL book 978.795/L1 H2t.

1876-1890. *Wyoming, Laramie County, Military Bounty Land Records* [Digital Capture], from the originals at the National Archives, Denver Branch. Digitized by the Genealogical Society of Utah, 2015. The federal government provided bounty land for those who served in the Revolutionary War, the War of 1812, the Mexican War, and Indian wars between 1775 and 1855. It was first offered as an incentive to serve in the military and later as a reward for service. This collection includes DGS #101289766 (Mining Applications, V. 36, 1876-1890), and DGS #101289767 (Mining Applications, v. 37, 1876-1890). To access the digital images, see the online FHL catalog https://familysearch.org/search/catalog/2526513.

1877-1920. *Wyoming Marriages* **[Online Database],** indexed at the FamilySearch.org website. Source: FamilySearch extractions from records on FHL film #9680959 at the Family History Library, Salt Lake City, UT. Each index record includes: Name, Birth year, Date of marriage, Place of marriage, and Name of Spouse. This database has 4,485 records. See https://familysearch.org/search/collection/1708702.

1878 Directory. See *Wolfe's Mercantile Guide, Gazetteer, and Business Directory of Cities, Towns, Villages, Stations, and Government Forts, Located Upon the Lines of the Following Named Railroads: Union Pacific, Omaha & Northwestern, Sioux City & Pacific, Omaha & Republican Valley, Colorado Central, Utah Northern, Utah Central, Utah Western, Utah Southern, Bingham Canon [sic] & Camp Floyd, Wahsath [sic] & Jordan Valley, and American Fork Railroad and Towns in the Black Hills* **[Printed Book & Digital Version],** compiled by J. M. Wolfe, publ. Omaha Republican Book and Job Printing House, 1878, 360 pages. FHL Filmed by the WY State Archives, 1974, 1 roll, FHL film #1004514. To access the digital images, see the online FHL catalog: www.familysearch.org/search/catalog/51112.

1880. *Wyoming Territory, 1880 Federal Census: Soundex and Population Schedules* **[Microfilm & Digital Capture],** from the original records at the National Archives, Washington, DC. Filmed by the National Archives, ca 1944. FHL has 2 rolls, as follows:
- Soundex: A000 thru Institutions, FHL film #378158.
- Population schedules: Entire territory, FHL #1255454.

To access the digital images (Population Schedules), see the online FHL catalog: www.familysearch.org/search/catalog/646360.
- See also, *1880 Wyoming Census Index* **[Printed Book],** edited by Ronald Vern Jackson, et al., an every-name index published by Accelerated Indexing Systems, Bountiful, UT, 1980, 266 pages. FHL book 978.7 X22w.

- See also, *1880 Wyoming Mortality Schedule* **[Printed Book],** edited by Ronald Vern Jackson, et al., published by Accelerated Indexing Systems, 1983, 31 pages (front matter), 3 pages (names). Includes deaths occurring prior to June 1, 1880. FHL book 978.7 X2.

"1885 Census, Fort Laramie, Wyoming" **[Printed Article],** name list in *Black Hills Nuggets*, (Rapid City Society of Genealogical Research, Rapid, City, SD), Vol. 4, No. 4 (Nov 1971). The location of the originals was not noted, but except for the entire territory census of 1869, this appears to be the only surviving portion of a territory-wide census taken in Wyoming.

1889 Qualified Electors, Grand Jurors, and Petit Jurors, Sheridan County, Wyoming **[Online Database],** indexed at the RootsWeb site for Sheridan Co WY. Archived at https://web.archive.org/web/20151221020819/www.rootsweb.ancestry.com/~wysherid/election.htm.

1890 Wyoming Veterans Census Index **[Printed Book],** edited by Ronald Vern Jackson, published by Accelerated Indexing Systems, Salt Lake City, UT, 1983, 57 pages (front matter), 19 pages (names). FHL book 978.7 X22j.

1890-1921. *Miscellaneous Records (Natrona County, Wyoming)* **[Microfilm & Digital Capture],** from the originals at the Natrona County Courthouse, Casper, WY. Includes deeds, affidavits, military discharges, physicians' certificates, etc. Filmed by the WY State Archives, 1970, 2 rolls, FHL film #973797 (Misc. Records, Vol. 1, 1890-1912); and FHL film #973798 (Misc. Records, Vol. 2-3, 1912-1921. To access the digital images, see the online FHL catalog: www.familysearch.org/search/catalog/87353.
- See also, *General Index, Natrona County, Wyoming, ca1890-1923* **[Microfilm & Digital Capture],** from the originals at the Natrona County Courthouse, Casper, WY. The records indexed include deeds (warranty, trust, quit claim, etc.), mortgages and releases, marriage records, bills of sale, leases, articles of agreement, some citizenship papers, power of attorney, homestead, certificate of incorporation, mining deed, brands, diplomas, and notice of tax sale. Filmed by the WY State Archives, 6 rolls, beginning with FHL film #973707 (General Index, grantor A-Z, et al). To access the digital images, see the online FHL catalog: https://familysearch.org/search/catalog/87365.

1892. *Cheyenne, Wyoming Directory* **[Online Database],** indexed at the Ancestry.com website. Source: R.L. Polk Co, publ. 1892. Each index record

→ **Sample page from the 1900 United States Federal Census.** A search was made for any person born between 1885 and 1895 in Wyoming. The results from that search included the above image from Fremont County, Wyoming. This page is from the enumeration of the Indian Population of the Shoshone Indian Reservation, specifically, the Arapahoe Indians living on that reservation. In 1900 only, Indian Population Schedules were added to the regular Federal Census schedules, at the end of a county list. Special censuses of Indians were usually conducted separately as Indians were specifically excluded from the census apportionment count per the U.S. Constitution of 1789. A ruling by the Supreme Court in 1924 declared that all American Indians were Citizens of the U.S., and as such, they were included as part of the general population in all federal censuses thereafter. This exact page from Fremont County, Wyoming can be accessed via the FHL catalog page URL shown below.

includes: Name, Location, City, State, and Year. This database has 3,742 records. See http://search.ancestry.com/search/db.aspx?dbid=5382.

1896 Directory. See *Directory of Lander, Lander Valley and the Mines and Other Useful Information: 1896* **[Microfiche],** from the reprint published by the Fremont Genealogical Society, Riverton, WY, 1990, 92 pages. Original published by Clipper Book and Job Print, Lander, WY, 1896. From Intro: "This consisted of Dubois, Lost Cabin, Thermopolis, Meeteetse and Burlington areas, or everything north of Lander to the Montana state line. Also all of the settlements towards Casper, Rawlins and Pinedale." Filmed by the Genealogical Society of Utah, 1990, 1 microfiche, FHL fiche #6075728.

→ **1900.** *Wyoming, 1900 Federal Census: Soundex and Population Schedules* **[Microfilm & Digital Capture],** from the original records at the National Archives, Washington, DC, filmed by the National Archives, ca1944, FHL has 17 rolls, including digitized population schedules:
- Population schedules: Albany, Bighorn, Carbon, Converse, Crook, Fremont, and Johnson Co., FHL film #1241826.
- Population schedules: Laramie, Natrona, Sheridan, Sweetwater, Uinta, and Weston Co.; Yellowstone National Park and Fort Yellowstone, FHL film #1241827.

To access the digital images (Population Schedules), see the online FHL catalog:
www.familysearch.org/search/catalog/655308.

1900-1952. *Wyoming, Index to Death Records* **[Digital Capture],** from records of the WY State Archives, digitized in 2017 by Reclaim the Records, Mill Valley, CA (As part of a larger set of WY vital records). The FHL has 14 digital file folders. To access the digital images, see the online FHL catalog: www.familysearch.org/search/catalog/2836155.

1901-2015. *Wyoming, Star Valley Independent Obituaries* **[Online Database],** digitized and indexed at the FamilySearch.org website. Each index record includes: Name, Event type, Event date, Gender, Relationship to the deceased, Birth date, Birthplace, Death date, and Death place. The obituary image has more information about a person. This database has 10,985 records. See
https://familysearch.org/search/collection/2103497.

"1906, First Census, Riverton, Fremont County, Wyoming" [Printed Article], name list in the *Fremont County Nostalgia News*, (Fremont County Genealogical Society, Riverton, WY), Vol. 12, No. 2 (Apr 1992).

1908-1909 Directory. See *Business Directory of Cheyenne, Wyo.: Laramie, Wyo.; Rawlins, Wyo.; Rock Springs, Wyo.; Green River, Wyo.; Evanston, Wyo.; Ogden, Utah; Preston, Idaho; Pocatello, Idaho; Brigham City, Utah; Logan, Utah; 1908-1909* **[Microfilm & Digital Capture],** from the original at Utah State Historical Society, Salt Lake City. Filmed by the Utah State Archives and Records Services, 1975, 1 roll, FHL film #1004510. To access the digital images, see the online FHL catalog:
www.familysearch.org/search/catalog/32287.

1908-1966. *Wyoming, Reclaim the Records, State Archives Vital Records* **[Online Database],** digitized and indexed at FamilySearch.org. This database includes Wyoming marriage, divorce, and death indexes spanning years 1908-1966 acquired by Reclaim the Records and shared with FamilySearch. Each records set and its respective years are as follows: Wyoming marriage index: 1980-1966, Wyoming divorce index: 1941-1952, and Wyoming death index: 1939-1952. The marriage index contains the following fields: last name, first name (either bride or groom depending on which index), spouse first initial, spouse last name, volume number, certificate number, and event date. The death index cards include the following fields: name, event place, cause of death, file number, certificate number, and age. The divorce index cards include the following fields: last name, first name, spouse last name, spouse first name, event place, event date, and certificate number. This database has 297,595 records, see
www.familysearch.org/search/collection/2837991.

1909 Gazetteer. See *Stockmen's Gazetteer of Wyoming, 1909* **[Microfilm],** from the original published by Given & Espy, Cheyenne, WY, 1909, 224 pages. Filmed by the State of Wyoming Microfilming Department, Cheyenne, WY, 1959. Contains cattle, sheep, and horse brands, arranged by type of brand and the Wyoming county, with the name of the person or company to which the brand belongs, and the town where they are located. FHL has 1 roll, FHL film #1759460. To see if this microfilm was digitized yet, see the online FHL catalog:
www.familysearch.org/search/catalog/651649.

1910. *Wyoming, 1910 Federal Census: Population Schedules* **[Microfilm & Digital Capture],** from the original records at the National Archives, Washington, DC. No Soundex was created for this state. Filmed by the National Archives, Series T624, 3 rolls, (NARA rolls 1745-1747), cataloged at the FHL as follows:
- Population schedules: Albany, Fremont, Big Horn, Carbon, and Johnson Co., FHL #1375758.
- Population schedules: Converse, Crook, Sweetwater, and Laramie Co., FHL #1375759.
- Population schedules: Natrona, Park, Sheridan, Uinta, and Weston Co. and Yellowstone National Park, FHL #1375760.

To access the digital images, see the online FHL catalog: www.familysearch.org/search/catalog/646895.
- See also, *1910 Wyoming Census Index: Heads of Households and Other Surnames in Households Index* **[Printed Book],** compiled by Bryan Lee Dilts, published by Index Publishing, Salt Lake City, UT, 1985, 245 pages. Transcribed from National Archives microfilm no. T624, rolls 1745-1747. FHL book 978.7 X2d.
- See also *Wyoming 1910* **[Printed Book],** a name index edited by Ronald Vern Jackson, published by Accelerated Indexing Systems, North Salt Lake, UT, 1986, 269 pages. FHL book 978.7 X22j.
- See also, *Colorado, Montana and Wyoming 1910 U.S. Federal Census Index* **[CD-ROM],** publ. Heritage Quest, Bountiful, UT, 2002. Extracted from the original records of the National Archives Series T624, this U.S. federal census index contains over 555,000 entries for all counties and cities in Colorado, Montana, and Wyoming. Indexed names include heads-of-household and any person with a different surname than the head. See FHL CD-ROM No. 1164.

"1911 Poll Tax & 1911 Dog Tax, Fremont County, Wyoming" [Printed Article], name list in *Fremont County Nostalgia News*, (Fremont County Genealogical Society, Riverton, WY), Vol. 10, No. 2 (Apr 1990).

***1917-1918 World War I Selective Service System Draft Registration Cards, Wyoming* [Microfilm],** from the original records at the National Archives, East Point, Georgia. The draft cards are arranged alphabetically by county draft board, and then alphabetically by surname of the registrants. Filmed by the National Archives, series M1508. FHL has 14 rolls, Beginning with FHL film #1993029 (Albany Co, A-O) To access the digital images, see the online FHL catalog: **www.familysearch.org/search/catalog/754904.**

- See also, ***Wyoming, World War I American Expeditionary Forces, Deaths, 1917-1919* [Digital Capture],** from records at the National Personnel Center, St. Louis, MO. Digitized by FamilySearch International, 2018. To access the digital images, see the online FHL catalog:
www.familysearch.org/search/catalog/3023960.

***1917-1935 City Directories, Casper, Wyoming, and Surrounding Area* [Microfilm],** from the original records located in various libraries and societies, original records published for years as noted below by R.L. Polk & Company. Filmed by Research Publications, Woodbridge, CT, ca 1995, 2 rolls, FHL #2310255-6.

***1920 Wyoming Federal Census: Soundex and Population Schedules* [Microfilm & Digital Capture],** from the original records at the National Archives, Washington, DC. Best copy available (original census schedules destroyed after microfilming). Filmed by the National Archives, ca1944. FHL has 22 rolls, as follows:
- Population schedules: Albany, Big Horn, Campbell, Carbon, and Crook Counties, FHL film #1822025.
- Population schedules: Converse, Goshen, Johnson, Fremont, Hot Springs, and Weston Counties, FHL film #1822026.
- Population schedules: Laramie, Lincoln, and Platte Counties, FHL film #1822027.
- Population schedules: Natrona, Niobrara, Washakie, Park, and Sweetwater Counties, FHL film #1822028.
- Population schedules: Sheridan, and Uinta Counties; and Yellowstone National Park, FHL film #1822029.

To access the digital images, see the online FHL Catalog page:
www.familysearch.org/search/catalog/558339.

1924-1989 Directories. See ***Polk's Laramie (Albany County, Wyoming) City Directory: Including Albany County, Containing an Alphabetical Directory of Business Concerns and Private Citizens, a Directory of Householders, Occupants of Office Buildings and Other Business Places, Including a Complete Street and Avenue Guide, a Directory of Rural Route* [Printed Book],** published by R. L. Polk and Company, Kansas City, MO. FHL has 1924-25, 1926-27, 1929-30, 1931-32 (fiche only), 1934-35, 1941, 1958, 1961, 1966, 1970, 1975, 1978, 1983, 1986, 1989. FHL book 978.795 E4pL.

1930. ***Wyoming, 1930 Federal Census: Population Schedules* [Microfilm & Digital Capture],** from the original records, series T626. Best copy available (original census schedules destroyed after microfilming). Filmed by the National Archives, ca1944. FHL has 2 rolls, population schedules, as follows:
- Population schedules: Albany, Big Horn, Campbell, Converse, and Crook Counties, FHL film #2342355.
- Population schedules: Carbon, Fremont, Goshen, Hot Springs, and Johnson Counties, FHL #2342356.

To access the digital images, see the online FHL catalog: **www.familysearch.org/search/catalog/1037545.**

1940. ***Wyoming, 1940 Federal Census: Population Schedules* [Digital Capture].** After microfilming, Congress allowed the Census Bureau to destroy the originals to free up space for WWII-related files. Digitizing of the 1940 census schedules microfilm images was done for the National Archives and made public on April 2, 2012. To access the digital images, see the online FHL catalog:
www.familysearch.org/search/catalog/2057800.

***1940 Federal Census Finding Aids* [Online Database].** The National Archives prepared a special website online with a detailed description of the 1940 federal census. Included at the site are descriptions of location finding aids, such as Enumeration District Maps, Geographic Descriptions of Census Enumeration Districts, and a list of 1940 City

Directories available at the National Archives. The finding aids are all linked to other National Archives sites. The National Archives website also has a link to 1940 Search Engines using Stephen P. Morse's "One-Step" system for finding a 1940 E.D. or street address conversion. See www.archives.gov/research/census/1940/general-info.html#questions.

1940-1947. *Wyoming, World War II Draft Registration Cards* **[Digital Capture],** from the originals at the National Personnel Records Center, St. Louis, MO. Draft registration cards of men who registered during World War II, with the exception of the fourth registration. Images courtesy of Ancestry. The event place is the residence of the registrant. Digitized by FamilySearch International, 2016. To access the digital images, see the online FHL catalog: www.familysearch.org/search/catalog/2659406.

- See also, *Wyoming, Military Records: World War II 4th Draft Registration Cards, 1942* **[Digital Capture],** from the originals at the National Personnel Center, St. Louis, MO. These cards represent older men, ages 45 to 65 in April 1942, that were registered for the draft. They had birth dates between 28 Apr 1877 and 16 Feb 1892. Includes name of individual, date and place of birth, address, age, telephone number, employer's name and address, name and address of person who would know where the individual can be located, signature, and physical description. Digitized by the Genealogical Society of Utah, 2015. To access the digital images, see the online FHL catalog: www.familysearch.org/search/catalog/2624866.

1941-1952. *Wyoming, Index to Divorce Records* **[Digital Capture],** from records of the WY State Archives, digitized in 2017 by Reclaim the Records, Mill Valley, CA (As part of a larger set of WY vital records). The FHL has 3 digital file folders. To access the digital images, see the online FHL catalog: www.familysearch.org/search/catalog/2836154.

1952-1956. *Wyoming, Index to Marriage Records* **[Digital Capture],** from records of the WY State Archives, digitized in 2017 by Reclaim the Records, Mill Valley, CA (As part of a larger set of WY vital records). The FHL has 13 digital file folders. To access the digital images, see the online FHL catalog: www.familysearch.org/search/catalog/2836153.

1965. See *Wyoming City Directories (Sheridan)* **[Online Database],** digitized and indexed at the Ancestry.com website. Source: 1965 Sheridan, WY Directory (publ. not noted). The entire text was scanned, with an OCR index. This database has 488 records. See http://search.ancestry.com/search/db.aspx?dbid=8986.

1997-Current. See *Wyoming Recent Newspaper Obituaries* **[Online Database],** digitized and indexed newspaper obituaries at the GenealogyBank website, including newspapers for Casper, Cheyenne, Laramie, Riverton, and Worland. See www.genealogybank.com/explore/obituaries/all/usa/wyoming.

Nationwide Chapter - Part 1
Maps, Descriptions & Internet Access
for the U.S. Federal Censuses, 1790-1950

Contents

Illustration - 1790 Census Page……………………………..218
1790 Federal Census……………………………………...219
1800 Federal Census…………………………………….. 221
1810 Federal Census……………………………………...223
1820 Federal Census……………………………………...225
1830 Federal Census……………………………………...227
1840 Federal Census……………………………………...229
1850 Federal Census……………………………………...231
1860 Federal Census……………………………………...233
1870 Federal Census……………………………………...235
1880 Federal Census……………………………………...237
State Censuses Taken in 1885…………………………… 239
    Table 5-1: 1885 State Census Publications……............. 240
1890 Federal Census……………………………………...241
    1890 Union Veterans & Widows Schedules…………......242
    Table 5-2: 1884-1896 State Censuses………………… 244
1900 Federal Census……………………………………...245
1910 Federal Census……………………………………...247
1920 Federal Census……………………………………...249
1930 Federal Census……………………………………...251
1940 Federal Census……………………………………...253
1950 Federal Census……………………………………...255
Census References……………………………….................257
Bibliography of U.S. Census Substitutes…………………259

1790 Census Pages, prepared for Nash County, North Carolina. There were no pre-printed forms, so the Asst. Marshal prepared the format for the name lists by hand. Note that the last column was the "Amount" (total number of persons in a household), a column added by the Asst. Marshal on his own. Also, note that this Nash Co NC Asst. Marshal arranged his names by the first letter of their surnames – evidence that these pages were copied from his original door-to-door name lists.

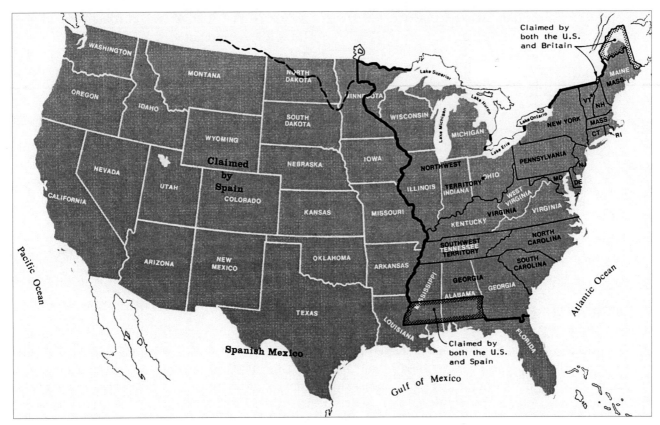

The U.S. in 1790. At the Treaty of Paris in 1783, the U.S. had agreed to meet later with Spain to settle a land dispute in the West Florida region; and also to meet with Great Britain to resolve the issue of the northern border of present Maine with present New Brunswick. Map Source: Page 1, *Map Guide to the U.S. Federal Censuses, 1790-1920* by William Thorndale and William Dollarhide.

1790 Federal Census

Location of Original Records: National Archives, Washington, DC.

U.S. Population: 3.9 million (3.2 free and .7 million slave).

1790 Census Legislative Act: 1 Stat. 101, 1 March 1790.

Responsibility: The President of the United States (George Washington), with authority delegated to the Secretary of State (Thomas Jefferson). Reporting to the Secretary of State, the U.S. Marshal of each U.S. Federal Court District hired and managed Assistant Marshals as the door-to-door census takers within his district. The Assistant Marshals were all political appointees (Mainly people loyal to the Federalist Party).

Census Day: the first Monday in August (2 Aug 1790). All of the questions asked by the census taker were related to a person's age or place of residence as of the census day. The original 1790 instructions were issued by Secretary of State Thomas Jefferson:

"...all the questions refer to the day when the enumeration is to commence; the first Monday in August next. Your assistants will thereby understand that they are to insert in their returns all the persons belonging to the family on the first Monday in August, even those who may be deceased at the time when they take the account; and, on the other hand, that they will not include in it, infants born after that day."

Time Allowed: Nine months. (Except VT had 5 months, and SC had 19 months).

States Included: 14 States. Of the two states late to join the Union, Rhode Island (the last of the 13 states to ratify the Constitution on 29 May 1790), was to be enumerated within the set nine months (1 Stat. 129, 5 July 1790). Vermont entered the Union as the 14th state on 4 Mar 1791 and had a census day of the 1st Monday in April 1791 (4 Apr 1791); the field count due within five months (1 Stat. 197, 2 March 1791). South Carolina's field count was extended to allow completion within nineteen months of the census day (1 Stat. 226, 8 November 1791).

Federal Court Districts: 16 Districts. There were fourteen (14) states at the time of the 1790 census, but the census was enumerated in sixteen (16) federal court districts. The districts lined up with the states, except that Maine was still part of Massachusetts and had its own census because it was a separate federal court district. The same was true of Kentucky, still part of Virginia but was a separate federal court district.

Territories Included: Congress believed there was no need for a census in the Northwest Territory because territories had no voting representation in Congress. But military captains in the Southwest Territory (which became Tennessee in 1796) took a count under the direction of the Governor

Surviving Censuses: Eleven (11) federal court districts: Connecticut, Maine, Maryland, Massachusetts, New Hampshire, New York, North Carolina, Pennsylvania, Rhode Island, South Carolina, and Vermont.

Census Losses: Five (5) federal court districts: Kentucky, Delaware, Georgia, New Jersey, and Virginia. These five states did not return the original 1790-1820 census manuscripts to Washington, DC as was specified in the 1830 law (4 Stat. 430, 28 May 1830).

Content of the Population Schedules: 5 columns. The 1790 format included:
- Name of a head of household
- Number of free white males under 16
- Number of free white males 16 or older
- Number of free white females of any age
- Number of slaves (omitted in places without slaves)

Microfilm of Originals & Digital Capture: The National Archives film for the 1790 census is contained on 12 rolls, series M637, beginning with FHL film #568141 (Connecticut). The microfilm was digitized by FamilySearch International. For a list of roll numbers, contents, and access to the digital images of each roll, see the online FHL catalog page:
https://familysearch.org/search/catalog/121535.

Printed Extract & Index: In 1908, the Census Bureau in Washington, DC undertook a project to extract and index the 1790 census name lists, a publication now commonly known as the *1790 Heads of Families*. It included one volume each for twelve of the sixteen federal court districts that were originally enumerated in the 1790 census. Although Virginia's 1790 census originals were lost, Virginia had extant tax lists covering all of its counties for the years immediately preceding 1790. The Census Office's 1908 publication used these tax lists to reconstruct the 1790 name lists for the lost Virginia census. A few 1790 counties of other states were also reconstructed from tax lists, including certain counties in North Carolina and Maryland. This 1790 census extract & index was printed in 1908, one volume per state; later microfilmed by the National Archives on three rolls as series T498. Search the FHL catalog for one of the 12 volumes. Search by: (Name of State) – 1790 Census. See www.familysearch.org/search/catalog/search.

Online Searching - 1790 Census Indexes and Digital Images. The 1790 Census was digitized from the National Archives microfilm, indexed, and made available at the following websites:
- Ancestry.com.
- FamilySearch.org.
- MyHeritage.com.
- Findmypast.com.
- GenealogyBank.com.
- HeritageQuestOnline-Subscribers Login.

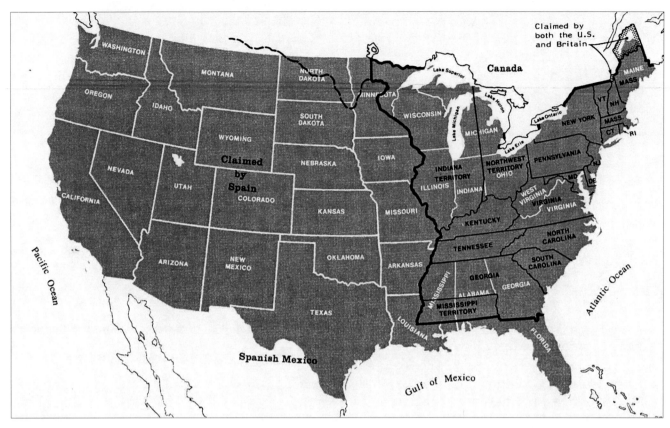

The U.S. in 1800. In the 1796 Treaty of San Lorenzo, the U.S. resolved the Spanish-U.S. disputed area by purchasing the area from Spain. In 1798, the area became Mississippi Territory. Map source: Page 2, *Map Guide to the U.S. Federal Censuses, 1790-1920* by William Thorndale and William Dollarhide.

1800 Federal Census

Location of Original Records: National Archives, Washington, DC.

U.S. Population: 5.3 million (4.4 million free and .9 million slave).

1800 Census Legislative Act: 2 Stat. 11, 28 February 1800.

Responsibility: The President of the United States (John Adams), with authority delegated to the Secretary of State (Charles Lee). Reporting to the Secretary of State, the U.S. Marshal of each U.S. Federal Court District hired and managed Assistant Marshals as the door-to-door census takers within his district. **Census day:** the first Monday in August (4 Aug 1800). All of the questions asked by the census taker were related to a person's age or place of residence as of the census day.

Time Allowed: Nine months.

1800 Jurisdictions: 21. Two new states were admitted to the Union since 1790: Kentucky, admitted in 1792; and Tennessee, previously the "Southwest Territory," admitted in 1796, for a total of 16 states in the Union. Still part of Massachusetts, the federal court district of Maine was enumerated separately from Massachusetts. The District of Columbia was included, separated from Maryland and Virginia. In addition, three territories were enumerated for the first time: Mississippi Territory, created in 1798 from lands obtained in a treaty with Spain; the Northwest Territory, created in 1787 (but not enumerated in 1790); and Indiana Territory, divided from the old Northwest Territory in early 1800, for a total of 21 jurisdictions.

Surviving Censuses: Thirteen (13) federal court districts: Connecticut, Delaware, District of Columbia (Washington Co DC only), Maine, Maryland, Massachusetts, New Hampshire, New York, North Carolina, Pennsylvania, Rhode Island, South Carolina, and Vermont.

Census Losses: Five (5) state/federal court districts; Georgia, Kentucky, New Jersey, Tennessee, and Virginia; and Three (3) Territories: Indiana Territory, Mississippi Territory, and Northwest Territory. These eight states/territories did not return the original 1790-1820 census manuscripts to Washington as was specified in the 1830 law (4 Stat. 430, 28 May 1830).

Content of the Population Schedules: 13 columns of questions were asked for the Head of Household, on one line, across one page, for the following:
- Name of a head of household
- Number of free white males, 0-9 years old
- Number of free white males, 10-15 years old
- Number of free white males, 16-25 years old
- Number of free white males, 26-44 years old
- Number of free white males, 45 & over
- Number of free white females, 0-9 years old
- Number of free white females, 10-15 years old
- Number of free white females, 16-25 years old
- Number of free white females, 26-44 years old
- Number of free white females, 45 & over
- Number of other free persons
- Number of slaves (omitted in places without slaves)

Microfilm of 1800 Originals & Digital Capture: The National Archives film for the 1800 census is contained on 54 rolls, series M32, beginning with FHL film #205618 (Connecticut). The microfilm was digitized by FamilySearch International. For a list of roll numbers, contents, and access to the digital images of each roll, see the online FHL catalog page:
https://familysearch.org/search/catalog/118365.

Online Searching, 1800 Federal Census Indexes and Digital Images:

- **Ancestry.com.** Subscription site, free database searching. Ancestry and FamilySearch share images and indexes. See www.ancestry.com/search/collections/1800usfedcenancestry.

- **FamilySearch.org.** Free database search, with images by FamilySearch, index by Ancestry. See https://familysearch.org/search/collection/1804228.

- **MyHeritage.com.** A Family Tree subscription site. All U.S. Federal Census Records are available to subscribers with a data plan. See www.myheritage.com/research/collection-10121/1800-united-states-federal-census.

- **Findmypast.com.** Monthly or annual subscriptions. Initial searches to U.S. Federal Censuses are free. See www.findmypast.com/articles/search-the-1800-us-census.

- **GenealogyBank.com.** Subscription site. Initial searches to the U.S. Federal Censuses, 1790-1940 are free. www.genealogybank.com/explore/census/all.

- **HeritageQuestOnline-Subscribers Login.** This is a library subscription service. Check with your local library to see if they subscribe to the ProQuest & HeritageQuest databases. Many subscribing libraries allow their library card holders remote access. See www.heritagequestonline.com/hqoweb/library/do/login.

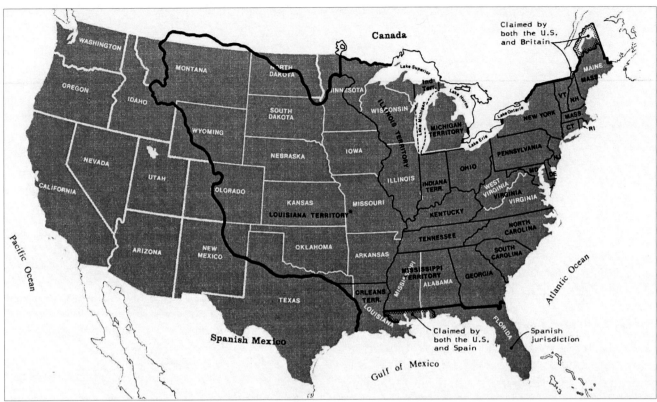

The U.S. in 1810. In 1803, the U.S. had purchased "The drainage of the Mississippi and Missouri Rivers" (Louisiana) from France. In 1804, the Louisiana Purchase was divided into Orleans Territory and Louisiana Territory, as shown on the map. In October 1810, in a proclamation by President James Madison, the U.S. arbitrarily annexed Spain's West Florida from the Mississippi River to the Perdido River. The area included Baton Rouge, Biloxi, and Mobile, but was not organized nor included in the 1810 census. Spain did not recognize the annexation, and continued their claim to West Florida in dispute with the U.S. Map Source: Page 3, *Map Guide to the U.S. Federal Censuses, 1790-1920* by William Thorndale and William Dollarhide.

1810 Federal Census

Location of Original Records: National Archives, Washington, DC.

U.S. Population: 7.2 million (6.0 million free and .9 million slave).

1810 Census Legislative Act: 2 Stat. 564, 26 March 1810.

Responsibility: The President of the United States (James Madison), with authority delegated to the Secretary of State (Robert Smith). Reporting to the Secretary of State, the U.S. Marshal of each U.S. Federal Court District hired and managed Assistant Marshals as the door-to-door census takers within his district.

Territories without a federal court district were enumerated by local militia captains, under the supervision of the Territorial Governor.

Census day: the first Monday in August (6 Aug 1810). All of the questions asked by the census taker were related to a person's age or place of residence as of the census day.

Time Allowed: In the first act, nine months; but extended to ten months (2 Stat. 658, 2 March 1811).

1810 Jurisdictions: 25. The 1810 federal census included one new state, Ohio, admitted in 1803, bringing the total to seventeen (17) states in the Union. The census also included the District of Columbia, the Federal Court District of Maine, and six (6) territories: Mississippi, Louisiana, Orleans, Michigan, Illinois, and Indiana territories, for a total of 25 jurisdictions.

Surviving Censuses & Census Losses: Seventeen (17) States & Territories had all or partial surviving censuses: Connecticut, Delaware, Illinois Territory (1 county only), Kentucky, Maine, Maryland, Massachusetts, New Hampshire, New York, North Carolina, Ohio (1 county only), Orleans Territory, Pennsylvania, Rhode Island, South Carolina, Vermont, and Virginia (about one fourth of VA's 135+ counties/independent cities survive). Eight (8) states, districts, or territories had complete losses: District of Columbia, Georgia, Indiana Territory, Louisiana Territory, Michigan Territory, Mississippi Territory, New Jersey, and Tennessee – the jurisdiction not returning the original 1790-1820 census manuscripts to Washington as was specified in the 1830 law (4 Stat. 430, 28 May 1830).

Content of the Population Schedules: 13 columns of questions were asked for the Head of Household, on one line, across one page, for the following:
- Name of a head of household
- Number of free white males, 0-9 years old
- Number of free white males, 10-15 years old
- Number of free white males, 16-25 years old
- Number of free white males, 26-44 years old
- Number of free white males, 45 & over
- Number of free white females, 0-9 years old
- Number of free white females, 10-15 years old
- Number of free white females, 16-25 years old
- Number of free white females, 26-44 years old
- Number of free white females, 45 & over
- Number of other free persons
- Number of slaves (omitted in places without slaves)

1810 was the first census in which the U.S. Marshals conducted non-population lists: A Census of Manufactures under the direction of the Secretary of the Treasury (Albert Gallatin) was authorized (2 Stat. 605, 1 May 1810). Any extant manufacturing lists are scattered among the population schedules, page locations given in Katherine H. Davidson and Charlotte M. Ashby, *Preliminary Inventory of the Records of the Bureau of the Census* (Washington: National Archives, 1964), pp. 132-134.

Microfilm of 1810 Originals & Digital Capture: The National Archives film for the 1810 census is contained on 72 rolls, series M252, beginning with FHL film #281229 (Connecticut). The microfilm was digitized by FamilySearch International. For a list of roll numbers, contents, and access to the digital images of each roll, see the online FHL catalog page:
https://familysearch.org/search/catalog/118496.

Online Searching - 1810 Federal Census Indexes and Digital Images. The 1810 Census was digitized from the National Archives microfilm, indexed, and made available at the following websites:

- **Ancestry.com.** Subscription site, free database searching. Ancestry and FamilySearch share images and indexes. See
www.ancestry.com/search/collections/1810usfedcenancestry.

- **FamilySearch.org.** Free database search, with images by FamilySearch, index by Ancestry. See
https://familysearch.org/search/collection/1803765.

- **MyHeritage.com.** A Family Tree subscription site. All U.S. Federal Census Records are available to subscribers with a data plan. See
www.myheritage.com/research/collection-10122/1810-united-states-federal-census.

- **Findmypast.com.** Monthly or annual subscriptions. Initial searches to U.S. Federal Censuses are free. See
www.findmypast.com/articles/search-the-1810-us-census.

- **GenealogyBank.com.** Subscription site. Initial searches to the U.S. Federal Censuses, 1790-1940 are free. www.genealogybank.com/explore/census/all.

- **HeritageQuestOnline-Subscribers Login.** This is a library subscription service. Check with your local library to see if they subscribe to the ProQuest & HeritageQuest databases. Many subscribing libraries allow their library card holders remote access. See
www.heritagequestonline.com/hqoweb/library/do/login.

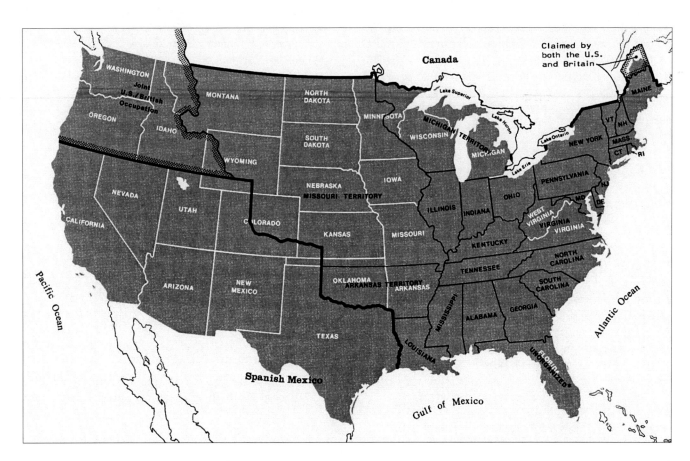

The U.S. in 1820: In the 1818 Anglo-American Convention, the United States and Great Britain agreed to a joint occupation of the Oregon Country/Columbia District. Both parties accepted the area as extending from the Continental Divide to the Pacific Ocean, and from about Latitude 54° in present British Columbia, to the Boundary Mountains (now Siskiyou Mountains) at Latitude 42°. Also in the 1818 treaty, Britain and the U.S. agreed to the 49th parallel as the international boundary from the Lake of the Woods (now Minnesota) to the Continental Divide. In 1819, the Adams-Onis Treaty settled the Purchase of Florida and set the Western boundary between Spanish and U.S. territory. However, the treaty was not ratified until 1821, and Florida was not a territory until 1822. Map Source: Page 4, ***Map Guide to the U.S. Federal Censuses, 1790-1920*** by William Thorndale and William Dollarhide.

1820 Federal Census

Location of Original Records: National Archives, Washington, DC.

U.S. Population: 9.6 million (8.1 million free and 1.5 million slave).

1820 Census Legislative Act: 3 Stat. 548, 14 March 1820.

Responsibility: The President of the United States (James Monroe), with authority delegated to the Secretary of State (John Quincy Adams). Reporting to the Secretary of State, the U.S. Marshal of each U.S. Federal Court District hired and managed Assistant Marshals as the door-to-door census takers within his district. Territories without a federal court district were enumerated by local militia captains, under the supervision of the Territorial Governor.

Census day: the first Monday in August (7 Aug 1820). All of the questions asked by the census taker were related to a person's age or place of residence as of the census day.

Time Allowed: In the first act, six months; but extended to thirteen months (3 Stat. 643, 3 March 1821).

1820 Jurisdictions: 27. Between 1810 and 1820, six (6) new states had been formed bringing the total to twenty-three (23) states in the Union: Orleans Territory became the state of Louisiana in 1812, followed by Indiana in 1816; Mississippi in 1817; Illinois in 1818; Alabama in 1819; and Maine in 1820. Add the District of Columbia and three (3) territories: Louisiana Territory was renamed Missouri Territory in 1812; Michigan Territory spanned the northern portion of the old Northwest Territory north of the states of Ohio, Indiana, and Illinois; and a new Arkansas Territory was created from the southern area of Missouri Territory in 1819; for a total of twenty-seven (27) census jurisdictions.

Surviving Censuses: Twenty-Three (23) states & territories: Connecticut, District of Columbia, Delaware, Georgia, Illinois, Indiana, Kentucky, Louisiana, Maine, Maryland, Massachusetts, Michigan Territory, Mississippi Territory, New Hampshire, New York, North Carolina, Ohio, Pennsylvania, Rhode Island, South Carolina, Tennessee (26 counties), Vermont, and Virginia.

Census Losses: Four (4) complete states & territories: Alabama, Arkansas Territory, Missouri Territory, and New Jersey. These states or territories did not return the original 1790-1820 census manuscripts to Washington as was specified in the 1830 law (4 Stat. 430, 28 May 1830). NOTE: In 1820, two federal court districts were in place in Tennessee, one with a U.S. Courthouse in Nashville, the other in Knoxville. The original censuses returned to Washington according to the 1830 law were twenty-six (26) western counties within the 1820 Nashville district only. The twenty (20) eastern counties enumerated within the 1820 Knoxville district were not received in Washington.

Content of the Population Schedules: 33 columns of questions were asked for the Head of Household, on one line, spread over two large pages of census schedules. The hand-drawn census forms had columns in the following order:
- Name of a head of household
- Number of free white males, 0-9 years old
- Number of free white males, 10-15 years old
- Number of free white males, 16-18 years old*
- Number of free white males, 16-25 years old*
- Number of free white males, 26-44 years old
- Number of free white males, 45 years & over
- Number of free white females, 0-9 years old
- Number of free white females, 10-15 years old
- Number of free white females, 16-25 years old
- Number of free white females, 26-44 years old
- Number of foreigners not naturalized
- Number of persons engaged in Agriculture
- Number of persons engaged in Commerce
- Number of persons engaged in Manufacture
- Number of male slaves (4 age categories)
- Number of female slaves (4 age categories)
- Number of free colored males (4 age categories)
- Number of free colored females (4 age cat.)
- Number of all other persons

* **NOTE:** any male in the 16-18 column was repeated in the 16-25 column.

Microfilm of 1820 Originals & Digital Capture: The National Archives film for the 1820 census is contained on 142 rolls, series M33, beginning with FHL film #281234 (Connecticut). To access the digital images, see the online FHL catalog: www.familysearch.org/search/catalog/120949.

Online Searching - 1820 Census Indexes and Digital Images. The 1820 Census was digitized from the National Archives microfilm, indexed, and made available at the following websites:

- **Ancestry.com.** Subscription site, free database searching. Ancestry and FamilySearch share images and indexes. See www.ancestry.com/search/collections/1820usfedcenancestry.

- **FamilySearch.org.** Free database search, with images by FamilySearch, index by Ancestry. See www.familysearch.org/search/collection/1803955.

- **MyHeritage.com.** A Family Tree subscription site. All U.S. Federal Census Records are available to subscribers with a data plan. See www.myheritage.com/research/collection-10123/1820-united-states-federal-census.

- **Findmypast.com.** Monthly or annual subscriptions. Initial searches to U.S. Federal Censuses are free. See www.findmypast.com/articles/search-the-1820-us-census.

- **GenealogyBank.com.** Subscription site. Initial searches to the U.S. Federal Censuses, 1790-1940 are free. www.genealogybank.com/explore/census/all.

- **HeritageQuestOnline-Subscribers Login.** This is a library subscription service. Check with your local library to see if they subscribe to the ProQuest & HeritageQuest databases. Many subscribing libraries allow their library card holders remote access. See www.heritagequestonline.com/hqoweb/library/do/login.

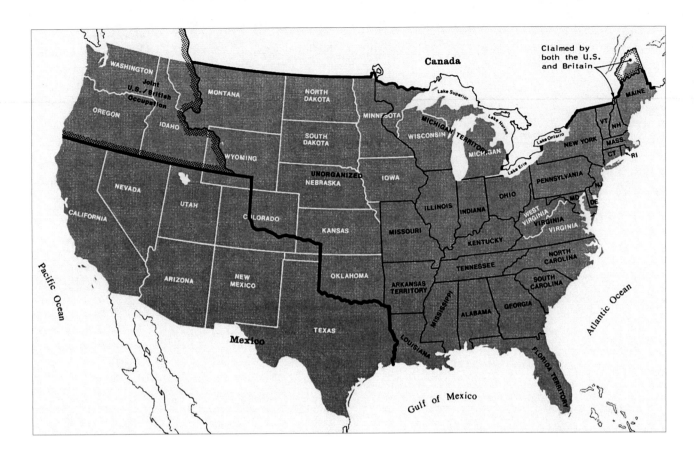

The U.S. in 1830. Missouri became a state in 1821, and Florida Territory was created in 1822. In 1828, Congress set aside specific areas of the Unorganized Territory as "Indian Territory." In doing so, about half of Arkansas Territory plus areas of present-day Kansas were designated as exclusive Indian resettlement areas. Indians were specifically excluded from the federal censuses until 1880, when separate schedules were compiled for several tribes. Map Source: Page 5, *Map Guide to the U.S. Federal Censuses, 1790-1920* by William Thorndale and William Dollarhide.

1830 Federal Census

Location of Original Records: National Archives, Washington, DC.

U.S. Population: 12.9 million (10.9 million free and 2.0 million slave).

1830 Census Legislative Act: 4 Stat. 383, 23 March 1830.

Responsibility: The President of the United States (Andrew Jackson), with authority delegated to the Secretary of State (Martin Van Buren). Reporting to the Secretary of State, the U.S. Marshal of each U.S. Federal Court District hired and managed Assistant Marshals as the door-to-door census takers within his district. Territories without a federal court district were enumerated by local militia captains, under the supervision of the Territorial Governor.

Census day: the first Monday in August (7 Aug 1820). All of the questions asked by the census taker were related to a person's age or place of residence as of the census day.

Time Allowed: In the first act, six months; but extended to twelve months (4 Stat. 439, 3 February 1831).

1830 Jurisdictions: 28. Between 1820 and 1830, one (1) new state was admitted to the Union. Missouri became a state in 1821, bringing the total number in the 1830 census to twenty-four (24) states. The treaty with Spain for the purchase of Florida was signed in 1819, but ratification did not occur until 1821. Florida Territory was created in 1822, its first federal census was taken in 1830.

Add the District of Columbia, Arkansas Territory, and Michigan Territory, for a total of twenty-eight (28) jurisdictions. An area commonly called the "Indian Territory" was created in 1828 from the western part of Arkansas Territory and parts of present-day Kansas, but no federal census was taken in that area until 1860 (for non-Indians only).

Census Losses: There were no statewide census losses for 1830.

Content of the Population Schedules: 57 columns of questions were asked for the Head of Household, on one line, spread over two large pages of census schedules. The columns were shown in the following order:
- Name of a head of household
- Number of free white males, 0-4 years old
- Number of free white males, 5-9 years old
- Number of free white males, 10-14 years old
- Number of free white males, 15-19 years old
- Number of free white males, 20-29 years old
- Number of free white males, 30-39 years old
- Number of free white males, 40-49 years old
- Number of free white males, 50-59 years old
- Number of free white males, 60-69 years old
- Number of free white males, 70-79 years old
- Number of free white males, 80-89 years old
- Number of free white males, 90-99 years old
- Number of free white males, 100 years & over
- Number of free white females, 0-4 years old
- Number of free white females, 5-9 years old
- Number of free white females, 10-14 years old
- Number of free white females, 15-19 years old
- Number of free white females, 20-29 years old
- Number of free white females, 30-39 years old
- Number of free white females, 40-49 years old
- Number of free white females, 50-59 years old
- Number of free white females, 60-69 years old
- Number of free white females, 70-79 years old
- Number of free white females, 80-89 years old
- Number of free white females, 90-99 years old
- Number of free white females, 100 years & over
- Number of male slaves (6 age categories)
- Number of female slaves (6 age categories)
- Number of free colored males (6 age categories)
- Number of free colored females (6 age cat.)
- Total Number of persons in this family
- Number of white persons who are deaf and dumb (3 age categories)
- Number of white persons who are blind
- Number of white persons who are aliens

Microfilm of Originals & Digital Capture: The National Archives film for the 1830 census is contained on 201 rolls, series M19, beginning with FHL film #2328 (Alabama). The microfilm was digitized by FamilySearch International. For a list of roll numbers, contents, and access to the digital images of each roll, see the online FHL catalog page:
www.familysearch.org/search/catalog/119992.

Online Searching - 1830 Census Indexes and Digital Images. The 1830 Census was digitized from the National Archives microfilm, indexed, and made available at the following websites:

- **Ancestry.com.** Subscription site, free database searching. Ancestry and FamilySearch share images and indexes. See
www.ancestry.com/search/collections/1830usfedcenancestry.

- **FamilySearch.org.** Free database search, with images by FamilySearch, index by Ancestry. See
https://familysearch.org/search/collection/1803958.

- **MyHeritage.com.** A Family Tree subscription site. All U.S. Federal Census Records are available to subscribers with a data plan. See
www.myheritage.com/research/collection-10125/1830-united-states-federal-census.

- **Findmypast.com.** Monthly or annual subscriptions. Initial searches to U.S. Federal Censuses are free. See
www.findmypast.com/articles/search-the-1830-us-census.

- **GenealogyBank.com.** Subscription site. Initial searches to the U.S. Federal Censuses, 1790-1940 are free. www.genealogybank.com/explore/census/all.

- **HeritageQuestOnline-Subscribers Login.** This is a library subscription service. Check with your local library to see if they subscribe to the ProQuest & HeritageQuest databases. Many subscribing libraries allow their library card holders remote access. See
www.heritagequestonline.com/hqoweb/library/do/login.

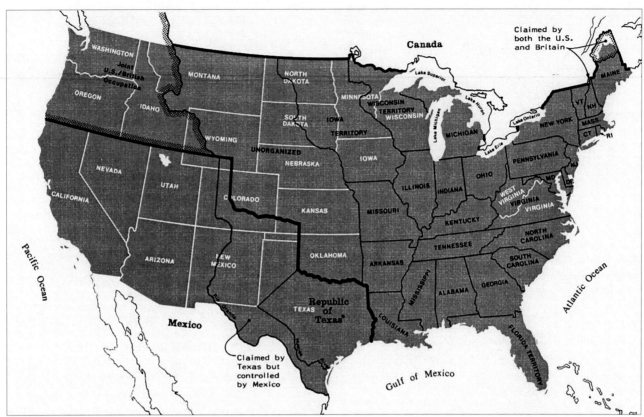

The U.S. in 1840: After defeating Mexico in battle, the Republic of Texas was formed in 1836, and was annexed to the U.S. as a state in 1845. The Republic's claim to lands extended to the Rio Grande, and that claim was to be the basis for the U.S. invasion of Mexico in 1846. Map Source: Page 6, ***Map Guide to the U.S. Federal Censuses, 1790-1920,*** by William Thorndale and William Dollarhide.

1840 Federal Census

Location of Original Records: National Archives, Washington, DC.

U.S. Population: 17.1 million (14.6 million free and 2.5 million slave).

1840 Census Legislative Act: 5 Stat. 331, 3 March 1840.

Responsibility: The President of the United States (Martin Van Buren), with authority delegated to the Secretary of State (John Forsyth). Reporting to the Secretary of State, the U.S. Marshal of each U.S. Federal Court District hired and managed Assistant Marshals as the door-to-door census takers within his district. Territories without a federal court district were enumerated by local militia captains, under the supervision of the Territorial Governor.

Census day: 1 June 1840. All of the questions asked by the census taker were related to a person's age or place of residence as of the census day.

Time Allowed: In the first act, nine months; but extended to eighteen months (5 Stat. 453, 1 September 1841).

1840 Jurisdictions: 30. As of the census day of 1 June 1840, two new states had been added to the U.S. since the 1830 federal census: Arkansas was admitted in 1836; and Michigan in 1837, bringing the total to Twenty-six (26) states in the Union. Territories added: Florida (created 1821), Wisconsin Territory (1836) and Iowa Territory (1838). Add the District of Columbia for a total of 30 census jurisdictions in 1840.

1840 Census Copies & Census Losses: A 2nd original copy of the 1840 census name lists was transcribed by the Clerk of the District Court in each district/state/territory. It was usually the clerk's copy that was sent to Washington, DC. There were no census losses for 1840.

Content of the Population Schedules: 66 columns of questions were asked for the Head of Household, spread over two large pages of census schedules. Unique to the 1840 census was an array of questions concerning a person's occupation; including persons engaged in mining, agriculture, commerce, manufacturing and trades; navigation of the ocean, navigation of canals, lakes, and rivers; and learned professionals and engineers. Also unique to the 1840 census was the special listing of any person in a household who was a Revolutionary War or other military pensioner. As a result, the 1840 census was the first to list the name of another person living in a household other than the head of the house. Columns included:

- Name of a head of household / Slave Owner (if slaves indicated).
  - Number of male slaves, in 6 age categories.
  - Number of female slaves, in 6 age categories.
- Name and age of each person receiving Revolutionary War/Military pension.
- Number of free white males, in 13 age categories.
- Number of free white females, in 13 age categories.
- Number of free colored males, in 6 age categories.
- Number of free colored females, in 6 age categories.
- Number of white persons who were deaf & dumb, in 3 age categories.
- Number of white persons who were blind.
- Number of white persons who were aliens (foreigners not naturalized).
- Number of persons engaged in:
  - Mining
  - Agriculture
  - Commerce
  - Manufacturing and Trades
  - Navigation of the Ocean
  - Navigation of Canals, Lakes, and Rivers
- Number of Learned Professionals and Engineers.
- Number of persons attending school.

Microfilm of Originals & Digital Capture: The National Archives film for the 1840 census is contained on 215 rolls, series M704, beginning with FHL film #2532 (Alabama). The microfilm was digitized by FamilySearch International. For a list of roll numbers, contents, and access to the digital images of each roll, see the online FHL catalog page: www.familysearch.org/search/catalog/120333.

Online Searching - 1840 Census Indexes and Digital Images. The 1840 Census was digitized from the National Archives microfilm, indexed, and made available at the following websites:

- **Ancestry.com.** Subscription site, free database searching. Ancestry and FamilySearch share images and indexes. See www.ancestry.com/search/collections/1840usfedcenancestry.

- **FamilySearch.org.** Free database search, with images by FamilySearch, index by Ancestry. See https://familysearch.org/search/collection/1786457.

- **MyHeritage.com.** A Family Tree subscription site. All U.S. Federal Census Records are available to subscribers with a data plan. See www.myheritage.com/research/collection-10124/1840-united-states-federal-census.

- **Findmypast.com.** Monthly or annual subscriptions. Initial searches to U.S. Federal Censuses are free. See www.findmypast.com/articles/search-the-1840-us-census.

- **GenealogyBank.com.** Subscription site. Initial searches to the U.S. Federal Censuses, 1790-1940 are free. www.genealogybank.com/explore/census/all.

- **HeritageQuestOnline-Subscribers Login.** This is a library subscription service. Check with your local library to see if they subscribe to the ProQuest & HeritageQuest databases. Many subscribing libraries allow their library card holders remote access. See www.heritagequestonline.com/hqoweb/library/do/login.

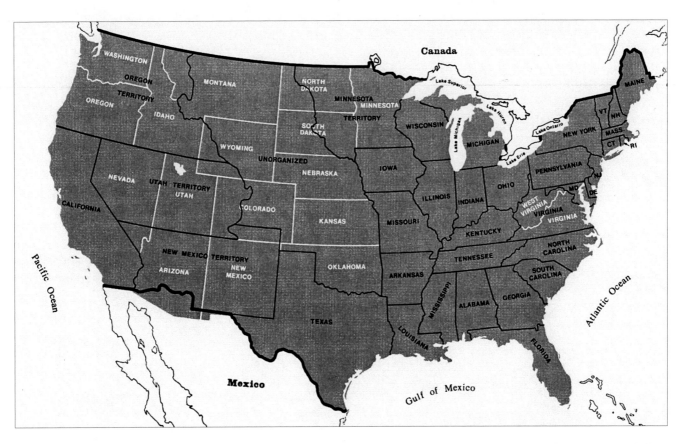

The U.S. in 1850. In 1842, the U.S. and Britain resolved the location of the northern New Hampshire-Maine border with New Brunswick. After the 1846 settlement of the Oregon Country boundaries with Britain; and the 1848 Mexican Cession, the U.S. land area dramatically increased in size. The United States of America now spanned "from Sea to Shining Sea." Map Source: Page 7, *Map Guide to the U.S. Federal Censuses, 1790-1920,* by William Thorndale and William Dollarhide.

1850 Federal Census

Location of Original Records: National Archives, Washington, DC.

U.S. Population: 23.2 million (20.0 million free and 3.2 million slave).

1850-1860-1870 Census Legislative Act: 9 Stat. 428, 23 May 1850.

Responsibility: The 1850 was the first census conducted under the direction of a **Census Office,** a new division under the U.S. Secretary of the Interior. Reporting to the Census Office, U.S. Marshals of the Federal Court Districts hired and managed Assistant Marshals as the door-to-door census takers within their districts. Territories without a federal court district were enumerated by local militia captains, under the supervision of the Territorial Governor.

Census day: 1 June 1850.

Time Allowed: Five months. However, California, Utah Territory, and New Mexico Territory were all given extra time to complete their censuses. Utah Territory's Census Day was moved to April 1, 1851.

1850 Jurisdictions: 36. Between 1840 and 1850 five new states were added to the Union: Florida and Texas, both admitted in 1845; Iowa in 1846; Wisconsin in 1848; and California in 1850, bringing the total to thirty-one (31) states in 1850. In addition, four new territories were included:

Oregon Territory, created in 1848; Minnesota Territory in 1849; and New Mexico Territory and Utah Territory, both created in 1850. Add the District of Columbia for a total of thirty-six (36) census jurisdictions.

1850 Census Copies: Three (3) sets of the 1850 census schedules were made: 1) The originals for one county remained at the county courthouse for public display. 2) The Supervising Assistant Marshal for a county made a second copy of each county set to be transmitted to the Secretary of State of the state or territory, and 3) a copy was made by the secretaries of state for transmittal to the Census Office/Secretary of the Interior in Washington, DC. The third copy is referred to as the Federal Copy, the same copy that was later microfilmed and digitized for public use.

Content of the Population Schedules: For the first time, the 1850 census schedules listed the name of every person in a household. Since there were both House Numbers and Family Numbers indicated on the census schedules, when more than one family lived in the same house, the head of each family would be clearly delineated as the first person listed for a family. The categories included a name; age as of the census day; sex; color; birthplace; occupation; value of real estate; whether married within the previous year; whether deaf, dumb, blind, or insane; whether a pauper; whether able to read or speak English; and whether the person attended school within the previous year. **Clues to Relationships:** Although relationships were not given, there can be clues based on the household listing parameters. For example, per the published instructions to the Assistant Marshals, all persons included within a family grouping were listed in a specified order: 1) Head of House, 2) Spouse of head of house, 3) Children of head of house, in order of birth; and 4) Other persons living with the family. Other relatives living with a family are not identified, but their surname and position in the household listing can reveal possible relationships, i.e., in-laws, married siblings, parents, grandparents, etc.

Persons with a different surname than the family group may be identified by their occupation (housekeeper, farm hand, laborer, etc.), which might explain their living arrangements.

Microfilm of Originals & Digital Capture: The National Archives film for the 1850 census is contained on 1,013 rolls, series M432, beginning with FHL film #2343 (Alabama). The microfilm was digitized by FamilySearch International. For a list of roll numbers, contents, and access to the digital images of each roll, see the FHL catalog page:
https://familysearch.org/search/catalog/121180.

Online Searching - 1850 Census Indexes and Digital Images. The 1850 Census was digitized from the National Archives microfilm, indexed, and made available at the following websites:

• **Ancestry.com.** Subscription site, free database searching. Ancestry and FamilySearch share images and indexes. See
www.ancestry.com/search/collections/1850usfedcenancestry.

• **FamilySearch.org.** Free database search, with images by FamilySearch, index by Ancestry. See
https://familysearch.org/search/collection/1401638.

• **MyHeritage.com.** A Family Tree subscription site. All U.S. Federal Census Records are available to subscribers with a data plan. See
www.myheritage.com/research/collection-10126/1850-united-states-federal-census.

• **Findmypast.com.** Monthly or annual subscriptions. Initial searches to U.S. Federal Censuses are free. See
www.findmypast.com/articles/search-the-1850-us-census.

• **GenealogyBank.com.** Subscription site. Initial searches to the U.S. Federal Censuses, 1790-1940 are free. www.genealogybank.com/explore/census/all.

• **HeritageQuestOnline-Subscribers Login.** This is a library subscription service. Check with your local library to see if they subscribe to the ProQuest & HeritageQuest databases. Many subscribing libraries allow their library card holders remote access. See
www.heritagequestonline.com/hqoweb/library/do/login.

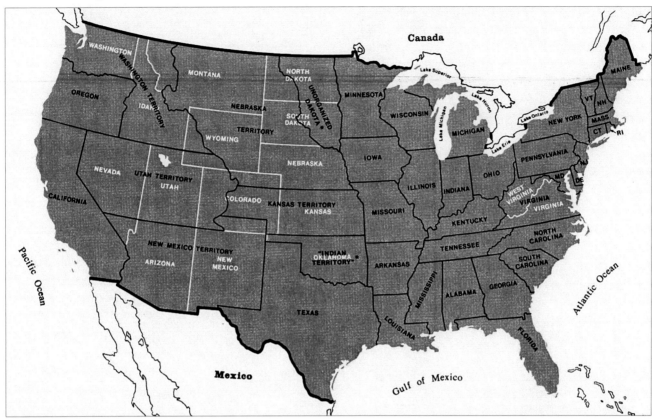

The U.S. in 1860. In a treaty ratified in 1854, the U.S. purchased a 45,000 square mile tract of land from Mexico, called the Gadsden Purchase. As the only benefactor of the tract, New Mexico Territory created Arizona County in the newly acquired area. Map Source: Page 8, *Map Guide to the U.S. Federal Censuses, 1790-1920,* by William Thorndale and William Dollarhide.

1860 Federal Census

Location of Original Records: National Archives, Washington, DC.

U.S. Population: 31.5 million (27.5 million free and 4.0 million slave).

1850-1860-1870 Census Legislative Act: Section 23, 9 Stat. 432, 23 May 1850.

Responsibility / Copies: The 1860 census was conducted under the direction of a **Census Office,** a division under the U.S. Secretary of the Interior. Reporting to the Census Office, U.S. Marshals of the Federal Court Districts hired and managed Assistant Marshals as the door-to-door census takers within their districts. Territories without a federal court district were enumerated by local militia captains, under the supervision of the Territorial Governor. **Mandated Copies:** Three (3) sets, to the county courthouse, the secretary of state of the territory or state, and the Census Office/U.S. Secretary of the Interior.

Census day: 1 June 1860. All of the questions asked by the census taker were related to a person's age or place of residence as of the census day.

Time Allowed: Five months.

1860 Jurisdictions: 40. Between 1850 and 1860, two (2) new states were added to the Union: Minnesota was admitted in 1858, and Oregon in 1859, for a total of thirty-three (33) states at the time of the 1860 federal census. Add the District of Columbia and five (5) territories: New Mexico

Utah, Washington, Nebraska, and Kansas territories. And, add one (1) more area between the Red River of the North and the Missouri River, enumerated as *Unorganized Dakota* (a name invented by the Census Office); for a total of 40 jurisdictions. The name lists for non-Indians in the unorganized "Indian Territory" were incorporated into the Arkansas schedules.

Content of the Population Schedules: The 1860 census schedule format had 14 columns, each person on one line, spread across a single schedule page, numbered as follows:
1. Dwelling houses numbered in the order of visitation.
2. Families numbered in the order of visitation.
3. The name of every person whose usual place of abode on the first day of June 1860, was in this family.
4. Age.
5. Sex.
6. Color: White, Black, or Mulatto.
7. Profession, Occupation, or Trade of each person, male and female, over 15 years of age.
8. Value of Real Estate.
9. Value of Personal Estate.
10. Place of Birth, Naming the State, Territory, or Country
11. Married within the year.
12. Attended School within the year.
13. Persons over 20 years of age who cannot read or write.
14. Whether deaf and dumb, blind, insane, idiotic, pauper or convict.

1860 Census and the Civil War Era. Name lists from the 1860 federal census can be used to find any soldier as a civilian just prior to his service. It may be possible to identify every future Union or Confederate soldier and their families about ten months before the Civil War began on 12 April 1861. Start a search in a major online database indexed at the National Park Service website. The ***Civil War Soldiers and Sailors Database*** contains information about the men who served in both the Union and Confederate armies during the Civil War. Other information at this website includes histories of Union and Confederate regiments, links to descriptions of significant battles, selected lists of prisoner-of-war records, and cemetery records. This database has 6.3 million records. See www.nps.gov/civilwar/soldiers-and-sailors-database.htm.

Microfilm of Originals & Digital Capture: The National Archives film for the 1860 census is contained on 1,013 rolls, series M432, beginning with FHL film #803001 (Alabama). The microfilm was digitized by FamilySearch International. For a list of roll numbers, contents, and access to the digital images of each roll, see the FHL catalog page: https://familysearch.org/search/catalog/121214.

Online Searching - 1860 Census Indexes and Digital Images. The 1860 Census was digitized from the National Archives microfilm, indexed, and made available at the following websites:

• **Ancestry.com.** Subscription site, free database searching. Ancestry and FamilySearch share images and indexes. See www.ancestry.com/search/collections/1860usfedcenancestry.

• **FamilySearch.org.** Free database search, with images by FamilySearch, index by Ancestry. See https://familysearch.org/search/collection/1473181.

• **MyHeritage.com.** A Family Tree subscription site. All U.S. Federal Census Records are available to subscribers with a data plan. See www.myheritage.com/research/collection-10127/1860-united-states-federal-census.

• **Findmypast.com.** Monthly or annual subscriptions. Initial searches to U.S. Federal Censuses are free. See www.findmypast.com/articles/search-the-1860-us-census.

• **GenealogyBank.com.** Subscription site. Initial searches to the U.S. Federal Censuses, 1790-1940 are free. www.genealogybank.com/explore/census/all.

• **HeritageQuestOnline-Subscribers Login.** This is a library subscription service. Check with your local library to see if they subscribe to the ProQuest & HeritageQuest databases. Many subscribing libraries allow their library card holders remote access. See www.heritagequestonline.com/hqoweb/library/do/login.

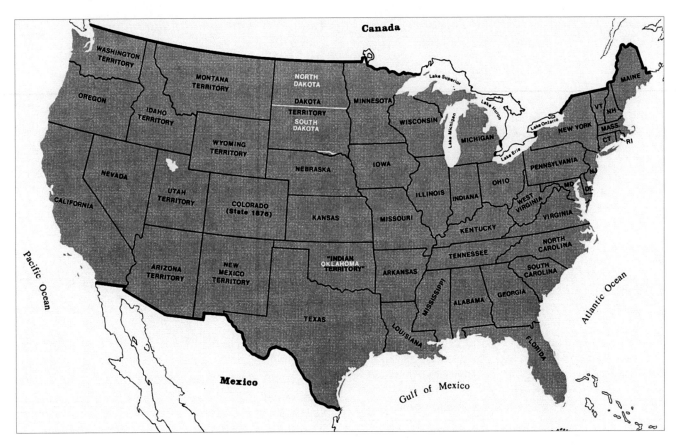

The U.S. in 1870. The huge tract of land known as Russian America was purchased by the U.S. in 1867. Congress renamed the area the Department of Alaska. (Not Shown on map). No federal census was taken in Alaska until 1900. Note that the map shows the area of Dakota Territory, which was divided into the states of North Dakota and South Dakota in 1889. Also shown is the unorganized "Indian Territory," the same area that became the State of Oklahoma in 1907. Map Source: Page 9, *Map Guide to the U.S. Federal Censuses, 1790-1920,* by William Thorndale and William Dollarhide.

1870 Federal Census

Location of Original Records: National Archives, Washington, DC.

U.S. Population: 38.6 million.

1850-1860-1870 Census Legislative Act: Section 23, 9 Stat. 432, 23 May 1850.

Responsibility / Copies: The 1870 census was conducted under the direction of a **Census Office,** a division under the U.S. Secretary of the Interior. Reporting to the Census Office, U.S. Marshals of the Federal Court Districts hired and managed Assistant Marshals as the door-to-door census takers within their districts. Territories without a federal court district were enumerated by local militia captains, under the supervision of the Territorial Governor. **Mandated Copies:** Three (3) sets, to the county courthouse, the secretary of state of the territory or state, and the Census Office/U.S. Secretary of the Interior.

Census day: 1 June 1870. All of the questions asked by the census taker were related to a person's age or place of residence as of the census day.

Time Allowed: Five months.

1870 Jurisdictions: 47. Between 1860 and 1870, the decade of the Civil War, four (4) new states were added to the Union for a total of Thirty-seven (37) states: Kansas became a state in 1861, West Virginia in 1863, Nevada in 1864, and Nebraska in 1867. Add the District of Columbia, New Mexico Territory, Washington Territory, and Utah

Territory; and add six (6) new territories: Dakota Territory and Colorado Territory in 1861; Arizona Territory and Idaho Territory in 1863; Montana Territory in 1864; and Wyoming Territory in 1868, for a total of forty-seven (47) jurisdictions. Left out of the 1870 Census was the Department of Alaska, acquired by the U.S. in 1867; and the "Indian Territory," also not enumerated in 1870.

Content of the Population Schedules. The 1870 format had 20 columns, each person on one line, spread across a single schedule page, as follows:
1. Dwelling houses – numbered in the order of visitation.
2. Families, numbered in the order of visitation.
3. The name of every person whose place of abode on the first day of June 1870, was in this family.
4. Age at last birthday. If under 1 year; give number in fractions, thus 9/12.
5. Sex – Male (M) Female (F)
6.. Color – White (W.), Black (B.), Mulatto (M.), Chinese (C.), Indian (I.)
7. Profession, Occupation, or Trade of each person, male and female.
8. Value of Real Estate.
9. Value of Personal Estate.
10. Place of Birth, Naming the State or Territory of U.S., or the Country, if of foreign birth.
11. Father of foreign birth.
12. Mother of foreign birth.
13. If born within the year, state month (Jan, Feb, &c)
14. If married with the year, state month (Jan, Feb, &c)
15. Attended school within the year.
16. Cannot read.
17. Cannot write.
18. Whether deaf and dumb, blind, insane, or idiotic.
19. Male Citizens of the U.S. of 21 years of age and up.
20. Male Citizens of the U.S. whose right to vote was denied.

Accuracy of the 1870 Census. After the Civil War, northern carpetbaggers were often used as census takers in the former Confederate states. They were not particularly interested in an accurate count of the southern population. Undercounting in the southern states was later estimated to be as much as 10-15 per cent of the population; while undercounting in the northern states was no more than 3-5 percent. In terms of completeness and accuracy, the 1870 Federal Census is now considered the worst one ever taken.

Microfilm of 1870 Originals & Digital Capture: The National Archives film for the 1870 census is contained on 2,322 rolls, series M593, beginning with FHL film #545500 (Alabama). The microfilm was digitized by FamilySearch International. For a list of roll numbers, contents, and access to the digital images of each roll, see the FHL catalog page: https://familysearch.org/search/catalog/122118.

Online Searching - 1870 Census Indexes and Digital Images. The 1870 Census was digitized from the National Archives microfilm, indexed, and made available at the following websites:

• **Ancestry.com**. Subscription site, free database searching. Ancestry and FamilySearch share images and indexes. See www.ancestry.com/search/collections/1870usfedcen.

• **FamilySearch.org**. Free database search, with images by FamilySearch, index by Ancestry. See https://familysearch.org/search/collection/1438024.

• **MyHeritage.com**. A Family Tree subscription site. All U.S. Federal Census Records are available to subscribers with a data plan. See www.myheritage.com/research/collection-10128/1870-united-states-federal-census.

• **Findmypast.com**. Monthly or annual subscriptions. Initial searches to U.S. Federal Censuses are free. See www.findmypast.com/articles/search-the-1870-us-census.

• **GenealogyBank.com**. Subscription site. Initial searches to the U.S. Federal Censuses, 1790-1940 are free. www.genealogybank.com/explore/census/all.

• **HeritageQuestOnline-Subscribers Login.** This is a library subscription service. Check with your local library to see if they subscribe to the ProQuest & HeritageQuest databases. Many subscribing libraries allow their library card holders remote access. See www.heritagequestonline.com/hqoweb/library/do/login.

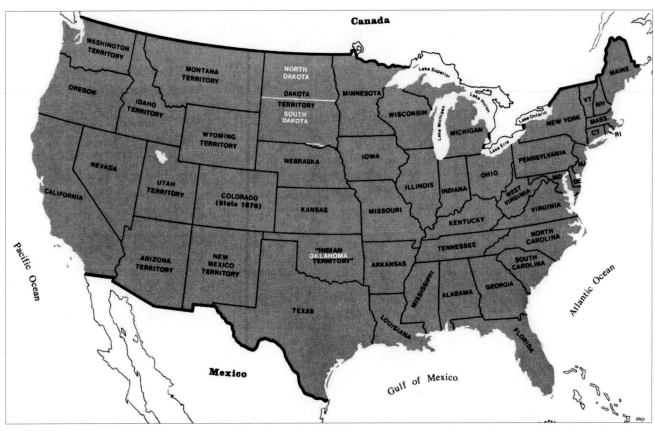

The U.S. in 1880. Note that the map shows the area of **Dakota Territory,** which was divided into North Dakota and South Dakota in 1889. Also shown is the so-called **"Indian Territory,"** the same area that became the State of Oklahoma in 1907.
Map Source: Page 9, *Map Guide to the U.S. Federal Censuses, 1790-1920,* by William Thorndale and William Dollarhide.

1880 Federal Census

Location of Original Records: In 1956, the National Archives transferred the original 1880 census volumes to state archives, state libraries, universities, or other repositories. These were the only population schedules handled in this way. For a review and state-by-state guide, see the GenealogyBlog article, *Repositories Holding 1880 Federal Census Originals.* The federal copies of the 1880 non-population schedules were also distributed to various non-federal repositories. For details, see the book, *The Census Book: Facts, Schedules & Worksheets for the U.S. Federal Censuses.*

U.S. Population: 50.2 million.

1880 Census Legislative Act: 20 Stat. 473, 3 March 1879, as amended by 21 Stat. 75, 20 April 1880.

Responsibility / Schedules / Copies: The 1880 census was conducted under the direction of the Superintendent of the Census (Census Office, U.S. Department of the Interior). For the first time, the Census Office hired and managed their own door-to-door enumerators for each state/territory. **Schedules:** Population, Mortality, Agriculture, and Industry. **Mandated Copies:** Two (2) sets, an abbreviated version (Short Form) to the county courthouse, and the original, full version to the Census Office/Secretary of the Interior.

Census day: 1 June 1880. All of the questions asked by the census taker were related to a person's age or place of residence as of the census day.

Time Allowed: field count due within 30 days, except communities over 10,000 in population due within two weeks.

1880 Jurisdictions: 47. Colorado was added to the Union in 1876, bringing the total to thirty-eight (38) states at the time of the 1880 census. Add the District of Columbia, and the territories of Arizona, Dakota, Idaho, Montana, New Mexico, Utah, Washington, and Wyoming Territory, for a total of forty-seven (47) jurisdictions. The population of the Department of Alaska was tallied, but no name list could be found. The Indian Territory was not enumerated. However, certain Indian Reservations were enumerated, e.g., Sisseton and Wahpeton Reservations, Dakota Territory.

Content of the Population Schedules. The census schedules listed the name of every person in a household with a census day of 1 June 1880. The categories included the following for each person: name and age as of the census day; month of birth if born during the year; relationship to the head of house; name of street and number of house; sex; color; birthplace; occupation; marital status; whether married within the previous year; whether temporarily or permanently disabled; whether crippled, maimed, or deformed; time unemployed during the census year; whether deaf, dumb, blind, or insane; whether able to read or write; birthplace of father and mother; and whether the person attended school within the previous year.

The 1880 Soundex Index. Soon after the creation of the Social Security Administration in 1935, clerical workers from the Works Progress Administration (WPA) were called upon to create an index to the 1880 census. A special system of coding names was created, called "Soundex." 3x5 index cards were prepared for each household which included children ten years of age or younger. The information on the Soundex index cards was extracted from the full census schedules and included the full name, age, and birthplace for a head of household, and included any other person living in the household, regardless of their age. Each head of household's surname was given a Soundex code, and the cards were then arranged in alphabetical order by the Soundex code number (A001-Z001) and after that by the first name of the head of the household.

Microfilm of Originals & Digital Capture: The National Archives film for the 1880 census is contained on 1,458 rolls, series T9, beginning with FHL film #1254001 (Alabama). The microfilm was digitized by FamilySearch International. For a list of roll numbers, contents, and access to the digital images of each roll, see the FHL catalog page: https://familysearch.org/search/catalog/1417529. For the 1880 Soundex Index, see https://familysearch.org/search/catalog/70449.

Online Searching - 1880 Census Indexes and Digital Images. The 1880 Census was digitized from the National Archives microfilm, indexed, and made available at the following websites:

- **Ancestry.com.** Subscription site, free database searching. Ancestry and FamilySearch share images and indexes. See www.ancestry.com/search/collections/1880usfedcen.

- **FamilySearch.org.** Free database search, with images by FamilySearch, index by Ancestry. See https://familysearch.org/search/collection/1417683.

- **MyHeritage.com.** A Family Tree subscription site. All U.S. Federal Census Records are available to subscribers with a data plan. See www.myheritage.com/research/collection-10129/1880-united-states-federal-census.

- **Findmypast.com.** Monthly or annual subscriptions. Initial searches to U.S. Federal Censuses are free. See www.findmypast.com/articles/search-the-1880-us-census.

- **GenealogyBank.com.** Subscription site. Initial searches to the U.S. Federal Censuses, 1790-1940 are free. www.genealogybank.com/explore/census/all.

- **HeritageQuestOnline-Subscribers Login.** This is a library subscription service. Check with your local library to see if they subscribe to the ProQuest & HeritageQuest databases. Many subscribing libraries allow their library card holders remote access. See www.heritagequestonline.com/hqoweb/library/do/login.

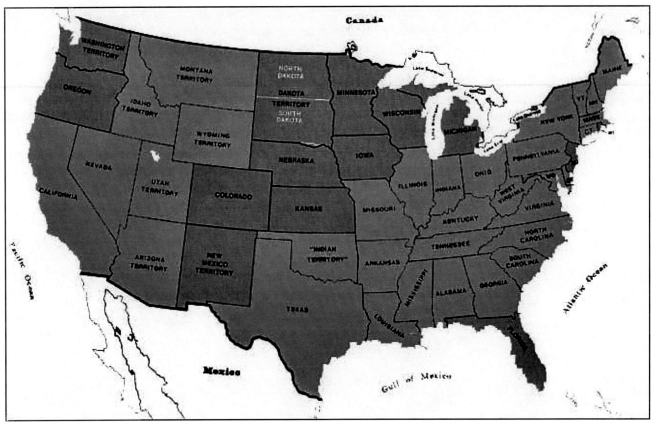

The U.S. in 1885. There were 14 states with 1885 state censuses: Colorado, Dakota Territory, Florida, Iowa, Kansas, Michigan (1884), Minnesota, Nebraska, New Jersey, New Mexico Territory, Oregon, Rhode Island, Washington Territory, and Wisconsin.
Map Source: Page 9, *Map Guide to the U.S. Federal Censuses, 1790-1920,* by William Thorndale and William Dollarhide.

State Censuses Taken in 1885

The 1890 federal census was mostly lost due to a 1921 fire in the Commerce Building in Washington, DC. To fill in the lost names, researchers need substitute name lists from the 1885-1895 period. There are many substitute name lists available, such as statewide tax lists, voter lists, etc. A recent publication has an annotated list of over 1,200 substitute name list databases from the period 1885-1895, see *Substitutes for the Lost 1890 Federal Census,* by William Dollarhide (publ. 2019, Family Roots Publishing Co., 103 pages). See
www.familyrootspublishing.com/store/product_view.php?id=3577.

Perhaps the best substitutes are the state censuses taken five years before the 1890 disaster. A total of fourteen (14) states/territories conducted a state census in 1885. Five of the states/territories had a census taken with federal assistance. The census act authorizing the 1880 census pledged the federal government to pay half the cost of a census taken by any state or territory in June or July 1885, if the format followed the same federal census form as 1880, and if a copy of all schedules were sent to Washington (Section 22, 20 Stat. 480, 3 March 1879). The five states/territories that took up the government's offer: 1) Colorado, 2) Dakota Territory, 3) Florida, 4) Nebraska, and 5) New Mexico Territory. These five were combined in a single printed index by the National Archives, with the title, *The 1885 Census*, see the FHL catalog page:
www.familysearch.org/search/catalog/2686600.

Another nine states/territories conducted an 1885 state census on their own, all done without federal assistance. These nine were: 1) Iowa, 2) Kansas, 3) Michigan (taken in 1884), 4) Minnesota, 5) New Jersey, 6) Oregon, 7) Rhode Island, 8) Washington Territory, and 9) Wisconsin.

The five states/territories done with federal assistance all followed the format of the 1880 federal census form; but the nine state censuses done without federal assistance were all conducted separately and with a design unique to that state/territory. Some list the names of the Heads of Household only; while others are an every-name listing similar to the federal layout.

There are some lost counties in the 1885 state censuses, but in general, they provide a good substitute for the lost 1890 census in 14 states.

Table 5-1: 1885 State Census Publications

States/Territories with an 1885 State Census	No. of Records or Images*	FHL Film No.	URL of Online Database or FHL catalog page for access to Digital Images
Taken with Federal Assistance:			
1. Colorado[1] - state copy	234,383	929067	www.familysearch.org/search/catalog/60816.
Colorado[1] - federal copy	195,979	498503	www.familysearch.org/search/collection/1807096.
2. Dakota Territory North[2]	151,500	--	https://library.ndsu.edu/db/census.
Dakota Territory South[2]	76,472	1405268	www.familysearch.org/search/catalog/361027.
3. Florida[3] - federal copy	309,323	888962	www.familysearch.org/search/catalog/82520.
Florida[3] - state copy (lost)	--	--	
4. Nebraska[4] - federal copy	747,367	499529	https://familysearch.org/search/collection/1810728.
Nebraska[4] - state copy (lost)	--	--	
5. New MexicoTerr.[5] - state copy	100,000 +/-	16610	www.familysearch.org/search/catalog/179492.
New Mexico Terr.[5] - Fed. copy	798*	--	www.familysearch.org/search/collection/2110742.
Without Federal Assistance:			
1. Iowa	1,737,228	1021316	https://familysearch.org/search/collection/1803643.
2. Kansas	94,071*	975699	www.familysearch.org/search/collection/1825188
3. Michigan (1884)	62,000*	--	https://michiganology.org/ (Search for 1884-1894 Census by County)
4. Minnesota	1,133,198	56733	https://familysearch.org/search/collection/1503044.
5. New Jersey	1,294,279	865499	www.familysearch.org/search/collection/1803972.
6. Oregon (Linn & Umatilla counties only)	--	--	Umatilla Co included in the Oregon Historical Records Index, see http://sos.oregon.gov/archives/Pages/records/aids-census_osa.aspx.
7. Rhode Island	321,999	953910	www.familysearch.org/search/collection/1794115.
8. Washington Territory	100,000 +/-	1841781	Indexed by county, part of the Washington State Archives – Digital Archives, see www.digitalarchives.wa.gov/Collections#RSID:3.
9. Wisconsin	407,138	1032695	https://familysearch.org/search/collection/1443713.

Table 5-1 Notes:

1. Colorado's 1885 federal copy is missing Fremont and Garfield counties, while the state copy has Fremont, but is missing Garfield and eighteen other counties.

2. The Dakota Territory 1885 census survives for 17 ND counties, and 20 SD counties. No federal copy of the Dakota Territory 1885 exists. The National Archives included only the SD portion as part of their printed index.

3. Florida's state copy of the 1885 census was lost. The federal copy is missing 4 counties.

4. Nebraska's 1885 state copy was lost. The federal copy of the Nebraska 1885 is missing one county.

5. New Mexico Territory's federal copy of the 1885 census is complete for all counties. The territorial copy is missing 4 counties.

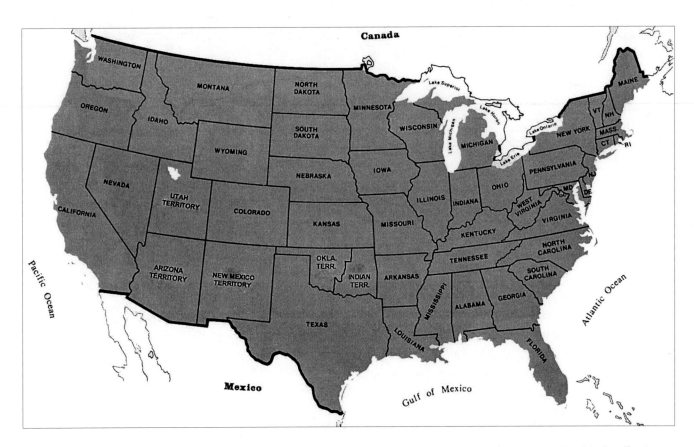

The U.S. in 1890. In May 1890, Congress created Oklahoma Territory, reducing the area of the unorganized Indian Territory. The areas of the two territories were merged in 1907 to become the State of Oklahoma. Idaho Territory became the state of Idaho on 3 July 1890, 3 days after the completion of the 1890 enumeration. And, Wyoming Territory became the state of Wyoming on 10 July 1890, 10 days after the 1890 enumeration. **Map Source:** Page 10, **Map Guide to the U.S. Federal Censuses, 1790-1920,** by William Thorndale and William Dollarhide.

1890 Federal Census

Loss of the Original Records: The original 1890 census population schedules (the name lists) were involved in a 1921 fire that took place in the Commerce Building in Washington, DC. The fire was contained to the basement storage area that held the entire collection of the 1890 federal census originals (the only copy). Fragments of the schedules that survived the 1921 fire are together on one roll of microfilm, all indexed, listing 6,160 persons out of the entire 1890 population of 63 million people. More of the bound volumes may have been harmed by water damage during the attempts to put out the fire, than were actually burned to ashes. There was some controversy about the handling of the remaining schedules, but several years after the fire, Congress permitted the Census Bureau to destroy the damaged remnants.

U.S. Population: 63.0 million.

1890 Census Legislative Act: 26 Stat. 760, 1 March 1890.

Responsibility / Schedules / Copies: The 1890 census was conducted under the direction of the Superintendent of the Census (Census Office, U.S. Department of the Interior). **Schedules:** Population, Mortality, Agriculture, Manufactures, Indians, and Union Veterans. **Mandated Copies:** One copy, to the Census Office/Secretary of the Interior. Counties could buy a Short Form copy of their schedules at cost.

Census day: 1 June 1890. All of the questions asked by the census taker were related to a person's age or place of residence as of the census day.

Time Allowed: field count due within 30 days, except communities over 10,000 in population, due within two weeks.

1890 Jurisdictions: 49. Between 1880 and 1890, six states were added to the Union: Montana, North Dakota, South Dakota, and Washington in 1889; Idaho and Wyoming in 1890, for a total of forty-four (44) states at the time of the 1890 census. Also enumerated: District of Columbia, Arizona Territory, New Mexico Territory, Oklahoma Territory, and Utah Territory, for a total of forty-nine (49) jurisdictions. Not enumerated: District of Alaska (statistics only), Indian Territory (some Indians were enumerated by tribe/nation), and Hawaii (not annexed to the U.S. until 1898).

Content of the Population Schedules. In 1890, the Census Office created a completely different method of recording the census enumeration, one that was unique to the 1890 census and never repeated. Up to 10 persons in one household were enumerated on both sides of one sheet of paper. The detailed information captured for every household was extensive, including the address of the house; the number of persons in the household; each individual by name; whether a soldier, sailor, or marine during the Civil War and whether Union or Confederate, or whether the widow of a veteran; relationship to head of family; race; sex; age; marital status; whether married during the previous year; if a mother, mother of how many children, and how many living; place of birth of the individual and his/her father and mother; if foreign born, how many years in the U.S.; whether naturalized or in the process of naturalization; a profession, trade, or occupation; the number of months unemployed during the previous year; ability to read and write; ability to speak English, if not, language or dialect spoken; whether suffering from an acute or chronic disease, if so, name of disease and length of time afflicted; whether defective in mind, sight, hearing, or speech, or whether crippled, maimed, or deformed, with the name of defect; whether a prisoner, convict, homeless child, or pauper; whether the home was rented or owned by the head or other member of the family, and whether it was mortgaged; whether a farmer, and if so, whether the farm was rented or owned; and if mortgaged, the post office address of the owner.

Microfilm of Originals & Digital Capture: The surviving fragments from the fire consist of a few names each from Perry Co Alabama, the District of Columbia, Muscogee Co Georgia, McDonough Co Illinois, Wright Co Minnesota, Hudson Co New Jersey, Westchester and Suffolk Co New York, Cleveland and Gaston Co North Carolina, Hamilton Co Ohio, Union Co South Dakota, and Ellis, Hood, Kaufman, Rusk and Trinity Co Texas. The remnants were filmed by the National Archives, 1962, Series M407, 6 rolls, beginning with FHL film #926497. To access the digital images, see the FHL catalog page: https://familysearch.org/search/catalog/231212.

1890 Union Veterans and Widows Schedules

In addition to the main population schedules, a special census listing was extracted from the 1890 population schedules for surviving Union soldiers, sailors, and marines (or their widows), and a portion of that special census survives. Census losses: Of the forty-nine (49) jurisdictions (states, territories, districts) in place in 1890, sixteen (16) of the Union Veterans Schedules jurisdictions were lost. The losses were alphabetically from Alabama through Kansas, and about half of the names for Kentucky. Surviving state listings begin with the partial list for Kentucky and are complete from Louisiana through Wyoming. Microfilm: *1890 Special Schedules Enumerating Union Veterans, and Widows of Union Veterans of the Civil War,* microfilmed on 118 rolls, series M123, beginning with FHL film #338160 (Kentucky). For access to the digital images of each roll, see the FHL catalog page:
https://familysearch.org/search/catalog/230777.

Content of the 1890 Veterans Schedules. The 1890 veterans format had 12 numbered columns, with space for up to 12 veterans per page. The top half of the format was as follows:
1. House No. (from Population Schedule).
2. Family No. (from Population Schedule).
3. Names of Surviving Soldiers, Sailors, Marines, & Widows. (This column had 2 lines: a widow's name, if applicable, on the top line, and a veteran's name on the bottom line).
4. Rank.
5. Company.
6. Name of Regiment or Vessel.
7. Date of Enlistment (day/month/year).
8. Date of Discharge (day/month/year).
9. Length of Service (Years/Months/Days).

The bottom half of the format was as follows:
10. Post Office Address.
11. Disability Incurred.
12. Remarks.

1890 Veterans Online Images and Indexes. This database has 990,276 records, see www.ancestry.com/search/collections/1890veterans. For the FamilySearch.org version, see www.familysearch.org/search/collection/1877095.

Online Searching - 1890 Census Indexes and Digital Images. The 1890 Census was digitized from the National Archives microfilm, indexed, and made available at the following websites:

- **Ancestry.com.** Subscription site, free database searching. Ancestry and FamilySearch share images and indexes. See www.ancestry.com/search/collections/1890orgcen.

- **FamilySearch.org.** Free database search, with images by FamilySearch, index by Ancestry. See https://familysearch.org/search/collection/1610551.

- **MyHeritage.com.** A Family Tree subscription site. All U.S. Federal Census Records are available to subscribers with a data plan. See www.myheritage.com/research/collection-10130/1890-united-states-federal-census.

- **GenealogyBank.com.** Subscription site. Initial searches to the U.S. Federal Censuses, 1790-1940 are free. www.genealogybank.com/explore/census/all.

- **HeritageQuestOnline-Subscribers Login.** This is a library subscription service. Check with your local library to see if they subscribe to the ProQuest & HeritageQuest databases. Many subscribing libraries allow their library card holders remote access. See www.heritagequestonline.com/hqoweb/library/do/login.

Related 1890 Resources Available

- *Censuses & Substitute Name Lists,* 52 books, Alabama to Wyoming, plus DC & U.S. Territories, publ. Family Roots Publ. Co., Orting, WA 2017-2018, www.familyrootspublishing.com/store/category.php?cat=3347.

- *Substitutes for the Lost 1890 Federal Census,* by William Dollarhide, publ. Family Roots Publ. Co., Orting, WA, 2019, 103 pages. This book continues the concept of the 52 books, *Censuses & Substitute Name Lists,* with bibliographic listings of databases with large numbers of names/events during the period 1885 to 1895. This book is the most comprehensive review of substitutes for the lost 1890 Census ever published, e.g., there are over 1,200 nationwide and statewide databases identified. Also, this new guidebook is abundantly and colorfully illustrated with actual database images, screen prints, and maps. See www.familyrootspublishing.com/store/product_view.php?id=3577.

- *First in the Path of the Firemen: The Fate of the 1890 Population Census, Part 1,* in *Prologue Magazine,* an online publication of the National Archives. See www.archives.gov/publications/prologue/1996/spring/1890-census-1.html.

- *First in the Path of the Firemen: The Fate of the 1890 Population Census, Part 2.* in *Prologue Magazine,* an online publication of the National Archives. See www.archives.gov/publications/prologue/1996/spring/1890-census-2.html.

Table 5-2: 1884-1896 State Censuses: Substitutes for the Lost 1890 Census

State	Year a Terr.	Year a State	Year in which a state census was taken								Notes
			1884	1885	1890	1891	1892	1894	1895	1896	
Alabama	1817	1819									
Alaska	1912	1959									
Arizona	1863	1912									
Arkansas	1819	1836									
California	—	1850									
Colorado	1861	1876		•							
Connecticut	—	1788									
Delaware	—	1787									
Distr. of Columbia	—	1791									
Florida	1822	1845		•					•		
Georgia	—	1788									
Hawaii	1900	1959		•					•		Kingdom of Hawaii
Idaho	1863	1890									
Illinois	1809	1818									
Indiana	1800	1816									
Iowa	1838	1846		•					•		
Kansas	1854	1861		•					•		
Kentucky	—	1791									
Louisiana	1809	1812									
Maine	—	1820									
Maryland	—	1788									
Massachusetts	—	1788									
Michigan	1805	1837	•					•			
Minnesota	1849	1858		•					•		
Mississippi	1798	1817									
Missouri	1805	1821									
Montana	1864	1889									
Nebraska	1854	1867		•							
Nevada	1861	1864									
New Hampshire	—	1788									
New Jersey	—	1787		•					•		
New Mexico	1850	1912		•							
New York	—	1788					•				
North Carolina	—	1789									
North Dakota	1861	1889		•							1885 Dakota Terr. - 17 cos.
Ohio	1787	1803									
Oklahoma	1890	1907			•						1890 Oklahoma Territory
Indian Territory	--	--			•						1890 Cherokee Nation
Oregon	1848	1859		•					•		1885 2 Counties. 1895 4 Cos.
Pennsylvania	—	1787									
Rhode Island	—	1790		•							
South Carolina	—	1788									
South Dakota	1861	1889		•					•		1885 Dakota Terr. - 20 Cos
Tennessee	1790	1796				•					
Texas	—	1845									
Utah	1850	1896									
Vermont	—	1791									
Virginia	—	1788									
Washington	1853	1889		•							
West Virginia	—	1863									
Wisconsin	1836	1848		•					•		
Wyoming	1868	1890									
Total Number of States			1	14	3	1	1	1	8	1	
			1884	1885	1890	1891	1892	1894	1895	1896	

The U.S. in 1900. This was the first federal census conducted in the District of Alaska as well as Hawaii Territory (neither are shown on the map). The areas of Oklahoma Territory and Indian Territory were merged in 1907 to become the state of Oklahoma. Both Arizona Territory and New Mexico Territory became states in 1912. **Map Source:** Page 10, **Map Guide to the U.S. Federal Censuses, 1790-1920,** by William Thorndale and William Dollarhide.

1900 Federal Census

Destruction of the Original Records: By the mid-1940s, the early original census schedules from 1790 through 1880 had already been transferred from the Census Bureau to the National Archives; but the original schedules from 1900 through 1940 were still stored on several floors of the Commerce Building.

To free up space, the Census Bureau undertook a major project to microfilm the census schedules of 1900 through 1940; and when the microfilming was complete, the original census schedules were destroyed. This was all done with the permission of Congress, who financed the microfilming project, and authorized the destruction of the originals.

U.S. Population: 76.2 million.

1900 Census Legislative Act: 30 Stat. 1014, 3 March 1899.

Responsibility / Schedules / Copies: The 1900 census was conducted under the direction of the Director of the Census (Census Office, U.S. Dept. of the Interior). **Schedules:** Population, Mortality, Agriculture, Manufactures, Indians, and Military & Naval. **Mandated Copies:** One copy, to the Census Office/Secretary of the Interior. Counties could buy a copy of their schedules at cost. (None did).

Census day: 1 June 1900. All of the questions asked by the census taker were related to a person's age or place of residence as of the census day.

Time Allowed: field count due within 30 days, except communities over 10,000 in population, due within two weeks.

1900 Jurisdictions: 52. Utah was admitted to the Union in 1896, bringing the number to forty-five  stars on the U.S. Flag. Seven more jurisdictions were enumerated: the District of Alaska, the District of Columbia, Arizona Territory, Hawaii Territory, Indian Territory, New Mexico Territory, and Oklahoma Territory. American Indians were enumerated within their tribal affiliations on *Indian Population* schedules. Non-Indians living within the bounds of any Indian Nation/Reservation were enumerated on standard *Schedule 1 - Population* forms.

Content of the Population Schedules. The 1900 census schedules listed every person in a household and included a name; relationship to the head of house; name of street and number of house; sex; color; the person's age, plus the exact month and year of birth; birthplace; if female, number of children, and number of children alive in 1900; occupation; marital status, and if married, number of years; number of years in the U.S.; birthplace of father and mother; whether parents were of foreign birth; whether able to read or write; whether a person could speak English; and whether the person attended school the previous year.

The 1900 Soundex Index. Soon after the creation of the Social Security Administration in 1935, clerical workers from the Works Progress Administration (WPA) were called upon to create an index to the 1900 census. A special system of coding names was created, called "Soundex." 3x5 index cards were prepared for each household in the U.S. The information on the Soundex index cards was extracted from the full census schedules and included the full name, age, and birthplace for a head of household, and included any other person living in the household, regardless of their age. Each head of household's surname was given a Soundex code, and the cards were then arranged in alphabetical order by the Soundex code number (A001-Z001) and after that by the first name of the head of the household.

Microfilm of Originals & Digital Capture: The National Archives film for the 1900 census is contained on 1,854 rolls, series T623, beginning with FHL film #1240001 (Alabama). The microfilm was digitized by FamilySearch International. For a list of roll numbers, contents, and access to the digital images of each roll, see the FHL catalog page:
https://familysearch.org/search/catalog/26038. At this writing, the digitizing project for the 1900 Soundex microfilm was still in progress. Check the catalog list for the rolls digitized and available to date, see **https://familysearch.org/search/catalog/33540.**

Online Searching - 1900 Census Indexes and Digital Images. The 1900 Census was digitized from the National Archives microfilm, indexed, and made available at the following websites:

• **Ancestry.com.** Subscription site, free database searching. Ancestry and FamilySearch share images and indexes. See
www.ancestry.com/search/collections/1900usfedcen.

• **FamilySearch.org.** Free database search, with images by FamilySearch, index by Ancestry. See
www.familysearch.org/search/collection/1325221.

• **MyHeritage.com.** A Family Tree subscription site. All U.S. Federal Census Records are available to subscribers with a data plan. See
www.myheritage.com/research/collection-10131/1900-united-states-federal-census.

• **Findmypast.com.** Monthly or annual subscriptions. Initial searches to U.S. Federal Censuses are free. See
https://search.findmypast.com/search-world-Records/us-census-1900.

• **GenealogyBank.com.** Subscription site. Initial searches to the U.S. Federal Censuses, 1790-1940 are free. www.genealogybank.com/explore/census/all.

• **HeritageQuestOnline-Subscribers Login.** This is a library subscription service. Check with your local library to see if they subscribe to the ProQuest & HeritageQuest databases. Many subscribing libraries allow their library card holders remote access. See
www.heritagequestonline.com/hqoweb/library/do/login.

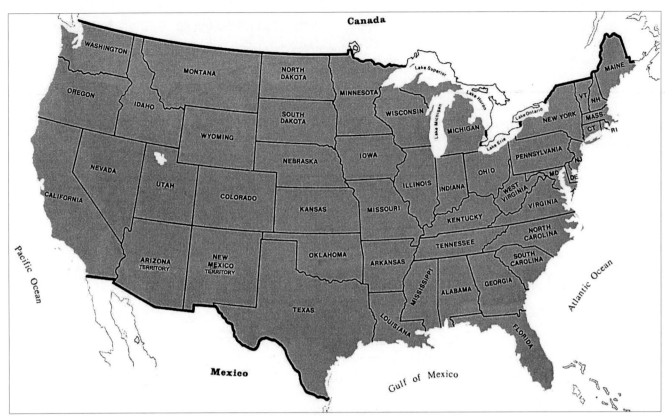

The U.S. in 1910. The areas of Oklahoma Territory and Indian Territory were merged in 1907 to become the state of Oklahoma. Jurisdictions enumerated in 1910 but not shown on the map: the District of Alaska, Hawaii Territory, and the Territory of Puerto Rico. **Map Source:** Page 10, **Map Guide to the U.S. Federal Censuses, 1790-1920.**

1910 Federal Census

Destruction of the Original Records: By the mid-1940s, the original census schedules from 1790 through 1880 had already been transferred from the Census Bureau to the National Archives; but the original schedules from 1900 through 1940 were still stored on several floors of the Commerce Building.

To free up space, the Census Bureau undertook a major project to microfilm the census schedules of 1900 through 1940; and when the microfilming was complete, the original census schedules were destroyed. This was all done with the permission of Congress, who financed the microfilming project, and authorized the destruction of the originals.

U.S. Population: 92.2 million.

1910 Census Legislative Act: 36 Stat. 1, 2 July 1909.

Responsibility / Schedules / Copies: The 1910 census was conducted under the direction of the Director of the Census (Census Bureau, U.S. Department of Commerce and Labor). **Schedules:** Population, Agriculture, Manufactures, and Military & Naval. **Mandated Copies:** One copy, to the Director of the Census. Counties could buy a copy of their schedules at cost. (None did).

Census day: 15 April 1910. All of the questions asked by the census taker were related to a person's age or place of residence as of the census day.

Time Allowed: field count due within 30 days, except communities over 5,000 in population, due within two weeks.

1910 Jurisdictions: 52. The areas of Oklahoma Territory and Indian Territory were merged in 1907 to become the state of Oklahoma – the 46th state in the Union. Also enumerated in 1910 were the District of Alaska, District of Columbia; and the territories of Arizona, Hawaii, New Mexico, and Puerto Rico.

Content of the Population Schedules. The 1910 census schedules listed every person in a household and included the name of a street, house number; and the name and age of each person; relationship to the head of house; sex; color; if female, the number of children, and number of children still living in 1910; marital status, and if married, number of years; year of immigration to the U.S.; whether a naturalized citizen, alien, or papers pending; language spoken; trade or profession, type of business, and whether an employee, employer, or working on one's own account; whether out of work, and if so, the number weeks out; birthplace of father and mother; whether able to read or write; whether the person attended school within the previous year; whether a person owned or rented a house; whether the house was mortgaged or mortgage free; whether a farm or a home; whether the person was a veteran; and whether the person was blind or deaf.

1910 Soundex & Miracode Indexes. The 1910 Soundex/Miracode indexes were compiled in 1962 for twenty-one (21) states by the staff of the Census Age Search section of the Bureau of the Census. The Soundex indexes were done on hand-entered index cards, similar to all of the other Soundex indexes; while the Miracode indexes were done using computers. The two systems are identical except for the citation to a page number (Miracode) or to a house number (Soundex).

1910 Soundex States: Alabama, Georgia, Louisiana (except Shreveport and New Orleans), Mississippi, South Carolina, Tennessee, and Texas.

1910 Miracode States: Arkansas, California, Florida, Illinois, Kansas, Kentucky, Louisiana (Shreveport and New Orleans only), Michigan, Missouri, North Carolina, Ohio, Oklahoma, Pennsylvania, Virginia, and West Virginia.

Microfilm of Originals & Digital Capture: The National Archives film for the 1910 census is contained on 1,784 rolls, series T624, beginning with FHL film #1374014 (Alabama). The microfilm was digitized by FamilySearch International. For a list of roll numbers, contents, and access to the digital images of each roll, see the FHL catalog page:
https://familysearch.org/search/catalog/297155. At this writing, the digitizing project for the 1910 Soundex & Miracode microfilm for all 21 states was still in progress. Check the catalog list for the rolls digitized and available to date, see
https://familysearch.org/search/catalog/297271.

Online Searching - 1910 Census Indexes and Digital Images. The 1910 Census was digitized from the National Archives microfilm, indexed, and made available at the following websites:

• **Ancestry.com**. Subscription site, free database searching. Ancestry and FamilySearch share images and indexes. See
www.ancestry.com/search/collections/1910uscenindex.

• **FamilySearch.org**. Free database search, with images by FamilySearch, index by Ancestry. See
https://familysearch.org/search/collection/1727033.

• **MyHeritage.com**. A Family Tree subscription site. All U.S. Federal Census Records are available to subscribers with a data plan. See
www.myheritage.com/research/collection-10132/1910-united-states-federal-census.

• **Findmypast.com**. Monthly or annual subscriptions. Initial searches to U.S. Federal Censuses are free. See
www.findmypast.com/articles/search-the-1910-us-census.

• **GenealogyBank.com**. Subscription site. Initial searches to the U.S. Federal Censuses, 1790-1940 are free. www.genealogybank.com/explore/census/all.

• **HeritageQuestOnline-Subscribers Login.** This is a library subscription service. Check with your local library to see if they subscribe to the ProQuest & HeritageQuest databases. Many subscribing libraries allow their library card holders remote access. See www.heritagequestonline.com/hqoweb/library/do/login.

The U.S. in 1920. Arizona and New Mexico both became states in 1912 bringing the total number to forty-eight (48) states at the time of the 1920 Census. Add eight (8) jurisdictions: The District of Columbia, Hawaii Territory and Alaska Territory; plus the insular territories of Guam, American Samoa, the Panama Canal Zone, Puerto Rico, and the U.S. Virgin Islands, for a total of 56 jurisdictions. The population of the U.S. Territory of the Philippines was not enumerated except for U.S. Military & Naval personnel stationed there. The population of the U.S. Territory of Wake Island was mostly military or civilians working for the military, thus part of the Military & Naval enumeration. For convenience, the U.S. Territory of Midway Atoll was enumerated as part of Honolulu Co HI. **Map source:** *National Atlas of the United States,* 1997-2014 edition.

1920 Federal Census

Destruction of the Original Records: In the 1940s, the Census Bureau undertook a major project to microfilm the census schedules of 1900 through 1940; and when the microfilming was complete, the original census schedules were destroyed. This was all done with the permission of Congress, who financed the microfilming project, and authorized the destruction of the originals.

U.S. Population: 106.0 million.

1920 Census Legislative Act: 40 Stat. 1291, 3 March 1919.

Responsibility / Schedules / Copies: The 1920 census was conducted under the direction of the Director of the Census (Census Bureau, U.S. Department of Commerce). **Schedules:** Population, Agriculture, Manufactures, and Military & Naval Forces. **Mandated Copies:** One copy, to the Director of the Census. Counties could buy a copy of their schedules at cost. (None did).

Census day: 1 January 1920. All of the questions asked by the census taker were related to a person's age or place of residence as of the census day.

Time Allowed: field count due within 30 days, except communities over 2,500 in population, due within two weeks.

Content of the 1920 Population Schedules: The 1920 Census Form had 29 numbered columns, labeled as follows: 1) Street Address, 2) House Number or Farm, 3) Dwelling Number in order of visitation, 4) Family Number in order of Visitation, 5) Name of Person whose place of abode on January 1, 1920, was in this Family 6) Relationship to the Head of House, 7) Home Owned or Rented, 8) If Owned, free or mortgaged, 9) Sex, 10) Color or Race, 11) Age at last birthday, 12) Marital Status: single, marriage, widowed, or divorced, 13) Year of Immigration to the U.S., 14) Naturalized or Alien, 15) Year Naturalized, 16) Attended School (in the past Six months), 17) Can Read, 18) Can Write, 19) Place of Birth of Person, 20) Mother Tongue of Person, 21) Place of Birth of Father, 22) Mother Tongue of Father, 23) Place of Birth of Mother, 24) Mother Tongue of Mother, 25) Can Speak English, 26) Trade or Profession, 27) Type of Business, 28) Employer, Employee, or Works on Own Account, and 29) No. of Farm Schedule.

1920 Soundex Index. The original records were microfilmed in the early 1940s and subsequently destroyed by the Census Bureau. The microfilm was later transferred to the National Archives, Washington, DC. Before the originals were destroyed, clerical workers from the Works Progress Administration (WPA) were called upon to create a comprehensive index to the 1920 census. The index was completed for every household in America. A special system of coding names was created, called "Soundex." 3x5 index cards were prepared for each household in the U.S. The information on the Soundex index cards was extracted from the full census schedules and included the full name, age, and birthplace for a head of household, and included any other person living in the household, regardless of their age. Each head of household's surname was given a Soundex code, and the cards were then arranged in alphabetical order by the Soundex code number (A001-Z001) and after that by the first name of the head of the household.

Microfilm of Originals & Digital Capture: The National Archives film for the 1920 census is contained on 2,076 rolls, series T625, beginning with FHL film #1820001 (Alabama). The microfilm was digitized by FamilySearch International. For a list of roll numbers, contents, and access to the digital images of each roll, see the FHL catalog page:
https://familysearch.org/search/catalog/489386.

Online Searching - 1920 Census Indexes and Digital Images. The 1920 Census was digitized from the National Archives microfilm, indexed, and made available at the following websites:

• **Ancestry.com**. Subscription site, free database searching. Ancestry and FamilySearch share images and indexes. See
www.ancestry.com/search/collections/1920usfedcen.

• **FamilySearch.org**. Free database search, with images by FamilySearch, index by Ancestry. See
https://familysearch.org/search/collection/1488411.

• **MyHeritage.com**. A Family Tree subscription site. All U.S. Federal Census Records are available to subscribers with a data plan. See
www.myheritage.com/research/collection-10133/1920-united-states-federal-census.

• **Findmypast.com**. Monthly or annual subscriptions. Initial searches to U.S. Federal Censuses are free. See
www.findmypast.com/articles/search-the-1920-us-census.

• **GenealogyBank.com**. Subscription site. Initial searches to the U.S. Federal Censuses, 1790-1940 are free. www.genealogybank.com/explore/census/all.

• **HeritageQuestOnline-Subscribers Login.** This is a library subscription service. Check with your local library to see if they subscribe to the ProQuest & HeritageQuest databases. Many subscribing libraries allow their library card holders remote access. See
www.heritagequestonline.com/hqoweb/library/do/login.

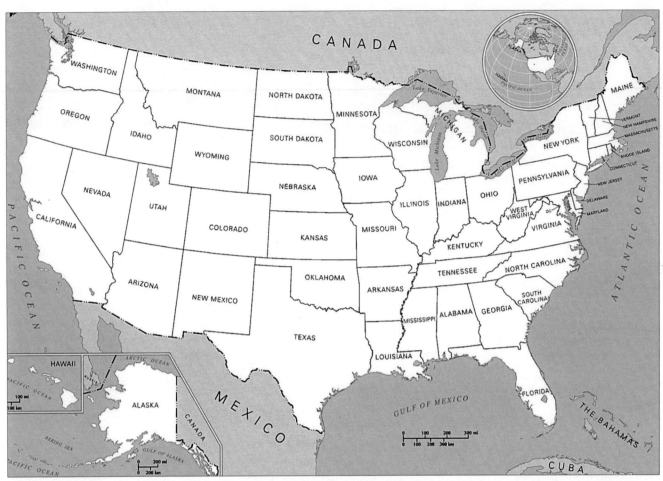

The U.S. in 1930. There were a total of forty-eight (48) states at the time of the 1930 Census. Add eight (8) jurisdictions: The District of Columbia, Hawaii Territory and Alaska Territory; plus the insular territories of Guam, American Samoa, the Panama Canal Zone, Puerto Rico, and the U.S. Virgin Islands, for a total of 56 jurisdictions. The population of the U.S. Territory of the Philippines was not enumerated. For convenience, the U.S. Territory of Midway Atoll was enumerated as part of Honolulu Co HI. Added to the insular territories was an enumeration of U.S. citizens employed at Consular Services around the world.
Map source: *National Atlas of the United States,* 1997-2014 edition.

1930 Federal Census

Destruction of the Original Records: In the 1940s, the Census Bureau undertook a major project to microfilm the census schedules of 1900 through 1940; and when the microfilming was complete, the original census schedules were destroyed. This was all done with the permission of Congress, who financed the microfilming project, and authorized the destruction of the originals.

U.S. Population: 122.7 million.

1930 Census Legislative Act: 46 Stat. 21, 18 June 1929.

Responsibility / Schedules / Copies: The 1930 census was conducted under the direction of the Director of the Census (Census Bureau, U.S. Dept. of Commerce). **Schedules:** Population, Agriculture, Unemployment, and Mines. **Mandated Copies:** One copy, to the Director of the Census. Counties could buy a copy of their schedules at cost. (None did).

Census day: 1 April 1930. All of the questions asked by the census taker were related to a person's age or place of residence as of the census day.

Time Allowed: field count due within 30 days, except communities over 2,500 in population, due within two weeks.

Content of the 1930 Population Schedules: The 1930 Census Form had 32 numbered columns, labeled as follows: 1) Street Address, 2) House number (in cities or towns), 3) Dwelling Number in order of visitation, 4) Family Number in order of Visitation, 5) Name of person whose placed of abode on April 1, 1930, was in this family 6) Relationship to the Head of House, 7) Home owned or rented, 8) Value of home if owned, or monthly rental if rented, 9) R=Radio set, 10) Live on a farm? 11) Sex, 12) Color or race, 13) Age at last birthday, 14) Marital status (S, M, Wd, D), 15) Age at first marriage, 16) Attended school (in the past 6 months), 17) Can Read and write, 18) Person's birthplace, 19) Father's birthplace, 20) Mother's birthplace, 21) Language spoken before coming to U.S., 22) Year of immigration to United States, 23) Naturalization (Na=Naturalized, Pa=First Papers, Al=Alien) 24) Can speak English 25) Occupation, 26) Industry, 27) Class of worker (E=Employer, W=Wage or salary worker, O=Working on own account, NP=Unpaid worker, member of the family), 28) At work yesterday? 29) If not, Line No. on Unemployment schedule, 30) Veteran? 30) What War? and 32) No. of Farm Schedule.

1930 Soundex Index. The original population schedules were microfilmed in the 1940s and subsequently destroyed by the Census Bureau. The microfilm was later transferred to the National Archives, Washington, DC. Before the originals were destroyed, clerical workers from the Works Progress Administration (WPA) were called upon to create a partial index to the 1930 census. The 1930 Soundex index was completed for the southern states of Alabama, Arkansas, Florida, Georgia, Louisiana, Mississippi, North Carolina, South Carolina, Tennessee, and Virginia, plus seven counties in Kentucky and seven more in West Virginia. The information on the Soundex index cards was extracted from the full census schedules and included the full name, age, and birthplace for a head of household and included any other person living in the household, with the person's relationship to the head of household.

1930 Census Publications with Digital Images

Microfilm of Originals & Digital Capture: The National Archives film for the 1930 census is contained on 2,667 rolls, series T626, beginning with FHL film #2339736 (Alabama). The microfilm was digitized by FamilySearch International. For a list of roll numbers, contents, and access to the digital images of each roll, see the FHL catalog page:
https://familysearch.org/search/catalog/1037623.
At this writing, the digitizing project for the 1930 Soundex microfilm was still in progress. Check the catalog list for the rolls digitized and available to date, see https://familysearch.org/search/catalog/1037621.

Online Searching - 1930 Census Indexes and Digital Images. The 1930 Census was digitized from the National Archives microfilm, indexed, and made available at the following websites:

- **Ancestry.com.** Subscription site, free database searching. Ancestry and FamilySearch share images and indexes. See
www.ancestry.com/search/collections/1930usfedcen.

- **FamilySearch.org**. Free database search, with images by FamilySearch, index by Ancestry. See
https://familysearch.org/search/collection/1810731.

- **MyHeritage.com.** A Family Tree subscription site. All U.S. Federal Census Records are available to subscribers with a data plan. See
www.myheritage.com/research/collection-10134/1930-united-states-federal-census.

- **Findmypast.com.** Monthly or annual subscriptions. Initial searches to U.S. Federal Censuses are free. See
www.findmypast.com/articles/search-the-1930-us-census.

- **GenealogyBank.com.** Subscription site. Initial searches to the U.S. Federal Censuses, 1790-1940 are free. www.genealogybank.com/explore/census/all.

- **HeritageQuestOnline-Subscribers Login.** This is a library subscription service. Check with your local library to see if they subscribe to the ProQuest & HeritageQuest databases. Many subscribing libraries allow their library card holders remote access. See
www.heritagequestonline.com/hqoweb/library/do/login.

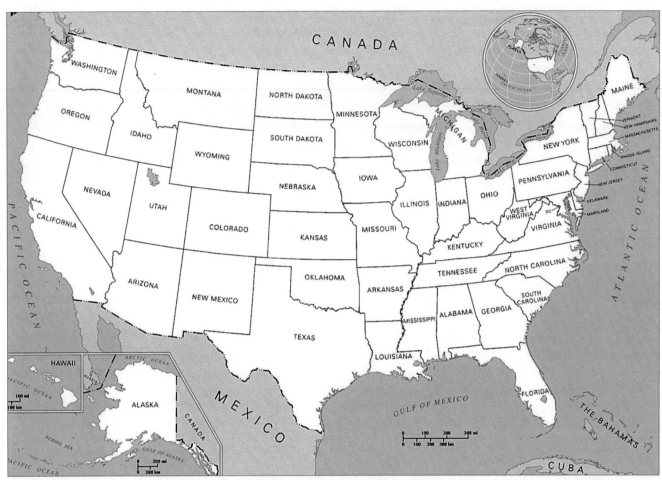

The U.S. in 1940. There were a total of forty-eight (48) states at the time of the 1940 Census. Add eight (8) jurisdictions: The District of Columbia, Hawaii Territory and Alaska Territory; plus the insular territories of Guam, American Samoa, the Panama Canal Zone, Puerto Rico, and the U.S. Virgin Islands, for a total of 56 jurisdictions. The population of the U.S. Territory of the Philippines was not enumerated. **Map source:** *National Atlas of the United States,* 1997-2014 edition.

1940 Federal Census

Destruction of the Original Records: In the 1940s, the Census Bureau undertook a major project to microfilm the census schedules of 1900 through 1940; and when the microfilming was complete, the original census schedules were destroyed. This was all done with the permission of Congress, who financed the microfilming project, and authorized the destruction of the originals.

U.S. Population: 132.1 million.

1940 Census Legislative Act: 46 Stat. 21, 18 June 1929; as amended by 54 Stat. 162, 25 April 1940.

Responsibility / Schedules / Copies: The 1940 census was conducted under the direction of the Director of the Census (Census Bureau, U.S. Dept. of Commerce). **Schedules:** Population, Agriculture, Manufactures, Housing, Businesses, Mines. **Mandated Copies:** One copy, to the Director of the Census. Counties could buy a copy of their schedules at cost.

Census day: 1 April 1940.

Time Allowed: field count due within 30 days, except communities over 2,500 in population, due within two weeks.

Content of the 1940 Population Schedules: The 1940 Census Form had 34 numbered columns, labeled as follows: **Location:** 1) Street, avenue, road, etc., 2) House number. **Household Data:** 3) No. of household in order of visitation, 4) Home owned

(O) or rented (R), 5) Value of Home or Monthly rental if rented, 6) Farm? Yes or No. 7) **Name** of each person whose usual place of residence on April 1, 1940, was in the household *[Be sure to include: 1. Persons temporarily absent from household. Write "Ab" after names of such persons. 2. Children under 1 year of age. Write "Infant" if child has not been given a first name. Enter ⊠ after name of person furnishing information]*. **Relation:** 8) Relation of the person to the head of household, as wife, daughter, father, mother-in-law, grandson, lodger, lodger's wife, servant, hired hand, etc., **Personal Description:** 9) Sex, 10) Color or Race, 11) Age at last birthday, 12) Marital status. **Education:** 13) Attended school or college at any time since March 1, 1940? 14) Highest grade of school completed. **Place of Birth:** 15) If born in U.S. give state, territory or possession. If foreign born, give country in which birthplace was situated on Jan. 1, 1937. **Citizenship:** 16) Citizenship of the foreign born. **Residence, April 1, 1935:** 17) City- Town-Village, 18) County, 19) State-Territory- Country, 20) On a Farm? Y or N. **Employment Status** (Persons 14 years old and over): 21) At work for pay last week? 22) If not, assigned to WPA, CCC, etc.? 23) Seeking work (Y or N), 24) Have a job, business, etc.? (Y or N), 25) Engaged in home housework (H), in School (S), Unable to work (U), or Other (O), 26) Number of hours worked last week, 27) Duration of unemployment in weeks, 28) Occupation, 29) Industry, 30) Class of worker, 31) No. of weeks worked in 1939, 32) Amount of money, wages, salary, or commissions received, 33) Did this person receive income of $50.00 or more from money wages or salary (Y or N), 34) No. of Farm schedule.

1940 Census Extraction Form. A 2-page PDF file is available at the National Archives website. The 1940 format was designed to fit on a standard legal-size sheet of paper (8-1/2" x 14"). Side 1 of the form has columns 1 to 34. Side 2 has Supplementary Questions for Persons Enumerated on Lines 14 and 29 (columns 35 to 50); Side 2 also has a key to Symbols and Explanatory Notes. To access the webpage and download the form, see www.archives.gov/files/research/census/1940/1940.pdf.

Digital Capture: Just prior to the 1 April 2012 opening date of the 1940 population schedules, approximately 4,400 rolls of microfilm were digitized by the National Archives. The images were made available to several interested websites for shared indexing. Upon the opening date, 3.84 million digitized images of the 1940 census were made accessible to the public online.

Online Searching - 1940 Census Indexes and Digital Images. The 1940 Census was digitized from the National Archives microfilm, indexed, and made available at the following websites:

• **Ancestry.com.** Subscription site, free access to indexes and images. See www.ancestry.com/search/collections/1940usfedcen.

• **FamilySearch.org.** Free access to images and indexes. See https://familysearch.org/1940census.

• **MyHeritage.com.** A Family Tree subscription site. Free access to images and indexes. See www.myheritage.com/research/collection-10053/1940-united-states-federal-census.

• **Findmypast.com.** Monthly or annual subscriptions. Free access to images and indexes. See www.findmypast.com/articles/world-records/full-list-of-united-states-records/census-land-and-substitutes/us-census-1940-free-access?rc=1.

• **GenealogyBank.com.** Subscription site. Initial searches to the U.S. Federal Censuses, 1790-1940 are free. www.genealogybank.com/explore/census/all.

• **HeritageQuestOnline-Subscribers Login.** This is a library subscription service. Check with your local library to see if they subscribe to the ProQuest & HeritageQuest databases. Many subscribing libraries allow their library card holders remote access. See www.heritagequestonline.com/hqoweb/library/do/login.

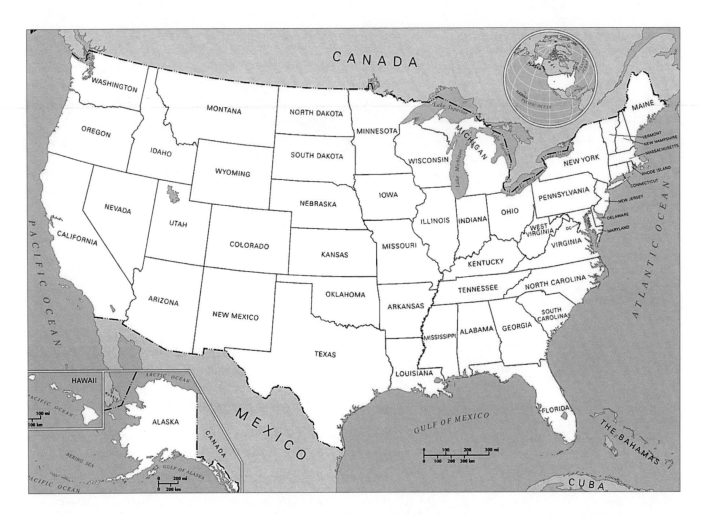

The 1950 census encompassed the 48 states (and DC) of the continental United States, plus the Territories of Alaska, Hawaii, American Samoa, Panama Canal Zone, Guam, Puerto Rico, and the U.S. Virgin Islands. The 1950 census also made special provisions/schedules for the enumeration of American citizens living abroad (and their dependents), including the armed forces of the United States, employees of the United States Government, and the crews of vessels in the American Merchant Marine at sea or in foreign ports. Also enumerated were any American citizens living on small islands claimed by the U.S., such as the Corn Islands, Midway Atoll, Wake Island, Canton Island, and Johnston Atoll. Also in 1950, the Trust Territory of the United States (1947-1986) was enumerated. (The Trust Territory included the main Micronesian island groups of the Northern Mariana Islands (later a U.S. Commonwealth Territory), the Marshall Islands (later the main population of the Federated States of Micronesia); and Palau, the western chain of the Caroline Islands (later the Republic of Palau). **Map source:** *National Atlas of the United States,* 1997-2014 edition.

1950 Federal Census

U.S. Population: 150.7 million.

Destruction of the Original Records: After microfilming, the Census Bureau destroyed the original schedules of the 1950 census. All the related microfilm and original published materials of the 1950 census were transferred to the National Archives in 2000.

1950 Census Legislative Act: 46 Stat. 21, 18 June 1929; as amended by an act dd 7 September 1950 to add or exclude certain schedules.

Responsibility: The 1950 census was conducted under the direction of the Director of the Census (Census Bureau, U.S. Department of Commerce).

Census day: 1 April 1950. All of the questions asked by the census taker were related to a person's age or place of residence as of the census day.

Time Allowed: field count due within 30 days, except communities over 2,500 in population, due within two weeks.

Content of the 1950 Population Schedules: The 1950 census questionnaire had 20 numbered columns, labeled as follows:
For Head of Household: 1) Name of street, avenue, or road. 2) House (and apartment) number. 3) Serial number of dwelling unit. 4) Is this house on a farm (or ranch)? (Yes or No). 5) If No in item 4 – Is this house on a place of three or more acres? (Yes or No).
6) Agriculture Questionnaire Number.
For All Persons: 7) Name: What is the name of the head of this household? What are the names of all other persons who live here? List in this order: The Head, His wife, Unmarried sons and daughters (in order of age), Married sons and daughters and their families, Other relatives, Other persons, such as lodgers, roomers, maids or hired hands who live in, and their relatives.
8) **Relationship** of person to head of household, as Head, Wife, Daughter, Grandson, Mother-in-law, Lodger, Lodger's wife, Maid, Hired Hand, Patient, etc.
9) **Race:** White (W), Negro (Neg), American Indian (Ind), Japanese (Jap), Chinese (Chi), Filipino (Fil), Other race-spell out. 10) **Sex:** Male (M), Female (F), 11) How old was he on his last birthday? (If under one year of age, enter month of birth as April, May, Dec., etc.). 12) **Marital Status:** Is he now married, widowed, divorced, separated, or never married (Mar, Wd, D, Sep, Nev). 13) **Place of Birth:** What State (or foreign country) was he born in? If born outside Continental United States, enter name of Territory, possession, or foreign country. Distinguish Canada-French from Canada-other. 14) If foreign born – Is he naturalized? (Yes, No, or AP for born abroad of American Parents).
For Persons 14 years of Age and Over: 15) What was this person doing most of last week – working, keeping house, or something else? (Wk, H, Ot, or U for unable to work). 16) If H or Ot in Item 15 – Did this person do any work at all last week, not counting work around the house? (Include work for pay, in own business, profession, or farm, or un-paid family work (Yes or No). 17) If No in Item 16 – Was this person looking for work? (Yes or No). 18) If No in Item 17 – does he have a job or business? (Yes or No). 19) If Wk in Item 15 or Yes in item 16 – How many hours did he work last week? (Number of hours). 20a (Occupation): What kind of work was he doing? 20b (Industry): What kind of business or industry was he working in? 20c) Class of Worker: Private (P), Government (G), Own business (O), Without pay (family or farm business) (NP).

1950 Census Publications

Digital Capture: Prior to the April 2022 opening date of the 1950 population schedules, approximately 5,000 rolls of microfilm will be digitized for the National Archives. The images will be made available to several interested websites for shared indexing. Soon after the opening, expect the FamilySearch digitized images of the 1950 census to be made accessible online. To find the images, start with a FamilySearch catalog search, see www.familysearch.org/search/catalog/search.
For the "Place" use "United States," then click on **Search**. At the list of categories, look for "United States – Census – 1950."

Online Searching - 1950 Census Indexes and Digital Images. The 1950 Census will be digitized from the National Archives microfilm, indexed, and made available at the following websites:

- **Ancestry.com.** Subscription site, free database searching. See www.ancestry.com/search/places/usa.

- **FamilySearch.org.** Free database and index search. See www.familysearch.org/search/collection/location/1.

- **MyHeritage.com.** A Family Tree subscription site. All U.S. Federal Census Records are available to subscribers with a data plan. See www.myheritage.com/research/category-1100/us-census.

- **Findmypast.com.** Monthly or annual subscriptions. Initial searches to U.S. Federal Censuses are free. See https://search.findmypast.com/search-world-records-in-census-land-and-substitutes.

- **GenealogyBank.com.** Subscription site. Initial searches to the U.S. Federal Censuses, 1790-1950 will be free. www.genealogybank.com/explore/census/all.

- **HeritageQuestOnline-Subscribers Login.** This is a library subscription service. Check with your local library to see if they subscribe to the ProQuest & HeritageQuest databases. Many subscribing libraries allow their library card holders remote access. See www.heritagequestonline.com/hqoweb/library/do/login.

Census References

Alterman, Hyman, *Counting People: The Census in History,* New York: Harcourt, Brace & World, 1969.

Barrows, Robert C., "The Ninth Federal Census of Indianapolis: A Case in Civic Chauvinism," *Indiana Magazine of History* 73 (1977).

Bureau of the Census, *200 Years of U.S. Census Taking: Population and Housing Questions, 1790-1990,* Washington: GPO, 1989. Reprint, Bountiful, UT: AGLL, 1996.

Davidson, Katherine H. and Charlotte M. Ashby, *Preliminary Inventory of the Records of the Bureau of the Census, National Archives Preliminary Inventory No. 16,* Washington: NARS, 1964. Reprint, 1997.

Dollarhide, William, *Substitutes for the Lost 1890 Federal Census,* Orting, WA: Family Roots Publ. Co., 2019. See www.familyrootspublishing.com/store/product_view.php?id=3577.

Dollarhide, William, *1790-1940 Census: A Quick Look – A Genealogists' Insta-Guide,* 16 Census years, 4-8 pages each, UV Coated Card Stock, publ. Family Roots Publ. Co., 2018. See www.familyrootspublishing.com/store/category.php?cat=3443.

Eckler, A. Ross, *The Bureau of the Census,* New York: Praeger, 1972.

Forstall, Richard L., *Population of States and Counties of the United States: 1790-1990.* Washington: U.S. Bureau of the Census, 1996.

Holt, W. Stull, *The Bureau of the Census: Its History, Activities and Organization,* Washington: Brookings Institution, 1929.

Rossiter, W. S., *A Century of Population Growth: From the First Census of the U.S. to the Twelfth, 1790-1920.* Washington: GPO, 1909. Reprint, Orting, WA: Heritage Quest, Press, 1989.

Russell, Donna Valley, ed., *Michigan Censuses, 1710-1830 Under the French, British, and Americans,* Detroit: Detroit Society for Genealogical Research, 1982.

Scott, Ann Herbert. *Census U.S.A.: A Fact Finding for the American People, 1790-1970,* New York: Seabury Press, 1968.

Thorndale, William and William Dollarhide, *Map Guide to the U.S. Federal Census, 1790-1920,* Baltimore: Genealogical Publishing Co., Inc., 1987-2018. 393 census year maps show the changing county boundaries for 3,142 counties, old and current boundaries on the same map, see www.familyrootspublishing.com/store/product_view.php?id=67.

Wright, Carroll D., *The History and Growth of the United States Census: Prepared for the Senate Committee on the Census,* GPO, Washington, DC, 1900, 967 pages. To access a digital version of this classic, see the FHL catalog page: www.familysearch.org/search/catalog/1912123.

Census Legislation, 1790-1940

A Census Bureau website identifies the titles and dates of each legislative act authorizing a census, beginning with the 1789 Constitution of the United States, followed by all census acts 1790 to the Present. There is a link to a downloadable PDF for census years, organized as follows:

1789-1820. For the complete 1789 U.S. Constitution, and legislative acts for the 1790, 1800, 1810, and 1820 censuses. see www.census.gov/history/www/reference/legislation/legislation_1789_-_1820.html.

1830-1900. For the legislative acts for the 1830, 1840, 1850-1860-1870, 1880, 1890, and 1900 censuses, see www.census.gov/history/www/reference/legislation/legislation_1830_-_1899.html.

1910-1940. For the legislative acts beginning with the *Act to Provide a Permanent Census Office* (March 6, 1902); and for the legislative acts for 1910, 1920, 1930, and 1940 Censuses; plus other census and apportioning acts, see www.census.gov/history/www/reference/legislation/legislation_1902_-_1941.html.

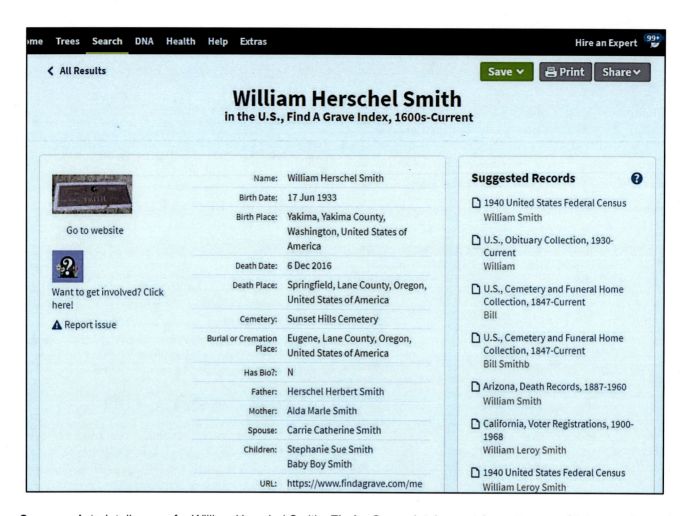

Screen print, details page for William Herschel Smith, *Find a Grave* database at Ancestry.com. Click on a photo of a grave marker to go to the Find a Grave webpage with much more information, including more photos, names of relatives, and citations of sources.

Nationwide Chapter - Part 2
Bibliography of U.S. Census Substitutes

Part 1 of this chapter identified the U.S. Federal Censuses, 1790-1950. This Part 2 section identifies *U.S. Census Substitutes*, i.e., alternative name lists that give the same information as a census: a name, place of residence, date of residence, and often much more data.

The Shotgun Approach

There are some huge genealogy look-up sites on the Internet. The main sites all provide the means of searching for a name or a place, starting with the U.S. Federal Censuses. They are the first search screens we can use to find an ancestor and a place of residence when little is known about a person at the onset. Get your shotgun out – you can now begin with a global search at one or all of the following look-up websites:

FamilySearch.org. This is a free site. Some census searching uses Ancestry.com indexes, and full access to the census records at Ancestry may require a membership. FamilySearch has over 6 billion records accessible for free.

Ancestry.com. This is the largest subscription site. An initial search is free. Ancestry has over 20 billion records from over 80 countries worldwide.

MyHeritage.com. This is a subscription site based in Israel, with a huge collection of Family Trees and genealogical databases for the entire world. For the US alone, MyHeritage boasts 3,228 collections with 2.57 billion records, including the U.S. Federal Censuses, 1790-1940.

Findmypast.com. This is a subscription site, owned by the British Brightsolid company. Worldwide, this site has over 4 billion records, including U.S. Federal Census Records, 1790-1940; and holds the PERiodical Source Index (PERSI) Database.

GenealogyBank.com. This is a subscription site, specializing in newspapers online. They have over 9,000 U.S. newspaper databases, with many millions of digitized/indexed newspaper pages They also have the entire set of the U.S. Federal Censuses, 1790-1940. The initial searches at the Home page are free.

The Sniper Approach

The Shotgun Approach is fine when all you have is the broad side of a barn as a target. But experienced Internet genealogists have learned that even the best search algorithms will not turn up every possible result. In fact, the global search/shotgun approach needs refining, because the numbers of unnecessary results have to be sifted out.

The best way to overcome the shotgun overkill is to focus on searching individual record collections. To be more precise, get your Sniper Scope out and start looking beyond the general search box to find specific records available, i.e., look for specific *U.S. Census Substitutes*. These include nationwide lists of births, marriages, deaths, & burials; plus lists of military units, veterans, immigrations, naturalizations, tax records, or other national databases that reveal much more than just the place of residence for a person.

After reviewing the census substitutes available for each of the 50 states, DC, and 7 U.S. Territories, it is time to see what nationwide databases are available. The 292 most important of these U.S. Census Substitutes are identified below in chronological order:

♦ ♦ ♦ ♦ ♦

1600s–2000s. *U.S., Find a Grave Index* **[Online Database],** this is a gravestone, tombstone, and memorial photo collection; digitized, indexed, with over 150 million names. Owned by Ancestry.com, *Find a Grave* has over 200,000 volunteer contributors, who not only tromp through cemeteries all across the country and write down the names and dates from the tombstones, but usually take photographs of them as well. Information for every grave includes a Given name, Surname, Birth date, Death date, Photo (if applicable), and the cemetery name and place. The site allows for contributors to add information, cite sources, add photos, and make links to other relatives elsewhere in the database, Compared with the *Social Security Death Index (SSDI)* with over 93 million names beginning in 1962; the *Find a Grave* database has over 150 million names, some as early as 1607. See http://search.ancestry.com/search/db.aspx?dbid=60525.

1600s-2000s. *Billion Graves Index* **[Online Database],** this is a gravestone, tombstone, and memorial photo collection, digitized and indexed online at the FamilySearch.org website The size of this database is smaller (over 19 million items) but most of the graves are unique to this website. Updates to the database are available periodically. See
https://familysearch.org/search/collection/2026973.

1600s-2000s. *Global, Gravestone Photograph Index* **[Online Database],** This is a third-party database available at Ancestry.com, operated by Charles Sale, Gravestone Photographic Resource website (of England?). The inclusive dates of the Ancestry title is 1285-2014, and that would mean gravestones most likely in Europe, probably concentrated in the UK. The only way to find out if this database has value is to do a search for surnames of interest and see what happens. This database has 876,327 records, see
www.ancestry.com/search/collections/9740.

1600s-1900s. *U.S. and Canada, Passenger, and Immigration Lists Index* **[Online Database],** indexed at the FamilySearch.org website. Original data: Filby, P. William, ed., *Passenger, and Immigration Lists Index, 1500s-1900s.* Farmington Hills, MI, USA: Gale Research, 2012. A database with over 5.2 million names cannot be ignored, but the fact is, some of the entries in this database are of poor value – most of the dates of "immigrations" came from a range of years of the title of a book, e.g., *Nova Scotia Immigrants to 1867.* Of the 4,500 surname Jones entries in that book, all of them are listed as having arrived in Nova Scotia "between 1598 and 1867." See
http://search.ancestry.com/search/db.aspx?dbid=7486.

1600s-1700. *American Marriages Before 1699* **[Online Database],** digitized and indexed at Ancestry.com. Original data: Clemens, William Montgomery. *American Marriage Records Before 1699.* Pompton Lakes, NJ: Biblio Co., 1926. Researched and compiled by William M Clemens in the 1920's, this volume of marriage records contains over ten thousand entries. Although primarily listing Massachusetts marriages, there are thousands of entries from other states, including New York and Pennsylvania. See
www.ancestry.com/search/collections/2081.

1607-1943. *U.S., Encyclopedia of American Quaker Genealogy, Vol I–VI* **[Online Database],** digitized and indexed at the Ancestry.com website. Source: 6-vol. digitized set, *Encyclopedia of American Quaker Genealogy,* by William Wade Hinshaw, reprinted, 1991-1994, GPC, Baltimore, MD. Copyists abridged the relevant details onto cards which were assembled into alphabetical order by surname, within each meeting. Each entry includes vital details (births, marriages, deaths) and other facts related to membership. Records may include: Name, Birth date, Birthplace, Death date, Death county and state, Marriage date, Marriage county and state, Children, and Residence. Some minutes are supplemented by details from family bibles, burial registers, and data from headstones. This database has 356,712 records:
http://search.ancestry.com/search/db.aspx?dbid=3753.

```
FCMM-WGI
Card #1
SMITH, Isabel  d. 8-13-1931 bur Earlham Cem., Richmond, Ind.

SMITH, Marie Isabel b. 7-12-1932
```

- See also, *U.S., Hinshaw Index to Selected Quaker Records, 1680-1940* **[Online Database],** digitized and indexed at the Ancestry.com website. Source: *Unpublished Quaker Records,* by William Wade Hinshaw, originals at Swarthmore College, Swarthmore, PA. This index contains records which were extracted from the minutes of 300 meetings from the East Coast to Nebraska. These meetings are not included in the *Encyclopedia of American Quaker Genealogy,* Vol. I-VI, 1607-1943. They are primarily from meetings in Indiana (86 meetings), Iowa (84 meetings), Kansas (49 meetings), Pennsylvania (13 meetings), and New Jersey (4 meetings). There are also extracts from a few meetings in the following states: Arizona, California, Colorado, Idaho, Illinois, Michigan, Minnesota, Missouri, Nebraska, Oklahoma, South Dakota, and Wisconsin. Each index record includes: Name, Birth date, State, and Monthly meeting. The document images may have more information about a person/family. This database has 887,019 records. See
http://search.ancestry.com/search/db.aspx?dbid=2705.

✓ **NOTE:** The significance of the Hinshaw Quaker lists is that Quakers did not believe in civil marriages or civil vital records registration. They believed that the local Quaker Meeting House was the place to record such events, which they all did profusely. Their thousands of records books were all stored in fire-proof

safes, and virtually all of the books are extant. The Quaker records are a genealogical gold mine. However, there is a caution about Quaker dating: These records span the time before and after the 1752 calendar change in Great Britain and America. Quakers used only numbers to represent years, months, and days. In 1752 the 1st day of a year changed from the 25th of March (1st month) to the 1st day of January (1st month). For an article on the subject, see
www.genealogyblog.com/?p=18500.

1620-1896. *Mayflower Births and Deaths, Vol. 1 and 2* **[Online Database],** digitized and indexed at Ancestry.com. Original data: Roser, Susan E. *Mayflower Births and Deaths: From the Files of George Ernest Bowman at the Massachusetts Society of Mayflower Descendants. Volumes 1 & 2.* Baltimore, MD: Genealogical Publishing Company, Inc., 1992. This database contains birth and death details for descendants of passengers on the Mayflower extracted from the files of George Ernest Bowman, founder of the Massachusetts Society of Mayflower Descendants. In 1896, Bowman compiled more than 20,000 pages of research on descendants of the original Mayflower colonists. Together, the two volumes include details on about 50,000 Mayflower descendants, often extending to the seventh or eighth generation. Details contained in the entries vary but may include the following: name, Relationship, parents' names, spouse's name, birth date, birthplace, death date, and death place. This database has 45,912 records, see
www.ancestry.com/search/collections/3718.

1631-1976. *U.S., Adjutant General Military Records* **[Online Database],** indexed at the Ancestry.com website. This database contains a collection of adjutant general reports and other records containing lists of military personnel from various states in the U.S. Along with a book listing Officers and Enlisted Men of the United States Navy Who Lost Their Lives During the World War [WWI], this database contains state adjutant general reports, officers lists, national guard and reserve lists, rosters, and various other legislative and military-related records from the following states: Arkansas, Connecticut, Florida, Georgia, Idaho, Illinois, Indiana, Iowa, Kansas, Kentucky, Maine, Maryland, Massachusetts, Minnesota, Missouri, Nebraska, Nevada, New Hampshire, New Jersey, North Dakota, Ohio, Oklahoma, Rhode Island, Vermont, and Washington. The records vary, as does the material in them. Many include lists of military service personnel, and you may find information such as name, rank or office, residence, unit, birthplace, date of commission, and summary of service. The records can be searched by name, year, and state of service or browsed by volume title and year. This database has 1,349,679 records. See
http://search.ancestry.com/search/db.aspx?dbid=1873.

1695-1954. *U.S., French Catholic Church Records (Drouin Collection)* **[Online Database],** indexed at the Ancestry.com website. Source: In the 1940s the Institut Généalogique Drouin in Québec began microfilming records pertaining to French Canadians throughout French Canada and former French jurisdiction in America. The entire Drouin Collection contains vital records, notarial records, and other miscellaneous records from Québec, Ontario, Acadia, and the U.S. This database contains only the records from the French Catholic parish locations now in the U.S. areas of Alabama, Arkansas, Illinois, Indiana, Louisiana, Maine, Massachusetts, Michigan, Missouri, New York, and Pennsylvania. This database has 228,368 records:
http://search.ancestry.com/search/db.aspx?dbid=1111.

1700s-1900s. *American Genealogical-Biographical Index (AGBI)* **[Online Database],** indexed at the Ancestry.com website. Source: Godfrey Memorial Library, Middletown, CT. One of the most important genealogical collections, the American Genealogical-Biographical Index, or AGBI, is the equivalent of more than 200 printed volumes. This database contains millions of records of people whose names have appeared in printed genealogical records and family histories. With data from sources largely from the last century, each entry contains the person's complete name, the year of the biography's publication, the person's state of birth (if known), abbreviated biographical data, and the book and page number of the original reference. In addition to family histories, other genealogical collections are indexed. These include the *Boston Transcript* (a genealogical column widely circulated), the complete 1790 U.S. Federal Census, and published Revolutionary War records. This database has 3,685,947 records. See
http://search.ancestry.com/search/db.aspx?dbid=3599.

1700s-1900s. See *Biography & Genealogy Master Index (BGMI)* **[Online Database],** indexed at the Ancestry.com website. Source: Book, same title, publ. Gale Research, 2008. Millions of Americans have been profiled in collective biography volumes such as *Who's Who in America* and *Women of Science*. In addition to providing the individual's name, birth, and death dates (where available), the source document is included. Sources for this index vary from *Who's Who of*

American Women and *National Cyclopedia to American Biography* to *Directory of American Scholars* and *American Black Writers*. This database has 5,168,959 records. See
http://search.ancestry.com/search/db.aspx?dbid=4394.

1700s-1900s. *North America, Family Histories* **[Online Database],** digitized and indexed at the Ancestry.com website. Database, same title, acquired by Ancestry, 2016. (no compiler noted). This collection contains genealogical research privately published in nearly one thousand family history books. The primary focus is on North American families from the 18th and 19th centuries, especially those with Revolutionary War and Colonial ties. The following details, when available, have been indexed from the books in this collection. Additional information may be found by viewing the images of the published books. Indexed Details: Name, Birth date and place, Baptism date and place, Marriage date and place, Death date and place, Burial date and place, Names of parents and spouses. To find the title of a book included in this database, use the Browse this Collection feature. This database has 4,252,238 records. See
http://search.ancestry.com/search/db.aspx?dbid=61157.

1733-1990 U.S. Marriages **[Online Database],** indexed at the FamilySearch.org website. This database is a name index to a small set of marriage records from a few states within the United States. Taken from microfilm copies at the Family History Library in Salt Lake City, this database has 5,167 records. See
https://familysearch.org/search/collection/1675543.

1740-1892 Draper Manuscript Collection **[Microfilm],** from originals at the Wisconsin State Historical Society, Madison, WI. The collection consists of nearly 500 volumes of manuscripts, papers, and books collected by Lyman Draper about the history of the trans-Allegheny West, a region including the western areas of the Carolinas and Virginia, all the Ohio River Valley, and part of the upper Mississippi Valley from the 1740s to 1830. Some series are titled by geographic area, some by the names of prominent frontier leaders, and some by topic. The bulk of the collection consists of notes from interviews, questionnaires, and letters gathered during Draper's extensive travels and research to learn about frontier history. For an information page at the Wisconsin State Historical Society's website, see
www.wisconsinhistory.org/military/draper.

1763-1924. *U.S., College Student Lists,* **[Online Database],** indexed at the Ancestry.com website. Source: American Antiquarian Society, Worcester, MA. This database contains a variety of publications listing the names of college students, faculty, alumni, and others associated with universities, colleges, medical schools, and seminaries. They include catalogs of students and officers, histories, biographical sketches, retrospectives, memorials, registers, anniversary books, annual reports, addresses and commencement exercises, alumni lists, lists of lectures and courses, board proceedings, catalogs of fraternity members, and other items. The majority of the books are from the 19th century, especially the first half of the century. They come from 36 states, most in the New England area, though there are volumes from Ohio, California, Tennessee, Georgia, and even a few from Canada. The books' contents vary, but they might list names, homerooms, extra-curricular activities, hometowns, death dates, and other details. This database has 1,516,361 records. See
http://search.ancestry.com/search/db.aspx?dbid=2207.

```
1891-92                    Bowdoin College

Thomas R Croswell, Ph.D., 300 West Mission St., Santa Barbara,
    Ret.
Henry E. Cutts, A.M., 130 Cedar St., New York, N. Y.   Chem.
Edwin C. Drew, Esq., 129 Spring St., Portland, Me.   Law.
Fred W. Dudley, Wolfboro, N. H.   Ed.
Algernon S. Dyer, A.M., Bar Mills, Me.   Ret.
Samuel H. Erskine. Damariscotta, Me.   Ret.
Fred O. Fish, Esq., Room 619, 53 State St., Boston, Mass.   Law.
Edward N. Goding, Esq., 73 Tremont St., Boston, Mass.   Law.
Charles H. Hastings, Library of Congress, Washington, D. C.   Lib.
Emerson Hilton, Esq., Damariscotta, Me.   Law.
Weston M. Hilton, Esq., Damariscotta, Me.   Law.
Henry W. Jarvis, Esq., 640 Tremont Bldg., Boston, Mass.   Law.
Dr. John F. Kelley.  Address unknown.
Charles S. F. Lincoln, M.D., 38 College St., Brunswick, Me.   Ret.
Everett G. Loring, 57 Oak Ave., Hempstead, N. Y.   Ret.
George C. Mahoney, M.D., 97 College Ave., W. Somerville, Mass. M
Wilbert G. Mallett, A.M. Farmington, Me.  Ed.
```

1765-1935. *U.S., School Catalogs* **[Online Database],** digitized and indexed at the Ancestry.com website. Source: Educational Institutions, American Antiquarian Society. This database contains a variety of publications listing names of students, faculty, alumni, and others associated with U.S. educational institutions and associations. These include colleges and universities, seminaries and theological institutes, normal schools, medical schools, academies, military schools, and others, as well as various fraternities, societies, and associations. Records include catalogs, obituary records and necrologies, class histories, speeches and addresses, commencement exercises,

class reports, registers, prospectus, circulars, proceedings, annual reports, magazines, and other documents. The majority of the books are from the 19th century, especially the middle and later half of the century. They come from 43 states. Each index record includes: Name, Publication year, Publication place, School name, and Residence place. The documents images may have more information. This database has 5,378,762 records. See
http://search.ancestry.com/search/db.aspx?dbid=2203.

1768-1921. *United States, Burial Registers for Military Posts, Camps, and Stations* **[Online Database],** digitized and indexed at the FamilySearch.org website. This collection corresponds with NARA publication M2014, one roll consisting of two volumes of burials, most occurring between 1860 and 1890. Records are arranged by place of burial, then date of death. This database has 16,152 records. See
https://familysearch.org/search/collection/2250027.
- See also, *U.S. Military Burial Registers, 1768-1921* **[Online Database],** digitized and indexed at Ancestry.com. This database has 15,757 records, see
www.ancestry.com/search/collections/1103.

1775-1783 Revolutionary War Compiled Service Records **[Online Database],** digitized and indexed at the FamilySearch.org website. Service record cards of approximately 80,000 individual soldiers who served in the Revolutionary War. The cards are arranged under the designation "Continental Troops" or under a state name, then by organization, and then alphabetically by soldier's surname. Corresponds to NARA Publication M881: Compiled Service Records of Soldiers Who Served in the American Army During the Revolutionary War, 1775-1783. Index courtesy of Fold3.com. This database has 1,997,022 records. See
https://familysearch.org/search/collection/1849623.
- See also, *U.S. Compiled Revolutionary War Military Service Records, 1775-1783* [Online Database], This database has 362,434 records, see
www.ancestry.com/search/collections/1309.
- See also, *Rosters of Revolutionary War Soldiers and Sailors, 1775-1783* **[Online Database],** digitized and indexed at FamilySearch.org. Includes published state rosters of Revolutionary War soldiers from the states of Alabama, Connecticut, Massachusetts, New Jersey, Vermont, and Virginia. This database has 1,113,260 records, see
www.familysearch.org/search/collection/2546162.

1775-1783. *U.S., Revolutionary War Rolls* **[Online Database],** digitized and indexed at Ancestry.com. Personnel, pay, and supply records of American Army units in the Revolutionary War, These rolls are organized by state and name of (regiment, battalion, guard, company, etc.). This database has 1,392,626 records, see
www.ancestry.com/search/collections/4282.
- See also, *Revolutionary War Rolls, 1775-1783* **[Online Database],** digitized and indexed at the Fold3.com website. 3,690 images, see
www.fold3.com/title_469/revolutionary_war_rolls.
- See also, *Abstract of Graves of Revolutionary Patriots* **[Online Database],** indexed at Ancestry.com. Original data: Hatcher, Patricia Law. *Abstract of Graves of Revolutionary Patriots.* Vol. 1-4. Dallas, TX, USA: Pioneer Heritage Press, 1987.The source for each grave entry is part of the record page for that person. This collection of abstracts of grave sites contains information originally published in the Senate documents of the National Society, Daughters of the American Revolution, as well as the Society magazine. Veterans and patriots of the Revolutionary War whose graves were found between 1900 and 1987 are included, each entry has the name of the patriot, the cemetery in which the headstone is found, and occasionally others who are located nearby or opposite the grave. This database has 57,498 records, see
www.ancestry.com/search/collections/4110.

1775-2006. *U.S. Veterans' Gravesites* **[Online Database],** a free VA website to locate any U.S. Veteran's grave, including veteran burials from the time of the Revolutionary War. Burial locations of veterans and their family members include those in VA National Cemeteries, State Veterans Cemeteries, Department of Interior Cemeteries; and for many veterans buried in private cemeteries when the grave is marked with a government grave marker. This database has 6,402,238 records, see
http://gravelocator.cem.va.gov.
- See also, *U.S. Veteran' Gravesites, ca. 1775-2006* **[Online Database],** indexed at Ancestry.com. See
www.ancestry.com/search/collections/8750.

1776-1835. *UK, American Loyalist Claims* **[Online Database],** digitized and indexed at Ancestry.com. Original data: American Loyalist Claims, 1776–1835. AO 12–13. The National Archives of the United Kingdom, Kew, Surrey, England. Following the American Revolutionary War (1775-1783), also known as the American War of Independence, British commissioners were appointed to examine claims of losses sustained by those loyal to the British crown or "Loyalists" during and following the war. Records in this database relate to Loyalist claims and cases heard by the American Loyalist Claims Commission. These documents include books of evidence and memorials given by witnesses, accounts of losses (which can provide detail about places and possessions), evidence of claims, correspondence, indentures, and other documents collected over the course of these examinations. Documents may mention names, residences (place and year), accounts of battles, estimates of losses, references to other documents presented in support of claims, power of attorney, and other details giving an account of both the Loyalist's claims and life in America before and during the Revolutionary War. This database has 30,752 records: www.ancestry.com/search/collections/3712.

1776-1938. *Daughters of the American Revolution Lineage Books (152 Vols.)* **[Online Database],** indexed at the Ancestry.com website. Source: DAR, Washington, DC. These lineage books contain information submitted by tens of thousands of individuals with connections to Revolutionary War patriots. This collection now contains nearly 2.4 million names and is a valuable collection for anyone with ancestors who fought in the American Revolution. This database has 333,348 records. See http://search.ancestry.com/search/db.aspx?dbid=3174.

1776-1941. *U.S., Navy Casualties Books* **[Online Database],** indexed at the Ancestry.com website. Source: Navy Dept Library, Washington, DC. This database contains a number of books documenting naval history stretching back to the U.S. Navy's early days. Most are casualty lists. These include details on sailors and officers who were killed, wounded, missing in action, or taken prisoner. Not all deaths are war related. Records include lists of personnel who drowned, were lost in shipwrecks, or died from other accidents or misadventure. Content of the records varies, depending on the year and type of record, but you may find the following details: Name, Rate, Date (death, wounded, MIA, etc.), Ship or station, and Cause of death. Some lists will include next of kin and their address, and some record enlistment details. Aside from casualties, some books contain lists of medical corps members and recipients of citations, medals, or awards. While predominantly Navy, these records may include some Army and Marine Corps personnel. This database has 322,387 records. See http://search.ancestry.com/search/db.aspx?dbid=2324.

1787-1906. *United States, New England, Petitions for Naturalization* **[Online Database],** indexed at the FamilySearch.org website. This collection consists of naturalization documents filed in the National Archives Northeast Region which includes Maine, Massachusetts, New Hampshire, Rhode Island, and Vermont. The majority of the records cover the date range of 1787-1906. This database has 954,378 images: https://familysearch.org/search/collection/2064580.

1789-1858. *U.S. War Bounty Land Warrants* **[Online Database],** digitized and indexed at Ancestry.com. Source: National Archives microfilm series M829. This database contains bounty land warrants issued to veterans of the U.S. Revolutionary War between 1789 and 1833, and to veterans of the War of 1812 between 1815 and 1858. It also contains some related papers of the Revolutionary War warrants that date to as late as 1880. Bounty land warrants were certificates given to eligible veterans granting them rights to free land on the public domain. Warrants usually contain the following information: Date of issuance, Name and rank of veteran, State from which enlisted, and Name of heir or assignee, if applicable. This database has 76,126 records, see www.ancestry.com/search/collections/1165.

1789-1984. *Search Historical Documents* **[Online Database],** digitized and indexed at the Genealogy-Bank.com website, over 225,675 historical documents, published since 1789. Includes military records, casualty lists, Revolutionary and Civil War pension requests, widow's claims, orphan petitions, land grants, and other interesting historical documentation. See www.genealogybank.com/gbnk/documents.

1790-1974. *Selected U.S. Naturalization Records - Original Documents* **[Online Database],** indexed at the Ancestry.com website. Source: This database contains images of original naturalization records (primarily Declarations and Petitions) from U.S. District and Circuit courts. Specifically, California, Colorado, Louisiana, Maryland, Montana, New York, Oregon, Pennsylvania, South Carolina, Alabama, Florida, Georgia, Kentucky, Mississippi, North Carolina, South Carolina, Tennessee, Virginia, and Washington. This database has 1,543,305 records. The original images are no longer available at Ancestry – they are indexed in the 1794-1995 index series, see http://search.ancestry.com/search/db.aspx?dbid=1192.

U.S. Census Substitutes • 265

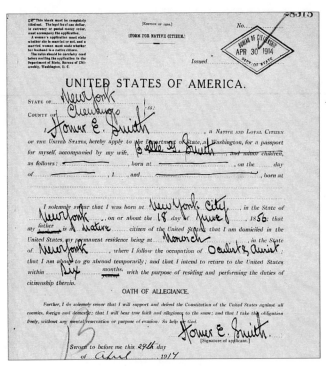

Sample of Passport Application

1790-1909. *U.S. Patent and Trademark Office Patents* [Online Database], digitized and indexed at the Ancestry.com website. Source: National Archives, Records of the U.S. Patent and Trademark Office. In 1790 the government created the federal patent system, laying the foundation for the patent system we use today. The existence of the patent system lends support to invention, research, and science. Studying patents from the past and present can provide an interesting historical perspective of the world our ancestors lived in. The database contains: Patent number, Current U.S. Classification, Name of patentee, Patent date, and Patent place. This database has 3,577,054 records. See http://search.ancestry.com/search/db.aspx?dbid=1314.

1791-1906 *New England Naturalization Index* [Online Database], digitized and indexed at the FamilySearch.org website. This database is an index to naturalization documents filed in courts in Connecticut, Maine, Massachusetts, New Hampshire, Rhode Island, and Vermont from 1791 to 1906. The documents and the index are in the National Archives-New England Region. The index consists of 3x5 cards arranged by state and then by name of petitioner. This database has 615,903 records. See
https://familysearch.org/search/collection/1840474.

1791-2014. *U.S., Officer Down Memorials* [Online Database], indexed at Ancestry.com. The Officer Down Memorial Page, Inc., (ODMP) is a non-profit organization dedicated to honoring America's fallen law enforcement heroes. Each entry provides details on one officer and may include: name, title, department, department state, date of death, place of death, age, tour of duty (length of service), badge, incident date, and photo. This database has 21,927 records, see
www.ancestry.com/search/collections/2373.

1794-1995. *U.S. Naturalization Records Indexes* [Online Database], digitized and indexed at the Ancestry.com website. Source: National Archives microfilm, index cards to naturalization records of various district courts of the U.S. (in several states). Each index record includes: Name, Birth date, State, and Locality, court. This database has 2,494,749 records, see
http://search.ancestry.com/search/db.aspx?dbid=1192.

← Sample. ***1795-1925 Passport Applications* [Online Database],** indexed at the FamilySearch.org website. This collection contains United States Passport Applications from two different NARA collections: M1490, and M1372. This database has 1,614,325 records. See
https://familysearch.org/search/collection/2185145.

1795-1972. *U.S., Naturalization Records - Original Documents* [Online Database], digitized and indexed at the Ancestry.com website. Includes the original documents of Declaration of Intentions and other naturalization papers. Each index record includes: Name, Age, Birth date, Birth location, Arrival year, Issue date, State, Locality/Court. The document images have much more information. This database has 775,142 records. See
http://search.ancestry.com/search/db.aspx?dbid=1193.
- See also, ***U.S., Naturalization Records, 1840-1957* [Online Database],** digitized and indexed at Ancestry.com. Source: National Archives microfilm series for all U.S. district courts. This major extraction of naturalization records from all states was a cooperative effort of a dozen genealogical groups across the country. Naturalization records include Declarations, Petitions, and Certificates. A description of the naturalization process is at the Ancestry webpage. This database has 1,042,040 records, see
www.ancestry.com/search/collections/1193.

1796-1907. *U.S. General Land Office Records* [Online Database], indexed at the Ancestry.com website. Source: Bureau of Land Management, General Land Office Records (Automated Records Project, Federal Land Patents, State Volumes). This database contains approximately 2.2 million land patents, primarily cash and homestead, from 1820-1908 for the following states: Alabama, Arkansas, Florida, Illinois, Indiana, Iowa, Louisiana, Michigan, Minnesota, Mississippi, Missouri, Montana, Ohio, and Wisconsin. A land patent is a document recording the passing of a land title from the government, or other proprietor, to the patentee/grantee. This is the first-title deed and the true beginning of private ownership of the land. The patent describes in legal terms the land to which the title is given. Information recorded in these records includes: Name of patentee(s), Issue date, State of patent, Land office issuing the patent, Acres of land, Legal land description – state, county, township, range, meridian, section, aliquot parts, block, survey number, etc. Accession number (a code used to uniquely identify a patent), Metes and bounds (whether the Metes and Bounds method was used to legally describe the patent), Cancelled (whether the patent was cancelled or not; if 'yes,' more info may be found in the Comments field), U.S. reservations (whether the government has retained some rights or interest in the land), Mineral reservations (whether the land included the reservation of mineral rights for mining, agriculture, manufacturing, or any other purpose), Authority (laws and statutes under which the land was acquired), Document number (the primary identification number given to the original General Land Office document), and Comments. This database has 2,340,335 records. See http://search.ancestry.com/search/db.aspx?dbid=1246.

1796-2010. *RootsWeb Death Index* **[Online Database],** indexed at the Ancestry.com website. This database is also accessible at the RootsWeb site. Each index record includes: Name, Death date, Death place, and a link to the RootsWeb website. This database has 572,438 records. Archived at https://web.archive.org/web/20120415174556/http://search.ancestry.com/search/db.aspx?dbid=70171.

1798-1958. *U.S. Marine Corps Muster Rolls* **[Online Database],** digitized and indexed at Ancestry.com. Source: National Archives microfilm series T1118 & T977. Muster Rolls are lists of the members of a specific military unit within militia, National Guard, regular army or navy, or volunteer army or navy. Usually these refer to a company, but they may also refer to a regiment, or to a special detachment, such as a band. For the early years, the Marine Corps rosters may have one particular marine listed once, showing his Name, Rank, Enlistment date, Muster roll date, and Station (Ship, Base, etc.), all under the name-designation of the unit to which he was assigned; later rosters may have a person listed several times for different events taking place during his tour of duty, e.g., promotions, change of duty or venue, training school attendance, etc. Officers assigned to the unit are listed first, followed by the enlisted members. This database has 39,841,896 records, see www.ancestry.com/search/collections/1089.

- See also, *Muster Rolls of the Marine Corps, 1798-1937* **[Online Database],** digitized and indexed at FamilySearch.org. Source: National Archives microfilm series T1118, 1798-1892, 123 rolls; and T977, 1893-1940, 460 rolls. The muster rolls from T1118, 1798-1892 have been indexed. Those from T977 are not complete in this publication. The records are arranged chronologically by month, then by post, station, or ship. See www.familysearch.org/search/collection/1916228.

1798-1914. *U.S. Army, Register of Enlistments* **[Online Database].** Digitized and indexed at the Ancestry.com website. The Regular Army is comprised of career soldiers and maintained through peacetime. Therefore, this database will not usually include individuals who enlisted as part of a reserve, during wartime for limited periods of time, or in a military unit raised by a state. Data in these registers was compiled from a variety of other military records, including enlistment papers, muster rolls, and unit records. Information listed on these records includes: Name of enlistee, Age at time of enlistment, Birthplace, Date of enlistment, Enlistment place, Occupation, Physical description (eye color, hair color, complexion, and height), Rank, company, and regiment, Date and cause of discharge, and Remarks. Some of this information is only viewable at the register image. Also, the register images are usually two pages long, viewed side-by-side. These records are arranged chronologically and alphabetically by first letter of the surname. This database has 1,378,006 records, see http://search.ancestry.com/search/db.aspx?dbid=1198.

1798-1914 Registers of Enlistments in the U.S. Army **[Online Database],** indexed at the FamilySearch.org website. Images and index of men who enlisted in the United States Army, 1798-1914. The registers may provide all or part of the following information: name, rank, regiment, company commander, regimental commander, height, weight, color of eyes, hair, complexion, age, occupation, county or state of birth, date and place of enlistment, miscellaneous remarks. Additional records include Indian Scouts, Philippine Scouts, Hospital Stewards, and Records of Prisoners. This database has 1,401,585 records. See www.familysearch.org/search/collection/1880762.

1798-1937 U.S. Marine Corps Muster Rolls **[Online Database]**, digitized and indexed at the Ancestry.com website. Information in the database includes a Name, Rank, Enlistment date, Muster date, and Station. This roll was used as the basis for pay due the marines. Names of commissioned officers were listed first, followed by names of noncommissioned officers and then privates. Shown on the form are the date and place of enlistment of each individual, by whom enrolled and for what period of time. Remarks might contain a "record of events" column describing the activities engaged in by the unit. This database has 5,794,949 records. See
http://search.ancestry.com/search/db.aspx?dbid=1089.

1800-1900 Revolutionary War Pension Files **(Online Database]**, digitized and indexed at the FamilySearch.org website. This collection includes an estimated 80,000 pension and bounty-land warrant application files based on the participation of American military, naval, and marine officers, and enlisted men in the Revolutionary War. The records in this collection include entire pension files for soldiers and sailors who served in the Revolutionary War. The size of the files range from a handful of pages to hundreds of pages. Unlike Selected Records, which were typically chosen subjectively for genealogical content, these records reveal more details about each veteran's history and service, as well as more information about his family, state of health, and life after the war. If you know the state for which a man served, you can locate him through the alphabetical hierarchy in the browse menu. Select the state, the first letter of his last name, then locate his surname, followed by his given name. This database has 6,959,032 records. See
https://familysearch.org/search/collection/1417475.
- see also, *U.S., Revolutionary War Pension and Bounty-Land Warrant Application Files, 1800-1900* **[Online Database]**, digitized and indexed at Ancestry.com. This database has 83,050 records, see www.ancestry.com/search/collections/1995.

1800-1908. U.S. Military and Naval Academies, Cadet Records and Applications **[Online Database]**, digitized and indexed at the Ancestry.com website. Source: Application papers and Registers of the US Military Academy, West Point, NY; and US Naval Academy, Annapolis, MD; now at the National Archives. Each index record includes: Name, Year, Volume, Record set, and Location. The document images have more information about a person. This database has 124,311 records. See
http://search.ancestry.com/search/db.aspx?dbid=1299.

1800-2010. RootsWeb Cemetery Index **[Online Database]**, indexed at the Ancestry.com website. This database is also accessible at the RootsWeb site. Each index record includes: Name, Death date, Burial place, Cemetery, and a link to the RootsWeb site. This database has 886,303 records. Archived at
https://web.archive.org/web/20160415014826/http://search.ancestry.com/search/db.aspx?dbid=9192.

1800s-Current. Newspapers.com Obituary Index **[Online Database]**, indexed at Ancestry.com. Newspapers.com™ is a separate genealogical feature, operated by Ancestry.com. This database consists of facts extracted from obituaries found on Newspapers.com™ dating from the early 1800's to current. Details present may include: Name of the deceased, Gender of the deceased, Birth date and place and/or age at death, Marriage date and place, Death and/or burial date, Residence and/or death place, Obituary date and place, Names of parents, spouse, children, and/or siblings, and other original publication details This database is presented as an index only, with a link to the digitized page on Newspapers.com™. Clicking on the link will open the image on the Newspapers.com™ site, which may require an additional upgrade or subscription. The source of the original data is included with each entry. This database has 835,278,762 records, see
www.ancestry.com/search/collections/61843.

1801-1872. U.S., Revolutionary War Pensioners, 1801-1815, 1818-1872 **[Online Database]**, digitized and indexed at Ancestry.com. Source: National Archives microfilm series M1786 (1801-1815) and T718 (1818-1872). This database contains Treasury Department pension payment records for payments made semiannually from 1801 to 1872. Entries contain: Name of pensioner, Name of veteran, and name and location of pension agency though which payment was made. When an heir or legal representative claimed an unpaid balance due the pensioner at the time of death, the date of death of the pensioner is given and the date of the final payment made to the family or heirs. Additional information such as rank of veteran, amount of monthly or half yearly allowance, and quarter and year of last payment, may also be listed on the record. This database has 216,962 records, see www.ancestry.com/search/collections/1116.

- See also, *U.S. Pensioners, 1818-1872* [Online Database], digitized and indexed at the Ancestry.com website. This database contains Treasury Department pension payment records for payments made semiannually from 1818-1871. See http://search.ancestry.com/search/db.aspx?dbid=1116.

- See also, *Revolutionary War Pension Payment Ledgers, 1818-1872* [Online Database], digitized at the FamilySearch.org website. Images of pension payment ledgers created by the Treasury Department to record semiannual payments to veterans and widows of the Revolutionary War from 1818-1872. A few records for the War of 1812 are also included. A coverage table for localities and dates can be found under User Guidance. Click the Learn More link to access this table and more information regarding how to use this collection. This collection is from Record Group 217, Records of the Accounting Officers of the Department of the Treasury and is National Archive Microfilm publication T718. This database has 8,955 images. See https://familysearch.org/search/collection/2069831.

1801-1900. *Search Historical Books* [Online Database], digitized and indexed at the GenealogyBank.com website, over 14,250 book titles, all published before 1900. See www.genealogybank.com/gbnk/books.

1804-1984. *U.S., County and Regional Histories and Atlases* [Online Database], indexed at the Ancestry.com website. Source: Gale County and Regional Histories and Atlases Collection. Detroit, Michigan: Gale Research Company. This image only database contains more than 2,200 volumes of county and regional histories from eight states: California, Illinois, Indiana, Michigan, New York, Ohio, Pennsylvania, and Wisconsin. Most of the books are from the mid to late 19th or early 20th century. In them you will find history, biographical sketches, maps, business notices, statistics and population numbers, pictures, descriptions of industry and business, stories of early settlement and pioneers, colleges and universities, military history, geography, and plenty of other details. Browse the collection, organized by state, then title of the history book. See http://search.ancestry.com/search/db.aspx?dbid=4078.

1806-1916 *U.S. Returns from Military Posts* [Online Database], digitized and indexed at the Ancestry.com website. Army Regulations stipulated that every post was to submit a return to the Adjutant General, usually at monthly intervals. The returns showed the units stationed at each post; the strength of each unit; names and duties of the officers; number present and absent; listing of official communications received, and record of events. While most of the records in this collection consist of monthly post returns, some additional records, such as morning reports, field returns, rosters of officers, and other related papers, have been mixed in. These additional records provide supplemental information or act as substitutes for missing returns. Records are available for military posts in all 50 states, Washington D.C., Cuba, Panama Canal Zone, Philippine Islands, Puerto Rico, Canada, China, and Mexico. This database has 3,993,758 records, see http://search.ancestry.com/search/db.aspx?dbid=1571.

1812-1815. *War of 1812 Pension Files* [Online Database], digitized and indexed at the Fold3.com website. The documents in this collection include full pension application files for soldiers and sailors who served in the War of 1812, as well as for their widows and children, or other heirs. The first applications were filed by servicemen who were disabled as a result of their service, or by widows who lost a husband in the war. See www.fold3.com/title_761/war_of_1812_pension_files.

1812-1815. *U.S., War of 1812 Service Records* [Online Database], digitized and indexed at Ancestry.com, from the original records at the National Archives, filmed as series M602. Each record includes the soldier's name, company, rank at time of induction, rank at time of discharge, This database has 582,266 records, see www.ancestry.com/search/collections/4281.

- See also, *United States War of 1812 Index to Service Record, 1812-1815* [Online Database], digitized at the FamilySearch.org website. Military service records for the War of 1812 are comprised of cards created from muster, pay, receipt and other rolls for soldiers and sailors who served in the war. The information includes name, service dates, terms of service, monthly pay, where they served, and notes of interest. This database came from Fold3 and has 622,984 images. See https://familysearch.org/search/collection/1916219.

1812-1910. *War of 1812 Index to Pension Application Files* [Online Database], digitized and indexed at the FamilySearch.org website. Name index and images of the jacket-envelope that contains the pension application files located in the National Archives. The envelope will provide soldier name and military service information as well as widow name and pension and bounty land numbers. This collection is part of Records of the Veterans Administration, National Archives Microfilm publication M313. This database has 91,259 records. See
www.familysearch.org/search/collection/1834325.
- See also, *War of 1812 Pension Application Files Index, 1812-1815* [Online Database], digitized and indexed at Ancestry.com. This database has 90,807 records, see
www.ancestry.com/search/collections/1133.

1812-1934. *Registers of Patients at Naval Hospitals* [Online Database], indexed at the Ancestry.com website. Dept of Navy records at the National Archives. This database contains registers of patients on ships and at Navy and Marine Corps hospitals and dispensaries. They vary in form and content but usually list the patient's name, rate or rank, age, birthplace, and the disease or injury and the disposition of the case (discharge to duty or another hospital; discharge for disability; or death). Later volumes include case numbers. Registers are included for sites both in and outside the United States. This database has 296,830 records. See
http://search.ancestry.com/search/db.aspx?dbid=9268.

1814-1992. *U.S. Navy and Marine Corps Registries* [Online Database], digitized and indexed at Ancestry.com. Original data: U.S., Navy and Marine Corps Registries, 1814-1992. Navy Department Library - Naval History and Heritage Command, Washington, D.C. This collection includes registers of officers of the US Navy and Marine Corps. Each index record includes: Name, Rank, and Ship or Station. Because this collection uses OCR technology, Ancestry.com encourages users to correct any errors found in the data by going to the image and editing the name in the correction panel at the bottom of the page. This database has 10,476,374 records, see
www.ancestry.com/search/collections/60656.

1815-1858. *U.S. Army Indian Campaign Service Records Index* [Online Database], digitized and indexed at Ancestry.com. Source: National Archives microfilm series M243, M256, M629, M907 & M908. This database contains alphabetical card indexes to compiled service records of Volunteer soldiers who:
- Belonged to units from Alabama and served during the Cherokee disturbances and removal, 1836-1839
- Belonged to units from Georgia and served during the Cherokee disturbances and removal, 1836-1839
- Belonged to units from North Carolina and served during the Cherokee disturbances and removal, 1836-1839
- Belonged to units from Tennessee or the Volunteer Field and Staff of the Army of the Cherokee Nation and served during the Cherokee disturbances and removal, 1836-1839
- Served in various Indian wars or participated in the quelling or solving of Indian disturbances or problems, 1815-1858
The "Cherokee disturbances and removal" are often referred to in these records as the Cherokee war. Each index card provides the following information: Name of the soldier, His rank, Unit in which served, and Name of the war or disturbance in which served. There are cross-reference cards for soldiers' names that appear in the records under more than one spelling. This database has 111,013 records, see
www.ancestry.com/search/collections/61592.

1815-1869 Freedmen's Bureau Marriages [Online Database], digitized and indexed at the FamilySearch.org website, this database consists of unbound marriage certificates, marriage licenses, monthly reports of marriage, and other proofs of marriages, as part of the records of the Bureau of Refugees, Freedmen, and Abandoned Lands, compiled between 1861 and 1872. This database has 7,796 records. See
https://familysearch.org/search/collection/1414908.

1815-1926 Old War Pension Index [Online Database], digitized and indexed at the FamilySearch.org website. This is a card index at the National Archives for service in the Regular Army, Navy or Marine Corps between 1783 and 1861. Taken from the National Archives microfilm, series T316. This database has 28,984 records. See
https://familysearch.org/search/collection/1979425.

1815-2011. *U.S. GenealogyBank Historic Newspaper Marriages* [Online Database], digitized and indexed at FamilySearch.org. Index to marriages from thousands of historic newspapers throughout the United States. Records are being published as they become available. This database has 16,335 records, see
www.familysearch.org/search/collection/2603807.

1815-2011. U.S. GenealogyBank Newspaper Obituaries [Online Database], digitized and indexed at FamilySearch.org. Index and images of obituaries from thousands of newspapers throughout the United States. Records and images are being published as they become available. This database has 1,567,543 records: www.familysearch.org/search/collection/2860782.

1818-1864 Final Payment Vouchers Index – Military Pensions [Online Database], digitized and indexed at the Fold3.com website. Pension payment records are not typically found in pension application files. These cards were created as an index for the final payments made to either the veteran or his widow. They provide additional details on where a family may have moved in the early to mid-19th century, death dates of veterans, widows, or dependent children, and sometimes the maiden name of a widow. This database has 68,769 records. See www.fold3.com/title_654/final_payment_vouchers_index_for_military.

1818-1919. U.S. and U.K., Quaker Published Memorials [Online Database], digitized and indexed at Ancestry.com. This database contains memorial volumes with death dates and other details for members of the Society of Friends (Quakers) from both the U.S. and the UK. Memorial books contain obituary information on prominent Quakers who have died. Some entries simply include the name, age, and death date; while others provide short biographical sketches that can be rich in personal detail. The database includes memorials from the *Annual Monitor* (London), the *American Annual Monitor*, a series entitled *Piety Promoted*, and memorials of deceased Friends published by various Yearly Meetings, located at three Quaker colleges (Swarthmore, PA; Guilford College, Greensboro, NC; and Haverford College, PA). This database has 55,135 records, see www.ancestry.com/search/collections/2581.

1820-1874 Index to Passenger Arrivals, Atlantic and Gulf Ports [Online Database], digitized and indexed at the FamilySearch.org website, a card index to passengers arriving at 70 ports along the Atlantic and Gulf Coast (New York excluded). Taken from the National Archives originals, Washington, DC. This database has 1,023,459 records. See https://familysearch.org/search/collection/1921756.

1820-1880. Dutch Immigrants to America [Online Database], digitized and indexed at Ancestry.com. Source: *Immigrants to America,* by Robert P. Swierenga, The information was extracted from the National Archives passenger lists of ships arriving at various Atlantic and Gulf ports. The list includes vessels disembarking at Baltimore, Boston, New Orleans, New York, Philadelphia, and other smaller ports. The passenger lists used in this compilation includes approximately 100,000 separate ship manifests. Each index record includes a name; gender; age; occupation; last residence; port of embarkation; port of arrival; date of arrival; intended destination; family status; National Archives microfilm series number; National Archive microfilm roll number; name of vessel. This database has 56,306 records, see www.ancestry.com/search/collections/7914.

1820-1908 Bureau of Land Management Tract Books [Online Database], digitized at the FamilySearch.org website. 3,907 tract books containing official records of the land status and transactions involving surveyed public lands arranged by state and then by township and range. These books indicate who obtained the land and include a physical description of the tract and where the land is located. The type of transaction is also recorded such as cash entry, credit entry, homesteads, patents (deeds) granted by the Federal Government, and other conveyances of title such as Indian allotments, internal improvement grants (to states), military bounty land warrants, private land claims, railroad grants, school grants, and swamp grants. Additional items of information included in the tract books are as follows: number of acres, date of sale, purchase price, land office, entry number, final Certificate of Purchase number, and notes on relinquishments and conversions. Original documents are located at the Bureau of Land management in Springfield, Virginia. This database has 942,374 images. See www.familysearch.org/search/collection/2074276.

1821-1916 U.S. Returns from Regular Army Infantry Regiments [Online Database], digitized and indexed at the Ancestry.com website. This database primarily contains monthly returns from U.S. Regular Army infantry regiments received by the Adjutant General's Office from June 1821 to December 1916. It also includes other forms and correspondence filed with these returns. The Regular Army monthly returns reported on the strength of each regiment, including total numbers of men present, absent, sick, or on extra daily duty, as well as giving a report of officers and some categories of enlisted men by name. Later returns included an accounting of strength in terms of horses and artillery. These records can be searched by name, year, and regiment. They can be browsed by regiment or year. Forms changed several times over the years, so

the information recorded about regiments and individuals varies. This database has 3,413,553 records, see
http://search.ancestry.com/search/db.aspx?dbid=2229.

1821-1923. *U.S., High School Student Lists* **[Online Database],** digitized and indexed at the Ancestry.com website. Source: American Antiquarian Society, Worcester, MA. This database contains a variety of publications listing the names of students, faculty, alumni, and others associated primarily with preparatory and similar schools, including academies, high schools, seminaries, reform schools, institutes, industrial schools, military academies, dance schools, grammar schools, Latin schools, and others. Some of these institutions evolved from a high school to university level. The majority of the books are from the 19th century. They come from 35 states, plus Washington, D.C. Most are from the New England area, though there are volumes from Ohio, California, Hawaii, New Mexico, and even a few volumes for schools in other countries. Each index record includes: Name, Publication year, Publication state, School name, Residence, and Title. The document images may include more information. This database has 645,940 records. See
http://search.ancestry.com/search/db.aspx?dbid=2395.

1988 Colorado Springs Directory

1822-1995. *U.S. City Directories* **[Online Database],** digitized and OCR indexed at the Ancestry.com website. This database is a collection of directories for U.S. cities and counties in various years. The database currently contains directories for all states except Alaska. Each index record includes: Name, Gender, Spouse, and Publication title (and state, city, year of publication). This database has 1.56 billion records.
http://search.ancestry.com/search/db.aspx?dbid=2469.

1822-2012. *U.S. Index to Quaker Obituary Notices* **[Online Database],** digitized and indexed at Ancestry.com. This Haverford College Quaker Collection contains an index of death notices and obituaries from Quaker periodicals, dating from the 1820s. The titles of those periodicals are listed below. Some titles changed over time as they merged with others and acquired different editorial staff.
- *The American Friend,* 1894-1960 (Five Years Meeting, Orthodox)
- *Evangelical Friend,* 1905-1914, 1929-1994 (Ohio)
- *Friend Bulletin,* 1934-2008 (Pacific Yearly Meeting)
- *Friends Weekly Intelligencer,* 1844-1853 (Philadelphia, Pa.- Hicksite)
- *Friends Intelligencer,* 1853-1885 (Philadelphia, Pa.)
- *Friends Intelligencer and Journal,* 1888-1901 (Philadelphia, Pa.)
- *Friends Intelligencer,* 1902-1955 (Philadelphia, Pa.)
- *Friends Review,* 1848-1894 (Philadelphia, Pa.)
- Friends Journal, 1955-2012 (Philadelphia, Pa.)
- Quaker Life, 1960-2012 (Friends United Meeting, Indiana)
- *Western Friend,* 2008-2012 (Pacific, North Pacific & Intermountain Yearly Meetings)

Each index card typically includes Name of the deceased, birth, and death years (where available), and the title of the periodical the death notice appeared in, including page number. If you are interested in requesting a copy of the original entry contact Special Collections at Haverford College Magill Library. They offer some research and copying services. For more information, visit their website. Most entries in periodicals include the name of the meeting attended by the deceased and may include internment information. This database has 79,196 records, see
www.ancestry.com/search/collections/5349.

1825-1889. *U.S., Naval Hospital Tickets and Case Papers* **[Online Database],** digitized and indexed at Ancestry.com. Source: National Archives Record Group 52, ARC ID 2694723. This database is a collection of U.S. Navy hospital tickets, medical case papers, and similar documents. "Hospital tickets" requested that men be transferred from ships or stations to hospitals for treatment. "Case papers" describe hospital treatment and a history of the case. These records include the Civil War and both sailors and

Marines. They also refer to hospitals both stateside and abroad. Hospital tickets and case papers can include the following details: Name of the patient, Rate or rank, Age, Nativity, Date, and place of shipping abroad, Medical history, Present diagnosis, and List of clothing. Use the Browse this Collection to select a specific hospital. This database has 107,683 records: www.ancestry.com/search/collections/2999.

1830-1848. *Membership of The Church of Jesus Christ of Latter-day Saints* **[Online Database],** indexed at the Ancestry.com website. Source: 50 vol. set, same title, compiled by Susan Easton Black, publ. BYU Religious Studies Center, 1989. This database contains details extracted from membership records for the Church of Jesus Christ of Latter-day Saints for the years 1830–1848. Details vary depending on circumstances in the member's life, but they may include the following: name, gender, father, mother, spouse, names of children, birth, marriage, and death dates, residences, burial location, and church ordinances. This database has 104,231 records. See http://search.ancestry.com/search/db.aspx?dbid=5333.

1830-1875 Virginia Revolutionary War Pension Application Files **[Online Database],** digitized at the FamilySearch.org website. Records of the half pay pensions of Virginia soldiers and sailors based on service in the Revolutionary War. The Virginia General Assembly granted the payment of half pay for life to the state's military and naval officers and others who served until the end of the war in state units within the state's borders or in the Continental Army. This collection is part of Records of the Veterans Administration, NARA Microfilm publication M910. This database has 10,771 images. See https://familysearch.org/search/collection/2070137.

1832-1971. *U.S., Appointments of U. S. Postmasters* **[Online Database],** indexed at the Ancestry.com website. Source: National Archives microfilm series M841 (Records of the Post Office Dept). This database is a collection of 181 volumes of post office appointments and vacancies. The records show the date of establishment and discontinuance of post offices, changes of names of post offices, and names and appointment dates for their postmasters. The database also includes dates of Presidential appointments of postmasters and their confirmation dates by the Senate. Starting in 1870, the records contain names of post offices where discontinued post office's mail was sent. From 1832 until 1950, these records were kept by assistants to the Postmaster General. From 1950 to 1971, the Bureau of Post Office Operations compiled the records. Up to 1930, the records are arranged by location and then alphabetically by name of post office. After 1930, there are two types of records. They are arranged alphabetically by name of post office and alphabetically by the appointment's name. The records include: Name, Appointment date, Vacancy cause, Vacancy date, Post office location, State, County, and Volume. This database has 1,514,110 records. See http://search.ancestry.com/search/db.aspx?dbid=1932.

1834-1897 Russians to America Index **[Online Database],** digitized and indexed at the FamilySearch.org website. See https://familysearch.org/search/collection/2110813.

1835. *U.S., The Pension Roll of 1835* **[Online Database],** digitized and indexed at Ancestry.com. Original data: United States Senate. *The Pension Roll of 1835*. 4 vols. 1968 Reprint, with index. Baltimore: Genealogical Publishing Company, 1992. In 1834 and 1835, the U.S. Senate passed a series of resolutions requiring the Commissioner of Pensions to compile a list of the pensioners who were drawing military pensions for service in the Revolutionary War. Each listing included the pensioners name, "rank, annual allowance, the sums which they have severally received, the laws under which their pensions have been granted, the State or continental line in they which they served, the date when placed upon the roll, their ages [although age was not always given], and the States and Counties in which they severally reside." The date of the commencement of the pension was also noted, and there was also a field for remarks that in some cases included the pensioner's death date. In cases where the pension was transferred to a different state or if the residence was out of state. Pensioners were required to appear before a government agent to collect their pension. In cases where the distance was too great, or the pensioner too infirmed to travel, an agent, possibly a family member, could be engaged to appear in his stead, sometimes for a fee. Some states included the name of the agent or legal representatives. The volumes in this collection are broken down by state, then county, and surname. This database has 55,234 records, see www.ancestry.com/search/collections/60514.

1835-1974. *Reports of Deaths of American Citizens Abroad* **[Online Database],** digitized and indexed at the Ancestry.com website. This database was compiled from reports of deaths of U.S. citizens (non-military) collected by Consuls of the U.S. State Department. Each record may include: Place and date of record, Name of deceased, Occupation, Nativity (which may

include birth date and place), Last known address in the U.S., Date of death, Age, Place of death, Cause of death, Disposition of the remains, Names of friends and family members who were informed of the death, had a copy of the report sent to them, or was traveling or residing abroad with the deceased, and Miscellaneous remarks. The image of the report may include more details about the person. This database has 213,880 records. See
http://search.ancestry.com/search/db.aspx?dbid=1616.

1840. *A General Index to a Census of Pensioners for Revolutionary or Military Service, 1840, Containing All of the Names of Military Pensioners, Including the Head of the Household With Whom the Pensioner was Living in 1840, if Different, and a Page Reference to Find the Names in the* **Census [Printed Book, Microfilm & Digital Capture],** compiled from the original 1841 book by the Genealogical Society of Utah, published by Genealogical Publishing Co., Baltimore, MD, 1965, 382 pages, FHL book 973 X2pc index. The 1965 edition of this index did not include all information from the original edition. The first publication of this index was printed for the Census Office in 1841 by printers Blair and Rivis, Washington, DC. Copies of the original index are rare and found today at only a few libraries, such as the Library of Congress. The first known reprint of the index was done in 1949, and includes the original title, *A Census of Pensioners .. with their Names, Ages, and Places of Residence, as Returned by the Marshals of the Several Judicial Districts Under the Act for Taking the Sixth Census.* The reprint was in two volumes, Vol. 1, A-L; Vol. 2, Mc-Z, FHL book 973 X2pc 1840. Also on microfilm, FHL film #899835. To access the digital images, see the online FHL catalog:
www.familysearch.org/search/catalog/282860.

1840s-2000s. *U.S., Western States Marriage Index* **[Online Database],** indexed at the FamilySearch.org website. This is a marriage index to over 700,000 marriage entries from county records in 12 western states: Alaska, Arizona, California, Colorado, Idaho, Montana, Nevada, New Mexico, Oregon, Utah, Washington, and Wyoming. This index was created by volunteers at Brigham Young University-Idaho and the Snake River Family History Center. See
www.familysearch.org/search/collection/1854302.

1842-1947. *U.S., Evangelical Free Church of America, Swedish American Church Records* **[Online Database],** digitized and indexed at Ancestry.com. Original data: Archives of the Evangelical Free Church of America. Swedish American Baptisms, Marriages, Deaths, and Burials. Minneapolis, MN, USA. Indexes have been provided for baptisms, marriages, burials, and membership records (arrivals, dismissals, and member lists), as well as congregational histories, meeting minutes, and biographical files of church leaders. The member lists in particular have a wealth of information, including vital dates and emigration information. Some member lists may include the location in Sweden an individual or family was originally from. Records are mainly written in English or Swedish. This database has 7,854 records, see
www.ancestry.com/search/collections/61616.

1845-1920. *U.S., Published Quaker Family Histories* **[Online Database],** digitized at Ancestry.com. This is an image-only database. Source: Friends Historical Library, Swarthmore College, PA. Use the Browse This Collection feature to scan through the contents list. This database has 17,950 records, see
www.ancestry.com/search/collections/34683.

1846-1848. *United States Mexican War Index and Service Records* **[Online Database],** indexed at the FamilySearch.org website. Military service records for the Mexican War (1846-1848) are comprised of cards created from muster, pay, receipt and other rolls for soldiers and sailors who served in the war. The information includes name, service dates, terms of service, monthly pay, where they served, and notes. This database has 211,909 images. See
https://familysearch.org/search/collection/1987567.

***1846-1851 Passengers Arriving in New York from Ireland* [Online Database],** digitized and indexed at the MyHeritage.com website. The Center for Immigration Research (CIR) at the Balch Institute created this series to promote access to information about immigrants from Ireland to the United States during the era of the Irish Potato Famine, 1846-1851. It was extracted from ship passenger lists in the records of the U.S. Customs Service (NARA Record Group 36). Questions Asked: Name, Age, Town of Last Residence, Destination, Passenger Arrival Date, Codes Passenger's Sex, Occupation, Literacy, Native Country, Transit Status, Travel Compartment Passenger, Port of embarkation, Identification Number for the Ship Manifest, Other Voyages (of the Ship), and Passenger List (for that voyage on that ship). This database identifies 604,596 persons who arrived in the Port of New York, 1846-1851, the years of the Irish Potato Famine. After locating a name of a person of interest, the database can be searched for the passenger list for one ship, allowing a researcher to locate other possible family members. See
www.myheritage.com/research/collection-10031/passengers-arriving-in-new-york-from-ireland-1846-1851.

1846-1851 Famine Irish Passenger Index **[Online Database],** digitized and indexed at the FamilySearch.org website. Records for passengers who arrived at the Port of New York during the Irish Famine 1846-1851. Created by the Balch Institute for Ethnic Studies, Center for Immigration Research. This database has 604,596 records. See
www.familysearch.org/search/collection/2110821.

1846-1923 Mormon Battalion Pension Applications **[Online Database],** digitized and indexed at the FamilySearch.org website. This database is for Mexican War pension files for the 500 members of The Mormon Battalion. The files are arranged in alphabetical order by the name of the veteran. Index courtesy of Fold3. This database has 26,830 records.
https://familysearch.org/search/collection/1852758.

1846-1867. *Freeman's Bureau Marriage Records* **[Online Database],** digitized and indexed at Ancestry.com. Source: National Archives microfilm series M1875. The Bureau of Refugees, Freedmen, and Abandoned Lands, also known as the Freedman's Bureau, was established in the War Department by an act of Congress on March 3, 1865. The Bureau was responsible for the supervision and management of all matters relating to refugees and freedmen, and of lands abandoned or seized during the Civil War. While the Bureau's mission was to provide relief and help freedmen become self-sufficient, it also solemnized marriages that freedmen had entered into during slavery where the state or other local agencies made no provisions for such an act for persons of color. This database contains Freedmen Bureau marriages that were recorded from 1861-1869. Record types include marriage certificates, marriage licenses, monthly reports of marriages, and other proofs of marriage. Information available on these records may vary from state to state and between record types. However, the following is a list of the type of information that may be found among these records: Names of the bride and groom, Ages of the bride and groom, Date of marriage, Where married, By whom married, Number of male and female children, Color of bride and groom, and Complexion of parents. States represented in this collection are Alabama, Arkansas, Delaware, District of Columbia, Florida, Kentucky, Louisiana, Mississippi, Missouri, South Carolina, Tennessee, and Virginia. This database has 9,613 records, see
www.ancestry.com/search/collections/1231.

1847 - Current. *U.S., Cemetery and Funeral Home Collection* **[Online Database],** indexed at the Ancestry.com website The collection contains recent cemetery and funeral home records. In addition to names, dates, and places of birth, marriage, and death, these records may even suggest other documentation of an individual's death - a death certificate in another county because the hospital was located there; church or cemetery records (by identifying the place of burial or the officiating minister); or records of a coroner's inquest because the death was sudden or unexpected. This database has 53,612,283 records, see
www.ancestry.com/search/collections/2190.
- See also, *U.S., Cemetery Index from Selected States, 1847-2010* **[Online Database],** This collection of cemetery records was compiled by NamesInStone.com. The majority of records are from Utah. Records typically contain an individual's name, birth year, death year, and the name and location of the cemetery. This database has 354,365 records, see
www.ancestry.com/search/collections/60940.

1848-1934. *U.S., Civil War and Later Wars Index to Remarried Widow Pension Applications* **[Online Database],** digitized and indexed at Ancestry.com. Source: National Archives microfilm series M1785. This database features a card index to pension claims made by widows of veterans of the Civil War and later wars. The cards typically include the name of the claimant, name of the soldier, military unit, the widow's certificate number, date of the claim/filing, and remarks. This database has 105,725 records, see
www.ancestry.com/search/collections/2402.

1850. *U.S. Federal Census, Slave Schedules* **[Online Database],** digitized and indexed at FamilySearch.org. Name index and images of slave schedules listing names of slave owners, and their (usually unnamed) slaves by age, gender, and color. This was the first time that slave information was captured as a separate schedule. There are Slave Schedules only for the slave-holding states of Alabama, Arkansas, Delaware, District of Columbia, Florida, Georgia, Kentucky, Louisiana, Maryland, Mississippi, Missouri, New Jersey, North Carolina, South Carolina, Tennessee, Texas, Utah, and Virginia. This database has 3,587,571 records, see
www.familysearch.org/search/collection/1420440.

1850-1885. *U.S. Federal Census Mortality Schedules* **[Online Database],** digitized and indexed at Ancestry.com. Source: National Archives collections for each state, 1850-1880; and 3 states for 1885. Part of the U.S. Federal Censuses from 1850-1880 included a mortality schedule enumerating the individuals who had died in the previous year. Because each of the

censuses from 1850-1880 began on June 1, "previous year" refers to the 12 months preceding June 1, or June 1 (of the previous year) to May 31 (of the census year). This database contains an index to individuals enumerated in these mortality schedules. In addition, each individual is linked to the census image on which they appear. Not all information that is recorded on the actual census is included in the index. Questions asked in the mortality schedules: Deceased's name, Sex, Age, Color (White, black, mulatto), Whether widowed, Place of birth (state, territory, or country), Month in which the death occurred, Profession, occupation, or trade, Disease or cause of death, Number of days ill, Parents' birthplaces (added in 1870), Place where disease was contracted and how long the deceased was a resident of the area (added in 1880). This database has 1,607,736 records, see
www.ancestry.com/search/collections/8756.

- See also, **U.S., Federal Census Mortality Schedules Index, 1850-1880** [Online Database], indexed at Ancestry.com. Source: Accelerated Indexing Systems, 1999 index. This database has 492,925 records, see www.ancestry.com/search/collections/3530.

- See also, **U.S. Federal Census, Mortality Schedules, 1850** [Online Database], digitized and indexed at FamilySearch.org. This is a name index and images of mortality schedules listing inhabitants of the United States who died between June 1849 and May 1850. This was the first time a mortality schedule was included with the general population census schedule. Searchable data and browse are available for the following: Alabama, Arkansas, Connecticut, Delaware, District of Columbia, Georgia, Illinois, Indiana, Iowa, Kentucky, Louisiana, Maine, Maryland, Massachusetts, Michigan, Mississippi, New Hampshire, New Jersey, New York, North Carolina, Ohio, South Carolina, Tennessee, Texas, Utah, and Virginia. This database has 257,789 records, see
www.familysearch.org/search/collection/1420441.

1850-1897 Germans to America Index [Online Database], digitized and indexed at the FamilySearch.org website. Includes data files relating to the immigration of Germans to the United States for arrivals 1850-1897. Created by the Balch Institute for Ethnic Studies, Center for Immigration Research. This database has 4,048,907 records. See
www.familysearch.org/search/collection/2110801.

1850-2010. U.S., Department of Veterans Affairs BIRLS Death File [Online Database], indexed at the Ancestry.com website. Original data: Beneficiary Identification Records Locator Subsystem (BIRLS) Death File. Washington, D.C.: U.S. Department of Veterans Affairs. This index contains birth and death dates for more than 14 million veterans and VA beneficiaries who died between the years 1850 and 2010. The majority of information in the index comes from the BIRLS Death File; however, the veteran's name has been added by cross-referencing the Social Security Number in the BIRLS Death File with the Social Security Death Index. This database has 14,465,014 records. See
http://search.ancestry.com/search/db.aspx?dbid=2441.

1851-2003. Historical Newspapers, Birth, Marriage, & Death Announcements [Online Database], digitized and indexed at the Ancestry.com website. This database is a collection of birth, marriage, and death announcements for the following years and major newspapers:
 - *The New York Times* (1851-2003)
 - *The Los Angeles Times* (1881-1985)
 - *The Boston Globe* (1872-1923)
 - *The Chicago Defender* (1921-1975)
 - *The Chicago Tribune* (1850-1985)
 - *The Hartford Courant* (1791-1942)
 - *The Washington Post* (1877-1990)
 - *The Atlanta Constitution* (1869-1929)

The newspaper announcements were digitized by Ancestry, then indexed with an OCR index. This database has 1,582,938 records. Archived at
https://web.archive.org/web/20110210170748/http://search.ancestry.com/search/db.aspx?dbid=50000.

1855-1891 Naval Enlistment Rendezvous [Online Database], digitized and indexed at the FamilySearch website. This database consists of enlistment registers of men who enlisted in the United States Navy from January 6, 1855 to August 8, 1891. The registers include name of naval rendezvous, name of sailor, date and term of enlistment, rating, previous naval service, place of birth, age, occupation, and personal description. Taken from the National Archives, Record Group 24, records of the Bureau of Naval Personnel. This database has 262,742 records. See
https://familysearch.org/search/collection/1825347.

1855-1900 Italians to America Index [Online Database], digitized and indexed at the FamilySearch.org website. Data files relating to the immigration of Italians to the United States for arrivals 1855-1900. Created by the Balch Institute for Ethnic Studies, Center for Immigration Research. This database has 845,368 records. See
www.familysearch.org/search/collection/2110811.

1857-1935. Israel, Index to Records from U.S. Consular Posts in Jerusalem, Jaffa, and Haifa [Online Database], digitized and indexed at Ancestry.com. Original data: National Archives,

Records of the Foreign Service Posts of the Department of State, 1788-1990. Few of the original records were indexed, and many were disposed of in 1950. After a survey of these records by members of the Jewish Genealogy Society of Greater Washington (JGSGW) in 1995, the volumes of records with the most significant genealogical material were indexed. Only those names assumed to be Jewish were included in the index. Records of genealogical value selected for indexing include: Birth, marriage, death, Probate and wills of American citizens, Records of passports issued, visas (required as of 1917) and related matters of immigration and naturalization, Registers of visitors, American citizens, and children born of American parents; Property disposal and settlement of estates, General correspondence and miscellaneous records concerning the protection of American citizens and their interests. This database has 9,107 records, see www.ancestry.com/search/collections/1470.

1860. *U.S. Federal Census, Slave Schedules* [Online Database], digitized and indexed at FamilySearch.org. Source: National Archives microfilm series M653. This is a name index and images of slave schedules listing names of slave owners, and their (usually unnamed) slaves by age, gender, and color. This was the first time that slave information was captured as a separate schedule. There are Slave Schedules only for the slave-holding states of Alabama, Delaware, the District of Columbia, Florida, Georgia, Kentucky, Louisiana, Maryland, Mississippi, Missouri, North Carolina, South Carolina, Tennessee, Texas, and Virginia. This database has 4,429,408 records, see www.familysearch.org/search/collection/3161105.

1860-1889. *U.S., Registers of Deaths in the Regular Army* [Online Database], digitized and indexed at Ancestry.com. Original data: *Registers of Deaths in the Regular Army, compiled 1860–1889.* 18 volumes. National Archives, Washington, D.C. This database contains death registers for U.S. Army Regulars. (Regulars were professional soldiers who served in the standing army, as opposed to volunteers, who were typically recruited for a specific conflict.) These registers were compiled by the Adjutant General's Office. They vary some by date, but they may list the following details: name, rank, unit, age, birthplace, length of service, date, place, and cause of death, and race or nationality. This database has 25,801 records, see www.ancestry.com/search/collections/2128.

1860-1918. *U.S., Indexed County Land Ownership Maps* [Online Database], digitized and indexed at the Ancestry.com website. This database contains approximately 1,200 U.S. county land ownership atlases from the Library of Congress' Geography and Maps division, covering the years 1860-1918. The original microfilms have recently been rescanned to improve image quality and legibility where possible. These maps can be searched by State, County, Year, and Owner's name. This database has 6,940,589 records. See http://search.ancestry.com/search/db.aspx?dbid=1127.

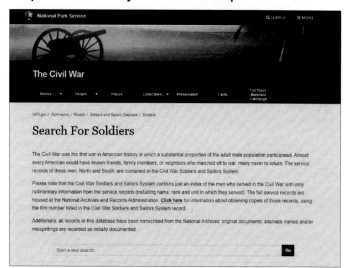

1861-1865. *Index to Soldiers & Sailors of the Civil War* [Online Database], a searchable name index to 6.3 million Union and Confederate Civil War soldiers is available online at the National Park Service website. A search can be done by surname, first name, state, or unit. Historians have determined that 4.3 million soldiers and sailors were in uniform during the Civil War, by both sides. The fact that this major database has 6.3 million soldier/sailor entries would seem to indicate that there are some duplicates. As it turns out, any soldier who used more than one name had more than one index card. And, if a soldier served with more than one unit, that soldier had an index card for each unit. See www.nps.gov/civilwar/search-soldiers.htm.

- See also, ***United States Civil War Soldiers Index, 1861-1865* [Online Database],** a searchable name index to 6.3 million Union and Confederate Civil War soldiers is available online at the FamilySearch website. Source: NPS database. The Index of soldiers who served in the Civil War, 1861-1865, was culled from 6.3 million soldier records in the General Index Cards to the Compiled Military Service Records at the National Archives. Each record provides the full name, regiment, whether Union or Confederate, the company, the soldier's rank, and sometimes alternate names. This database has 6,282,360 records: https://familysearch.org/search/collection/1910717.

- See also, ***U.S., Civil War Soldiers, 1861-1865* [Online Database],** indexed at Ancestry.com. This database has 6,261,619 records, see www.ancestry.com/search/collections/1138.

1861-1865 U.S. Civil War Soldier Records and Profiles **[Online Database],** digitized and indexed at the Ancestry.com website. This database has over 4.2 million soldier records, mostly culled from Adjutant General state lists rather from the General Index cards to Compiled Service Records. The numbers match with what historians say is the total number of soldiers who fought in the Civil War for both sides. Includes the interlinked records of 4,225,076 soldiers, 4,681 regimental rosters; 3,839 regimental chronicles, 1,010 officer profiles, 3,398 battle synopses, and 23,121 soldier photographs. The Ancestry.com version of this database is located online at:
http://search.ancestry.com/search/db.aspx?dbid=1555.

✓ **NOTE:** The *U.S. Civil War Soldier Records and Profiles* database at the Ancestry.com site was obtained from Historical Data Systems, Inc. of Duxbury, MA. Their interactive database goes by the name, *American Civil War Research Database*. Unlike the Ancestry version, the original database allows interaction with anyone wishing to add or correct information at any point. Profiles, or capsule biographies, are featured wherever they can be found, and users are encouraged to add biographies for an ancestor at this very affordable subscription site: **www.civilwardata.com**.

1861-1865. Compiled Service Records, Union & Confederate Soldiers **[Online Database].** This fully searchable database contains digitized images of the card abstracts of a soldier's Compiled Service Record, with information collected from original muster rolls, returns, rosters, payrolls, appointment books, hospital registers, prison registers and rolls, parole rolls, and inspection reports. Located at the Fold3.com site, both Union and Confederate records can be searched at one search screen. This database is the source of the Index to Soldiers and Sailors of the Civil War, online at the National Park Service and FamilySearch sites. That index found 6.3 million compiled service records. This database is made up of the images and includes a whole new index that can be compared with the earlier S&SCW index. See **www.fold3.com/category_19**.

1861-1865 Service Records of Confederate Soldiers **[Online Database],** digitized and indexed at the MyHeritage.com website. This index includes records from the Confederate government and the states of Alabama, Arkansas, Florida, Georgia, Kentucky, Louisiana, North Carolina, South Carolina, Tennessee, Texas, and Virginia. The records are card prison registers and rolls, parole rolls, inspection abstracts of original muster rolls, returns, rosters, payrolls, appointment books, hospital registers, Union reports, etc. A given soldier may have multiple documents. This database has 11,793,958 images. See
www.myheritage.com/research/collection-10027/service-records-of-confederate-soldiers.

1861-1865 Civil War Service Records of Confederate Soldiers **[Online Database],** digitized and indexed at the FamilySearch.org website. Confederate service records of soldiers who served in organizations raised by the Confederate Government. The records include a jacket-envelope for each soldier, labeled with his name, his rank, and the unit in which he served. The jacket-envelope typically contains card abstracts of entries relating to the soldier as found in original muster rolls, returns, rosters, payrolls, appointment books, hospital registers, Union prison registers and rolls, parole rolls, inspection reports; and the originals of any papers relating solely to the particular soldier. For each military unit, the service records are arranged alphabetically by the soldier's surname. The Military Unit field may also display the surname range (A-G) as found on the microfilm. This collection is a part of RG 109, War Department Collection of Confederate Records and is National Archive Microfilm Publication M258. Index courtesy of Fold3. See
https://familysearch.org/search/collection/1932383.
- See also, ***U.S., Union Soldiers Compiled Service Records, 1861-1865*** **[Online Database],** digitized and indexed at Ancestry.com. This database has 837,569 records, see
www.ancestry.com/search/collections/2344.
- See also, ***U.S., Confederate Soldiers Compiled Service Records, 1861-1865*** **[Online Database],** digitized and indexed at Ancestry.com. This database has 2,049,383 records, see
www.ancestry.com/search/collections/2322.

1861-1865 Confederate Navy and Marine Service Records **[Online Database],** digitized at the FamilySearch.org website. Records consist of card abstracts of vessel papers, pay rolls, muster rolls, hospital and prison records including documents relating to service in the Confederate Navy and Marine Corps. This is NARA microfilm publication M260 and is from Records Group 109 War Department Collection of Confederate Records. There are 21,519 images. See
www.familysearch.org/search/collection/2019254.

1861-1865 Civil War Prisoner of War Records **[Online Database],** digitized and indexed at the Ancestry.com website. This database contains records relating to Civil War Prisoners of War (POW). The database is comprised of four National Archives (NARA) microfilm series (M1303, M598, M2702, and M918). Microfilm series M1303 contains records relating to Federal or Union POWs that were held by Confederate authorities at Camp Sumter, Andersonville, Georgia between February 1864, and April 1865. Records contained in this series include: 1) Register of departures of prisoners from Andersonville. 2) Register of admittances to the prison hospital. 3) Register of prisoners confined at the prison hospital. 4) Register of prisoners' deaths and burials. 5) Burial lists of prisoners. 6) Lists of prisoners claiming reimbursement for money taken from them by Confederate authorities. 7) Consolidated monthly strength reports of prisoners. 8) Series of provision returns of the prison hospital. 9) Name index to the original hospital register of admittances. And 10) Partial name index to one of the burial lists. The register is generally organized alphabetically by name of prison or hospital and then alphabetically by name of the deceased. This database has 1,565,511 records, see http://search.ancestry.com/search/db.aspx?dbid=1124.

1861-1865 Records of Confederate Prisoners of War [Online Database], digitized at the FamilySearch.org website. This is an image-only database with images of 427 volumes of Confederate Prisoners of War records, most of which are from the War Department's Office of the Commissary General of Prisoners. Others are from the Surgeon General's Office, a few Army commands and individual prison camps. The collection consists mainly of lists and registers and is part of RG 109, War Department Collection of Confederate Records. This database has 51,108 images, see www.familysearch.org/search/collection/1916234.

1861-1865. U.S., Confederate Army Casualty Lists and Reports [Online Database], digitized and indexed at Ancestry.com. Source: National Archives microfilm series M836. Estimates of Confederate casualties (killed, wounded, and missing) during the Civil War range from 335,000 to 450,000 and even higher. This database includes lists and narrative reports reporting casualties sustained by Confederate Army units during the war. Records of casualties were submitted to the Confederate Office of the Adjutant and Inspector General so Confederate leadership could assess the strength of their forces. Records in this database are organized first by the state where an engagement took place and then by battle or engagement. The format of the documents varies, but they will typically include the date and name of and engagement and names, ranks and organization, and types of casualties. This database has 74,656 records, see www.ancestry.com/search/collections/2401.

- See also, ***United States, Register of Confederates and Civilians Who Died in the North, 1861-1865*** [Online Database], digitized and indexed at the FamilySearch.org website. Includes Confederate soldiers, sailors, and citizens who died in federal prisons and military hospitals in the North, 1861-1865. The register was compiled in 1912 in the Office of the Commissioner for Marking the Graves of Confederate Dead. The register is arranged by place of death then alphabetically by name. A table of contents will be found at the beginning of the volume. This database has 25,511 records. See https://familysearch.org/search/collection/2250054.

1861-1865 Civil War Confederate Papers of Citizens or Businesses [Online Database], digitized and indexed at the FamilySearch.org website. Approximately 650,000 vouchers and documents pertaining to goods and services rendered to the Confederate Government by individuals and businesses. The collection is arranged alphabetically in over 350,000 jackets. The collection is located in RG 109, War Department Collection of Confederate Records and is National Archive Microfilm Publication M346. Index courtesy of Fold3. This database has 2,040,863 records. See https://familysearch.org/search/collection/1937233.

1861-1865 U.S. Colored Troops Military Service Records [Online Database], digitized and indexed at the Ancestry.com website. This database contains compiled military service records for United States Colored Troops that volunteered to serve with the Union in the American Civil War. Though some African-American units had been raised and seen fighting prior to this, President Lincoln did not authorize the use of colored troops in combat until 1863, after the Emancipation Proclamation. The Bureau of Colored Troops was established by the United States War Department in May 1863 and was responsible for recruiting African-American soldiers to fight. About 175 regiments composed of 178,000 African-American troops served the Union in the final two years of the Civil War. See http://search.ancestry.com/search/db.aspx?dbid=1107.

- See also, ***US, African American Civil War Sailor Index, 1861-1865*** [Online Database], digitized and indexed at Ancestry.com. Source: National Park Service. This database has 68,536 records, see www.ancestry.com/search/collections/9748.

1861-1865 Official Records of the Union and Confederate Armies **[Online Database],** digitized and indexed at the Ancestry.com website. This database contains the 70-volume printed collection of official records of the Union and Confederate Armies from the American Civil War. Examples of record topics covered in this collection includes: 1) Formal reports. 2) Operations. 3) Correspondence. 4) Orders, and 5) Returns. This database has 113,833 records, see http://search.ancestry.com/search/db.aspx?dbid=1203.

1861-1865 Civil War Records of Confederate Non-regiment Soldiers **[Online Database],** digitized and indexed at the FamilySearch.org website, this is a database of Confederate service records of general and staff officers and non-regimental enlisted men who did not serve in any particular regiment, company or special corps. The records include a jacket-envelope for each soldier, labeled with his name, rank, and unit in which he served. Each record typically contains card abstracts of entries relating to the soldier as found in original muster rolls, returns, rosters, payrolls, appointment books, hospital registers, Union prison registers and rolls, parole rolls, inspection reports; and the originals of any papers relating solely to the particular soldier. For each military unit, the service records are arranged alphabetically by the soldier's surname. Taken from the National Archives microfilm, series M331. Index courtesy of Fold3, this database has 498,640 records. See
https://familysearch.org/search/collection/1932377.

1861-1865 Confederated Officers Card Index **[Online Database],** digitized at the FamilySearch.org website, consists of images of index cards of Confederate Officers acquired from the Military Order of the Stars and Bars. This database has 207,550 images. See https://familysearch.org/search/collection/2145147.

1861-1865. U.S., Registers of Deaths of Volunteers **[Online Database],** indexed at the Ancestry.com website. Source: Adjutant General's records at the National Archives. This database contains registers listing volunteer Union soldiers who died during the Civil War. Registers were compiled by the Adjutant General's Office and list soldiers from the following states: Connecticut, Illinois, Indiana, Iowa, Kentucky, Maine, Massachusetts, Michigan, Missouri, New Hampshire, New Jersey, New York, Ohio, Pennsylvania, Vermont, and Wisconsin. There are also separate registers of colored troops. Records are grouped by state of enlistment and then alphabetically by first letter of the surname; names within each letter group are listed chronologically. The registers list Name, Rank, Company, Date of death, Place of death, Cause of death, and Remarks (these often name the attending surgeon). These records include soldiers killed in the Sultana steamboat disaster. This database has 249,612 records. See
http://search.ancestry.com/search/db.aspx?dbid=2123.

1861-1865. U.S., Civil War Roll of Honor **[Online Database].** Original data: Quartermaster General's Office. Roll of Honor. Names of Soldiers Who Died in Defense of the American Union. Volumes VIII-XXVII. Washington, D.C.: Government Printing Office, 1867. This database contains the names of over 203,000 deceased Civil War soldiers interred in U.S. cemeteries. Records in this database are organized first by volume and then by burial place. It may contain the following information: Name of soldier, Age, Death date, Burial place, Cemetery, Rank, and Regiment. This database has 203,022 records, see
www.ancestry.com/search/collections/61388.

1861-1865 Civil War Unfiled Papers of Confederate Soldiers **[Online Database],** digitized and indexed at the FamilySearch.org website, this database consists of unfiled papers and slips of Confederate service records of soldiers that were not interfiled in the compiled service records: card abstracts of entries relating to the soldier as found in original muster rolls, returns, rosters, payrolls, appointment books, hospital registers, Union prison registers and rolls, parole rolls, inspection reports; and the originals of any papers relating solely to the particular soldier. Taken from the National Archives microfilm, series M347. The index by Fold3, this database has 924,845 records. See
https://familysearch.org/search/collection/1932387.

1861-1866 Union Provost Marshal Files of Individual Civilians **[Online Database],** digitized at the FamilySearch.org website. The U.S. Provost Marshal served as military police for the Union Army. Records in this collection deal with deserters, Confederate spies, civilians suspected of disloyalty, civilian passage through military zones, etc. Taken from the National Archives publication M345. This database has 502,960 records. See
https://familysearch.org/search/collection/1834304.
- See also, *U.S., Union Provost Marshal Files of Individual Civilians, 1861-1866* [Online Database], digitized and indexed at Ancestry.com. This database was acquired from FamilySearch. This database has 502,957 records, see
www.ancestry.com/search/collections/60371.

1861-1866 Union Provost Marshal Files of Two or More Civilians **[Online Database]**, digitized at the FamilySearch.org website. The U.S. Provost Marshal served as military police for the Union Army. Records in this collection deal with deserters, Confederate spies, civilians suspected of disloyalty, civilian passage through military zones, etc. Taken from the National Archives publication M416. This database has 107,471 records, see
https://familysearch.org/search/collection/1845948.
- See also, *U.S., Union Provost Marshal Files of Two or More Civilians, 1861-1866* **[Online Database]**, digitized and indexed at Ancesty.com. (Database acquired from FamilySearch). This database has 107,471 records, see
www.ancestry.com/search/collections/60372.

1861-1867. *U.S., Union Provost Marshals' Papers* **[Online Database]**, digitized and indexed at Ancestry.com. Source: National Archives microfilm series M345. Documents in this database concern civilians who came in contact with the U.S. Army during and just following the Civil War. Documents include the following: correspondence, compensation and property claims, summonses, passes, reports on prisoners, receipts, applications to ship goods, requests for hearings, statements of witnesses, oaths of allegiance, parole documents, court findings and other papers, draft notices, licenses, and land forfeitures. In the records you will find names, dates, and details. Each document in this database relates to one civilian, and records are arranged alphabetically by the subject's name. This database has 236,494 records, see
www.ancestry.com/search/collections/2399.

1861-1904. *Headstones Provided for Deceased Union Civil War Veterans* **[Online Database],** from the original records at the National Archives, digitized and indexed by Ancestry.com. The searchable digitized cards have the following for each soldier: Name, rank, company, and regiment; burial place (cemetery, town, county, state); grave number, if applicable; death date; name of contractor that supplied the headstone; and date of contract in which the headstone was provided. In 1873, Congress allowed a headstone for any Union soldier buried in a National Cemetery, and in 1879, a headstone was allowed for any Union soldier buried in any cemetery. The card records are mostly for private cemeteries. This database has 170,057 records, see
http://search.ancestry.com/search/db.aspx?dbid=1195.

1861-1910 Navy Widows' Certificates **[Online Database],** digitized and indexed at the FamilySearch.org website. This collection consists of an index of approximately 20,000 approved pension application files of widows and other dependents of US Navy veterans who served between 1861 and 1910. The applications are commonly referred to as "Navy Widows' Certificates." Applications prior to approval were termed "originals." When claims were approved, a new file number was issued, and they were referred to as "certificates." Taken from National Archives microfilm, series M1279. Index courtesy of Fold3, this database has 1,003,115 records. See
https://familysearch.org/search/collection/1852605.

1861-1910. *U.S. Navy Pensions Index* **[Online Database],** Indexed at Ancestry.com. From case files of disapproved or approved Pension Applications of Widows and Other Dependents of Civil War and Later Navy Veterans, National Archives. Information contained in this index includes: File number, Name of widow or veteran making application, Alias name (if applicable), Publication number, Whether approved or disapproved, Certificate number, Fiche number, and Additional information. This database has 81,655 records, see
www.ancestry.com/search/collections/1357.

1861-1917 Civil War and Later Pension Files **[Online Database],** digitized and indexed at the FamilySearch.org website. Each card gives the soldier's name, application number, certificate number, and regiment in which the soldier served. In some cases, the soldier's rank, terms of service, date of death, and place of death are given. The index cards refer to pension applications of veterans who served in the U.S. Army between 1861 and 1917. The majority of the cards are from the Civil War era. Index courtesy of Fold3, this database has 2,990,891 records. See
https://familysearch.org/search/collection/1471019.

1861-1932. *United States Cancelled, Relinquished, or Rejected Land Entry Case Files* **[Online Database],** digitized at the FamilySearch.org website. Includes serialized land entry case files that were cancelled, relinquished, or rejected by the General Land Office. The applications include homesteads, mining claims, and land preemptions. This collection includes Kansas land offices at Dodge City and Topeka and Nebraska land offices at Alliance, Broken Bow, Lincoln, North Platte, O'Neill, and Valentine. The records are at the

NARA Regional Center in Kansas City, Missouri. This collection is being published as images become available. The database has 253,348 images. See https://familysearch.org/search/collection/2170637.

1861-1934 General Index to Pension Files [Online Database], digitized images at the FamilySearch.org website, containing the card index to pension files held at the National Archives. Most of the files are for Union Civil War service but also include the War with Spain, Philippine Insurrection, and Boxer Rebellion, National Archives microfilm, series T288. This database has 3,404,743 records. See
https://familysearch.org/search/collection/1919699.

1861-1934 Civil War Widows and Other Dependents Pension Files [Online Database], case files digitized and indexed at the FamilySearch.org website. This database consists of approved pension case files of widows and other dependents of soldiers submitted between 1861 and 1934 and sailors between 1910 and 1934. Some files may be for service in the War with Spain. The files are arranged numerically by certificate number. Taken from the original files located at the National Archives, record group 15, Veterans Administration. Index courtesy of Fold3, this database has 3,080,277 records. See
https://familysearch.org/search/collection/1922519.

Sample page, U.S. IRS Tax Assessment Lists from New York, District 29, Annual Lists: 1864-1866

1862-1874 Internal Revenue Assessment Lists [Online Database], digitized at the FamilySearch.org website. This is an Image-only database of internal revenue assessment lists (annual, monthly, and special) arranged by state and collection district. These records are the result of the Internal Revenue Act of July 1, 1862 authorizing the collection of monthly and annual taxes on goods, services, licenses, income, and personal property. The assessments were used to raise money for the Civil War. The tax assessments were organized by collection districts, which could cover any number of counties, part of a city or township, or part of a county. The boundaries of some districts changed part way through the civil war. "A guide for all counties" that distinguishes which records cover which localities is included for all States where more than one district is present, and the guide was present in the images. Also, for the purposes of this browse, a county label has been included. Patrons researching any counties that became part of West Virginia should search in both Virginia (M793) and West Virginia (M795) for those records, regardless of date. Images for collection districts are found under every county included within the boundaries of the district in question. Hence, the same images are listed under multiple counties. This database has 403,116 records. See
www.familysearch.org/search/collection/2075263.

↑ Sample. ***1862-1918 U.S. IRS Tax Assessment Lists*** [Online Database], digitized and indexed at the Ancestry.com website. On July 1, 1862, Congress passed the Internal Revenue Act, creating the Bureau of Internal Revenue (later renamed to the Internal Revenue Service). This act was intended to "provide Internal Revenue to support the Government and to pay interest on the Public Debt." Instituted during the height of the Civil War, the "Public Debt" at the time primarily consisted of war expenses. The Internal Revenue Act also established the Office of Commissioner of Internal Revenue and allowed the country to be divided into collection districts, of which assessors and collectors were appointed. Taxable goods and services were determined by legislative acts passed throughout the years. All persons, partnerships, firms, associations, and corporations submitted to the assistant assessor of their division, a list showing the amount of annual income, articles subject special taxes and duties, and the quantity of goods made or sold that were charged with taxes or duties. The assistant assessors collected and compiled these lists into two general lists. These lists were: 1) A list of names of all individuals residing in the division who were subject to taxation. 2) A list of names of all individuals residing outside the division, but who were owners of property in the division. These lists were organized alphabetically according to surname and recorded the value, assessment, or enumeration of taxable income or items and the amount of tax due. After all examinations and appeals, copies of these lists were given to the tax collector. See http://search.ancestry.com/search/db.aspx?dbid=1264.

1862-1899 Final Statements [Online Database], digitized and indexed at the Fold3.com website. The "Final Statement" was issued when a soldier died while in service and discharged by "reason of death." A copy was forwarded to the Adjutant General's Office. A document lists personal information, including cause, place, and date of death; and often a physical description, birthplace, and next of kin. Also included are often an inventory of possessions at time of death, heir's receipts for effects, paymaster's receipts for money owed, and forms for effects and pay when no heirs are stated. This database has 55,377 records. See www.fold3.com/title_749/final_statements_18621899

1862-1960. *U.S. Burial Registers, Military Posts and National Cemeteries* **[Online Database],** indexed at Ancestry.com. Source: National Cemetery Administration, Washington, DC; and Dept of the Army, Office of the Quartermaster General, National Archives. Many veterans of the U.S. armed services are buried in cemeteries established or maintained by the National Cemetery Administration (NCA) or the U.S. Army. The NCA maintains 131 national cemeteries and other smaller burial grounds. The Department of the Army is responsible for Arlington and the U.S. Soldiers' and Airmen's Home National Cemetery. These records also include burial details for soldiers who were disinterred and moved to military cemeteries sometime after their death. Burial ledgers and other records in this database vary, but they may include the following details: name, rank, company, regiment, date of death, cause of death, age at death, date of burial, grave mark/number, grave location, and original place of burial. This database has 556,034 records, see www.ancestry.com/search/collections/3135.

1862-1985. *U.S., Select Military Registers* **[Online Database],** digitized and indexed at Ancestry.com. This database contains registers of U.S. military personnel stationed in the United States. The majority of this collection covers U.S. Army and Navy personnel, though lists for the Air Force, Marine Corp, National Guard, and the Reserves are included as well. The database does not include all possible years for each publication listed. All records will list the subject's name. Depending on the register type, other details you may find include the following: rank, unit, service history, birthdate, birthplace (home address), education level, promotion dates, awards, and retirement date. The original image may add more information. This database has 4,783,212 records, see www.ancestry.com/search/collections/2345.

1863-1865. *Civil War Service Records of Union Colored Troops* **[Online Database],** digitized and indexed at the FamilySearch.org Website. Includes Union service records of soldiers who served in the United States Colored Troops. The records include a jacket-envelope for each soldier, labeled with his name, his rank, and the unit in which he served. The jacket-envelope typically contains card abstracts of entries relating to the soldier as found in original muster rolls, returns, rosters, payrolls, appointment books, hospital registers, prison registers and rolls, parole rolls, inspection reports; and the originals of any papers relating solely to the particular soldier. For each military unit, the service records are arranged alphabetically by the soldier's surname. The Military Unit field may also display the surname range (A-G) as found on the microfilm. This collection is a part of RG 94, Records of the Adjutant General's Office, 1780's-1917 and include NARA microfilm publications pertaining to the compiled service records of the United States Colored Troops. Index courtesy of Fold3. This database has 2,319,767 records. See https://familysearch.org/search/collection/1932431.

- See also, *U.S., Colored Troops Military Service Records, 1863-1865* **[Online Database],** digitized and indexed at Ancestry.com. This database has 239,118 records, see
www.ancestry.com/search/collections/1107.

Sample page, Civil War Draft Registration, Kentucky.

1863-1865. *U.S. Civil War Draft Registration Records* **[Online Database],** digitized and indexed at the Ancestry.com website. There were four drafts between 1863 and 1865. Historically, the 1863 draft was one of the most tenuous moments in the Union outside of the battles fought on Northern soil. Most of the concern was due to the draft riots that took place in New York in 1863. These records include 631 volumes of registries and are basically lists of individuals who registered for the draft. The records are split into two different classes, Class I are those aged 20-35 as well as those 36-45 and unmarried. Class II is everyone else that registered. The registry contains information including: Class, Congressional district, County, State, Residence, Name, Age on July 1, 1863, Race, Profession, Marital status, Birthplace, Former military service, and Remarks. These are records from the Provost Marshal General's Bureau, Record Group 110, National Archives, Washington, DC, with the title, Consolidated Lists of Civil War Draft Registrations, 1863-1865. This database has 3,176,682 records, see
http://search.ancestry.com/search/db.aspx?dbid=1666.

1863-1878. U.S., *Freedmen Bureau Records of Field Offices* **[Online Database],** indexed at the Ancestry.com website. This database contains records relating to the Bureau from the following field offices: Florida, Georgia, Tennessee, New Orleans, Louisiana, North Carolina, Virginia, and Washington, D.C., The database also contains records relating to the Bureau for the following states from the Adjutant General's office in Washington, D.C.: Kansas, Kentucky, Louisiana, Mississippi, Missouri, and South Carolina. Types of records found in this database include: Labor Contracts, Letters, Applications for Rations, Monthly Reports of Abandoned Land, Monthly Reports of Clothing and Medicine Issued, Statistical School Reports, Court Trial Records, Hospital Records, Lists of Workers Complaints Registered, and Census Returns. This database has 549,014 records. See
http://search.ancestry.com/search/db.aspx?dbid=1105.

1863-1959. *U.S., Register of Civil, Military, and Naval Service* **[Online Database],** digitized and indexed at the Ancestry.com website. Source: Publication , same title, Dept of Commerce, Bureau of the Census. In 1816, Congress authorized the publication of a list of all federal employees every two years. It appeared in book form under the title *Register of Officers and Agents, Civil, Military, and Naval, in the Service of the United States*. This collection includes 77 volumes of registers for years ranging from 1863 to 1959 (see the browse table for each year available). Registers include the name of each government employee, office held, where employed, where born, whence appointed, and pay received, as well as information regarding the Navy, such as names and conditions of all ships and vessels belonging to the U.S. and when and where they were built. This database has 3,783,772 records. Archived at
https://web.archive.org/web/20170105103058/http://search.ancestry.com/search/db.aspx?dbid=1105.

1864-1866 *Civil War Service Records of Union Soldiers (Confederate Prisoners)* **[Online Database],** digitized and indexed at the FamilySearch.org website. Includes Union service records of Confederate prisoners of war who enlisted and served in the 1st- 6th U.S. Volunteer Infantry Regiments. The records include a jacket-envelope for each soldier, labeled with his name, his rank, and the unit in which he served. The jacket-envelope typically contains card abstracts of entries relating to the soldier as found in original muster rolls, returns, rosters, payrolls, appointment books, hospital registers, Union prison registers and rolls, parole rolls, inspection reports; and the originals of any papers relating solely to the particular soldier. For each military unit, the service records are arranged alphabetically by the soldier's surname. The Military Unit field may also display the surname range (A-G) as found on the microfilm. This collection is a part of RG 94, Records of the Adjutant General's Office, 1780's-1917 and is National Archive Microfilm Publication M1017. This database has 119,672 records. Index courtesy of Fold3. See
https://familysearch.org/search/collection/1932430.

1864-1968 Deceased Physician File (AMA) **[Online Database],** digitized at the FamilySearch.org website, a name index, and images of the deceased physician card file from the American Medical Association (AMA), which are physician biographic records of decedent records from 1864 to 1968. This database has 707,724 images. See
https://familysearch.org/search/collection/2061540.

1865-1867 Civil War Confederate Applications for Pardons **[Online Database],** digitized and indexed at the FamilySearch.org website. Includes applications for pardons submitted to President Andrew Johnson by former Confederates, excluded from the proclamation of May 29, 1865. The case files include affidavits, oaths of allegiance, recommendation for clemency, and other papers. Taken from the National Archives microfilm, series M1003. Index courtesy of Fold3. This database has 79,992 records. See
https://familysearch.org/search/collection/1936545.

1865-1872. ***United States, Freedmen's Bureau, Records of the Commissioner*** **[Online Database],** digitized at the FamilySearch.org website. The bureau was created in 1865 at the end of the American Civil War to supervise relief efforts including education, health care, food and clothing, refugee camps, legalization of marriages, employment, labor contracts, and securing back pay, bounty payments and pensions. These records include letters and endorsements sent and received, account books, applications for rations, applications for relief, court records, labor contracts, registers of bounty claimants, registers of complaints, registers of contracts, registers of disbursements, registers of freedmen issued rations, registers of patients, reports, rosters of officers and employees, special and general orders and circulars received, special orders and circulars issued, records of claims, court trials, property restoration, and homesteads. This database has 71,886 records. See
https://familysearch.org/search/collection/2431126.

1865-1872. ***United States, Freedmen's Bureau, Records of the Assistant Commissioner*** **[Online Database],** digitized at the FamilySearch.org website. Includes records of the Assistant Commissioner of the Bureau of Refugees, Freedmen, and Abandoned Lands (often called the Freedmen's Bureau). This database has 392,161 images. See
https://familysearch.org/search/collection/2427901.

1865-1872. ***United States, Freedmen's Bureau, Hospital and Medical Records*** **[Online Database],** digitized at the FamilySearch.org website. Includes an index of patient registers, registers of sick and wounded, prescription books, and other medical records from freedmen hospitals and dispensaries. This database has 44,734 images. See
https://familysearch.org/search/collection/2432992.

1865-1872. ***United States, Freedmen's Bureau, Records of the Superintendent of Education and of the Division of Education*** **[Online Database],** digitized at the FamilySearch.org website. These records include letters and endorsements sent and received, account books, applications for rations, applications for relief, court records, labor contracts, registers of bounty claimants, registers of complaints, registers of contracts, registers of disbursements, registers of freedmen issued rations, registers of patients, reports, rosters of officers and employees, special and general orders and circulars received, special orders and circulars issued, records relating to claims, court trials, property restoration, and homesteads. This database has 162,191 images. See
https://familysearch.org/search/collection/2427894.

1865-1874. ***United States, Freedmen's Bank Records*** **[Online Database],** digitized and indexed at the FamilySearch.org website, this is a name index and images of registers for 67,000 people who opened accounts in the Freedman's Savings and Trust Co. This database has 478,086 records. See
https://familysearch.org/search/collection/1417695.

1866-1916. ***U.S., Buffalo Soldiers, Returns From Regular Army Cavalry Regiments*** **[Online Database],** digitized and indexed at Ancestry.com. Source: National Archives microfilm series M744. This collection includes the monthly returns from the 9th and 10th Calvary Units of the U.S. Army up to 1916. These two units were the first peacetime units of enlisted African-Americans and the enlisted men were known as "Buffalo Soldiers." Both units were formed in 1866 with white officers commanding the enlisted men. The units went on to fight in the Indian Wars and the Spanish-American War during that era. The monthly returns were used to report on the strength of each regiment, including total numbers of men present, absent, sick, or on extra duty, as well as happenings during the month. Officers were listed by name, as were enlisted men who were absent, on special duty, or who joined or left the unit during the month. Later returns included strength reports in terms of horses and artillery. Returns include: Names of regimental commanders; Names of all officers and reasons for loss or gain, if applicable; Names of company commanders, Stations of the regiment and companies; Names of absent enlisted men, 1857-1904, and reason for absence; Names of enlisted men lost and gained, 1821-1914, and reasons; Names of enlisted men on extra or daily duty, 1857-1873, and nature of duty; Record of events information, 1832-1916; Total strength of both officers and enlisted men by rank, 1819-1857; Total strength of horses by company, 1846-1916; and Total strength of artillery pieces by company, 1857-1912. This database has 227,634 records, see www.ancestry.com/search/collections/1934.

1866-1938 U.S. National Homes for Disabled Volunteer Soldiers **[Online Database],** digitized and indexed at the Ancestry.com website. The following is a list of the names of the twelve National Homes covered in this database as well as which records and years there are included for each: 1. Bath Branch, Bath, New York – Historical Registers and Indexes to Historical Registers, 1876-1934; Register of Deaths and Index to Register of Deaths, 1879-1929. 2. Battle Mountain Sanitarium, Hot Springs, South Dakota – Historical Registers and Indexes to Historical Registers, 1907-1934. 3. Central Branch, Dayton, Ohio – Historical Registers and Indexes to Historical Registers, 1867-1935. 4. Danville Branch, Danville, Illinois – Historical Registers and Indexes to Historical Registers, 1898-1934. 5. Eastern Branch, Togus, Maine – Historical Registers and Indexes to Historical Registers, 1866-1934; Hospital Index, A-Z; Burials Records, 1892-1932; Death Records, 1893-1899. 6. Marion Branch, Marion, Indiana – Historical Registers and Indexes to Historical Registers, 1890-1931. 7. Mountain Branch, Johnson City, Tennessee – Historical Registers and Indexes to Historical Registers, 1903-1932. 8. Northwestern Branch, Milwaukee, Wisconsin – Historical Registers and Indexes to Historical Registers, 1867-1934. 9. Pacific Branch, Los Angeles, California – Historical Registers and Indexes to Historical Registers, 1888-1933. 10. Roseburg Branch, Roseburg, Oregon – Applicants, 1894-1918; Admissions 1908-1932; Deaths, 1894-1937. 11. Southern Branch, Hampton, Virginia Historical Registers, and Indexes to Historical Registers, 1871-1933. 12. Western Branch, Leavenworth, Kansas – Historical Registers and Indexes to Historical Registers, 1885-1934. Information recorded includes: Name of soldier, Name of home or branch, Date of admission, Birthplace, Rank, Company and regiment, Date and place of enlistment, Date and place of discharge, Physical description (height, complexion, eye, and hair color), Occupation, Marital status, and Religion. See http://search.ancestry.com/search/db.aspx?dbid=1200.

1866-1938 National Homes for Disabled Volunteer Soldiers **[Online Database],** digitized and indexed at the FamilySearch.org website. Images and partial index of historical registers of residents (a record of veterans admitted) for twelve regional homes. Pages in the registers were divided into four parts for each veteran: military history, domestic history, home history, general remarks. Content for these sections includes such information as rank, company, regiment, discharge, when admitted to home, birthplace, age, religion, residence, marital status, name, and address of nearest relative, pension information, date and cause of death, and place of burial. This collection is part of Record Group 15 Records of the Veterans Administration and is NARA microfilm publication M1749. This database has 384,887 records. See www.familysearch.org/search/collection/1916230.

1867-1931. *United States Births and Christenings* **[Online Database],** indexed at the FamilySearch.org website, this database is a name index to small sets of birth, baptism, and christening records from a few states within the United States. Taken from the microfilm copies at the Family History Library in Salt Lake City, this set has 20,946 records. See https://familysearch.org/search/collection/1808995.

1867-1961. *U.S., Select Deaths and Burials* **[Online Database],** indexed at the FamilySearch.org website, this database is a name index to small sets of death and burial records from a few states within the United States. Taken from the microfilm copies at the Family History Library in Salt Lake City, this set has 3,863 records. See https://familysearch.org/search/collection/1675539.

1868-1970. *U.S. Evangelical Covenant Church, Swedish American Church Records* **[Online Database],** digitized and indexed at Ancestry.com. The records in this collection consist of administrative records from select affiliates of the Evangelical Covenant Church in America. Indexes have been provided for baptisms, marriages, burials, and membership records (arrivals, dismissals, and member lists), as well as congregational histories and biographical files of church leaders. The member lists in particular have a wealth of information, including vital dates and emigration information. Some member lists may include the location in Sweden an individual or family was originally from. Records are written in either English or Swedish. See www.ancestry.com/search/collections/61586.

1872-1878. See *United States, Freedmen's Branch Records* **[Online Database],** digitized at the FamilySearch.com website. The records of the Freedmen's Branch in the Office of the Adjutant General are part of Records of the Bureau of Refugees, Freedmen, and Abandoned Lands. This database has 61,984 images. See
https://familysearch.org/search/collection/2333780.

1875-1940. See *U.S., Evangelical Lutheran Church of America, Records* **[Online Database],** digitized and indexed at the Ancestry.com website. Source: Births, Marriages, Deaths, ELCA, Chicago, IL. This collection contains images and an index to baptism, confirmation, marriage, and burial records from more than 2,000 Evangelical Lutheran Church in America (ELCA) congregations. The information contained in the records varies from congregation to congregation (and sometimes from minister to minister). In some ethnic congregations, you may run into records in German, Danish, or some other language. Search the index, or browse through the collection, organized by state, then city of a church. This database has 8,094,994 records:
http://search.ancestry.com/search/db.aspx?dbid=60722.

1876-2004. *U.S. Professional Baseball Player Profiles* **[Online Database],** digitized and indexed at Ancestry.com. Original data: Baseball Almanac, with images reproduced courtesy of the Library of Congress, Washington, D.C. For over a century baseball has often been referred to as the country's national pastime. This database is an index to over 15,000 professional baseball players who played between 1876 (the year the National League was founded) and 2004. Information listed in the index for each individual includes: First and last names, Birth first and last names, Nickname, Birthdate, Birthplace, Death date, Death place, College attended, Height, Weight, Date of first game, Date of final game, How bats, How throws, and Date and round drafted. This database has 13,622 records, see
www.ancestry.com/search/collections/8666.

1879-1903. *United States, Records of Headstones of Deceased Union Veterans* **[Online Database],** digitized and indexed at the FamilySearch.org website. Images of card records used to provide headstones for deceased Union veterans. Most burials occurred in private cemeteries though some may have occurred in National Soldier's Home cemeteries. Gravestones were provided to Union soldiers who died between 1861 and 1903. Some cards may include War of 1812 veterans. The gravestones were provided between 1879-1903 by the United States government. Some of the names on the cards may be difficult to read. This database has 169,253 records. See
www.familysearch.org/search/collection/1913388.

1880s-1920s. See *U.S. Property Owners Index and Maps* **[Online Database],** digitized and indexed at the MyHeritage.com website. The Historic U.S. Maps – Name Index has thousands of maps with the names of property owners. Includes maps from Arkansas, Colorado, Illinois, Indiana, Iowa, Kansas, Michigan, Minnesota, Missouri, Nebraska, North Dakota, Oklahoma, South Dakota, and Wisconsin. See
www.myheritage.ee/research/collection-10094/us-property-owners-index-maps.

1880-1999 & 1900-2012. See *U.S., School Yearbooks* **[Online Database],** digitized and indexed at the Ancestry.com website. Source: Various school yearbooks from across the United States. There are 51,000 yearbooks with more than 7 million photos. Each index record includes Name, Birth year, School, School location, year, and Yearbook title. The images may have more information about a person. This database has 678,321,057 records. See
http://search.ancestry.com/search/db.aspx?dbid=1265.

1883. See *List of Pensioners on the Roll, January 1, 1883, Vols. 1-5* **[Online Database],** digitized and indexed at the Ancestry.com website. Includes the name of each pensioner, the cause for which pensioned, the post-office address, the rate of pension per month, and the date of original allowance. See
http://search.ancestry.com/search/db.aspx?dbid=31387.

1885-1940 Indian Census Rolls **[Online Database],** digitized and indexed at the Fold3.com website. Most rolls include the English and/or Indian name of the person, roll number, age or date of birth, sex, and relationship to head of family. Beginning in 1930 the rolls also show the degree of Indian blood, marital status, ward status, place of residence, and sometimes other information. Includes persons who maintained a formal affiliation with a tribe under Federal supervision are listed on these census rolls. This database has 424,217 records. See
www.fold3.com/title_84/indian_census_rolls_18851940.
- See also, *U.S., Native American, Census Rolls, 1855-1940* **[Online Database],** digitized and indexed at FamilySearch.org. Native American census rolls for various tribes. Original records are NARA Series M595. This NARA series also includes some vital records. This database has 5,620,882 records, see
www.familysearch.org/search/collection/2761958.

- See also, ***U.S., Native American Birth and Death Records, 1885-1940*** **[Online Database]**, digitized and indexed at FamilySearch.org. Source: National Archives series M595. This database has 78,133 records, see www.familysearch.org/search/collection/2765178.

1887-1926. ***Mexican War Pension Index*** **[Online Database]**, digitized and indexed at the FamilySearch.org website. This is a card index to Mexican War pension files located at the National Archives for service between 1846 and 1848. Taken from National Archives microfilm, series T317. The database has 51,620 records. See https://familysearch.org/search/collection/1979390.

1887-1942. ***Remarried Widows Index to Pension Applications*** **[Online Database]**, digitized and indexed at the FamilySearch.org website. This collection consists of two card indexes to widows who had applied for a pension renewal. The first covers service between 1812 and 1860 (National Archives microfilm, series M1784). The second covers service in the Civil War and later (National Archives microfilm, series M1785). This database has 52,939 records. See https://familysearch.org/search/collection/1979426.

1888-1895. ***U.S., Special Census on Deaf Family Marriages and Hearing Relatives*** **[Online Database]**, digitized and indexed at Ancestry.com. The Volta Bureau, located in Washington, D.C., was founded in 1887 by Alexander Graham Bell. The Bureau served as a center of information for deaf and hard of hearing persons. Bell had a deaf wife and taught at a day school for deaf children. As a center of information, one of the things the Bureau did was promote research in regard to marriages of the deaf in America. This work was primarily undertaken by Dr. E. A. Fay. The federal government, seeing a need for an official supplement to the 1890 U.S. census, even appointed Dr. Fay as its special agent for collecting such statistical information. This database contains the questionnaires issued by Dr. Fay to deaf couples in America. The questionnaires were completed during the years 1889-1894. Information recorded on these forms includes: Names of husband and wife, Whether deaf or hearing, Age at which deafness occurred and the cause of deafness, If attended school, Occupation, Details relating to the couple's marriage (including date and place), Details relating to couple's children (number deaf or hearing, names, dates of birth or death, cause of death, etc.), and Details relating to husband's and wife's parents, and brothers and sisters. This database has 10,482 records: www.ancestry.com/search/collections/1582.

1889-1904 ***U.S. Index to General Correspondence of the Record and Pension Office*** **[Online Database]**, digitized index cards at the FamilySearch.org website. The Record and Pension Office was in charge of military and medical records of volunteer forces, medical records of the Regular Army, and any business pertaining to these records. However, during the years 1889-1904, generally the Record and Pension Office only had responsibility over records of volunteer forces. Records relating to the Regular Army were in the charge of the Adjutant General's Office. Records that related to both the volunteer forces and the Regular Army were under the Record and Pension Office. Correspondence received by the Record and Pension Office was numbered consecutively according to time of receipt. Replies and other abstracts and copies of the communication were filed together with the incoming correspondence. Name and subject index cards to these files were created as a finding aid. This finding aid is what is reproduced in this database. Most of the index cards are arranged according to the Soundex system, and thereunder alphabetically according to soldiers' surnames. A card listing all of the variant spellings precedes such index cards. Other index cards were filed according to names of volunteer organizational units or subjects. These cards are also filed according to the Soundex system but appear after the cards containing the names of soldiers. Organizational units were often filed by the name of the officer who commanded the unit. Each index card lists the Name of the soldier, and Organization in which he served. Name of person or office making the inquiry, and Subject of inquiry, see www.familysearch.org/search/collection/1834308.

- See also, ***Index to General Correspondence of the Pension Office, 1889-1904*** **[Online Database]**, digitized and indexed at the FamilySearch.org website. Name index and images of the name and subject index to correspondence of the Records and Pension office. The index is part of RG 94, Records of the Adjutant General's Office, National Archives microfilm series M686, located at the National Archives, Washington, DC. This database has 858,866 records, see www.familysearch.org/search/collection/1834308.

1889-1970. ***U.S. Sons of the American Revolution Membership Applications*** **[Online Database]**, digitized and indexed at the Ancestry.com website. Applications require a pedigree and accompanying information to demonstrate a generation-by-generation link to a patriot ancestor. Genealogical information submitted may include references to Revolutionary

War pension files, baptismal records, marriage records, cemetery records, census records, family Bible records, deeds, court records, documented family and local histories, and copies of applications to other lineage societies. Applications also typically include a short summary of the ancestor's service. This database has 1,268,400 records, see
http://search.ancestry.com/search/db.aspx?dbid=2204.

1890 Federal Census, Special Schedules of Union Veterans and Widows of Union Veterans [Microfilm & Digital Capture]. Over 99 percent of the 1890 census was destroyed as a result of a fire that took place in January 1921 in Washington, DC. In addition to the population schedules, a special census listing was extracted from the 1890 population schedules for surviving Union soldiers, sailors, and marines (or their widows), and a portion of that special census survives. **Content:** The schedules listed the name of each soldier, sailor, marine, or widow of a veteran in a household; the veteran's rank; company; regiment or vessel; dates of enlistment and discharge; length of service in years, months, and days; post office address; nature of disability, if any; and remarks. **Census losses:** Of the forty-nine states and territories enumerated in 1890, sixteen of the states' Union Veterans' schedules (alphabetically from Alabama through Kansas) were apparently lost in the fire, as were about half of the names for Kentucky. State listings begin with the partial list for Kentucky and are complete from Louisiana through Wyoming. Microfilm: The 1890 Special Schedules Enumerating Union Veterans and Widows of Union Veterans of the Civil War were microfilmed on 120 rolls, series M123, beginning with FHL film #338160 (Kentucky). To access the digital images, see the online FHL catalog:
https://familysearch.org/search/catalog/230777.
- See also, ***1890 Federal Census, Union Veterans and Widows of the Civil War*** [Online Database]. Digitized and indexed images are available online at the FamilySearch website for the schedules enumerating Union veterans and widows of veterans of the Civil War for the states of Kentucky through Wyoming. Except for some miscellaneous returns, data for the states of Alabama through Kansas do not exist. Some returns include U.S. Naval Vessels and Navy Yards. The schedules are from Record Group 15, Records of the Veterans Administration, microfilmed by the National Archives as Series M123. All 118 rolls in this series were digitized. This database has 897,849 records. See
https://familysearch.org/search/collection/1877095.

1890 Veterans Schedules [Online Database]. The 1890 Special Schedules Enumerating Union Veterans and Widows of Union Veterans of the Civil War was digitized and indexed at the Ancestry.com site. See
http://search.ancestry.com/search/db.aspx?dbid=8667.

1891-1892 Confederate Citizens File [Online Database], original papers digitized and indexed at the Fold3.com website. The papers reproduced in this publication were created or received by the Confederate War and Treasury departments. Most are alphabetized vouchers that came into the custody of the US War Department after the Civil War. After being assembled in 1891-92, they were used to facilitate post-war claims cases filed by Southern citizens. The vouchers show goods furnished or services rendered by private citizens and firms to the Confederate government, establishing the disloyalty of Southern claimants. This database has 2,118,605 records. See
www.fold3.com/title_60/confederate_citizens_file/.

1892-1896. ***Rosters and Applications, United Confederate Veterans*** [Microfilm & Digital Capture]. The rosters include name, company or rank, regiment, state and remarks, and name and location of the camp. The applications include extensive information about a veteran's family, residence, and military service. The Rosters and applications are organized by camp numbers. Filmed by the Genealogical Society of Utah, 6 rolls, beginning with FHL film #1685779 (Rosters, Applications, Letters, Camp No. 1-212 1892-1893). To access the digital images, see the online FHL catalog:
https://familysearch.org/search/catalog/582952.
- See also, ***Rosters, United Confederate Veterans, 1895-1899*** [Microfilm & Digital Capture], from the originals at the Jackson Barracks Military Library, New Orleans, LA. This organization was established in New Orleans in June of 1889 by veterans of the Confederate Army. These rosters of members are arranged by state and camp. The contents include name, company or rank, number of regiment, state and service, rank of officers and their camps, and remarks. Filmed by the Genealogical Society of Utah, 1990, 2 rolls, FHL film #1710607 (Alabama-Mississippi); and FHL film #1710608 (Missouri-West Virginia). To access the digital images, see the online FHL catalog:
www.familysearch.org/search/catalog/590459.

1892-1924 Ellis Island Passenger Arrival Records [Online Database], indexed at the Statue of Liberty-Ellis Island Foundation website. The Ellis Island Passenger Arrival Records contains details for more than 24 million passengers and crew who arrived through the Port of New York at Ellis Island between January 1, 1892 and December 31, 1924. This index is a free search at the Statue of Liberty-Ellis Island Foundation website. Information in the index contains passenger name, residence, year of arrival, and age on arrival. The records also provide ethnicity, exact date of arrival, gender, marital status, name of ship, and port of departure. In addition to the passenger index, the Ellis Island website provides digital images of passenger ships and original passenger manifests that include even more details for each passenger, their final destination in America, physical conditions, education, and more. But first, check the Passenger Arrival index here. See **www.ellisisland.org/.**

1892-1926. *Index to Indian Wars Pension Files* **[Online Database],** digitized and indexed at the FamilySearch.org website, a card index to pension files for service in the Indian Wars between 1817 and 1898. Taken from the National Archives microfilm, series T318, this database has 51,709 records. See **https://familysearch.org/search/collection/1979427.**

1894-1954. *Border Crossings from Canada to United States* **[Online Database],** indexed at the FamilySearch.org website, this database is an index of aliens and citizens crossing into the U.S. from Canada via various ports of entry along the U.S.-Canadian border between 1894 and 1954. This database has 204,822 records. See **https://familysearch.org/search/collection/1803785.**

1896-2003. *U.S., Selected Quaker College Yearbooks and Alumni Directories* **[Online Database],** digitized and indexed at the Ancestry.com website. This database contains alumni directories and yearbooks from Guilford College in North Carolina and Earlham College in Indiana. Yearbook entries vary some but may provide at least a name, hometown, photograph, and other details. Seniors sometimes get more detailed entries. Entries in the alumni directory provide a name and years the alumnus attended school. Some also include an address, occupation, and other details. This database has 521,947 records. See **http://search.ancestry.com/search/db.aspx?dbid=2888.**

1898. *Index to Service Records, War with Spain, 1898* **[Online Database],** digitized and indexed at the FamilySearch.org website, a name index to compiled service records of volunteer soldiers who served during the War with Spain. Taken from the National Archives originals from the Adjutant General's Office. This database has 302,679 records. See **https://familysearch.org/search/collection/1919583.**

- See also, **U.S., Spanish American War Volunteers Index to Compiled Military Service Records, 1898 [Online Database],** digitized and indexed at Ancestry.com. This database has 300,059, see **www.ancestry.com/search/collections/2400.**

1898 *Dawes Packets* **[Online Database],** records of the Dawes Commission in negotiation with the five civilized tribes, digitized and indexed at the Fold3.com website. This series contains the original applications for tribal enrollments under the act of June 28, 1898, as well as supporting documents such as birth and death affidavits, marriage licenses, transcripts of testimony taken by the Commission, correspondence relating to the status of the application, and decisions and orders of the Dawes Commission. This database has 882,753 records, see **www.fold3.com/title_70/dawes_packets.**

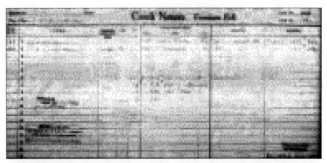

1898-1914 Enrollment Cards for the Five Civilized Tribes **[Online Database],** the "Dawes Enrollment Cards" were digitized and indexed at the Fold3.com website. Enrollment cards were created by the Dawes Commission to record information about family groups within the Cherokee, Choctaw, Creek, Chickasaw, and Seminole nations. They list family relationships, degree of native blood, age, tribal enrollment, and other data useful to establishing family connections and Native American ancestry. This database has 76,037 records. See **www.fold3.com/title_69/dawes_enrollment_cards/.**

1898-1932. *U.S., Navy Burial Records* **[Online Database],** indexed at the Ancestry.com website. Source: Dept of the Navy records, National Archives. This database contains registers and lists from Navy ships, hospitals, training centers, and other installations. The lists provide details on the disposition of remains of the dead. They typically contain at least: name, rank or rate, and place and date of death. They may also list birth date, cause of death, whether a patient in hospital, name, and address for next of kin, place and date of burial, nativity/birthplace/where from, even date of funeral and who was notified about the death. Not all of the people on these lists are Navy personnel. Family members or other civilians who were treated at Navy facilities might be included, as well as members of the United States Marine Corps. Though this collection is not comprehensive, it does include a broad range of facilities, from a Marine brigade field hospital in Tientsin, China, to a tuberculosis sanatorium in Colorado. This database has 4,052 records. See http://search.ancestry.com/search/db.aspx?dbid=3014.

1899-2012. *Obituaries, American Historical Society of Germans from Russia* **[Online Database],** digitized and indexed at the FamilySearch.org website. Includes an index and images of obituaries collected by the American Historical Society of Germans from Russia. This database has 2,090,258 records. See https://familysearch.org/search/collection/2367299.

1901-2010. *U.S. Navy Support Books* **[Online Database],** indexed at the Ancestry.com website. Similar to Navy cruise books, Navy support books are "yearbooks" for Navy units that cover an operational deployment, training group, base, or similar group or institution. For example, in this collection you'll find copies of the U.S. Navy and Marine Corps Registry and books for the U.S. Navy Preparatory School, Navy ROTC programs at various colleges and universities, U.S. Naval Officer Candidate School, U.S. Naval Training Centers, U.S. Merchant Marine Academy, mobile construction battalions, recruiting depots, naval air stations, and others. This database has 959,335 records. See http://search.ancestry.com/search/db.aspx?dbid=2323.

1903-1957. *Border Crossings from Mexico to United States* **[Online Database],** indexed at the FamilySearch.org website, this database is an index of aliens and citizens crossing into the U.S. from Mexico via various ports of entry along the U.S.-Canadian border between 1895 and 1956. This database has 3,610,754 records. See https://familysearch.org/search/collection/1803932.

1903-1959. *U.S. Subject Index to Correspondence and Case Files of the Immigration and Naturalization Service* **[Online Database],** Digitized and indexed at Ancestry.com. Source: National Archives microfilm series T458. This database has case files as kept by the Immigration and Naturalization Service for various individuals pertaining to immigration, emigration, and naturalization. Includes surnames, port and date of entry, date of birth and whether or not they came alone or with relatives. In rare cases, there can be a very substantial abstract of the correspondence or case file in the index. This database has 331,285 records, see www.ancestry.com/search/collections/1946.

1903-1962. *U.S., Select Crew Lists and Manifests* **[Online Database],** indexed at the Ancestry.com website. Source: National Archives microfilm of crew lists and manifest from ports in several states. The captain or master of each vessel was required to submit crew lists to the Immigration and Naturalization Service (INS) upon arrival. This data collection contains crew arrival and departure lists for selected U.S. ports. In later years crews may have arrived by airplane rather than by ship. See the browse menu for the list of ports and years included. This database has 2,454,823 records. See http://search.ancestry.com/search/db.aspx?dbid=9220.

1905-1937. *Panama Canal Zone, Employment Records and Sailing Lists* **[Online Database],** digitized at the FamilySearch.org website. Includes employee records (service history cards), sailing lists of contract laborers, and employee identification records (metal check cards and applications) from Record Group 185 Records of the Panama Canal, 1848-1999, located in Archives II in College Park, Maryland. This database has 118,532 images. See https://familysearch.org/search/collection/2193241.

1905-1990. See *Associated Press, Name Card Index to AP Stories* **[Online Database],** digitized and indexed at the Ancestry.com website. Source: Associated Press Corporate Archives, New York, NY. Each index record includes: Name, Classification number, Publication date, Location, and Subject. This database has 2,169,301 records. See http://search.ancestry.com/search/db.aspx?dbid=50018.

1906-1991. *Panama Canal Zone, Index to the Gorgas Hospital Mortuary Registers* **[Online Database],** indexed at the FamilySearch.org website. Includes an index to the mortuary's registers of military personnel, canal employees and canal zone civilians processed through the Gorgas Hospital Mortuary, acquired from the National Archives. The records are from Record Group 185 Records of the Panama Canal. Additional information about this collection may be found on the National Archives website. This database has 26,212 records. See https://familysearch.org/search/collection/2127918.

1907-1918. *U.S., Consular Registration Certificates* **[Online Database],** indexed at the Ancestry.com website. Source: Dept of State records, National Archives. Whether naturalized or native born, American citizens who intended to stay in a foreign country for a protracted length of time were required to register with the American consulate and file an "Affidavit to Explain Protracted Foreign Residence and to Overcome Presumption of Expatriation." This collection covers the years 1907–1918 and includes certificates filed by citizens at U.S. consulates and legations. The forms may provide the following details: Name of registrant, Consulate where registered, Date and place of birth, General travel data, Names, places of birth, and residences of spouse and children, and Registrant's current place of residence. This database has 82,464 records. See
http://search.ancestry.com/search/db.aspx?dbid=2995.

1907-1933. *Veterans Administration Pension Payment Cards* **[Online Database],** Images of cards used by the Bureau of Pensions and Veterans Administration to record the payment of pensions to veterans and widows. Card images were digitized at the FamilySearch website. The National Archives film series M850 was used to digitize the images. This database has 1,786,095 images and 1,428,203 indexed names. See
https://familysearch.org/search/collection/1832324.

1908-1922 *Investigative Case Files of the Bureau of Investigation* **[Online Database],** digitized and indexed database at the Fold3.com website. These case files cover important investigations by an agency of the US government later known as the FBI, called the Bureau of Investigation. They include tales of espionage during World War I, case files for German aliens who were politically suspect, records pertaining to Mexican neutrality, and reports dealing with alleged violations of Federal laws. This database has 2,313,321 records. See
www.fold3.com/title_74/fbi_case_files/.

1910-1949. *U.S., Consular Reports of Births* **[Online Database],** digitized and indexed at the Ancestry.com website. Source: National Archives, Records of the Department of State. This database includes birth reports from U.S. Consulates abroad between the years of 1910 and 1949. The report form is called a Consular Report of Birth Abroad and is primary proof of the individual's American citizenship. To qualify, the child must have either two U.S. citizen parents with one of the parents having resided in the U.S. prior to the child's birth, or one of the child's parents must be a U.S. citizen who has resided in the U.S. for a specified number of years previous to the child's birth. The database includes records of proof of birth filed by Americans living abroad, as well as delayed filings of births of children born to American parents. Each index record includes: Name, Gender, Birth date, Father, and Mother. The images of the consular report forms have much more information. This database has 104,878 records. See
http://search.ancestry.com/search/db.aspx?dbid=1664.

- See also, *U.S. Consular Reports of Marriages, 1910-1949* **[Online Database],** digitized and indexed at Ancestry.com. Source: National Archives, Records of the Department of State. Contained in this database are reports of U.S. citizens' marriages abroad submitted by U.S. Consulates between the years 1910 and 1949. Marriage ceremonies conducted outside the U.S. are subject to the laws of the country in which the individuals are married by civil or religious officials. Once the marriage has taken place, officers at the U.S. Consulate authenticate the foreign marriage document and report it, hence the collection of forms in this database. If the spouse is a foreign National, they can then apply for U.S. citizenship. Some of the records are also accompanied by a letter regarding the status of the spouse's passport application (whether it has been granted or denied). This database has 37,000 records, see **www.ancestry.com/search/collections/1652.**

1911-1954. *United States, New England Passenger and Crew Lists* **[Online Database],** digitized at the FamilySearch.org website. This collection contains passenger and crew lists from vessels arriving at various ports in New England from 1918-1954. It corresponds with NARA Publication A3468: Passenger and Crew Lists of Vessels Arriving at Providence, Davisville, Melville, Newport, Quonset

Point, and Tiverton, Rhode Island; Fall River, Massachusetts; and New London, Connecticut. This database has 179,903 images. See https://familysearch.org/search/collection/2072112.

1914-1946. *U.S., Photographs of Military Ships by the Bureau of Ships* **[Online Database],** digitized and indexed at Ancestry.com. Source: National Archives microfilm series M1157and M1222. This database contains thousands of photographs of military ships dating from 1914 to 1946. These ships and photographs were under the jurisdiction of the Bureaus of Engineering and Construction and Repair before coming under the Bureau of Ships in 1940. Each photograph has a Ship Name and Date of Photo associated with it. The photographs are searchable by these fields, or by a Keyword (such as *Arizona* to locate the photo above). This database has 36,567 records, see www.ancestry.com/search/collections/1173.

1914-1965. *U.S., Departing Passenger and Crew Lists* **[Online Database],** indexed at the Ancestry.com website. Source: combined microfilm publications of the National Archives for several states and cities. These passenger and crew departure lists from both ships and aircraft were recorded on a variety of forms that were then turned over to the Immigration and Naturalization Service. Details requested on the forms varied, but they typically include the name of the vessel, departure date, ports of departure and destination, shipmaster, full name, age, gender, physical description, military rank (if any), occupation, birthplace, citizen of what country, and residence. For military transports, you may find the next of kin, relationships, and address listed as well. Later manifests may include visa or passport numbers. This database has 7,811,023 records. See http://search.ancestry.com/search/db.aspx?dbid=60882.

1916-1925. *U.S., Consular Registration Applications* **[Online Database],** digitized and indexed at the Ancestry.com website. Dept of State, National Archives. This database consists of applications of US citizens to stay in a foreign country for an extended period of time. Applications included in this collection pertain to both native-born and naturalized American citizens. Two different applications were used depending on the citizenship type. Information found in this collection will include: Name of registrant, Consulate at which he registered, His date and place of birth, General travel data, Names and places of birth and residence of his spouse and children, and registrant's current place of residence. The document images have more information about a person. This database has 45,028 records. See http://search.ancestry.com/search/db.aspx?dbid=2133.

1917-1918. *World War I Draft Registration Cards* **[Online Database],** digitized and indexed at the FamilySearch.org website. Name index and images of draft registration cards for World War I. Three registrations occurred between 1917 and 1918. The 1st was held 5 Jun 1917 for men ages 21-31. The 2nd was held 5 Jun 1918 for men who turned 21 since the 1st registration. The 3rd started 12 Sep 1918 for men ages

18-45. The collection includes cards for 24 million men. The cards are arranged by state, by city or county, by local draft board, then alphabetical by surname. The draft registration cards are part of Record Group 163, Records of the Selective Service System (WWI), 1917-1939, and is National Archives Microfilm publication M1509. This database has 24,867,345 records. See www.familysearch.org/search/collection/1968530.

- See also, *World War I Draft Registration Cards, 1917-1918* **[Online Database]**. A fully searchable database to 24.8 million draft registrants is online at Ancestry.com.
http://search.ancestry.com/search/db.aspx?dbid=6482.

- See also, *U.S. WWI Civilian Draft Registrations, 1917-1918* **[Online Database]**, indexed at Ancetry.com. From an index compiled by Ray Banks, *World War I Civilian Draft Registrations*. This database has 1,231,099 records, see www.ancestry.com/search/collections/3172.

1917-1919. *U.S., YMCA World War I Service Cards* **[Online Database]**, includes index and images of approximately 27,600 index cards kept by the Kautz Family YMCA Library at the University of Minnesota. Cards include the names of individuals who served with the YMCA in WWI. Cards are arranged alphabetically by surname and often include information such as age, home address, and occupation. This database has 27,352 records, see www.familysearch.org/search/collection/2513098.

1917-1919. *U.S., World War I Naval Deaths* **[Online Database]**, indexed and digitized at Ancestry.com. Original data: McHenry, Kathy. U.S. Naval Deaths, World War I. Although the United States Navy did not take part in many World War I battles, thousands of American sailors died fighting for their country during the war. This database collects from disparate sources the death records for sailors who died between 1917 and 1919. Each record reveals the sailor's name, rank, branch of service, death date, and cause of death. Additionally, the sailor's enlistment address is given along with the nearest living relative. This database has 7,273 records, see www.ancestry.com/search/collections/4022.

1917-1919. *American Soldiers of World War I (Deaths)* **[Online Database]**, Original data: Haulsee, W.M., *Soldiers of the Great War. Vol. I-III.* Washington, D.C.: *Soldiers Record,* 1920. This database is a record of the American soldiers who lost their lives in World War I. The work is arranged alphabetically by state. For each soldier who fought and died in this Great War his picture, name, rank, and means of death (killed in action, died of disease, died of wounds, died of accident, or wounded in action) is provided. While the pictures under each state are not arranged alphabetically, there is an alphabetical listing following the pictures for each state, arranged first by mean of death, then rank, and finally last name. This listing is the official list of men who lost their lives in World War I compiled from the Official Bulletin provided by the government. In addition to the pictures of all the deceased men of this war, this work also provides a parallel record of war events among the leading countries involved in the war from 1914 to 1918. These countries include the United States, Great Britain, Belgium, France, Germany, Austria-Hungary, Italy, Balkans, Turkey, and Russia. This database is a great source of information for both historians of World War I and family historians who are seeking information about their relatives who served and died in this war. Volume 1: Alabama – Maryland. Volume 2: Massachusetts – Ohio. Volume 3: Oklahoma - Wyoming and Supplement. This database has 89,332 records, see
www.ancestry.com/search/collections/61470.

- See also, *U.S., World War I American Expeditionary Forces Deaths, 1917-1919* **[Online Database]**, digitized and indexed at FamilySearch.org. This collection contains information regarding soldiers who lost their lives while serving with the American Expeditionary Forces (AEF) during World War I. Each officer's entry includes their name, rank, and organization that they were assigned to at the time of their death, and the date of death. Each enlisted man's entry includes the above information as well as their military serial number. This database has 76,128 records, see
www.familysearch.org/search/collection/2996059.

1917-1918. *U.S., Residents Serving in Canadian Expeditionary Forces* **[Online Database]**, digitized and indexed at Anceatry.com. Source: National Archives textual records, Records of the Selective Service System (World War II). Rather than wait for the United States' own declaration of war or military preparations, some U.S. citizens opted to join with Allied forces engaging the enemy during World War I. These records consist of lists of United States residents serving primarily in the Canadian Expeditionary Force. There is a small section of records of United States residents serving in the Australian Imperial Force. Each entry contains the name of the resident, his address in the United States, date and place of birth, nationality, marital status, occupation, and place and date of entering service. This database has 23,291 records, see www.ancestry.com/search/collections/9177.

1917-1919. *U.S., Residents Serving in the British Expeditionary Forces* **[Online Database],** digitized and indexed at Ancestry.com. Source: National Archives textual records, Records of the Selective Service System (World War II). These records consist mainly of cards listing British citizens residing in the United States who served with the British Expeditionary Force in the World War I era. Each entry contains the name of the resident, address in the United States, date and place of birth, nationality, marital status, occupation, and place and date of entering service. This database has 13,565 records, see www.ancestry.com/search/collections/9178.

1917-1940. *U.S., Veterans Administration Master Index* **[Online Database],** indexed at FamilySearch.org. This collection contains an index to veterans who served at any time during World War I and who made (or whose heirs made) pension or benefits claims of the Veterans Administration between 1917 and 1940. Each card contains the name of the veteran as well as other personal identifying information such as home address at the time of enlistment, date of birth, and date of death. Additionally, the cards may provide the following service information: rank, branch of service, service number, date of entry and discharge, claim number, insurance number(s), cross-reference to the beneficiary of the veteran, and first organization the veteran was assigned. This database has 6,931,032 records, see www.familysearch.org/search/collection/2968245.
- See also, *U.S. Veterans Administration Master Index, 1917-1940* **[Online Database],** indexed at Ancestry.com, a database provided to Ancestry.com by FamilySearch.org and the non-profit Reclaim the Records organization (who found these records hiding in the St. Louis National Personnel Records Center and using the Freedom of Information Act, was able gain access to digitize the entire collection. The Ancestry.com database has 5.67 million records, see www.ancestry.com/search/collections/61861.

1917-1954. *U.S., Jewish Welfare Board, War Correspondence* **[Online Database],** digitized and indexed at Ancestry.com. From the original records at the American Jewish Historical Society, New York, NY. This database contains correspondence to and from JWB workers relating to Jewish personnel in the armed forces. Documents include letters, telegrams, memos, newspaper clippings, staff/member lists, photos, reports, minutes, and other correspondence. The records include names, dates, and places recorded in the documents, as well as valuable historical context and insight. While the bulk of the records come from the WWII years, some come from WWI and the Korean War era as well. This database has 453,840 records, see www.ancestry.com/search/collections/1865.

1917-1954. *WWI, WWII, and Korean War Casualty Listings* **[Online Database],** indexed at the Ancestry.com website. Original data: American Battle Monuments Commission: World War I List; World War II Listing; Korean War Listing. Each index record includes: Name, Birth date, State registered, Death date, Death country, Death description, War, Title, Rank, Service, Service ID, Notes (may contain unit, dates of service, awards, and more). This database has 137,572 records. Archived at https://web.archive.org/web/20170623085409/http://search.ancestry.com/search/db.aspx?dbid=8853.

1918 Index to Naturalizations of World War I Soldiers **[Online Database],** digitized and indexed at the FamilySearch.org website, a card index to over 18,000 naturalizations of soldiers who served in World War I. From the National Archives microfilm, series M1952. Index courtesy of Fold3. See https://familysearch.org/search/collection/1858291.

1918-1940. *New England Seamen's Identification Cards,* **[Online Database],** digitized at the FamilySearch.org website. This collection contains identification cards of Seamen departing from or arriving at the following ports: Boston, Vineyard Haven, Salem/Beverly, Marblehead, Fall River, New Haven, Portland, and Providence. The record includes name, age, place of birth, parent's birthplace, naturalization data, physical description, photo, and signature. The records can be found at NARA Northeast Region facility in Waltham, Massachusetts. This database has 104,825 images. See https://familysearch.org/search/collection/2191222.

>   VA-81, Squadron
>
> Meeks, Howard (n), AT2, Rt #1, Box 252 Greenville, N.C.
> Miller, Walter A., AN, Box 142, Salembury, N.C.
> Morgan, Alvin E., ADR2, 311 S. Hill St., Gastonia, N.C.
> Newkirk, Charles E., ATN3, Rt. 1, Box 245, Smithfield, N.C.
> Norum, Gene H., AT1(P2), 134 Zabbar Rd., Pawla, Malta
> Olivier, Philippe A., AT2, 614 Mandalay Ave., Clearwater Beach, Fla.
> Ovist, Gerald E., AN, 4431 N. Troy St., Chicago, Ill.
> Ozmun, Richard C., AN, 309 N. Linden, Northfield, Minn.
> Parker, William A. Jr., ADJ3, 1505 A St., N.E., Washington, D.C.
> Pfadenhauer, Stephen F., AE1, 2025 Hopkins St., Orange Park, Fla.
> Poirier, David (n), ATN3, 421 Winnebago St., Park Forest, Ill.
> Prince, Freddie G., YNSN, 411 1/2 Broad St., Jacksonville, Fla.
> Pullen, David H., AMH3, Big Creek, Miss.
> Ray, Paul F., AT2, 10024 Mark Twain, Detroit, Mich.
> Robinson, David C., AMS3, 344 E. Hearon St., Paris Lamar, Texas
> Rooney, Robert A., ADJ3, 2307 Loyola St., New Orleans, La.
> Rose, William E., AE2, Box 146, Sinton, Texas
> Sawyer, Lawrence P., SD3, 508 Beeche Dale Rd., Portsmouth,
>
> Westerman, William R., LTJG, 1600 Montclain St., Ann Arbor, Mich.
> Martin, Joseph H., LTJG, 604 Delaware Ave., Norwood, Penna.
> Owen, Robert S., LTJG, 7118 Atlantic, Va Beach, Va.
> Parks, John H., LTJG, 515 Delaware Ave., Va. Beach, Va.
> Caldwell, William A., LTJG, 9156 Anthony Land, Va. Beach, Va.
> Bissell, Chesney O., LTJG, 809 9th St., Va. Beach, Va.
> Bolton-Smith, Carlile Jr., ENS, 3007 Que St., N.W., Washington 7, D.C.
> Carter, Lloyd S., AECS, 9321 Oyster Rd., Lynnhaven, Va.
> Thompson, Robert D., ADC, General Del., Stanford, Mich.
> Golbinec, Rudolph P., ATC, Rt. 2, Box 114B London Bridge, Va.
> Lindstrom, Harold R., AQC, 47766 Myrtlewood Rd., Jacksonville, Fla.
> Grantham, Wilbur M., ATC, 417D Painter St., Norfolk, Va.
> Bratcher, Paul D., AMC, 508 Delaware Ave., Va. Beach, Va.
> Poston, James C., AECA, 8048 Lourdes Dr., N., Jacksonville, 5, Fla.
> Dittmar, Robert E., AMCA, 166 N. Walnut St., East Orange, N.J.

Sample page from U.S. Navy Cruise Books, USS Forrestal CVA-59 – 1961.

1918-2009. *U.S. Navy Cruise Books* **[Online Database],** indexed at the Ancestry.com website. Source: Navy Dept Library, Washington, DC. This database contains U.S. Navy cruise books for various years and ships from 1918 to 2009. They include the volumes in the Navy Department Library's collection, the nation's largest cruise book collection. Cruise books are yearbook-style books put together by volunteers on board ship to commemorate a deployment. They usually include portraits of the sailors, officers, and other personnel aboard the ship, accompanied by the individual's surname and naval rate. Portraits are generally organized alphabetically by surname within each division or department. Other features may include candid photographs of crew members at work and recreation, details and history of the ship, and short biographies on captains, commanders, and other prominent officers. Cruise books are created for private distribution. They are not official Navy publications, and the Navy does not stock, sell, or republish these books. This can make copies of some books, especially older volumes, extremely rare. This collection is searchable by ship name, ship ID, year, and name of crew member. This database has 4,670,671 records. See
http://search.ancestry.com/search/db.aspx?dbid=2348.

1925. *U.S., Official National Guard Register* **[Online Database],** indexed at Ancestry.com. Original data: Secretary of War, Militia Bureau. Official National Guard Register for 1925. Washington, D.C.: Government Printing Office, 1925. This is a listing of the officers and sergeant instructors of the National Guard for all the states in 1925. Database information includes name, rank, regiment, company, birth date, birthplace, state, and page number. The records also include information on the organization of the unit and each person's complete military record up to that point. Also, it contains educational information on many, specifically college and military training. In addition to states, the database covers the territories of District of Columbia, Hawaii, Alaska, and Puerto Rico. This database has 13,824 records:
www.ancestry.com/search/collections/4996.

1925-1941. *Applications for Headstones for Military Veterans* **[Online Database],** digitized images at the FamilySearch.org website, applications for headstones received by the Cemeterial Division of the Quartermaster General. Most are for veterans of the Civil War or later. A few may cover earlier wars. Taken from the National Archives microfilm, series M1916, this database has 644,338 records. See
https://familysearch.org/search/collection/1916249.
- See also, *Headstone Applications for Military Veterans, 1925-1963* **[Online Database],** indexed at Ancestry.com. This database contains application forms for headstones for deceased members and veterans of the U.S. armed services. Applications were made between 1925 and 1963, but they include veterans in conflicts going back to the Revolutionary War. Forms vary, but they may contain the following

details: name, birthdate, enlistment date, rank, discharge date, death date, cemetery name, cemetery place, marker type, religious emblem, medals, name, and relationship of applicant. This database has 1,958,218 records, see
www.ancestry.com/search/collections/2375.

1928-1962. *U.S. National Cemetery Interment Control Forms* **[Online Database]**, digitized and indexed at the Ancestry.com website. Source: Records of the Quartermaster General at the National Archives. The cards in this database are "control forms" for burial lots in national cemeteries. They list details for U.S. Military personnel interred in national cemeteries, including the following: Name, Birth date, Rank, Serial number, Units served in, Wars served in, Enlistment, discharge, and other service details, Dates of death and interment, Gravesite, and Next of kin. The cards may have much more information, including details about the gravestone order, and may also list a spouse's burial location if buried in the same cemetery. This database has 826,157 records. See
http://search.ancestry.com/search/db.aspx?dbid=2590.

1929. *U.S. World War I Mothers' Pilgrimage* **[Online Database]**, digitized and indexed at Ancestry.com. Original data: *List of Mothers and Widows of American Soldiers, Sailors, and Marines Entitled to Make a Pilgrimage to War Cemeteries in Europe.* Washington, D.C.: Government Printing Office, 1930. In the late 1920s the War Department of the United States compiled a list of mothers and widows of deceased soldiers killed in World War I and offered to send them to their loved one's final resting place in Europe. This database contains the names those women who were entitled to make the pilgrimage, as shown by department records on 15 November 1929. Each record provides the name of widow or mother, city and state of residence, and relationship to the deceased. Plus, information regarding the decedent's name, rank, unit, and cemetery is provided. This database has 22,124 records, see
www.ancestry.com/search/collections/4224.

1930. *U.S., Census of Merchant Seamen* **[Online Database]**, digitized and indexed at FamilySearch.org. Source: National Archives microfilm series M1932. This database includes a name index and images of the Merchant Seamen schedules from the 1930 Federal Census. This database has 62,527 records, see
www.familysearch.org/search/collection/1821205.

1930-1949. *U.S., California, List of United States Citizens Arriving at San Francisco* **[Online Database]**, This collection contains passenger lists of United States citizens returning to San Francisco, California, 1930-1949. Passenger lists are arranged chronologically and by ship name. Source: National Archives microfilm series M1439. This database has 438,171 records, see
www.familysearch.org/search/collection/2822767.

1930-Current. *U.S., Obituary Collection* **[Online Database]**, indexed at the Ancestry.com website. Source: Ancestry's obituary collection, extracted from newspapers from all over the country. More source information is at each entry. Each index record includes: Name, Gender, Residence (at time of death), Death place, and Obituary date. This database has 178,827,563 records. See
http://search.ancestry.com/search/db.aspx?dbid=7545.

1934-1963 *Alcatraz, California, U.S. Penitentiary Prisoner Index* **[Online Database]**, digitized and indexed at the Ancestry.com website. Contained in this collection is an index to inmates held at the Alcatraz U.S. Penitentiary (USP), California, from 1934 to 1963. After locating the inmate identification number in this index, the inmate's case files can then be requested from the National Archives and Records Administration (NARA) Pacific Regional Office. The listing covers approximately 1,550 men incarcerated at Alcatraz including "Scarface" Al Capone and Robert Franklin Stroud, the "Birdman of Alcatraz." The inmate files are meant to document the prisoner's time while in the penitentiary and can include biographies, family histories, medical and psychiatric information, mail sent and received, number of visitors, legal documents, conduct records, mug shots, rap sheets, and the like. See
http://search.ancestry.com/search/db.aspx?dbid=34666.

U.S. Census Substitutes

See More	View all related information
NAME:	Helen Bryan Smith
GENDER:	Female
RACE:	White
BIRTH DATE:	21 Jan 1898
BIRTH PLACE:	Lisbon, Florida
DEATH DATE:	Sep 1937
FATHER:	John C Bryan
MOTHER:	Annie McKinly
SSN:	255050134
NOTES:	Nov 1936: Name listed as HELEN BRYAN SMITH; 30 Dec 1987: Name listed as HELEN SMITH

Sample, U.S. Social Security Applications and Claims Index – details on one person. (Ancestry.com).

1936-2007. U.S., Social Security Applications and Claims Index [Online Database], indexed at the Ancestry.com website. Source: Social Security Administration. This database picks up where the *Social Security Death Index (SSDI)* leaves off by providing more details than those included in the SSDI. It includes information filed with the Social Security Administration through the application or claims process, including valuable details such as birth date, birthplace, and parents' names. Each index record includes: Applicant's full name, Social Security Number (SSN), Gender, Race, Birth date, Birth place, Father, Mother, Type of claim, and Notes (may include details on changes made to the applicant's record, including name changes or when a claim was made for disability or retirement benefits, or when a claim was made by a surviving family member for death or survivor benefits). This database has 117,554,105 records. See
http://search.ancestry.com/search/db.aspx?dbid=60901.

1937-1985. *Associated Press, Stories and News Features* **[Online Database],** indexed at the Ancestry.com website. Source: Associated Press Corporate Archives, New York, NY. This collection includes AP news stories (1937-85), which were selected by news librarians for microfilming to create an internal news archive of over 700 reels. The set was not meant to be complete but to include only those stories of national or international importance. Most stories take the form of "wire copy," the version that AP sent via teletype to its newspaper members for publication. As newspapers were free to edit stories for their own purposes, the wire copy may differ from published newspaper accounts. During the period 1937 to 1950, the clippings were sometimes microfilmed instead of the wire copy. This database has 704,997 records. See
http://search.ancestry.com/search/db.aspx?dbid=50017.

1937-1985. *Associated Press, Subject Card Index to AP Stories* **[Online Database],** indexed at the Ancestry.com website. Source: Associated Press Corporate Archives, New York, NY. Each index card contains a subject or a country name and a list of AP stories in which that subject is found. Next to each story listing is the date the story was released by AP (generally in the Day/Month/Year format) and a classification number. This number is the key to connecting the index card with a corresponding AP story. This database has 493,916 records. See
http://search.ancestry.com/search/db.aspx?dbid=1308.

1938-1946 *U.S. World War II Army Enlistment Records* **[Online Database],** is a searchable database of the extracted records for 8.3 million men and women who enlisted in the U.S. Army during World War II. Information may include: Name of enlistee, Army serial number, Residence (county and state), Place of enlistment, Enlistment date, Grade, Army branch, Component, Term of enlistment, Birthplace, Year of birth, Race and Citizenship, Height and weight, Education, Marital status, and the box and reel no. of the microfilmed records. The database is available at the Ancestry.com site. See
http://search.ancestry.com/search/db.aspx?dbid=8939.

- See also, *1938-1946 World War II Army Enlistment Records* **[Online Database],** digitized and indexed at the FamilySearch.org website. Name index to Army Serial Number Enlistment Card Records, excluding officers, in the United States Army including the Women's Army Auxiliary Corps and the Enlisted Reserve Corps circa 1938-1946. The index is part of Record Group 64: Records of the National Archives and Records Administration. This index is not complete and may contain scanning errors. Database courtesy of the National Archives. This database has 9,038,855 records. See
www.familysearch.org/search/collection/2028680.

1938-1949 U.S. World War II Navy Muster Rolls [Online Database], is a searchable database at the Ancestry.com website, for the 1938-1949 Navy muster rolls. Muster rolls were quarterly lists of enlisted naval personnel attached to each ship, station, or activity. Information usually available on muster rolls includes: Name of enlistee, Rating (Occupation/Specialty), Service number, Date reported for particular duty or on board, Date of enlistment, Name of ship, station, or activity, Ship number or other numeric designation, and date of muster roll. This database has 33,037,784 records, see
http://search.ancestry.com/search/db.aspx?dbid=1143.

1939-1945 *U.S. Rosters of World War II Dead* [Online Database], digitized and indexed at the Ancestry.com website. This database contains the names of those who died in World War II from all U.S. armed services. Names are listed in alphabetical order according to surname. Information available in this database includes (listed in order as it appears on the image from left to right): 1) Name of permanent interment site. 2) Name. 3) Rank. 4) Service Number. 5) Name of temporary interment site. 6) Religion. 7) Race. And 8) Disposition. This database has 357,086 records, see
http://search.ancestry.com/search/db.aspx?dbid=1102.

1939-1954. *Jewish Transmigration Bureau Deposit Cards* [Online Database], digitized and indexed at Ancestry.com. Source: American Jewish Joint Distribution Committee Archives. The Transmigration Bureau was a non-profit service agency established in New York City on June 21, 1940 by the American Jewish Joint Distribution Committee (JDC) in order to deal with emigration of Jews from Germany, Austria, former Czechoslovakia, Holland, Belgium, and Luxembourg. In 1940, JDC was assisting refugees in transit in more than forty countries in eastern and Western Europe, Asia, and Latin America. The Transmigration Bureau's primary purpose was to accept monetary deposits made by American friends and family to pay the full or partial travel costs of the Jews emigrating from the European countries. In the same month that the Transmigration Bureau was established, JDC's European headquarters transferred from Nazi-occupied Paris to neutral Lisbon. JDC leased every available ship to enable the thousands of refugees arriving in Lisbon to proceed to safe havens in North and South America, and many of the émigrés found on the Transmigration Bureau Deposit Cards left from that port. This database has 59,396 records, see
www.ancestry.com/search/collections/1355.

1940-1958. *U.S., Marine Corps Casualty Indexes* [Online Database], indexed at the Ancestry.com website. This database is also accessible at the Marine Corps History Division website. Each index record includes: Name, Casualty date, Casualty type, Unit, Service No., Collection title, Location, Item No., and a link to the Marine Corps website. This database has records. This database has 115,570 records, see
http://search.ancestry.com/search/db.aspx?dbid=70837.

1940-2003. *U.S. Index to Alien Case Files* [Online Database], digitized and indexed at FamilySearch.org This is an index to Alien Case Files housed at the National Archives Regional Office in Kansas City, Missouri. Under the Alien Registration Act of 1940, immigrants in the United States were required to register and be fingerprinted. The Immigration and Naturalization Service (INS) – now the U.S. Citizenship and Immigration Service (USCIS) – drew upon the 1940 Alien Registration Form (AR-2) to create Alien Case Files beginning in 1944. Immigrants recorded in these files come from all over the United States. Some files from aliens living in the immigration districts of Guam; Honolulu, Hawaii; Reno, Nevada; and San Francisco, California are housed in the National Archives Regional Office in San Bruno, California and may not be included in this index. This database has 456,334 records, see
www.familysearch.org/search/collection/2540918.

1941-1945. *Japanese Americans Relocated During World War II* [Online Database], digitized and indexed at Ancestry.com. Source: National Archives, Records of the War Relocation Authority. This database contains information collected by the War Relocation Authority (WRA) on over 100,000 Japanese-Americans who were relocated during World War II. Evacuees were taken from Washington, Oregon, and California and placed in the following relocation centers: Tule Lake Center, California; Manzanar Center, California; Minidoka Center, Idaho; Central Utah Center, Utah; Granada Center, Colorado; Colorado River Center, Arizona; Gila River Center, Arizona; Heart Mountain Center, Wyoming; and Rohwer Center, Arkansas; Jerome Center, Arkansas; The following information was collected about the relocated citizens and recorded on WRA Form 26 (all of this information is available in this database): Name of evacuee, Relocation project and assembly center assigned to, Sex, Marital status, Race of evacuee and spouse, Birth year, Age, Birthplace, Previous address, Birthplace of parents, Father's occupation, Evacuee's occupation, Religion, Education, Whether attended Japanese language school, Highest grade completed,

Language proficiency, Foreign residence, Indication of military service, Public assistance, Pensions, Physical defects, Indication of an alien registration number and/or Social Security Number. This database has 109,377 records, see
www.ancestry.com/search/collections/8918.

- See also, *U.S. War Relocation Authority Centers, Final Accountability Rosters, 1942-1946* [Online Database], digitized and indexed at FamilySearch.org. Source: National Archives microfilm series M1865. These rosters are alphabetical lists of evacuees housed in relocation centers from 1942-1946. This project was completed in cooperation with Densho: The Japanese American Legacy Project. This database has 96,910 records, see
www.familysearch.org/search/collection/2729264.

1941-1945 *World War II Prisoners of War of the Japanese* [Online Database], indexed at the FamilySearch.org website. Includes an index of military personnel and civilians who were prisoners of the Japanese during World War II, acquired from the National Archives. The index includes name, rank, service number, branch of service, source of information, unit information as available from parent unit to subordinate unit and notes. Additional information about this collection may be found on the National Archives website. This database has 29,879 records. See
https://familysearch.org/search/collection/2127320.

1941-1945. *World War II Navy, Marine Corps, and Coast Guard Casualties* [Online Database], digitized and indexed at the Ancestry.com website. Source: Records of the Bureau of Navy Personnel, National Archives. The records include the following casualty categories: Killed in action, died of wounds, or lost lives as result of operational movements in war zones, Missing in action or during operational war missions, Wounded in action or during operational war missions, Died or killed in Prisoner of War status, Released from Prison Camps. Men who served in these military branches but died in the U.S. as a result of disease, homicide, or suicide are not included in this list. Information available for each casualty includes: Name of military personnel, Rank of military personnel, Name, address, and relationship of next-of-kin. The records are arranged first by state. then by casualty type, then alphabetically by surname of personnel. This database has 150,715records. See
http://search.ancestry.com/search/db.aspx?dbid=1122

1941-1946. *U.S. WWII Military Personnel Missing In Action or Lost At Sea* [Online Database], digitized and indexed at Ancestry.com. Original data: Department of Defense Prisoner of War/Missing Personnel Office. This database contains a listing of U.S. soldiers, sailors, marines, and civilians (presumably mainly military employees and contractors) who have been reported by the U.S. government as Missing in Action (MIA) or Buried at Sea from World War II. The "Buried at Sea" category includes individuals aboard ships that sank due to enemy action and whose bodies were never recovered. Thus, very few persons categorized as "Buried at Sea" actually received a formal burial service. For this reason, Ancestry has chosen to instead use the term "Lost at Sea." Information listed in this database includes: Name of military personnel; Date of loss; Branch of service; Rank; Service Number; Status: either "Lost at Sea" or "Missing in Action." This database has 80,427 records, see
www.ancestry.com/search/collections/1199.

1941-1946. *World War II Prisoners of War* [Online Database], digitized and indexed at Ancestry.com. Source: National Archives, Records of the Provost Marshal General. This database contains information on approximately 140,000 U.S. officers and soldiers, as well as U.S. and some Allied civilians who were prisoners of war (POWs) during World War II (specifically 7 Dec 1941-19 Nov 1946). Information in this database was originally taken from records and reports created by the International Committee of the Red Cross. Generally, the type of information you will find in this database for an individual includes: Name of prisoner or internee; Race; State of residence; Report date; Latest report date; Grade or rank; Service branch; Arm or service; Area served; Detaining country; Camp (the numbers listed at the end of the camp name are latitude and longitude coordinates); Status; and Report source. This database has 143,374 records, see
www.ancestry.com/search/collections/8919.
- This database is also available at FamilySearch.org:
www.familysearch.org/search/collection/2039747.

1941-1957. *World War II and Korean Conflict Veterans Interred Overseas* [Online Database], Original data: National Archives: *Register, World War II Dead Interred in American Military Cemeteries on Foreign Soil and World War II and Korea Missing or Lost or Buried at Sea.* The most destructive and far-ranging war in human history, World War II claimed the lives of countless millions. This database is a listing of American servicemen who fought in the Second World War or the Korean Conflict and were interred outside of the contiguous forty-eight states. Each entry provides the individual's name, rank, unit, death date, and location of interment (listed as monument). Additionally, place of induction into the service is provided along with a list of awards presented by the military. This database has 159,582 records, see www.ancestry.com/search/collections/4283.

1942. *World War II Draft Registration Cards, 1942* **[Online Database],** digitized and indexed at the FamilySearch.org website. Includes a name index and images of cards for men, age 45-64 (born 1877-1897), included in the fourth draft conducted on April 27, 1942. The indexed portion of this publication currently includes the states of Arkansas, California, Connecticut, Delaware, Hawaii, Illinois, Indiana, Louisiana, Maryland, Michigan, Nevada, New Jersey, New York Bronx, New York Kings, New Hampshire, New York Manhattan, Massachusetts, New York Queens, New York Staten Island, Ohio, Oklahoma, Pennsylvania, Rhode Island, Texas, Vermont, Virginia, West Virginia, and Wisconsin. Index and images for Alaska, Idaho, Oregon, and Washington courtesy of Ancestry.com. This database contains 15,292,577 records. See
https://familysearch.org/search/collection/1339071.
- See also, *World War II Draft Registration Cards, 1942* **[Online Database],** digitized and indexed at Ancestry.com, see
www.ancestry.com/search/collections/1002.

1942-1946 *Japanese Americans Relocated During World War II* **[Online Database],** indexed at the FamilySearch.org website. Includes a name index of Japanese Americans living in Washington, Oregon, and California who were relocated during World War II acquired from the National Archives, part of Record Group 210, Records of the War Relocation Authority. Additional information about this collection may be found on the National Archives website. This database has 109,368 records. See
https://familysearch.org/search/collection/2043779.

1942-1948. See *U.S., World War II Cadet Nursing Corps Card Files* **[Online Database],** digitized and indexed at the Ancestry.com website. National Archives, Records of the Public Health Service. This database contains membership cards providing details on women who joined the Cadet Nurse Corps created during World War II. After the United States entered World War II, the military's needs quickly brought on a nursing shortage. To address the need, federal funding, administered by the Public Health Service, began flowing to nursing schools in 1942, and in 1943 Congress authorized the Cadet Nurse Corps. The Corps offered scholarships for tuition and fees, stipends, and uniforms to women ages 17–35 who went to nursing school and committed to serve in the nursing profession for the duration of the war. The Corps did not discriminate on race and graduated almost 125,000 nurses. Each index record includes: Name, Age, Birth date, Issue date, Educational institution, and School location. The images of the membership cards contains more details. This database has 390,020 records. See
http://search.ancestry.com/search/db.aspx?dbid=2251.

1942-1949. *U.S., Headstone, and Interment Records for U.S. Military Cemeteries on Foreign Soil* **[Online Database],** digitized and indexed at Ancestry.com. Source: National Archives, Records of the American Battle Monuments Commission. The American Battle Monuments Commission is responsible for 24 American cemeteries located in foreign countries. This collection includes burial cards for veterans buried in overseas cemeteries during and after World War II through 1949. The cards include the headstone inscription, which typically includes the name of the deceased, rank, military unit, state of residence, and date of death. Other information provided is the service number, name of the cemetery and grave number, gender, race, creed, decorations, temporary cemetery information, and the name and address of the next of kin. This database has 93,053 records, see
www.ancestry.com/search/collections/9170.

1942-1954. *U.S, WWII Hospital Admission Card Files* **[Online Database],** indexed at Ancestry.com. Original data: Hospital Admission Card Files, Records of the Office of the Surgeon General, National Archives, College Park, MD. The files contain records pertaining to mostly U.S. Army personnel wounded in battle during World War II and the Korean War. The records contain various medical treatment information about each patient including diagnoses, operations, and dates and places of hospitalization. The original records do not contain the name of the hospital patient, but list military service number, age, race, sex, place of birth, rank, and unit. The names of some patients were identified and added to the record by comparing the service number to other military record collections available on Ancestry. This database has 6,886,199 records, see
www.ancestry.com/search/collections/61817.

1942-1994. *U.S., Navy and Marines Awards and Decorations* **[Online Database],** digitized at Ancestry.com. Original data: Awards Information Management System (AIMS) Files, General Records of the Department of the Navy, National Archives, College Park, MD. These awards consisted of individual awards approved for sailors, marines, and Department of Navy civilians and unit awards approved for Navy and Marine Corps activities. This database has 1,804,597 records, see www.ancestry.com/search/collections/61823.

1944-1948. *U.S., New York, Index to Passengers Arriving at New York City* **[Online Database],** The collection is arranged in Soundex order. The images are originally part of NARA collection M1417 (rolls 7 and 35 are missing). This database has 1,125,332 records: www.familysearch.org/search/collection/3029266.

1948-2002. *U.S., Selected Jewish Obituaries* **[Online Database],** This is a database of over 8,800 obituary notices for the Chicago, Illinois area, compiled by Richard Hoffman. For each entry, the index contains the deceased's name, date of death, and other information such as the deceased's age, birthplace, maiden name, and occasionally the name of the cemetery. This database has 17,134 records, see www.ancestry.com/search/collections/1478.

1949-1963. *U.S. Navy Muster Rolls* **[Online Database],** digitized at Ancestry.com. This is an image-only database. Browse the image sets, organized by year. Arranged by two-year chronological subseries (1949-1950, 1951-1952, 1953-1954, 1955-1956, and 1957-1958), followed by single-year subseries (1959-1971). Each subseries is arranged by "activity number," a unique number assigned to each ship, unit, and command within the Navy. Each activity's muster rolls are arranged in chronological order by quarter, typically with enlisted personnel arranged by rate and thereunder alphabetically by surname. Beginning in the spring of 1956, officers precede enlisted personnel, with officers arranged either alphabetically by surname or hierarchically by rank. Personnel diaries, which precede each quarter's muster rolls, are arranged chronologically by date. This database has 2,444,510 records, see www.ancestry.com/search/collections/61718.

1949-1969. *U.S. Cemetery Abstracts* **[Online Database],** digitized and indexed at FamilySearch.org. Abstracts from cemeteries in the United States, compiled by various missions of the Church of Jesus Christ of Latter-day Saints. The collection also includes records from Bahamas, Bermuda, Canada, New South Wales, and New Zealand. This database has 468,634 records, see www.familysearch.org/search/collection/2579610.

1950-1953. *American Prisoners of War During the Korean War* **[Online Database],** indexed at the FamilySearch.org website. Name index of American prisoners of war during the Korean War, compiled by the Army Staff. This database has 4,714 records. See https://familysearch.org/search/collection/2043777.

1950-1953. See *Korean War Dead and Army Wounded* **[Online Database],** indexed at the FamilySearch.org website. Includes an index to the casualties of Army personnel during the Korean War. Includes dead, missing, wounded, or captured soldiers. The records are from Record Group 407 Records of the Adjutant General's Office. Additional information about this collection may be found on the National Archives website. This database has 109,961 records: https://familysearch.org/search/collection/2127897.

1950-1954. *Korean War Repatriated Prisoners of War* **[Online Database],** indexed at the FamilySearch.org website. Includes an index to Korean War former prisoners of war acquired from the National Archives. The records are from Record Group 15, Records of the Veterans Administration. The event date is the date of release and event place is the prisoner of war camp. Additional information about this collection is at the National Archives website. This database has 4,447 records. See https://familysearch.org/search/collection/2127902.

1950-1957. *Korean War Battle Deaths* **[Online Database],** indexed at the FamilySearch.org website. Includes an Index of military personnel who died (battle deaths) during the Korean War. The records are from Record Group 330 Records of the Office of the Secretary of Defense. Additional information about this collection may be found on the National Archives website. The event date is the date died or declared dead. This database has 33,642 records. See https://familysearch.org/search/collection/2127893.

1950-1993. *U.S. Public Records Index, Volume 1* **[Online Database],** indexed at the Ancestry.com website. Source: Voter Registration Lists, Public Record Filings, Historical Residential Records, and Other Household Database Listings. This Index is a compilation of various public records spanning all 50 states in the United States, including White pages, Directory assistance records, Marketing lists, Postal

change-of-address forms, Public record filings, and Historical residential records. Each index record may include: A person's first name, middle name or initial and last name, A street or mailing address, A telephone number, A birth date or birth year, and An age. This database has 418,687,293 records. See
http://search.ancestry.com/search/db.aspx?dbid=1788.

1950-1993. *U.S. Public Records Index, 1950-1993, Volume 2* **[Online Database],** indexed at the Ancestry.com website. This database has 402,469,185 records. See
http://search.ancestry.com/search/db.aspx?dbid=1732.

1954-1970. *National Register of Scientific and Technical Personnel Files* **[Online Database],** indexed at the FamilySearch.org website. Includes a name index from registers of specialized personnel from the National Science Foundation. It includes professionals in the field of biology, chemistry, economics, geology, mathematics, psychology, meteorology, physics, anthropology, political science, and sociology. This database has 125,530 records. See
https://familysearch.org/search/collection/2126719.

1956-1998. *Casualties of the Vietnam War* **[Online Database],** indexed at the FamilySearch.org website. This index consists of two files, the Combat Area Casualities Current File, 6/8/1956-1/21/1998 and the Combat Area Casualties Returned Alive File, 5/1/1962-3/22/1979 to Vietnam War dead, missing and prisoners of war occurring in Cambodia, China, Laos, North Vietnam, South Vietnam, and Thailand. The files were acquired from the National Archives "Access to Archival Databases" (AAD). The records are from Record Group 330 Records of the Office of the Secretary of Defense. The event date is either date of death or declared dead from the current file or date released or returned from the returned alive file. The database has 58,965 records. See
https://familysearch.org/search/collection/2127907.

1956-2003. *Military Personnel Who Died During the Vietnam War* **[Online Database],** indexed at the FamilySearch.org website. Includes records of military personnel who died in the Southeast Asian combat area during the Vietnam War acquired from the National Archives. Additional information about this collection may be found on the National Archives website. This database has 58,230 records. See
https://familysearch.org/search/collection/2127916.

1961-1981. *Casualties of Army Personnel, Dependents and Civilian Employees* **[Online Database],** digitized and indexed at the Ancestry.com website. This database contains information relating to U.S. Army personnel and their dependents (including active duty personnel, retired or separated personnel, reservists, and civilian employees) who were casualties (either killed or wounded) between 1961 and 1981. Although this database includes casualties worldwide, about 85 percent of the records are connected to the Vietnam Conflict, and therefore, are likely to be located in Southeast Asia. Information found in this database includes the name of the individual, country of casualty, military grade, military component, and a dozen other categories about the person. This database has 70,010 records. See
http://search.ancestry.com/search/db.aspx?dbid=8849.

Albert Smith	
United States Social Security Death Index	
Age:	54
Given Name:	Albert
Surname:	Smith
Birth Date:	22 Sep 1925
State:	New York
Previous Residence Postal Code:	95705
Event Date:	May 1979

Sample, *1862-2014 U.S. Social Security Death Index (SSDI)* – details on one person. (FamilySearch.org). **NOTE:** See the *1936-2007 Social Security Applications and Claims Index*, which may add more information about a person than the SSDI.

1962-2014 U.S. Social Security Death Index (SSDI) **[Online Database],** is included at the FamilySearch website. The SSDI usually includes the decedent's name, birth, and death date (month & year only for early years), social security number, and place of last residence of persons who died from 1962, the year when SSA first began computerizing the records. See
https://familysearch.org/search/collection/1202535.
- See also, *1962-2014. U.S. Social Security Death Index (SSDI)* **[Online Database],** is also found at the Ancestry.com site. See
http://search.ancestry.com/search/db.aspx?dbid=3693.
- See also, *1962-2011. U.S. Social Security Death Index (SSDI)* [Online Database], is also found at the Genealogybank.com site. See
www.genealogybank.com/gbnk/ssdi.

1970-2009. *United States Public Records* **[Online Database],** indexed at the FamilySearch.org website. This collection is an index of names, birthdates, addresses, phone numbers, and possible relatives of people who resided in the United States between 1970 and 2009. These records were generated from telephone directories, property tax assessments, credit applications, and other records available to the public. This database has over 897,849 records. See https://familysearch.org/search/collection/2199956.

1971-1994. *U.S., F.B.I. Deceased Criminal Identification Files* **[Online Database],** indexed at Ancestry.com, from records of the Bureau of Investigation, now at the National Archives, Washington, DC. Includes Name, Birthplace, Birthdate, Gender, Race, Death date, Eye color, Hair color, Height, and Weight. This database has 19,807 records, see
www.ancestry.com/search/collections/60578.

1980-2014. *United States, GenealogyBank Obituaries* **[Online Database],** indexed at the FamilySearch.org website. Index to obituaries from thousands of newspapers throughout the United States. Records are being published as they become available. This database has over 34.1 million records. See https://familysearch.org/search/collection/2333694.

1993-2002. *U.S. Phone and Address Directories* **[Online Database],** indexed at the Ancestry.com website. Source: 1993-2002 White Pages. Little Rock, AR, USA: Acxiom Corporation. Each index record includes: Name, Address, City, State, Zip code, Phone number, Residence years, and View neighbors. This database has 313,280,384 records. See
http://search.ancestry.com/search/db.aspx?dbid=7339.

1995-Current. *Obituary Daily Times Index* **[Online Database],** indexed at the Ancestry.com website. This index is also accessible at the RootsWeb site. Each index record includes: Name, Age at death, Birth date, Death date, Publication of record date, Publication of record place, and a link to the RootsWeb website. This database has 16,094,500 records. See
http://search.ancestry.com/search/db.aspx?dbid=70050.

2001-2012. *U.S. Casualties From Iraq and Afghanistan Conflicts* **[Online Database],** digitized and indexed at Ancestry.com. This collection includes casualties suffered by the U.S. military during wars primarily in Iraq and Afghanistan. **Operation Iraqi Freedom** (OIF) casualties include military deaths reported from March 19, 2003 to 2012. **Operation Enduring Freedom** (OEF) casualties include military deaths reported from October 10, 2001 to 2012. Most of these deaths were in Afghanistan. **Operation New Dawn** (OND) casualties include military deaths reported from 2010 to 2012. Information provided about casualties includes: Name, , Branch of Service, Component (Regular Active Duty, Reserve, or National Guard), Rank, Pay Grade, Conflict, Unit, Unit location, Death date, Casualty location, Incident date, Incident location, Hostile, Age, Gender, Race/ethnicity, Home residence, and Occupation, This database has 6,498 records, see
www.ancestry.com/search/collections/1568.

2002-2015. *U.S., Newspaper Marriage Index* **[Online Database],** indexed at the Ancestry.com website. Source: Ancestry extractions from hundreds of online newspapers. This collection contains recent engagement, marriage, wedding, and anniversary announcements. Each index record includes: Name, Wedding date, Spouse, Newspaper title, and Newspaper location. This database has 293,15 records.
http://search.ancestry.com/search/db.aspx?dbid=1594.

2005-2015. See *U.S., Newspaper Birth Index* **[Online Database],** indexed at the Ancestry.com website. Source: Ancestry extractions from hundreds of online newspapers. This collection contains recent newspaper birth announcements. Each index record includes: Name, Residence, Parents, and Newspaper location. This database has 173,291 records. See
http://search.ancestry.com/search/db.aspx?dbid=1592.